AF180222

Labour Law in Canada

Labour Law in Canada

by

Donald D. Carter
Geoffrey England
Brian Etherington
and
Gilles Trudeau

This book was originally published as a monograph in the International Encyclopaedia of Laws/Labour Law and Industrial Relations

Fifth edition

2002

Kluwer Law International
The Hague – London – New York

Butterworths
A Member of the LexisNexis Group

Published by:
Kluwer Law International
P.O. Box 85889, 2508 CN The Hague, The Netherlands
sales@kli.wkap.nl
http://www.kluwerlaw.com

Sold and Distributed in Canada by:
Butterworths Canada Ltd.
75 Clegg Road
Markham, Ontario
L6G 1A1, Canada
http://www.lexisnexis.ca

Sold and Distributed in North, Central and South America by:
Kluwer Law International
101 Philip Drive, Norwell, MA 02061, USA
kluwerlaw@wkap.com

Sold and Distributed in all other countries by:
Kluwer Law International
Distribution Centre, P.O. Box 322, 3300 AH Dordrecht, The Netherlands

A C.I.P. Catalogue record for this book is available from the Library of Congress

Printed on acid-free paper

Cover design: The Bears Communications, Amsterdam

ISBN 90 411 1750 4 (Kluwer)
ISBN 0 433 43012 5 (Butterworths)

Kluwer Law International incorporates the imprint of Martinus Nijhoff Publishers

The Authors

Brian ETHERINGTON is a graduate of McMaster University in arts and Queen's University in education and law. He also holds an LL.M. degree from Yale. He is a professor of law at the University of Windsor where he teaches labour law, labour arbitration, personal employment law and criminal law. He has written about, and acted as a consultant on, employment, administrative, constitutional, criminal, and trade and labour law issues. He is also a labour arbitrator, and has served as editor-in-chief of the *Canadian Labour and Employment Law Journal* since 1995.

Gilles TRUDEAU holds a bachelor degree in Industrial Relations and a licence in law from the Université de Montréal. In 1985, he received his S.J.D. from Harvard Law School. Since 1979, he has been professor of labour law and industrial relations at École de relations industrielles, Université de Montréal. From 1995 to 1999 he served as director of that institution. His major fields of research and publication include labour standards, industrial discipline and international labour law. He also acts as a labour arbitrator in Quebec and the federal jurisdiction.

General Acknowledgement

The authors acknowledge with gratitude the essential contribution of Professors Harry W. Arthurs, Judy Fudge, and Harry J. Glasbeek to this edition of the book. Their authorship of earlier editions has, not only provided us with the essence of this edition, but has also established for us a high standard of scholarship to which to aspire. Their contribution is greatly appreciated.

General Acknowledgement

Acknowledgement from Brian Etherington

I want to thank a number of people who were instrumental to the completion of my contribution to this edition. First, I want to thank my co-authors, who were truly a pleasure to work with, and add a special thanks to Don Carter for asking me to take part at the outset. Don was my first labour law teacher and has been a true friend and mentor in the years since that class. I owe a large debt to several fine student researchers, most notably Jack Huber, Jennifer Myers, Sarah Rimmington and Tarne Whitely. I also wish to thank the Law Foundation of Ontario for its funding of my research. And finally, I want to thank my family – Marilyn, Darrell, Craig and Laura – for being so supportive throughout my academic endeavours, and for putting up with my absences on so many Sundays to enable me to complete this project.

Acknowledgement from Brian Etherington

Table of Contents

Table of Contents

List of Abbreviations

Law Reports and Periodicals

Can. Bar Rev.	*Canadian Bar Review*
C.L.L.C.	Canadian Labour Law Cases
C.L.L.R.	Canadian Labour Law Reporter
C.L.R.B.R.	Canadian Labour Relations Boards Reports
D.L.R.	Dominion Law Reports
I.L.M.	International Legal Materials
L.A.C.	Labour Arbitration Cases
O.L.R.B.Rep.	Ontario Labour Relations Board Monthly Report
O.R.	Ontario Reports
Rel. Ind.	*Relations industrielles*
R.J.Q.	*Recueils de jurisprudence du Québec*
U.B.C.L.R.	*University of British Columbia Law Review*
U. of T.L.J.	*University of Toronto Law Journal*
T.A.	*Tribunal d'arbitrage* (Quebec)
T.T.	*Tribunal du travail* (Quebec)

Statutes

S.C.	Statutes of Canada
R.S.C.	Revised Statutes of Canada
S.B.C.	Statutes of British Columbia
R.S.B.C.	Revised Statutes of British Columbia
S.O.	Statutes of Ontario
R.S.O.	Revised Statutes of Ontario
S.Q.	Statutes of Quebec
R.S.Q.	Revised Statutes of Quebec
S.N.S.	Statutes of Nova Scotia
S.S.	Statutes of Saskatchewan
C.c.B.-C.	*Code civil du Bas-Canada*
C.c.Q.	*Code civil du Québec*

List of Abbreviations

LABOUR RELATIONS BOARD AND COURTS

B.C.I.R.C.	British Columbia Industrial Relations Council
B.C.L.R.B.	British Columbia Labour Relations Board
C.L.R.B.	Canada Labour Relations Board
O.L.R.B.	Ontario Labour Relations Board
Q.L.C.	Quebec Labour Court
S.L.R.B.	Saskatchewan Labour Relations Board
Alta. S.C.	Alberta Supreme Court
Alta. L.R.B.	Alberta Labour Relations Board
B.C.S.C.	British Columbia Supreme Court
B.C.C.A.	British Columbia Court of Appeal
Fed.C.A.	Federal Court of Appeal
N.B.S.C., App.Div.	New Brunswick Supreme Court, Appeal Division
Nfld.C.A.	Newfoundland Court of Appeal
Ont.C.A.	Ontario Court of Appeal
Ont. Div. Ct.	Ontario Divisional Court
Ont.H.C.	Ontario High Court
P.C.	Judicial Committee of Privy Council
Q.S.C.	Quebec Superior Court
Q.C.A.	Quebec Court of Appeal
S.C.C.	Supreme Court of Canada

Introduction

I. General Observations

1. To speak of the Canadian system of labour law, however defined, is in a sense to mislead. In effect, there are at least eleven functioning labour relations systems in Canada, embracing the ten provinces and the federal (national) sphere. Moreover, each system is composed of a number of statutes which regulate collective bargaining, employment standards, pay and employment equity and occupational health and safety. At the centre of each system is a statute which governs labour relations in the private sector generally. But often, as well, special provision is made for one sector of the labour market, such as construction, or even a single major undertaking, such as the development of a new energy resource. And almost always, special legislation deals with labour relations in the civil service, and with various private sector and municipal activities which are perceived to be of special concern to the public.

Nor is this list exhaustive: common law (or, in Quebec, civil law) principles play an important role, especially in relation to the rules of industrial conflict, as does the federal criminal law; administrative and judicial pronouncements are of vital importance in the authoritative interpretation of all aspects of law; and labour law necessarily intersects with other aspects of the general legal system, including the Constitution and the Charter of Rights and Freedoms.

Finally, to a greater or lesser extent, most aspects of Canadian labour law presuppose that employers, employees and unions, at the level of the individual enterprise, or, occasionally of local labour markets in a particular industry, will generate their own 'law' through formal agreements and informal understandings and customs.

2. The picture, then, is one of great complexity and diversity. The problem of the editors is to present this picture in a way which simplifies it, yet remains accurate. We have tried to do this by identifying common policy themes and typical legal solutions, and recording significant departures. We have generally looked to the four jurisdictions of Quebec, Ontario, British Columbia and the national government, both because they embrace the largest numbers of workers, and because they offer interesting comparisons and contrasts. Reference is made to the law of other jurisdictions where unusual provisions exist. Unfortunately, we can do no more than sketch in the 'law' of the parties themselves, but we try to do so at least where its absence would make the formal system incomprehensible. This selective approach, we trust, will accurately and sufficiently inform the foreign, or non-expert Canadian, reader.

But we do not intend that our work should be regarded as definitive text for domestic, professional consumption.

II. General Background Information

§1. Geographic Setting

A. Size

3. In terms of land mass, Canada is the second largest country in the world. However, its rather sparse population of approximately 30 million is widely dispersed across its enormous land mass (each province having one or two principal cities) except for a dense area of settlement in the highly industrialized crescent which reaches from Montreal through Toronto, along the northern and western shores of Lake Ontario to the Niagara frontier with the United States.

B. Boundaries

4. Canada is bounded on the east and west by the Atlantic and Pacific oceans, respectively. It shares its northern border in the Arctic with the former Soviet Union, and its southern border, along 49° latitude and the Great Lakes – St. Lawrence river system, with the United States. Its extended and open frontier with the United States has had important historic and contemporary influences on Canadian economic, social and political development. Its boundary with the former Soviet Union and its proximity to both Europe and Asia are also facts of profound geopolitical significance.

C. Transportation and Communications

5. The pattern of settlement and population distribution have made east–west communications a matter of vital national concern. There is a heavy dependency on railways for moving wheat and other natural resources from the middle of the continent to the oceans and inland seas for export, but also for purposes of domestic trade. An east–west pipeline also exists for the purposes of moving gas and oil from production fields on the western plains to major users, primarily in the industrial east–central region. Roads, rivers and canals complement the railways and pipelines.

Establishment and maintenance of east–west transportation and communications has been an important national priority. However, the existence of Canada's much larger neighbour to the south, the United States, has led to the development of transportation and communication lines on a north–south axis. This has promoted continental integration between Canada and the United States which, in turn, has led to tensions between proponents of nationalism and continentalism over transportation, economic, financial and cultural policies.

In 1988 there was a shift toward a greater economic connection with the United States when the federal government negotiated a free trade deal with the American government. At the time there was great debate about the extent to which closer economic ties would erode Canadian culture and the ability of Canadian governments to maintain independent domestic policies concerning social welfare and regulation of the workplace. The pressure towards greater economic continentalism increased, however, as the governments of Canada, the United States and Mexico concluded the North American Free Trade Agreement (NAFTA) in 1993. The extent of the impact of these agreements on social policy and trade and communication patterns is as yet unclear.

D. Physical Resources

6. From earliest times there has been a considerable dependence on the great natural endowments of the country – principally wheat, timber and minerals, and more recently oil and gas – which have been largely destined for export rather than domestic consumption. Development of a modern industrial economy has been impeded not merely by the relatively small and scattered population, and problems of east–west transportation, but as well by the high degree of foreign ownership, principally by United States and multinational firms. Attempts to reverse this pattern are to some extent inhibited by difficulties of accumulating domestic capital and of interrupting existing patterns of ownership and development without losing the benefits of foreign investment. Moreover, the free trade agreement with the United States and Mexico has impeded the ability of Canadian governments to regulate or limit foreign investment by placing restrictions on their capacity to differentiate between foreign and domestic businesses in their regulation of economic activity. The NAFTA has also created an incentive for manufacturers located in Canada, both domestic and foreign controlled, to relocate in the United States and Mexico to lower costs of production.

§2. Governmental Structure

A. The Constitution[1]

7. Canadian constitutional principles are essentially derived from the United Kingdom. To a significant extent, therefore, they are either found in historical British texts or subsist merely in unwritten conventions. However, the British inheritance has been modified by Canadian constitutional convention, and certain important legislative texts of specific Canadian significance.

1. *See* generally P. Hogg, *Constitutional Law of Canada*, 4th edn. (Toronto, 1996).

8. The most important of these texts is the Constitution Act of 1867 which established the Canadian federation. This constitutional document, originally enacted by the Parliament of the United Kingdom, and known as the British North America Act, allocated powers to the federal and provincial governments, partly defined the rights of linguistic minorities, and identified certain major governmental institutions. In 1982, the Canadian Constitution was 'patriated' by legislation passed in the United Kingdom at the request of the Canadian Parliament and with the concurrence of all save one of the Canadian provinces. At the same time, provision was made for the subsequent amendment of the Constitution Act within Canada, and a Charter of Rights and Freedoms was entrenched in the Constitution.

9. Other important constitutional documents include legislation by which various territories were joined to the original federation, by which federal and provincial governments have organized elections and their respective public services, and by which protection is secured for civil and minority rights. Particularly significant in this latter respect is the Canadian Bill of Rights, adopted in 1960, by which the federal government undertook to limit its own legislative authority to the extent necessary to secure respect for certain fundamental libertarian principles.[1] However, like all other legislation – but unlike the new Charter[2] – the Canadian Bill of Rights is subject to amendment or repeal by Parliament.

1. Canadian Bill of Rights, S.C. 1960, c.44.
2. S.33 of the Charter provides for the suspension by legislative declaration of certain of its provisions for limited periods of up to five years.

B. Federalism

10. The Constitution Act, as amended and judicially interpreted, creates a federal state comprising ten provinces – Prince Edward Island, Newfoundland, Nova Scotia, New Brunswick, Quebec, Ontario, Manitoba, Saskatchewan, Alberta and British Columbia – and three territories in the northern part of Canada with limited local autonomy. The three territories are the Yukon, the Northwest Territories and Nunavut. Nunavut is the newest territory, created in 1999 from the eastern part of the Northwest Territories pursuant to a 1993 land claims settlement between the federal government and the Arctic Inuit as a method of fulfilling a long-held aspiration of the Inuit of the eastern and central Arctic to control their own destiny.

11. To the federal government is theoretically assigned the responsibility for 'peace, order and good government', as well as residual authority over all matters not falling within exclusive provincial competence, including national defence, interprovincial and international trade and communications, criminal law, fiscal matters and a comprehensive taxing power. However, provincial authority, nominally limited to 'matters of a purely local and private nature' and 'civil rights within the province', has been expanded through a process of judicial interpretation to embrace many of the concerns of modern social and economic legislation.[1]

1. *See infra*, ch. V, §1, for an analysis of constitutional jurisdiction over labour relations.

12. As a practical matter, there exists something of a constitutional stalemate between apparently broad federal powers, especially powers of taxation and spending, and provincial assertion of responsibility for costly programmes of social welfare and for regulation of economic activity (such as collective bargaining) which obviously affects the national economy. This stalemate has tended to be resolved through formally negotiated schemes of interprovincial cooperation and revenue sharing, or by informal understandings. The Supreme Court has, however, sustained the constitutional right of the federal government to respond to the 'emergency' of double-digit inflation, by establishing a system of wage and price controls, overriding normal collective bargaining procedures under provincial legislation.

13. But the major issue for Canadian federalism has been the emergence of strong regional pressures, and particularly of a genuine separatist movement in Quebec. These, in turn, have produced demands for formal redefinition, and perhaps even dissolution, of the Canadian federation.

In order to bring about the full and active participation of Quebec in Canada's constitutional evolution, the federal and ten provincial governments have attempted to negotiate a constitutional accord which provides for the recognition of Quebec as a 'distinct society' in Canada. The attempts have not been successful so far. However, it appears likely that any satisfactory constitutional accord would involve some devolution of existing federal powers to the provinces and a major reorganization of central institutions.

C. Formal Structure

1. The legislative power

14. The formal head of the federal government is the Governor-General (and of the provincial government, the Lieutenant Governor) representing the Queen of the United Kingdom, who is also the Queen of Canada. However, the real head of government is the federal Prime Minister (or the provincial Premier) who, in the parliamentary tradition, enjoys the support of a majority of members in the federal Parliament (or provincial legislatures).

15. The federal Parliament is bicameral. The lower house, the House of Commons, like the provincial legislatures (which are unicameral), is elected by universal suffrage, almost exclusively in single member constituencies. The upper house, the Senate, with limited powers, comprises members appointed by the federal government, on a basis which ensures regional representation. If significant constitutional reform concerning the powers of the federal and provincial governments takes place, it is likely that the composition and function of the senate will be radically transformed.

2. The executive

16. The Prime Minister (or provincial Premier) is by constitutional convention leader of the party with the most elected members. A cabinet is formed by the

Prime Minister from amongst the elected members of her/his own party, or any other party which formally agrees to participate in the government. Cabinet ministers are occasionally appointed from the non-elective Senate at the federal level, but are otherwise expected to seek and secure election as soon as possible after appointment. The maximum term of office for a government is five years, but the Prime Minister may seek earlier dissolution and a new electoral mandate; in fact the usual term of office is about four years. Most federal and provincial governments have enjoyed clear majorities, often successively renewed for extended periods of time. However, there have been a few instances of formal coalitions and, more recently, minority governments dependent upon the tacit and informal support of one or more rival parties.

17. The cabinet not only controls the legislative process, but it also directs the activities of the civil service. The civil service is, almost entirely, recruited to permanent government service up to and including the most senior administrative officials. Thus, the civil service is expected to survive intact any changes in government, although ministers have small personal staffs and may recruit key senior people into the civil service on a permanent or temporary basis, especially in policy-sensitive roles.

In theory, the civil service is responsive to policy laid down by the government in legislation or through cabinet orders. In practice, the civil service obviously has a great influence on both the formation and implementation of policy.

3. Administrative agencies

18. Much modern legislation is administered neither by the ministries of government, nor by the courts, but rather by specialized and expert administrative tribunals. These are, typically, established by statute and often operate (as for example in labour relations) with a high degree of autonomy from executive interference. By statute or practice, they are reasonably – not entirely – immune from changes in government although not, of course, from explicit changes in legislation.

19. The powers and prestige of such tribunals varies greatly. Some perform relatively low-level routine tasks; some are responsible for major sectors of public policy, including the elaboration of specific rules within very general lines laid down by legislation, and other tasks of investigation, adjudication and enforcement. Their pervasive presence can be attributed to a desire to secure expertise, informality and flexibility in the administration of modern social and economic legislation.

20. The right to seek judicial review is generally afforded to persons dissatisfied with the action of an administrative tribunal. Except where otherwise stipulated, this review usually does not involve an appeal on the merits, but rather is limited to questions of conformity to the mandate conferred upon the administrative agency by parliament, and adherence to fair procedures.[1]

1. There is a constitutionally guaranteed minimum of review of 'jurisdictional' issues.

4. The judiciary and legal system

21. Except for Quebec, the law in all Canadian jurisdictions is rooted in the traditions of the English common law, with an overlay of legislation passed by the competent authority, parliament or the provincial legislature. Quebec private law is based on French civil law notions, incorporated into the Quebec Civil Code; in other respects (particularly as regards commercial affairs and administrative law) Quebec law resembles that of the other jurisdictions.[1]

1. *See infra* ch. VI, §3, for an overview of the sources of Quebec private law relating to the employment relationship and, more generally, to labour relations.

22. Appeals from the courts of all jurisdictions, including Quebec, may ultimately be taken to the Supreme Court of Canada, which has a discretionary jurisdiction to entertain the appeal, or to leave unreviewed the decision of the province's highest court. Thus, the Supreme Court of Canada has the final word in all common or civil law controversies, in the interpretation of all federal and provincial statutes, and in the adjudication of constitutional disputes.

The federal government is authorized to make appointments to the Supreme Court of Canada. However, there has been pressure from the provinces to amend the Constitution Act so as to require the federal government to fill vacancies in the Supreme Court of Canada by selecting a name from a list submitted by the provinces.

23. Typically, the superior courts of the provinces are organized into trial and appellate divisions, all of whose judges are appointed by the federal government. In addition, there are minor and specialized courts in various provinces whose judges are provincial appointees, while a federal trial and appellate court (below the Supreme Court of Canada) has exclusive competence in certain specialized areas under federal jurisdiction, including the review of decisions of federal administrative tribunals.

24. There is a historic prejudice against the establishment of specialized courts, except in Quebec where a specialized court administers some parts of labour relations law. The role played by such courts in other countries is, in Canada, largely discharged by administrative tribunals.

§3. Informal Political Structures

25. Traditionally there have been three major political parties in Canada – Liberals, Conservatives and the labour-affiliated New Democratic Party (N.D.P.). Recently, however, there has been a rise in regional parties with a populist base on the federal scene. These are the Reform Party from the western provinces, which espouses a conservative populist agenda, and the Bloc Québécois, which is based in Quebec and supports separatism for that province.

The Liberal and Conservative parties dominated the federal parliamentary process from Confederation to the 1993 election. However, since the 1993 election one of the two largest regional parties, the Bloc Québécois and the Reform Party, has formed the official opposition, replacing the Conservatives who seem to have fallen out of favour federally despite forming many provincial governments during the 1990s. The N.D.P. has formed several provincial governments, as has the Social Credit (a minor conservative party), and various other regional parties. Principal amongst those is the Parti Québécois (P.Q.) – a social democratic party committed to the separation of Quebec from Canada – which assumed office in Quebec from 1976 to 1985 and regained power in Quebec in the 1990s.

The two traditionally strong national parties are essentially centrist. They draw upon regional, ethnic or religious blocs, to some extent, but seek to make broad, 'consensus' appeals to the entire electorate.

The N.D.P. (and, in Quebec, the P.Q.) differs slightly in espousing a social democratic philosophy. The N.D.P. enjoys formal affiliation with the labour movement (but does not receive the automatic allegiance of its members) while the P.Q. has the informal support of many Quebec unions. However, neither N.D.P. nor P.Q. governments have moved far from the general trend of Canadian private sector labour legislation, although introducing various legislative reforms and occasionally adopting somewhat more pro-labour positions in particular disputes.

Underlining, perhaps, the limited range of political attitudes towards labour relations is the fact that two of the most significant confrontations between governments on the one side and public and para-public workers on the other have occurred in British Columbia and Quebec. The right-wing Social Credit party formed the government of the former province and the social democratic P.Q. in the latter. The convergence of political views of the various parties in Canada was perhaps accentuated in the late 1990s when provincial governments of all stripes, Conservatives in Ontario, P.Q. in Quebec, and N.D.P. in Saskatchewan, had major confrontations with public sector workers concerning government policy to downsize and privatize in the interests of deficit reduction and tax cuts.

§4. Political Culture

26. Cutting across formal and traditional organizations and loyalties are important themes which dominate Canadian political life.

27. Nationalism and regionalism are both important factors in the Canadian political calculus. Nationalism, on the one hand, has sought to foster a Canadian identity, to resist or turn back foreign (United States) penetration of the Canadian economy and Canadian cultural life, and to rally all segments of the population around the theme of national unity. There has been a recent resurgence in Canadian cultural and economic nationalism in response to the federal government's free trade agreements with the United States and Mexico. The Canadian labour movement has been especially vocal in opposing closer economic ties with these two countries.

Fears about a race to the bottom in labour standards and social dumping were prevalent in the objections of labour in the U.S. and Canada to the NAFTA.[1] Those opposed to the agreement feared that low wages and inadequate protection of labour rights and standards in Mexico would create incentives for capital flight to Mexico resulting in loss of jobs in both northern countries and social dumping. Social dumping occurs where companies invest or threaten to invest where wages and conditions are cheapest due to inadequate protection of labour rights and standards, thereby forcing workers in countries with higher wages and standards to lower their standards and conditions of employment to remain competitive with the labour in the low standard country. While Mexican law provides for labour rights and standards comparable and in some cases superior to Canadian and U.S. labour law, recent studies have concluded that those standards lack effective enforcement in Mexico.[2] Hence the fears of social dumping and pressures for 'downward harmonization' of social policy and labour standards.

It was this type of concern that led Bill Clinton during the 1992 presidential election to promise that if elected he would insist on the negotiation of a side agreement to deal with labour's concerns before agreeing to implement the NAFTA. In September of 1993 the three countries signed the North American Agreement on Labor Cooperation (NAALC),[3] commonly known as the labour side accord. However, the NAALC was generally castigated by spokespersons for labour in both Canada and the U.S. as being quite inadequate to prevent a race to the bottom and social dumping. Several advocates of greater international protection of labour rights and standards have joined in those criticisms.[4] One has to look at both the substance and processes of the labour side accord to assess its capacity to preserve and promote labour rights and standards.

The main source of criticism of the NAALC is its failure to establish minimum labour standards or effective means for transnational enforcement of labour rights and standards. However, the side accord was not a surprise in this respect. Unlike the European Union and its constituting treaties, NAFTA is a free trade treaty and not a treaty of association.[5] As such, the three parties recognized that there might have to be some concessions to absolute sovereignty but were not prepared to accept the kind of threat to national sovereignty that would be represented by agreement to international standards to supersede domestic standards or the delegation of authority over labour issues to some form of international labour commission.[6] Instead the NAALC was designed to provide for a framework for cooperation, consultation and information sharing among the three parties. Rather than committing to maintain particular international standards each country simply promises to enforce its own domestic labour laws.[7] The oversight mechanisms which allow signatories to the accord to enforce this commitment against another signatory rely heavily on cooperation and consultation and are quite restrictive in terms of the type of violations of labour rights and standards which can actually lead to some form of adjudication and sanctions.

The accord does contain a statement of international labour rights but its effect would appear to be merely hortatory. Article 1 of the agreement notes that one of the objectives of the NAALC is to 'promote, to the maximum extent possible, the labor principles set out in Annex 1'.[8] There are eleven basic principles identified in Annex 1:

1. freedom of association and protection of the right to organize;
2. the right to bargain collectively;
3. the right to strike;
4. prohibition of forced labour;
5. labour protections for children and young persons;

6. minimum employment standards;
7. elimination of employment discrimination;
8. equal pay for women and men;
9. prevention of occupational injuries and illnesses;
10. compensation in cases of occupational injuries and illnesses;
11. protection of migrant workers.[9]

However, the accord states these principles as general aspirations and they are not enforceable obligations. The agreement does not require any party to pass new legislation to bring domestic policy into line with these principles, nor does it prohibit a signatory from changing its existing laws in a way which may depart from these principles.[10] The side accord states expressly that no country is required by the agreement to alter its labour standards in any way.[11]

Nevertheless some early assessments of the first five years of experience under the NAALC have concluded that the procedures for complaint and cooperation under the agreement hold potential for the protection of labour standards through increased public awareness concerning the labour standards practices of corporations and countries operating under the agreement.[12]

1. North American Free Trade Agreement (NAFTA), 17 December 1992, 32 I.L.M. 289, 309.
2. Adams and Singh, 'Early Experience with NAFTA's Labour Side Accord' (1997) 18 *Comp. Lab. L. J.* 161: La Botz, *Mask of Democracy: Labor Suppression in Mexico Today* (1992); Bierman and Gely, 'The Labor Side Agreement: The North American Agreement on Labor Cooperation: a New Frontier in North American Labor Relations' (1995) 10 *Conn. J. Int'l L.* 533, at 541–9.
3. North American Agreement on Labor Cooperation (NAALC), 13 September 1993, Can.–Mex–U.S., 32 I.L.M. 1499 (1993) (hereinafter NAALC).
4. Adams and Singh, *op. cit.*, at 162–3; and Robinson, 'The NAFTA Labour Accord in Canada: Experience, Prospects, and Alternatives' (1995) 10 *Conn. J. Int'l. L.* 475.
5. Bierman and Gely, *op. cit.*, at 535.
6. McKenniry, 'Labor in the International Economy' (1996) 22 *Can–U.S. L. J.* 183, at 188; Trudeau, 'Les modes de régulation internationale du travail et de l'emploi' in *L'Intégration économique en Amérique du Nord et les relations industrielles*, Blouin and Giles (ed.), (Québec: Les Presses de l'Université Laval, 1998) 201, at 215–25.
7. NAFTA, *op. cit.*, at preamble and Art. 3. Each party agrees to 'promote compliance with and effectively enforce its labor law through appropriate government action'. In addition each country is required to ensure that 'due consideration' is given to request for an investigation of an alleged violation of that country's labour laws. Article 4 also requires that appropriate access to administrative, quasi-judicial or labour tribunals is ensured to persons with a legally recognized interest under the country's law. See Bierman and Gely, *op. cit.*, at 537; Moreau and Trudeau, 'La clause sociale dans l'Accord de libre-échange nord-américain' (1995) *Revue internationale de Droit Économique* 393; Verge, 'Les dilemmes de l'ANACT: ambiguïté ou complémentarité?' (1999) *Rel. Ind.* 223.
8. *Ibid.*, Art. 1(b), at 1503.
9. NAALC, *op. cit.*, Annex 1, at 1515–16.
10. Adams and Singh, *op. cit.*, at 165. Adams and Singh suggest that these principles should be viewed as voluntary standards which each country should promote in accordance with their own laws, customs and history, similar to the treatment of the standards of the International Labour Organization.
11. NAALC, *op. cit.*, Art. 2, at 1503.
12. Compa, 'NAFTA's Labour Side Agreement Five Years On: Progress and Prospects for the NAALC' (1999) 7 C.L.E.L.J. 1: Adams, 'Using the North American Agreement on Labour Cooperation to Achieve Industrial Relations Reform' (1999) 7 C.L.E.L.J. 31.

28. Regionalism, historically strong but quiescent in the post-war period, has recently revived. For the western and Atlantic regions, the concern is essentially to obtain a 'fair share' of the benefits of a national economy, which is perceived to be dominated by the central provinces of Ontario and Quebec. For Quebec, in turn, regionalism fuelled by similar concerns is compounded by a desire for autonomy based on the distinctive French language, history, culture and ethnic roots of the majority (80 per cent) of its population. But even within the regions, within the individual provinces, there exist tensions between the centre and the periphery. Both nationalism and regionalism influence government policies, business decisions and patterns of union organization.

29. To some extent associated with the theme of regionalism is that of populism, which tends to manifest itself in a dislike of elites, experts and bureaucracies – which, in turn, are also perceived to reside at the centre rather than the periphery. Populism, of both the left and right, has had some influence on political developments in the western provinces and Quebec and is increasingly likely to exert a greater influence on the national government.

30. The debate over public versus private control of the economy has become increasingly polarized, at least at the rhetorical level, amongst political parties, as well as between business and labour organizations. While it has long been accepted in practice that Canada is a mixed economy, several political parties, supported by business interests, have called for a reduction in government regulation and ownership of industry. Once elected, these parties have begun a programme of privatizing crown (government-owned) corporations and deregulation.

31. In the post-war period, the three major political crises of direct relevance to the conduct of labour relations involved government attempts to limit spending as part of an anti-inflationary strategy. In October 1975, the federal government enacted pervasive anti-inflation legislation which had the effect of limiting maximum salary increases which could be gained through collective bargaining. This measure, which applied to both public and private employment, provoked an unprecedented and only modestly successful 'National Day of Protest', a one-day work stoppage called by the labour movement. The termination of the anti-inflation programme in 1978 seemed to signal a restoration of the relative consensus amongst the political parties on labour relations issues. However, a second round of anti-inflationary initiatives, directed against public expenditure and affecting workers in public and para-public employment, precipitated a further crisis in 1982 and 1983. In both British Columbia and Quebec, widespread, and often illegal, strikes protesting against these initiatives resulted in a direct confrontation between the labour movements of the two provinces and the governments responsible. In each case, draconian proposals were somewhat modified, but the government's objectives were largely attained, while those of the labour movement were not. At the federal level, and in other provinces, unions appeared to have reluctantly acquiesced in slightly less extreme schemes of financial restraint. This acquiescence, in the end in all provinces, resulted from the combined interaction of an acceptance of labour's weakness in the face of considerable unemployment, a fear of legal sanctions and increasingly hostile public opinion. In the 1990s there have been several repetitions of these types of confrontation between governments and unions in the public and quasi-public sectors, particularly in the Ontario, Quebec and federal jurisdictions. Unfortunately for labour, they have had similar results to earlier confrontations. Ontario was a major battleground with social contract legislation which placed severe limitations on collective bargaining in the public and quasi-public sectors during the early 1990s. This was followed by province-wide strikes among public servants and teachers in the mid-1990s resulting from the clash between unions and a Conservative government intent on cutting public spending and privatizing the delivery of many services. There were similar struggles in Quebec and Saskatchewan between nurses and governments in the late 1990s.

It is unclear whether these major intrusions by government into the realm of collective bargaining in pursuit of macroeconomic objectives are to be viewed as isolated phenomena or as signals of an impending radical revision of the assumptions upon which labour law rests. In the 1980s changes to labour relations legislation in British Columbia[1] and Saskatchewan[2] suggested a shift away from enhancing trade union power towards enhancing the promotion of business flexibility. In the early 1990s there was a brief interruption in this trend with the election of N.D.P. governments in Ontario, Saskatchewan and British Columbia. However, at the end of the millennium the legislative pendulum appears to be swinging back in favour of the prominence of business interests with the election of a very pro-business Conservative government in Ontario, which made labour reform to promote the interest of business its first legislative priority,[3] and the election of Conservative governments in Nova Scotia and New Brunswick in 1999.

1. Industrial Relations Act, R.S.B.C. 1979, c.212, as amended by S.B.C. 1987, c.24 (repealed in 1992 by N.D.P. government and replaced by what is now the Labour Relations Code, R.S.B.C. 1996, c.244. and the Employment Standards Act, R.S.B.C. 1996, c.113).
2. The Trade Union Act, R.S.S. 1978, c.T-17, as amended by S.S. 1983, c.81.
3. Labour Relations Act, 1995, S.O. 1995, c.1.

32. Finally, as in most developed countries, political debate has increasingly focused in Canada on how to compete with Third World countries while still retaining the standard of living to which Canadians have become accustomed. The increasing globalization of the economy has led to a restructuring of the Canadian economy and a polarization of the labour market. The Economic Council of Canada has called this latter phenomenon 'good jobs, bad jobs'. Non-standard work (casual, part-time and own-account self-employment) is proliferating at the expense of standard (full-time, full-year) work, which is resulting in a related decline in middle-level income earners.[2] Women and young workers tend to dominate these 'bad jobs'.

1. Economic Council of Canada, *Good Jobs, Bad Jobs* (Ottawa: Ministry of Supply and Services, 1990).
2. *Collective Reflection on the Changing Workplace: Report of the Advisory Committee on the Changing Workplace* (Ottawa: Public Works and Government Services Canada, 1997).

§5. The People of Canada

A. Generally

33. The outstanding characteristic of Canada, a new country, is its ethnic diversity. The francophone population, largely derived from the original French colonial settlement, comprises about 24 per cent of the population and is located almost entirely in Quebec or on its boundaries in adjacent provinces. Relatively small and isolated francophone communities exist elsewhere across the country.

34. In the balance of the population United Kingdom ancestries predominate, but 'other' ethnic elements exist in very great and ever increasing numbers. The latter originally settled in the western agricultural communities, but since World War I have tended to concentrate in the largest urban centres. Large Mediterranean and central European immigrant groups have been complemented by recent arrivals from the Caribbean, the Indian subcontinent, and south–east Asia. All of these groups have been encouraged to maintain their cultural integrity through newspapers, and cultural and social organizations.

35. Relatively small, but recently resurgent, communities of aboriginal peoples are scattered across the country and exist in some concentration in the three northern territories.

B. The Workforce

36. There is much discussion in Canada today of a shortage in the skills necessary for a high value-added manufacturing based economy. The general educational system has come under increasing criticism for failing to provide both the skills and general literacy level needed for Canada to compete in a global market. Traditionally, it is immigrants who have made up deficiencies in both the skilled, and especially the unskilled, labour force. However, recently immigration has been increasingly subject to attack.

37. Since the beginning of the 1980s Canada has experienced an official unemployment rate of over 8 per cent, with rates of approximately 10–12 per cent during the recessions of the early 1980s and 1990s. This situation is, in part, attributable to the fact that the federal government has eschewed any remnants of a full employment policy. The problem is endemically severe in the depressed Atlantic provinces, in Quebec, and amongst young people. There are also suggestions that rates have moved down to the 8 per cent range in the late 1990s due more to great increases in the numbers of 'own account self-employed' and part-time employment rather than any significant growth in permanent full-time employment. By 1993 almost one in four jobs (23 per cent) was a part-time job and by 1994 17 per cent of workers in Canada worked part-time.[1] A 1998 study done for the federal department of Human Resources Development showed that by 1997 10 per cent of all employment was comprised by 1.5 million own-account self-employed persons, those who are self-employed but do not employ other persons. Between 1976 and 1995 self-employment almost doubled while total employment grew by less than 40 per cent during that time period.[2] This increase in self-employment is also consistent with a growing trend among large manufacturers and service providers towards the vertical disintegration of production processes. Vertical disintegration means that some aspects of production and labour needs are provided by subcontracting, franchising and outsourcing, which provides large firms with more flexibility in providing for their labour needs and enables them to make production processes more efficient.[3] Nevertheless, there is great potential for this shift to own-account self-employment, usually out of necessity on the worker's part, to mask the real unemployment rate at any given point in time.

1. *Report of the Advisory Group on Working Time and the Distribution of Work* (Ottawa: Human Resources Development Canada, 1994), at 31.
2. Evaluation and Data Development, Strategic Policy Branch, *Own-Account Self-Employment in Canada: Lessons Learned, Final Report* (Ottawa: Human Resources Development Canada, February 1998).
3. See Collins, 'Independent Contractors and the Challenge of Vertical Disintegration to Employment Protection Laws' (1990) 10 *Oxford J. of Leg. Studies* 353 for a description of similar developments in the British context.

38. While there is free movement of labour amongst the provinces, and indeed considerable internal migration, there has never been a coherent national human resources policy embracing both immigration and the internal redeployment of labour. Amongst the obstacles to such a policy are the constitutional and political limits of federal power, linguistic and social barriers to movement, and the cost of movement attributable to distance. What have emerged, instead, are various schemes for regional development designed to provide employment in areas of economic depression. These too have foundered to some extent because of disparities of natural endowment, distances from markets, problems of capital accumulation and the existence of established patterns of trading and production across the country.

The Charter of Rights and Freedoms adopted in 1982 purports to guarantee 'mobility rights', to entrench language and minority education rights at a provincial level to a limited extent, and to enshrine in principle a commitment to the reduction of regional economic differences and differences in essential public services. It remains to be seen whether any of these new constitutional commitments will, in the long run, have an impact upon national human resources policy.

39. In common with most industrialized countries, Canada has experienced a considerable reallocation of jobs within the employed labour force. The percentage of workers employed in service industries has expanded greatly, from 34.2 per cent in 1981 to 71 per cent in 1989. Whereas one in three Canadian workers worked in the manufacturing sector in the 1950s, by 1994 that figure had declined to one in six workers, largely due to increases in technology that enable fewer workers to produce much more than in the past.[1]

1. *Report of the Advisory Group on Working Time and the Distribution of Work* (Ottawa: Human Resources Development Canada, 1994), at 2.

C. Income Distribution

40. Canada is one of the world's richest countries. However, while spared the most extreme disparities of wealth and poverty, it can hardly be said that Canada is an egalitarian society. Moreover, since the 1980s, polarization and inequality have increased.

Apart from the effects of progressive taxation (at a maximum marginal rate of about 50 per cent) and of transfer payments through the social welfare system, there exists no programme of income equalization or of guaranteed minimum incomes.

41. Despite some fluctuations, ironically most favourable during the period of anti-inflation controls, the percentage of the gross national product attributable to the labour sector has grown relatively slowly (46.1 per cent in 1939, to 48.7 per cent in 1955 to 58.3 per cent in 1983). Within the labour sector there has probably been some relative improvement in the position of workers in service occupations, especially in the public sector, in recent years. However, a combination of inflation, unemployment and government restraint policies led to a decline in workers' real incomes during the early 1980s. This decline has continued throughout the 1980s and in to the 1990s as both private sector and government employers have adopted a policy of concession bargaining to meet both the competition from the Third World and reduce government deficits.

42. In heavily unionized sectors, gains secured through collective bargaining have tended to be adopted by non-union firms seeking to avoid unionization. It is therefore difficult to assess the extent to which unionized workers enjoy any advantage in relation to wages and working conditions. This difficulty is compounded by the highly decentralized and diversified pattern of collective negotiations in Canada in most industries.

D. Union Membership

43. Union membership in Canada grew significantly from 1940 to 1980, after a low point in the depression years of the 1930s, as a result of rapid advances in the private sector during the war years and the immediate post-war period and a surge of public sector organization in the late 1960s and early 1970s. In the 1980s, for a while, increases in union membership in the public sector offset losses in manufacturing due to extensive redundancies. However, government policies, including hiring freezes and privatization, have led to stagnation in public sector union membership. The profound increase in employment in the hard-to-organize service sector and the continuing decline in employment in the manufacturing sector has resulted in a slow decline in union membership in Canada (as a per cent of non-agricultural workers) from almost 40.0 per cent in 1983 to 32.5 per cent in 1998 (or 25.6 per cent of the total workforce at the beginning of 1998). The total union membership of 3,938,000 in 1998 was the lowest level in ten years. The largest decline has been from 1992 to 1998, a decline of 151,000 members.[1]

1. Workplace Information Directorate, *Directory of Labour Organizations in Canada 1998* (Ottawa: Human Resources Development Canada, 1998) at 7.

44. Concentrations of union membership are found in particular industries, such as mining, construction, petrochemical, transport and communications, steel and manufacturing (especially in larger establishments). The fast-growing 'white collar' service sector of the labour market, however, has been traditionally difficult for unions to penetrate. Their only substantial successes in this field have been amongst government employees who were only permitted to be unionized in the late 1960s. As compared with the private sector, unionization is high in the public sector. Nevertheless, during the period of decline in union membership from 1992 to 1998 the major public sector unions have experienced a disproportionate share of the decline, due primarily to trend towards downsizing and privatization among Canadian governments in the 1990s.

III. General Notions and Special Definitions

§1. 'Labour Law' Defined

45. Canadian labour law, as is characteristic of most aspects of law in systems derived from the common law, lacks precise definition of either its general boundaries or its specific concepts and institutions. However, most lawyers, legal academics and lay practitioners who use the term 'labour law' refer to the system of rules governing collective relations amongst management, trade unions, their members and the institutions involved in such relations.

46. This emphasis upon collective relations is significant in view of the fact that most Canadian workers are employed under a regime of individual contracts, rather than collectively bargained terms. It suggests, first, that legal and other professionals have been preoccupied with the collective, largely to the exclusion of the individual. Perhaps the explanation for this lies in the relative financial attractions of professional work in relation to group interests. Second, it suggests that there is an affinity between the collective and 'law' which, impliedly, does not exist between the individual and 'law'. This affinity approximately reflects reality: although most ordinary workers may have enjoyed contractual rights in theory, in practice they secured effective legal protection only with the advent of the collective regime. Third, to the extent that 'law' represents a social good, an aspiration for which to strive, it would seem that the collective is regarded as normatively preferable to the individual.

47. At the same time, the reluctance – now, perhaps, changing – to address the legal position of individual workers has led to the relative underdevelopment of legal scholarship and representational skills and resources in matters which are vitally important to the majority of Canadians who are not union members. In their relations with their employers, individual workers are governed by the rules of contract, sometimes embraced by the term 'employment law'. But their employers are, in turn, bound by statutes and regulations relating to minimum wages, benefits and working conditions, occupational health and safety standards, prohibitions against discrimination and, increasingly by pay and employment equity legislation which is designed to redress systemic discrimination. These rules, emanating from government, are sometimes generically grouped as 'employment standards legislation'. And, providing protection both for workers and others who encounter financial disaster, there is a system of 'social security legislation' embracing pensions, unemployment insurance, public health care and other welfare payments.

There is no logical reason why 'labour law' should not embrace employment law, labour standards legislation and social security, as well as the law of collective relationships – especially because of the interaction and overlap amongst these systems. But relatively little progress has been made in their functional and conceptual integration. This monograph, while focusing upon collective 'labour law' will also deal extensively with individual 'employment law' and, to a lesser extent, with labour standards legislation: 'social security' will be dealt with only peripherally.

48. Finally, although labour policies in the public sector have come, in recent years, increasingly to resemble those in the private sector, typically they do not provide the same degree of access to economic sanctions as characterizes the private sector labour policies. Public sector policies will not be dealt with in this work and no attempt will be made to explore either the special public sector adaptations of general private sector policies, or the influence of public sector models upon the private sector.

§2. General Notions of Collective Labour Law

49. Canadian labour law, in the collective sphere, draws heavily upon that of the United States, but is characterized by indigenous institutions, preoccupations and practices. As in the United States workers enjoy a statutorily protected right to organize for collective bargaining. Their bargaining representative, selected by a majority of the workers in an appropriate bargaining constituency, may require the employer to bargain in good faith, with a view to concluding a collective agreement binding on all employees. And if no agreement is negotiated, the employees may have recourse to a strike, or the employer to a lockout, as a bargaining sanction.

50. Two distinctively Canadian features of collective labour law are both concerned with reducing industrial conflict. No strikes are permitted while a collective agreement is in effect (arbitration being required instead) or, after the expiry of the agreement, until extensive peacekeeping procedures have been exhausted.

51. The primary feature of English common law which has survived in the collective sphere is the use of ordinary private law principles to regulate industrial conflict. These principles (tort and contract) have been modified (to a certain extent) by specially designed legislative rules. English common law principles also dominate the field of individual 'employment law'. In both cases, integration between the common law and the modern collective labour legislation has been difficult to accomplish. In Quebec, integration of the Civil Code (Quebec's equivalent to the common law of other Canadian provinces) and statutory regimes offers similar problems.

§3. Definitions

I. General

52. The following terms are widely used in discussions of labour law in Canada. However, they are not terms of art which have precise definitions, except to the extent that particular statutes in which they appear lay down such definitions. And even such statutory definitions generally have an overlay of judicial or administrative interpretation.

2. *Arbitration*

53. Arbitration is a process of independent, third party adjudication. The 'third party' may be a single neutral individual selected by agreement of the parties (or in default of such agreement, by a government agency) or a tripartite body similarly selected, but comprising, as well as the neutral, equal numbers of partisan nominees. 'Rights arbitration' (or 'grievance arbitration') refers to the adjudication of disputes relating to alleged violations of a collective agreement. It is the most widespread method of deciding such disputes, and is the sole method legislatively prescribed in most jurisdictions. In some jurisdictions grievance arbitrators have also been given the jurisdiction to resolve employment law disputes arising under other employment law statutes. 'Interest arbitration' refers to the adjudication of terms of a collective agreement when the parties are unable to agree upon its (re)negotiation. Interest arbitration is legislatively compelled in a few key industries and occupations, but the parties seldom voluntarily opt for interest arbitration or abandonment of the right to strike or lockout which otherwise resolves such disputes.

3. *Bargaining units*

54. The concept of bargaining unit is central to Canadian labour relations, for it performs two key functions. The bargaining unit is the constituency, defined by the labour relations board or agreed upon by the parties, within which the union must demonstrate majority support in order to be certified as the exclusive bargaining agent for all present and future employees within its boundaries. It may embrace workers sharing a single craft (a 'craft unit') or those whose common denominator is participation in a particular operation, plant or industry (an 'industrial unit'). In some industries, bargaining is conducted in 'multi-employer' or 'industry-wide' units. In each case, the bargaining unit must be 'appropriate for collective bargaining', i.e. the workers must have a common interest in the outcome of negotiations. Typically, however, bargaining units are defined on the basis of a single employer at a single location.

Once certified, the design of the bargaining unit influences the conduct of collective bargaining. Perhaps most importantly, the determination of the appropriate unit affects the degree of economic pressure which the parties may bring to bear against each other. In the vast majority of circumstances, economic action is limited to the bargaining unit.

4. *Boycott*

55. A boycott is the abstention from dealing with an employer, or from handling goods destined for or produced by him, in aid of collective bargaining (or other) demands by those organizing the boycott.

5. Certification

56. Certification is the process by which the labour relations tribunal determines that a trade union is entitled to act as the exclusive bargaining agent of employees in a bargaining unit. Entitlement normally depends upon majority support, as demonstrated by either a secret ballot vote in favour of, or membership in, the trade union. Occasionally, absent such majority support, a union may nonetheless be certified if the employer has improperly interfered in its attempts to organize in such a manner as to render it unlikely that a secret vote or other measures of support will reflect the true wishes of the affected employees.

6. Collective agreement

57. A collective agreement is a document recording the terms and conditions of employment and the rights and duties of the employer, trade union and employees in a bargaining unit. In almost all Canadian jurisdictions, it is legally enforceable only through arbitration procedures initiated by the employer or the trade union, and is deemed to contain certain statutory provisions – a minimum term of one year, the prohibition of strikes and lockouts during that term, and a requirement for the submission to arbitration of all disputes concerning its interpretation or alleged violation.

7. Collective bargaining

58. Collective bargaining is the process whereby an employer and a trade union seek to negotiate a collective agreement. In almost all jurisdictions, this process must be undertaken 'in good faith' and requires 'every reasonable effort to make a collective agreement'.

8. Conciliation

59. Conciliation is a process of non-coercive, third party intervention designed to assist parties in resolving differences. In the majority of Canadian jurisdictions, conciliation must be attempted before the parties are legally free to break off negotiations, or to have recourse to economic sanctions. Historically, conciliation was undertaken by *ad hoc* tripartite boards whose findings were made public. Today, this process has largely been replaced by one employing professional mediators who work with the parties on an informal, confidential basis, and seldom make normative reports.

9. Employee/employer

60. The relationship of employer and employee subsists when one of several different tests (laid down by a legislature, court or labour relations board) are met:

(a) the employer has the right to direct the manner of execution of work of the employee, or (b) the employee is a member of the employer's enterprise or organization, or (c) the various incidents of their relationship place the employee in a position of economic dependence upon the employer, such that he could profit from participation in collective bargaining. In some Canadian jurisdictions, this latter category is legislatively enlarged by the inclusion of 'dependent contractors' who have some of the characteristics of independent entrepreneurs, but who ultimately exhibit the requisite degree of economic dependence. Only 'employees' have the right to engage in collective bargaining under most labour legislation, and only 'employees' can claim the benefit of most protective labour legislation.

10. Employers' associations

61. An employers' association is an organization of employers formed for the purposes of collective bargaining with trade unions. In some Canadian provinces, such associations may be 'accredited', a process analogous to 'certification' for trade unions, and thus gain certain legal rights to speak authoritatively for their members.

11. Labour relations tribunal

62. Labour relations tribunals (which are called labour boards in most jurisdictions) are administrative agencies, established by statute, to regulate the relationship between employers and trade unions. In most jurisdictions, the membership of the labour relations board is tripartite, embracing labour, management and neutral members. Either by statute or tradition, members enjoy some security of tenure, and independence of decision. While their precise jurisdictions vary, all have the power to determine disputes relating to union certification and to remedy unfair labour practices, some also have the power to deal with violations of collective agreements and to curb illegal strikes, lockouts and picketing. Orders of a labour relations board are enforceable in the regular courts as orders of those courts. They are also, typically, subject to limited judicial review by the courts.

12. Lockout

63. A 'lockout' is generally defined as a temporary economic sanction imposed by an employer, the notional analogue to a strike, in order to pressure a trade union to accede to his collective bargaining demands. In Ontario, however, it also includes a refusal by an employer to continue to employ employees, in order to interfere with their right to engage in trade union activities.

13. Management

64. 'Management' embraces those individuals in a firm who have effective direction of the work of other employees. Members of management are precluded from participating in the organization of trade unions by other employees, and except in a few jurisdictions, may not themselves form trade unions.

14. Mediation

65. 'Mediation' and 'conciliation' are often used interchangeably, although in some jurisdictions they denote slightly different methods of intervention to promote dispute settlement.

15. Picketing

66. Picketing is a tactic for pressuring an employer involved in a labour dispute. It customarily advertises the existence of a dispute by means of the attendance of workers carrying signs or distributing leaflets. Picketing may be intended as an appeal to the public for support, to employees to maintain their solidarity, or to other workers to decline employment or to refuse to enter the employer's premises.

16. Strike

67. A strike is the concerted cessation of work by employees. By statutory extension, the term may also include various forms of partial cessation, including a slowdown.

17. Trade union

68. A trade union is an organization of employees formed for purposes that include the regulation of relations between employers and employees.

18. Unfair labour practices

69. Unfair labour practices are illegal tactics by an employer or a trade union which interfere with the right of employees to organize in the trade union of their own choice, to enjoy representation by that trade union for collective bargaining purposes, or otherwise involve violation of the prohibitions of the Labour Relations Act.

19. Union security

70. Union security provisions in a collective agreement are intended to protect the union's institutional arrangements. Minimal arrangements may provide for a 'voluntary dues checkoff', a commitment by the employer to deduct from the pay of each consenting employee, and remit to the union, union dues. The 'Rand formula', or 'agency shop', requires the employer to deduct dues, or a sum in lieu thereof, from the pay of all employees in the bargaining unit – whether union members or not – in recognition of the union's obligation to bargain for all. Other arrangements may require union membership as a condition of continuing employment ('union shop') or of initially securing employment ('closed shop').

20. Voluntary recognition

71. Except in Quebec, a union may gain the right to act as an exclusive bargaining agent other than by certification, if the employer voluntarily agrees to recognize its status.

§4. Explanation of References

72. Each Canadian province, as well as the national government, has enacted a general statute regulating private sector labour relations. These are variously entitled 'Labour Relations Acts', 'Labour Codes' or 'Trade Union Acts', and are referred to in footnotes by the name of the jurisdiction only, e.g. 'Manitoba, s.72'. The following is a complete list of these statutes. (In each case, reference is made to the latest comprehensive enactment, or to its most recent decennial consolidation. Reference to subsequent amendments is provided in footnotes to the text, where appropriate.)

Canada Labour Code, R.S.C. 1985, c.L-2, as am. R.S.C. 1985 (1st Supp.) C.9., R.S.C. (2nd Supp.) c.32, R.S.C. (3rd Supp.) c.24, c.43; R.S.C. (4th Supp.) c.26.
Alberta Labour Relations Act, R.S.A. 1980, c.L-1.2.
British Columbia Labour Relations Code, R.S.B.C. 1996, c.244.
Manitoba Labour Relations Act, C.C.S.M. 1987, c.L10.
New Brunswick Industrial Relations Act, R.S.N.B. 1973, c.I-4, as am. By N.B.A. 1994, c.42, N.B.A. 1996, c.5, N.B.A. 1997, c.6.
Newfoundland Labour Relations Act, R.S.N. 1990, c.L-1, as am. By S.N. 1991, c.21, c.47, S.N. 1993, c.58, S.N. 1997, c.14, c.44.
Nova Scotia Trade Union Act, R.N.S. 1989, c.475, as am. By S.N.S. 1994, c.35.
Ontario Labour Relations Act, 1995, S.O. 1995, c.1, as am. By S.O. 1997, c.4, c.31, S.O. 1998, c.8.
Prince Edward Island Labour Act, R.S.P.E.I. 1988, c.L-1, as am. By S.P.E.I. 1990, c.27, S.P.E.I. 1991, c.19, S.P.E.I. 1994, c.32.
Quebec Labour Code, R.S.Q., c.C-27.
Saskatchewan Trade Union Act, R.S.S. 1978, c.T-17, as am. By S.S. 1994, c.47.

All other statutes are referred to by title, year of latest consolidation, revision or relevant amendment, and chapter number, e.g. Rights of Labour Act, R[evised] S[tatutes] of O[ntario] 1990, c.R-33.

References to cases in footnotes are to the following series of reports:

D.L.R.	Dominion Law Reports
O.R.	Ontario Reports
S.C.R.	Supreme Court Reports
C.L.R.B.R.	Canada Labour Relations Board Reports
C.L.L.C.	Canadian Labour Law Cases
O.L.R.B.	Ontario Labour Relations Board Reports
L.A.C.	Labour Arbitration Cases
R.J.Q.	*Recueils de jurisprudence du Québec*
T.A.	*Tribunal d'arbitrage*
T.T.	*Tribunal du travail*
C.S.	*Cour supérieure*
C.A.	Cour d'Appel
B.R.	Banc de la Reine
D.T.E.	Droit du travail Express
R.J.D.T.	*Recueil de jurisprudence en droit du travail*

IV. The Canadian Labour Movement

73. The beginnings of the Canadian labour movement antedate the establishment of the Canadian Confederation in 1867. As early as 1794 employees of the North West Fur Trading Company went on strike for higher wages. However, only with the introduction of industry at the beginning of the nineteenth century was a true labour movement begun. Journeymen and craftsmen in the few urban areas, particularly in the building, printing, clothing and shoe trades, began to organize for the purpose of mutual aid and protection and to achieve by united action such objectives as the ten-hour day, higher wages and better working conditions. In 1830, for example, the journeymen shoemakers in Toronto went on strike against 'scanty wages . . . beds of straw . . . and tyrannical oppression'. The union movement grew slowly before 1840 owing to depression and labour surpluses but gained momentum in the years prior to confederation, a period which was further characterized by the affiliation of Canadian unions with their British and American counterparts. This growth brought unionism into collision with the law.

74. Union organizers were subject to prosecution for the common law crime of conspiracy. The freedom of workers to associate and to alter conditions of work was restricted by legislation modelled upon the English Combinations Act of 1800, such as the Nova Scotia statute of 1816, which prohibited unlawful meetings and combinations for the purpose of regulating wages. Union organizational activities were interdicted as well. In the old Province of Canada, the Master and Servant Act declared the persuasion of labourers 'to confederate for demanding extravagant or high wages' to be unlawful. The common law prohibition against restraint of the course of free trade also affected the civil status of unions. As a result of common law prohibitions, the trade unions were unable to use the courts to enforce any contractual rights they might have achieved, or to protect their property.

75. In the years following confederation, labour began to develop a new assertiveness and unity. Local labour councils sprang up in the cities and in 1873, representatives of 35 unions formed the first central labour council, the Canadian Labour Union. The C.L.U. resolved to promote union membership, to bring unorganized workers into the C.L.U., and to provide financial assistance to striking unions. Realizing that efforts in these directions would be in vain in view of the existing state of the law, it resolved further to:

> '... agitate such questions as may be for the benefit of the working classes, in order that we may obtain the enactment of such measures by the Dominion or

local legislatures as will be beneficial to us, and win the repeal of all oppressive laws now existing.' (Canadian Labour Union, *Proceedings*, September 1873)

This organization petered out in 1877, but it must be credited with arousing in government an awareness of the grievances and aspirations of this segment of the electorate.

76. In the 1870s the federal government intervened to limit the availability of criminal sanctions to inhibit trade unionism. In part, this reflected the evolution of English law, in part, local political realities. Popular working class support for the nine-hour day movement in 1872, and public reaction against the arrest of the strike committee of the Toronto Typographical Union on conspiracy charges, moved Parliament to enact legislative reforms. Trade unions were encouraged to register under a new Trade Unions Act, and thereby to escape the taint of illegality which the common law had assigned them as 'conspiracies in restraint of trade'.[1] The Criminal Law Amendment Act of the same year legalized all strikes except those in which the means employed were calculated to coerce the employer or to prevent him carrying on his business. However, these reforms were not nearly so far reaching in practice as they were held out to be. Whilst the legislation provided that the common law doctrines of criminal conspiracy and restraint of trade did not apply to registered trade unions, the vast majority of trade unions did not register under the federal legislation. Moreover, common law tort doctrines, initially developed in England, were available to restrain trade union activity where the criminal law no longer operated.

However, further amendments in 1875 and 1876 narrowed the definition of criminal conspiracy for the purposes of trade combinations to the performance of acts expressly punishable by law. In 1890, the refusal to work with a workman or for an employer was expressly legalized. By the end of the nineteenth century, the doctrine of criminal conspiracy had ceased to be of practical significance in relation to ordinary labour-management disputes,[2] although it has become, and remains, a central theme in relation to the regulation of business competition.[3]

1. Mark Chartrand, 'The First Canadian Trade Union Legislation: An Historical Perspective' (1984) 16 *Ottawa Law Review* 267; Eric Tucker, 'That Indefinite Area of Toleration': Criminal conspiracy and Trade Unions in Ontario, 1837–77' (1991) 27 *Labour/Le Travail* 15.
2. Now Criminal Code, R.S.C., 1985 c.C-46, ss.465–7.
3. The Competition Act, R.S.C. 1985, c.19 (2nd Supp.) s.19 outlaws conspiracies to suppress competition in the supply of goods and services. However, labour union activities are expressly protected. C. Backhouse, 'Labour Unions and Anti-Combines Policy' (1976) 14 *Osgoode Hall L.J.* 113.

77. Another significant development of the 1870s was the definition of the permissible limits of picketing, or 'watching and besetting' as it is called in the Criminal Code. From the outset, violent and coercive conduct was outlawed while the peaceful communication of appeals was permitted. However, when the Criminal Code of 1892 was enacted, the peaceful picketing proviso was omitted. Until it was restored in 1934,[1] the courts tended to deal severely with all forms of picketing, no matter how innocuous.

1. Now Criminal Code, s.264(2)(c) and 423(1)(f), (2), R.S.C. 1985, c.C-46, as amended.

78. If the 1870s were a period of legal reform and symbolic advance for the cause of trade unionism the next two decades were to represent a considerable setback. The 'long depression' (mid-1870s to mid-1890s), and the growth of manufacturing on an industrial scale, combined to create abysmal working conditions and nullify the bargaining power of the individual employee. By 1889, as the report of the Royal Commission on the Relations of Capital and Labour disclosed, employers deemed it their prerogative to discipline workers by administering beatings, by imprisonment and by fines; factories were often unsanitary; employees were required to sign agreements to work on religious holidays; the 60-hour week prevailed; and the penalty for joining a union was dismissal and blacklisting. These practices stimulated the growth of unionism in the worst years of the depression, and led to the establishment of the Trades and Labour Congress of Canada and the more militant Knights of Labour. By the end of the century, then, it was becoming clear that the repeal of criminal prohibitions against unionism did not automatically place labour organizations on an equal footing with employers.

79. Unions grew as resource development and national transportation were emphasized as key elements in the emerging national economy. Several provincial governments enacted legislation authorizing third party intervention in order to resolve disputes in industries considered essential for the fragile provincial economies – typically, coal mines, railways and public utilities. These provincial experiments in third party arbitration and conciliation were modelled on legislation enacted in other Commonwealth jurisdictions, and proved to be unsuitable for resolving industrial disputes in Canada prior to the turn of the century. For example, much of this legislation became operative only with the consent of both parties – a condition which usually led the stronger party (typically the employer) to refuse consent.

80. Industrial disputes in the western provinces which threatened the federal government's policy of western settlement led to the enactment of three federal statutes – the Conciliation Act,[1] the Railway Labour Disputes Act,[2] and the Industrial Disputes Investigation Act,[3] 1907. The first authorized voluntary third party conciliation of industrial disputes, the second enabled one of the parties to initiate conciliation and investigation of the dispute by an *ad hoc* tripartite board which was required to issue a normative report, and the third, borrowing the main features of its immediate predecessor, added a prohibition against industrial action by the disputants during the *ad hoc* board's investigation. Like its provincial antecedents, the Industrial Disputes Investigation Act was directed to industries considered to be essential for the Canadian economy. However, unlike the provincial statutes the federal legislation introduced features of Canadian labour relations policy which continue to exist to date – in particular, the requirement that the parties refrain from using economic sanctions until the conciliation board has exhausted its investigation. Furthermore, this statute clearly signalled a conscious policy choice on the part of the federal government to avoid the use of compulsory and binding interest arbitration to settle labour disputes.

1. S.C. 1900, c.24.
2. S.C. 1903, c.55.
3. S.C. 1907, c.20.

81. Although weakened by constitutional attack,[1] the Industrial Disputes Investigation Act dominated Canadian labour relations policy until the end of the Second World War. In theory the legislation provided for the legitimacy of collective bargaining and the propriety of even-handed government intervention to assist in the establishment of a permanent, bilateral relationship. However, in practice, the Industrial Disputes Investigation Act neither forced employers to bargain with trade unions nor established the terms and conditions of employment. Under this legislation collective bargaining and its outcomes were viewed as essentially private matters between employers and employees.

1. In 1925, in *Toronto Electric Commissioners* v. *Snider*, [1925] A.C. 396, the Privy Council confined the operation of the Act to industries within the federal sphere. However, most provinces soon passed enabling statutes extending the reach of the statute.

82. During the first third of the twentieth century the Canadian economy described a cyclical pattern of growth and recession. The strength and size of the Canadian labour movement tended to ebb and flow with the economy. Moreover, the trade union movement was weakened by internal controversies over international versus national unionism, over the issue of social reform versus higher wages as prime union objectives, over organization of unskilled industrial workers versus organization of skilled craftsmen. Rival labour organizations were formed.[1]

Throughout this period Canada experienced a large increase in industrialization. Foreign investment attracted by extensive natural resources provided the capital required to stimulate economic growth while immigration opened up the west, swelled the unskilled labour force and created larger domestic markets for industry. Between 1901 and 1915 capital investment in Canadian manufacturing quadrupled and, as the capital requirements of industrial enterprises expanded, these enterprises became organized increasingly along corporate lines. In these same years, the number of workers employed in manufacturing rose from 340,000 to 600,000. Labour organization grew even more dramatically, especially during World War I, as union membership swelled from 50,000 in 1901 to 175,000 in 1915 to 250,000 in 1919.

1. *See* generally Abella, *Nationalism, Communism, and Canadian Labour* (Toronto, 1973).

83. The First World War proved to be extremely important for the Canadian trade union movement. Workers exploited their new-found strength (which was attributable to the brief period of full employment caused by the surge in war production) by engaging in industrial action. The number of workers involved in strikes grew from 43,000 in 1912 to 150,000 in 1919. When the war ended workers were determined to ensure that employers did not take advantage of the changed economic conditions to roll back their collective bargaining gains. This resulted in widespread confrontations between workers, employers and public authorities.

The postwar discontent and conflict is symbolized by the Winnipeg General Strike of 1919. The vast majority of the city's workers demanded union recognition, collective bargaining and the maintenance of working conditions obtained during the war. The entire city was brought to a virtual standstill until the federal government intervened to break the strike. Not only did the federal government use its immigration and criminal powers to deport and imprison strike leaders, it called in armed mounted police reinforced by federal troops.[1] In the end the strike was crushed, as was labour militancy across the country. Throughout the 1920s substantial segments of the industrial workforce remained unorganized and little improvement in working conditions was achieved. Working conditions deteriorated during the depression of the 1930s as the massive unemployment caused the power of the unions (together with their membership) to decline dramatically. Unprotected by collective organizations, the lives of individual workers and their families grew increasingly desperate.

1. David Bercusson, *Confrontation at Winnipeg* (Montreal, 1974).

84. Throughout these two decades, the federal legislation – the 1907 Industrial Disputes Investigation Act – had limited impact. The fundamental problem of industrial relations remained the gross disparity of bargaining power between employers and employed. Given this disparity, employers could ultimately afford to ignore conciliation efforts, to disregard concessions sought, and occasionally secured, by workers in favourable market conditions, and even to make it impossible for workers to bargain collectively. Workers who joined unions were threatened with discharge and then fired; they were easily replaced from the ranks of the unemployed. When unions were formed, employers simply refused to deal with them. And when strikes occurred, either to secure union recognition or for better conditions, employers were almost always able to replace the strikers and to outlast them in any endurance contest.

85. Increasingly, in the 1930s, industrial strife began to centre on the very basic issue of whether workers would be prevented from associating together for purposes of collective bargaining – not by legislation as in the early days, but by the harsh economic realities. As this issue was being thrashed out on picket lines and street corners throughout North America, unions and employers both began to resort increasingly to coercive and violent tactics. Added to the debilitating effects of the depression, this industrial warfare was doubly damaging.

86. In 1935 the US Congress passed the National Labour Relations Act (also called the 'Wagner Act' after its sponsor, Senator Wagner of New York) which exerted a profound, if somewhat delayed, influence on Canadian labour relations policy. This statute explicitly recognized the right of employees to belong to the trade union of their choice and to participate in the process of collective bargaining through that union. To make effective these rights, the statute forbade certain unfair labour practices commonly practised by employers to thwart unionization and imposed upon employers the duty to bargain in good faith with the union selected by their employees.

87. These elements of the Wagner Act did not come to Canada for almost a decade. In the interim, Canadian unionists continued to struggle against both intransigent governments and employers for the basic right of association and for the fruits which could be won through the practice of collective bargaining. Perhaps the most dramatic episode in this struggle came in 1937 when the Premier of Ontario threatened to use the provincial police to end a strike at the General Motors plant in Oshawa where the company refused to recognize the newly organized United Automobile Workers. This threat, in turn, precipitated both a cabinet crisis and considerable public protest. In the end, a facesaving compromise emerged in which the union gained some of its demands, but not formal recognition. The incident, however was regarded as a moral victory for industrial unionism and a spur to further organization.

88. From the mid-1930s onwards there was an attempt by the recently established industrial union movement to organize the semi-skilled workers employed in the new mass production industries on an industrial basis. Between 1935 and 1937 union membership increased from 280,000 to 383,000. Moreover, organized labour began to pressure both the federal and provincial governments for legislative protection of the freedom of association. Between 1937 and 1939 a number of provinces enacted statutes which announced the basic right of association and attempted to protect employees from employer retaliation on the basis of trade union membership. In 1939 the federal government followed suit by amending the Criminal Code to prohibit discrimination or discharge of workers because of their union membership.[1] However, these statutes proved ineffective as they were enforceable only through criminal prosecution. Both the federal and provincial enactments deviated from the Wagner Act in that they failed to provide an administrative tribunal whose function it was to police the provisions of the statute.

1. Now Criminal Code, R.S.C. 1985, c.C-46, s.425.

89. The Second World War was a period of rapid industrialization and trade union growth. Trade union membership almost doubled from 362,000 in 1940 to 711,000 in 1945, as the labour shortage and general economic recovery proved conducive to trade union organization. Initially the federal government responded to the increased demand for legislative recognition of trade unions and collective bargaining by issuing exhortary regulations declaring the freedom of association and extolling the benefits of collective bargaining. However, employers refused to bargain with trade unions unless compelled to do so by the union's economic sanctions. As the war continued the failure of the federal government to provide legislative backing for union representation and collective bargaining led to repeated outbursts of industrial unrest. In 1943 the crisis reached its peak as the steel industry was shut down by a nation-wide walkout and one out of every three workers was on strike.

90. The need to move to an American-style statute became increasingly obvious. In 1943, Ontario became the first jurisdiction to adopt a fully fledged collective bargaining statute, although its enforcement was entrusted to the Ontario Labour Court (a division of the High Court of Justice), rather than to an administrative board. Experience under the Ontario statute was short lived, as the federal government preempted the field of collective bargaining in 1944 by enacting P.C. 1003, regulations made under the War Measures Act, which covered virtually all significant industry and economic activity. The federal regulations welded features of the Wagner Act to the long-established Canadian policy of third party conciliation and investigation during a compulsory cooling off period. In particular, P.C. 1003 established a representative tribunal (the National War Labour Relations Board) to administer a regime of collective bargaining which included bargaining unit determination and certification, unfair labour practices and a ban on industrial action during the currency of a collective bargaining agreement. Following the repeal of the federal wartime regulations in 1948, virtually all provinces (and the federal government) adopted Wagner-style labour relations statutes, covering all employees in the private sector.

91. Following World War II, the Canadian labour movement continued to grow. Organized workers constituted 27.9 per cent of the total non-agricultural paid workforce in 1946, and by 1958 the figure was 34.2 per cent. During the period 1959–64, however, unions experienced a reversal of their previous potential for growth, falling to a low of 29.4 per cent in 1964, but later regained momentum. In 1971, organized workers constituted 33.3 per cent of the workforce, a percentage that continued to grow in the 1970s. Since the 1980s, union membership in Canada has experienced a gradual but slow decline. In 1998, 32.5 per cent of non-agricultural paid workers were unionized, down from 37.9 per cent in 1984. In part, this is due to the changing structure of the Canadian economy which is shifting from goods producing, which is relatively heavily unionized, to the provision of services. With the exception of the public service, unions have not made major inroads in the service sector. In the 1990s downsizing and privatization of parts of the public service have played a major role in the decline in union density.

92. The strength of the unions is concentrated in a few important areas of the economy. The table shows the heavy concentration of union membership in sectors such as construction, transportation and utilities and the public sector, and the

Rates of Unionization by Industry, 1992

Industry Group	*Paid Workers*	*Union Membership*	*Unionization Rate (%)*
Agriculture	143,100	2,400	1.6
Forestry	53,600	28,500	53.1
Fishing and trapping	13,100	7,000	53.5
Mines, quarries, oil wells	139,300	40,900	29.4
Manufacturing	1,727,800	608,100	35.2
Construction	516,100	336,500	65.2
Transportation, communications and other utilities	865,100	462,200	53.4
Trade	1,941,600	231,500	11.9
Finance	484,700	22,800	4.7
Real estate operators and insurance agencies	236,300	5,600	2.4
Service industries	3,954,900	1,413,500	35.7
Public administration	813,200	643,800	79.2
Total	10,888,800	3,802,800	34.9

Note: Excludes pensioners, unemployed and members in the Territories.
Source: CALURA Labour Unions, 1992, Appendix 1.5.

relative low level of membership in the rapidly expanding financial, service and trade sectors. In 1966, 39.2 per cent of all union members were employed in manufacturing but that had fallen to 16 per cent by 1992. In contrast, the numbers for percentage of union members who were employed in the services sector went from 9 per cent in 1966 to 37.2 per cent in 1992.

93. Institutional reorganization has accompanied overall union growth since the 1930s. The conservative Trades and Labour Congress of Canada (T.L.C.) had largely concentrated upon the organization of workers on a craft-by-craft basis, thus largely ignoring unskilled and semi-skilled employees in mass-production industry. Its constituent unions were largely affiliated with international unions who were associated with the American Federation of Labour (A.F.L.). In the late 1930s a new, vigorous, and less restrictive, philosophy of 'industrial' organization soon produced the Congress of Industrial Organizations (C.I.O.) in the United States and the Canadian Congress of Labour (C.C.L.) in Canada. Competition between the A.F.L.–T.L.C. and the C.I.O.–C.C.L. persisted for almost 20 years, and counterpoised not only two approaches to organization but also the 'business' unionism of the older group and the broader social and political objectives of the newer. Finally, in an effort to end this rivalry, merger movements on both sides of the border produced the A.F.L.– C.I.O. and the unified Canadian Labour Congress (C.L.C.). In 1981–2, however, the C.L.C. suffered the defection of almost all construction unions, which established a new Canadian Federation of Labour (C.F.L.). A small grouping of purely Canadian unions, the Confederation of Canadian Unions (C.C.U.), has also emerged.

Public sector unions are beginning to outpace the private sector, typically international, unions which historically dominated the labour movement. This, plus the increasing demands for autonomy by Canadian divisions within large international unions, has precipitated a reconsideration of the structure of the labour movement.

94. A description of the Canadian labour movement would not be complete without a few words on the diversity and distinctiveness of Quebec's labour movement. At the beginning of the century, even while Canadian locals of international unions were organizing employees in Quebec, another form of unionism, vigorously encouraged by the Catholic Church and largely inspired by its social doctrine, emerged. In the beginning, the Catholic unions offered an alternative to the more militant American-based international unions, not only by advocating collaboration rather than confrontation with employers, but also by providing an institution with which French Canadian workers could preserve their own cultural identity. However, as the pace of industrialization increased in Quebec, the Catholic unions, now formed into the Confédération des travailleurs catholiques du Canada (C.T.C.C.), became more militant with their involvement in a few but important industrial conflicts, one of them being the famous asbestos strike of 1949. With the advent of the so-called *Révolution tranquille*, the C.T.C.C. cut its remaining ties with the Catholic Church in 1960 and became the Confédération des syndicats nationaux (C.S.N.).

95. In the same year, the election of a new liberal government, led by Premier Jean Lesage, generated important changes in Quebec society. This new government enacted progressive labour legislation extending the right to strike to all public sector employees with the exception of firefighters and police. This period was also the beginning of a new era in the Quebec's search for national autonomy, marked by the appearance of a strong separatist movement and the resurgence of a widespread nationalistic fervour within the population. The C.S.N. was a major beneficiary of these social changes, attracting most of Quebec's public sector employees to its ranks.

96. In the early 1970s, the C.S.N. adopted a more radical stance in its public sector negotiations with Quebec's Liberal government led by Robert Bourassa. The C.S.N., along with two other important central union organizations, the Fédération des travailleurs et travailleuses du Québec (F.T.Q.) and the Centrale de l'enseignement du Québec (C.E.Q), joined in a *front commun* that would represent all public sector employees in their negotiations with the government. In 1972, the *front commun* staged a general strike of 300,000 public sector employees that was ended by special back-to-work legislation. In the aftermath Quebec's three most prominent labour leaders were sent to jail for encouraging a defiance of the back-to-work legislation.

The leftist ideology embraced by the C.S.N. during this period was revealed in several booklets denouncing capitalism, American imperialism in Quebec, and the close relationship between employers and the state. This ideology was not exclusive to the C.S.N. though, since the C.E.Q. and even, to some extent, the more business oriented F.T.Q. were making similar public statements at that time.

The 1970s also witnessed important ruptures within Quebec's labour movement. A significant faction of the C.S.N.'s private sector membership, displeased by the C.S.N.'s move to the left, formed a new confederation of unions, the Centrale des syndicats démocratiques (C.S.D.). Moreover, the C.S.N. and F.T.Q. had begun a bitter struggle, punctuated with violent outbursts, over exclusive representation rights in the construction industry.

97. The radical inclinations of both the C.S.N. and F.T.Q. have become more restrained with the economic crisis and neo-liberal ideology brought in by the early 1980s. Their Marxist ideology has gradually given way to a more pragmatic stand. However, the three largest labour organizations, the F.T.Q., C.S.N. and C.E.Q. still play an important role within the coalition of social forces advocating national autonomy for Quebec while at the same time resisting a full implementation of the neo-liberal model.

98. Today, the labour movement in Quebec remains much more diversified than its Canadian counterpart. The F.T.Q., the provincial federation formed from locals of international and Canadian unions, still constitutes the largest labour organization, representing more than 35 per cent of total union membership in Quebec.[1] Its strong stand in favour of Quebec sovereignty and its policy disagreements with the C.L.C. over union jurisdictional claims in Quebec, has in the past generated serious tensions between the F.T.Q. and the C.L.C. Nowadays, the F.T.Q. benefits from a special status with the C.L.C., enjoying a large degree of autonomy.[2]

With approximately 25 per cent of total union membership, the C.S.N. constitutes the second largest labour organization in Quebec. Although it still addresses broader social issues – as do the F.T.Q. and C.E.Q. – the C.S.N. has gradually concentrated its action on bread and butter issues. The same could be said of the C.E.Q., the Quebec's federation of teachers' unions, which represents almost 10 per cent of total union membership in Quebec.

The C.S.D., with only about 4 per cent of Quebec's union membership, enjoys a much lower profile than the three larger union organizations. Mention should also be made of those unions falling outside any of these labour organizations. In Quebec, even more than in the rest of Canada, independent unions have an important presence, representing approximately 25 per cent of all union members in the province.

In 2000, the C.E.Q. changed its name to become the Centrale des Syndicats du Québec, thereby reflecting a new policy of diversifying its membership.

1. The figures on Quebec union membership are drawn from Shaw, 'La présence syndicale au Québec en 1997', *Le Marché du Travail*, September 1998, 6–10.
2. G. Murray and P. Verge, *La représentation syndicale* (Sainte-Foy: Les Presses de l'Université Laval, 1999) 30.

99. In the 1960s efforts to bring labour unions into politics (which had begun as early as 1870) culminated in the affiliation of many labour organizations with the N.D.P. In the post-war period, too, government began to recognize organized labour as a factor of importance in the community, frequently consulting with the C.L.C. and C.S.N. on issues of national economic policy, and other matters of general interest to the trade union movement. Most importantly, until recently, collective bargaining has been accepted throughout the country, and by many of the largest employers, as a legitimate (if not altogether affirmative) public policy. However, the increasing emphasis on global competition and the demands by employers for greater flexibility in the organization of production is putting pressure on the post-war settlement.

100. But all has not been well for the Canadian labour movement. Although its membership has expanded in absolute terms over the past generation, the fact remains that labour unions have failed – except in one or two areas – to increase the proportion of workers who are members. Union density has declined to about one-third of those eligible for unionization in the public and private sector. The movement is continuing to enjoy only limited success in organizing the rapidly growing clerical and technical occupations. Although unions claimed dramatic advances in membership in public administration in the 1970s and 1980s, claiming membership rates of 90 per cent in the late 1980s, by 1992 union density in that sector had stabilized at 78 to 79 per cent.[1] Within the area of private sector white collar employment, the banks became a particular focus of organizational efforts in the 1970s and 1980s. However, despite favourable legal interpretations, of the 168 local branches certified between 1977 and 1985, only 67 survived into 1986 and the numbers have continued to decline since that time.

1. *Calura Report*, 1992 (Statistics Canada – Cat. 71–202, 1992) Charts 1.10 and 1.10a, 22–3.

101. Political issues have reappeared on the primary agenda of the labour movement. In 1944, the first C.C.F. (social democratic) provincial government was elected in Saskatchewan, and it promptly enacted an advanced labour relations statute. That statute remained one of the most progressive pieces of labour legislation in Canada until it was radically altered by the newly elected Conservative government in 1984. In the 1970s, the New Democratic Party, which had succeeded the C.C.F., elected provincial governments in Saskatchewan, British Columbia and Manitoba. N.D.P. provincial governments have generally enacted labour legislation which was more favourable to organized labour than have governments of other political persuasions. However, such reforming legislation did not succeed in cementing the bonds between the political and collective bargaining wings of the labour movement, at least in part because of differences over the appropriate degree of government intervention into the collective bargaining process, although for other reasons as well. In the mid-1980s, Conservative provincial governments politicized collective bargaining by enacting legislative changes which significantly shifted the legal balance in favour of employers. This served to strengthen the bonds between the N.D.P. and the labour movement. By the end of 1992, three provinces, Ontario, British Columbia and Saskatchewan, had N.D.P. governments and the labour movement in these provinces began to press for labour relations reform favouring trade unions. However, despite significant labour law reforms in Ontario in 1993 which shifted the legal balance somewhat in favour, several major public and private sector unions had a falling out with the N.D.P. government following its enactment of social contract legislation. The legislation limited compensation in the public service and placed significant restraints on public sector collective bargaining. The rift caused some unions to speak out against the N.D.P. and refuse to support it in the 1995 Ontario election. That election saw the rise to power of a very conservative Progressive Conservative government. The first order of business of the new Conservative government was repeal of the N.D.P. reforms and enactment of the new Labour Relations Act, 1995 which was more favourable to employers than what had existed prior to the N.D.P. reforms of 1993.

102. The introduction of wage controls has repeatedly been a catalyst for propelling Canadian labour into more concerted political activity. The significance of wage controls for politicizing collective bargaining was demonstrated in both world wars and more recently in 1975, 1982 and the early 1990s. In 1975 the federal government introduced the Anti-Inflation Act,[1] which imposed a system of rigid wage controls as well as a regime of ineffective price controls. Labour responded to this perceived attack on its freedom of action by withdrawing from consultation and cooperation with the government, engaging in a one-day general strike (Day of Protest) on 14 October 1976, and embarking on a short-lived campaign for tripartisism. These actions were largely ineffective. Finally, in the 1979 federal election, after the expiry of the wage control programme, the Canadian Labour Congress announced its intention to work in active support of the New Democratic Party. Prior to 1979, labour support for the N.D.P. had been sporadic, uneven, and dependent upon the sympathies of local unions. The formal affiliation of the C.L.C. with the N.D.P. had hitherto produced few initiatives to actually translate support in principle into a sizeable number of labour votes. In 1979, the C.L.C. finally attempted to deliver those votes, but its efforts were only marginally effective, if at all. Nor have subsequent efforts been more so. However, the opposition of several major unions, including the C.A.W., to the Ontario N.D.P. because of their social contract legislation in the early 1990s, may have contributed to its defeat and the election of the Conservatives in 1995.

By contrast, in 1982 when the federal government imposed wage controls on its public sector workers, the largest federal public sector union opted to argue in the courts that the federal legislation was void as it infringed the newly entrenched Charter of Rights and Freedoms, rather than engaging in political action. Ultimately the Supreme Court of Canada dismissed the challenge, as it decided that the Canadian Charter of Rights does not protect the freedom to bargain collectively or the right to strike.[2]

1. Anti-inflation Act, S.C. 1974–75–76, c.75.
2. *P.S.A.C.* v. *The Queen In Respect of Canada* (1987) 87 C.L.L.C. 14,022; [1987] I.S.C.R. 424.

103. Finally, questions of internal structure and external international affiliation, which have plagued the Canadian labour movement since its inception, have recently emerged with renewed vigour.[1] In 1984 the Canadian council of the large and influential United Automobile Workers split from the international union to form the Canadian Automobile Workers. The move to full Canadian autonomy by 140,000 automobile workers has prompted other Canadian divisions of large American unions to consider severing their ties with their larger and dominant American parents.

This development has resulted in a major restructuring of the Canadian labour movement characterized by a much higher degree of structural independence from its American counterpart. Thus, in 1997, 65.4 per cent of union membership belonged to Canadian unions compared to 29.9 per cent who were members of Canadian locals of American unions, a complete reversal of the situation prevailing less than two decades before.[2]

1. *See infra.*
2. Murray and Verge, *op. cit.*, 29–30.

104. Job satisfaction and enrichment have become increasingly matters of concern both within and beyond the labour movement; attention has been focused especially on restive young workers. Since the mid-1970s corporate managers have attempted to address the problem of worker dissatisfaction by concentrating on worker motivation and morale and, in this way, win employee commitment to, and participation in, the corporation's goals for working life. One of the most prevalent techniques for enhancing job satisfaction is the introduction of Quality of Work Life programmes. These programmes have, however, elicited a divided response both from workers and within the Canadian literature. Many workers have rejected such programmes as failing to address the fundamental problems of control in the workplace and the distribution of monetary benefits. Moreover, such programmes have been seen as techniques for avoiding the union and creating an increased identification between smaller work teams and the employer.

105. Job security, pay equity for female employees and indexed pension plans have moved to the forefront of the collective bargaining agenda over the past two decades. However, many of the major breakthroughs in these areas have not come through collective bargaining, but rather through legislation.

106. Upheavals in the Canadian economy since the late 1970s have confronted Canadian labour with an urgent and dramatic concern: structural unemployment. Shifts in world trading patterns, the rise of Third World manufacturing and high technology competition, the transformation of domestic industries by the computer and 'chip' revolutions, have caused a massive – and many fear, permanent – loss of manufacturing jobs in Canada.

Service sector employment has been outpacing employment in the manufacturing sector since the late 1960s. By 1988, 71 per cent of Canadian workers were employed in the service sector and it is estimated that in the near future 80 per cent of Canadian workers will toil in the service sector in direct contact with customers, users or beneficiaries.

Federal government policies of deregulation and privatization, coupled with trade liberalization with the United States and Mexico, are placing increased pressure on the sectors from which unions have traditionally drawn their members. The short-run effects for Canadian labour have been traumatic. Principal amongst these are the shrinkage of important unions whose members are employed in 'smoke stack' industries.

As well, the increasing polarization of the labour market, which the Economic Council of Canada has called the 'good jobs, bad jobs' phenomenon,[1] bodes ill for organized labour. According to the Council, there has been a rapid growth in non-standard forms of employment, which include part-time, short-term, own-account self-employment and temporary help agency work. In 1997 these forms of work represented nearly approximately one-third of total employment. By 1995 Statistics Canada reported that approximately one-fifth (19 per cent) of all paid workers reported that they were self-employed.[2] Generally, non-standard workers earn less than others in full-time, more permanent jobs in the same occupations and the same industries and they have fewer fringe benefits. These forms of work are extremely difficult to organize under existing labour law, which, in part, helps to explain why women workers who tend to dominate non-standard forms of employment are not unionized to the same extent as men workers. In 1997, 29.6 per cent of women, as opposed to 32.4 per cent of men, were unionized in Canada.[3]

These changing features of the labour market place the Canadian labour movement at a milestone in its evolution. The unanswered question remains whether it will adapt and succeed in maintaining and increasing its membership despite these structural changes, or will it follow the downward trend that has characterized the Canadian scene during the last five to ten years and the American labour movement for more than three decades.[4]

1. Economic Council of Canada, *Good Jobs, Bad Jobs* (Ottawa: Minister of Supply and Services, 1990).
2. *Collective Reflection on the Changing Workplace: Report of the Advisory Committee on the Changing Workplace* (Ottawa: Public Works and Government Services Canada, 1997).
3. Murray and Verge, *op. cit.*, 26.
4. *Ibid.*, 25–6.

107. The deep recessions which framed the 1980s and the early 1990s have inflicted wounds upon most Canadian unions which at the end of 1999 have had neither the time nor the conditions to heal. While the Canadian labour movement has travelled a long and difficult road since it was first, formally established, as the Canadian Labour Union, in 1873, the problems confronting the country as a whole virtually guarantee that its aspirations will inevitably outstrip its achievements.

V. The Role of Government Institutions in the Shaping and Administration of Labour Law and Industrial Relations Policy

§1. Constitutional Background

108. There are two constitutional limitations to government action (or inaction) in the field of labour law and industrial relations. First, as has already been mentioned, the new Charter of Rights and Freedoms may constrain legislative, executive and administrative action designed to regulate the behaviour of labour or management.[1] The influence of the Charter will be indicated at appropriate points, *infra*. More generally, legislation may be attacked on the ground that it has not been enacted by the appropriate level of government – either the federal government or the provinces.

1. Notably in *R.W.D.S.U., Local 580* v. *Dolphin Delivery*, [1986] 2 S.C.R. 573 the Supreme Court of Canada held that the Charter did not apply to judicial action absent an additional governmental connection.

109. Jurisdiction over industrial relations is divided between the two levels of government on the basis of the nature of the activity involved. The federal government has jurisdiction over interprovincial and international trade, transportation and communications, defence-related industries (e.g. uranium), a few other anomalous industries and, of course, industrial relations in the federal public service. Only about 10 per cent of Canadian private sector employees fall under federal jurisdiction. All others, embracing those who work in all major manufacturing sectors, mining and other natural resource industries (other than uranium mining), construction, service industries etc. fall within provincial jurisdiction.

110. However, some collective bargaining relationships have emerged which do not conform to the demarcation of constitutional responsibilities. For example, local trucking comes under provincial jurisdiction and interprovincial and international trucking comes under federal jurisdiction, but collective bargaining in the trucking industry has sometimes embraced trucking of both sorts. In such situations, the division of constitutional responsibility has often created difficulties which can be resolved only by intergovernmental cooperation.

111. The federal government, however, has several potentially important possibilities for expansion of its present, secondary role in industrial relations. First, although the term has not been given a generous interpretation, courts have held that when the activity of an enterprise is 'necessarily incidental' to a federal undertaking, federal labour legislation governs.[1] Second, although again the matter is somewhat unclear and conservatively stated, the courts have conceded that the federal government enjoys power to deal with a national economic crisis, such as inflation, by enacting legislation which overrides otherwise valid provincial collective bargaining statutes. The Supreme Court of Canada sustained the federal Anti-Inflation Act of 1975 on this basis.[2]

Third, perhaps most importantly, the federal government can exert leadership and exercise moral suasion by the way it conducts labour relations within its own jurisdiction. Indeed, it did this by using its broad wartime powers to launch the first nation-wide collective bargaining scheme in 1944, again by enacting in 1967 an advanced statute which introduced collective bargaining in the federal public service, in 1968 by sponsoring the far-reaching Task Force on Labour Relations which, in turn, laid the groundwork for substantial changes in both federal and provincial collective bargaining legislation, and in 1977, by according individual workers within its jurisdiction a statutory right to adjudication in the event of unjust dismissal. More recently, the federal government exercised its leadership role both with respect to the provincial governments and the private sector, by imposing wage restraints on federal public sector employees and revoking their right to strike.[3]

1. *See* e.g. *Letter Carriers* v. *C.U.P.W.* (1973) 40 D.L.R. (3d) 105 (S.C.C.); *Northern Telecom* v. *Communications Workers*, [1980] 1 S.C.R. 115.
2. *Re Anti-Inflation Act*, [1976] 2 S.C.R. 373.
3. *See* Dickson C.J.'s dissent in *P.S.A.C.* v. *The Queen in Respect of Canada* (1987) 87 C.L.L.C. 14,022; [1987] 1 S.C.R. 424.

112. Two further constraints of a quasi-constitutional nature may be mentioned. First, as a matter of general constitutional law, federal legislation which 'occupies the field' has been held to preempt provincial legislation directed to the same end. However, although the federal government has enacted valid legislation regulating federal elections, a provincial statute limiting union political activity in both provincial and federal elections has been upheld.[1] Similarly, although the federal Criminal Code generally deals with matters of public order, and has specific provisions relating to picketing, provincial authority over labour (and other) demonstrations has been upheld, and there is little doubt that the provinces' attempt to regulate picketing by administrative, civil and quasi-criminal sanctions are likewise valid.[2]

1. *Oil Workers* v. *Imperial Oil* (1963) 41 D.L.R. (2d) 1 (S.C.C.).
2. *A.G. Canada* v. *Dupond* (1978) 84 D.L.R. (3d) 420 (S.C.C.).

113. Although the Charter of Rights and Freedoms has generated a great deal of litigation during its short history (since 1982), its legal effect on industrial relations has been marginal. In principle, the Charter guarantees certain fundamental freedoms (including the freedoms of expression, peaceful assembly and association), legal rights (including guarantees of procedural due process) language, equality and mobility rights. These rights and freedoms provide a standard against which to judge the validity of both preexisting and new laws and the manner of their enforcement. Thus, legal challenges based on the Charter have become an everyday occurrence; however, courts, labour boards and arbitrators have overwhelmingly deferred to the legislative compromise and administrative policies designed and implemented to date.[1] By contrast with its minimal legal impact, the Charter has had an important political effect, for both employers and individual employees have sought to use it to challenge aspects of the collective bargaining legislation, which before the entrenchment of the Charter, were taken to be firmly established elements of Canadian labour relations policy.[2]

1. This deferential tone was established early in a trilogy of Supreme Court of Canada decisions which considered Charter challenges based on freedoms of association and expression against legislative restrictions on the right to strike. The decisions are *Ref. re Alberta Public Service Employee Relations Act*, [1987] 1 S.C.R. 313; *Public Service Alliance of Canada* v. *A.G. of Canada*, [1987] 1 S.C.R. 424; and *Gov't of Saskatchewan* v. *RWDSU*, Local 544, [1987] 1 S.C.R. 460. The legislative restrictions on strike activity were upheld in all three cases and in the main decision, *Ref. re Alberta Public Service Employee Relations Act*, the majority suggested that it would be unwise for the Court to question the wisdom of legislative choices in the complex area of labour relations policy. *See also* the discussion of the significance of the Supreme Court's 1999 ruling that limitations on labour leafleting activity of workers on a lawful strike in British Columbia violated the freedom of expression of workers under the Charter, U.F.C.W., *Local 1518* v. *Kmart Canada Ltd.*, [1999] (Sept. 9/99) S.C. File no. 26209.
2. *See* Etherington, 'An Assessment of Judicial Review of Labour Laws Under the Charter: Of Realists, Romantics, and Pragmatists' (1993) 24 *Ottawa Law Review* 685, for a discussion of the impact of the Charter on Canadian labour law.

114. The determination of whether a particular provision or action offends the Charter is a two-step process. First, a court must determine whether or not a Charter-protected right has been infringed upon. Second, even if an apparent legislative intrusion upon rights and freedoms is identified, it may nonetheless be permitted in the following circumstance. The Charter itself states that its protections are 'subject . . . to such reasonable limits prescribed by law as can be demonstrably justified in a free and democratic society'. Thus, the government will be afforded an opportunity to demonstrate, through evidence or argument, that a given 'reasonable limit' upon, for example, picketing – as the exercise of freedom of expression – is warranted.[1]

1. In *Dolphin Delivery, supra* para. 108, the Supreme Court stated that although peaceful picketing is prima facie protected by the Charter, limitations on secondary picketing are demonstrably justified.

115. In addition, despite a judicial finding that a Charter-protected right has been infringed by government activity, the federal Parliament or a provincial legislature may expressly declare that a given law shall operate notwithstanding certain provisions of the Charter. Such a declaration will have effect for renewable periods of up to five years. Thus, a government which is determined to impose a particular legislative policy in labour relations may legally do so, the Charter to the contrary notwithstanding, provided it is prepared to risk the possible adverse political consequences of a declaration.[1]

1. Shortly after the Charter was adopted, the government of Quebec secured adoption of such a declaration, in connection with legislation affecting public and parapublic employees. In Saskatchewan the provincial government enacted a statute containing such a declaration to end the strike by the Saskatchewan Government Employees' Union, see the S.G.E.U. Dispute Settlement Act, s.1984–85–86, c.111. However, the use of s.33 is no longer necessary to ensure the constitutionality of legislation prohibiting workers from exercising their collective bargaining rights since the Supreme Court of Canada ruled that freedom of association guaranteed by the

Charter does not include either collective bargaining or the right to strike in *Reference Re Public Service Employees Relations Act (Alta.)* (1987) 87 C.L.L.C. 14,021; [1987] 1 S.C.R. 313.

116. Finally, several technical problems remain in connection with the practical application of the Charter. These include the scope of remedies available to the courts in enforcing the Charter (in addition to declaring offending legislation invalid) and the impact of the Charter on non-governmental action. The remedial power of the courts includes striking down legislation, the severance of an offending provision and the suspension of a declaration of invalidity for a period to allow the appropriate governmental authority to amend the offending legislation. In addition, the Supreme Court of Canada held that a court has a limited power to extend legislation and legislated benefits in narrowly defined appropriate circumstances.[1] The decision of the Supreme Court of Canada in *Dolphin Delivery*[2] established that the Charter does not apply to a court order giving effect to the common law tort of inducement of breach of contract used to restrain a trade union from secondary picketing.

In addition, so far the courts have been unanimous in holding that the Charter does not apply to negotiated union security arrangements contained in collective agreements between unions and private sector employees.[3]

However, the Charter applies both to collective agreements negotiated by a governmental employer and to grievance arbitration in the public sector. In *Lavigne* v. *Ontario Public Service Employees Union*[4] the Supreme Court of Canada held that the Charter applied to a union security provision contained in a collective agreement negotiated by and binding upon a governmental actor. Moreover, in four decisions dealing with the constitutionality of mandatory retirement policies,[5] the Supreme Court of Canada drew a distinction between the exercise of government control over the ordinary operations of a public agency and the ultimate control exercised by government over public agencies through the power of the purse and limited the application of the Charter to instances of the first form of control. The result of this distinction was that the Charter did not apply to the actions of universities because of their independence from government control despite their reliance on government financing. However, it did apply to the collective agreements of community colleges because of the greater degree of direct government control in the governance of community colleges.

1. *Schacter* v. *Canada* (1992) 92 C.L.L.C. para. 14,036 (S.C.C.).
2. *Dolphin Delivery, supra.*
3. *Re Bhindi and B.C. Projectionists* (1986) 29 D.L.R. 51 (B.C.C.A.).
4. (1991) 91 C.L.L.C. para. 14,029; [1991] 2 S.C.R. 211.
5. *Harrison* v. *University of British Columbia* (1991) 91 C.L.L.C. para. 17,001; [1990] 3 S.C.R. 451; *Douglas College* v. *Douglas/Kwantlem Faculty Association* (1991) 91 C.L.L.C. para. 17,002; [1990] 3 S.C.R. 570; *Vancouver General Hospital* v. *Stoffman* (1991) 91 C.L.L.C. para. 17,003; [1990] 3 S.C.R. 483; *McKinney* v. *University of Guelph* (1991) 91 C.L.L.C. para. 17,004; [1990] 3 S.C.R. 229.

117. A further possible limitation on federal action is the Canadian Bill of Rights which prevails over ordinary federal statutes, unless express provision is made to the contrary. An attempt to use the Bill of Rights to strike down federal legislation which allegedly interfered with freedom of association was unsuccessful.[1] While the Bill of Rights was not repealed when the Charter was adopted in 1982, arguments under the latter are likely to be more frequent, and more compelling, than under the former. The Charter, moreover, affects provincial legislation, as the Bill of Rights does not.

1. *Swait* v. *Maritime Trustees* (1966) 61 D.L.R. (2d) 317 (Que. C.A.).

§2. The Role of Government Institutions

A. The Legislature

118. Subject to the Charter, the federal Parliament and provincial legislatures have plenary authority to shape Canadian labour law within their respective constitutional spheres. If fully exercised, legislative power can displace ordinary rules of civil or common law, considerably limit judicial review, and authorize or limit administrative and tribunal action.

But legislative power is not unconstrained. Labour law is politically charged: extreme measures may bring unwanted consequences. Labour law is complex: it has ramifications for many parts of the legal system which must be carefully considered. And for these reasons labour law legislation tends to be episodic and piecemeal and it tends to receive low legislative priority. When significant labour law reforms are enacted, they are often anticipated by considerable study and consultation, not to say by changes in actual behaviour. Such reforms are also often met by strong political reactions, depending upon public perceptions concerning the extent to which they alter the existing balance (or imbalance) between protection for the interests of labour and employers. The political reactions to significant labour law reforms in Ontario, first by the N.D.P. government in 1993 and later the Conservative government in 1995, were far more extensive and intense than reaction to reforms during the previous 45 years because of the perceptions of employers (in 1993) and unions (in 1995) that they would have a significant detrimental impact on their ability to protect their interest.

1. Kevin Burkett, 'The Politicization of the Ontario Labour Relations Framework in the 1990s' (1998) 6 *Can. Lab. & Emp. L. J.* 161.

B. The Courts

1. The superior courts

a. Appellate courts

119. At the apex of the judicial system is the Supreme Court of Canada. It has a discretionary jurisdiction to accept appeals from all other federal or provincial appellate courts, and its interpretations of the Constitution and of legislation, and decisions on matters of civil or common law, have authoritative effect across the country. Consequently, its impact on the development of labour law is potentially great.

120. Each province also has a general appellate court, usually referred to as the 'Court of Appeal', whose decisions on all matters are final, unless appealed successfully to the Supreme Court of Canada. Usually, these courts are not involved in matters of labour law until they have been litigated at a lower level. However, the Federal Court of Appeal (which unlike the provincial appellate courts has a limited jurisdiction in relation to certain federal matters) does have the primary obligation of reviewing the decisions of various federal labour tribunals.

b. The trial courts

121. Each province has a general trial court, variously named 'the Supreme Court', 'the Superior Court', 'the High Court', or 'the Court of Queen's Bench'. (There is also a federal Trial Court, but its role in labour law is insignificant.) These provincial courts have a residual jurisdiction to decide all controversies, whether under federal or provincial law, not expressly assigned elsewhere. They play a major role in shaping labour law in two areas.

122. First, ordinary lawsuits involving principles of common or civil law are normally brought in these courts. These include the enforcement of individual employment contracts, and claims for damages or injunctions arising out of industrial action. Litigation amongst union members, or relating to union property, is also found in these courts.

123. Second, decisions of labour tribunals operating under provincial law are usually subject to review by, and enforcement proceedings in, the provincial trial courts. (In Ontario, a special Divisional Court, comprising three High Court judges, is assigned the task of review.)

124. Thus, whether exercising original or reviewing jurisdiction, the provincial trial courts, in theory, have the power to shape the development of labour law in virtually all matters of significance. This power is, however, limited by several constraints. First, legislatures have increasingly confined the role of the court by assigning responsibility for industrial action to labour relations tribunals, and by expressly limiting the right of the courts to review various tribunal decisions. Second, the costs, formality and delays of conventional litigation create some disincentives to the use of these courts in labour matters. And third, perhaps aware of the first two matters, the courts themselves are developing procedural rules and substantive doctrines which somewhat limit their role in labour law.[1]

1. The most notable S.C.C. decisions on deference to labour tribunals on matters of original jurisdiction are *St. Anne Nackawic Pulp & Paper Co.* v. *C.P.U., Local 219*, [1986] 1 S.C.R. 704; and *Weber* v. *Ontario Hydro*, [1995] 2 S.C.R. 929. The most notable decision on deference to labour tribunals on judicial review applications is *C.U.P.E., Local 963* v. *New Brunswick Liquor Corporation*, [1979] 2 S.C.R. 227.

2. The lower courts

125. The provinces are authorized to establish minor courts of civil and criminal jurisdiction. These play some role in labour law, although largely in its ongoing administration rather than in the adumbration of broad principles, or in the announcement of authoritative interpretations, functions reserved to the superior trial, and especially appellate, courts.

126. Small claims courts deal with most claims for unpaid wages. Lower criminal courts, variously named, deal with prosecutions for violations of the federal Criminal Code (e.g. by violent conduct during a strike) or of federal or provincial labour legislation. However, such prosecutions are relatively rare and reserved for the worst offenders, no doubt because they normally require the consent or permission of the labour relations board or Minister of Labour and it is felt that such prosecutions are not conducive to future good labour relations between the parties.

C. The Executive

1. The cabinet

127. In any parliamentary system, the cabinet as a whole is ultimately responsible for the development, enactment and administration of legislation. This is particularly true in such a politically sensitive area as labour policy. Thus, the cabinet will carefully set legislative proposals originating in the ministries and, on occasion, even decide whether to intervene *ad hoc* in a dispute with high public visibility. Moreover, the cabinet will play a mediative role amongst the various ministries concerned with labour matters.

128. Subject to cabinet control, the ministries themselves are charged with both the origination and review of policies, and their daily execution. The distribution of responsibility amongst the ministries concerned with labour matters differs from jurisdiction to jurisdiction.

2. The Ministry of Labour

129. Typically the Ministry of Labour has the main responsibility for collective bargaining policy, although administration and enforcement of the general private-sector labour relations statute is almost inevitably undertaken by an independent labour relations board.

In addition, the Ministry of Labour may be responsible for such matters as manpower policy, human rights legislation, occupational health and safety, trade licensing and training, some forms of social insurance, and legislation regarding individual (as distinct from collective) employment rights.

3. The Ministry of Justice or of the Attorney-General

130. In almost all Canadian jurisdictions, the chief legal minister is responsible for drafting legislation, including labour legislation and for undertaking court proceedings on behalf of the government. These functions may be undertaken in close cooperation with the relevant ministry, or even delegated to the department in question.

4. Other ministries

131. No consistent pattern exists by which labour relations-related responsibilities are distributed amongst other ministries. At the federal level, for example, the Ministry of Finance is responsible for anti-inflation initiatives, including wage and price controls, the Ministry of Human Resources and Development Canada for employment and human resources policies, the Ministry of Health and Welfare for some employment-related schemes of social insurance, etc. In some provinces, responsibility for anti-discrimination legislation may be vested in the Attorney-General or another minister, while responsibility for occupational health and safety, trade training and licensing may be assigned elsewhere.

D. The Labour Relations Board

132. In every Canadian jurisdiction, except Quebec, the private-sector labour relations statute establishes a labour relations tribunal which is charged with administering and enforcing the statute in relation to union certification, unfair labour practices, and in some cases, industrial conflict and regulation of internal union affairs. In Quebec, such functions are still divided between a Labour Court/ *Tribunal du travail* and departmental officials called Labour commissioners/ *commissaires du travail*. However, this will change in the near future since the legislature of the province adopted, in June 2001, an Act to amend the Labour Code, to establish the Commission des relations du travail and to amend other legislative provisions,[1] thereby creating a labour board similar to those existing elsewhere in Canada, will be established. It is expected that these legislative amendments will come into force in the middle of the year 2002.

In British Columbia, the labour relations board has reached its fullest flowering and enjoys plenary independent authority as well over conciliation, strikes, picketing and grievance arbitration, *inter alia*. Other labour relations tribunals enjoy some, but not all, of these responsibilities.

1. S.Q. 2001, c.27.

133. The organization and membership of the labour relations tribunal varies from jurisdiction to jurisdiction. In the federal jurisdiction and some provinces, the tribunal has tripartite membership, i.e. a presiding officer who is a neutral, and equal numbers of management and labour representatives. However, the boards of some provinces are comprised of neutral members only.

134. Labour relations tribunals have at their disposal sizeable supporting staffs. The staff are, typically, used to make inquiries concerning facts which will determine union bargaining rights, but also to investigate and seek to dispose amicably of complaints made under the Act against employers or unions. Some labour relations tribunals also control a staff of employees whose function it is to conciliate interest disputes.

135. While much of the non-contentious business of the tribunals is disposed of through informal processes of investigation, or *pro forma* disposition by the tribunal itself, a certain number of cases are inevitably submitted for formal adjudication. Following adjudication, most labour relations tribunals enjoy the power to make remedial orders to secure compliance with statutory policies. These orders are, typically, registrable in, and enforceable as orders of, the superior courts.

In almost all jurisdictions, violation of the governing labour relations statute or orders of the tribunal, is also a quasi-criminal offence. However, prosecution is usually possible only with the prior consent of the tribunal, which is loathe to give consent except in egregious cases. Indeed, neither unions nor employers evince much interest in criminal prosecution, and the criminal courts are seldom involved in labour relations matters.

VI. Sources of Labour Law

§1. Methods of Legal Analysis

136. As a practical matter, the vast bulk of disputes which may arise between an employer and his employees or their union are settled bilaterally, and not always in accordance with legal norms. The predominant influence in such settlements is the desire to preserve an amicable and mutually profitable relationship.

137. However, if such settlement proves impossible, and recourse to law is necessary, the courts almost inevitably have the last word. In certain areas, they possess original jurisdiction to decide issues of constitutional or private law in labour relations; otherwise, they may possess power to review or hear appeals from legal decisions in other forums. In the latter case, however, whether because of the limited scope of review, or as a result of diffidence about intervention, or – by far the most important factor – because the parties choose not to resort to courts – the 'law' of other forums is, in fact, of primary importance. This is significant because the procedures of dispute resolution, the norms of decision-making, the modes of reasoning, the methods of proof, and the remedial powers of these other forums may often differ considerably from those of the courts.

§2. The Constitution

138. Both the federal division of powers and the Charter function primarily to delimit legislative and governmental powers, rather than as source of law operating directly upon the parties. Although the Charter has not played a significant role to date in defining the content of our labour relations law, as noted earlier it is still somewhat unclear what the courts will define as governmental action and, thus, subject to Charter scrutiny. So far the courts have been unwilling to scrutinize the internal affairs of trade unions simply because they have been accorded exclusive bargaining rights under collective bargaining legislation. This does not mean, however, that in the future the courts will not intervene under the Charter in some areas to enforce constitutional standards of freedom of expression and association by awarding 'such remedy as the court considers appropriate and just in the circumstances'.[1] For example, in 1999 the Supreme Court of Canada ruled that restrictions on picketing under the British Columbia Labour Relations Code violated the freedom of expression of workers on lawful strike protected by the Charter because it prohibited them from peaceful leafleting activity at secondary locations of their employer in support of their strike.[2]

1. Charter, s.24(1).
2. *U.F.C.W., Local 1518* v. *Kmart Canada Ltd.* [1999] 2 S.C.R. 1083.

§3. Common Law

A. General

139. In the absence of legislation, common law governs wherever the courts choose to intervene. There are several areas of importance, primarily on issues related to industrial conflict, where the court has intervened in labour law through application of the common law. In Quebec, however, private law principles have been enacted in a comprehensive legislated code.[1] Therefore, in the absence of statutory law, the general jurisdiction courts have no choice but to apply and interpret the Code provisions relevant to the cases that are brought before them.

1. Civil Code of Quebec, S.Q. 1991, c.64, as amended.

B. Tort or Delict

140. The law of industrial conflict (in all provinces except British Columbia) has been in large measure the law of tort or delict. The legality of strikes and picketing has been measured by general doctrines of civil liability, although it must be said that the development of these doctrines was largely influenced by the fact that they evolved in the context of industrial relations controversies; indeed, they are relatively seldom employed elsewhere. Moreover, even tort doctrines draw upon standards of behaviour which are implicit, or explicit, in legislatively enacted collective bargaining schemes. More recently the labour boards in several other jurisdictions, most notably Ontario and the federal jurisdiction, have been given increasing powers to regulate and give remedies for industrial conflict which is contrary to their statutory regimes. In Quebec, the provisions of the Civil Code dealing with civil liability resulting from wrongful conduct apply to industrial conflicts. Damages, and especially injunctions, are the remedies sought from the courts usually to restrain illegal strikes, picketing or boycotting.

C. Contract or Obligation

141. Contract law is the primary source of law governing relationships between non-unionized workers and their employers, although the existence of a formal written contract is, in fact, relatively rare amongst ordinary employees. The extent to which the advent of a regime of collective bargaining displaces the common law of contract has been a matter of considerable ongoing controversy, although the trend has clearly been in favour of displacement of the common law of contract by the statutory regime for collective bargaining and grievance arbitration once the initial hiring has taken place. There have also been ongoing questions concerning the relevance of common law contract principles to the interpretation and enforcement of collective agreements by arbitrators.

The relationship amongst union members is, in part, also viewed as a contractual matter, the 'contract' being the union constitution.

D. Property

142. Property law is relevant in so far as an employer asserts his rights as a property owner *vis-à-vis* a union or his employees. For example, he may complain that union organizers have trespassed on his property, or that picketing is conducted in such a way as to interfere with access to property. Property law may also govern disputes amongst union members over the ownership of union assets.

E. Judicial Review of Administrative Decisions and Arbitration Awards

143. To the extent that judicial review is not grounded in explicit statutory arrangements, common law principles govern the procedures by which courts review the decisions of administrative tribunals and of arbitrators, and the scope of such review. Quebec public law follows the same principles.

§4. Legislation

144. Legislation is supreme over all other legal sources, displaces common law to the extent it explicitly or implicitly can be read as doing so, and also defines the power of administrative tribunals. However, even apart from constitutional and Charter considerations, legislation must inevitably be interpreted. Thus, the role of the courts, particularly in reviewing the decisions of administrative tribunals, but also in determining the continued survival of common law principles, limits the practical extent of legislative supremacy. At times, the courts have been highly interventionist, disputing the interpretations of labour legislation adopted by administrative tribunals. Legislatures have responded, on occasion, either by limiting or entirely eliminating judicial review, or by enacting amendments expressly restoring the original administrative interpretation.

§5. Subordinate Legislation

145. Often, legislation lays down broad lines of policy, leaving details to be worked out over a period of time, especially in the light of changing circumstances, or where technical or scientific matters are at issue. Where these details of regulation are required to be given legal force, the governing statute generally provides for the enactment of 'subordinate legislation' (rules or regulations) by the responsible department or administrative agency, subject usually to (formal) approval of the cabinet. Examples of such subordinate legislation include the procedural rules of the labour relations tribunal, health and safety standards in particular industries, and levels of benefits and standards of entitlement in social security schemes.

§6. Administrative Decision-making

146. Labour relations tribunals have developed an extensive jurisprudence of decisions by them in interpretation of the Labour Relations Act and its subordinate procedural rules. These decisions, which are contained in various series of reports, are extremely important in understanding the actual operation of the legislation, and often involve significant declarations of policy, especially where legislation is itself couched in general terms. These decisions are subject to judicial review, although the scope of review has been statutorily narrowed in some jurisdictions and the Supreme Court of Canada has stated that courts should generally be deferential to the expertise of specialist labour tribunals on judicial review applications.[1] Despite this, judicial review continues to shape labour relations board's decisions.

A labour relations tribunal may also announce, through a published policy statement not made in the context of a specific case, that it intends to exercise (or has exercised) its decision-making discretion in a particular manner. Such announcements enable the parties to conduct themselves in a manner consistent with the board's policy.

A labour relations tribunal is, however, not legally bound by its own prior decisions or announced policies. Nonetheless, it will generally adhere to such precedents until it is demonstrated that they were erroneous, or have become obsolete.

1. *C.U.P.E., Local 963* v. *New Brunswick Liquor Corporation*, [1979] 2 S.C.R. 227.

§7. Collective Agreements

147. Collective agreements are a primary source of law which define the rights of unions and employers who are parties to the agreement, and of the employees governed by them. They are often documents of considerable length and complexity, and deal with such matters as the wages to be paid for various jobs, discipline, working conditions, the assignment of work, 'fringe benefits' such as pensions, insurance, paid vacations and holidays (over the statutory minimum), and the prerogatives of the employer and union. Of overriding significance are clauses – whose inclusion is typically required by statute – providing for the recognition of the union as the exclusive bargaining agent of the employees, requiring the submission of all disputes during the term of the agreement to arbitration, and prohibiting strikes and lockouts for the duration of the agreement. Occasionally required by statute, but almost inevitably included by agreement of the parties, is a clause which stipulates that an employee may not be disciplined or discharged except for 'just cause'.

148. Disputes over the meaning of the collective agreement are generally not justiciable in the civil courts. In all Canadian jurisdictions, parties to a collective agreement are either compelled or permitted to submit their disputes over the application, interpretation or alleged violation of a collective agreement to arbitration. In some provinces, notably British Columbia, the parties have the additional option of submitting their dispute to the labour relations tribunal, which may either resolve it through mediation, itself adjudicate the matter, or remit it to arbitration.

149. In most jurisdictions, the awards of arbitrators are subject to judicial review, generally on grounds of procedural impropriety, or because the arbitrator has exceeded her/his powers or has assigned meaning to the language of the agreement it cannot (in the court's view) reasonably bear. As a practical matter, despite proclamations of deference by the courts, the possibility of judicial review allows courts to require arbitrators to adhere fairly closely to a common law contractual approach. Departures from such an approach are most likely to succeed if they are explicitly licensed by the agreement itself, or, as in British Columbia, by governing legislation which directs arbitrators to decide cases according to 'principles consistent with the industrial relations policy of [the British Columbia Labour Relations Code]' and 'not . . . a strict legal interpretation of the issue in dispute'.

150. Awards of arbitrators are published, and tend to be cited as persuasive (but not binding) authority by other arbitrators. However, it is ultimately the language of the agreement which governs the award, provided it is sufficiently clear and unequivocal.

§8. Industrial Custom and Practice

151. Although in fact many features of the ongoing relationship between a union and employer, or between an employer and his individual, non-organized employees, is governed by custom and practice, custom and practice are not generally *per se* enforceable in arbitration, labour relations tribunal or court proceedings (unless, of course, they are expressly or impliedly given binding effect by language in the collective agreement or contract of employment). However, in the 1980s and 1990s there has been much greater legal recognition of the significance of past practice through acceptance of the applicability of the doctrine of estoppel in grievance arbitration proceedings.[1] Where the past practice or custom can be found to be consistent enough to constitute representation by conduct by the employer that it will continue, it may estop the employer from changing that practice until the next round of collective bargaining.

In addition, to the extent that they can be proved to, noted by, or lie within the expert knowledge of, an arbitrator or labour relations tribunal, industrial custom and practice may serve several important functions. They may supplement and help to give meaning to general language in a collective agreement. They may illuminate or help to determine the credibility of contentious evidence. They may also guide the parties in the bilateral resolution of their differences, before they seek adjudication by a third party.

Processes of daily administration of an employment relationship not only adhere to, but obviously in turn generate, informal practices, customs and understandings. The 'web of rules' thus produced is part of the true law of the workplace, and is as functionally significant as if it were legally binding.

1. The pivotal decision on this issue is *C.N.R. Co.* v. *Beatty* (1981) 34 O.R. (2d) 385 (H.C.).

§9. Bibliography

G. Adams, *Canadian Labour Law* (Aurora. Ont.: Canada Law Book, 2nd edn., looseleaf, 1993).

J.C. Anderson, M. Gunderson, and A. Ponak (eds.), *Union-Management Relations in Canada* (Don Mills, Ont.: Addison-Wesley, 3rd edn., 1995).

E.A. Aust, *The Employment Contract* (Cowansville, Qué.: Les Editions Yvon Blais Inc., 2nd edn., 1993).

D.J.M. Brown and D.M. Beatty, *Canadian Labour Arbitration* (Aurora. Ont.: Canada Law Book, 3rd edn., looseleaf, 1992).

Canadian Industrial Relations, *The Report of the Task Force on Labour Relations* (H.D. Woods, Chairman, 1968) (and 23 published studies).

A.W.R. Carrothers, E.E. Palmer, and W.B. Rayner, *Collective Bargaining Law in Canada* (Toronto: Butterworths, 2nd edn., 1986).

R.P. Chaykowski and A. Verma (eds.), *Industrial Relations in Canadian Industry* (Toronto: Dryden, 1998).

J.E. Dorsey, *Canada Labour Relations Board: Federal Law and Practice* (Toronto: Carswell, 1983).

J.L. Dubé and N. Di Iorio, *Les normes du travail* (Les Editions Revue de Droit, Université de Sherbrooke, 2nd edn., 1992).

G. England, I. Christie and M. Christie, *Employment Law in Canada* (Toronto: Butterworths, 3rd edn., looseleaf, 1993).

C. Foisy, D. Lavery and L. Martineau, *Canada Labour Relations Board Policies and Procedures* (Toronto: Butterworths, 1986).

R. Gagnon, L. LeBel and P. Verge, *Droit du Travail* (Sainte-Foy: Les Presses de l'Université Laval, 2nd edn., 1991).

D. Harris, *Wrongful Dismissal* (Toronto: DeBoo, 3rd edn., looseleaf, 1984).

Labour Law Casebook Group, *Labour and Employment Law: Cases, Materials and Commentary* (Kingston: Queen's I.R.C., 6th edn., 1998).

G. Hébert, *Traité de négociation collective* (Boucherville: Gaétan Morin Éditeur, 1992).

H.A. Levitt, *The Law of Dismissal in Canada* (Aurora, Ont.: Canada Law Book, 2nd edn., 1992).

F. Morin and J.-Y. Brière, *Le droit de l'emploi au Québec* (Montréal: Wilson et Lafleur Ltée, 1998).

E.E. Palmer and B.M. Palmer, *Collective Agreement Arbitration in Canada* (Toronto: Butterworths, 3rd edn., 1991).

J. Sack, C.M. Mitchell and S. Price, *Ontario Labour Relations Board Law and Practice* (Toronto: Butterworths, 3rd edn., looseleaf, 1996).
K.P. Swan and K.E. Swinton, *Studies in Labour Law* (Toronto: Butterworths, 1983).
P. Weiler, *Reconcilable Differences* (Toronto: Carswell, 1980).

Part I. The Individual Employment Relationship

Chapter I. Definitions and Concepts

152. Before turning to the core of the material to be dealt with in the two chapters of this part, attention must be drawn to the fact that, in Canada, there is no overriding theory which unifies the doctrines governing employment contracts made between individuals and those made between employers and unions, i.e. collective agreements. In the common law provinces, the law relating to the individual contract of employment is inherited from England and modified for Canadian conditions. In Quebec, however, the general law of contract, found in the Civil Code, applies to individual contracts of employment since employment contracts are viewed as just another type of contract. Nevertheless, some specific provisions of the Code do deal just with the contract of employment. Despite the quite different legal foundation for the individual contract of employment in Quebec, many of Quebec's rules are similar in effect to those that apply in the rest of Canada. In the following analysis references will only be made where these rules diverge. The collective bargaining regime is indigenous and, although often the same semantics seem to be used when it is legally analysed, many of the assumptions of the common law have been abandoned or, at least, perceptibly changed. From a doctrinal point of view, the accommodation between the two regimes has not been worked out with precision. In this part the individual contract of employment is the focus. It is to be remembered, however, that, even though the law relating to this aspect of labour relations has a role to play when collective bargaining law governs the relationship between employers and employees, it will not necessarily be the same role, either theoretically or functionally.

§1. The Central Place of the Contract of Employment

A. The Ubiquity of the Concept

153. The term contract of employment denotes an essential concept in labour law. There must be a relationship recognized by law to be one of contract between an employer and employee before any of the incidents of labour law will be applicable. This is so whether the labour law sought to be applied relates to the making, administering or enforcing of agreements between employers and trade unions, or to the exercise of rights and imposition of obligations arising out of long established rules of custom or the common law in respect of working conditions, or to the rights arising under legislation dealing with working conditions. It is so, even though some of the legislation, such as workers' compensation statutes, refers to 'workers' rather than 'employees' in describing its scope and it is so when a statute defines 'employee' for its own limited purposes. The interpretation of such statutory provisions has been to require the establishment of a contract of employment whatever the terminology used to describe the persons covered by them,[1] unless there is a specific legislative direction to the contrary.[2]

1. E.g. *Re The Employment Relationship* (1974) 1 W.C.R. 127 (Workmen's Compensation Board of B.C.), 'workmen' interpreted; *Re Telegram Publishing* (1973) 3 L.A.C. (2d) 175 (Carter), 'employee', in Employment Standards Act, R.S.O. 1970, c.147 interpreted.
2. In many jurisdictions the collective bargaining legislation specifically provides that persons who otherwise would not be treated as employees by the law of the contract of employment should be treated as such for the purposes of collective bargaining law: e.g. Saskatchewan, s.2(f) British Columbia s.1(1); Ontario, s.(1)(i).

B. Working Definition

154. At common law, the contract of employment is, in simple terms, an agreement by one party, the employee, to serve the other party, the employer, the consideration being remuneration for those services. Quebec civil law defines the contract of employment in a similar fashion, contemplating an agreement where a person agrees to work for a limited period of time under the direction or control of another person for remuneration.[1] These definitions are widesweeping, including many relationships which in other jurisdictions might be classified separately.

1. The *Code civil du Québec* defines the contract of employment in s.2085.

155. In Canada, both the common law and the civil law of Quebec make no distinction in principle between full-time and part-time employees, between regular and casual employees or between probationary and seniority rated employees. In as much as collective bargaining and legislative provisions create special duties, rights and obligations in respect of probationary, part-time and casual employees, this has no effect on the legal classification of such employees. Similarly, the Supreme Court of Canada ruled in 2000 that persons who work for the government are considered to have contracts of employment with the crown which include all the usual incidents of regular employment contracts found in the private sector.[1] Although many of the terms and conditions of employment of crown employees are dictated by statute rather than by contract negotiations, nonetheless the contract of employment provides the gateway into, and the foundation of the employment relationship between, the crown and its employees. Again, sometimes persons are spoken of as 'office' holders. Whatever special meaning attached to that term, today it has no special magic in labour law. An 'office' holder will be classified as an employee on the basis of the same principles, which apply to persons who do not hold an 'office'. Being an 'office' holder may have other implications such as, for instance, bearing the burden of special obligations if the 'office' is that of a director of a corporation, or of not being able to claim certain expenditures against earned income as a taxpayer, or of entitling the holder of the 'office' to be treated in a procedurally fair manner in dismissal and disciplinary proceedings under general administrative law, but such incidents are not germane to legal classification.[2] Finally, several Canadian courts have recognized a special status of 'intermediate' for workers whose contracts fall marginally beyond the normal borderline of 'employee' status as outlined below. It has been held that 'intermediate' status entitles the worker to reasonable notice of termination and protection against summary dismissal without 'just cause' and obliges the worker to act in the best interests of the employer. In these ways, 'intermediate' status resembles a regular employment contract.[3] It remains to be seen how far courts will extend the definition of 'intermediates'.

1. *Wells* v. *Newfoundland* (2000) 46 C.C.E.L. (2d) 165 (S.C.C.), [1999] 3 S.C.R. 199.
2. Statutes in respect of companies usually define 'officer' as including presidents, directors, secretaries, treasurers, general managers. E.g. The Business Corporations Act, R.S.O. 1990, c.B-16, s.1(1). For the purposes of the Income Tax Act, S.c.1970–71–21, c.63, s.248(1) defines 'office' as the position of an individual who has been appointed to have an ascertained income, e.g. a judge.
3. E.g. *Erb* v. *Expert Delivery Ltd.* (1996) 14 C.C.E.L. (2d) 158 (N.B.Q.B.) where truck drivers who were not 'employees' because they owned their own vehicles were nonetheless entitled to reasonable notice of termination as 'intermediates'.

156. On the other hand, there are many relationships which apparently fall within the scope of the contract of employment as described but which are not categorized as employment relationship for the purposes of labour law. Much will depend on the weight given to certain aspects of the context in which the services rendered for remuneration are given. This issue is explored in §2.

157. Note also that many persons who do render services in a way which would normally qualify them as employees are specifically excluded from the operation of statutes which purport to govern employment relationships. Typically, collective bargaining statutes exempt persons who may be termed 'professionals' such as doctors, lawyers, dentists and the like from their operation. Also they often do not apply to other persons who work under contracts of employment such as agricultural or domestic workers or to members of the police force, firefighters or teachers. Frequently, other statutory schemes create special industrial relations' systems for such groups. It is impossible to catalogue the great number of special legislative schemes here, but a perusal of the sections relating to coverage in the basic collective bargaining legislation will indicate whether or not such special legislation exists.

158. Finally, many persons who are legally classified as working under contracts of employment are excluded from statutes which provide that employees shall be paid a prescribed minimum wage, shall not be paid more than a prescribed period of notice of vacation, etc. Typically, such employees include domestic, agricultural and horticultural workers. Again, a compilation is impractical in this work, but the basic standard statutes to which reference will be made below ought to be consulted. An exclusion from statutory benefits which directly or indirectly discriminates against members of a protected group under section 15 of the Charter and Rights and Freedoms must be justified under section 1 of the Charter or be struck down as unconstitutional. Section 1 provides that Charter rights may be abridged 'subject only to such reasonable limits prescribed by law as can be demonstrably justified in a free and democratic society'. For example, the domestics exclusion arguably might be found unconstitutional if it is the case that the vast majority of domestics are women, for then the exclusion would indirectly discriminate against females.

C. Apprenticeships

159. Apprentices form a special category of employees worthy of separate treatment. An apprenticeship may have to be served as a condition of admission to an occupational field. Once it was common for an apprentice not to receive any remuneration apart from this instruction and supervision and support and maintenance. Today, the apprentice receives, like other employees, remuneration. Because of the special nature of this contract of employment, many of the incidents normally associated with the contract of employment – to be considered below – do not apply as a matter of common law. For example, in the common law provinces, unless there is a covenant or a contract to the contrary, misconduct on the part of the apprentice does not permit an employer to terminate the contract. Neglect, intoxication, incompetence, disobedience of orders will not normally provide grounds for dismissal. Termination of the contract, without a custom or covenant to the contrary, is to be by mutual consent. If an apprenticeship is wrongfully terminated, the apprentice may sue for damages for the remuneration for the amount of time which the apprenticeship still had to run (subject to the duty to mitigate such loss by accepting other employment) and also, in appropriate cases, for the value of injured future prospects.[1] Contrary to the situation in France where the rules relating to apprenticeships have been codified in the *Code du travail*, Quebec's Civil Code provides no specific rules dealing with apprenticeship. Therefore, the working conditions of an apprentice are found in the particular contract of employment concluded with the employer. The rights and obligations of each party to the contract are established both by the agreement of the parties, but also by reference to the customs and rules of the particular trade or occupational field since they are deemed to be implicitly included in the agreement.

In all jurisdictions there are statutes governing apprenticeships.[2] In all provinces but Ontario, boards are created which are empowered to make recommendations and/or regulations, in respect of specified occupations, which govern the requirements of training, impose duties on employers to instruct, require registration of apprenticeship agreements; they may provide for a system of granting proficiency certificates and even specify some conditions of employment.

1. *Dunk* v. *George Welder*, [1970] 2 All E.R. 630 (C.A.).
2. E.g. Manitoba Apprenticeship and Trade Qualifications Act S.M. 1998, c.54. In Ontario, the two relevant Acts are the Trades Qualification and Apprenticeship Act R.S.O. 1990, c.T-17 and the Apprenticeship and Certification Act, 1998, S.O. 1998, c.22.

D. The Service Characteristic

160. As described, the contract of employment is an agreement to render services in return for remuneration. It must not be thought, however, that this economic element is the sole characteristic of the employment contract. Rather, the essential consideration which an employer bargains for under an employment contract is the right to demand obedience from the employee. Given the constantly changing nature of the work environment, it is impossible for the employer, at the date the contract is made, to predict exactly what the employee will be required to do in the future. The employer's contractual right to have its instructions obeyed provides the employer with the flexibility it needs to accommodate to changing circumstances. Furthermore, the subject matter of any employment contracts is a human being, not a commodity such as wheat. The employee's right to have his/her personal dignity and autonomy respected sits uneasily with the employer's right to command; the potential clearly exists for these interests to clash. On several occasions, the Supreme Court of Canada has explicitly acknowledged this human rights dimension to the employment relationship by giving judicial recognition to the fact that work provides an important psychological benefit to the employee, in addition to economic benefits, which merits protection against employer abuse.[1] Nor must the reality be overlooked that under most employment contracts the employee is in a position where most of the onerous obligations under the contract will be imposed on her or him. Thus, while it is true that, for the purposes of legal classification, the relationship is one of ordinary contract (that is, an enforceable agreement entered into on a voluntary basis by the two parties), it differs from such an ordinary contract in that one party will be assumed to have accepted more burdensome duties of performance than the other. On a strictly analytical basis this is not a valid distinction between a contract of employment and other kinds of contracts. After all, employees are free to negotiate terms which would diminish their obligation to serve. The reality is otherwise. The need for collective bargaining arises out of this reality. Further, where collective bargaining does not occur, legislatures will step in to ensure that employees are guaranteed certain minimal conditions – a 'floor of rights' so to speak – regardless of their strength to obtain these by free contract negotiations. To return: the essence of the contract of employment being the rendering of services at the command of the employer, such contracts will, by implication, impose obligations of a special kind on the employee. These implied obligations will be discussed below. Note that today we eschew the language of master and servant which used to describe these relationships because it implies a relationship between superiors and inferiors. The modern terminology of contract of employment suggests a freedom and equality which better reflects our aspirations. But the language of master and servant is useful because it explains the existence of many of the incidents of the contract of employment. They stem from the duty to serve: obedience, cooperation, good faith and fidelity from the employee are to be expected. They would not be considered integral to the relationship if employment were regarded as just another contractual arrangement. One would expect the corresponding employer obligations to relate to the provision of an appropriate environment for the rendering of services. Additional obligations do not flow naturally from the contract of employment. It is pertinent, therefore, to underline the importance of the characteristic of service.

1. E.g. *Machtinger* v. *HOJ Industries Ltd.* (1992) 40 C.C.E.L. 1 (S.C.C.), [1992] 1 S.C.R. 986, involving a harsh notice of termination clause; *Wallace* v. *United Grain Growers Ltd.* (1997) 97 C.L.L.C. 210029 (S.C.C.), [1998] 3 S.C.R. 701, involving bad faith discharge; *Re Rizzo and Rizzo Shoes Ltd.* (1998) 33 C.C.E.L. (2d) 173 (S.C.C.), [1998] 1 S.C.R. 27, involving frustration of the employment contract by bankruptcy.

§2. Distinguishing the Contract of Employment from other Contracts to Provide Service

A. Why Distinguish?

161. It has been seen that a determination of whether or not there is a contract of employment is crucial to the issue of the applicability of collective bargaining legislation, minimum conditions' statutes, workers' compensation law and the incidents attached to the contract of employment. It is also vital to such questions as to whether or not social welfare benefits are obtainable and as to whether or not claims of expenditures may be made against taxable income. In addition, the attribution of vicarious liability for the acts of another may depend on the existence of a contract of employment between the defendant and the wrongful actor.

B. Relationships that Need to be Distinguished

162. There are several contractual relationships recognized by the common law and the Quebec Civil Code which, on their face, bear a close resemblance to contracts of employment in that they too are contracts to provide services for a fee. First, there is the independent contractor agreement. This is traditionally described as being a contract with a person who agrees to perform tasks to produce a particular result. The notion is that how the result is produced is a matter within the performer's discretion. Moreover, an independent contractor is an entrepreneur who runs his or her own business rather than an employee who is part and parcel of his or her employer's business. The assumption of Canada's capitalistic economy is that protective employment legislation should not shield independent contractors against market risks because untrammelled competition between entrepreneurs is the powerhouse of wealth generation from which society as a whole benefits. Nevertheless, the distinction is easier to draw in theory than is practice, for Canada is currently experiencing a proliferation of self-employment, particularly of a part-time or casual nature, which is frequently characterized by a high degree of economic dependence and subordination on the part of the worker to the 'employer' more akin to employee status than that of the swashbuckling entrepreneur. One explanation for this development is that the forces of the 'new economy' are pressuring Canadian employers to reduce their labour costs in order to compete with overseas companies and one way of doing this is to substitute cheaper, non-employee labour for regular employees.[1] The challenge for courts and tribunals is to determine the extent to which the traditional tests for 'employee' status ought properly to be stretched in order to encompass such dependent contractors. Secondly, the *agency* agreement is to be kept separate from the contract of employment. The salient differentiating feature is that an agent brings her or her principal into contractual relations with others. The agent is usually given power to use his or her judgement and discretion as to how to bring this about. It is self-evident that it will be very difficult to distinguish independent contractors and agents from each other and, more importantly, from employees, because services are rendered for consideration in all of these relationships. It has been suggested that employees are persons who work under a contract of service whereas independent contractors and agents work under a contract for services.[2] But this seems merely to restate the problem in a different way; it does not resolve it.

1. *See Rights and Responsibilities in a Changing Workplace: A Review of Employment Standards in British Columbia* (Victoria: Ministry of Skills, Training and Labour, 1994, chaired by M. Thompson), at 32–3.
2. E.g. *Cassidy* v. *Ministry of Health*, [1951] 1 All E.R. 574 (C.A.).

163. Other relationships which need to be differentiated from the employment one include bailment, partnership and landlord and tenant. Typically, in a bailment for hire, chattels are left with a bailee. He or she is often entitled to use the chattel for some specific purpose in return for the payment of money, often periodically payable. The question of whether or not such a relationship is in fact a contract of employment will arise where the use of the chattel by the bailee is alleged to be for the benefit of the owner-bailor of the chattel. The hire of a car might be such a situation.

164. A partnership is the carrying on of business by two or more people for profit. It is sometimes the case that although the relationship is said to be a partnership, it is more fairly characterized as a contract of employment because it involves the rendering of services by one party to another for remuneration.

165. The last group of relationships which it is necessary to discuss here is that of landlord and tenant. An issue may arise where a person who is unquestionably an employee occupies a dwelling of her or his employer and the question is whether or not landlord and tenant law applies to such occupation. The difficulty then will not be whether or not such occupation can be distinguished from a contract of employment but rather whether or not the occupation is primarily to further the employer's interest in which case the employee will not be a tenant for landlord and tenant law. Here the question is whether the character of the employment is such that it prevents the employee from claiming another status under law. This problem, being different in kind, will not be treated again in this work.

C. The Criteria Used to Make the Distinctions

166. As has been noted, the most important characteristics of the contract of employment are, first, that it is a contract of service under which the employee is subordinate to the authority of the employer and, secondly, that the employee is not running his or her own business but is part of the employer's business. It follows that the nature of the service becomes crucial. Reference here is not being made to the tasks which are to be performed, the product to be produced or the result to be reached. Rather the emphasis is on the essence of the relationship: does it more closely approximate one in which the person performing the task is a servant *vis-à-vis* the hiring entrepreneur rather than an equal, contracting person operating her or his own business in much the same way as the hiring entrepreneur? Line drawing will necessarily be imprecise. It can be shown that the original concept of master and servant (with its attendant notions that to be a servant was to be legally classified as having a status in society with duties, rights, obligations and privileges which were not negotiable) still pervades legal thinking when the determination of whether or not a relationship is a contract of employment is to be made. Master and servant law assumed that the master had control over the servant. The test of control is of great importance today when deciding whether or not a contract of employment exists. But the notion of control is itself an elusive one. When society was much less industrialized than it is now, it was practical to assume that, in the much smaller and simpler enterprises which then existed, the master was the servant's equal in his understanding of the task to be performed. Under such conditions the control test was applicable. The court could look at whether or not the alleged servant had any real discretion as to what he or she was asked to do and as to how to do it. If the answer were that he or she possessed such discretion, no master and servant relationship would exist. The utility of this test decreased as the mode of organization of enterprises and technical developments made it increasingly less likely that the employer would have any skill or competence in, or experience of, the many tasks which had to be performed in daily operations. Today, control is understood in a different sense, namely does the employer control the residual 'when and where' of employment?[1] Thus, if a university administrator has the power to direct a professor how many courses he or she must teach, how many committees he or she must sit on, how much research must be done, when he or she must attend the workplace to complete his or her duties, then the relationship will be one of employee status even though the administrator cannot dictate precisely how these various tasks are to be accomplished. Nevertheless, the test of control over the way tasks are to be performed remains useful. Accordingly, where the degree of the supervision makes it clear that the working person does not have the power to exercise any discretion in mode of performance nor to delegate his or her duties, there will be an employment relationship.[2] These inquiries are, therefore, still made in the cases.

Other criteria of this kind include the ownership of the tools used. If the person for whom the work is to be done supplies the tools, this may be taken as an indication that the performer is an employee rather than an independent contractor who is self-employed. But, while complete control over the mode of production indicates the existence of a contract of employment, incomplete control over how the work is to be done, or ownership of the tools by the performer of the work, does not mean that there is no contract of employment. The courts, acknowledging the new modes of organization in enterprise, have sought alternative and complementary tests, but these do not provide precise guidelines. A variant which has been offered is the organization test: to determine whether or not a person is an employee is to depend on a judgement as to whether the person is part and parcel of the organization.[3] By definition, this includes a lot of people who are not strictly controlled in the mode of carrying out their tasks, permitting doctors, professional people of all kinds, skilled craftspeople, etc., to be treated as employees. But, once again, this test provides no mathematically exact means of differentiating people who have contracts of employment from persons who are self-employed and Canadian courts have cautioned against attempting to apply it mechanistically.[4] A formula much in use in Canada is that offered by Lord Wright in *Montreal* v. *Montreal Locomotive Works*:[5]

> 'In earlier cases a single test, such as the presence of absence of control, was often relied on to determine whether the case was one of master and servant . . . In the more complex conditions of modern industry, more complicated tests have often to be applied. It has been suggested that a fourfold test would in some cases be more appropriate, a complex involving (1) control; (2) ownership of the tools; (3) chance of profit; (4) risk of loss.'

Elsewhere in his judgment, Lord Wright explained that these factors are relevant in so far as they help answer the fundamental question 'whose business is it?':

> 'In this way, it is in some cases possible to decide the issue by raising as the crucial question whose business is it, or in other words by asking whether the party is carrying on the business, in the sense of carrying it on for himself or on his own and not merely for a superior.'

Similarly, under the Quebec civil law, employer control or worker subordination to the employer in the performance of the job are criteria used to distinguish an employment relationship from entrepreneurship.[6] Indeed, the test set up by the Privy Council in *Montreal Locomotive Works* has often been referred to by Quebec courts in applying civil law principles. The uncertainty of the law is compounded by the fact that courts and tribunals frequently blend selected components of the various tests. The elastic nature of the above-mentioned tests affords courts and tribunals ample leeway to apply them in a purposive sense, namely by asking the question whether or not it accords with the underlying policy goals of the statute or common law doctrine in question to rule that a person is an employee. Prior to 1997, decision-makers did not always openly admit that the policy approach was the crucial, or even an operative factor in their rulings. However, the policy approach was explicitly endorsed by the Supreme Court of Canada in 1997.[7] Although that case arose in the context of collective bargaining legislation, the principle appears to hold good for other protective employment statutes as well as common law doctrines such as vicarious liability or reasonable notice of termination For example, in *Imperial Taxi Brandon (1983) Ltd.* v. *Hutchison*,[8] the Manitoba Court of Appeal held that a taxi driver was an employee under the Employment Standards Act and the Payment of Wages Act, even though he did not receive a wage check from the company, because he fell squarely within the mischief at which the Acts are aimed:

> 'The purpose of the employment standards legislation is to prevent the exploitation of those who, to earn a living, have no choice other than to follow the direction of an employer as to the hours they must work, and the manner in which the work is to be done. It is with the statutory purpose in mind that the definition in the legislation must be construed.'

By focusing on the policy nature of the inquiry, it becomes possible to infuse a measure of rationality, orderliness and predictability into the law which otherwise too often disappears in the hodge-podge of 'tests' and 'facts' in each case.

1. E.g. *Truong* v. *British Columbia* (1998) 32 C.C.E.L. (2d) 291, at 306 (B.C.S.C.).
2. E.g. *Pacific Logging Company* v. *The Queen*, [1974] 5 W.W.R. 523 (B.C.Co.Ct.).

3. *Stevenson, Jordon and Harrison Ltd.* v. *MacDonald and Evans*, [1952] I T.L.R. 101 *per* Denning L.J. (C.A.).
4. E.g. *Wiebe Doors Services Ltd.* v. *M.N.R.*, [1986] 5 W.W.R. 450, at 459 (F.C.A.); *Pointe-Claire (City)* v. *S.E.P.B. Local 57*, [1997] 1 S.C.R. 1015, at 1047 (S.C.C.).
5. [1947] 1 D.L.R. 161, at 169 (P.C.).
6. *Quebec Asbestos Corporation* v. *Couture*, [1929] S.C.R. 166; *Lemay Construction Ltée* v. *Poirier*, [1965] B.R. 565.
7. *Pointe-Claire (City)* v. *S.E.P.B. Local 57*, [1997] 1 S.C.R. 1015, at 1047; Gilles Trudeau 'Temporary Employees Hired Through A Personnel Agency: Who Is The Real Employer?', (1997) 5 *Canadian Labour and Employment Law Journal* 359.
8. (1987), 46 D.L.R. (4d) 310 (Man.C.A.), *per* Twaddle J.A. *See also Cormier* v. *Alta. Human Rights Commission* (1984) 6 C.C.E.L. 60, at 61 (Alta.Q.B.), in the context of the human rights legislation.

D. Application of the Criteria

167. No useful purpose would be served by cataloguing decisions on the question of whether or not a contract of employment existed.[1] The tests used are different in kind and each requires a weighing of facts, while leaving much discretion to the judges to weigh the significance of the various facts in the light of the policy goals of the particular statute or common law doctrine in question. But some feeling for the flavour of decision-making may be gained by considering a few examples. A court, using the control test fairly rigidly, found that salesmen were servants.[2] They worked on commission and could choose their own routes, subject to veto by the hirer, who also had the right to stipulate which merchandise to push, how to keep books of account and who required full-time devotion to the sale of its goods. Drivers of mobile canteens who worked under not very different conditions were held to be independent contractors on an appeal from a determination under an Employment Standards Act.[3] This was done even though the appeal board noted that many of the circumstances of the relationship indicated an employment contract. The test apparently used was the four-fold one from *Montreal Locomotive Works* set out above. A court applied a mixed test to determine the status of a painter who had worked under a contract of employment with his hirer prior to the creation of the relationship in question. He performed the same tasks, but he could do them whenever he felt like it. He had to provide his own transport. He was held to be an employee rather than an independent contractor.[4] But people who manage general stores held under franchises have been held to be employees for the purpose of minimum standards' legislation, even though their earnings were tied to profits and they had a good deal of discretion in the day-to-day running of the store. Factors which led to those decisions included the nature of the right of selection and termination of the store operators by the franchisors, the contractual requirement to take a certain amount of stock, etc.[5] Two final examples: a court held a 13-year-old newsboy who collected and delivered papers for which he was remunerated on the basis of number delivered to be an independent contractor.[6] Crucial to the decision seemed to be the fact that the boy had a choice as to which method he used to deliver the papers: on foot, by bicycle, by wagon or by motor vehicle. He also was to seek new subscribers and customers for his route. A strict adherence to the control test seems to have governed the decision. Contrast this with a case in which persons, known as district circulation managers for a newspaper, were held to be employees. They contracted with the supervised carriers: they assumed responsibility for the wholesale value of the newspaper they accepted for distribution. Their remuneration was held to be a guaranteed lump sum although the agreement had tied remuneration to the value of the newspapers sold. The expenses of running the district managers' offices were shared by them with the newspaper owners. These factors were evaluated in light of the *Montreal Locomotive Works*' test, where control ostensibly matters less, and led to the determination that there was a contract of employment between the district managers and the newspaper.[7]

1. A complete analysis can be found in G. England, I. Christie and M. Christie, *Employment Law in Canada*, 3rd edn. (Markham: Butterworths, 1998, looseleaf), ch. 2.
2. *Wright* v. *Jeffrey*, [1937] 1 D.L.R. 227 (Ont.C.A.).
3. *Re Appeal, Employment Standards: Gil's Lunch Service Limited*, October 1970 (Frank G. Harrington).
4. *Armstrong* v. *Mac's Milk* (1975) 7 O.R. 2(d) 478 (Ont.H.C.).
5. E.g. *Becker Milk* (1973) 1 L.A.C. (2d) 337 (Carter). Similar facts led to the same conclusion in *Commission des normes du travail* v. *Laiterie Perrette Ltd.*, Q.S.C., D.T.E. 84T–761.
6. *Elliott* v. *Preston and Bartholomew*, [1957] O.W.N. 205 (Ont.C.C.).
7. *Telegram Publishing* (1973) 3 L.A.C. (2d) 175 (Carter).

E. Significance of the Context as a Criterion

168. The cases typically arise in two contexts. One, where a person who has rendered services seeks to have some of the guaranteed benefits of minimum standards' legislation apply to him or her. The other is where a person other than the one who actually inflicted injury is being sought to be made responsible vicariously for the injury-causing action. The nature of these cases and the seemingly agreed upon notion that employers cannot be expected to exercise the same amount of control over their employees as they could in times gone by, have influenced decision-makers to look more towards tests such as the *Montreal Locomotive Works* one than to the control one. The minimum standards legislation is designed to ensure certain terms and conditions. They are to be the bare minima which must obtain in workplaces where employees are in poor contractual bargaining positions. The central notions behind vicarious liability are to be discussed below but they include (i) that those who profit from the work done at their behest should bear the cost of harm inflicted on strangers by the profit-earning operation, and (ii) that the injured strangers should have a means of redress available against someone economically capable of compensating them. In both sets of situations important social objectives could be undermined by a restrictive reading of the definition of the contract of employment. Accordingly, as we saw above, decision-makers apply the tests in order to further the policy goals of the statute or common law doctrine in question.

F. Who is the Employer?

169. There are some other situations which give rise to the question of whether or not a contract of employment exists. One of these is where a person who is unquestionably an employee under a contract with employer A is sent to B to do some work and, while he or she does this, causes injury. There could be an issue as to whether A or B should be held vicariously responsible for the damage caused. Circumstances in which employees are lent in this way can vary a great deal, but there are some which recur more often than others in the reported decisions. They include the lending of vehicle drivers, crane operators, seafarers to operate charter vessels and doctors by one hospital to another. The courts have traditionally approached the question by asking in whose employ the servant was at the time he or she inflicted injury.

170. The task facing the courts in these kinds of cases is complicated by the fact that there is often a contract between employer A and B, setting out the conditions of the lending of A's employee and/or equipment. Such a contract is of itself not dispositive of the question of who the employer is, even if the contract states that, say B, shall be the employer for certain purposes and time;[1] other terms of the contract may affect the determination. This will be so because they may specify the amount of control which A and B shall have, who is to pay for what aspects of the servant's remuneration and other such indicia of the existence of an employment relationship. Thus much will depend on the facts of the particular case, but some general observations can be offered to aid in predicting of the outcome of such cases.

1. *Mersey Docks and Harbour Board* v. *Coggins & Griffith*, [1974] A.C. 1 (H.L.).

171. The same developments in jurisprudence which were noted above, from adherence to a restricted notion of control to the use of an approach which recognizes the modes of organization of modern enterprise, can be recognized. Early on, there was a readiness by the courts to say that B had become the responsible employer where most of the direction as to how the work was to be done was given by B.[1] However, more recently, the courts have held that the original employer, usually referred to as the general employer, has a very heavy burden to discharge in order to prove that a transfer has taken place to the borrowing employer, referred to as the temporary employer.[2] It seems that part of this shift in emphasis is due to the fact that many of the borrowed employees are not subject to control in the carrying out of their tasks, being highly skilled. Thus, the courts have come to look to such criteria as: who can actually dismiss the employee, who is the real paymaster, for what length of time is the borrowed service to continue? Such questions will, more frequently than not, lead to the conclusion that the lending employer has remained the responsible employer. Furthermore, the general employer normally will be in the best position to appraise the safety risk of its own employees and, therefore, will be able to take out insurance coverage against negligence on the part of its employees and pass on the cost of the premium to the temporary employer as part of the price for the job.[3]

1. E.g. *Canadian Northern Transfer* v. *Toronto Storage* (1924) 55 O.L.R. 352 (Ont.C.A.).
2. *Mersey Docks and Harbour* v. *Coggins*, *supra*; *McKee* v. *Dumas* (1976) 12 O.R. (2d) 670 (Ont. C.A.); *City of North York* v. *Kent Chemical Industries* (1985) 32 A.C.W.S. (2d) 271; *James Street Hardware & Furniture Co. Ltd.* v. *Spizziri* (1985) 51 O.R. (2d) 641 (Ont.H.Ct.).
3. See J. Denis Hynes, 'Chaos and the Law of the Borrowed Servant: An Argument for Consistency' (1994) 1 *The J. of Law and Commerce* 1.

172. It is interesting to observe that in dealing with similar facts Quebec courts, applying civil law principles deeply rooted in French law, have reached exactly the same conclusion as other Canadian courts have through common law principles. According to Quebec civil law, the borrowing employer will be held vicariously responsible for damages caused as a temporary employer only if the borrowed employee falls under his or her immediate control in the performance of his or her tasks.[1]

1. For an example of the application of that rule, *see Lemay Construction Ltée* v. *Poirier et al.*, [1965] B.R. 565.

173. To establish an employment relationship there must be a contract between identifiable individuals. Difficult questions may arise because it is not clear whom the actual employer is when services are rendered for the benefit of a number of associated businesses. An enterprise may, for reasons such as limiting commercial liability, minimizing the incidence of taxation, enhancing efficiency by, say, separating storage from distribution in its operations, etc., organize itself so that several separate legal entities are created, although the business is, in functional terms, one. Workers may be asked to do work for several of the legal entities. At common law, one of these entities will have to be capable of being classified as an employer before the incidents of the contract of employment will be applicable.[1] Such a determination will have to be made on the basis of such tests as control, ownership of tools, the fourfold test of *Montreal Locomotive Works*, and so forth. Moreover, some courts have gone so far as to treat as a single employer two or more related employers which operate under common control or direction, so that all the relevant employers are jointly and severally liable for the employee's entitlements.[2] This can assist the employee particularly when his/her main 'employer' has become insolvent; the employee can simply collect from other 'employers' within the group.

Interestingly, this approach incorporates into the common law the 'related employer' provision found in several provinces' employment standards and collective bargaining Acts. For example, section 11 of the Nova Scotia Labour Standards Code provides,

> 'Where, in the opinion of the Director or the Tribunal, associated or related activities, or businesses, are carried on, concurrently or constructively, by or through more than one corporation, individual, firm, syndicate or association, or any combination thereof, under common control or direction, the Director or the Tribunal may treat the corporations, individuals, firms, syndicates or associations or any combination thereof as constituting one employer for the purposes of this Act.'

These statutory provisions give the decision-maker discretion to issue a single employer declaration. Typically, an order will be granted where either the intent or the effect of the employers' corporate structuring is to undermine the policy goals of the Act.

1. *Holland* v. *Saltair Beach Resort*, [1951] 1 W.W.R. (N.S.) 816 (B.C.C.A.).
2. E.g. *Sinclair* v. *Dover Engineering Ltd* (1987) 11 B.C.L.R. (2d) 176 (S.C.), affm'd 49 D.L.R. (4d) 297 (B.C.C.A.); *Gray* v. *Standard Trustco Ltd* (1995) 8 C.C.E.L. (2d) 46 (Ont.Gen.Div.)

174. In the same vein, a problem could arise when an employer sells its business: who will be responsible for existing obligations to the employee? Frequently, of course, the matters will be controlled by the contract between the seller and buyer of the business. But they may not be. Further, there may be occasions where the employee will not want to bring an action against the seller of the business because of the financial difficulties of the seller. Again, some jurisdictions have copied collective bargaining legislation. There it is provided that unions, faced with a change of ownership of an undertaking with which they have an agreement about working conditions will, in given circumstances, have that agreement continue to operate *vis-à-vis* the successor owner. Some minimum standards' statutes have similar provisions to ensure the continuation of availability of benefits to employees. Thus, section 12 of the Nova Scotia Employment Standards Code states,

> 'If an activity, business, trade or undertaking is disposed of, transferred or sold in any manner or amalgamated, whether by agreement, will, instrument, transfer, including transfer of shares, or by operation of law, the period of employment of an employee of the activity, business, trade or undertaking at the time of such disposition, transfer, sale or amalgamation, shall be deemed to have been employed with the disposee, transferee, purchaser or amalgamation and the continuity of employment not broken.'

Again, the courts have also addressed the issue by ruling that there is an implied term in the employment contract of the worker and the new employer that the worker's prior service with the previous employer will be counted towards his/her continuous employment for the purpose of all contractual benefits, unless the new employer 'squarely' notifies the worker to the contrary when their contract of employment is made.[1] In Quebec, the Civil Code goes a step further, providing that the contract of employment 'is not terminated by alienation of the enterprise or any change in its legal structure by way of amalgamation or otherwise'. In such circumstances, the contract of employment is as binding on the successor as on the former employer.[2]

1. *Tayolor* v. *Dallas Investments Ltd.* (1993) 93 C.L.L.C. 14045, at para. 12271 (Alta.Q.B.).
2. C.c.Q., s.2097.

175. Sometimes a claim will be made that a person who ran a one-person company was an employee of that company. This is possible because a company is a juristic person separate and distinct from the incorporators. The problem is most likely to arise where dependants wish to make a workers' compensation benefit claim or the like. In such a case there can be no argument that the person is under the control of the company as to either what work can be done or how it ought to be done. On the basis of such a test, the director/worker cannot claim an employment relationship. It is also difficult to succeed on the basis that the relationship is one of such dependency that there is in fact an employment relationship. This latter argument would fly in the face of the fact that the company was formed to serve the needs of the director/worker. Yet such a person may well be classified as an employee if the context warrants, once again highlighting the fact that the semantic tests used by decision-makers are driven by the need to satisfy sometimes unstated policy objectives. Thus, in one such case, the Privy Council refused to pierce the corporate veil and held that the one-man company was the employer of the one man who had formed it, had appointed himself as a life-long director of it and had then employed himself as a servant. The need of a widow and children were thus met (as well as those of an arbitrary company law rule).[1] In a very similar case, the chairman of a workers' compensation board held that the failure to register the one-man company as an employer under the scheme (as well as not seeking protection as a sole proprietor), showed that the intent of the guiding soul of the company was to avoid having to pay premiums under the scheme. Such an attitude was seen as leading to an undermining of this socially beneficial compensation scheme. Thus, it would be dysfunctional to permit dependants to collect compensation on the basis that the deceased had been an employee. It would mean that a business person had obtained free insurance, because the normal rule that the scheme did not punish an employee for the employer's failure to pay premiums would have been applied to benefit a person who should not, whatever his classification would have been for other purposes, be regarded as an employee under this statute.[2] That is, a contrary position to that adopted by the Privy Council in respect of the corporate veil and the existence of an employment relationship was taken because different purposes were sought to be served.

1. *Lee* v. *Lee's Air Farming*, [1960] 3 All E.R. 420 (P.C.).
2. *Re A One-Man Company* (1975) 2 W.C.R. 41 (Workmen's Compensation Board of B.C.).

§3. Formation of Contracts of Employment

A. Types of Contract of Employment

176. A contract of employment is, in some respects, similar to other kinds of contract. That is, it is a voluntarily entered into agreement, between two capable parties, with an intention to create legal relations. There will have been an offer of certain terms and an acceptance thereof, and consideration must be proved before the contract can be enforced. It should be noted, however, that in Quebec, under the Civil Code, the concept of consideration does not apply in the same way. At common law, all the criteria listed above must be met. They are usually very easy to establish where an employment relationship is alleged to exist. But there is at least one significant difference between a contract of employment and other contracts. In the ordinary contract, even one which provides for a fixed period of duration, performance will terminate the contract. A contract of employment is, typically, one of indefinite duration, which terminates upon appropriate notice being given.

177. It was common for English courts to read a contract of employment of indefinite duration as being a yearly contract, that is, a contract for at least one year certain. The effect of this was that it could not be terminated until that year had elapsed. Should the yearly hiring continue beyond the first year, without any express arrangements being made by the parties, the employment would be considered a yearly one. This was known as the presumption of yearly hiring. It was always a weak presumption, one which could be easily rebutted by, say, showing that the method of payment of wages had reference to a different time period than a year. The presumption had its origins in a society whose economic base, being primarily agricultural, was markedly different to our present one. Indeed, at a time when the presumption of yearly hiring was still part of the formal statement of the rules relating to employment relationships, society was changing so fast that a number of courts had already begun not to treat contracts of indefinite duration as yearly contracts.[1] As early as 1898, the Supreme Court of Canada rejected the notion that the presumption of a yearly hiring was a rule of law. It held that the nature of the contract had to be deduced from surrounding facts, not by presumption of law.[2] It was not until 1969 that an English Court of Appeal finally stated that in England the presumption of yearly hiring was no longer effective.[3]

1. M.R. Freedland, *The Contract of Employment* (Oxford, 1976) 143–6.
2. *Bain* v. *Anderson and Anderson Furniture* (1898) 28 S.C.R. 481.
3. *Richardson* v. *Koefod*, [1969] 3 All E.R. 1264 (C.A.).

178. Once the presumption of yearly hiring is not applied to a contract of employment of indefinite duration, the question arises as to how such a contract is to be treated. One tendency has been to regard it as a periodic hiring, the length of the period being ascertained by reference to the incidents of the contract especially the method of payment of wages. For example, an indefinite hiring in which wages are paid on a monthly basis could be treated as hiring for a month, which is renewed every month for a month. But the notion that employment contracts are of this nature is at a variance with the common understanding of both employers and employees, namely that the relationship is a continuing one. Accordingly, the prevailing and better view is that such contracts are to be treated as being of indefinite duration, terminable by reasonable notice. We will return, later, to the nature of reasonable notice but it suffices to note that the method of payment of wages was a significant factor.

179. It is also possible to have a contract of employment for a fixed term. Under such a contract the relationship cannot be ended by either party until the specified period expires, unless the conduct of one of the parties is such as to amount to a repudiation of the contract. Not every provision for a fixed term will characterize the contract as being one, which cannot be ended by the giving of reasonable notice. The particular circumstances of the contract, including the express provision for a fixed term, will be weighed. Similarly, the parties can create an employment contract for the purpose of having performed a defined task. Again, the contract will terminate lawfully by its own terms when the task has been completed.

180. According to the Quebec Civil Code, a contract of employment is like any other kind of contract and will be validly formed if it meets the following conditions: (i) the parties are legally capable of contracting; (ii) their consent has been legally given; and (iii) both the object and the cause or consideration of the contract are not prohibited by law or contrary to public order.[1] The contract can be for a fixed period or for an indeterminate duration.[2] The parties can expressly specify that the contract will be for a fixed term. In such a case, the contractual relationship will come to an end upon the expiration of the term unless the parties tacitly or expressly renew their agreement. Unless proven otherwise, the renewed employment contract is presumed to be of an indeterminate duration.[3] In that case, each party can terminate the agreement upon reasonable notice.[4]

1. C.c.Q., s.1385.
2. C.c.Q., s.2086.
3. C.c.Q., s.2090.
4. C.c.Q., s.2091.

B. The Requirement of Writing

181. The contract of employment may be formed in the same way as all other contracts: the parties may write down the terms of their agreement, they may merely express their agreement orally, or the relationship can be inferred as having been created by the conduct of the parties. The latter is very common. Typically, an employee will commence work and obey the employer's commands, as well as receive certain benefits. On the other hand, contracts of employment concerned with managerial-type employees will often be in writing. The law does not require that they should be so unless they are to last for a term longer than a year. Except in Quebec, where contracts are entered into on the basis that they are not to be completed within the space of one year, the seventeenth-century English Statute of Fraud's[1] Canadian equivalents[2] must be satisfied. These requirements are that the agreement must be in writing, or some memorandum or note of it must exist, before an action can be brought on it. Further, the party who is made a defendant to the action must have signed the agreement, memorandum or note; the plaintiff need not be a signatory. Where a memorandum or note is relied upon, it need not be in a particular form. The signed minutes of a company's books or a letter from a principal to an agent accepting the terms negotiated by that agent, may satisfy the statute. But the memorandum or note must contain the material terms of the agreement. What is material is a question of fact but, at the very least, there must be an indication of the essence of the bargain between the parties and the condition in respect of which the action is brought must be in writing. Note here that failure to comply with the writing requirements does not render the contract void, merely a particular term or terms unenforceable.

1. Statute of Frauds (1677) 29 Car. II. c.3.
2. E.g. the Statute of Frauds, R.S.O. 1990, c.S-19.

182. The rationale behind the Statute of Frauds was that parties in a dispute about an agreement should not be in a position where they had to rely on differing and fading memories, making it easy to perjure themselves about the terms of the agreement. Those dangers increase as the length of the contractual relationship increases. Binding the parties to what they had written down made some sense but the mechanism used was crude. For example, the resolution of a dispute which takes place a day after entering an agreement which was to last for more than a year hardly requires protection against failing memories. Or, conversely, a dispute about an agreement which was not, at the time of entering, meant to last for as long as a year, but which had continued for much longer, could be enforced regardless of the lack of writing which supposedly protects against defective memory and the possibility of perjury. Further, the Statute of Frauds frequently has the very opposite effect to its intended one. More often than not the party relying on the failure of writing is a defendant who seeks to escape the obligations he or she has taken on under the agreement. Such a defendant will not have to say that he or she has not agreed to the term with which he or she is now charged, but merely that it is not contained in writing signed by him or her. Inevitably, the courts' disapproval of the Statute of Frauds led to the development of many means to avoid its literal application. Some of these included: (i) inroads on the parole evidence rule which theoretically forbids the use of parole evidence to complement evidence which must be in writing and (ii) the reading-in of implied terms into a memorandum or note, thus amplifying the ambit of the available writing. A detailed discussion of these judicial tools of avoidance is out of place here; attention must be reserved for the reading given to the Statute of Frauds in the particular context of contracts of employment. It is a narrow one. Such contracts are read as not being caught by the statute (that is, to be enforced they do not require writing), if either party's obligations under the agreement can be performed within one year of entering into the agreement, even if the agreement stipulates that it was to last longer than one year. All that needs to be shown is that it is possible, regardless of the parties' intentions, that one party's obligations may be discharged within one year.[1] Thus, even if the contract of employment is said to be for the life of the employee, the contract will not need to meet the requirements of the Statute of Frauds because the employee might die within a year of entering into such an agreement.[2] Similarly, a contract of indefinite duration does not have to meet the Statute of Frauds criteria to be enforceable because, as was noted above, it can be terminated by reasonable notice (provided the reasonable notice in the particular case does not exceed one year).[3] This is of particular importance now that the presumption of yearly hiring is a thing of the past. It seems as if the only contracts of employment which have to be in writing for the purposes of enforcement are those which are specifically stated to be for more than one year and where performance by neither party can be discharged within a year. It has been held in England that, when such a rare case arises, the contract must be in writing even though one of the terms of the contract says that it could be terminated by notice within one year.[4] This seems a strange view of the law, one which ought not to be followed in Canada.

1. *Cemco Electrical Manufacturing* v. *Von Snellenberg*, [1947] S.C.R. 121; *Mott* v. *Troot*, [1943] S.C.R. 256.
2. *Campbell* v. *Business Fleels*, [1954] O.R. 87 (C.A.); *Cemco supra* note 1.
3. *Harvard* v. *Freeholders Oil*, [1952] 6 W.W.R. (N.S.) 413 (Sask.Q.B.); *Dalimore* v. *Canada Permanent Trust*, [1947] O.W.N. 682 (H.C.).
4. *Dobson* v. *Collis* (1856) H. & N. 81; *Hanau* v. *Ehrlich*, [1912] A.C. 39 (H.L.).

183. Some western provinces of Canada have similar legislative provisions to those of the Statute of Frauds in respect of the contract of employment. They are found in specialized statutes, that is, statutes not dealing with all of the incidents of the contract of employment.[1] This has raised the question of whether or not the requirement of writing applied to terms other than those covered by the particular statute. In one Saskatchewan case it was held that the requirement of writing should be so restricted, but the Saskatchewan Wages Recovery Act was amended to overcome this defect.[2] The other statutes, however, are still in the form which gave rise to the judicial decision in Saskatchewan. Another aspect of these statutes is that they are phrased differently from the Statute of Frauds. The latter requires writing whenever the contract is not to be performed within the space of one year; the western statutes demand writing where a contract is to last longer than one year, no matter when it commences. This could make for different application.

1. E.g. Saskatchewan Wages Recovery Act, R.S.S. 1978, c.W-1, s.4.
2. *Edwards* v. *Grosser & Glass*, [1936] 3 W.W.R. 670 (Sask.C.A.).

184. It is important to note that to hold that a plaintiff cannot succeed because there is no adequate writing does not necessarily mean that the plaintiff fails altogether. For instance, an employee may still recover wages for work proved to have been performed (even though he or she cannot prove the terms of the agreement relating to wages by reference to the agreement), by way of the remedy of *quantum meruit*. This will be discussed below.

185. The Statute of Frauds has no equivalent in Quebec law. Quebec's civil law requires the consent of the parties 'legally given' as a condition to the validity of a contract, but does not require this consent to be confirmed in writing unless otherwise stated.[1] This general rule applies equally to employment contracts.[2] However, when available, such written documentation could be of great help if it becomes necessary to prove the content of the agreement before a court.

1. C.c.Q., s.1385.
2. S.2089 of the *Code civil du Québec* allows the parties to an employment contract to reach an express agreement prohibiting the employee from competing with her/his former employer for a limited period of time, but such a restrictive covenant must be stated in writing.

186. Some special relations are required to be in writing by statute, not because of their duration but because their contents have been considered to be worthy of particular attention. Reference has already been made to apprenticeship contracts. No list of special cases is being offered here, but note that frequently teachers' contracts are required to be in writing.[1] As we shall see below, in some instances statutes will provide that certain terms of the contract must be reduced to writing after the contract has been entered into, notably in situations where the calculation of remuneration has to be accounted for and where the conditions relating to safety have to be revealed.

1. The Education Act, R.S.O. 1990, c.129, s.258(2) which provides that, where there is no written memorandum of the agreement, a contract embodying the terms and conditions contained in the form of contract prescribed for a full-time teacher will be assumed to regulate the contract. *See also*: The Public Schools Act, R.S.M., 1987, c.P-250, s.92(1); The Education Act, R.S.S. 1978, (Supp.) c.E-o.1, s.198(8); The School Act, S.A. 1988, c.S-3.1, s.78(5)(a).

C. Capacity to Contract

1. Minors

187. At common law, all adults have the same capacity to enter into contracts of employment, subject to the rules relating to immigrants, discussed below. But minors or infants, that is, persons below the age of 18, have attracted special rules. First, a contract entered into between an adult and an infant is not enforceable unless the contract (i) provides goods and services which can be classified as 'necessaries' at law (food, clothing, and lodging, which are suitable to the infant's station in life and required at the time when they are tendered),[1] (ii) is, on the whole, beneficial to the infant. It was held long ago that contracts of apprenticeship and employment were, prima facie to be regarded as being of the second kind, viz., contracts which on the whole benefited the infant.[2] Of course, certain adverse provisions in such a contract might render it disadvantageous to the infant and, hence, not binding on him or her.[3]

1. *Chapple* v. *Cooper* (1844) 153 E.R. 105 (Exch.); *Nash* v. *Inman*, [1908] 2 K.B. 1 (C.A.).
2. *De Francesco* v. *Barnum*, [1886–90] All E.R. Rep. 414 (Ch.).
3. E.g. *Toronto Marlboro Major Junior 'A' Hockey Club et al.* v. *Tonelli et al.* (1977) 18 O.R. (2d) 21 (Div.Ct.), *affm'd* 23 O.R. (2d) 193 (C.A.) where the employment contract of an up and coming hockey star was held to be non-beneficial to him, and therefore void, because of the unduly one-sided balance of benefits in favour of the club.

188. The Quebec Civil Code states as a general rule that all persons are capable of contracting except those whose incapacity is expressly stipulated by law.[1] Such is the case of infants and young persons who generally remain minors until they reach the age of 18.[2] This incapacity is established for their benefit so that a person capable of contracting could not invoke the incapacity of the other party to escape from his or her contractual duties.[3] It means also that the contract remains valid and enforceable as long as the minor does not resort to his or her right to have it annulled. A court will relieve a minor from his or her contractual agreement only if it is convinced that the minor, while not being represented by his or her tutor, gave his or her consent to an unfavourable deal.[4] This rule applies generally to any type of contract, including the contract of employment. However, section 156 of the Civil Code states that persons 14 years of age or over are deemed to be of full age for all acts pertaining to their employment.[5] Consequently, such young workers are treated by the law in the same manner as any other employee unless otherwise provided by specific legislation.[6]

1. C.c.Q., s.154.
2. C.c.Q., s.153.
3. C.c.Q., ss.1420 and 163.
4. C.c.Q., s.163.
5. C.c.Q., s.156.
6. For example, the Education Act (R.S.Q., c.I-13.3, s.14) states that school attendance on full-time basis is mandatory until the child attains 16 years of age.

189. It is clear that the special rules relating to the enforceability of infant contracts were the result of the perceived need to protect people of tender years from being exploited. It is equally clear that the judicial reasoning that contracts of service are on the whole beneficial to infants create a risk that minors could be taken advantage of by employers. The abuses of child labour have been well documented and, as a result, modern legislatures have limited the capacity of infants to enter employment relationships. The statutes are too numerous to list and differ so much in detail that only a general picture can be presented. Typically, they define 'child' as a person of a particular age or less, and 'adolescent' or 'young person' as a person of an age less than 18 but older than a 'child'. They go on to prohibit employment for each grouping in certain industries altogether. In other occupations they permit employment only where certain conditions are satisfied so that the work will not interfere with school attendance and effort; permission of the parents may have to be obtained; the work must be adjudged, by the appropriate ministry, not to be dangerous to the physical well-being of the child, the work must not be performed at certain hours (usually not between midnight and early morning sometimes not in the early evening), unless there is special parental permission; the work must not be a hazard to the mental well-being of the child, by say, being associated with 'morally' unattractive behaviour (as in the business of hotel keeping, entertainment and the running of licensed premises). A common exception to prohibitions in respect of child employment is found in employment in a family undertaking.

2. *Migrants*

190. As was the case with respect to minors, migrants are people whose status affects their right to enter into employment relations. The federal Immigration Act 1976,[1] which came into effect on 10 April 1978, has specific provisions aimed at dovetailing immigration objectives with employment policies. Accordingly, it has special rules about persons who are not Canadian citizens or permanent residents of Canada and who seek employment in Canada. The Act eschews discrimination against them on the basis of race, nationality or place of origin, but it has regard to the employment prospects of such persons and of the effect of such employment on Canadian citizens' and permanent residents' prospects for employment. Immigrants must therefore obtain an employment authorization before they will be given the necessary visa permitting them to enter the country. Typically, an employer will have determined that he has a need for a particular worker or group of workers who are not presently Canadian citizens or permanent residents. The employer may have been contacted by such prospective employees or have decided that the skills he requires can only be found outside Canada. Once the employer has made a decision to employ such a person or persons, the employer must detail the qualification and experience of the applicant and provide other information to an immigration officer which enables that officer to consider whether or not (i) the employer has made reasonable efforts to hire citizens or permanent residents, (ii) the job offered is a good one in the sense that the conditions of employment are ones which would be acceptable to Canadian citizens and permanent residents. The immigration officer is to consult with the National Employment Services office in the pertinent geographical area when making these assessments. The National Employment Service operates as a placement office.

1. Immigration Act, R.S.C. 1985, ch. I-2.

191. Another aspect of the law relating to immigration which shows its integration with employment law is that no employment authorization may be granted to workers whose employment will affect the settlement of a labour dispute at the intended place of employment or the employment of a disputant.

192. There are exemptions to the need for an employment authorization.[1] They include diplomats, sports' teams, certain entertainers, foreign representatives, trade representatives of foreign countries, companies' and unions employees who come for less than 90 days, and other such special cases. Of greatest practical importance is the list of approximately 60 occupations, including defined professionals and technicians, investors, traders and intra-company transferees, who are exempted from the usual requirements under Chapter 16 of the North America Free Trade Agreement. Usually, any exemption must be renewed annually.

1. The categories are listed in the Immigration Regulations, S.O.R. 78–172, s.19(1) and (2) and s.20.

3. Collective agreements as a restraint on capacity to contract

193. If employees' conditions of work are governed by a collective agreement, the employer and his employees cannot enter into agreements to change such conditions, unless the collective agreement provides to the contrary. This underscores the difference made to the employment relationship when it comes to be governed by the collective bargaining regime. Whereas the legal capacity to enter into, and to vary, contracts is unlimited outside this sphere, employees are restricted in their right to negotiate as individuals once collective agreement-making has taken place. This restriction of capacity to contract is justified on the basis that a greater advantage for many can be obtained by not permitting individuals to undermine the solidarity of collective action.

D. Purpose of Contract

194. As in all other contract situations, a contract of employment, otherwise validly formed, may be held to be unenforceable or even void if the purpose of entering into the relationship was to engage in conduct which offends public policy, such as when it contravenes the criminal law, a statutory provision or the rules governing restraint of trade, or where the contract offends public morality.[1] What effect the particular offence against public policy has on the contract depends on the nature of the conduct and on whether or not it can be severed from the remainder of the contract, permitting the remainder a life of its own. The principles of severance in respect of the restraint of trade doctrine will be reviewed briefly below.

1. E.g. *Dann* v. *Curzon* (1911) 104 L.T. 66 (K.B.).

195. It remains to note that it may be that contracts, which on their face are employment ones, may be held to be void if the obligations on the apparent employee go far beyond those which may be required of a servant. A contract of slavery is apparently not enforceable. But it is far from clear when the imposed obligations will lead courts to say that the alleged contract of employment is unenforceable. The only attempt at propounding a test came in a nineteenth-century case in which the issue was not directly before the court. The following formulation was offered:

> 'The law of England allows a man to contract for his labour, or allows him to place himself in the service of a master, but it does not allow him to attach to his contracts of service any servile incidents – any elements of servitude as distinguished from service.'[1]

This authority is not used by modern Canadian courts to strike down contractual terms that unduly favour the employer, Today, the closest approximation to the old 'servile incidents' rule is the doctrine of unconscionability. This doctrine allows courts to rescind an employment contract, which has been made by parties having unequal bargaining power and whose provisions are unfairly one-sided. Despite the potential breadth of the doctrine, the courts have applied it narrowly to situations where the employer deliberately exploits a known, special vulnerability of the employee so as to win oppressively one-sided terms, especially if the worker has not received professional legal counsel. For example, a separation agreement under which a worker gave up his right to sue for wrongful dismissal in return for an unreasonably low amount of money was rescinded because the employer knew the worker was depressed and anxious following her termination, in desperate financial straits and had not consulted a lawyer.[2] So far the courts have refused to presume the presence of a special vulnerability from the fact that the contractual terms in question are unduly harsh or from the fact that the employment relationship is inherently unequal; the presence of such a vulnerability must be demonstrably proven by the employee.[3] Clearly, this narrow approach reflects the courts' concern to safeguard the principle of 'freedom of contract' against the risk of undue encroachment. Two other doctrines resemble somewhat the old 'servile incidents' principle. First, the doctrine of duress allows a court to rescind a contract that has been procured by a threatened unlawful act, provided that the plaintiff gives notice of avoidance within a reasonable time of the duress having lifted. This doctrine is rarely applied to the employment relationship. Second, the doctrine of undue influence also permits the courts to rescind a contract where one party has been usually swayed by the other. So far, undue influence has been restricted to relationships such as patient and doctor, lawyer and client, guardian and ward and even husband and wife.

1. *Davies* v. *Davies* (1887) 36 Ch. D. 359, *per* Bowen, L.J. (C.A.). The passage was also cited with approval, but again by way of an aside in *Horwood* v. *Millar's Timber & Trading*, [1971] 1 K.B. 305 (C.A.).
2. *Blackmore* v. *Cablenet Ltd.* (1994) 8 C.C.E.L. (2d) 174 (Alta.Q.B.).
3. *Boisonault* v. *Block Bros. Realty Ltd.* (1987) 47 Man. R. (2d) 148, esp. 154 (Man.Q.B.), where the Court upheld a provision which entitled to company to retain 50 per cent of sales made by the plaintiff after his employment terminated.

196. The Quebec Civil Code states that a lawful object and cause are essential to the validity of a contract and, if not present, the contract is void.[1] The object of a contract is 'the judicial operation envisaged by the parties at the time of its formation, as it emerges from all rights and obligations created by the contract'.[2] For instance, in a contract of employment, the main object would be the work to be performed and the remuneration to be paid. The cause of the contract, which does not need to be expressed, 'is the reason that determines each of the parties to enter into the contract'.[3] Both the cause and the object of the contract must be lawful and not contrary to public order.[4] According to the Quebec Civil Code, a contract between two persons of full age is valid even if its terms are unduly harsh for one of them. Section 1405 clearly specifies that the exploitation of one of the parties by the other does not vitiate the contract, thereby safeguarding the principle of 'freedom of contract'. However, distinct rules govern the 'contract of adhesion', a contract the essential terms of which are imposed by one of the parties without the possibility of negotiating them. These rules aim at protecting the weaker party against an abusive application or interpretation of what is otherwise a valid contract. Section 1437 of the Code goes as far as to state that an abusive term of a contract of adhesion is null or the obligation arising from it can be reduced. Depending upon the circumstances of its conclusion, a contract of employment could well be considered a contract of adhesion.[5]

1. C.c.Q., ss.1411 and 1413.
2. C.c.Q., s.1412.
3. C.c.Q., s.1410.
4. C.c.Q., ss.1411 and 1413.
5. C.c.Q., ss.1379, 1435–8.

E. Requirements of Fairness in Formation of Contracts of Employment

1. The human rights statutes

197. The essence of the employment relationship being that it is a voluntarily negotiated contract, it follows that employers and employees are free to determine with whom they form such a relationship. The economic reality is that this gives the employer a great advantage: complete freedom in the selection of employees, in normal market conditions, will, for the most part, benefit employers in the bargaining game. The freedom to select has been restricted to a considerable extent by legislative support for the countervailing policy of preventing a variety of discriminatory practices.

198. Every legislature has enacted human rights legislation.[1] Such statutes prohibit discriminatory conduct of various kinds, especially in relation to hiring and during employment. Each jurisdiction's statute must therefore be examined for the precise scope of the prohibitions. It is impractical to cover anything but the more basic aspects of the enactments.[2] All of the statutes prohibit discrimination on the basis of race, or the basis of one or more of national origin, place of origin, ethnic origin, or origin of ancestry, colour and religion (sometimes referred to as creed), and physical or mental handicap. Discrimination on the basis of sex and marital status is not permitted, nor is discrimination on the basis of age allowed. The age groups which are protected (by not permitting an employer to take account of age when hiring or dealing with employees) vary from jurisdiction to jurisdiction, some providing protection to persons between the ages of 45 and 65, others to those between 18/19 and 65. In addition to these commonly specified grounds, there are noteworthy special heads of non-discrimination in various provinces. These include, depending on the jurisdiction, political beliefs, pregnancy/childbirth, criminal convictions, family status, language, source of income and social origin. As well, sexual orientation is a protected ground throughout Canada. In some jurisdictions, this has been achieved by express legislative inclusion. However, even in the absence of such legislation, the Supreme Court of Canada has ruled that provincial human rights Acts are to be read as implicitly encompassing sexual orientation in order to comply with section 15 of the Charter.[3] Transgendered and transsexual persons are also protected in all jurisdictions under the heads of either 'disability' or 'sex'.

1. Canadian Human Rights Act, R.S.C. 1985, c.H-6; Human Rights, Citizenship and Multiculturalism Act, R.S.A. 1980, c.H-11.7; Human Rights Code, R.S.B.C. 1996, c.210; The Human Rights Code, C.C.S.M., c.H-175; Human Rights Act R.S.N.B. 1973, c.H-11; Human Rights Act, R.S.N.S. 1989, c.214; Ontario Human Rights Code, R.S.O. 1990, c.H-19; Human Rights Act, R.S.P.E.I. 1988, c.H-12; Charter of Human Rights and Freedoms, R.S.Q., c.C-12; The Saskatchewan Human Rights Code, S.S. 1979, c.S-24. This modern concept of 'substantive equality' is aimed at ensuring that all persons can fully participate in employment. *See Promoting Equality: A New Vision*, Report of the Canadian Human Rights Act Review Panel, Chair G. La forest (Ottawa, Department of Justice, 2000), esp. chs. 1–3.
2. The most elaborate recent examination of the law and policy of contemporary human rights Acts is *Promoting Equality: a New Vision*, Report of the Canadian Human Rights Act Review Panel, Chair Laforest J. (Ottawa: Canadian Human Rights Commission, March 2000).
3. *Vriend* v. *Alberta*, [1998] 1 S.C.R. 493.

198A. The purpose of the human rights legislation is to eliminate not only wilful discrimination where an employer deliberately penalizes a person out of distaste for his or her protected characteristics but also the results of past discriminatory practices and attitudes of employers and society as a whole. To achieve this purpose, the legislation distinguishes between two forms of discrimination.[1] First, 'direct' discrimination prohibits employer rules or practices that on their face discriminate against minorities, for example, 'no Catholics need apply for this vacancy'. Second, 'indirect' discrimination prohibits employers from having rules or practices that, while neutral on their face, have a disproportionately severe impact on a protected person. For example, a rule requiring minimum eyesight, health or fitness standards would exclude disabled persons from the job even though the rule does not explicitly state that disabled persons need not apply. The doctrine of 'indirect' discrimination is very important because it opens to review a broad swathe of employer rules and practices, including recruitment and promotion policies, shift scheduling, job assignments, seniority systems, wage payment systems, leaves of absence, insurance benefit packages, performance appraisal systems, retirement systems, and the physical environment of the workplace.

1. The leading authority is *Ontario Human Rights Commission* v. *Simpson-Sears Ltd.* (1985) 23 D.L.R. (4d) 321 (S.C.C.), [1985] 2 S.C.R. 536.

198B. In all Canadian jurisdictions, a discriminatory rule or practice is allowed if it constitutes a 'bona fide occupational requirement' (BFOR), or words to that effect.[1] In order to establish the BFOR defence, an employer must prove, first, that it introduced the rule or practice honestly and in good faith, genuinely believing that it was necessary for the efficient and safe performance of work. Secondly, the employer must prove that the rule or practice is objectively necessary to assure the efficient and safe performance of the job.[2] Employers must adduce concrete evidence to support a BFOR; mere subjective impressions, which are often based on cultural stereotypes, will not suffice.[3] Not surprisingly, the fact that an employer's customers or clients may have discriminatory tastes and prefer not to deal with minorities will not ground a BFOR. Furthermore, the BFOR defence cannot succeed unless the employer proves that it has reasonably accommodated the employee up to the point of undue hardship. This is an important requirement. For example, a disabled employee who is too weak to do the lifting component of a job could be excluded from it were it not for the requirement employer's duty to reasonably accommodate the employee by examining the feasibility of assigning the lifting component to another employee or installing a mechanical lifting device. Prior to 1999, the obligation to reasonably accommodate only arose in cases of 'indirect' discrimination,[4] save in Manitoba, Ontario and the federal jurisdiction where the legislation expressly required an employer to reasonably accommodate an individual as part of the BFOR defence. This limitation caused considerable technical uncertainties for lawyers and their clients as well as frustrating the remedial goal of the human rights Acts. Therefore, in 1999 the Supreme Court of Canada ruled that in all provinces the legislation implicitly requires the employer to prove that it has reasonably accommodated the employee as a condition precedent to establishing a BFOR.[5]

1. E.g. British Columbia Human Rights Code, R.S.B.C., c.210, s.13(4). The precise formulation of the defence varies between the provinces but there are no practical differences.
2. *Ontario Human Rights Commission* v. *Etobicoke (Borough)*, [1982] 1 S.C.R. 202, at 208.
3. For example, in *Carson* v. *Air Canada* (1982) 3 C.H.H.R. D/818 (Can. H.R.T.), an airline company could not justify its policy of not hiring pilots below age 28 because it failed to adduce evidence showing that age 28 was the correct cut-off date for it to amortize the recruiting and training costs of pilots.
4. *Central Alberta Dairy Pool* v. *Alberta (Human Rights Commission)*, [1990] 2 S.C.R. 489.
5. *B.C. Public Service Employment Relations Commission* v. *B.C. Government and Service Employees Union*, [1999] 3 S.C.R. 3.

198C. The duty of reasonable accommodation under the human rights Acts is a revolutionary development in Canadian employment law. The duty requires the employer to attempt to accommodate the employee's protected characteristics short of causing the firm or other employees an undue hardship. In other words, the duty seeks to strike a balance of proportionality between the business interests of the employer and the personal interests of the employee. The human rights tribunals are permitted to go the very heart of traditional managerial prerogatives and determine whether the employer's judgements are substantively and procedurally fair having regard to the parties' respective interests. All areas of managerial decision making are susceptible to review, including recruiting and promotion policies and procedures, leaves of absence, performance appraisal, insurance benefits packages, compensation systems, shift scheduling, job assignment, discipline and dismissal procedures, seniority systems, the physical design of the workplace.[1] This marks a major breakthrough in the traditional attitude of the law which was to defer to management's expertise in sensitive areas of business operations. Potentially, the influence of the duty will spread beyond the frontiers of the human rights Act into other areas of labour law such as the common law contract of employment. Indeed, one court has already ruled that an employment contract cannot be frustrated by the illness of the employee at common law unless the employer has reasonably accommodated the employee prior to invoking termination.[2] Previously, the common law did not require an employer to consider changing an employee's job duties or work schedule as a prerequisite to finding frustration.[3] Furthermore, the duty of reasonable accommodation will likely intensify the pressure on the courts to imply a general duty of fairness on employers under the employment contract.[4] The duty also binds any trade union that has bargaining rights in the workplace as well as all employees in the bargaining unit. Thus, the union is obliged to cooperate with management in devising methods to accommodate protected employees. The effect is to give the union a voice in decision-making in highly sensitive areas of business operations.[5] Potentially, this experience of joint partnership may make employers less reluctant than was historically the case to defend their prerogatives in regular collective bargaining.

1. For a detailed analysis of the duty, *see* England *et al.*, *op. cit.*, vol. 1, at paras. 5.106–5.1109.
2. *Antonacci* v. *Great Atlantic and Pacific Co. of Canada* (1998) 98 C.L.L.C. 210017, at para. 141098 (Ont.Gen.Div.).
3. E.g. *Condor* v. *Barron Knights Ltd.*, [1966] 1 W.L.R. 87.
4. *See infra.* para. 302A.
5. E.g. *O.P.E.I.U. Local 267* v. *Domtar Inc (No. 4)* (1990) 12 C.H.R.R. D/161 (Ont.Bd.Inq.). *See also* M. Lynk and R. Ellis, 'Unions and the Duty of Accommodation' (1992) 1 C.L.L.J. 238.

199. Special mention must also be made of the so-called 'employment equity' approach to redressing existing discrimination. This approach requires employers proactively to redesign the composition of their workforce to achieve equality, under the supervision of a state agency, within designated time limits. The only 'employment equity' Act currently in force in Canada is in the federal jurisdiction. The federally enacted Employment Equity Act[1] requires employers who employ one hundred or more employees on, or in connection with, a federal work, undertaking or business to file reports with the Minister of Employment and Immigration concerning the number of persons employed, and to identify those employees who belong to groups which might be disadvantaged in respect of employment opportunities: women, aboriginal peoples, disabled people and people who, by race or colour, belong to visible minorities. The employer is required to develop an 'employment equity plan' for ensuring that employment practices which create barriers are removed and that designated groups receive proportional representation.[2] As part of such a plan, the employer must, *inter alia*, 'consider' establishing 'short term' (i.e. between one and three years) numerical goals for hiring and promoting protected groups. However, the Act does not require the employer to take measures that would cause the firm 'undue hardship', to hire or promote unqualified persons, to create new vacancies, or to override pre-existing seniority rights in layoffs and recall.[3] There are two primary methods for enforcing the Act. First, the employer must file an annual progress report with the Minister who has the discretion to publicize the results. Bad publicity, it is thought, will be a disincentive to renegade employers. Of greater potency is the Minister's authority to pass on a report to the Canadian Human Rights Commission for the latter body could use it to launch a complaint of systemic discrimination against the employer under the Canadian Human Rights Act.[4] The latter Act provides Human Rights Tribunals with an arsenal of remedies to 'make whole' the effects of unlawful discrimination, including the imposition of hiring and promotion quotas for protected groups.[5] The second enforcement method is to impose an administrative fine on employers who fail to comply with the Act. The imposition of such a fine is at the discretion of the Minister. Such a fine cannot exceed $10,000 for a single violation and $50,000 for repeated violations.[6] These fines are administrative, not criminal in nature. The advantages of administrative penalties are that the parties' ongoing relationships will not be soured by the stigma of criminality, and that the criminal law burden of proof of 'beyond any reasonable doubt' would be too difficult to surmount in many cases of subtle discrimination. In Ontario, similar legislation was introduced in 1993 by the left-wing N.D.P. government but it was repealed by the Progressive Conservative government in 1995 in response to widespread public opposition to the Act.[7]

1. S.C. 1995, c.44.
2. S.10(2) describes in detail what the plan must contain.
3. Ss.6 and 8(1)–(3).
4. A review of the Act's operation up to 1992 concluded that these disincentives were insufficient to deter violators and recommended that the Act be given sharper teeth: *A Matter of Fairness: Report of the Special Committee on the Review of the Employment Equity Act* (Ottawa: Queen's Printer, 1992), 29.
5. A Canadian Human Rights Commission's decision to force an employer to make one in four of its new hirings a woman until women constituted 13 per cent of the internal workforce – the proportion of jobs held by women in Canada as a whole – has been upheld by the Supreme Court or Canada; *see Canadian National Railway Co.* v. *Canadian Human Rights Commission* (1987) 87 C.L.L.C. 17,022; [1987] 1 S.C.R. 1114.
6. Ss.35 and 36.
7. Employment Equity Act, S.O. 1993, c.35, repealed by S.O. 1995, c.4, s.1.

200. There are other exceptions to human rights legislation bans on discrimination in addition to the defence of 'bona fide occupational requirement' described above. The most important one is the permission granted to non-profit organizations whose major objective is to further the interests of a particular religion, ethnic group, or the like, to discriminate to this end.[1]

1. In some jurisdictions, any educational non-profit organization may be exempt from the legislation, e.g. Nova Scotia, Ontario, Prince Edward Island.

201. Typically, the operation of human rights legislation requires the lodging of a complaint with a commission set up under the statute. The commission will then dispatch an investigating officer and/or conciliator. Sometimes the commission is empowered to initiate such an investigation without receiving a complaint. The officer will make a report (usually to the pertinent Minister), unless a settlement is effected. Where that report indicates that there are grounds for believing that proscribed discrimination has occurred, a board or tribunal may be set up. The carriage of the hearing of the matter before such a board or tribunal may be left to the complainant in some cases, to the commission itself in others. The board or tribunal is given an arsenal of remedies, including the powers to order that the discriminatory practice cease, to reinstate or re-engage employees who have been wrongfully terminated, and to award financial and other remedies to 'make whole' the harm caused by the discrimination. Under the 'make whole' approach, compensation is based on the principle of placing the victim, or victims of the discrimination in the financial position they would have been in had the discrimination never occurred.[1] This is broader than the common law measures of damages in wrongful dismissal which restricts damages to the period of notice of termination and the general contract law measure of damages which is to give the plaintiff the value of the promise that has been broken. Compensation can be awarded not only for economic losses such as wages and benefits but also for psychological harm. As well, the 'make whole' process allows the adjudicator to apply so-called 'affirmative action' measures to eradicate systemic discrimination in the workplace, including setting hiring and promotion targets[2] for protected groups and establishing sensitivity training seminars for supervisors and other employees. An order of a human rights tribunal may be given effect by registering it in an appropriate superior court, giving it the standing of a judgment and making it enforceable as such. In some cases, the board or tribunal merely may make a recommendation leaving it to the commission to make an order, and in Alberta, by leaving it to the appropriate ministry to determine whether the steps leading to enforcement will be taken. The procedures for enforcing human rights complaints have been criticized on several grounds,[3] foremost among which is the unreasonably lengthy delays in processing claims to adjudication. Indeed, in many provinces, it is not unusual for three years to elapse between the date of filing the complaint and the date of adjudication. Other criticisms include the provision of inadequate education services by the commissions, undue conservatism on the part of the schemes' administrators, inadequate public input into the process, unduly low damages awards by tribunals and inadequate training of human rights administrators in the complexities of human rights law.[4] In addition to providing for 'make whole' remedies, the human rights Act also establish offences in respect of which criminal prosecutions may be launched, although this means of enforcement is seldom employed, particularly because a minister's consent has to be obtained and this makes such a route unattractive. There are not all that many hearings before boards or tribunals considering the great number of potential situations in which prohibited practices might occur. But this does not mean that the existence of the legislation is unimportant. To the contrary, its educational effect is very significant and may well have led, in the employment field, to a much greater awareness of the need to provide equality of opportunity than existed before.[5]

1. E.g. *Mckee* v. *Hayes-Dana Inc* (1993) 17 C.H.R.R. D/84 (Ont.Bd.Inq) where a foreman who was unlawfully laid off at age 57 was awarded compensation for loss of future earnings and benefits up to retiring age of 65 because there was little chance he would ever find replacement work. For a detailed explanation of the 'make whole' approach, *see* England *et al.*, *op. cit.*, vol. 1, paras. 5.168–5.179.
2. As in *C.N.R. Railway Co.* v. *Canadian Human Rights Commission*, [1987] 1 S.C.R. 1114, where the employer was ordered to make one in four of its new hirings a woman until women constituted 13 per cent of the internal workforce – the proportion of jobs held by women in Canada as a whole. *See also National Capital Alliance on Race Relations* v. *The Queen* (1997) 97 C.L.L.C. 230015 (Can. H.R.T.).

3. R.B. Howe and M. Andrade, 'The Reputations of Human Rights Commissions in Canada' (1994) *Can. Jo. of Law and Society* 1. *See* the sweeping recommendations for reform contained in *Promoting Equality, op. cit.*
4. *Ibid.*
5. There are other statutes proscribing discrimination in employment. Of particular importance are the Fair Wages and Hours of Labour Act, R.S.C. 1985. c.F-1 (requires federal government contractors to stipulate non-discriminatory practices in their dealings with sub-contractors); the Employment Insurance Act, S.C. 1996, c.23 (requires non-discriminatory practices in placement of people). In addition, collective bargaining legislation proscribes discriminatory practices by employers and unions whose practices could vitally affect employment opportunities because of the creation of a closed shop or modification thereof.

202. Employers cannot select employees by reference to criteria which offend human rights legislation; the advertising and posting of vacancies must comply with such legislation. Sometimes it is provided directly that the publishers of the invitation to treat (as advertisements and postings are usually treated as a matter of law) may not publish discriminatory material. Furthermore, employment agencies cannot discriminate against workers whom they assign to their clients.

2. *Investigation and testing*

203. It has been noted that employers can defend themselves against a charge of discrimination if the basis for the discrimination is related to a bona fide occupational requirement. In determining whether or not an applicant is qualified for a position, the employer might make inquiries into a person's background and/or ask the applicant to submit to a test. In Manitoba, the right of an employer to make pre-employment investigations is fettered by a statute, requiring that an employee who is to be investigated must be given notice of that fact and that only certain types of information may be sought.[1] The employee is entitled to examine the file containing the results of the investigation. There are, however, relatively broad categories of information that an employer can seek out that are not covered by the Act, for example, the worker's age, marital status, number of dependants, paying habits, outstanding credit obligations and cost of living obligations. Moreover, the Act does not apply to anyone who earns more that $12,000 per annum. In other jurisdictions, prospective employees are protected from such potential invasions of their privacy in a rather fragmented way. Thus, protection against some practices could come from human rights legislation, from special statutes relating to the storage of computer data, or from the obligations of confidence imposed by the law of contract and/or tort on potential informants. Note that in Saskatchewan, where the Human Rights Code prohibits pre-employment inquiries with respect to physical disabilities, a special exemption order has been issued to permit employers to ask job applicants about disabilities which would interfere with their ability to do their job. But such inquiries are to be strictly limited.

1. The Personal Investigation Act, R.S.M. 1987, c.P-34.

204. In relation to pre-employment testing of an employee's health, intelligence, general aptitude or integrity, the risk exists that such tests may discriminate against disabled persons or against those from a different cultural milieu than Canada. If a test does have a discriminatory impact, the employer must establish that the test is a bona fide occupational requirement and that it has attempted to reasonably accommodate the employee to the point of undue hardship. In particular, the employer must be able to prove that the test is both 'reliable' and 'valid'. A 'reliable' test is one where the degree of statistical error in measuring the desired criteria must be within tolerable statistical limits. A 'valid' test is one where satisfactory performance in the tested criteria will result in satisfactory performance of the job itself. The difficulties that can occur in determining the 'reliability' and 'validity' of pre-employment tests are illustrated in *Persad* v. *Sudbury Regional Police Force (No. 2)*.[1] There, an East Asian argued that a cognitive ability test – the department used the well-known 1922 Otis Self-Administered test – was discriminatory because it had the effect of excluding a disproportionately large number of visible minorities from the police force. The Board of Inquiry had to scrutinize and pronounce upon a substantial body of complex expert evidence from professionals in the field before ruling that the test was not culturally biased against visible minorities. In effect, the tribunal became the 'judge' of scientific debates between professionals. The American jurisprudence demonstrates how such inquiries can often become battlefields between the experts.[2] As yet, Canada has not experienced the full impact of this tendency.

1. (1992) 19 C.H.R.R. D/334 (Ont.Bd.Inq.).
2. *See*, for example, P.N. Cox, *Employment and Discrimination Law* (New Hampshire: Butterworths, 1991), ch. 11.

205. There has been much debate as to whether or not employers should be entitled to test would-be employees and/or employees to determine whether or not they use proscribed drugs. In the context of this discussion, the issue is whether or not human rights issues are raised. Employers argue that they should be entitled to subject would-be employees and/or employees to such tests to protect the public, the safety of workers and the stability of production. Human rights activists point to the intrusive nature of the tests (urine and blood samples are to be used), their scientific frailty, the potential for abuse, unwarranted disclosures and the possibility of breaks in the chain of custody of samples. These are all cited as making the human rights and privacy costs too great when compared to the public and private benefits obtainable.[1] The human rights legislation does not directly regulate the use of mandatory drug testing. However, the general proscription of discrimination on the basis of physical and mental handicap prevents employers from randomly initiating drug testing. Thus, in order to establish the bona fide occupational requirement defence, the employer must be able to adduce objective evidence that a worker's drug use undermines his or work performance or poses a significant threat to the health and safety of others. An employer cannot justify drug testing on the basis of stereotypical assumptions such as the perception that all drug users are criminals.[2] Instead, the employer must normally observe that a worker's job performance has actually deteriorated before subjecting him or her to a drug test. Moreover, the courts have struck down work rules requiring employees to self-disclose any previous drug problems, the rationale being that some forms of drug dependency can be rehabilitated completely with the passage of time so that the worker in question would pose no more serious threat than any other employee.[3]

Nevertheless, the employer is given greater leeway to apply mandatory drug tests in highly safety-sensitive industries such as long distance trucking, but even there the particular test used must be reliable and there must not be any less intrusive means of testing for drug use available. In most jurisdictions, the Human Rights Commissions publish guidelines on the circumstances under which drug testing of employees is permissible.[4] Before an employer can dismiss an employee for drug abuse, the employer must have reasonably accommodated that employee up to the point of undue hardship. Reasonable accommodation usually entails supporting the employee through a rehabilitation programme.[5] Only if the employee has clearly demonstrated that he or she cannot perform the job satisfactorily and cannot be expected to remediate in the future can dismissal be invoked.[6]

1. *See* H. Glasbeek and D. McRobert, 'Privatising Discipline: The Case of Mandatory Drug Testing' (1989) 9 *Windsor Yearbook of Access to Justice* 30, esp. 41–6; S. Macdonald, M. Shain and S. Wells, 'Assessing the Justifiability of Workplace Interventions: the Case of Drug Testing' (1998) 6 C.L.E.L.J. 369.
2. *Canada (Human Rights Commission)* v. *Toronto Dominion Bank* (1998) 98 C.L.L.C. 230030 (F.C.A.).
3. *Ibid.*
4. E.g. Ontario Human Rights Commission, *Policy on Drug and Alcohol Testing* (Toronto: Ontario Human Rights Commission, 1992).
5. *Entrop* v. *Imperial Oil Ltd.* (1996) 96 C.L.L.C. 230045 (Ont.H.Ct.).
6. E.g. *Handfield* v. *Board of School Trustees School District No. 26* (1995) 95 C.L.L.C. 230015 (B.C.H.R.C.).

3. Employment agencies

206. An industry has grown up in which agents undertake to put employers in touch with employees for the purposes of entering into contracts of employment. Such agencies may be acting, as a matter of law, as either the agents of the prospective employer or employees. They may bind their principals if they were acting within their ostensible authority. As they are thus in a position to discriminate in relation to employment on proscribed grounds, they have been made subject to the human rights statutes in all provinces. In addition, because they are also in a position to take what is deemed to be unacceptable advantage of persons' lack of information about the labour market, several provinces have passed statutes directly regulating the conduct of employment agencies.[1] The usual form of regulation is to require that the agency must apply for an operating licence. The licensees are normally not permitted to charge employees for services rendered. An assumption seems to have been made that the employer should bear the burden of this cost of enterprise, except in Ontario where a small fee may be charged. The charging of a fee to employees leads to fines and, possibly, loss of licence to operate. In addition to such controls, the agencies may be required to keep records and to provide employees referred to employers with pertinent information about the nature of the employment.

1. British Columbia Employment Standards Act, R.S.B.C. 1996, c.113, s.1; Manitoba Employment Services Act, R.S.M. 1987, c.E-100; Ontario Employment Agencies Act, R.S.O. 1990, c.E-13; Saskatchewan Employment Agencies Act, R.S.S. 1978, c.E-9.

4. Fair practices and collective bargaining

207. The practices in respect of fairness in hiring have to conform to the legislation set out above, even when the employer and employees have entered into a collective agreement. In addition, the union, which as a matter of law is one of the parties to the collective agreement, may have insisted on inserting clauses in the collective agreement, which bolster its security. Sometimes, a union may have inserted a clause requiring that only union members should be hired, or that anyone hired must become a union member within 30 days of joining the bargaining unit, or that persons who were already members must maintain their membership, or, at the very least, that non-union member employees should pay union dues. Such clauses will limit the hiring freedom of the employer, an inhibition which is accepted by the collective bargaining schemes because of the importance they place on the policy of promoting union formation and stability. But, having put the unions in a position where they can, and do, directly affect employment prospects, unions have been made subject to rules of the same nature as are found in human rights legislation, as well as other constraints. This will be discussed in greater detail below.

5. Impact of the Charter of Rights and Freedoms

208. The Charter applies to governments and their instrumentalities, and prohibits discrimination on similar grounds to those commonly found in human rights' statutes. It does not provide for exceptions as those statutes generally do. The Charter's relationship to human rights legislation has already been, and will probably continue to be, the subject of litigation. Note that the Charter asserts that equal treatment without discrimination on the stated grounds shall be accorded before and under the law to all individuals and that all benefits of the law shall be bestowed without discrimination.[1] This section came into effect in April 1985. Judicial interpretation of the impact of the Charter on human rights legislation will also be affected by section 1 of the Charter of Rights and Freedoms which allows limitations on rights and freedoms which may be reasonably justified in a free and democratic society.

1. S.1.

209. The Charter directly governs any statute or statutory regulation that is discriminatory in nature. Less obviously, perhaps, human rights Acts themselves may be challenged as violating the Charter. For example, the courts have ruled that the provincial human rights Acts of some provinces which define 'age' as exempting persons aged 65 or over are constitutional in so far as they permit employers to force people to retire at age 65. This result is to be welcomed because compulsory retirement involves balancing complex interests such as income security, labour mobility, productive efficiency, etc. which the judiciary is poorly placed to deal with.[1] In addition, the Charter may apply directly to an employer if it is exercising statutory authority in administering its personnel policies.[2]

1. E.g. *McKinney* v. *University of Guelph* (1991) 91 C.L.L.C. para. 17,004; [1990] 3 S.C.R. For a detailed analysis of the treatment of compulsory retirement under general human rights Acts and at common law *see* G. England *et al., op. cit.*, vol. 2, ch. 12, 111.

2. *Lavigne* v. *Ontario Public Service Employees Union* (1991) 81 D.L.R. (4d) 545 (S.C.C.), [1991] 2 S.C.R. 211; *Douglas College* v. *Douglas/Kwantlen Faculty Association* (1990) 91 C.L.L.C. 17002 (S.C.C.), [1990] 3 S.C.R. 570.

210. Despite the potential for Charter challenges to human rights abuses, one major limitation must be emphasized; Charter litigation is very lengthy and expensive and is beyond the financial resources of most ordinary employees. It is only where a union or a special interest group becomes involved that Charter litigation becomes financially feasible. Plainly, this limitation applies to all common law litigation to enforce rights in the contract of employment. Nevertheless, since Charter challenges frequently have to be resolved by the highest courts in the lands – provincial courts of appeal or even the Supreme Court of Canada – the delay and financial costs are more excessive than unusual. For the ordinary worker who is not unionized, his or her only realistic forum for enforcing employment rights is the administrative procedure established under employment standards and other protective legislation which is specially designed to achieve speed, informality and cheapness.

Chapter II. Rights and Duties of the Parties to the Employment Relationship

§1. The Roots of such Rights and Duties

211. At common law, the terms of any contract may be expressly spelt out, provided by statute or a court may imply them. In the case of employment contracts, it is rare that a comprehensive statement of the parties' rights and obligations will be expressed in a contractual document, save in the case of senior managers, professionals, stage personalities and sports stars. Instead, for most ordinary workers any written employment contract will rarely include more than the most rudimentary matters such as the nature of the job duties, wages, hours of work and perhaps annual vacations. Indeed, employment contracts are often purely verbal, with nothing being written down. One explanation for this dearth of written terms is that employment contracts are often of indefinite duration so that it is impossible for the parties, in a constantly changing economic and technological environment, to predict in advance exactly what their respective rights and obligations will be. Another explanation is that employers, who typically have the superior bargaining power, like to retain the power to amend and create terms as future circumstances dictate. The flesh and blood of the employment contract derives from other sources. One is the employment standards and other protective employment legislation whose terms are compulsorily imposed into the employment contract and cannot be abridged by agreement of the parties themselves. Terms also derive from company personnel manuals, works rule books and other memoranda that may be incorporated into the contract either expressly by provision to that effect in the contract itself or in the documentation in question, or impliedly by the practice of applying the documentary provisions. Yet another source of terms is judicial implication. Courts distinguish between two kinds of implied terms. First, there are implied terms of fact. Here, the terms are implied into the contract in order to give effect to the unstated factual intentions of the parties. Thus, the court asks whether an officious bystander, watching the parties enter into the contract, would have said: 'Of course, they meant to include a provision to this or that effect'.[1] In this way, the process of implying terms is supposed to conform to freedom of contract. In reality, however, employers and employees may often not have thought of the matter at all and the process of implication is based on what the courts perceive the parties' relationship ought to resemble as a matter of public policy. The second kind of implied term is the implied term of law. Here, the courts frankly acknowledge that terms are implied into the contract as a matter of public policy. In practice, the two kinds of implied terms frequently blend and it is difficult to distinguish the precise basis for the implication.[2] Be that as it may, the outcome of the process is that the implied term has become an important vehicle for judicial policy-making in the formulation of rights and obligations under the employment contract. Indeed, the golden thread that runs through the history of the employment contract in Canada is how the courts are continually re-formulating the implied obligations of the parties in order to give effect to the changing standards of personnel practice and community values about how work relationships should be structured. Nowhere is this more evident than in the case of the employer's implied duty to give 'reasonable' notice of termination; the 'reasonableness' test has become a veritable catch-all a wide variety of judicial policy preferences, as we shall see below.[3] Some commentators have argued that such is the importance of judicial fiat in creating standardized implied terms in employment contracts that it is appropriate to regard the employment relationship as being one of 'status' rather than 'contract'. Although the 'status' point is valuable in manifesting the important role of judicial policy-making in the process of designing a 'model' employment relationship, it must not be taken too far. After all, an implied term is always superseded by an express term so that the parties are free – in theory if not in reality, given the bargaining power disparity between employers and workers – to bargain modifications to the standardized implied terms. Regardless of what the precise theoretical nature of the implication process may be, there is no doubt that its yield is a set of standardized implied terms that favours the employer to a substantially greater extent than the employee, as we shall see below.

1. *Shirlaw* v. *Southern Foundries* (1926) Ltd., [1939] 2 K.B. 296 at 227, *per* Mackinnon, L.J. (C.A.) aff'd. [1940] A.C. 701 (H.L.). A Canadian authority emphasizing the supremacy of this method is *Olympic Industries Inc.* v. *McNeill*, [1994] 3 W.W.R. 268, at 275 (B.C.C.A.).
2. E.g. *Wiebe* v. *Central Transport Refrigeration (Manitoba) Ltd.*, [1994] 6 W.W.R. 305, at 319–20 (Man.C.A.), in the context of the employer's implied obligation to give reasonable notice of termination.
3. *Infra*, para. 337 and the following.

212. In Quebec, the Civil Code expressly defines what a contract of employment is and what broad obligations it must cover. According to section 2085 C.c.Q., three fundamental elements must be present in a contractual arrangement for it to be a contract of employment: (i) performance of work, (ii) done for remuneration, (iii) under the direction or control of the employer. The contract of employment can be either for a fixed term or an indeterminate term (section 2086 C.c.Q.). The employer is bound to allow the performance of the work, to pay the remuneration agreed upon and to protect the health, safety and dignity of the employee (section 2087 C.c.Q.). The employee, for his part, is obliged to carry on his work with prudence and diligence, to act faithfully and honestly and not to use any confidential information he may obtain in the course of his duties (section 2088 C.c.Q.). If the contract of employment is for an indeterminate term, either party may terminate it by giving notice of termination to the other party in reasonable time, given all the circumstances of the case. Beyond these broad obligations that the Civil Code attaches to any contract of employment, the actual working conditions such as remuneration, fringe benefits and working hours are established through negotiation between the parties. Freedom of contract prevails to a large extent in Quebec civil law as well as in Canadian common law. As in the rest of Canada, in Quebec the contract of employment is rarely expressed in written form. This is why most of its terms must be implied by the courts. The Civil Code states that a contract binds the parties not only as to what they have expressed but also as to 'what is incident to it according to its nature and in conformity with usage, equity or law' (section 1434 C.c.Q.). Finally, it must be emphasized, as will be seen below, that in Quebec, as in other provinces, numerous terms of the contract of employment are provided by statute.

§2. The Employer's Duties and Obligations

A. The Duty to Pay Remuneration

1. The foundation of the duty

213. The essence of the contract of employment is that the employee is to render services in return for remuneration. In many cases, the contract itself will specifically provide that remuneration must be paid, the amount which is to be paid, how it is to be paid, and so forth. Where there is no expression of such terms they will be implied if the circumstances of the relationship are such that they indicate an understanding by both parties that there should be payment for the services. It may seem strange to put the proposition in this form but, in the past, courts have held that where there is no express agreement to pay remuneration and the circumstances surrounding the agreement are ambiguous, there ought to be no implication that wages are due. The doubt about the parties' understanding of the bargain usually arises in cases where the employer provides board and lodging and other such benefits to a person who renders services, or where the parties cohabit or are related in some way.[1]

1. *Reeve* v. *Reeve* (1858), 1 F. & F. 280 (N.P.); *Bradshaw* v. *Hayward* (1842), Car. & M.591 (N.P.); *R.* v. *Inhabitants of Sow* (1817) 1 B. & Ald. 178; *Osborn* v. *Guy's Hospital (Governors)* (1726) 2 Stra. 728.

214. It follows that if the parties have explicitly agreed that the employer shall have discretion as to whether or not there shall be payment for the services, there will be no enforceable contractual obligation to pay remuneration. Such arrangements are rare and are sometimes termed engagements of honour to differentiate them from contracts of employment.[1] But it does not follow that if there is no enforceable contract of employment in existence there will be no obligation to pay remuneration to a person who has rendered services. There may be a variety of reasons for the unenforceability of a contract. To take but one, refer to paragraph 181 in which it was noted that a failure to comply with the requirement of writing necessitated by the Statutes of Frauds, might lead to unenforceability. Another such situation might arise where there had been a fundamental mistake by the parties in respect of the bargain they thought they had struck. In such circumstances, services might well have been rendered on the basis that the contract was an enforceable one. At common law, remuneration may then be ordered by the courts on a *quantum meruit* basis. Although there is some confusion in analysis about the origin and scope of this remedy,[2] the best view is that it is a remedy based on general restitutionary principles.[3] The calculation of the remuneration to be paid by way of *quantum meruit* is done on the basis of inferences drawn from the circumstances of the parties' understandings and agreements. The awarding of pay on the basis of *quantum meruit* thus involves the same exercise as is involved in implying a term into a valid contract although analytically it is a different process. Note that the notion of *quantum meruit* may also be employed to award remuneration for services rendered when an employer's conduct is of such a kind that the employee is entitled to treat it as a repudiation of the contract and accordingly to exercise her or his right to rescind it. If the contract is not rescinded, the employee must seek compensation under the contract and a differing means of calculating the sum due will be used, frequently leading to a very different result.[4] The nature of the right of the employer and the employee to sue under the contract will be discussed below.

1. E.g. *Loftus* v. *Roberts* (1902) 18 T.L.R. 532 (C.A.). Sometimes the problem arises in situations where the employer, in addition to the agreed-to remuneration, promises to pay more. The question then becomes whether or not a new contract has been entered into; if it has not, there will be no obligation to pay the extra remuneration, it merely being a promise of honour: *Stylk* v. *Myrick* (1809) 170 E.R. 1168 (N.P.); *Hartley* v. *Ponsonby* (1857) 119 E.R. 1471; *Powell* v. *Braun*, [1954] All E.R. 484 (C.A.).
2. It is sometimes suggested that *quantum meruit* is available where there is a contract on foot; *see Way* v. *Latilla*, [1937] 3 All E.R. 759, but this is analytically unsound.
3. This appears to be the modern Canadian position e.g. *Hill* v. *Develcon Electronics Ltd.* (1992) 37 C.C.E.L. 19 (Sask.Q.B.).
4. *Planch* v. *Colburn* (1831) 8 Bing. 14.

215. Despite the fact that *quantum meruit* is a common law notion, equivalent outcomes can be reached under Quebec civil law principles. For instance, a person who is enriched at the expense of another without justification or cause is required to indemnify the other for her or his correlative impoverishment.[1] This principle could apply to a situation where a person is enriched by the professional services of another in the absence of an enforceable contract providing for remuneration to the professional.[2] Courts may also order remuneration for work performed according to a contract of employment that has then been annulled because of its failure to meet conditions essential to its formation. Even though such a contract is deemed to have never existed, the Civil Code allows the continuing nature of the contract of employment to be taken into account.[3]

1. This rule is derived from Quebec case law based on French law prior to the *Code Napoléon*. It has been codified in the *Code civil du Québec*, ss.1493 to 1496.
2. This was the case in *Ville de Louiseville* v. *Ferrons*, [1947] B.R. 438.
3. *See* s.1700, C.c.Q.; *see* Jean-Louis Baudouin and Pierre-Gabriel Jobin, *Les obligations* (Cowansville: Les Editions Yvon Blais Inc., 5th edn., 1998) 617–19.

2. When the obligation to pay matures

216. The agreement may expressly provide when remuneration shall be paid and it might be that the parties agree that there shall be payment before services have been rendered. Failing such an express term, it has been the common law view that remuneration is payable in arrears. It will be paid at the end of agreed upon periods. Such agreement may, of course, be implied. If such a period is not completed at the time of termination of the contract of employment for reasons other than a breach of contract by the employer, at common law, and according to Quebec civil law, there will be no obligation to pay for the uncompleted period of service.[1] But legislation may have alleviated this potential problem in some provinces. Employment standards Acts in all Canadian jurisdictions provide that wages must be paid at fixed (or shorter) intervals.[2] Further, it is enacted that if a contract is terminated, the employer must, within a given time span, pay all wages due to the employee, without any deductions.[3] The rationale is that the employer, as the party with the deeper pocket, can most comfortably launch civil proceedings to recover sums owed to it by the employee rather than vice versa. Frequently, the legislation will specify exceptional circumstances in which an employer can make deductions. Under the Canada Labour Code, for example, the permissible deductions are (i) those required by another statute; (ii) those required by a court order or a collective agreement; (iii) overpayments of wages; (iv) amounts prescribed by regulation; (v) and any other amount authorized in writing by the employee.[4] The statutory prohibition against deductions pre-supposes that the amounts have been earned in the first place and therefore constitute 'wages' within the meaning of the Acts. Accordingly, it will not be an illegal deduction if the amount in question is discounted from the initial calculation of wages. Theoretically, a question remains: are all wages due upon termination the wages which would be due if the common law applied, that is, wages due for completed periods only? In practice, it is not a major problem. It is likely that employers accept an obligation to pay for all services rendered, regardless of whether or not remuneration is thus paid for incomplete periods. Further contracts usually terminate upon the giving of reasonable notice. Reasonable notice, more often than not, will be a complete pay period.

1. *Cutter* v. *Powell* (1795) 101 E.R. 573; for a rare 'modern' application, *see Ord* v. *Public Utilities Cm'n of Mitchell*, [1936] 1 D.L.R. 540 (Ont.S.C.).
2. E.g. British Columbia Employment Standards Act, R.S.B.C. 1996, c.113, s.17.
3. E.g. Alberta Employment Standards Code, S.A., 1996, c.E-10.3, s.11, s.25(1).
4. S.254.1(3).

217. Sometimes, regardless of the periods at the end of which remuneration is to be paid (by dint of legislation or as a result of the apparent agreement of the parties), a contract may be read as being one which requires a certain amount of service to be given before any contractual obligation to pay remuneration arises. Typically, this will be the case in services to be rendered by a seafarer or by a worker hired to bring in the harvest.[1] The courts' appreciation of custom in the undertaking and of the understanding of the parties will control the outcome of such cases. Suffice it is to say that it will be rare in modern times to read a contract as one which requires performance in its entirety before remuneration for services rendered has to be paid.

1. *Cutter* v. *Powell*, *supra*; *La Plante* v. *Kinnon* (1915) 8 W.W.R. 6 (Sask.C.A.); *Abramoff* v. *Podraiz*, [1902] 2 W.W.R. 6 (Sask.C.A.).

3. The effect of illness

218. Because the contract of employment is one of rendering services, it follows that where an employee becomes so ill that he or she becomes incapable of doing any work at all or, at least, not for a protracted period, the contract will have been frustrated. This will be considered again when termination of the contract of employment is discussed below, in paragraphs 323–327.

219. Where an illness is of a temporary duration, the courts have treated the contract as continuing with certain rights and obligations being suspended for the duration of the absence e.g. the employee's duty to work and the employer's duty to pay wages. As well, the employment standards Acts may prohibit dismissal for defined short-term illnesses.[1] More importantly, the human rights legislation comes into play if the illness constitutes a protected 'disability' as defined in the Acts. As we saw in paragraph 198, the employer cannot dismiss an employee by reason of 'disability' unless the employer can prove that the lack of capability is a bona fide occupational requirement and that it has attempted to reasonably accommodate the employee up to the point of undue hardship, for example, by allowing him or her reasonable time off to recover and by considering amending his or her job duties, work schedule and physical environment in order that he or she can still perform some work. Regarding payment of wages, the courts have permitted recovery of wages for such periods of illness, even though no work was done by the employee. In a 1903 case, the Supreme Court of Canada justified the recovery of wages for an employee who had not rendered services during a temporary illness, in part, on the basis that common humanity required such an approach.[2] The analytically sounder rationalization was that there was an obligation to pay employees during temporary periods of illness on the basis that employees do not warrant their good health and that as long as they are willing to render the services due under the contract of employment there is no breach of contract disentitling them from remuneration.[3] Hence, the stress is on the temporary nature of illness. It follows that, should the employer be forced to hire a substitute to perform the necessary work because of the length of absence of the ill, but willing, employee, the obligation to pay may well have ended. In contrast, the approach of the English Court of Appeal in its 1982 decision in *Mears* v. *Safecar Security Ltd.*[4] is less generous to the employee than the older authorities. There, the Court of Appeal held that there is no presumption in favour of implying a requirement on the employer to provide sick pay. Rather, in the absence of express provisions on point, the burden falls on the employee of proving that there is a reliable past practice in the organization from which it can be deduced that the both sides intended that sick pay be payable. Modern Canadian courts have yet to pronounce upon the *Mears* ruling. Under Quebec civil law, too, there is no clear rule requiring the payment of wages for a temporary period of illness.

1. The Canada Labour Code, R.S.C. 1985, c.L-2, which only covers federal undertakings, prohibits employers from dismissing employees who have been sick for no longer than 12 weeks and requires them to treat the period of absence as continuous employment time for the purposes of calculating seniority and other benefits. The Quebec Labour Standards Act, R.S.Q., c.N-1.1., s.122.2, prohibits employers from dismissing, suspending or transferring an employee on the

ground that s/he was absent by reason of illness or accident for no longer than 17 weeks in the preceding 12 months.
2. *Dartmouth Ferry Commission* v. *Marks* (1903–4) 34 S.C.R. 366 (S.C.C.).
3. *See also Cuckson* v. *Stones* (1859) 120 E.R. 902 (K.B.); *Marrison* v. *Bell*, [1939] 2 K.B. 187 (C.A.); *Orman* v. *Saville Sportswear*, [1960] 3 All E.R. 105 (Q.B.).
4. [1982] I.C.R. 626, at 649–51 (C.A.).

220. Perhaps the dearth of modern authorities is explained by the fact that employers and employees usually agree expressly that there shall be remuneration paid during absences due to illness. Such agreements stipulate that a certain number of sick days will be allowed to an employee per year. Sometimes the sick leave plan is cumulative. That is, unused sick days are added (sometimes at the rate of one and half days for each day not used) until a maximum period of continuous sick leave is reached. When the plan is not a cumulative one, sick leave entitlement not used during the prescribed period (usually a year) is lost. An employee entitled to paid sick leave may be fully or partially remunerated. Occasionally the plan provides that the employee has to undergo a waiting period before sickness payments begin. These may then be retroactive to the date of the commencement of absence. If the sick leave agreement is of the indemnity insurance kind, the waiting period is nearly always written in and is often quite long. Under such schemes, the employer and/or employee contribute to the purchase of an insurance plan to obtain coverage for either long or short-term illness. A maximum period of entitlement to benefit is usually prescribed. The entitlement is usually a proportion of weekly earnings, tailored in some way to ensure that the total amounts recovered from the sick leave plan and other benefit schemes do not exceed normal earnings. Furthermore, workers forced to be absent from work by illness may receive compensation under the workers' compensation Acts (so long as the illness was contracted during the course of their employment) or under the federal Employment Insurance Act. Also, there is legislation entitling disabled persons to a government-funded pension under the Canada Pension Plan.[1]

1. On the social security legislation that applies in Canada, *see* Gilles Trudeau, 'Discontinuité d'activité et garanties sociales: réflexions à partir du cas canadien' in *L'insécurité de l'emploi. Acte du séminaire international de droit comparé du travail, des relations professionnelles et de la sécurité sociale* (Bordeaux: Université Montesquieu – Bordeaux IV, 2000) 183–212.

221. Conceivably, an employee would be better off relying on his common law right of remuneration during a temporary illness than relying on an agreed upon number of sick days under a sick leave plan. It is likely, however, that, where there is such an agreed upon entitlement to sick leave pay, courts would read down the common law entitlement to coincide with such agreed upon terms.

4. Form of remuneration

222. When we speak of remuneration today, we automatically think of monetary payments. But it is, of course, possible to pay in other ways, for instance, by providing employees with goods, lodging, stocks, shares and the like. Indeed, this mode of payment led to abuses in the nineteenth century. Employers paid employees by giving them goods, but cheated them by overvaluing these goods; or they paid them with vouchers which entitled them to buy goods from the employer; or arranged with innkeepers that wages should be paid at the inn, tempting the workers to spend a larger portion of their wages on drink than they otherwise might. These means came to be termed as payment in 'truck' and necessitated the enactment of Truck Acts. These have modern equivalents in Canada.[1] Typically, they protect all workers or only those who are within the scope of minimum employment standards' statutes. The protection afforded is to require that all payments are to be in cash or by cheque. Deductions made from wages by the employer for the purchase of shares, options and the like in the employing company are not permissible. Where the employee agrees to it, it is permitted to make deductions for payments to charities, for insurance schemes, for union dues or plans which benefit the employee.

1. E.g. Alberta Employment Standards Code, S.A., 1996, c.E-10.3, s.11.

5. *Legislative standards in respect of remuneration*

a. Minimum wage legislation

223. All jurisdictions have enacted minimum wage legislation. In Alberta, for example, the basic minimum wage is currently $5.90 per hour.[1] The variations in the amount of the minimum wage and the groups who are either excluded altogether or who receive a reduced minimum wage are many. Nevertheless, there are some common features. Typically, a board or commission is created which has power to make general or specific orders. These orders will prescribe that no employee within its scope is to earn less than a particular hourly rate for work done. A general order will regulate all the employees covered by the empowering legislation; a specific order will be aimed at workers in one or more particular industries. In some jurisdictions, the board merely recommends and orders are issued by the Lieutenant-Governor in Council, in others, the board makes recommendations to the Lieutenant-Governor in Council who may then authorize the board to make an order, in others, the Lieutenant-Governor in Council will set minimum wages by regulation. Whatever may be the formalities of the process, the practical result seems to be that setting the minimum wages boils down a political game of 'follow the leader'. This is unfortunate since setting an overly generous minimum wage appears to have the undesirable consequence of reducing employment and training opportunities for low paid workers.[2]

1. E.g. Alberta Employment Standards Regulation, R.S.A. 1980, c.E-10–2, Alta. Reg. 14/97, ss.7–13, as am. by Alta. Reg. 114/2000.
2. The economics literature is reviewed in England *et al.*, *op. cit.*, vol. 1, paras. 8.85–8.88.

224. Although the kinds of employees covered by the various statutes differ from province to province, they often exclude domestic servants and various classes of agricultural workers. Also specifically excluded may be members of the family of the employer, some professional employees, and employees in industries which, in the particular jurisdiction, require special economic treatment, e.g. fishing, timber. Students working part-time or seasonally, or employees in recreational camps, are often excluded or have special rates apply to them. Minimum wages are set on the basis of an hourly rate. It is common to prescribe that where workers work less than three (or in some cases four) hours they shall nonetheless be paid a minimum of three hours' (or four hours') wages. There are also differences in rates depending on age. Typically a rate is set for adults and for persons under 17 or 18 years of age. Often salespersons are specifically covered by minimum wage regulations, even where their wages are calculated on a commission basis. Frequently there are specific provisions, which exclude gratuities from the definition of wages, thus ensuring that people in service industries are paid the minimum rate by their employers. A common provision is that the value of board and lodging which is provided by an employer may not be calculated as being part of the minimum remuneration which must be paid unless the minimum wage legislation specifically permits a certain part of the due wage to be so paid or authorization is obtained from the appropriate agency or minister. Such provisions are, in effect, exemptions from the protection afforded against payment in truck.

225. In addition, safeguards for employees are provided by requiring that contracts for public works done for the government must stipulate that fair wages[1] or in some cases, at least minimum wage rates be paid to employees.[2]

1. Wage (Public Construction) Act, S.B.C. 1979, c.426; The Government Contracts Hours and Wages Act, R.S.O. 1990, c.G-8.
2. The Construction Industry Wages Act, R.S.M. 1987, c.C-190; Minimum Wage for Categories of Employees in Crown Construction Work Regulation – Employment Standards Act, N.B. Reg. 90–149.

b. Equal pay legislation

226. Consonant with the principles evinced in human rights legislation, all jurisdictions provide that there should be no differentiation in rates of pay on the basis of sex. Sometimes the provisions are found in the minimum standards statute, sometimes in the human rights statute, sometimes in a special piece of 'pay equity' legislation. The process and remedies will vary accordingly. Where the minimum standards statute operates, the Director will have a complaint investigated, a settlement attempted and/or an order made. Such an order may include, in addition to providing for payment making up for the proved discrimination in respect of wages, a fine. There may be provision for bringing an action in a civil court. Where the human rights legislation applies, the processes described earlier will apply. Sometimes the minimum standards and the human rights legislation (by implication, perhaps) may both proscribe discrimination in pay on the basis of sex. The usual rule is that where proceedings have been commenced under the human rights statute, no action may be initiated under the minimum standards one. Another common provision is that the recovery of wages due because of sex discrimination is limited to 12 months of pay.

227. Although the principle underlying equal pay seems uncontroversial, its effectuation is not easy. The language of the governing statute may be vital. Thus, when the ruling statutes provided that there was to be no differentiation in rates for males and females doing identical or substantially identical work, it was held that relatively slight variation in duties and services permitted the employer to use different wage rates for employees.[1] As a consequence, some statutes were amended and provided that there should be equal pay where the same work was done by male and female employees in the same place of employment. The same work was deemed to be done where the duties to be performed required the exercise of similar skill, the use of equal effort and the acceptance of equal responsibility.[2] Although this formulation could be read as requiring identical duties to be performed, it was not so read by either courts or other decision-makers.[3] On the whole, equal pay proponents were able to draw some comfort from the statutory interpretation which evolved in this way but, nonetheless, the statutory regimes discussed do not have the language which permits the conquering of a pervasive difficulty.

1. *Re Harris and Bell Canada* (1975) 58 D.L.R. (3d) 610 (Fed.C.A.).
2. E.g. Saskatchewan Labour Standards Act, R.S.S. 1978 c.L-1, s.17, considered in *Pasqua Hospital* v. *Harmatiuk* (1987) 87 C.L.L.C. 17021, affg 4 C.H.R.R. D/1177 (Sask.Bd.Inq.)
3. *Ibid.* To the same effect, *see R.* v. *Howard Ex p. Municipality of Metro Toronto*, [1970] 3 O.R. 555 (C.A.); *Board of Governors of Riverdale Hospital* (1973) 73 C.L.L.C. para. 14,174 (Ont.C.A.); *Derouin Opticians Ltd.* v. *Fraser* (1983) C.L.L.C. 14.028 (Ont.S.C.); *Salor Sales Ltd.* v. *Department of Labour* (1983) 83 C.L.L.C. 17,018 (Sask.C.A.).

228. The major drawback with the above-mentioned legislation is that it is ineffective in organizations where the vast majority of employees are female so that there are few, if any, males doing the same or similar work with whom the females can be compared. Consequently, there is much support for the notion that the statutes ought to provide that there should be equal pay for work of equal value. Presumably, if the productivity of women in 'ghettoized' work is of the same value to an employer as work done by men in his employ, equal rates ought to be offered other things being equal. The difficulty with giving this principle practical scope is manifest. Thus, the federal Human Rights Act, after providing that there should be equal pay for males and females doing work of equal value, goes on to say that in assessing the value of work performed the criterion to be applied is the composite of skill, effort and responsibility required in the performance of the work.[1] This formula necessitates a similar inquiry which other statutes mandate and does not solve the ghetto problem without more.

1. Canadian Human Rights Act, R.S.C. 1985 c.H-6, s.11; *see* Equal Wage Guidelines, 1986, SOR/86–1082 which spell out in detail how skills, efforts and acceptance of responsibility ought to be assessed.

229. Inequality in wage rates is still permitted, despite similarities in skill, effort and responsibility, where a seniority system requires it, or a merit system has been agreed upon, or a payment by quantity-produced system exists or where the discrimination can otherwise be shown not to be based on the criterion of sex.

230. The main weakness with this model of equal pay legislation is that it is complaints based. As with most employment protection legislation, non-unionized employees are reluctant to file complaints against their employer either because they do not know their legal rights or because they are afraid of retaliation or because of both factors. One solution is to enact proactive equal pay Acts which require employers to achieve pay equality within specified deadlines and to report periodically on progress to a government agency. Accordingly, statutes have been enacted in Manitoba, Ontario, Nova Scotia, Prince Edward Island, Quebec and New Brunswick which all are proactive in nature. In these provinces (with some minor exceptions) it is no longer be necessary to wait for a disadvantaged person or group to come forward and prove to a tribunal that there is a failure to award women equal pay for work of equal value to that done by men.[1] Although these schemes are referred to as 'pay equity', this nomenclature is misleading in so far as it implies that the Acts' purpose is to eradicate wage differentials. Rather, 'pay equity' Acts aim to achieve the more modest goal of eliminating gender discrimination in the job evaluation process.[2] Thus, the Acts are not designed to tackle the fundamental cultural and economic forces that have resulted over the years in females being segregated in relatively low paid occupations. One suspects that the title 'pay equity' was chosen by governments for its political appeal.

1. Manitoba Pay Equity Act, S.M. 1985–86, c.21; New Brunswick Pay Equity Act, S.N.B. 1989, c.P-5.01; Nova Scotia Pay Equity Act, R.S.N.S. 1989, c.337; Equity Act, R.S.O. 1990, c.P-7; Prince Edward Island Pay Equity Act, R.S.P.E.I. 1988, c.P-2; Quebec Pay Equity Act, S.Q. 1996, c.43. For a detailed analysis of these, and other equal pay Acts *see* England *et al.*, *op. cit.*, vol. 1, paras. 8.260–8.345.
2. The best account of the economic and moral arguments for and against 'pay equity' legislation is P. England, *Comparable Worth: Theories and Evidence* (New York: De Gruyter, 1992).

231. A detailed analysis of the pay equity legislation is beyond the scope of this essay. Commonly, the Acts require that the jobs in an employer's establishment be divided into job classes. Once so divided, they are to be designated as either male or female job classes. A class will be designated male or female if it is predominantly peopled by men or women. The content of the term 'predominantly' varies from jurisdiction to jurisdiction. Manitoba stipulates that if a class is 70 per cent male or female it is predominantly male or female; Nova Scotia, Prince Edward Island and Quebec set the figure at 60 per cent, while Ontario and New Brunswick provide that for a class to be a male one, 70 per cent of its members must be men and, for it to be a female one, 60 per cent of its members must be female. Furthermore, in most of these provinces, the designation of a job class is not determined by numerical ratios alone, but account can also be taken of 'historical incumbency', namely whether the jobs in question have been occupied predominantly by men or women in the past. This avoids the risk that an employer might staff a traditionally female, and therefore low paid, job by a majority of males in order to forestall an impending pay equity inquiry. In Ontario Quebec and Prince Edward Island, the scope for designating a job class is further widened by requiring that account be taken of 'gender stereotypes of fields of work'.

232. Once job classes have been designated, the jobs in it are to be evaluated on the basis of a gender-neutral job evaluation scheme. This done, the compensation paid to the female job classes is to be compared to that in those male job classes which, as a result of evaluation, are deemed to be comparable. Any discriminatory pay practices which are revealed are to be rectified. The critical feature is that the designation, evaluation and redress must take place without the pre-condition that an individual or a trade union file a complaint. Instead, there is an obligation on employers to develop a pay equity plan within designated time limits.

233. There are many obvious points of difficulty for implementation.[1] Job evaluation systems have been in wide use for a long time. Employers constructed them to suit their purposes. Work organization reflects these schemes. To impose gender-neutral criteria on schemes which continue to flourish and which were designed with different purposes in mind is to create a contested terrain.[2] This is particularly so because gender-neutral evaluation schemes are to have regard to skill, responsibility and working conditions, criteria which normally underpin extant job classification and wage rate practices. Similarly, the designation of job classes is crucial to the exercise. If a job class turns out to contain a large number of people of lower skill and pay rates, as well as some highly paid people (e.g. all library workers, as opposed to librarians), the appropriate male comparator group may be a lowly paid one. Struggles on this front are inevitable where the scheme is a job-to-job comparison one.[3] This is so in Ontario, but not in Manitoba and Quebec, which employ an average pay line method to adjust wages. Thus, whereas in Ontario, once discrimination is found, it may be adjusted by paying the highest ranked woman at the same rate as the lowest paid worker in the male comparator class, in Manitoba and Quebec a job class receives an increase to bring it up to the average pay line of the employer's establishment. Furthermore, difficulties are encountered where an employer does not hire any men with whom females' jobs can be compared. This problem normally arises in occupations which historically have been dominated by women, e.g. nursing. Here, the Ontario statute used to contain a 'proxy' system whereby comparisons could be made with male pay rates in force in other organizations, thereby extending pay equity comparisons into the external labour market. However, the depth of penetration into the external labour market was limited by requiring that the 'proxy' employer be within the Ontario public service, that it perform similar work within the same geographic area as the seeking employer and that its collective bargaining or compensation system be similar to that of the seeking employer. These provisions, however, were repealed after three years of operation.[4] Also, defining the section or sections of an organization for pay equity purposes can be problematic. For instance, in multiplant enterprises the scope for achieving pay equity could be severely limited if the inquiry were limited to a single plant because the employer could concentrate low paying within that plant, or there might be insufficient male jobs within that plant to compare the female jobs with. To minimize these risks, the pay equity Acts create multiplant 'establishments' within a defined geographical area within which pay equity plans must be devised. In a similar vein, a purposive definition is applied to determining who is the 'employer' for pay equity purposes, the goal being to enlarge the scope for making male/female job comparisons. Thus, a municipality has been ruled to be the 'employer' of nurses as well as police officers so that the jobs of nursing and policing could be evaluated.[5] If a business is sold, merged, amalgamated or otherwise disposed of such that, at common law, the employment relationship would have terminated, the pay equity Acts of Ontario and Quebec contain express 'successorship' provisions which bind the new employer to any pay equity plans or other pay equity proceedings that were in place prior to the disposition. In other provinces without this provision, the courts appear willing to go to great lengths to 'pierce the corporate veil' in order to further the goal of achieving pay equity. Thus, the Nova Scotia Court of Appeal has ruled a pay equity plan in place for school cross-walk superintendents employed by a municipality continued to bind a contractor to whom school cross-walk services were contracted out.[6] Last, but by no means least, all schemes are complicated by the fact that different kinds of pay equity plans may emerge where the workers are represented by trade unions. Plans may be bargained. The legislation typically contains detailed procedures for balancing the interests involved.

1. *See* generally the various guidelines in the *Pay Equity Implementation Series, Pay Equity* (Toronto: Pay Equity Commission, 1994). For a detailed account of the jurisprudence, *see* England *et al.*, *op. cit.*, vol. 1, paras. 8.260–8.345. *See also* S. Handman and K. Jensen, 'Pay Equity in Canada: An Overview' (1999) 7 C.L.E.L.J. 65.
2. Useful advice on how to conduct a gender-neutral job evaluation is contained in N. Weiner and M. Gunderson, *Pay Equity: Issues, Options and Experience* (Toronto: Butterworths, 1990) chs. 2 and 4.
3. *See*, for example, *P.S.A.C.* v. *Canada (Treasury Board)*, [1999] F.C.J. 1531 (Tr.Div.), examined by P. Hughes, '*P.S.A.C.* v. *Canada (Treasury Board)*: The Long and Winding Road to Equity' (2000) 8 C.L.E.L.J. 55.
4. The 'proxy' system was originally enacted in Part III.2 of the Pay Equity Act (1993, c.4, s.13). It was repealed by S.O. 1996, Sched. J. s.4. The repealing Act was ruled unconstitutional in *S.I.E.U. Local 204* v. *A-G Ontario* (1997) 97 C.L.L.C. 230035 (Ont.Gen.Div.). This decision is currently under appeal.
5. *Haldimand-Norfolk Regional Board of Commissioners of Police* v. *Ontario Nurses Association* (1989) 30 C.C.E.L. 139 (Ont.Div.Ct.). *See also Kingston – Frontenac Children's Aid Society (No. 2)* (1992) 3 P.E.R. 117 (P.E.H.T.); *Oshawa Times* v. *Southern Ontario Newspaper Guild* (1994) 4 P.E.R. 21 (P.E.H.T.).
6. *Dartmouth (City)* v. *Nova Scotia (Pay Equity Commission)* (1995) 134 N.S.R. (2d) 308 (N.S.C.A.).

234. Not all employers are covered by the pay equity statutes. In all but Ontario and Quebec, only workers in the public sectors fall under the umbrella of the legislation. Even then, in New Brunswick, only the non-managerial segments of the provincial government public service are covered. Presumably, it is thought that the costs of implementing pay equity Acts would unduly impair the economic competitiveness of Canadian private sector employers.

235. In Ontario and Quebec, the scheme covers both the broader public sector and the private one. All establishments with over 10 employees are to be covered. A timetable was set to give everyone time to make the necessary adjustments. In Ontario, for example, two years after proclamation the broader public sector was to submit pay equity plans; employers of more than 500 people in the private sector were given three years, four years if they had between 100 and 499 employees. For those with payrolls of 50–99, five years was the period stipulated, while it was six for those with 10–49 employees. In the last two categories, it was left to employees to initiate complaints if the employers did not act of their own volition. Despite the much greater scope of the Ontario and Quebec legislation, there are still many gaps. Thus, in Ontario, 13 per cent of female workers are employed in situations where there are fewer than 10 workers, a category to which the statute does not apply.

c. Statutory protection for part-time workers

236. Like most mature economies, Canada has experienced a dramatic increase in the incidence of part-time work in the last 20 years.[1] It must not be thought that part-time work is always being forced down the gullets of unwilling workers. On the contrary, for many workers part-time status is highly desirable because it provides them with the flexibility to do other things with their lives. However, part-time workers currently are being disadvantaged by the fact that they usually receive less pay for doing the same work, or work of equal value, as full-timers; they often are excluded from important fringe benefits such as medical/dental insurance, life insurance, death and disability insurance, pensions; and they often denied access to the same training and career development opportunities as full-timers. So far, only two Canadian provinces have legislated comprehensive safeguards against these abuses. First, in Saskatchewan the Labour Standards Act requires employers to provide part-time employees who work for fewer than 30 hours per week with the same insurance coverage, on a pro-rated basis, in respect to life insurance, dental care, prescription drugs and death and disability benefits as full-timers are entitled to.[2] The pro-rating formula is that an employee who works on average between 15 and 30 hours per week is entitled to 50 per cent of the level of benefits received by full-timers, increasing to 100 per cent if the employee works on average 30 or more hours per week. However, the Act only protects part-timers who have a regular attachment to the firm. Thus, the employee must have completed 26 weeks with the same employer during which he or she must have worked at least 390 hours, in addition to having worked at least 780 hours in the previous year for that employer. Casual workers, therefore, are denied protection. Moreover, the Act does not apply to small firms which employ fewer than 10 full-time employees, the rationale being that the costs of equalizing benefits would be unduly costly to such firms which often operate at the margins of profitability. In Quebec, legislation takes a somewhat broader approach by prohibiting employers from paying any employee a lower rate of wage than that granted to other employees for the 'sole reason' that the employee in question 'usually works less hours per week'.[3] This prohibition, however, does not apply to an employee whose remuneration is more than twice the rate of the minimum wage. As yet other provinces have not followed the lead of Quebec and Saskatchewan. The only other significant protection available to part-timers is the requirement in the pension benefits Acts of all provinces (save Newfoundland) that an employer allow part-timers to participate in any private occupational pension plan, on a pro-rated basis, where such a plan has been introduced for full-timers.[4] However, this legislation does not require an employer proactively to introduce a pension plan where none otherwise existed for full-timers.

1. The explanations and consequences of this circumstance are examined in the *Advisory Group Report* (Ottawa: Ministry of Supply and Services, 1994). *See also* the seminal study by Wallace,

Part Time Work in Canada: Report of the Commission of Inquiry into Part Time Work (Ottawa: Labour Canada, 1983).
2. Saskatchewan Labour Standards Act, R.S.S. 1978, c.L-1 s.45.1 and Labour Standards Regulations 1995, c.L-1, Reg. 5, s.2(f).
3. An Act Respecting Labour Standards, R.S.Q., c.N-1.1, s.41.1.
4. E.g. Canada Pension Benefits Standards Act, R.S.B.C. 1985, c.P-7.01, s.5(1).

6. *Important benefits related to remuneration*

a. Unemployment insurance

237. The power to enact legislation with respect to unemployment insurance has, since 1940, rested with the federal legislature. That power to legislate has been implemented.[1] The scheme created is complex and can only be described in outline.

238. Persons who lose their jobs are entitled to receive unemployment benefits. The amounts of those benefits and the periods for which they are payable are laid out in the Act. Entitlement to benefits depends, principally, on the length of employment prior to becoming unemployed.

1. Employment Insurance Act, S.C. 1996, c.23.

239. Prior to 1992, there was a tripartite contributory scheme with the federal government, employers and employees paying into the unemployment insurance fund. In 1992, a new contributory scheme was announced under which the federal government ended its contributions and, instead, redirected what used to be its contributions to job training programmes. This was part and parcel of a new ideological approach to labour markets, as well as an attempt at controlling the expenditures of the federal government.[1]

1. On this new ideological approach, *see* Jean Charest and Gilles Trudeau, 'De l'assurance-chômage à l'assurance-emploi. Un baromètre de l'évolution des politiques sociales canadiennes' (1999) *Bulletin de droit comparé du travail et de la sécurité sociale*, 69–91.

240. Employees have their contributions deducted at source by their employers. The premium rate for each employee is fixed periodically by the Employment Insurance Commission subject to the approval of the Governor in Council on the recommendation of the Ministers of Finance and the Minister of Employment and Immigration.[1] The Act states that the rate is to be fixed in order that there will be enough revenue 'over a business cycle' to fund the scheme and in order to 'maintain relatively stable levels throughout the business cycle'.[2] Currently the employee must contribute $2.40 for every $100 earned up to a ceiling of $39,000. Insurable earnings are the earnings gained from all sources by the employee, but, as stated, there is a ceiling of $39,000 on the amount of earnings in respect of which contributions need be made.

1. Employment Insurance Act ss.66 and 82.
2. Employment Insurance Act s.66(a) and (b).

241. Currently, the employer's premium rate is 2.25 per cent of its employees' annual insurable earnings. Where an employer has privately provided for a wage scheme whereby employees will be indemnified for loss of wages due to illness or pregnancy, the employer may have the premiums payable to the employment insurance fund reduced on the basis that the unemployment benefits which would otherwise have been payable are reduced.

242. In order to qualify for benefits, an employee must show that he or she was employed for a designated number of hours based on where the employee resides and the unemployment rate in the geographical area in question.[1] Under the predecessor statute, qualification depended on the employee working for a minimum period of 52 weeks continuous employment with an employer. This disadvantaged casual employees who work intermittently and so could not accrue the requisite period of continuous service. As well, the new scheme takes account of the employee's 'need', so to speak, by reducing the amount of working hours required in areas of relatively high unemployment. Currently in areas where the unemployment rate is 6 per cent or less, the requisite qualifying hours are 700 but for areas where the unemployment rate is 13.1 per cent or over, it decreases to 420 hours. In between this maximum and minimum there are seven variations depending on the local unemployment level. Canada's national unemployment rate at the date of writing is marginally below 7 per cent. Possibly, the minimum qualifying hours requirement could be challenged as violating section 15 of the Charter on the ground that it indirectly discriminates against women. This is because mothers with child-rearing duties may find it more difficult to accrue the requisite number of hours worked than would males, who usually do not take as much time off work as women to look after their children. If this argument were accepted, the government would have to justify the discrimination under section 1 as being fair and reasonable in a democratic society. As yet, the courts have not ruled on the matter.

1. Employment Insurance Act ss.7–11.

243. There is generally a two-week waiting period before benefit are payable. Currently, the amount of benefit to be paid to a qualified claimant is 55 per cent of the average weekly pay of the claimant during the qualifying period up to the ceiling of $413 per week. The recent trend is to reduce the level of benefits. Thus, in the late 1970s the benefit level had been 66 per cent, but this was reduced to 60 per cent in the late 1980s and then to 57 per cent after 1993. However, low income families earning less than $25,921 per year who have children can receive a Canada Child Tax Benefit which can have the effect of exceeding the 55 per cent ceiling.[1] On the other side of the coin, the 55 per cent ceiling is reduced for an employee who has drawn regular unemployment insurance benefits in the past. The amount of the reduction is 1 per cent for every 20 weeks of regular benefits subject to maximum reduction level of 5 per cent.[2]

1. Employment Insurance Act s.16.
2. Employment Insurance Act s.15.

244. Claimants are not entitled to unemployment benefits if they do not show that they are ready, able and willing to take suitable employment.[1] They can furnish evidence of their readiness to return to work by showing that they are making reasonable efforts to find employment. The claimants may be asked to register with the government or private placement agencies. The claimants are given a span of time in which to search for a job compatible with their training and experience. After such a reasonable period, they may be asked to reduce their expectations in respect of both congeniality and pay.

1. Employment Insurance Act s.27(1).

245. The employment insurance scheme is to some extent integrated with collective bargaining schemes by disallowing claims made by persons whose unemployment is attributable to a labour dispute at the place where they were employed.[1] This disentitlement is removed if the former employees accept a job elsewhere, intending not to return to their former employment. They can then receive benefits for the period of their unemployment. They may also be so entitled where they can show that they did not finance or were directly involved in the dispute, which led to the interruption of work. Difficult questions used to arise as to what a labour dispute was, how long it was, what direct involvement was, and the like. These difficulties were alleviated somewhat by a Supreme Court of Canada decision which held that it was not consonant with reality to assume that, just because an employee paid dues to a union on strike, the employee was supporting the particular local on strike and, therefore, was a participant in the labour dispute.[2] On the other hand, another attempt by the Supreme Court of Canada to assist unionist unemployment claimants has not fared well. The Court had held that disentitlement to benefits of an employee who had participated in a labour dispute ended when there was no longer any dispute between the parties, even though a large-scale return to production had not yet been achieved. This was to help workers as, often, full-scale resumption takes a while to achieve after agreement to end the dispute has been reached. But a regulation was passed to set aside the effect of this decision.[3]

1. Employment Insurance Act s.36.
2. *Hills* v. *Attorney-General Canada*, [1988] 1 S.C.R. 513.
3. *Canada Employment and Immigration Commission* v. *Caron et al.* (1991) 91 C.L.L.C. 14,007; [1991] 1 S.C.R. 48; Reg 49 (U.I.C.) 18 November 1990.

246. As well, claimants will not get benefits for the periods of unemployment during which they were imprisoned for a criminal offence or were out of Canada. Moreover, unless a pregnant woman is able to bring herself within the specific provisions relating to maternity leave, she cannot claim compensation as if she were an insured worker asking for the basic benefits available under the scheme.

247. A pregnant woman who has a major attachment to the workforce – the claimant must have worked for 600 hours during the shorter of either the last 52 weeks or the start of her last claim – is entitled to a maximum of 17 weeks of maternity benefits, less the two weeks waiting period, for a maximum of 15 weeks.[1] The benefits may, but do not have to, be claimed as early as eight weeks before the expected confinement date or the actual confinement date, whichever is the earlier. In addition, 'parental benefits' can be collected for up to 35 weeks by biological or adoptive parents or their partners while they are caring for a newborn or adopted child. These 'parental benefits' can be claimed by one parent or shared between the two partners. 'Parental benefits' for biological parents and their partners are payable from the date of the child's birth, and for adoptive parents and their partners from the date the child is placed with them.

1. Employment Insurance Act s.22.

248. Prior to 1992, there was a provision which gave either of two adopting parents 15 weeks of unemployment insurance benefits if he or she chose to stay home with the adopted child. No such leave was offered to natural parents. This was successfully challenged as violating the Charter of Rights and Freedoms guarantee of equal treatment. Moreover, the Court held that a court had the power to force the government to provide benefits. This was appealed by the government. Before the Supreme Court of Canada could pronounce on this issue, the government changed the Unemployment Insurance Act (as it was then called).[1] Today, the Employment Insurance Act provides that maternity benefits should stay as they are and that each of the natural parents of a new-born child or of an adopted child could have up to 35 weeks of unemployment insurance benefits by way of parental leave.[2]

1. *The litigation culminated in Shachter* v. *Canada et al.* (1992) 92 C.L.L.C. para. 14,036 (S.C.C.); [1992] 2 S.C.R. 679.
2. *See* para. 247, *supra*, and the Employment Insurance Act s.23.

249. Claimants may be 'disqualified' – in the sense that their benefits, though accrued, are temporarily withheld – for specified periods of time. This may occur where a claimant fails, due to her or his own actions or lack thereof, to seek re-employment in the expected manner. The disqualification from benefits is for a maximum period of 6 weeks where the employee has failed to cooperate with the Employment Insurance Commission in seeking replacement work, but this can increase to anywhere between 7 to 12 weeks where the employee has failed to seek suitable replacement work.[1] Temporary disqualification also is imposed where an employee loses her or his employment because he or she was justifiably dismissed because of her or his misconduct.[2] Furthermore, an employee who voluntarily resigns is denied benefits altogether unless the quit was for 'just cause', e.g. if the employer unilaterally changes the terms or conditions of employment in a significant way, harasses the employee (sexually or otherwise), endangers the employee's health or safety or assigns excessive amounts of overtime.[3] Arguably, the total disentitlement for a voluntary quit is another step on the road to using the employment insurance scheme increasingly as a disciplinary tool in tough economic environments, alongside the reduction of the benefit level from 66 per cent in the late 1970s to 55 per cent today.

1. Employment Insurance Act ss.27–8.
2. Employment Insurance Act s.30.
3. *Ibid.*

250. The Canada Employment and Immigrant Commission deals with the claims made for benefits. Accordingly, it makes decisions as to entitlement, including assessing the time of insured employment, whether the claimant is disentitled because of, say, her or his unwillingness to accept employment, her or his absence from the country, or participation in a labour dispute, whether and for how long the claimant should be disqualified because her or his loss of job is due to misconduct, and so forth. The Commission is a crown corporation and is tripartite in nature. All four members are appointed by the Governor in Council. One is named as chairperson and chief executive. One is selected after consultation with employer organizations, the other after consultation with employee organizations. Many offices throughout the land carry out the functions of the Commission.

251. A claimant or employer may appeal any decision of the Commission to a Board of Referees. These boards are selected from panels of employers, employed and insured persons' representatives established by the Commission. An appeal from a Board of Referees lies to an umpire, a person appointed from among the judges of the Federal Court of Appeal. There is no appeal from the umpire's decision, except in as much as this is permitted by the Federal Court Act. There is a separate appeal in respect of determinations made with respect to employee and employer premiums and insurable employment. The appellate tribunal is the Tax Court of Canada. No appeal lies from its decisions, except in so far as this allowed by the Federal Court Act.

(1) Work sharing agreements and unemployment insurance benefits

252. The continuing rise in unemployment levels in the late 1980s and early 1990s led the federal government to develop a scheme with the goal of sustaining employment in those circumstances in which an employer would lay off people for a relatively short period. The purposes included the maintenance of a stable workforce by preventing the erosion of workers' skills while on lay-off and by avoiding the disbursement of the workforce which inevitably occurs when lay-offs are instituted. The scheme developed consists of a work-sharing system subsidized by the employment insurance fund. Section 24 of the Employment Insurance Act empowers the Commission to establish the mechanism. An agreement may be reached between an employer and its employees to permit employees facing short-term employment losses to work fewer hours than comprise an ordinary week of work, while all keep their jobs. The agreement may be presented to the Commission for review. If it is accepted, employees will be entitled to their unemployment insurance benefits less an amount that bears the same ratio to the claimant's rate of weekly benefits that the amount of their gross earnings for the shortened work-week bears to their ordinary week gross earnings. Participation in such a work-sharing programme does not affect the employees' eligibility for regular unemployment insurance benefits should they lose their jobs after the work-sharing programme has begun.

253. Because of the federal government's objective to further training, it provided money to claimants who were likely to remain claimants for some time to help them take up jobs which were deemed to be socially useful to a community. A claimant's participation in such a project is voluntary. If the claimant agrees he or she will be paid her full benefits while he or she does the job, or if the normal job rate is greater than the benefit to which he or she is entitled, the pay-out will be increased to that extent. If the claimant leaves such a job, he or she will not be disqualified from receiving unemployment insurance benefits as if he or she had voluntarily quite a traditional job. In addition, where an unemployed person is attending an approved training course under the National Training Act, he or she will be deemed unemployed and entitled to receive benefits for the normal period. This period may be extended if the course period extends beyond the entitlement period. The employment insurance funds may also help pay relocation childcare expenses, and the like, for a person attending such a training course.

254. In view of the fact that Canada's unemployment insurance benefits are low – relative to European countries at least – trade unions sometimes attempt to improve through collective bargaining the position of their members when laid off. They reach agreements which require an employer to pay an amount of money, that, together with the laid off employee's unemployment insurance benefit, will yield something close to that employee's ordinary wages. Typically, the employer's contribution to this supplementary unemployment benefit (SUBs, as they are known) diminishes with the lapse of time.

b. Pension plans

255. It is trite that providing for income after termination of one's working life is a major concern of employed persons. There are both public and private schemes of arrangements which seek to provide such security.

(1) Canada Pension Plan[1]

256. This is an earnings-related scheme under which employers and employees pay in to a federally administered plan an equal amount of money each year as specified by law. At the date of writing, an employee must contribute 4.3 per cent of his or her wages up to a maximum contribution level of $1496.40 per year. The first $3500 of an employee's annual wages are exempted from the levy and no contribution need be made for earnings above the level of $34,800 per year. The employer makes the appropriate deductions from the worker's pay cheque and returns them (together with income tax and employment insurance contributions) to the Minister of Revenue. These contributions are calculated to render a specified benefit upon retirement, normally 25 per cent of a person's average pensionable earnings.[2] Thus, a portion of the year's maximum pensionable earnings (those earnings subject to contribution) will be payable upon retirement, or age 65 if the employee continues to work beyond that age. The year's maximum pensionable earnings are adjusted annually by reference to a cost-of-living index. Thus, both contributions and benefits rise or fall with cost-of-living changes.

1. R.S.C. 1985, c.C-8. For a detailed analysis, *see* L.E. Coward, *Mercer Handbook of Canadian Pension and Welfare Plans*, 9th edn. (Don Mills: C.C.H. Canadian, 1988) ch. 17.
2. The formula for calculating benefit levels is found in s.46 of the Canada Pension Plan.

257. The plan applies to nearly all workers. Self-employed persons earning no more than $3200 are exempt. If their earnings are more than that, they are to pay the combined contributions of employers and employees. Some employed persons are excepted employees under the plan: migratory workers who do not spend at least 25 working days a year with the same employer or who do not earn at least $250 per year from the same employer; casual workers (e.g. baby-sitters, lawn-cutters); provincial and foreign government employees unless their employers agree that they should be covered by the federal plan; exchange teachers and persons employed by their spouses, as well as people belonging to religious orders which have taken a vow of poverty are excepted from the operation of the plan.

258. Where a contributor becomes disabled to the extent that he or she is unable to become regularly employed, a disability pension will be paid to the contributor who has made contributions for a specified period. The plan also provides for a survivor's pension. This means that the spouse of a pensioner is entitled to receive the pension if he or she survives the original contributor unless the contributor dies within one year of the marriage having taken place and the Minister is not satisfied that the contributor was not at the time of her or her marriage in such a state of health as to lead to the belief that he or she would be alive one year after the marriage. Survivor pensions cease to be paid upon the death of the survivor or remarriage. Where the subsequent marriage ends, the original survivor's pension may be reinstituted (or the pension which is payable because of the death of the later spouse, if that is how the marriage ended).

259. A contributor's pension rights are fully portable as he or she moves from employment to employment. In order to avoid harsh results because of irregularity in employment or low payment circumstances, benefits are calculated on the basis that the average earnings of a contributor can be computed by permitting the contributor to drop out of the data base 15 per cent of the months of lowest average monthly earnings.

260. Finally, it is to be noted that initially there was some doubt as to whether the federal legislature could pass legislation with respect to the retirement income of survivors and disabled persons. This was eventually clarified by amendment to section 94A of the British North America Act, which left intact the provincial jurisdiction of the provinces to legislate with respect to pensions. Quebec has taken advantage of this. Initially it was not satisfied with the proposed Canada Pension Plan because of its perceived incapacity to provide supplementary benefits. It had instituted its own scheme. It continues to do so. This scheme is now, in all essentials, the same as the federal scheme described above.[1]

1. An Act Respecting the Quebec Pension Plan, R.S.Q., c.R-9.

(2) Old age security pension

261. Everyone who has resided in Canada for 40 years after reaching the age of 18 is entitled to a full benefit under this pension plan upon reaching 65. Any one with lesser residence but with at least 10 years' residence after the age of 18 will get a pro-rated amount. The pension is payable as a flat rate, regardless of income or wealth of the recipient. It can only be received for six months if the recipient lives out of Canada unless he or she has resided in Canada for at least 20 years after the age of 18. The amount payable is adjusted in line with quarterly fluctuations in the Consumer Price Index.

262. To supplement the old age security when some people were ineligible for Canada or Quebec pension plan benefits, the guaranteed income supplement was instituted. Today, all persons in receipt of the old age security pension are eligible for a guaranteed income supplement. It is an additional amount allowed if the income of the applicant justifies it. That is, it is a means-tested pension.

263. Another supplement to the old age security pension is the spouse's allowance. It guarantees to one-pensioner couples (that is, where one spouse is of the age 60–64), the income that two-pensioner couples would receive by way of the old age security plus guaranteed income supplement. Both the guaranteed income supplement and spouse's allowance are reduced if the recipients earn income above a certain amount.

264. Last, but by no means least, account must also be taken of provincial guaranteed basic income programmes, which complement the federal measures. The variety of these provincial schemes prevents a detailed discussion here.

(3) Private occupational pension plans

265. Approximately 47 per cent of the workforce is covered by private sector plans. They are most commonly found in collective agreements in the unionized sector of the economy. Further, workers in the public sector are more likely to have a pension plan than in the private sector. Pension schemes may consist of employee, employer or employer–employee contributions to a fund. The variety of plans is great, being tailored to the particular profiles and aspirations of distinct groups.[1] Thus, there is the money purchase plan in which the contributions are predetermined but the retirement income is directly related to the profitability of the investment. A profit sharing plan is one in which the contributions are made by the employer on the basis of a percentage of the employer's profits. The retirement income of an employee is calculated on a points system based on her or his years of service and earnings. A flat benefit plan is one which guarantees an income of an amount based on so many dollars per month of service or some such equivalent. Typically, the employer is the sole contributor and his contributions vary with the profile of his workforce. Unit benefit plans are the most common. Under these the benefit payable varies with the employee's earnings. Typically both the employee and the employer make contributions, the employee's contributions being certain, the employer's varying with the benefits which become payable. These benefits are calculated by taking a percentage of the employee's earnings (usually around 2 per cent), multiplying this by the number of years of service and multiplying this by an

1. For a detailed analysis of the types of plans and the legal framework *see Employment Benefits and Pensions Guide*, vols. 1 and 2 (Don Mills: C.C.H. Canadian, looseleaf).

266. The funds created are administered by insurance or trust companies, sometimes banks, specialized pension counsellors or, increasingly, the employers themselves. There is some concern over the adequacy of the plans. In particular, the plans usually provide that employees must remain with a particular employer for a particular time before they become entitled to benefits paid into the plan by the employer. This is known as the vesting period. (The employee, of course, can recover any benefits he or she has paid in out of his or her own pocket notwithstanding that he or she has not yet worked until the designated vesting date.) The mobility of employees, both voluntary and involuntary, can thus lead to a denial of their pension rights. To alleviate the situation, legislation has reduced the minimum vesting periods.[1] Initially, the statutes specified that an employee's pension rights were vested after 10 years of service and the reaching of age 45. Workers well placed to bargain brought down the vesting period in their own plans. Gradually legislatures are beginning to do this for all of the plans in their jurisdiction. Currently most jurisdictions have a minimum vesting period of two years continuous employment with the employer,[2] but in Alberta and New Brunswick the period is five years.[3] Furthermore, the legislation typically provides that an employee cannot take out her or his contributions after vesting. Contributions are said to be 'locked in'. The legislation confirms the common law position that if an employee leaves before her or his pension benefits have vested, he or she is entitled to a return of whatever contributions he or she made plus interest. The employer contributions, however, are not returnable even though they could be classified as deferred wages. The legislation also prescribes that employees are to be informed of their rights and interests in the employer plans, puts conditions on how pension funds may be invested in order to maintain solvency and also dictates how the assets of a pension plan are to be distributed when it is wound up. Finally, another major difficulty is the fact that because plans are devised on an employer-by-employer basis, they are rarely portable from one employer to another. This means that individuals may participate in a number of different plans over their working lives; this does not yield the best possible return on the contributions made.

1. E.g. Ontario Pension Benefits Act, R.S.O. 1990, c.P-8, ss.36, 37 and 63, under which benefits vest after two years of continuous employment with the employer.
2. As in Ontario, *supra*, note 1.
3. Alberta Employment Pension Plans Act, S.A. 1986, c.e-10.05, ss.23(1), (2) and 25; New Brunswick Pension Benefits Act, S.N.B. 1987, c.P-5.1, ss.35(2) and (6) and 56.

267. There are great pressures to change both the private and public sector pension regimes.[1] Employees would like shorter vesting periods, greater portability and more protection against erosion of benefits earned by inflation. Very few plans provide adequate protection against cost-of-living increases. In 1992, for example, only 19.8 per cent of pension plans contained some formula for automatic indexing to inflation, with such provisions being concentrated in the public, not the private sector.[2] Efforts are being made to institute at least partial indexation. Thus, the Freedland Report recommended that employers be required to ensure that their pension plans contained an annual inflation adjustment of 75 per cent of the C.P.I. increase for each year minus 1 per cent, with a ceiling of 10 per cent. This formula was thought to avoid imposing an undue burden on employers in periods of high inflation.[3] In addition, the federal government, with the use of tax incentives, has encouraged individuals to put their savings into private, individualized registered retirement savings plans. A surplus (that is, a pool of money greater than that needed to guarantee the promised benefits of the plan) may exist in employer-sponsored plans because of a combination of inflation, higher interest rates, successful investments and a reduced payroll. It is a complicated question whether the surplus so created should belong to the employer to do with as it likes (on the basis that the employer would have to top-up the fund if the contributions were to fall short of actuarial needs) or to the employees (because the surplus money can be regarded as deferred wages).[4] The current legal response amalgamates the pension benefit legislation and the common law of contracts and trusts. Briefly put, the employer must prove initially that it is entitled to any surplus under the plan by application of the usual principles of the law of contracts and trusts.[5] If that hurdle can be surmounted, the employer must then obtain the approval of a government-appointed pension administrator. Typically, such approval will only be given if the administrator decides that the employees have been given full information about the proposed reversion, that the surplus actually exists and that the pension plan is otherwise adequately funded in order to meet its liabilities. In addition, the pension benefits legislation addresses the problem of the exclusion of part-time workers (most of whom are female) from participation in pension plans. Thus, an employer is required to permit part-timers to join any pension plan that is in force for full-time employees, provided that the part-time worker in question has accrued a minimum period of continuous employment with the employer and has actually worked for a minimum number of hours. In most provinces, the minimum period of continuous employment is 24 months and the part-timer must have earned at least 35 per cent of the year's maximum pensionable earnings.[6] Last, but by no means least, all pension benefits Acts require that pension plans be registered with a government agency and make adequate funding of the plan a condition precedent to registration. Accordingly, employee are guaranteed that the pension fund will be able to meet its financial obligations to retired persons. Indeed, Ontario goes further by establishing a pension benefits guarantee fund maintained by the province which secures pension rights when an employer becomes insolvent and its pension plan is wound up by a declaration of the Commissioner of Pensions.[7]

1. The major weaknesses with the current system are examined by M. Friedland, *Report of the Task Force on Inflation Protection for Employment Pension Plans* (Toronto: Queens Printer, 1988).
2. *Pension Plans in Canada* (Ottawa: Statistics Canada, 1 January 1992), at 40.
3. *Supra*, note 1.
4. The balance of interests is examined in the *Freedland Report*, vol. 2, at 209 and 212–14. *See also* B. Adell, *Pension Plan Surpluses and the Law: Finding a Path for Reform* (Kingston: Queen's University Industrial Relations Center, 1988).
5. The best accounts of the common law position are *Bathgate* v. *National Hockey League Pension Society* (1992) 98 D.L.R. (4d) 326 (Ont.Div.Ct.) and *Schmidt* v. *Air Products of Canada Ltd.*, [1994] 2 S.C.R. 611.

6. E.g. Canada Pension Benefits Standards Act, R.S.C. 1985, c.P-0.01, s.15.
7. Ontario Pension Benefits Act, R.S.O. 1990, c.P-8, s.83. The Fund was created in 1980.

7. Collective agreement decrees: a legislative regime unique to Quebec

268. A unique feature of the Quebec industrial relations regime lies in its legislation providing for the extension by government regulation of the provisions of a collective agreement to employers and employees not named in the collective agreement. A decree extends the effect of a collective agreement to all employers and employees within 'any trade, industry, commerce, or occupation' specified by the decree.[1] The vast majority of the provisions of a collective agreement can be extended by governmental decree, including those respecting wages, hours of work, paid vacation, social security benefits, classification of operations and those determining the various classes of employees and employers.[2] The decree makes these provisions mandatory for all employers and employees within a stated economic sector, whether unionized or not, and no private agreement can provide for working conditions less favourable than those contained in the decree.[3]

1. An Act Respecting Collective Agreement Decrees, R.S.Q., c.D-2, s.2. *See* generally, J.-L. Dube, *Decrets et comités paritaires* (Sherbrooke: Les Editions Revue de Droit, Université de Sherbrooke, 1990) and G. Hebert, *Traité de négociation collective* (Boucherville: Gaetan Morin editeur, 1992), 1022–34.
2. *Ibid.*, ss.9 to 9.2.
3. *Ibid.*, ss.11 to 13.

269. Three general conditions are necessary to have a collective agreement extended by decree. First, a collective agreement must have been concluded by two contracting parties, which can be, on the one side, a single union or a federation of unions and, on the other side, a single employer or a group of employers generally represented by an association. The contracting parties do not have to be representative of the employees and the employers of the economic sector. Moreover, it is not required that their bargaining takes place within the framework defined by the Labour Code. The second condition is a petition presented to the Minister of Labour by any party to the agreement for the extension of its provisions. The third and final condition is that the government must pass a decree extending the provisions of the agreement if it deems that the provisions of the agreement meet the conditions which the Act states for its extension. The government may also modify a decree and repeal it at any time. The decree is administered by a parity committee that includes representatives of the parties to the collective agreement and representatives of those employees and employers that are not parties to the collective agreement, but which are appointed by the Minister of Labour. Any person who violates the provisions of a decree commits a penal infraction and may be fined accordingly.

270. This decree system, which had been inspired by some earlier European models, was enacted in 1934 and at that time was seen as a means to improve the conditions of a working class that had been severely hit by the economic crisis of the 1930s. It was also seen as a legislative measure that would favour unionization and collective bargaining by preventing unionized employers from having to compete on the basis of wages and labour costs with non-unionized employers in the same economic sector. In the beginning, this regime was very successful, but was later superseded by the collective bargaining legislation introduced in Quebec and Canada in 1944 which was perceived by employees and unions as being more favourable. However, the extension of collective agreements by decree continued to exist and the regime was not significantly modified before 1996. Until the end of the 1960s, when specific legislation was enacted to regulate labour relations in the construction industry, working conditions in that industry were established by collective agreement decrees. In the following decades, and despite a few difficult periods, the number of decrees in force in Quebec remained relatively stable, covering between 5 and 10 per cent of the workforce. Decrees were mainly found in industries where competition was high among a large number of small-size enterprises, such as the garment industry and the service sector. Important amendments were made to the decree system in 1996, particularly with respect to the criteria used by the government when deciding to extend a collective agreement.[1] A number of them were redefined to take the context of increased international competition into account. Thus, the Minister of Labour may recommend that the government extend a collective agreement if he deems, among other things,

> 'that the provisions of the agreement (a) have acquired a preponderant significance and importance for the establishment of conditions of employment; (b) may be extended without any serious inconvenience for enterprises competing with enterprises established outside Quebec; (c) do not significantly impair the preservation and development of employment in the defined field of activity; and (d) do not result, where they provide for a classification of operations or for various classes of employees, in unduly burdening the management of the enterprises concerned.'

These amendments, which can be seen as an illustration of how sensitive state regulation governing the employment relationship may be to economic globalization, have been followed by a significant decrease in the number of decrees adopted. From 29 decrees in 1996, the figure decreased to 20 decrees in 2000, three years only following the amendments. Most striking is the fact that the decree system has almost completely lost its influence in the manufacturing sector, as only four decrees remained in force as of 30 June 2000.[2]

1. An Act to Amend the Act Respecting Collective Agreement Decrees, S.Q. 1996, c.71.
2. On that point, *see* Guylaine Vallée and Jean Charest, 'Globalization and the Transformation of State Regulation of Labour: The Case of Recent Amendments to the Quebec Collective Agreement Decrees Act' (2001) *The International Journal of Comparative Labour Law and Industrial Relations* 79.

B. The Duty to Provide Work

271. Unless the contract of employment is one determinable at will, the parties may only end it by giving appropriate notice of termination, or by properly treating a breach of the contract by the other party as one which repudiates the contract.

Thus, when an employer for some reason does not want work done, a question may arise as to whether or not he can insist both that the contract continue on foot and not provide work to be performed by the employee. Quebec provides a quite different legal answer to this fundamental question than is found in the common law provinces. The Quebec treatment of this issue is discussed below in paragraphs 278 *et seq.*

272. At common law, the starting point is that an employer is under no duty to provide actual work. If no attempt is made to end the contract, it would appear to follow that the employer should remain obliged to pay the non-working employee the agreed upon remuneration.[1] There are, however, two exceptions where the employer will be required to provide an opportunity to work. First, this is so where the employee's remuneration depends on the number of things he or she makes or sells. In such cases the employer may be required to provide that amount of work which will enable the employee to earn the average level of remuneration he or she had earned when work was being made available. In contracts which provide that a piece-worker or commission employee is to receive a guaranteed minimum wage, the employer need only provide sufficient work to permit the guaranteed amount to be earned, rather than an amount equivalent to a higher average. When there is no such guaranteed minimum income, arguably the statutory minimum wage rates provide a limit to the employer's obligation to provide work. Secondly, the employer is obliged to provide work where the employee claims that at least as real a benefit of the contract as remuneration is the publicity and experience which performance will bestow on her or her. Typical of such claims are those of stage performers, sportsmen or managers in particular trades. The courts have occasionally held that in such cases the employer has a duty to provide work.[2]

1. *Driscoll* v. *Australian Royal Mail Steam Navigation* (1895) 1 F. & F. 458 (N.P.); *Collier* v. *Sunday Referee Publishing*, [1940] 2 K.B. 647.
2. E.g. *Cranston* v. *Canadian Broadcasting Corp.* (1994) 2 C.C.E.L. (2d) 301, at 309 (Ont.Gen. Div.); *Clayton and Waller* v. *Oliver*, [1930] A.C. 209 (H.L.); *Hall* v. *British Essence* (1946) 62 T.L.R. 542.

273. The reason that the employer is under a duty to pay an employee, even though he does not require her or him to work, is that it would be a very one-sided contract if the employer had no obligation to provide work or to pay wages while the employee had to remain available and willing to perform. The courts have suggested that the contract would lack mutuality. However, if the surrounding circumstances are such that an inference can be drawn that the parties had agreed that the employer could refuse both to provide work and to pay if certain contingencies materialized, then normal contract interpretation permits a suspension – as opposed to a termination – of the contract. Put another way, if the contract of employment impliedly makes it a condition precedent to the right to receive wages that work actually be performed, the employer need not pay wages during downtime. Although in the earlier English case of *Devonald* v. *Rosser*[1] it was held that the employer had a heavy burden to discharge when seeking to prove that a custom neither to provide work nor to pay wages existed when the suspension of the contract was due to lack of orders for the employer's goods, modern English and Canadian courts have found in favour of employers who have neither provided work nor paid wages where production was halted because machinery needed repair, where safety conditions warranted it or where profitability concerns justified it. Indeed, it appears that in Canada the employer's right to withhold wages during economic downtimes is considered a normal inference to be drawn from the circumstances of employment relationships and that the old common law precedents cited above, although intact, have little application. Nevertheless, it does not follow that employers have an implied contractual right to lay off without pay during tough economic times. Canadian courts consistently hold that a lay-off operates as a termination of the employment contract, requiring the employer to provide the requisite notice or pay in lieu thereof, unless the contract contains an express term permitting such a lay-off or a reliable past practice exists in the firm from which an implied term permitting unilateral lay-off can be deduced.[2] The courts are reluctant to imply such a term because it would deprive the employee of monies he or she needs to weather the storm of being unemployed. In sum, an employer cannot unilaterally lay off an employee without terminating the contract and paying severance benefits (in the absence of an express or implied term in the contract to the contrary) but the employer can cease providing working opportunities without incurring a duty of compensation to the employee under the wage and benefit provisions in the employment contract.

1. [1906] K.B. 728 (C.A.).
2. E.g. *Martellaci* v. *CFC/INX Ltd.* (1998) C.C.E.L. (2d) 75, at 83 (Ont.Gen.Div.Ct.).

274. In contrast to contracts of employment which rarely regulate expressly how lay-offs are to be handled, collective agreements frequently contain comprehensive provisions on the matter. Under collective agreements, it is clear that lay-offs are temporary suspensions of the employment relationship. Normally, elaborate seniority provisions are brought into play, seeking to guarantee as much job security as possible to the most senior employees when the employer determines that he will not provide work to the same extent as before. This is so commonplace that minimum standards legislation does not require termination notice to be given where there is a short-term lay-off as defined in the statute. In British Columbia, for instance, a 'temporary' lay-off is defined as one which does not last beyond 13 weeks in any period of 20 weeks employment.[1]

1. British Columbia Employment Standards Act, R.S.B.C. 1996, c.113, s.1.

275. Similarly, where the parties to a collective agreement agree that the employer may (provided that he does not discriminate between employees) reduce the number of working hours, such a reduction, which results in less work being provided, may take place without imposing an obligation to pay remuneration for anything but the hours actually worked. Where the agreement has no such express provisions, arbitrators have still held that reduction of the hours worked will permit the employer to pay only for the hours worked. To overcome the notion that this offends the common law, it may be argued that grievance arbitrators, who have developed the collective agreement jurisprudence and who are very familiar with industrial customs, have regarded employees working under collective agreements as hourly employees. If this is so, no violence is done to the legal doctrine by permitting the employer to reduce the amount of work available by an hourly diminution and paying accordingly. But, conceptually, this is not very satisfying. It is difficult to think of employees who have obtained the security which goes with a collective agreement as being as insecure as hourly employees. Further, the minimum standards legislation provides for a minimum period of notice which must be given to all employees who have worked for longer than three months. Such provisions negate the notion that, with some rare exceptions, any employees are hired by the hour. In sum, it is fair to say that the precepts of the common law of employment relating to the duty to provide work just simply do not apply when collective bargaining has taken place.

276. It has already been noted in paragraph 272 that there are some occupations such as stage performing in which the opportunity to perform is the essence of the contract and where, therefore, a failure to provide work will be a breach of contract.

277. In similar vein, it may be that a failure to provide work of the calibre that an employee had a right to expect will be deemed to be such an insult that an employee will be entitled to resign and sue for damages for wrongful dismissal under the 'constructive dismissal' doctrine. Thus, in one case where an employer reassigned an employee job duties that substantially eroded his previous level of responsibility and prestige but gave him an increase in wages, the court held that the employer had nonetheless committed a fundamental breach of the employment contract.[1] Similarly, an employer was held to have fundamentally breached the employment contract of a chief executive officer by withdrawing all his work duties and leaving him to twiddle his thumbs in his office, even though he continued to receive full wages.[2] These decisions illustrate how modern Canadian courts are more willing than before to recognize that the psychological component of a job can be just as important to an employee – if not more so – than wages and benefits. Interestingly, this reasoning would support the view that an employee who is forced to accept a promotion or face dismissal could refuse and sue for constructive dismissal if he or she genuinely obtained an irreplaceable level of job satisfaction from the old position. However, no Canadian court has so far adopted Lord Denning's view that all workers have an implied right to work and obtain job satisfaction under their employment contracts.[3] Although this precept has not found a following as yet in Canada or England, nonetheless it is of potential interest in view of the widespread attention alienation in the workplace is attracting amongst human resource experts.

1. *Wedding* v. *Motorola Canada Ltd.* (1998) 99 C.L.L.C. 210008, at para. 141052 (B.C.S.C.). However, on the facts of the case the plaintiff condoned the breach and lost his right to sue.
2. *Park* v. *Parsons Brown and Co.* (1989), 27 C.C.E.L. 224 (B.C.C.A.). However, the Court emphasized the economic harm the executive would suffer to his professional reputation if the word got out among his peers that he was not being assigned work.
3. *Langston* v. *A.U.E.W.* [1974] I.C.R. 180 at 190, *per* Lord Denning but the point was considered doubtful in *Langston* v. *A.U.E.W. (No. 2)*, [1974] I.C.R. 510 at 522 (an appeal to the Industrial Court from the original decision).

278. In Quebec, in order to determine the extent of the employer's duty to provide work, one must look first to the Civil Code rather than the case law as is done in the common law jurisdictions. Section 2087 of the Code makes it clear that allowing the performance of the work agreed upon is one of the basic duties that the contract of employment imposes on the employer. The failure to do so, either in quality or in quantity, even where remuneration is maintained, would amount to a repudiation of the contract and the employee could treat it as such.

279. In Quebec and the common law jurisdictions, the parties to a contract of employment can expressly define the extent of the employer's obligation to furnish work. They may well establish the amount and the type of work to be provided by the employer, the hierarchical authority attached to it, and other conditions of employment. For example, the parties could even allow the employer to suspend unilaterally the contract, with or without remuneration, in the event of a lack of work. Indeed, as mentioned before (paras. 274–6), this is what the contracting parties generally do in collective agreements. Collective agreements also specify under which conditions employers may proceed to a lay-off or, more generally, suspend their duty to provide work. In the absence of express contractual provisions dealing with the provision of work, trade usage or custom becomes very important and, if proven, may well allow a court to imply a right of the employer to temporarily suspend its obligation to provide work.[1]

1. In *Laurier Auto inc.* v. *Paquet*, [1987] R.J.Q. 804, the Quebec Court of Appeal stated that the notion of temporary lay-off applied to the individual contract of employment even though the Civil Code does not contemplate this question. This statement was revisited two years later in *Surveyer, Nenniger, Chênevert Inc.* v. *Thomas* (D.T.E. 89T-640), when the Court of Appeal stated that the notion of lay-off does not exist in the Civil Code. The employer can resort to a lay-off only if the contract of employment expressly provides for it.

280. An employee may decide not to contest the employer's failure to provide the amount or the type of work that the parties agreed upon. Accordingly, if the employee continues to work under the changed terms for a significant period of time without protest, he or she is deemed to have accepted, or 'condoned', the employer's breach of the employment contract.[1] In the case of an employee's refusal, the contract of employment is deemed to be breached at the employer's initiative and amounts to a wrongful dismissal unless the employer shows just cause for doing so. The employee can either remain at work under the changed terms and sue for damages for breach of contract – obviously a rare occurrence due to the risk of retaliation by the employer – or, more realistically, resign and sue for damages for 'constructive dismissal'.

1. As in *Wedding* v. *Motorola Canada Ltd.* (1998) 99 C.L.L.C. 210008, examined in para. 277, *supra*, where the plaintiff continued working under the new terms for approximately one year without protest.

C. Responsibility for the Employee's Conduct

1. Master's tort theory

281. At common law, there are two ways in which an employer can be made responsible for the acts of his employees which cause harm to others. First, the employer may be held liable to redress the damage because the employer is adjudged to be personally at fault. That is, the employer is said to owe a 'duty of care' under the law of tort to the injured party, which duty is breached because he should have prevented a situation arising in which the employee could inflict injury.[1] When this argument is relied on, the so-called 'master's tort theory' is being espoused. The justification for this approach is that although the employer has a need to act – which need can only be implemented through other persons such as its employees or contractors – the employer nonetheless cannot delegate its duty under the law of tort to take care. Generally, this theory is not favoured by the courts.[2] Where it is applied, the theory leaves much discretion to the courts as to when a duty is of a non-delegable kind. This problem is exacerbated by the fact that there is no rationale for imposing a duty on the employer rather than the actor. If judicial discretion is to be exercised it is always helpful to have a principled reason for exercising it one way rather than another. Accordingly, the second theory for holding the employer responsible for the conduct of his employees is that the employer should be made liable for the acts of others not because they were, in effect, the employer's acts but, rather, because it is socially useful to make the employer vicariously liable. Most plaintiffs will, as a matter of practicality, not care on which theoretical basis an employer is held responsible, but it will make a difference where the employee would not have been liable to the plaintiff. When this occurs, the master's tort theory is manifestly more useful to the plaintiff as the employer may still be in breach of a non-delegable duty of care.[3]

1. *Twine* v. *Bean's Express*, [1946] 1 All E.R. 202.
2. E.g. *Co-operation Insurance Assoc.* v. *Kearney* (1965) 48 D.L.R. (2d) 1 (S.C.C.); [1965] S.C.R. 106.
3. *Broom* v. *Morgan*, [1953] 1 Q.B. 597 (C.A.).

282. In Quebec, the position is similar. According to the general regime of civil liability established by the Civil Code, an employer, as any other person, may be held responsible for any injury its tortious act causes to another person.[1] In order to obtain compensation, a plaintiff has to establish that the employer is personally at fault.[2] However, because an employer often has to act through others, fault might have to be established by reference to the acts of those persons with sufficient authority to be considered as a representative of the employer. It is important to note that, from a theoretical point of view, in such case, it is not the personal fault of the representative that ought to be demonstrated, but that of the employer as being represented by another person. In practice, however, it may be difficult to establish personal fault even by reference to a representative, but in such cases an employer may be held vicariously liable for the acts of its employees or agents. In such cases, it is not the personal fault of the employer that must be established, but rather the fault of the employee or agent for which the employer is vicariously liable.

1. C.c.Q., s.1457.
2. For instance, an employer could be held responsible for its negligence in carrying on its business: *Bergevin* v. *Ford Marechal Inc.*, [1981] C.S. 1181; it could also be responsible for having selected an incompetent agent: *La commission scolaire régionale Honoré – Mercier* v. *St-Onge*, [1980] C.A. 248.

2. Vicarious liability

283. The notion that the employer should be responsible for the tortious acts of its employees is, at first glance, an anomaly in the law of torts. It is so because it is normally deemed to be necessary to establish that a defendant was at fault before he may be held liable to compensate an accident victim. To attribute the fault of an employee to the employer strikes a discordant note. Yet the concept of liability without fault is not unknown to the law.[1] Justification for holding an employer vicariously liable has to be found. Several are available.[2] One is that the employer has control over its employees. Therefore, the employer ought to be responsible for their conduct while under management control. In as much as this implies that the acts of the employee are really the acts of the employer, this is but another version of the master's tort theory. However, if the employer is held liable, even though it is not in any way careless in the way that it chose his employees, organized their work, supervised their activity, etc., the liability must be based on the notion that, because the employer is in control, it is the actor which must be saddled with taking precautions to avoid harm to others. That is, it is not enough to engage competent employees and the like: strangers are entitled to hold the employer responsible for tortious conduct of his employees which affect them because the employer is in a better position to prevent such faulty conduct than anyone else. Associated with this reasoning are other lines of argument. For example, it appears reasonable that a person who benefits from all the activity which creates risk, should be held responsible when that risk materializes. The argument is that an employer benefits directly from the labour of others, unlike the rest of society, which also benefits but does so only indirectly. Furthermore, economic efficiency seems to require the redistribution of the loss caused by the enterprise of the employer, and the employer is much better situated than anyone else in the causal chain to spread the loss to the broad community by purchasing insurance to cover the risk in question and passing on the cost of its premiums through its pricing practices. Moreover, if the employer is made vicariously liable, the victim is assured of finding a defendant who is capable of paying. Also, the plaintiff is relieved of what would otherwise be serious evidentiary problems in proving fault; generally, the victim will more easily be able to prove an employee at fault than an employer.[2] Amongst these rationales for holding employers vicariously liable, none predominates in judicial reasoning, although the 'loss distribution' rationale appears to be especially forceful. The co-existence of these various *raisons d'être* for the doctrine has led to some rather unclear guidelines as to when an employer will be held vicariously liable.

1. E.g. the famous Rule in *Rylands* v. *Fletcher* is often cited as an illustration, even though in practice it may be doubted that it operates as a no-fault doctrine.
2. On vicarious liability generally, *see* P. Atiyah, *Vicarious Liability in the Law of Torts* (London, 1967). Atiyah examines the policy interests underlying the doctrine at 31–5.

284. An employer will be held vicariously liable for the tortious conduct of its employees and agents only if they were acting within the scope of their employment. This formulation is obviously wider than one which would limit liability to tortious acts committed when the employee was complying with the mode of performance demanded by the employer. That is, the employer may be vicariously liable even for unauthorized means of carrying out the work.[1] Clearly, this runs counter to the notion that employers are made vicariously responsible because of their right to control. The rule can be harmonized, however, with the other rationales for vicarious liability described in the previous paragraph. Nonetheless, because the courts are sometimes unclear on what is a proper basis for founding vicarious liability, there are endless battles about whether or not the employee was on a 'frolic of her or his own' when the injury was inflicted;[2] or about whether or not the fact that the employer had actually prohibited the particular conduct which caused the injury precluded a finding a vicarious responsibility;[3] or about whether or not intentional wrongdoing by an employee can render an employer vicariously liable.[4] Detailed examination of the law on these points is beyond the scope of this essay. Suffice it to say that the resolution of such matters ultimately depends on which of the justifications for the doctrine of vicarious liability a particular court favours. One potentially large loophole in the doctrine of vicarious liability must be addressed. The courts have held that an employee who tortiously injures a third party during the course of his or her employment will normally be deemed to have breached the implied term in his or her employment contract to perform the job in a non-negligent manner. The employer – or more likely its insurance company to whom the employer's rights are subrogated under insurance law – can sue the employee for damages which will generally represent the monies paid out to the third party victim.[5] Plainly, this doctrine circumvents the loss distribution rationale of vicarious liability. Fortunately, such actions are rare, due to a 'gentlemen's understanding' on the part of insurance companies that to sue the worker in such circumstances would not be in the spirit of vicarious liability. In its 1993 ruling in *London Drugs Ltd.* v. *Kuehne and Nagel International Ltd.*,[6] La Forest J suggested, by way of *obiter dictum*, that employment contract law should be modified to preclude an employer for suing an employee for breach of the implied duty not be negligent where insurance coverage is in place and provided that the degree of the employee's negligence is not 'gross'. It remains to be seen whether future courts will adopt this view. It would be far simpler, of course, to reverse the *Lister*[7] doctrine by express legislative enactment.

1. *See R.* v. *Levy Bros.* (1961) 26 D.L.R. (2d), 760, at 762 (S.C.C.); [1961] S.C.R. 189.
2. E.g. *Krokosz Estate* v. *Soucy Estate* (1992) 82 Man. R. (2d) 124, at 131 (QB); *Hall* v. *Halifax Transfer* (1959) 18 D.L.R. (2d) 115 (N.S.S.C.); *Bamert* v. *Parks* (1965) 50 D.L.R. (2d) 313 (Ont. C.C.); *Hamilton* v. *Farmers'*, [1953] 3 D.L.R. 382 (N.S.S.C.).
3. *Hamilton* v. *Farmers'*, *ibid.*; *Longdo* v. *McCarty and Gordie's Auto Sales* (1979) 28 N.B.R. (2d) 56 (N.B.Q.B.).
4. *Brezinski* v. *Schultz and Healy Hotel Ltd.*, [1975] 3 W.W.R. 467 (Sask. Q.B.); *Smart* v. *McCarty and Control Investments* (1980) 33 N.B.R. (2d) 27 (N.B.Q.B.); *Bourgeault* v. *McDermid & Miller* (1982) 140 D.L.R. (3d) 176 (B.C.S.C.).
5. *Lister* v. *Romford Ice and Cold Storage Ltd.*, [1957] A.C. 555 (H.L.); *D.H. Overmyer of Canada Ltd.* (1975) 65 D.L.R. (3d) 717 (B.C.C.A.).
6. (1993) 43 C.C.E.L. 1, at 82–5 (S.C.C.); [1992] 3 S.C.R. 299.
7. *Supra*, note 5 and accompanying text.

285. The basis for vicarious liability is expressed in terms of liability for the conduct of agents as well as employees. The word 'agent' encompasses both employees and independent contractors in as much as agency denotes a contract to have work performed by another. Where such work is done in a representative capacity, it is appropriate, as a matter of linguistic convenience, to refer to the performer as an employee or an agent, whereas if the performer can be classified as a principal in her or his own right, it is best to describe him or her as an independent contractor. As between an employee and an agent, it is customary to reserve the term agent for those representatives who are employed on a casual, rather than a continuous, basis.

286. This categorization is obviously imprecise. The determination of whether or not a person acts as a principal rather than as a representative involves the analysis discussed above. When the purpose of categorization is to decide whether an employer ought to be made vicariously liable, the underlying justifications for the existence of the doctrine will play a determining role. Thus, whereas it was once thought that an employer could only be held liable for the tortious acts of an independent contractor where the task to be performed was inherently ultra-dangerous,[1] the physical diminution of control over the enterprise and the attendant devaluation of the control test led to an ever increasing approximation in treatment of employees and independent contractors. Thus the initial starting position has been modified and employers may be held vicariously liable for the conduct of independent contractors in an increasing number of circumstances: hospitals are often held responsible for work performed by consulting medical practitioners;[2] occupiers will be responsible to some lawful entrants on their land who are injured by independent contractors working on that land;[3] most importantly, employers will be held responsible for not providing a safe system of work or for not ensuring compliance with statutory safety standards.[4] Such duties are said to be non-delegable. Manifestly, the increased scope of vicarious liability in respect of independent contractors reflects the augmented importance of the rationale that (i) the reaper of profits should bear the cost, and (ii) loss-distribution principles dictate a finding of vicarious responsibility. As these principles are imprecise in scope, it follows that there will still be many occasions where an employer will be permitted to say that an independent contractor should, as a principal, be the sole person to bear the burden of causing harm.[5] In such cases the courts will justify their decision by reasoning that the employer's duty was a delegable one and that it had been properly delegated.

1. *City of St. John* v. *Donald*, [1926] 2 D.L.R. 185 (S.C.C.); [1926] S.C.R. 371; *Savage* v. *Wilby*, [1954] 3 D.L.R. 204 (S.C.C.); [1954] S.C.R. 376; *Holinary* v. *Hawkins and Neilsens' Maintenance* (1966) 52 D.L.R. (2d) 289 (Ont.C.A.).
2. E.g. *Hopital Notre-Dame de l'Esperance* v. *Laurent*, [1978] 1 S.C.R. 605, in which it was held that the hospital was not liable for the acts of a consultant surgeon, because the hospital exercised no control over the performance of the work. This position, however is in some doubt: *compare Yeprimian* v. *Scarborough General Hospital* (1980) 110 D.L.R. (3d) 513 (Ont.C.A.) where it was held that a hospital could only be liable for specialists whom it employed, even if the specialist has admitting and other privileges at the hospital.
3. *Francis* v. *Cockrell* (1870) 5 Q.B. 501 (Exch.).
4. *Wilsons & Clyde Coal* v. *English*, [1938] A.C. 57 (H.L.).
5. *Davie* v. *New Merton Board Mills*, [1959] A.C. 604 (H.L.); *Howard* v. *Morgan Trust Co.* (1983) 25 C.C.L.T. 65.

287. In Quebec, the incorporation of the rules of vicarious liability in the Civil Code has provided a somewhat clearer and more definitive approach than in the common law provinces where the rules have evolved through the case law. Nevertheless, Quebec still closely parallels the common law. The employer is responsible for the fault of the employee in the performance of his or her job although the employer is not personally at fault.[1] According to the Quebec Civil Code, three conditions must be met in order to hold the employer vicariously liable: (i) the fault of the agent or the employee; (ii) the fact that the person at fault is the agent of the employer; and (iii) the fault occurred in the performance of the agent's duties.[2]

1. C.c.Q., s.1463.
2. *See* Jean-Louis Baudoin and Patrice Deslauriers, *La responsabilité civile*, 5th edn. (Cowansville: Les Editions Yvon Blais Inc., 1998) 417–66.

288. The first condition is straightforward. There is no need to prove the personal fault of the employer as the employer is simply held responsible for the agent or employee's personal fault. The second and third conditions are more problematic and they have been the subject of debates in Quebec case law. The Code does not define what 'agents' or 'servants' means. It seems clear today that these terms encompass any person who performs work for another person while being under the control of the latter. No contractual relationship or remuneration need to be proven; the mere fact that one person acts for another and remains under her or his control during the performance of his or her duties suffices. In principle, the employer would not be made vicariously liable for the conduct of an independent contractor since in such a case the former does not retain control over the latter in the performance of the job. The question is not settled in case law regarding professional employees. The issue is whether the employer should be held vicariously liable where the provision of professional services is governed by a profession's code of conduct rather than by the employer.

289. The third condition of vicarious liability is that the employee's fault must occur in the performance of her or his job. It is impossible to draw from Quebec's case law a precise definition of what constitutes an act performed in the course of an employee's duties. Courts have dealt with several issues related to the matter such as the fact that the employee's conduct was criminal, occurred outside the regular hours or location of work, amounted to gross negligence or constituted insubordination. None of these facts appears to be determinative. The only criterion that has been held significant is whether or not the employee or the agent was acting for the benefit of the employer when the fault took place. Once these three conditions are met, the employer is held vicariously liable for the damages caused by the faulty conduct of the employee. This liability is absolute and the employer cannot escape from it by showing that the employee had been carefully selected, or was properly supervised. The employer, however, is entitled to recover any damages paid from the employee who is at fault, but such recourse may not be practical.

D. Duty to Provide a Safe Work Environment

1. The common law duty

290. As indicated in section C, the common law doctrine of vicarious liability makes employers liable for the acts of their employees which cause harm to strangers and for the conduct of independent contractors who cause harm to the employer's employees. Yet, oddly, the courts historically had refused to make employers responsible for injuries caused to their employees by fellow employees. The contract of employment was interpreted as including a term implied by law that employees agreed to run the risk of injury due to the acts of fellow employees. This was the common employment doctrine. It was eventually repealed by statute. In the meanwhile, the courts came to realize the harshness of the doctrine and, in typical common law fashion, developed a tool to overcome the problem without having to disavow the existing law. They simply held that an employer had a positive legal duty to all his employees to provide a safe system of work. This duty is spelt out as requiring an obligation (i) to provide competent fellow workmen, (ii) to provide safe tools, machinery and equipment, (iii) to provide a safe place of work and safe access to that place of work and (iv) to provide a safe system of working.[1] These being the employer's personal responsibilities, they cannot be delegated to competent managers. Similarly, the hiring of independent contractors ought not to discharge these duties of employers, although, as we have seen, reliance on others may sometimes permit the employer to claim that they have discharged their obligations.[2]

1. *Wilson* v. *Tyneside Window Cleaning*, [1958] 2 Q.B. 110 (C.A.); *Wilsons and Clyde Coal* v. *English*, [1938] A.C. 367 (H.L.); *Marshment* v. *Borgstrom*, [1942] S.C.R. 374.
2. *Davie* v. *New Merton Board Mills, supra.*

291. In Quebec, the Civil Code imposes a similar obligation on the employer to provide a safe working environment for employees. Section 2087 states that the employer is bound 'to take any measures consistent with the nature of the work to protect the health, safety and dignity of the employee'. The specific content of this broad duty is, however, detailed in a specific statute.[1]

1. *See* An Act Respecting Occupational Health and Safety, R.S.Q., c.S-2.1.

2. Workers' compensation legislation

292. There is relatively little jurisprudence in Canada relating to the employer's implied duty to provide a safe work environment because, from early on in this century, statutory schemes of workers' compensation schemes have replaced judicial action for damages as a recovery mechanism. All provinces have such statutes and they provide that workers shall be compensated for personal injuries arising out of, or incurred in the course of, their employment. There are various categories of disablement for which benefits are paid. Within each category, the methods of calculation vary from jurisdiction to jurisdiction. No full account can be given.[1] By way of indication, it is noted that payments may be made for (i) temporary total disability, (ii) temporary partial disability, and (iii) permanent disability. Wage loss benefits are usually a percentage of the average wage rate of the injured worker. The period over which this is calculated varies between jurisdictions. In some jurisdictions an approach is taken which calculates the worker's wage rates less what he or she is earning now, or deemed to be capable of earning, and to pay a percentage of that amount. Some jurisdictions provide for a minimum level of benefits. While there is no maximum prescribed, each jurisdiction has a ceiling on the average earnings, which can be used as a yardstick to set the periodic payments which are to be paid to a successful claimant. Where a worker is not totally disabled but can only work at a job which pays a lower rate for a while, the formula used to calculate payments may be a different one from that used for the calculation of temporary total disability payments. Where the injury has stabilized and it is clear that the recovery will never be complete, a payment will be made for permanent disability. In some jurisdictions this may lead to the payment of a lifetime pension. Arguably, this could be said to unjustly enrich an employee who is in a 'dying industry' and who otherwise would have been terminated for redundancy in the foreseeable future. Be that as it may, difficulties of classification arise as to whether the permanent disability is a total or a partial one. Different methods of calculating benefits are used. If it is a total permanent disability, the means employed to determine temporary disability periodic payments are adopted; if it is a partial permanent disability, an assessment is made based on schedules, e.g. a loss of a kidney may be equivalent to a 15 per cent disability.

1. Workers' compensation legislation is a subject of great political concern and the various legislatures move from one set of provisions to another continuously. All that can be done is to give this skeletal outline and suggest consultation of guides and books. The law is examined in detail in T.G. Ison, *Workers' Compensation in Canada* (Toronto: Butterworths, 2nd edn., 1989). The best policy analysis remains P.C. Weiler, *Reshaping Workers Compensation for Ontario* (Toronto: Ministry of Government Services, 1980).

293. Diseases arising out of working conditions are also compensable, but on a much less universal scale. Although details differ, in general the statutes provide that certain diseases are compensable if it can be shown that the worker was employed in a particular industry at a relevant time. That is, schedules in the statutes list a number of diseases and go on to say that there is a presumption that the suffering of such a disease is compensable if the worker was employed in a scheduled industry. In some provinces, the worker must have been so employed at any time in the 12 months previous to the manifestation of the disabling disease, in others there is no time limit. Where the disease complained of is not listed in such a schedule, the burden is on the worker-applicant to show that the disease is work related.

294. The schemes are funded in part on a collective basis. The industries covered by the statutes are grouped by type, the relevant employers paying into collective fund for their industry groups. The sum levied from each employer is calculated on the basis of the estimated payroll for the coming year. The Workers' Compensation Board (as the administrative agency running the scheme is usually called) calculates the contribution rate on the basis of the known hazard in a particular group of industries. At the end of the year, an accounting is done to readjust the rate based on actual payroll, to adjust for particularly hazardous enterprises in a group. In addition, the legislation may impose an extra financial burden on individual employers with a poor health and safety record. This individualized approach has the benefit of preventing renegade employers from operating unsafely in order to obtain a comparative advantage from the majority of employers in the group who operate at a higher safety level. On the other hand, the risks of individualized rating are that the employer may coerce employees into remaining at work when they are sick instead of leaving the workplace and claiming compensation; the employer might contest more claims than would otherwise have been the case; and the amount of the extra premium for being 'unsafe' is too low to provide an effective disincentive to renegade employers.[1] As yet Canadian studies have not conclusively established whether or not the benefits of individualized rating outweigh the costs. The Workers' Compensation Boards may also have the power to provide for preventive regulation. Clearly, there ought to be an effective incentive for employers to cooperate in such efforts. However, it is fair to assert that the preventive efforts of the schemes have been rather insipid. Generally, they have consisted of setting up advisory bodies, mainly comprised of appropriate employers, which publicize obvious safety problems.

1. T. Ison, 'The Significance of Experience Rating' (1986) 24 *Osgoode Hall L.J.* 723.

295. The statutory schemes thus provide compensation without workers having to establish that their employers or fellow employees were at fault, although employees may be denied compensation if it is found that the injury was caused by their serious misconduct and the injury was not serious. A majority of the statutory schemes provide that certain excluded employers are liable to compensate their employees on a negligence basis. That is, such employees must establish fault.[1] By generally removing fault notions, the compensation schemes have reduced a significant stumbling block to the recovery of compensation, but areas of dispute remain. Thus, the questions of whether the injury arose out of or in the course of employment, whether the disease is a compensable one, the extent of disability, etc. are all potentially contentious issues.

1. This means that the employee must prove a defect in the machinery, faulty process organization or injury caused by the negligence of the employer or of those for whom he is responsible. The employee's own negligence may bar his or her cause of action or diminish the amount of damages recoverable.

296. With the advent of the Charter of Rights and Freedoms some people have argued that the preemptive nature of the workers' compensation schemes has robbed them of a valuable right, namely, that of seeking redress for work-related injuries in court by way of a tort action, that is, by way of proving fault. The reasoning is that being limited to the workers' compensation machinery denies employees the equality guaranteed by section 15 of the Charter because other similarly injured persons, albeit injured in other circumstances, have a right to sue in court. In addition, they argue, this pre-emption also denies them the protection of life, liberty and security promised by section 7 of the Charter. The Newfoundland Court of Appeal has rejected these arguments and has upheld the statutory bar against alternate legal remedies.[1] However, the Court emphasized by way of *obiter dictum* that this so-called 'historical trade off' will only prevail for as long as the Workers' Compensation Acts continue to provide reasonably adequate financial relief to injured workers. This decision was upheld by the Supreme Court of Canada without comment on the fairness of the current 'trade off'. Therefore, the constitutionality of the statutory ban on alternate actions could become judicially contested in the future if compensation levels under the legislation are significantly reduced.

1. *Re a Constitutional Reference on the Validity of s.32 and s.34 of the Workers' Compensation Act* (1987) 67 Nfld and PEI Rep. 16, affm'd [1989] 1 S.C.R. 923.

297. In Ontario and Quebec, large governmental-type operations, such as railways, federal telephone companies, steamship companies and the like are exempted from paying into the Workers' Compensation Accident Fund, but participate in the scheme by contributing to its administrative cost. Their employees are paid compensation by the Workers' Compensation Board on the same basis as all other covered employees.

3. Developing occupational health and safety legislation

298. Workers' compensation operates to a relatively small degree as a preventive mechanism against unsafe working conditions and practices by means of the collective and individual experience and penalty rating of employers with high accident rates. However, the major preventive mechanism is found in omnibus occupational health and safety statutes. Historically, it was left initially to private contract-making between the parties, then to a series of special statutes which imposed penalties for breaching standards externally imposed in respect of specified pieces of equipment and conditions (guards on machines, pressure of boilers). This was an *ad hoc* system. Today, the growing awareness of the dangers posed to workers by the use of toxic substances in manufacturing processes has led to the enactment of comprehensive health and safety legislation.[1] These statutes impose a set of obligations on both employers and workers in order to attain certain standards of safety in the work environment. Usually, there is provision for regulations to be passed after appropriate recommendations by a designated agency. The agency will be given the task of evaluating the feasibility of imposing safety standards in the work place. It is given research facilities. The amount of money given in this respect is of the utmost importance in view of the difficulties inherent in setting appropriate exposure levels to the thousands of chemical substances in use in manufacturing. The agency is aided by an inspectorate which not only has the task of enforcing the existing standards, but also has to report on the need for more regulation or deregulation. The enforcement process involves consultation with the employers and employees, the making of recommendations, the possible imposition of fines and, where there is immediate danger, ordering the cessation of work until the premises comply with essential safety standards.[2] As well, these statutory schemes seek to improve the safety of the work environment by placing an onus on employers and employees to create an internal responsibility system. The essential components of this internal responsibility system are that employees have an effective right to participate in health and safety decisions, an effective right to know what health and safety hazards exist and an effective right to refuse unsafe work.[3] The right to participate is achieved by providing for joint employer–employee safety committees. In some jurisdictions the appropriate minister is given power to appoint committees comprised of an equal number of employer and employee representatives where the minister deems it desirable, in others it is mandated that, where the workforce exceeds a certain number, a joint committee of this kind must be appointed. Committees of this kind must make inspections regularly, educate and train people in health and safety matters, make joint recommendations, and call in government inspectors where needed, or where no agreement as to appropriate action can be reached. Accordingly, employers are under an obligation to make available to the committee information as to levels of exposures of particular workers, new substances introduced into the plant, medical advice respecting employees, etc. Generally, these committees are not authorized to *compel* an employer to take a particular action. Instead, the government inspector is armed with the legal authority to order that the employer make the workplace safe and it is the freedom to call in such an inspector that generally gives the committees its only 'teeth'. However, in the early 1990s Ontario revolutionized the traditional system by permitting the committees themselves, and even in some circumstances the employee representatives on the committee acting unilaterally, to order employers to cease and desist unsafe operations. It remains to be seen whether or not other provinces will adopt this experiment.

1. E.g. Canada Labour Code, R.S.C. 1985, c.L-2, Part II; The Occupational Health and Safety Act, R.S.A. 1980, c.O-2.
2. The weaknesses of this legislative framework are examined by E. Tucker, 'The Persistence of Market Regulations of Occupational Health and Safety: the Stillbirth of Voluntarism' in G. England (ed.), *Essays in Labour Relations Law* (Don Mills: CCH Canadian Ltd., 1983) 244.
3. The critical role of the internal system in securing health and safety was recently emphasized in Nova Scotia by the Advisory Council, *Taking Responsibility: Proposed Changes to the Nova Scotia Occupational Health and Safety Act* (Halifax: The Advisory Council, 1995) 7.

299. In addition, the Health and Safety Acts commonly give workers an individual right to refuse to perform work that they honestly and reasonably belief is dangerous to themselves or other persons at the work site.[1] If the employee's supervisor feels that the worker's fear is misplaced, the joint committee, or a safety representative who may have been appointed in lieu of such a committee, may be asked to determine the issue. Failure to so resolve the problem at this level may lead to a government inspector being asked to adjudicate. Even where an inspector adjudges the situation to be safe, a worker may continue to refuse to work without being disciplined. Generally, the employer may not discipline an employee for a genuine and reasonable refusal to work. What is 'genuine' and 'reasonable' is the subject of evolving jurisprudence. The initial refusal will, it seems, be considered permissible if the employee had a bona fide apprehension of danger, even if the employee's judgement subsequently turns out to have been objectively incorrect.[2] Criteria such as familiarity with the job and workplace, anxieties arising out of previous unsafe occurrences or media accounts of danger, may be used to gauge whether a belief or perceived danger was appropriately held.[3] As the steps in the procedure are followed, adverse findings by supervisors, committees and inspectors will render it more likely that continuing refusals will amount to a willful act of disobedience for which discipline may be imposed, although it will not automatically be deemed appropriate to discipline such a refusing employee.[4] While an employer may not discipline a refusing employee, the employer may ask him or her to do other available work. Arguably, if a lower rate of pay applies to such other work, the diminution in pay amounts to a 'penalty'. British Columbia and Quebec provide that refusing workers be paid in the normal way. But if the employer does not provide work at all because of the refusal to work and it is clear that this failure is not due to an 'anti-safety animus', employees may not have any redress at all.[5] This may be a powerful disincentive to use the provisions at all. Note that the failure to provide work may also result from an inspector's order to halt production until compliance with the appropriate standard of safety is achieved. In British Columbia, it is provided that in such circumstances, employees are entitled to pay for the day of closure and three days following it. Another limitation on the right to refuse is that refusal to work is not permitted because a danger may potentially arise out of the work processes at some time; there must be a danger perceived as actually existing.[6] Last, in some provinces, including Alberta, the statute expressly compels an employee to cease performing work, regardless of his or her choice, if to continue working would cause an 'imminent' threat to the health or safety of himself or herself or to others.

1. E.g. Canada Labour Code ss.128–31. For a detailed elaboration of the law on point, *see* R. Brown, 'The Right to Refuse Unsafe Work' (1983) 17 *U.B.C. Law Rev.* 1.
2. E.g. *Elgaard* v. *Sidbec Dosco Inc.*, [1988] O.L.R.B. Rep. 1334.
3. E.g. *Canadian National Railways*; [1980] 2 Can. L.R.B.R. 344 (Can.); *Re Industrial Health and Safety Regulations* (1980) 5 W.C.R. 86 (B.C.).
4. *Re Pharand and Inco Metal*, [1980] 3 Can. L.R.B.R. 194 (Ont.).
5. *Canada General Electric Co. Ltd.*, [1981] O.L.R.B. Rep. 616 (Ont.); *Re Domtar Chemicals Ltd. and International Chemical Workers Union Local 682* (1975) 8 L.A.C. (2d) 346, 349 (Weatherill).
6. *Re Pharand and Inco Metal, supra*, note 4; *Re Miller and C.N.R.*, [1980] 2 Can. L.R.B.R. 344 (Can.).

300. At common law it was always open for an employee to refuse work in unsafe conditions.[1] But such a worker ran a great risk: if the refusal was held to be unreasonable by a court there was no question but that the employer's right to dismiss such an employee would be upheld. Further, even if the refusal was found to be reasonable, a dismissed employee, as will be seen below, could not be reinstated and his or her damages would not be assessed on a 'make whole' basis. In any event, it was not difficult for an employer to get rid of such a 'trouble-making' employee lawfully, if it saw fit to do so. Where an employee covered by a collective agreement refused to work, grievance arbitrators had advanced the common law rights a good deal. Arbitrators would uphold workers' refusals where they found that (i) they honestly believed their safety was endangered, (ii) they had effectively and reasonably communicated this fear to the employer, (iii) their belief was reasonable in the circumstances, and (iv) there was in fact sufficient danger to justify such refusal.[2] This test was more onerous than that required by the new statutory regimes and it appears that where there is a conflict between the two approaches, the legislative standards should be applied.[3]

1. E.g. *Ottoman Bank* v. *Chakarian*, [1930] A.C. 277 (P.C.).
2. *Re Steel Co. of Canada Ltd., and U.S.W.A. Local 1005* (1973) 4 L.A.C. (2d) 315 (Johnston).
3. *Re Beachvilime Ltd.*, and *Energy and Chemical Workers Union*, Local 32 (1981) 1 L.A.C. (3d) 22 (Palmer).

301. The efficacy of these elaborate schemes is still open to doubt.[1] What is clear is that the right to refuse is used mainly where collective agreements exist. As to the external regulatory machinery, much will depend on the political will supporting the work of the agencies, which are to set standards. Much depends on economic circumstances. These will dictate whether a standard can be imposed in view of the effect on the competitive position of an industry or people within it. Indeed, it has been forcefully argued by Professors Glasbeek and Rowland that a greater role should be played by the criminal law and, in particular, that criminal charges be brought against individual managers and members of the boards of directors of companies whose work practices kill and injure their workers.[2] As yet the potential for personal criminal liability has not been fulfilled. For example, criminal charges were recently brought against named managers of the Westray coal mine in Nova Scotia after an explosion in 1992 that killed 26 miners, but the legal complexities of applying criminal law to such 'accidents' proved to be so intractable that the prosecutions had to be dropped because of problems with legal technicalities.[3]

1. *See*, for example, E. Tucker, 'The Persistence of Market Regulations of Occupational Health and Safety: the Stillbirth of Voluntarism' in G. England (ed.), *Essays in Labour Relations Law* (Don Mills: CCH Canadian Ltd., 1983) 244; Advisory Council, *Taking Responsibility: Proposed Changes to the Nova Scotia Occupational Health and Safety Act* (Halifax: The Advisory Council, 1995); *Ontario Advisory Council on Occupational Health and Occupational Safety*; *Ninth Annual Report* (Toronto: Ministry of Supply and Services, 1987), esp. 49–57.
2. H. Glasbeek and S. Rowland, 'Are Injury and Killing at Work Crimes?' (1979) 17 *Osgoode Hall L.J.* 506.
3. The sorry saga is recounted by E. Tucker, 'The Westray Mine Disaster and its Aftermath: the Politics of Causation' (1995) 10 *Can. J. of Law and Society* 91.

302. The third and final pillar of the internal responsibility system is the right to know of workplace hazards. In 1987, after many meetings between employers, unions and all Canadian governments, an agreement was reached to implement national right to know legislation. It is to be known as the Workplace Hazardous Materials Information System (W.H.M.I.S.).[1] The concept is that all suppliers of what are defined to be controlled and hazardous substances, as well as employers who use them, are to make material safety data sheets available about such substances, indicating the chemical identity and level of concentration of the ingredients, or the fact that nothing is known about their toxicological properties when there is reason to believe that they may be harmful. As a matter of jurisdictional division, federal legislation addresses the regulation of controlled and hazardous substances put into circulation by suppliers and importers and provincial mirror image legislation speaks to the employers' duties and obligations. The Canada Labour Code regulates employers engaged in a federal work, undertaking or business. Suppliers and employers may apply for exemptions by arguing that they may be forced to disclose legitimate trade secrets. Even if they are granted such exemptions they must still provide hazard information about the undisclosed ingredients. The suppliers and importers (and employers where they are manufacturers of hazardous products) must make sure that all containers, vats, packages, etc., in which hazardous products are found are clearly labelled, giving warnings in words and pictures and advice as to how to deal with problems which the ingredients may create. Employers must ensure that the material safety data sheets are current and also are to provide training programmes for workers on how to use the knowledge which is to be made available.[2] In Ontario, the enabling legislation has imposed some additional obligations on employers. They are to provide an inventory of the substances in use in their workplaces and the material safety data sheets are to be made available to medical officers of health and to fire departments. Members of the public can gain access to the information by asking the appropriate medical officer of health to furnish them with it.[3]

1. For details of the scheme, *see* P. Simon, *Hazardous Products: Canada's WHMIS Laws*, 2nd edn. (Don Mills: CCH Canadian, 1989).
2. Hazardous Products Act, S.C. 1987, c.30, Part III.
3. Occupational Health and Safety Act, R.S.O. 1990, c.0.1, s.38.

E. A Duty of Fairness

302A. During the 1980s and 1990s, it appeared as though the courts were moving towards implying an independent term into the employment contract requiring the employer to treat the employee fairly in all aspects of the employment relationship. Many facets of a duty of fairness were regularly being applied under the rubric of other legal doctrines, such as 'just cause' for dismissal, estoppel, condonation, etc., as well as under the law of torts; a corresponding implied duty on the employee to advance the employer's business interests had long been recognized by the courts; employers were regularly being obliged to exercise express discretionary powers in the employment contract in a good faith and fair manner; employers generally expect as a matter of fact that they will treat their employees fairly and this is the factual understanding of most employees; employers arguably stand to achieve efficiency gains by treating their employees fairly; employers and employers acting statutory powers were bound under administrative law to treat their employees fairly in the procedural sense. It seemed only a matter of time before the courts would grasp the nettle and imply an independent duty of fairness in all employment contracts as a matter of law.[1] Indeed, the English House of Lords took this step in 1998 in *Malik* v. *B.C.C.I.*[2] However, in its landmark 1997 decision in *Wallace* v. *United Grain Growers Ltd.*, the Supreme Court of Canada held that no duty of fairness is implied into employment contracts as a matter of general law.[3] The Court reasoned that such an implied term potentially would impair management's flexibility by enabling aggrieved workers to challenge in the courts almost any management decision. This risk appears to be overstated given the high costs of civil litigation and the deterrent effect of awarding loser costs. Furthermore, if the duty of fairness is defined relatively conservatively as requiring the employer's decisions to be rational (in the sense of furthering legitimate business reasons rather than being arbitrary, discriminatory or in bad faith), procedurally fair and – more controversially – substantively proportionate in terms of the relative degrees of harm likely to be sustained by each side, then the risk of widespread judicial second-guessing in substantive areas of management's expertise is minimized. The Supreme Court of Canada, however, sought a compromise by requiring employers to act in good faith and professionally in handling dismissals on pain of having the period of reasonable notice of termination extended.[4] In contrast, Mclachlan J. dissented in her ruling that an independent duty of fairness should be implied into all employment contracts. Clearly, there are obstacles with an implied contractual duty of fairness. One is the appropriate remedy. Ideally, specific performance appears to be the most appropriate remedy in that it would force the employer to act fairly, thereby having an educational effect as well as upholding the symbolic importance of the duty of fairness. However, courts traditionally have not granted specific performance to remedy breaches of employment contracts and the employer may simply 'go through the motions' of acting fairly in any case, thereby bringing the duty of fairness into disrepute. Therefore, punitive damages may be appropriate in order to deter employers from treating the duty lightly. Ideally, the courts should order employers to implement training programmes for their managers in treating people fairly, but it is questionable whether courts have the jurisdiction to make such orders. Another obstacle is how the duty of fairness would be applied where one employee claims that another employee, not a manager, has treated him unfairly. Ideally, if a duty of fairness is considered to be in the public interest, such a duty should be legislated as an employment standard so that it can be enforced through the relatively cheap and expeditious statutory procedures by a specialized tribunal which has the authority to make 'make whole' remedial orders.

1. For a detailed analysis of these development, *see* England *et al.*, *op. cit.*, vol. 2, paras. 10.19–10.39.2.
2. [1998] A.C. 20 (H.L.).
3. (1997), 97 C.L.L.C. 210029 (S.C.C.); [1998] 3 S.C.R. 701.
4. This aspect of the decision is examined *infra*, para. 338.

§3. The Employee's Duties and Obligations

A. Introduction

303. Duties and obligations may be imposed because they are explicitly agreed to by the parties in their contract of employment. They may also be implied. As we saw earlier, the process of implying terms into the employment contract, whether on the basis of 'fact' or 'law' or a combination of both, provides broad scope for judicial policy-making. Indeed, in common law jurisdictions, the courts have used the implied term to fashion a standardized set of rights and obligations for employees which often makes the employment relationship resemble one of 'status' as much as one based on free contracting.[1] The golden thread in the evolution of the law of employment contracts is that judges are continually remodelling the implied terms to reflect the changing standards of personnel practice and community perspectives on the nature of working relationships. The 'status' point must not be overplayed, however, for theoretically it is always open to the parties to modify an implied term by express provisions in their contract, although in reality the disparity of bargaining power between the parties would normally preclude an employee from opting out of his or her implied obligations.

1. As already seen in para. 212, in Quebec, the basic set of rights and obligations of both the employer and the employee is expressly defined by the legislator in the Civil Code.

304. The particular duties and obligations imposed on employees by implication of law ultimately derive from a bedrock duty of fidelity imposed on them towards their employer. The nature of this duty is explained as follows by Sanderman J of the Alberta Queens Bench Trial Division:

> 'It has long been accepted that . . . the employee is expected to serve his employer honestly and faithfully during the term of employment. This duty of fidelity permeates the entire relationship between the employer and the employee. It is a flexible concept that is paramount to the basic relationship . . . there is an implied obligation placed upon the employee to act in the best interests of his employer at all times. The employee shall not follow a course of action that harms or places at risk the interests of the employer.'[1]

There are few more ringing judicial acknowledgements of the primacy of managerial interests under the employment contract than this. There are two main subcategories of the duty of fidelity. First, there is the duty to obey and duty to use appropriate skill and care; secondly, there is the duty of good faith. Plainly, these categories overlap, but the nature of particular obligations which employees must honour can be usefully perceived by referring them to one of these two discrete subcategories. Further, the two subcategories are distinct in one important aspect, despite the potential for overlap. Thus the duties and obligations which will be discussed under the heading of good faith may require that an employee be held in breach of such duties and obligations where that breach causes damage to the employer after the contract has terminated or even that an employee comply with his or her duty of good faith after the contract has run its course. The duties to obey or to use appropriate skill and care can have no such post-contractual scope.

1. *C.R.C. – Evans Canada Ltd.* v. *Pettifer* (1997) 26 C.C.E.L. (2d) 294, at 303 (Alta.Q.B.).

305. Where an employee is in breach of an express or implied duty, the employer may have a cause of action in damages in respect of the loss occasioned. Such actions are rarely brought, however, since individual workers, at least between the lower and mid ranges of the organizational hierarchy, rarely have enough money to cover much more than minimal damages. More importantly, the employer can summarily dismiss an employee without notice or wages in lieu if he or she commits a serious breach of an implied obligation. The general laws of contract which govern the employment contract require that a breach of contract be sufficiently serious to constitute a 'repudiation' of the contract before the innocent party can elect to bring the contract to an end. The definition of 'repudiatory breach' is malleable and the courts in the employment sphere have applied it to reflect changing expectations about the nature of the working relationship.[1] Today, the term is generally interpreted as requiring that the penalty of dismissal be invoked only where there is substantial harm caused to the employer's interests – essentially this boils down to a doctrine of substantive proportionality, much like that which exists under human rights Acts for groups protected thereunder – and only where dismissal is invoked in a procedurally fair manner. The trend in Canada since the late 1960s has been to give increasingly more rights to employees in summary dismissal situations. Today, there is little difference between the common law standards governing dismissals for 'just cause' and the standards of 'just cause' fashioned by collective agreement arbitrators in the unionized sector. (The critical difference, of course, is at the remedial stage where a unionized employee normally wins reinstatement while a non-unionized worker only receives damages for lost wages and benefits over the period of notice of termination.) The precise requirements of 'just cause' at common law are examined later in this essay.

1. The balance of interests at stake in this situation are examined by England *et al.*, *op. cit.*, vol. 2, paras. 15.5–15.30.

B. The Duty to Obey

306. Refusal to obey the employer's instructions is commonly referred to as 'insubordination'. There are certain orders of an employer which an employee may lawfully refuse to carry out. These include commands to do something which is illegal and those which would jeopardize the physical well-being of the employee if obeyed.[1] As to the latter, the right to refuse an order to do unsafe work has already been discussed.[2] As previously indicated, modern health and safety Acts have made it somewhat easier for a worker to take such a stand. In addition, if an employer requires an employee to carry out her or his duties in an area where he or she is endangered because, say, her or his political or religious beliefs are anathema in the region, the employee is entitled to refuse to accept such an assignment.[3] However, if the employee can merely show that it is awkward for her or him to go to a particular place because of a language difficulty and because the local authorities do not like him, or her, the employer will be entitled to summarily dismiss such an employee. The argument is that, as long as there is no personal danger, the employee has to obey the employer's order.[4] That is, the duty to obey truly reflects the notion that the relationship is one of service.

1. E.g. *Ottoman Bank* v. *Chakarian*, [1930] A.C. 277 (P.C.), involving a refusal grounded on personal safety.
2. At paras. 299–300.
3. E.g. *Ottoman Bank* v. *Chakarian*, *supra*, note 1.
4. E.g. *Bouzourou* v. *Ottoman Bank*, [1930] A.C. 271 (P.C.).

307. Disobedience of an order will not automatically give the employer the right to summarily dismiss an employee. As noted above, modern courts impose that a balance of proportionality be struck between the employee's interests and those of the employer. In this context, the courts take account not only of the degree of economic harm caused to the employer by the disobedience but also of the fact that, symbolically, management's authority to command may have been undermined by an act of disobedience. The employer's right to control the workforce is, of course, the cornerstone of the employment relationship.[1] Thus, courts have held that disobedience must be willful in order to ground summary dismissal. The meaning of willfulness has not been clearly spelt out in the jurisprudence. It seems to require more than an intent to disobey the employer's command, although once this was a view expressed by the courts.[2] The term, as used in modern times, appears to connote some deliberate design or purpose to derogate from one's duty.[3] To pinpoint the nature of the intent required further is fraught with difficulty. It may well be easier to classify disobedience as being one, which offends the duty, imposed by law when it is accompanied by behaviour, which can be described as insolent. This was the case in *Markey* v. *Port Well Dry Docks*,[4] in which the employee not only refused to obey instructions but justified his conduct to his supervisor by telling him that he was incompetent, challenging him to a trade test and suggesting that, to prove who was more rational, they should be examined by a psychiatrist. The employee indicated that he, the employee, would come out 'the better'. In such a case, it is readily apparent that the reason for the disobedience was willfulness rather than any other basis. (Note that, apart from the disobedience, insolence itself may give the employer a right of discipline against an employee. This will be discussed below.) This kind of disobedience can easily be differentiated from those cases in which the refusal to abide by an order can be attributed to a reasonable misunderstanding about the nature of her or his duties by the employee.[5] Such a misunderstanding may arise not only where the employer's instructions are themselves unclear, but also if clear works rules have been inconsistently applied in the past so that workers do not know what is expected of them. The notion of seeking a balance of proportionality between the parties' interests is reflected in the courts' willingness to treat an act of insubordination as justifiable if the worker has a 'reasonable excuse'. Put another way, the courts insist that an employer's orders be 'reasonable' ones. For example, it has been ruled 'unreasonable' for an employer to order a senior manager to cease having an affair with a subordinate in his off-duty time because of the disproportionately severe impact of the order on the employee's privacy compared with the relatively insignificant threat to the employer's operations.[6] In Quebec, the case law on the employee's duty to obey has developed along similar lines.[7]

1. Thus we saw earlier in paras. 160 and 166 that the courts will not recognize an 'employment' relationship as existing unless management has the requisite degree of control over the where, when and how of employment.
2. *Turner* v. *Mason* (1845) 153 E.R. 411; *Clouston* v. *Corry*, [1906] A.C. 122 (P.C.).
3. *Bist* v. *London and South Western Railway*, [1907] A.C. 209 at 211, 213–14 (H.L.); *George* v. *Glasgow Coal*, [1909] A.C. 123 at 128–9 (H.L.).
4. [1974] 4 O.R. (2d) 12 (C.C.). *See also Pepper* v. *Webb*, [1969] 1 W.L.R. 514 (C.A.).
5. E.g. *Wilson* v. *K.P. Manufacturing (Calgary) Ltd.* (1998) 37 C.C.E.L. (2d) 202, at 208 (Alta. Q.B.); *Drudl* v. *Brick Warehouse Corp.* (1998) 99 C.L.L.C. 210012, at para. 141080 (B.C.S.C.). In both cases the employer's orders were insufficiently clear and precise to ground 'just cause'.
6. *Dooley* v. *C.N. Weber Ltd.* (1994) 3 C.C.E.L. (2d) 95 (Ont.Div.Ct.).
7. *See* A. Edward Aust, *The Employment Contract* (Cowansville: Les Editions Yvon Blais Inc., 1988) 95–100; George Audet, Robert Bonhomme, Clément Gascon and Magali Cournoyer-Proulx, *Le congédiement en droit québécois* (Cowansville: Les Éditions Yvon Blais Inc., 3rd edn., looseleaf) 4-10 to 4-14.

308. In as much as the contract of employment requires an employee to perform certain kinds of services, it precludes the employer from making demands on that employee which are not incidental to, or within the purview of, the agreed upon area of performance. If an employer's instructions violate the terms of the contract, and the breach in question is 'repudiatory' in nature, the employee can resign and sue the employer for damages for constructive dismissal. Where the terms of the contract are relatively specific, the scope of orders which require obedience will be comparatively easy to delimit,[1] but usually the parties are quite vague on the scope of an employee's duties, not least because employers want the flexibility to adjust job duties to changing economic and technological circumstances. Thus, the issue goes beyond simple scenarios such as whether it is part and parcel of a secretary's duties to make and get coffee for the employer, to file driver's licence applications, and the like. The hard cases typically arise when an employer changes production processes and directs an employee to take on a new task or to work different days and/or hours. The fundamental issue in all of these cases is where the courts will choose to draw the boundary of legitimate managerial prerogatives. We will examine the law on point in detail in the context of the 'constructive dismissal' doctrine. At this juncture, suffice it to say that modern Canadian courts are beginning to afford employers greater leeway than before to modify job duties and working practices in the face of increasing pressures on Canadian employers to be more flexible in order to meet the challenge of overseas competition. As yet, however, no Canadian court has gone so far as the English Court of Appeal when it held that there is an implied term in employment contracts obliging employees continuously to upgrade their skills and expertise in order to perform satisfactorily any new job assignments that the employer might thrust upon them.[2] Perhaps the strongest endorsement of managerial prerogatives by a recent Canadian court is the 1998 holding of an Ontario trial judge, Weekes J., that there is an implied term in the employment contract allowing the employer to modify even clear contractual provisions by giving the worker reasonable advance notice.[3] Furthermore, where the employer requires an employee to do different work, or to work a different shift or the like, the employee's claim that he or she is entitled to be given specific tasks at specific times, is not aided by the fact that, failing an agreement to the contrary, the employer is under no duty to provide work.[4]

1. As in *Stacey* v. *Consolidated Foods Corp. of Canada* (1987) 15 C.C.E.L. 13 (N.S.S.Ct., Tr.Div.).
2. *Woods* v. *W.M. Car Services (Peterborough) Ltd.*, [1982] I.C.R. 693 (C.A.), esp. *per* Walkins L.J. On the contrary, recent Canadian decisions require the employer to act reasonably in assisting the employee to adjust to technological changes, e.g. *Levesques* v. *Sherwood Credit Union* (2000) C.L.L.C. 210038, esp. paras. 141303–141304 (Sask.Q.B.).
3. *Fellowes-Strike* v. *Co-operators Group Ltd.* (1998) 98 C.L.L.C. 210024, at paras. 141140–141142 (Ont.Gen.Div.).
4. *See* para. 271 *et seq. supra*.

1. Duty to obey commands to work for a particular period: the statutes

309. A frequently contested issue is the reasonableness of an employer's demand that an employee work a certain number of hours. In the absence of a specific term in the contract or an established past practice on the matter from which a term can be implied into the contract, there would appear to be no limit to the number of hours that an employer can order an employee to work, given the fundamental 'service' character of the employment contract. The historical struggles for the ten-hour and then eight-hour days are testimony to that proposition. A modern court, however, inspired by the prevailing societal view that the personal dignity and autonomy of workers merits protection, would arguably imply a standardized term employment contracts that the working hours be reasonable. Today, this is largely of academic interest because employment standards Acts in all Canadian jurisdictions now provide for a maximum number of hours per week an employee may be required to work. This legislation aims to create new jobs as much as it seeks to protect employees against the physical and mental pressures of working too hard.[1] Indeed, one curious feature of the modern Canadian labour market is that excessively high amounts of work are being performed by relatively small numbers of employees with full-time jobs simultaneously with relatively high levels of unemployment and underemployment.[2] Nevertheless, most economists consider that the solution to this problem is not to legislate lower ceilings on permissible working hours; this would merely cause unduly impair on employer's flexibility and efficiency and discourage new firms from opening in the province in question. At best, it is thought that such legislation would have a 'modest' supporting role in tandem with other, more potent job creation policies such as reducing levels of taxation and eliminating import tariffs. There are two, often complementary methods used to limit the assignment of excessive work. First, the statutes define what constitutes 'standard working hours' and impose an overtime premium, usually time and one half, on work assigned above this trigger. Currently, five jurisdictions set the trigger at 40 hours per week and 8 hours per day, two set it at 48 hours per week and three provinces set it at 44 hours per week. The second method for reducing excessive working hours is for the legislation to fix a maximum of hours that can be worked within a defined period which the parties are not allowed to exceed even if they both want to. In the federal jurisdiction, for example, the limit is 48 hours per week.[3] As stated earlier, these two methods are often complementary. Furthermore, the statutes seek to balance the employer's interest in maintaining a reasonable modicum of flexibility in assigning working hours by creating exceptions where excessive work can be scheduled. For example, one common exception is where an emergency has been created by a breakdown in the plant or like catastrophe. Another is to exempt designated industries such as construction, taxi driving, logging and long distance trucking or for designated occupations such as salespersons, janitors and managers and supervisors. Also, extra hours may usually be worked where a permit is obtained from the appropriate director or board under the relevant legislation. It appears that such permits are granted very liberally by the authorities, to such an extent, it is sometimes alleged, as to deprive the legislation of much of its relevance.[4] As well, for employers whose cycle of work operations necessitate irregular shift schedules such as compressing the work week into four 10-hour days instead of five 8-hour days are generally permitted to 'average' actual hours worked over longer than usual periods of time in order to avoid the burden of paying the overtime premium.[5] Usually, approval of the Director of Labour suffices, but in 1994 British Columbia enacted the step of requiring that a vote of at least 65 per cent of the workforce must support the proposed schedule in addition to approval being given by the Director.[6]

1. For a detailed examination *see* England *et al.*, *op. cit.*, vol. 1, paras. 8.97–8.125.
2. *See Report of the Advisory Group on Working Time and the Distribution of Work*, A. Donner, Chair (Ottawa: Ministry of Supply and Services, 1994).
3. Canada Labour Code, R.S.C. 1985, c.L-2, s.117.
4. *Report of the Advisory Group on Working Time and the Distribution of Work*, A. Donner, Chair (Ottawa: Ministry of Supply and Services, 1994.) ch. 4 and 129–30. The recently announced amendments to the Employment Standards Act will eliminate the permit system and allow employers to schedule up to 60 hours of work per week subject to the written consent of the employee. The amendments are discussed in para. 310, *infra*.
5. E.g. Canada Labour Code, R.S.C. 1985, c.L-2, ss.169(2) and (3) and 170(2) and (3) and Canada Labour Standards Regulations, C.R.C. 1978, c.986, ss.4–6.
6. British Columbia Employment Standards Act, R.S.B.C., 1996, c.13, s.37(1). To similar effect, see Canada Labour Code, R.S.C. 1989, c.L-2, s.171 which requires 70 per cent employee support.

310. The future of the maximum hours of work legislation is uncertain in view of the increasing competitive pressure on Canadian employers under the conditions of the 'new economy'. Indeed, the liberal use of permit systems to circumvent the statutes amounts to a *de facto* recognition of the strength of the employers' concern in this regard.[1] A foretaste of what possibly lies in store is the recent proposal to amend the Ontario hours of work legislation. The government plans to allow the employer to schedule work in excess of the current daily and weekly ceilings, namely 8 hours per day and 48 hours per week, if the employee agrees in writing up to a maximum of 60 hours per week. The employee will be allowed, however, to retract his or her written authorization upon giving the employer two weeks notice.[2] The superior bargaining power of employers, at least in the non-unionized sector, will probably render the written authorization safeguard meaningless in reality. The new amendments also repeal the old permit system whereunder administrative consent could be given to employers to assign work in excess of the statutory ceilings without paying the overtime premium. There may be little practical difference for employees under the new regime since the scope for exempting employers from assigning hours in excess of the '8 and 48' cap under the old provisions was so broad (especially by virtue of the permit system) that most employees could face 60-hour work weeks anyway. The political symbolism of the amendments, however, is of greater potential significance in enunciating to the business community that Ontario is prepared to place employers' economic interests above employee rights. One wonders whether this heralds the future direction of labour standards Acts in the 'new economy'.

1. *See* note 5 and accompanying text in para. 309, *supra*.
2. Bill 47, the Employment Standards Act 2000, s.17. The new Act will come in force some time in the middle of 2001, save for its parental leave provisions which came into force on 31 December 2000.

311. Statutory restrictions are also placed on the employer's power to assign work in so far as employment standards legislation entitles employees to defined leaves of absence in specified circumstances. The commonly designated leaves of absence are (i) a weekly rest period, normally taken on Sundays; (ii) daily rest periods; (iii) designated holidays; (iv) annual vacations; (v) maternity and parental leave; (vi) bereavement leave; (vii) time off to vote in federal, provincial and municipal elections; (viii) sick leave; and (ix) educational leave. Space constraints preclude all but a brief outline of these statutory leaves.[1]

a. Weekly rest periods

Historically, Sunday was viewed as the weekly day of rest in Canada. The old federal Lord's Day Act passed in 1905 used to make it a criminal offence for employers not to close down on Sundays. Not surprisingly, however, twentieth-century lifestyles necessitated that a plethora of exceptions be made to this Act allowing employers to operate on Sundays. In 1985 the latter Act was ruled unconstitutional under the Charter of Rights and Freedoms because it violated the guarantee of freedom of religion by causing people to close on Sundays when their own religious tenets might cause them to close down on, say, Saturday.[2] In the meanwhile, provincial jurisdiction had passed pieces of legislation to protect vulnerable workers who preferred not to work on Sundays. This had been necessitated because well before the Lord's Day Act was struck down, so many exceptions to it had been created that very few workers who wanted Sundays off were protected. Consequently, these provincial statutes were challenged as offending the freedom of religion protected by the Charter. The Supreme Court of Canada held that Ontario's Retail Business Holidays Act, notwithstanding that it had secular purposes, violated the religious freedom of Saturday observers. Nonetheless the Court felt that this violation was justified because vulnerable workers needed protection from exploitation. The majority of the Court stressed that it upheld the legislation because the particular statute before it had allowed Sunday opening for small establishments with fewer than seven workers.[3] Despite this finding, provincial legislatures throughout Canada have been scrambling to find Charter-proof legislation to provide a day of rest without offending the guarantee of religious freedom. The trend is towards the elimination of Sunday observance. Nevertheless, the reality is that for most Canadians Sundays are the most convenient day for family members to enjoy leisure time together. Accordingly, the legislation in Manitoba and New Brunswick provides employees engaged in defined 'retail business establishments' – the retail sector is generally permitted to conduct operations on Sundays in most provinces – with the right to refuse to work on Sundays so long as the employee notifies the employer at least 14 days in advance. In Ontario, the position is similar except that the employee does not have an unqualified right to take Sunday off; rather, it must be 'reasonable' in all the circumstances for the employee to absent himself of herself.

b. Daily rest periods

In all but three Canadian jurisdictions, the employment standards Acts entitle employees to a break of at least 30 minutes in every five hours of work. Typically, exceptions are allowed to safeguard the employer's interest in flexibility, for example, where an emergency or an accident occurs or other unforeseeable and unpreventable exigencies occur.[4] Typically, an employee must also be guaranteed a minimum number of consecutive hours off work in any 24-hour period. In Ontario, for example, the proposed amendments to the Employment Standards Code will impose a minimum period of 11 consecutive hours off work in a period of 24 hours, unless there are 'exceptional circumstances' which justify making an exception.

c. Statutory holidays

All provinces and the federal jurisdiction designate several public holidays upon which an employer must give its employees a leave of absence or, if the employee comes to work, pay him or her a wage premium usually fixed at one and a half times regular pay.[5] The designated holidays vary between the province – as many as 13 different dates are recognized between the provinces – but the common ones are Christmas, Good Friday, Canada Day, Labour Day and New Year's Day. The rationale for the holiday provisions is somewhat obscure. The purpose does not appear to be to enhance the worker's health and well being by giving him or her temporary relief from the stresses of the workplace because the legislation commonly allows employees to work on a holiday. Rather, the purpose seems to be economic in nature, with many employees regarding statutory holidays as an earnings opportunity, not a leisure opportunity. Typically, the legislation contains detailed regulations about the amount of prior service an employee must perform in order to qualify for a holiday, how holiday pay is to be calculated, the possibility of the parties substituting alternate days for the designated holiday, and the circumstances under which exceptions are made to the holiday provisions.[6]

d. Annual vacations

In the federal jurisdiction and all provinces, the employer must provide its employees with an annual paid vacation, with most provinces fixing the pay rate at 4 per cent of the employee's regular earnings over the designated qualifying period.[7] In most provinces the vacation must be of two weeks duration, but in a minority of provinces this period increases with the length of seniority of the employees (as in Saskatchewan where an employee with 10 years' prior service is allowed four weeks vacation).[8] As with statutory holiday provisions described above, the purpose of the vacation provisions does not appear to be the enhancement of the employee's health and well-being by having time off work since the employee is generally allowed to work through his or her vacation. Again, there is detailed regulation on how much prior service an employee must perform in order to qualify for a vacation, how the vacation period is to be selected, whether the vacation must be taken in one lump sum or in broken time, how much advance notice the employee must give of the date the leave is to commence, when vacation pay can be given in lieu of time off, the deadlines for giving the employee his or her vacation pay, how the employee's rights are to be protected when an annual vacation day falls on a statutory holiday and what exemptions are made to the vacation provisions. The details on these matters vary enormously between the provinces, requiring that each Act be carefully scrutinized.[9]

e. Maternity and parental leave

All provinces and the federal jurisdiction satisfy the minimum requirements for maternity leave established under the I.L.O. Convention No. 103, namely 12 weeks unpaid leave at least six of which must follow the worker's confinement. In most jurisdictions, the length of maternity leave is 17 weeks,[10] but this increases to 18 weeks in a minority of provinces.[11] However, the period of leave may be extended in certain circumstances. One example where an extension can be granted is if the medical condition of the mother or the child requires it. Another more widespread example is that a pregnant mother is commonly entitled to add on to her basic maternity leave the period of 'parental leave' also provided under the legislation. Thus, in British Columbia, where the periods for maternity and parental leave are, respectively, 18 and 12 weeks, the pregnant worker can take a leave of 30 weeks' duration.[12] The trend seems to be to towards increasing the leave period. In Quebec, for instance, the maximum duration of parental leave was increased to 52 weeks in 1999, thereby entitling a pregnant mother to a total of 70 weeks' leave when the basic maternity leave period of 18 weeks is taken into account. Similarly, the proposed amendments to the Ontario Employment Standards Act will extend parental leave to 35 weeks (for a total of 52 weeks when the 17 weeks of maternity leave are taken into account). Maternity leave is unpaid in all Canadian jurisdictions following the rationale of I.L.O. Convention No. 103 that the state, not the employer, should carry the financial burden so as to avoid providing employers with an incentive to coerce employees into shortening their leave. As we saw earlier,[13] the employee is entitled to receive unemployment insurance benefits under the federal Employment Insurance Act. Because the level of these benefits are below the employee's actual wage level – normally, they cannot exceed 55 per cent of the employee's earnings – employers often agree (the more so in the unionized sector) to 'top up' state benefits to the level of the employee's actual earnings. The right to maternity and parental leave in all but three provinces is made dependent on the employee accruing a minimum period of prior continuous service with his or her employer, usually 12 consecutive months.[14] The Employment Standards Act generally contains detailed regulation on when a leave of absence must begin and end, how notice of an impending leave must be served and the procedures for medical certification of an employee's condition. Furthermore, the Employment Standards Acts commonly safeguard employees against being penalized by their employer on account of taking maternity or parental leave.[15] These provisions are of critical importance, for employers are known to dislike the presence of 'unreliable' workers, especially if they hold key positions. Regrettably, too many employers seek either to fire such individuals, or shuffle them into 'dead end' positions or coerce them into not becoming pregnant or taking a leave by threatening their job security or their other terms or conditions of employment. Accordingly, the legislation commonly contains broadly worded prohibitions against dismissing or otherwise jeopardizing any terms or conditions of employment of an employee because he or she exercises his or her rights to take maternity and parental leave.[16] The employer is required to reinstate the worker in his or her old job when the leave expires, or to re-engage him or her in a comparable position involving no loss of pay or benefits (for example, if the employee's old position has been made redundant). Plainly, the fact that an employee is on maternity or parental leave does not prevent the employer from firing him or her for an act of misconduct or from laying him or her off for bona fide business reasons. The employer must provide an employee on leave with a full opportunity to participate in any promotion competitions, training programmes or other career development schemes.[17] Also, an employer cannot rescind an employee's accrued seniority on the basis that he or she has been on leave. At first blush, it might appear to make sense that an employee's seniority for the purpose of insurance benefits depending on 'continuous service' should *not* continue to accrue during the period of leave, otherwise this would be irreconcilable with the principle that such leaves are deemed to be unpaid unless the employer expressly agrees to the opposite. Nevertheless, in several jurisdictions, not only is the leave deemed to count towards seniority for such a purpose but also the employer must continue to make contributions to the benefit plans so long as the worker remains willing to make his or her share of the contributions. When considering the rights of pregnant employees, account must also be taken of the Human Rights Acts. These Acts either expressly incorporate 'pregnancy' as a protected ground or, if not, pregnancy has been held to constitute 'sex' within the statutory definitions.[18] The courts have held that it will violate the Human Rights Act for an employer either to exclude a pregnant employee from an insurance plan such as long- or short-term disability benefits or to treat a pregnant employee less favourably than other workers under such a plan, for example, by 'topping up' state unemployment benefits for workers with non-pregnancy related sickness but not 'topping up' the benefits of pregnant workers.[19] In most provinces, either or both of the Human Rights Acts and the Employment Standards Act contain detailed exceptions where an employer is permitted to establish differential contribution and/or benefit rates under pension and other insurance plans for pregnant employees, basically where there is a bona fide actuarial reason for the differential treatment.[20] Examination of the details of those provisions is beyond the scope of this essay. Furthermore, the occupational health and safety legislation may come into play in pregnancy situations, for instance where a pregnant employee refuses to perform assigned tasks because she believes it will harm herself or the foetus, or where the employer refuses to permit a pregnant employee to continue working because the employer believes it will harm the employee or her foetus.

f. Miscellaneous leaves

All provinces and the federal jurisdiction entitle an employee to bereavement leave in the event of a death in the employee's immediate family. The statutes commonly define which persons comprise the employee's immediate family and there are some differences between the jurisdictions. The modern trend is to enlarge the definition so as to encompass common law and same sex partners provided that the relationship in question has a reasonable degree of longevity.[21] Bereavement leave is generally unpaid, with Quebec and the federal jurisdiction alone providing the exceptions. In addition, all jurisdictions provide the employee with time off work to vote in federal, provincial and municipal elections. Elsewhere in Canada, various other leaves of absence are provided, depending on the jurisdiction. For example, Quebec and British Columbia have been the pathfinders in enacting leaves for family emergencies such as the sickness of relatives or children.[22] In 1994, the federal government's Advisory Committee recommended that such leaves be provided in order to cater to the needs of the growing number of women, many of whom are single, in the labour force.[23] Sick leave, without pay, is provided for employees who have defined amount of prior service with their employer in only three jurisdictions, namely Newfoundland (5 days), Saskatchewan (12 days but increasing to 12 weeks for serious illnesses) and the federal jurisdiction (12 weeks). The only area where Canada's leave of absence legislation falls short of the International Labour Organization's recommendations is in respect to educational leave. No Canadian jurisdiction as yet has enacted a right to take leave, with or without pay, for educational purposes, even though paid educational leave is recommended in the I.L.O.'s 1974 Convention on Paid Educational Leave and even though the federal government's Advisory Committee endorsed such leave.[24] Finally, as far back as 1987 an Ontario government-sponsored report urged that legislation be enacted to provide an employee with at least 10 years' seniority with one week's unpaid leave of absence each year, increasing to a ceiling of four weeks' annual leave as the employee gets closer to retirement.[25] The rationale for this recommendation was to foster job creation, but an ancillary advantage is to provide employees nearing retirement with extra flexibility to prepare for their future. As yet, no Canadian province has enacted this leading-edge measure.

1. For a detailed examination, *see* England *et al.*, *op. cit.*, vol. 1, ch. 8, 1V, I–M.
2. *R.* v. *Big M Drug Mart Ltd.*, [1985] 1 S.C.R. 295.
3. *Edwards Books and Art Ltd.* v. *R.* (1986) 87 C.L.L.C. 14,001; [1986] 2 S.C.R. 713.
4. E.g. British Columbia Employment Standards Act, R.S.O. 1996, c.113, s.32(1).
5. E.g. Nova Scotia Labour Standards Code, R.S.N.S., 1989, c.246, ss.37–43.
6. For a detailed examination, *see* England *et al.*, *op. cit.*, vol. 1, ch. 8, 1V, I–K.
7. E.g. New Brunswick Employment Standards Act, S.N.B., 1982, c.E-7.2, s.24(1).
8. Saskatchewan Labour Standards Act, R.S.S., 1978, c.L-1, s.30(1).
9. For a detailed examination, *see* England *et al.*, *op. cit.*, vol. 1, ch. 8, 1V, I–L.
10. E.g. Newfoundland Labour Standards Act, R.S.N. 1990, c.L-2, s.40(2).
11. E.g. British Columbia Employment Standards Act, R.S.B.C., 1996, c.113, s.50(2) and (3).
12. British Columbia Employment Standards Act, R.S.B.C., 1996, c.113, s.51(1).
13. Para. 247, *supra.*
14. As in Nova Scotia Labour Standards Code, R.S.N.S., 1989, c.246, s.59(1). The exceptions are British Columbia, Quebec and New Brunswick where no prior service requirement exists.
15. E.g. Nova Scotia Labour Standards Code, R.S.N.S., 1989, c.246, s.59G.
16. *Ibid.*
17. This is made explicit under Canada Labour Code, R.S.C. 1989, c.L-2, s.209.3. Elsewhere, it is implied under the general prohibition.
18. *Brooks* v. *Canada Safeway Ltd.* (1989) 26 C.C.E.L. 1, at 17 (S.C.C.); [1989] 1 S.C.R. 1219.
19. *Ibid. See also Alberta Hospital Assn.* v. *Parcels*, (1992) 1 Alta. L.R. (3d) 332 (Q.B.); *Stagg* v. *Intercontinental Packers Ltd.* (1993) 18 C.H.R.R. D/392 (Sask.Bd.Inq.); *Crooks* v. *Ontario Cancer Treatment and Research Foundation* (1996) 96 C.L.L.C. 230044, esp. para. 145461 (Ont.Bd.Inq.), affm'd (1998) 98 C.L.L.C. 230011 (Ont.Div.Ct.).
20. E.g. Ontario Benefit Plans Regulations, R.R.O., Reg. 321, s.8(c), which creates exceptions to the general ban on 'sex' discrimination in benefit plans under the Employment Standards Act, R.S.O. 1990, c.E-14, s.33(2).
21. E.g. Saskatchewan Labour Standards Act R.S.S., c.L-1, s.29.3(1)(b)(ii).
22. British Columbia Employment Standards Act, R.S.B.C., 1996, c.113, s.52(b); An Act Respecting Labour Standards, R.S.Q., c.N-1.1, s.81.2.
23. *Advisory Group Report* (Ottawa: Ministry of Supply and Services, 1994) at 60–1.
24. *Ibid.*, at 61.
25. *Report on Hours of Work and Overtime: the Donner Report* (Toronto: Ministry of Labour, 1987) at 132.

C. The Duty to Exercise Skill and Care

312. It was once thought that the failure by an employee to exercise adequate skill and care entitled the employer to summarily dismiss an employee without notice or wages in lieu. The basis for this rule was that the employee, by accepting employment, had held out that he or she had the skill and competence to do the job.[1] This rationale is not consonant with modern employment conditions. As between the employer and a potential employee, the former is in the best position to assess the requirement of skill and capacities necessary to the work to be performed during the recruitment process. Further, even if the employee has the requisite skills when hired, quickly changing technological process and the inability of the employee to adapt to these may result in a 'faultless' incapacity of the employee. To hold fast to the old rule under these circumstances, except where the employee expressly holds out that he or she has a special kind of expertise, would be unwarrantedly draconian. This reasoning is in line with the arguments canvassed in respect of the duty to obey by which it was shown that, for disobedience to permit discipline, it has to be willful and/or insolent. Reasonable refusal is not enough. Similarly, lack of adequate skill by an employee who is doing her or his best no longer permits dismissal. This attitude is reflected in statutes, which provide for minimum notice (or wages in lieu) in respect of termination of employment. It does not follow that an employer cannot terminate an employee whose level of performance is deemed unacceptable. On the contrary, the employer can dismiss such a worker provided that the employer gives the proper notice of termination (or wages in lieu) as required under the employment standards Acts and the contract of employment. The only circumstances under which the common law and the employment standards Act permit summary dismissal for incompetence is where the degree of such incompetence is so manifestly gross as to be tantamount to deliberate neglect. As one employment standards Act referee explains,

> 'it is axiomatic that mere inefficiency on the job is not sufficient to constitute willful misconduct, unless the inefficiency is so extreme that a reasonable person could only conclude that it ceased to be mere inefficiency but rather became a calculated course of action deliberately aimed at harming the employer by disrupting the normal business production at the place of employment or being so reckless in one's action that such a result would naturally follow.'[2]

1. *Harmer* v. *Cornelius* (1858) 5 C.B. (N.S.) 236 at 247.
2. *Re: Reid Industries*, 6 December 1975 Ontario (McNish).

313. The fact that the employer cannot summarily dismiss an employee for non-deliberate incompetence short of gross negligence does not prevent the employer from pursuing other legal remedies against the worker. Rather, the employee's implied contractual duty to exercise reasonable skill and care, if breached, will entitle the employer to sue the employee for damages for any economic harm it has suffered as a consequence of the breach. For example, one employer was recently awarded $45,000 damages representing the cost of fixing up a concrete job which was ruined because of the employee's poor workmanship.[1] Of course, the worker often will not have enough money to make such litigation practicable. More importantly, if a third party is harmed by the employee's negligent acts and sues the employer for damages under the vicarious liability doctrine, the employer (or more likely its insurance company) can sue the employee to recover the monies it has paid out to the third party. We saw earlier that this view is repugnant to the policy goals of vicarious liability, especially the theory of loss distribution.[2]

1. *Petrone* v. *Marmot Concrete Services Ltd.* (1996) 18 C.C.E.L. (2d) 170, at 185 (Alta.Q.B.).
2. *See* para. 284, *supra.*

314. In Quebec, section 2088 of the Civil Code expressly states that the employee must carry on her/his work 'with prudence and diligence'. As well, the *Lister* doctrine described earlier continues to represent the law in Quebec.[1]

1. *See* para. 284, *supra.* Jean-Louis Baudouin and Patrice Deslauriers, *La responabilité civile*, 5th edn. (Cowansville: Les Éditions Yvon Blais Inc., 1998) 420.

D. The Duty of Good Faith and Fidelity

315. The phraseology itself suggests that this duty implied by law into the contract of employment has more to do with notions of service than cooperation. The duty is not to injure the employer by conduct, which amounts to an abuse of the trust reposed in the employee. A similar duty of loyalty towards the employer exists under the *Code civil du Québec.* According to the Code, the employee must 'act faithfully and honestly' and refrain from using 'any confidential information he or she may obtain in carrying on or in the course of his or her work'.[1] Moreover, the provision states that these obligations continue to be binding for a reasonable period of time following cessation of the contract. The specific applications of the duty of good faith and fidelity are similar in Quebec and the common law provinces.

1. S.2088, C.c.Q.

1. Trade secrets and confidential business information

316. Employees are only bound to serve their employer for the time they have agreed that services shall be rendered. Therefore, what an employee does in her or his own time is generally of no concern to the employer. Otherwise, it has been judicially said, the employee of modern days would be placed 'in a position little, if at all, better than the villein of former times'.[1] Nevertheless, the common law seeks to fix a balance of proportionality between the employee's interest in safeguarding his or her private life and the employer's interest in protecting itself against undue economic harm. Accordingly, the courts have recognized that there are some activities which an employee will not be permitted to engage in, even though he or she is acting outside of working time.

1. *Sheppard Publishing* v. *Harkins* (1905) 9 O.L.R. 504 at 508, *per* Anglin J. (D.C.), delivering the judgment of the court.

317. One such activity is where the employee discloses the employer's trade secrets or confidential business information to a competitor. Thus, in *Hivac* v. *Park Royal Scientific Instruments*,[1] employees who aided a rival employer in competition with the plaintiff-employer by selling their services and knowhow were held to be in breach of their contract of employment. This decision does not mean that an employee cannot take a second job in his or her spare time with a rival employer. Rather, the key point in *Hivac* is that the employees were using confidential business information obtained during their employment to benefit a rival. Clearly, an employee's duty to safeguard an employer's trade secrets and confidential business information persists even after the employment relationship has terminated. Although employees are normally allowed to compete with a former employer after their relationship has ended, it is impermissible for the employee to do so by using the former employer's trade secrets or confidential information. Not only is the employer allowed to pursue the usual contract law remedies against an employee who wrongfully misappropriates trade secrets or confidential information – including summary dismissal if the employee is still on payroll, damages for losses caused by the breach[2] and an interlocutory injunction to prevent further misappropriation[3] – but also special equitable remedies come into play. This is because the courts treat an employer's trade secrets and confidential information as a 'proprietary interest'. If the employer's property rights are violated, the courts deploy special equitable remedies to ensure that no other person can make an unjust enrichment from the employer's property. Accordingly, the courts allow the employer to sue the employee and any third party user of the confidential material for an accounting for all profits wrongfully made from such material.[4] Whether the employer will elect to sue in contract for damages caused by the wrongful disclosure, or in equity for an accounting of profits will depend on which avenue is most profitable to it in the circumstances. Furthermore, if an employer suspects that an employee has taken away confidential material after his or her employment has ended, the employer can apply *ex parte* to the court for a so-called *Anton Piller* order allowing the employer to enter the employee's premises in order to search for the confidential material designated in the court order.[5] Unsurprisingly, such draconian orders will only be granted in exceptional cases of impending irreparable harm to the employer's interests.[6]

1. [1946] 2 All E.R. 350. For a detailed examination of the law in this area, *see* England *et al.*, *op. cit.*, vol. 2, paras. 11.113–11.159.
2. As in *Sure-Grip Fasteners Ltd.* v. *Allgrade Bolt and Chain Inc.* (1993) 45 C.C.E.L. 276, esp. 289–94 (Ont.Gen.Div.); *Crawley* v. *Trans-Power Construction Ltd.* (1997) 23 C.C.E.L. (2d) 34 (B.C.S.C.).
3. The injunction can be obtained against the employee or any third party who is misusing the material e.g. *International Tools Ltd.* v. *Kollar* (1968) 67 D.L.R. 386 (Ont.C.A.).
4. E.g. *57134 Manitoba Ltd.* v. *Palmer* (1989) 37 B.C.L.R. (2d) 50 (C.A.); *Gotton Contractors Ltd.* v. *Manzo* (1992) 92 C.L.L.C. 14031, at para. 12184 (Ont.Gen.Div.).
5. *Anton Piller KG* v. *Manufacturing Processes Ltd.*, [1976] Ch. 55. *See* generally G. Takach, 'Exploring the Outer Limits: the Anton Piller Order in Canada' (1985) 23 *Alta. L.Rev.* 310.
6. *Ibid. See also MAI Systems Corp.* v. *Banwell Computer Services Inc.* (1991) 41 C.P.R. (3d) 57, at 66 (Ont.Gen.Div.).

318. An employee will only be liable if the information he or she discloses constitutes a trade secret or confidential business information as defined in law.

Unfortunately, the definition of a trade secret or confidential business information is sometimes unclear. The protected information may be either a formula, special material, a list or a technological or other business process.[1] It is essential that the employer wishes the secret to be kept and only shares it with those employees in whom it is necessary to confide. It is different from a copyrighted or patented idea in that anyone who comes by the confidential information or trade secret without in any way relying on the original possessor's knowledge or on that of those employees entrusted with it, is entitled to use it in any ways he or she likes.[2] One of the indicia to determine an employer's right to successfully obtain judicial protection is whether or not the divulged information was such that no other competitor in the field would be able to make the product or render the services without possession of the information. As it is not necessary that the subject matter of the trade secret be capable of being copyrighted or patented, it need not be completely original information, process or material.[3] Where competitors do not need knowledge of the trade secret to compete and/or the information about it is freely available, the plaintiff-employer will not get protection, nor will, in all likelihood, its employee be held to be in breach of the duty of good faith if the employee divulges such information.[4] The only judicially recognized exception where an employee is allowed to disclose confidential information is for the purpose of revealing an 'iniquity'.[5] The breadth of this exception remains untested in Canada. It would probably safeguard, for instance, a worker who 'blows the whistle' on an employer's misdeeds in a responsible manner to a responsible outsider, at least where those misdeeds are serious in nature.

1. Frequently cited check-lists include *R.* v. *Stewart* (1983), 24 B.L.R. 53, at 78 (Ont.C.A.); *Montour Ltee* v. *Jolicoeur* [1988] R.J.Q. 1323, at 1330 (S.C.); *Faccenda Chicken Ltd.* v. *Fowler*, [1987] Ch. 177 *per* Neill L.J. (C.A.).
2. *R.I. Crain* v. *Ashton*, [1949] O.R. 303, aff'd, [1950] O.R. 62 (C.A.); *Molnar Lithographic Supplies Ltd.* v. *Sikatory* (1974) 14 C.P.R. (2d) 197 (Ont.C.A.).
3. *Gibbons* v. *Drew Chemical* (1973) 8 C.P.R. (2d) 105 (B.C.S.C.).
4. *Cooperheat* v. *Slater* (1974) 13 C.P.R. (3d) 25 (H.C.).
5. E.g. *Initial Services Ltd.* v. *Putterill*, [1968] 1 Q.B. 396 (C.A.) where the employee was absolved for disclosing that his employer was fixing prices in breach of the anti-monopoly legislation.

319. Employers can also protect their business know-how by including express restrictive covenants in the employment contract which prevent employees from divulging or using information for their own or other people's benefit. These covenants may be expressed to apply both during the term of the employment contract as well as after the relationship has ended. In order to be avoid being struck down as unduly restraining trade, a restrictive covenant must satisfy four conditions.[1] First, it must protect an employer's legitimate 'proprietary interest' as judicially defined. This means that the clause must protect an employer's trade secrets, confidential information, goodwill etc. as defined in the preceding paragraph rather than merely attempt to eliminate competition by keeping an employee out of the labour market. Similarly, it has been held that a restrictive covenant cannot seek to prevent an employee from using general knowledge about the operation of the firm's product market, customer preferences, technical operations and general know-how about running the business.[2] Secondly, the restrictive covenant must be reasonable between the parties in regard to its geographical scope. This means that its spread must not exceed that which is necessary to safeguard the employer's legitimate 'proprietary interest'. For example, an accounting firm whose client base was limited to within city limits was disallowed from enforcing a restrictive covenant which precluded an accountant from practising within a 50-mile radius of the city.[3] Thirdly, the clause must be reasonable between the parties in regard to how long it is necessary to safeguard the employer's particular 'proprietary interest'. In the case of confidential client lists, a reasonable time is usually defined as that which is necessary for the replacement worker to establish a good working relationship with the plaintiff's former clients.[4] In the case of a secret recipe for a sauce or a beer, however, a lifetime's restraint may be justifiable. Fourthly, it must be in the overall public interest to uphold a particular restraint. For example, a clause which purported to prevent an obstetrician from practising in a defined location was ruled contrary to the public interest because there was a general shortage of substitute obstetricians to serve the public in the area in question.[5] Normally, ambiguities in a restrictive covenant will be interpreted *contra proferentem* the interests of the employer in acknowledgement of the latter's usual bargaining superiority in deciding the terms of the employment contract. If only part of a restrictive covenant is invalid, the courts may sever the offending part and uphold the remainder. However, if the clause would not make linguistic sense in the absence of the offending portion, the courts will not modify or add to the language in order to make it sensible in deference to the principle of freedom of contract.[6] Instead, the entire clause will be avoided. This is commonly referred to as the 'blue pencil' test. Last, but not least, is the curious holding that a restrictive covenant automatically by operation of law ceases to bind an employee who has been wrongfully dismissed by his or her employer.[7] This ruling is questionable since there appears to be no logical reason why a restrictive covenant cannot survive a repudiatory breach but an exclusion clause in a commercial contract can.[8] Moreover, the employee will presumably have received a wage premium in return for accepting the restrictive covenant in his or her employment contract yet the employer will not have received its *quid pro quo* after the contract has ended. Arguably, this is an unjust enrichment of the employee. Nevertheless, Canadian courts persist in applying the rule despite some recent judicial concerns with it.[9] The Quebec Civil Code formulates the same principles to regulate the inclusion of that type of restrictive covenants in the employment contract. Section 2088 of the Code makes it clear that the covenant must be limited 'as to time, place and type of employment, to whatever is necessary for the protection of the legitimate interests of the employer'. Moreover, the covenant must be stipulated in writing and in express terms. The burden of proof as to the validity of the covenant rests on the employer.

1. *Nordenfelt* v. *Maxim Nordenfelt Guns and Ammunition*, [1894] A.C. 535 (H.L.).
2. *Mercury Marine Ltd.* v. *Dillon* (1986) 30 D.L.R. (4d) 627 (Ont.H.C.).
3. *Ernst and Young* v. *Stuart* (1993) 46 C.C.E.L. 161 (B.C.S.C.). In contrast, a worldwide restraint was upheld in *Nordenfelt* v. *Maxim Nordenfelt Guns and Ammunition*, [1894] A.C. 535 (H.L.) because the employer sold machine guns throughout the world.
4. *Jostens Canada Inc.* v. *Gendron* (1994) 1 C.C.E.L. (2d) 275 (Ont.Gen.Div.).
5. *Sherk* v. *Horwitz*, [1972] 2 O.R. 451 (H.C.).
6. *R.C. Young Insurance Ltd.* v. *Bricknell*, [1955] 5 D.L.R. 490 (Ont.C.A.).
7. *General Billposting Co.* v. *Anderson*, [1910] A.C. 118 (H.L.).
8. *Photo Production Ltd.* v. *Securicor Transport Ltd.*, [1980] 1 All E.R. 556 (H.L.).

9. E.g. *Murrell* v. *Burns International Security Services Ltd.* (1994) 5 C.C.E.L. (2d) 123, at 130 (Ont.Gen.Div.).

320. The employee's duty to further the employer's business interests is applied more rigorously than normal if the employee is ruled to owe the employer a super-added 'fiduciary' duty. A fiduciary relationship is *uberrimae fidei*, requiring the employee to accord a greater than usual degree of trust and loyalty to his or her employer and to accord absolute primacy to the employer's interests. Thus, a fiduciary must proactively divulge to a prospective employer any negative aspects of his or her previous career in a recruitment interview whereas a regular employee generally need not.[1] Also, a fiduciary must proactively disclose any business opportunities that his or her employer could exploit[2] as well as any threats he or she perceives to the employer's business such as misdeeds committed by fellow employees or his or her own decision to quit the job.[3] Again, regular employees need not go this far in their employer's interests. Furthermore, a fiduciary is precluded from working in competition with his or her former employer for a reasonable time after their employment relationship has ended.[4] Again, regular employees are not bound by so stringent a limitation. Because a fiduciary relationship derives from the old laws of equity, the courts provide the aggrieved employer with special equitable remedies such as an accounting for profits in addition to the regular remedies for breach of the employment contract. The definition a 'fiduciary relationship' is imprecise. Normally, fiduciaries are limited to employees who occupy positions at the uppermost levels of the firm's hierarchy with authority to make independent and autonomous decisions about the fundamentals of the firm's business and employment interests.[5] One Ontario judge, Smith J., has usefully summarized a fiduciary as being someone who exercises a 'directing hand' over the firm's affairs.[6] Similarly, a more rigorous duty to further the employer's interests for employees at a management level must be implied within the general framework of section 2088 of the Quebec Civil Code.[7]

1. *Courtright* v. *Canadian Pacific Ltd.* (1983) 4 C.C.E.L. 152 (Ont.H.C.). *See* generally G. Davenport, 'To Speak or Not to Speak? What if there is no Question' (1998) 6 C.L.E.L.J. 185.
2. *Berkey Photo Canada Ltd.* v. *Ohlig* (1983) 2 C.C.E.L. 113, at 129 (Ont.H.C.).
3. *CRC Evans Canada Ltd.* v. *Peffifer* (1997) 26 C.C.E.L. (2d) 294 (Alta.Q.B.).
4. *Ibid.*
5. *International Corona Resources Ltd.* v. *LAC Minerals* (1989) 61 D.L.R. (4d) 14 (S.C.C.); [1989] 2 S.C.R. 574.
6. *R.W. Hamilton Ltd.* v. *Aeroquip Corp.* (1988) 65 O.R. (2d) 345, at 351 (H.C.) In a similar vein, *see Barton Insurance Brokers Ltd.* v. *Irwin* (1999) 40 C.C.E.L. (2d) 159, at 165 (B.C.C.A.).
7. Morin and Brière, *op. cit.* 280.

2. Inventions

321. Implicit in the discussion of the duty of good faith so far has been that whatever an employee does by way of obtaining benefits, he or she does for the employer. Accordingly, an employee can be made to account to the employer for profits he or she has made when using information, materials, or processes rightfully belonging to the employer.[1] So stringent is this implied duty that the employer will be entitled to any benefits from the employee's actions even if the employer would not have had the desire or the capacity to obtain the benefits in question by its own endeavours.[2] Furthermore, an employee who breaches this duty by making a secret profit out of his or her employment will generally provide cause for summary dismissal.[3] Only if the employee makes the profits when acting in his or her own time, relying on his or her own skills, knowledge and resources, will that employee be entitled to retain the profits.[4] A particularly difficult application of this principle is related to inventions. The English House of Lords has held that it is an implied term of the contract of employment that an employee is a trustee for her or his employer of any invention made in the course of his or her duty as an employee. unless such an implied term is displaced by a contrary agreement having legal effect.[5] In Canada, however, the presumption appears to be to the opposite, namely that an employee is prima facie entitled to the full benefit of any invention made in the course of his or her employment unless there is either an express term to the contrary or if there is a reliable past practice in the firm from which an implied term to the contrary can be deduced.[6] Arguably, the optimal solution would be to legislate some kind of sharing formula to permit the employee and the employee to divide the benefit of an invention according to the value of their respective inputs into the process. A vexed question under the common law doctrine is exactly when is an invention made in the course of an employee's employment. Relevant considerations are when and where the invention was made, whether the employer requested the employee to engage in inventing things, whose materials were used and the level of employment of the particular employee in relation to the invention.[7]

1. *William R. Barnes* v. *MacKenzie*, [1973] 2 O.R. 511 (H.C.); *Schavenburg Industries Ltd.* v. *Borowski* (1980) 8 Bus. L.R. 164 (Ont.H.C.).
2. E.g. *Bank of Montreal* v. *Ng* (1989) 62 D.L.R. (4d) 1 (S.C.C.); [1989] 2 S.C.R. 429.
3. E.g. *Connolly* v. *General Motors of Canada Ltd.* (1994) 50 C.C.E.L. 247 (Ont.Gen.Div.).
4. *Jones* v. *Linde Refrigeration* (1901) 2 O.L.R. 428 (C.A.); *Sheppard Publishing* v. *Harkins* (1905) 9 O.L.R. 504 (D.C.).
5. *Sterling Engineering* v. *Patchett*, [1955] 1 All E.R. 369.
6. *Comstock Canada* v. *Electec Ltd.* (1991) 38 C.P.R. (3d) 29 (Fed.Tr.Div.).
7. *W.J. Gage* v. *Sugden* (1967) 62 D.L.R. (2d) 671 (Ont.H.C.).

§4. Termination of Employment

322. The general rules of contract apply to the termination of contracts of employment. Thus a contract of employment may be terminated according to the terms relating thereto in the contract, by mutual agreement, by repudiation of the contract by one party to the contract which entitles the other party to elect to terminate it and sue for damages, by performance, by frustration, death of one of the parties, by the sale of the business, by bankruptcy, and by retirement. Some of these matters will be specifically discussed. At the outset, the crucial point deserves emphasizing that whatever legal protections against unlawful termination an employee may have at common law, in reality the expense of civil litigation to enforce such rights is beyond the resources for most middle and lower level employees. For such employees, the employment standards legislation is the only realistic source of legal rights. In recognition of this reality, we shall see that the common law principles have been modified by minimum standards legislation. Furthermore, the law in force in Quebec displays some particularities that require comment.

A. Frustration

323. At common law, a contract will be terminated automatically by operation of law as a result of frustration when it has become impossible of performance because of a supervening event, which is fortuitous and unforeseeable. A standard example is the case of a plant which has been burnt down, making work impossible.[1] But the event which allegedly frustrates the contract by rendering it impossible of performance must not have been the result of the conduct of the party seeking to rely on the frustration argument. Thus, a provincial government which passed legislation abolishing the plaintiff's position as an employee of the Public Utilities Board was precluded from defending his wrongful dismissal action by arguing that his employment contract had been frustrated by the legislation because the frustrating event had been self-induced; here, the government was acting as both legislator and employer.[2]

1. As in *Polyco Window Manufacturers Ltd.* v. *Saskatchewan (Director of Labour Standards)* (1994) 3 C.C.E.L. (2d) 101 (Sask.Q.B.), arising in the context of entitlement to the minimum notice period under the Labour Standards Acts.
2. *Wells* v. *Newfoundland* (2000) 46 C.C.E.L. (2d) 165, at 183 (S.C.C.); [1999] 3 S.C.R. 199.

324. The question of whether or not a contract has been rendered impossible of performance is a question of fact. No hard and fast rule can be formulated.[1] In some cases, the special nature of the contract may permit characterizing temporary illness or disability on the part of one of the parties as frustration of the contract. Typically, this will be so where the employees are skilled artists engaged for relatively short-term runs. In *Poussard* v. *Speirs & Pond*[2] there was an engagement of an opera singer for three months. Due to illness she could not rehearse, or appear on the first three nights of actual performances. The contract was held to be frustrated by her illness. Where the relationship is not of this kind, the question for a court or board to answer is whether or not an illness or disability has created a fundamentally different situation from that which existed at the outset of the contract. In one case, the employment contract of an employee with 27 years' seniority who occupied a position which could easily be filled by a temporary replacement and who had been unable to perform satisfactorily for two years due to work-related stress was held not to have been frustrated. A key fact was that it was reasonably foreseeable at the date of the trial that he would fully recover with a fairly short time.[3] Indeed, the Newfoundland Court of Appeal has opined that an absence from work due to illness normally must be between 18 to 24 months in order to frustrate the employment contract of an employee with substantial seniority.[4] Again, the medical prognosis must show that the employee will be able to recover within a reasonable period of time. Significantly, most courts assess the worker's medical prognosis at the date of the trial, not at the date of dismissal.[5]

1. *Thomas* v. *Lafleche Union Hospital Board* (1989) 15 A.C.W.S.L. (Sask.C.A.); *Hare* v. *Maple Leaf Mills Ltd.* (1984) 45 C.P.C. 223 (Ont.Co.Ct.).

2. (1876), 1 Q.B.D. 410. Contrast *Loates* v. *Maple* (1903) 88 L.T. 288 (K.B.) (three-year contract for jockey; incapacitated for two months; no frustration).
3. *Yeager* v. *R.J. Hastings Agencies Ltd.* (1985) 5 C.C.E.L. 266 (B.C.S.C.).
4. *White* v. *F.W. Woolworth Co.* (1996) 22 C.C.E.L. (2d) 110 (Newf.C.A.).
5. *Ibid.*

325. The influence of the human rights doctrine of reasonable accommodation has recently made itself felt on the common law doctrine of frustration. Historically, an employer was not obliged to consider modifying a worker's job duties or shift schedules so as to enable him or her to remain a productive member of the workforce; if the job could not be performed satisfactorily in its unchanged form due to illness, the contract would be frustrated.[1] However, in a landmark decision in 1998, Swinton J. of the Ontario General Division ruled that an employment contract cannot be frustrated by illness or disability at common law unless the employer has previously attempted to reasonably accommodate the employee up to the point of undue hardship in accordance with the requirements of the human rights legislation.[2] This decision testifies to the profound effect the human rights duty of reasonable accommodation will probably have throughout Canadian employment law.

1. E.g. *Condor* v. *Barron Knights Ltd.*, [1966] 1 W.L.R. 87.
2. *Antonnaci* v. *Great Atlantic and Pacific Co. of Canada* (1998) 98 C.L.L.C. 210017, at para. 141098 (Ont.Gen.Div.). *See also* paras. 198B and 198C, *supra*, where the human rights legislation is reviewed.

326. If an employee is terminated for an illness that constitutes a protected 'disability' under the Human Rights Acts, the employee can launch an action under the special machinery provided under those Acts. As we saw earlier, the basic rule is that an employer cannot terminate, or otherwise penalize an employee by reason of disability without proving that its health standards are a bona fide occupational requirement and that it has attempted to reasonably accommodate the employee up to the point of undue hardship.[1] Furthermore, we saw earlier that all jurisdictions have passed legislation which ensure that absence due to pregnancy and confinement shall not operate to frustrate a contract of employment.[2] It will be recalled that the protections enacted for employees who choose to take maternity and parental leaves are extensive.

1. *See* paras. 198A, 198B and 198C, *supra*.
2. This legislation is examined in detail in para. 311(5), *supra*.

327. When a contract of employment is frustrated it terminates at the time that the contract becomes impossible of performance. No requirement of notice has to be satisfied, not even the statutory 'floor' which is discussed below. Finally, where illness incapacitates employees but not to the point of frustration, the right to be paid wages during that period of illness or incapacity is determined on the bases discussed above.

328. In Quebec, the common law doctrine of frustration does not exist in the strict common law sense. Rather, according to Quebec's general law of contract, a debtor is liberated from his or her obligations if, without any act or fault on her or his part, performance of the contract has become impossible.[1] Only a superior force, that is a fortuitous, irresistible and unforeseeable event, will allow the debtor to escape from contracted duties. Thus, a fire or a natural disaster, such as flooding or an earthquake, would exonerate the employer whereas adverse economic conditions or financial difficulties, since they do not amount to a fortuitous event, would not relieve the employer of its contractual responsibilities. The employee's illness or disability does not always amount to a superior force that would free the employer from his contractual duties. However, section 2094 of the Civil Code states that one party to an employment contract may unilaterally terminate the contract without prior notice for serious cause. This includes the inability of an employee to perform his or her employment duties, as long as the inability is permanent or for a significant period of time. However, as elsewhere in Canada, human rights legislation in force in Quebec requires that the employer attempt to reasonably accommodate the disabled employee up to the point of undue hardship.

1. C.c.Q., s.1693.

B. Death

329. As the contract of employment is a personal one, death of either party terminates the contract at common law. Death does not extinguish the parties' rights, which had vested at that point such as, say, the right to wages. According to the Quebec Civil Code, the death of the employee terminates the contract of employment. Depending on the circumstances, the employer's death may also end the contract.[1] This is the case when the personal attributes of the employer are a central consideration in the agreement but, otherwise, the contract of employment continues to bind the employer's successors.

1. C.c.Q., s.2094.

C. Bankruptcy

330. Unless the contract of employment depended on the personal attributes and characteristics of the parties, there is nothing about the bankruptcy of either party which, *per se*, leads to termination of the contract. Indeed, the Supreme Court of Canada has held that it would be inconsistent with the goal of enhancing employee rights in bankruptcy situations to find frustration because it would deprive employees of the financial cushion provided by the notice periods provided for under their contracts of employment and the labour standards legislation.[1] According to Quebec civil law, bankruptcy does not *per se* terminate the contract of employment since it is not a fortuitous event. As in the common law jurisdictions, the employer must provide the affected employees with their common law and statutory notice periods and other severance benefits. Finally, bankruptcy law has an effect on the capacity of employees to recover arrears of wages. There are rules, interlocking with common law and minimum standards legislation, which govern the priority given to employees as creditors of a bankrupt employer.[2]

1. *Re Rizzo and Rizzo Shoes Ltd.* (1998) 33 C.C.E.L. (2d) 173 (S.C.C.); [1998] 1 S.C.R. 27.
2. For a detailed analysis, *see* England *et al.*, *op. cit.*, vol. 2, paras. 19.225–19.265.

331. The winding-up of a company, similarly, does not lead to the termination of the contract of employment. Instead, the employer must give the requisite notice of termination (or wages in lieu) under the employment contract and comply with the statutory minimum notice periods.[1]

1. *Canada (Att.Gen.)* v. *Standard Trust Co.* (1994) 8 C.C.E.L. (2d) 58, at 64–5 (Ont.Gen.Div.).

D. Dissolution of Firms

332. At common law, where one of the parties to a contract of employment dies, the employment contract will always be terminated. As we have seen above however, Quebec law may in the same circumstances hold the employer's successors liable. Of some interest is the fact that where a firm is dissolved because of a partner's death, Canadian common law takes an approach very similar to Quebec law. If the contract was of such a character as to make the personal attributes to the partners an essential element of the relationship then the result will be the same as if the contract had been concluded between two individuals viz., it will be considered frustrated.[1] Where the personal attributes of the partners were of no concern, as will most often be the case, the contract can only be terminated upon service of the requisite notice of termination (or pay in lieu) as provided under the contract and the statutory notice periods will apply.[2] Where a partnership's constitution has been changed by the retirement of one partner, the result will be the same, even though technically there has been a dissolution of the partnership. Where the retiring partner is replaced by another, the employee may treat this as a breach of contract because he or she cannot be forced to work with an employer he or she does not care for. But such a breach will be waived if the employee continues in service.[3] In any event, even if the employee should sue for damages for breach of contract in such circumstances, the amount awarded is likely to be nominal.[4] This legal reasoning is equally applicable in Quebec.

1. *Tasker* v. *Shepherd* (1861) 158 E.R. 237.
2. *Harvey* v. *Tivoli, Manchester* (1907) 23 T.L.R. 592 (D.C.).
3. *Hobson* v. *Cowley* (1858) 27 L.J. Ex. 205.
4. *Brace* v. *Calder*, [1895] 2 Q.B. 253 (C.A.); *Duplessis* v. *Irving Pulp and Paper Ltd.* (1982) 39 N.B.R. (2d) 584, 596–7 (N.B.Q.B.).

333. Where an employer's business is either sold, merged, amalgamated or otherwise transferred to a successor employer, common law would treat the contract as terminated; unilateral assignment of an employment contract is impermissible at common law.[1] However, as was noted earlier, minimum standards legislation provides that where there is a sale (which usually includes a lease, merger, amalgamation, a transfer or any other manner of disposition) of a business (which usually includes an activity, trade, undertaking or any part thereof), the employment shall not be deemed to be terminated and duties and obligations that the vendor owed to his employees shall now be borne by the purchaser.[2] Recently, the common law courts appear to have adopted this approach. They have presumed that the parties intend to preserve continuity of employment in circumstances where the new employer has acquired the business as a going concern, unless the new employer explicitly states at the date of the takeover that seniority must be rebuilt from scratch.[3] The *Code civil du Québec*, which came into force in 1994, brought about a major change in this area of law in Quebec. It states that the alienation of an enterprise, or any change in its legal structure, does not terminate the contract of employment.[4] In other words, the purchaser of an enterprise will be bound by the contracts of employment concluded by the vendor as long as the purchaser operates the same enterprise.[5] Under the former law, unless expressly stated in the contract of sale, the purchaser, not being an immediate party to these arrangements, was not bound by the contracts of employment of the vendor.

1. *Lingelbach* v. *James Tire Centers Ltd.* (1994) 7 C.C.E.L. (2d) 297, at 308 (Sask.C.A.).
2. *See* paras. 174–5, *supra.*
3. *Tayolor* v. *Dallas Investments Ltd.* (1993) 93 C.L.L.C. 14045, at para. 12271 (Alta.Q.B.); *Addison* v. *M. Loeb Ltd.* (1986) 53 O.R. (2d) 91 (N.R.C.A.).
4. S.2097, C.c.Q.
5. However, the provision does not prohibit the vendor from terminating his employees prior to the sale of his enterprise, as long as in doing so, he does not violate the contracts of employment (*see infra*, paras. 342–5). *See* Georges Audet, Robert Bonhomme, Clément Gascon and Magali Cournoyer-Proulx, *Le congédiement en droit québécois* (Cowansville: Les Éditions Yvon Blais Inc., 3rd edn., looseleaf) 8–13 to 8–15.

E. Termination by Notice

1. Common law

334. According to Canadian common law, a contract can be terminated because its object has been fulfilled, for example, if the contract is for the performance of a defined task or for the duration of a specified period. It can also be terminated at the will of either party, without the giving of prior notice, if the other party commits a repudiatory breach, for example, if the employee commits a serious act of misconduct or if the employer reduces the contractual wage rates. As well, a contract can be terminated by giving the requisite notice of termination expressed or implied under the contract, or wages in lieu thereof.[1]

1. For a detailed analysis of this topic, *see* England *et al.*, *op. cit.*, vol. 2, chs. 12, 13, 14, 15 and 16.

335. Sometimes the termination may be made conditional on the doing of an act on the part of the employee which is prejudicial to the employer in the employer's opinion. Courts hold that, in such cases, the employer must show that it exercised this discretion given by the terms of the contract in a bona fide and reasonable manner.[1] The requirement of reasonableness is significant in that it imposes an objective standard of behaviour on the employer and lends support to the view that there should be a standardized implied duty of fairness on employers under the employment contract in relation to all management decisions, not just dismissal.

1. *Greenberg* v. *Meffert* (1985) 18 D.L.R. (4d) 548 (Ont.C.A.); *Truckers Garage Ltd.* v. *Krell* (1994) 3 C.C.E.L. (2d) 157 (Ont.C.A.).

336. Where the contract contains express terms governing termination, these terms prevail over any implied terms but they cannot reduce the minimum statutory rights of the employee described below.[1] The express terms may state that the contract is for a definite duration, in which case it must run its full course. Alternatively, the contract may define the length of notice that must be given in order to terminate it. Where employers attempt to impose unduly harsh express termination clauses, the courts strive to circumvent them in acknowledgement of the reality that most employees do not have sufficient bargaining power to resist such clauses being inserted into the contract. Courts have used various techniques to achieve this purpose. One is to interpret harsh termination clauses *contra proferentem* the interests of the employer.[2] Another is the so-called 'changed subsratum' doctrine. This means that if an employee was originally hired in a relatively low level position under a contract containing a harsh notice clause but subsequently over the course of his or her career is promoted into higher positions, the employer must, at the date of each promotion, bring the harsh notice clause to the employee's attention so that he or she has the opportunity to bargain a more generous notice period, otherwise the harsh clause will be avoided.[3] As well, if the employer after the date of hiring attempts to include a new harsh termination clause in the contract, the courts will only allow that clause to stand so long as the employee provides fresh consideration to support the variation, is clearly notified that the clause is to have contractual force, is made to understand the full legal implications of the clause, and positively assents to having the clause included in the contract by words or deeds other than simply continuing to work without protest.[4] If an express termination clause is avoided in one of the above ways, the court can proceed to imply a reasonable notice period and, as we shall see below, reasonable notice periods can be relatively lengthy.

1. *Infra*, para. 346. *See Machtinger* v. *HOJ Industries Ltd.* (1992) 92 C.L.L.C. 14022 (S.C.C.), [1992] 1 S.C.R. 986, where the court held that the an express notice clause that is void as offending the statutory minimum notice period is replaced with an implied reasonable notice period.
2. E.g. *Shore* v. *Ladner Downs* (1997) 28 C.C.E.L. (2d) 151, at 155 (B.C.S.C.).
3. *Nardocchio* v. *C.I.B.C.* (1979) 41 N.S.R. (2d) 26 (S.C.).
4. E.g. *Wegg* v. *National Trust Co.* (1993) 47 C.C.E.L. 104 (Ont.Gen.Div.); *Jones* v. *Consumers Packaging Inc.* (1995) 14 C.C.E.L. (2d) 273 (Ont.Gen.Div.); *Ellision* v. *Burnaby Hospital Society* (1992) 92 C.L.L.C. 14042 (B.C.S.C.).

337. In the absence of express terms governing the notice period, the courts will imply a notice period into the contract. Strict contract law theory would appear to dictate that in implying a notice period, the courts should initially search for evidence of the parties' factual intentions on the matter, such as a past practice in the organization. While some courts have emphasized that this is the proper approach to implying notice periods,[1] the majority of judges proceed directly to implying a reasonable notice period as a matter of law based on a variety of policy interests. The theoretical aspect of the debate cloaks an underlying practical concern. Thus, judges who endorse the factual intent basis of implying the notice period do so because it usually produces a shorter notice period than the reasonableness method and they are concerned with the possible negative economic effects of awarding excessively long notice periods.[2] Be that as it may, there is no doubt that the yield of the reasonableness method is to produce increasingly lengthy notice periods. In the 1960s the courts astonished the legal community by making awards of 12 months' notice, thereby demolishing the pre-existing 'unofficial' ceiling of 6 months. By the 1990s, awards of 24 months' duration has become commonplace. Today, some courts have awarded as much as 30 months' reasonable notice.[3] Even that figure has been exceeded where the employer has handled the dismissal in a bad faith or unprofessional manner, under the so-called *Wallace* doctrine.[4] The reasonableness test has become a catch-all vehicle for effectuating a broad range of policy factors which the courts, from time to time, regard as being worthy of advancement. Not surprisingly, this makes it very difficult to predict exactly what the reasonable notice period will be and most cases are settled in negotiations without going to trial. The main policy interests are as follows:

(1) providing the employee with a financial cushion to enable him or her to weather the storm of unemployment. This is the paramount objective. Thus, the notice period will increase if the employee has little chance of finding a replacement job having regard to the state of the labour market for his or her trade or occupation and his or her personal attractiveness in that labour market, e.g. his or her age;
(2) recognizing the employee's seniority in his or her job. Typically, the courts award greater notice periods the longer an employee has been with the firm. In part, high seniority goes with high age and therefore can be regarded as a proxy for re-employability, but many courts reward seniority in its own right, possibly reflecting the notions of 'job property' and 'deferred wages' that are commonly thought to justify seniority;
(3) protecting the employee's expectations where he or she has been induced by the employer to quit a secure job;
(4) deterring bad faith, callous or unprofessional handling of dismissals on the part of the employer;[5]
(5) rewarding superiority based on job classes by attaching a notice premium to high status occupations;
(6) distributing part of the costs of terminations throughout the economy by making the employer pay high severance benefits the cost of which is passed on to its customers through higher prices;
(7) encouraging labour mobility.

At various times, other policies have been advanced by the courts. For example, it was once presumed that hiring would be on an annual basis.[6] Also, some courts have held that the length of the pay period determines the notice period, or that there is a 'rule of thumb' that an employee should receive one month's notice for each year of service.[7] Moreover, until recently some judges would reduce the notice period to take account of contributory blameworthiness on the employee's part under the so-called 'near cause' doctrine. Even though the latter doctrine would appear to be useful in giving the court the flexibility to apportion blame between the parties, the Supreme Court of Canada in 1998 disallowed it.[8] Furthermore, some courts responded to the recession that gripped Canada in the early 1980s by reducing notice periods to help employers withstand conditions of economic adversity but today this practice is rarely followed.[9] Of course, it might be revived if another serious recession occurred because the reasonableness test is highly responsive to changing social and economic conditions. Ultimately, each case depends on its own facts. Useful contemporary charts are provided by digest services. For practical purposes, such lists are more valuable than knowledge of the vague criteria provided by the case law and the generalized policies described above.[10] However, several general principles are sufficiently important to warrant detailed examination.

1. E.g. *Foster* v. *Kockums Cancar Division Hawker Siddeley Canada Inc.* (1993) 83 B.C.L.R. (2d) 207 (B.C.C.A.) *per* Southin J.A.
2. E.g. *Bartlam* v. *Saskatchewan Crop Insurance Corp.* (1993) 49 C.C.E.L. 141 (Sask.Q.B.). The economic consequences of unduly generous severance benefits are examined in E. Lazear, 'Job Security Provisions and Employment' (1990) 105 *Quarterly Jo. of Economics* 699; N. Leckie, *An International Review of Labour Adjustment Policies and Practices*, Working Paper Series No. 1993–15 (Kingston: Queen's University Industrial Relations Center, 1993).
3. *Kilpatrick* v. *Peterborough Civic Hospital* (1998) 36 C.C.E.L. (2d) 265 (Ont.Gen.Div.). *See also Donovan* v. *New Brunswick Publishing Co.* (1996) 469 A.P.R. 40 (N.B.C.A.), where 28 months was awarded; *Cowper* v. *Atomic Energy of Canada Ltd.* (1999) 43 C.C.E.L. (2d) 276 (Ont.S.C.J.) where 27 months was awarded.
4. E.g. *Clendenning* v. *Lownes Lambert (B.C.) Ltd.* (1999) 41 C.C.E.L. (2d) 58 (B.C.S.C.), where 42 months was awarded. The *Wallace* doctrine is examined *infra*, para. 338.
5. *Wallace* v. *United Grain Growers Ltd.* (1997) 97 C.L.L.C. 21029 (S.C.C.), [1998] 3 S.C.R. 701, examined *infra*, para. 338.
6. E.g. *Pollard* v. *Gibson*, [1924] 4 D.L.R. 54 (Ont.C.A.). But *see* now *Richardson* v. *Koefed*, [1969] 1 W.L.R. 1812 (C.A.).
7. E.g. *Sigmore* v. *C.A.S. Sports International Inc.* (1997) 32 C.C.E.L. (2d) 10 (Ont.Div.Ct.). However, the 'rule of thumb' approach has been overruled in *Minott* v. *O'Shanter Development Co.* (1999) 168 D.L.R. (4d) 270 (Ont.C.A.).
8. *Dowling* v. *Halifax (City)*, [1998] 1 S.C.R. 22, examined in G. England, '*Dowling* v. *City of Halifax*: the Shortest Hard Case Ever?' (1998) 6 C.L.E.L.J. 455.
9. *Bohemier* v. *Storwal International Inc.* (1982) 142 D.L.R. (3d) 8 (Ont.H.C.), varied 44 O.R. (2d) 361 (C.A.).
10. E.g. Ellen E. Mole, *Wrongful Dismissal Practice Manual* (Toronto: Butterworths, 1984, looseleaf).

338. The first of these general principles is the *Wallace* doctrine. This doctrine allows the court to extend the notice period if the employer has acted in bad faith, callously or otherwise unprofessionally in handling the dismissal.[1] Extensions usually range between five to eight months depending on the degree of blameworthiness of the employer's actions. The rationale is at least partially one of deterrence, for the courts have ruled that an improperly handled dismissal will result in an extension being granted even if the worker does not suffer any economic or mental harm as a result of the employer's actions. This is very significant because it shows that the courts regard the employee's right to be treated fairly and decently as a fundamental human right worthy of protection in and of itself. Therefore, it might be thought that the courts would have chosen to imply into all employment contracts a general right to be treated fairly in all aspects of the working relationship in all employment contracts instead of restricting the right to be treated fairly to dismissal situations and using the reasonable notice doctrine as the vehicle for enforcing the right. The reason the Supreme Court of Canada gave for not implying a generalized duty of fairness is that it did not want to make all areas of managerial decision making susceptible to challenge in the courts. Given the high costs of civil litigation, it is unlikely that frivolous actions would proliferate. Moreover, by attaching the duty of fairness to the reasonable notice doctrine, the courts may have created a loophole for employers who can easily oust a reasonable notice review by including an express notice clause in the employment contract. Possibly the courts may reconsider implying a generalized duty of fairness into the employment contracts if employers do thwart the *Wallace* doctrine by using express notice clauses.

1. *Wallace* v. *United Grain Growers Ltd.* (1997) 97 C.L.L.C. 21029 (S.C.C.), [1998] 3 S.C.R. 701.

339. The second general principle worthy of further consideration is that of awarding extra notice to employees in high status occupations. It was always regarded as axiomatic that high status workers should receive a notice premium because it was thought that the blow of unemployment would fall more heavily on them than on lesser minions. This proposition is dubious both morally and empirically. As well, the practice of awarding a notice premium could be regarded as part of the price high status workers should rightfully receive for incurring the opportunity costs of undergoing often lengthy and expensive educational and training periods. Be that as it may, in 1994 an Ontario trial judge, MacPherson J., disapproved of the principle and held that a low echelon employee whose chance of finding alternate employment is slim should receive the same notice period as a high echelon employee with a similarly low chance of finding a replacement position.[1] This decision caused considerable controversy before it was quashed by the Court of Appeal, which reinstated the old principle.[2] Today, therefore, high status workers continue to receive a notice premium. As for low echelon workers, they frequently receive lengthy notice periods of 12 months or more if their prospects of finding replacement work are minimal, but they cannot insist on being treated equally with high status employees. New Brunswick is unique in that the Court of Appeal has ruled that occupational status is irrelevant for both high and low status workers; instead, re-employability along with the other factors mentioned earlier are all that count.[3]

1. *Cronk* v. *Canadian General Insurance Co.* (1994) 94 C.L.L.C. 14032.
2. (1995), 95 C.L.L.C. 210038 (Ont.C.A.). *See also* G. England, 'Determining Reasonable Notice of Termination: the Implications of *Cronk* v. *Canadian General Insurance Co.*' (1996) 4 C.L.E.L.J. 115.
3. *Medis Health and Pharmaceutical Services Inc.* v. *Bramble* (1999) 99 C.L.L.C. 210045 (N.B.C.A.).

340. The final general principle that merits special consideration is the so-called 'range', or 'ballpark' doctrine. This doctrine held that a court should not interfere with a notice period proposed by an employer if it is within the reasonable range, or ballpark of what the courts might rule to be reasonable.[1] The risk with this doctrine, of course, is that it allowed employers to get away with making low end offers to employees. The courts in all provinces – rightly, it is submitted – have disapproved of the doctrine.[2]

1. E.g. *Allen* v. *Assaly Holdings Ltd.* (1991) 34 C.C.E.L. 81 (Ont.Div.Ct.).
2. *McCrea* v. *Conference Board of Canada* (1993) 45 C.C.E.L. 29, at 35–6 (Ont.Gen.Div.).

341. There is little point in examining the details of the cases in an essay such as this. However, the general flavour of the inquiry can be gleaned by randomly picking from the current list in one of the looseleaf services. A vice president finance aged 55 with 12 years' seniority received 18 months; a regional credit manager aged 36 with 2.75 years' seniority received 6 months; a personnel manager aged 51 with 28 years' seniority received 18 months; a sales manager aged 47 with 3.5 years' seniority received 8 months; an auto mechanic aged 26 with 6 years' seniority received 5 months; a supervisor aged 56 with 5.5 years' seniority received 9 months; a bartender aged 30 with 3 years' seniority received 3 months; a chef aged 48 with 7 months' seniority received 3 months; a forklift operator aged 50 with 16 years' seniority received 14 months; and an office supervisor aged 36 with 16 years' seniority received 12 months. Again, it must be emphasized that the majority of cases are settled in negotiations without ever reaching the courts. As well, the high costs of civil litigation mean for many workers that their common law right to reasonable notice exists only in theory for they simply cannot afford to enforce it.

342. Current Quebec law governing the termination of employment has the same effect as the common law in the rest of Canada, but its evolution has followed a slightly different path. The rules were clarified with the enactment of the new Civil Code that came into force in 1994. According to its section 2086, a contract of employment is for a fixed term or an indeterminate term. If a specific term is not expressly stated by the parties, the contract must necessarily be deemed to be of an indeterminate term.

343. The parties can specify that their contract is for a definite duration. In such a case, the contract ends upon the expiration of the term and neither party can terminate it without cause during its term. However, the agreement is tacitly renewed 'where the employee continues to carry on his work for five days after the expiry of the term, without objection from the employer'.[1] The Civil Code now expressly provides that the renewed contract is to be for an indeterminate term, altering the law under the old *Code civil du Bas-Canada* where the contract was presumed to be renewed for a similar term up to a maximum of one year.

1. C.c.Q., s.2090.

344. Generally, the individual contract of employment is of indefinite duration. Similar to the Canadian common law, Quebec civil law provides for the possibility of either party terminating the contract without cause by giving prior notice to the other party. According to the *Code civil du Québec*, this notice 'shall be given in reasonable time, taking into account, in particular, the nature of employment, the special circumstances in which it is carried on and the duration of the period of work'.[1] Furthermore, the Code prohibits the employee from waiving his or her right to be indemnified when insufficient notice of termination was given.[2]

1. C.c.Q., s.2091.
2. C.c.Q., s.2092.

345. What constitutes reasonable notice in Quebec depends on the circumstances of each case. Like the courts in Canada's common law jurisdictions, Quebec courts have considered factors such as the circumstances of hiring, the nature and the importance of the position, the fact that the employee had quit a secured position to accept the new one, the intentions of the parties, the difficulties of finding another equivalent job, the age of the employee and the length of services with the employer.[1] Quebec courts have sometimes viewed adverse economic conditions as justifying a longer period of notice, but on other occasions they have been sympathetic to the economic plight of the employer and have placed little emphasis on this fact when determining the proper length of notice.[2] It is interesting to note that Quebec courts have traditionally awarded shorter periods of notice than has been the case elsewhere in Canada. The length of the notice period seldom exceeds 12 months in Quebec.[3]

1. *See Columbia Builders Supplies*, *op. cit.*, para. 344; *Jolicoeur* v. *Lithographie Montréal Ltée.*, [1982] C.S. 230; Isabelle Jolicoeur, *L'évolution de la notion de délai-congé raisonnable en droit québécois et canadien* (Cowansville: Les Éditions Yvon Blais Inc., 1993).
2. *Surveyer, Nenniger et Chenevert inc.* v. *Short*, D.T.E. 88T-4 (Quebec C.A.).
3. *See* Georges Audet, Robert Bonhomme, Clément Gascon and Magali Cournoyer-Proulx, *Le congédiement en droit québécois* (Cowansville: Les Éditions Yvon Blais Inc., 3rd edn., looseleaf) ch. 5 and Annex I.

2. Statutes

346. Most legislatures have provided for minimum periods of notice, or wages in lieu, which must be given to employees covered by the particular statutes.[1] The details very enormously. Some minimum periods of notice are tied directly to the way wages are paid. Thus, if payment is made every week, a week's notice will be required. In the majority of jurisdictions, the minimum protection is only available to employees who have been employed for a specified length of time (usually three months). The amount of notice may vary with the length of time of service, increasing as length of employment increases (Alberta, Nova Scotia, Ontario, Saskatchewan, Quebec) or be specified independently of length of service (Canada, Prince Edward Island). Normally the employer is given the right to pay an amount equal to the wages that would ordinarily be earned by employees during the statutorily required notice period instead of giving notice. If the contractually agreed upon or customary notice in the industry is longer than the statutory minimum, the employee is to get the benefit of the longer notice period. Where the contract of employment provides for less than the statutory minimum, the provision is void and the employee is entitled to a period of reasonable notice which may be more than the minimum statutory provision. Except in Quebec, where section 2092 of the Civil Code prohibits such a clause, the parties may, however, stipulate expressly that no period of notice greater than the statutory minimum is to be read into the contract of employment.[2]

The employer is not required to give the statutory notice in a variety of circumstances which are the equivalents of frustration or conduct by the employee which amounts to a breach entitling the employer to repudiate the contract. Thus, impossibility of performance may avoid the need to give notice. Where there is an established practice which permits an employer to require an employee to retire at a particular age the statutory provision will not apply. Nor will it where the employer has just cause to terminate the contract, or where the employer has offered reasonable alternative work to an employee, or different work as a result of an application of an agreed upon seniority system and the employee refuses to accept such new work. The statutory notice period does not normally apply where an employee is put on temporary lay-off, as this is not a permanent termination of the contract, provided this is not a breach of the contract or, if it is a breach, it is one which is waived. Where an employee has been asked to return after a temporary lay-off and refuses to do so after a specified time (usually seven days), the employer can terminate the contract without giving notice. Quebec, Nova Scotia and the federal jurisdiction now provide a remedy for unjust discharge even where the employee has been given proper notice. In these jurisdictions, the employer must establish just cause to end the employment relationship. Significantly, the primary remedy for unjust dismissal is reinstatement. Traditionally, reinstatement is unavailable in a common law wrongful dismissal suit. Unfortunately, it has proven difficult to enforce reinstatement in the non-organized sector where there is no trade union to ensure that the employer does not retaliate against the reinstated employee.[3] In addition, adjudicators under these schemes can select from an arsenal of remedies including reinstatement subject to conditions, re-engagement in different positions and compensation assessed on a make whole basis rather than limited to the common law notice period. Eligibility for this remedy varies among jurisdictions. The federal jurisdiction requires only one year of employment, Quebec requires three years, and Nova Scotia requires more than ten years of employment.[4] Also, lay-offs caused by economic conditions are excluded from adjudicative review provided that they are genuinely for economic reasons and not a subterfuge for discarding an unwanted employee. As yet other Canadian provinces have failed to enact unjust discharge statutes. This is perhaps because the non-organized have no collective voice in the political forum. After all, it is unlikely that trade unions would lobby for the enactment of such measures when the effect would be reduce the incentive to unionize and win just cause protections under a collective agreement.

1. E.g. Alberta Employment Standards Code, S.A. 1988, c.E-10.1, ss.55–62.
2. *Machtinger* v. *HOJ Industries Ltd.* (1992), 92 C.L.L.C. 14,022 (S.C.C.), [1992] 1 S.C.R. 986.
3. For this, and other difficulties with the implementation of these provisions, *see* G. England, 'Section 240 of the Canada Labour Code: Some Current Pitfalls' (1999) 27 *Man.L.J.* 17.
4. *See infra*, paras. 353–69.

a. Group termination

347. In addition to these statutory protections for individuals, employees are also given some legislative aid in mass lay-offs involving large numbers of employees. Most jurisdictions provide that where an employer intends to lay off more than 50 employees in a four-week period (10 in Nova Scotia and Quebec), the employer is to notify the appropriate ministry. This notice must also be given to the employees concerned, individually or by public notification. Thus the employees will be given at least four weeks' notice. As the number of intended lay-offs increases, so does the period of required notice. For instance, in Manitoba, if more that 50 but fewer than 100 employees are to be laid off, 10 weeks' notice is required, 14 weeks if there are more than 100 but fewer than 300 employees and 18 weeks if there are more than 300 employees. Pay instead of notice may be given. The employer is required to collaborate with the appropriate ministry in finding employment for the laid off people. The intent behind notifying the ministry is to assist labour market organizational efforts. At the federal level and in Manitoba and Quebec joint committees of employers and worker representatives are to be created to determine whether or not the termination can be avoided or, at least, lessened in effect. At the federal level, if the joint consultation fails, an independent arbitrator may be appointed to attempt to find a solution. The arbitrator, however, is not empowered to block the lay-off. These joint employer–employee committees are symbolically important in that they acknowledge that employees have a moral right to participate in their employment destiny without necessarily having to do so through the agency of a trade union using the collective bargaining mechanism.[1] In Quebec, a collective fund may be established for the purpose of the reclassification and indemnification of employees where the minister, having been notified of a group termination, thinks this to be appropriate.

1. *See* R. Adams, *The Unorganised: A Rising Force*, McMaster University Research and Working Paper Series No. 21, April 1983, at 13.

b. Severance pay

348. In Ontario and the federal jurisdictions, an additional payment is to be made to employees upon termination.[1] It is referred to as severance pay to differentiate it from payment of wages in lieu of notice. The latter, as noted earlier,[2] is deemed to be a contractual term, its precise content being a matter of interpretation and modified by statute. Severance pay, notionally, might be treated as deferred pay. This view is favoured in respect of provisions for severance payment found in collective agreements. The idea is that such employees' gains are secured by the trading off of other bargaining items in negotiation.[3] Such provisions are obtained only by the relatively powerful unionized bargaining units. In 1990, 45.1 per cent of collective agreements covering 500, or more, employees provided for severance pay plans; 41.4 per cent did not. The percentage is much lower in smaller units.[4] The common law has never implied a term to the effect that deferred wages should be paid as severance pay in addition to notice or pay in lieu thereof, presumably because individual employees could not have such bargaining strength attributed to them. This is why statutory entitlements were necessitated.

1. Ontario Employment Standards Act, R.S.O. 1990, c.E-14, s.58; Canada Labour Code, R.S.C. 1985, c.L-2, ss.235–7.
2. *Supra*, paras. 337–8.

3. *Report of the Commission of Inquiry into Redundancies and Lay-Offs* (The Carrothers Report) (Ottawa: Labour Canada, 1970) para. 495.
4. *Provisions in Major Collective Agreements in Canada Covering 500 or More Employees* (Ottawa: Bureau of Labour Information, Labour Canada), April 1990.

349. Another way to conceptualize severance pay is as a windfall, something to tide terminated workers over until they are employed again. Entitlement would cease where need ceased. However, this is not how the statutes creating severance pay schemes operate. Rather, having set criteria for payment, they provide for specific amounts of payment. The nature of the criteria which act as prerequisites reveal two distinct philosophies underlying the schemes. In Ontario, severance pay becomes payable where 50 or more employees are terminated in a period of six months or less, or one or more employees are terminated by an employer with a payroll of more than $2.5 million per annum. In both cases, however, an employee must have been employed for five years to be entitled to these severance payments. Temporary absence due to illness or injury does not disqualify an employee. The termination must be the result of the permanent discontinuance of all or part of the employer's business. The severance payment to be made shall amount to one week's regular wages for each year of employment of the terminated employees up to a maximum of 26 weeks. The purport of the legislation is to overcome some of the great hardships which resulted out of the increased number of plant closures in Ontario which were not redressed by the notice requirements or pension coverage. The legislation reflects an attempt to make closure, especially by branch-plant organizations which might close as a result of rationalizing investment decisions made elsewhere, somewhat less attractive by making employers share in the community burdens created by unemployment, while still not making it as expensive as to inhibit investment unduly. The scheme thus applies to employees who lose their jobs as a result of other employees exercising their seniority rights, or who are laid off and become entitled to a reduced pension benefit. But employees who refuse alternative offers of reasonable employment by the employer, or who do not exercise their seniority rights or who retire on full pensions are not entitled to severance pay. Moreover, where the discontinuance of business is due to economic loss due to a lockout or a strike, there shall be no entitlement to severance pay. Severance pay is thus linked to the Ontario legislature's effort to exercise some influence over private policies. At the federal level, the emphasis is a different one. Entitlement to severance pay arises upon termination (contrast lay-off as defined by the regulations under the statute) of any employee who does not retire on a full pension and who has had 12 months continuous employment with the employer. While this may also have been drafted, in part, as a disincentive to employers, the fact that group termination is not required, that the employer's business need not be discontinued, that the prerequisites are so limited, all indicate that the federal legislature is guided by another motive. This appears to be the notion that an employee develops a proprietary right in a job, so that when tenure is ended compensation is warranted. This concept is but feebly acknowledged in common law and the federal legislation is thus a significant signpost. But – perhaps because of the conceptual difference – the federal benefits are meager compared to the Ontario ones.

F. Termination for Just Cause

350. In Quebec and the common law jurisdictions, there is no need for an employer to give notice of termination where the employer has just cause to dismiss an employee by reason of the latter having committed a 'repudiatory' breach of the employment contract. The earlier examination of the legally implied obligations of an employee made it clear that failure by an employee to obey may amount to a repudiatory breach of contract entitling the employer to treat the contract as at end forthwith.[1] The definition of 'repudiatory' is extremely malleable and has enabled courts to fashion standards of just cause according to changing social and economic circumstances. Today, the common law standards are virtually identical to the arbitral standards of just cause fashioned by collective agreement arbitrators in the unionized sector. Indeed, sometimes courts explicitly cite arbitral authorities in their judgments. It is generally regarded as desirable that equal standards of industrial discipline should be applied to all sectors of the workforce. The main components of just cause are as follows:

(1) The employer's decision must be rational in the sense that the employee's conduct must cause demonstrable and substantial harm to the production process or to management's symbolic authority to command before cause will be grounded.[2] Clearly, this means that bad faith, arbitrary or discriminatory dismissals are unlawful for the essence of the latter is that the employer's decision is not based on advancing its legitimate business interests.

(2) The penalty of dismissal must not be disproportionately severe on the worker in relation to the degree of harm sustained by the employer as a result of the employee's behaviour. A key feature of this concept of proportionality is that the so-called 'corrective', or 'rehabilitative' philosophy of industrial discipline. This holds that an employee must be afforded a fair chance to improve his or her level of performance before dismissal can be invoked. Typically, this requires that the employer provide the employee with a clear understanding of the performance expectations; notify the employee clearly of the precise areas of his or her deficiency; notify the employee clearly that his or her job is in jeopardy unless he or she improves; apply a system of graduated penalties beginning with formal warnings followed by unpaid suspensions prior to invoking dismissal; and make reasonable efforts to assist the employee to reach the desired performance levels. Of course, if the circumstances show that the employee will not take the chance of self-improvement, for example, if the employee continues to deny any wrongdoing on his or her part, corrective measures can be dispensed with. Similarly, the concept of proportionality implies that corrective measures are not required where the employee's actions severely damage the employer's operations. Proportionality also implies that account be taken of mitigating factors such as provocation or other blameworthiness of the employer's part or domestic problems on the employee's part.

(3) The employer's actions must be procedurally fair. Traditionally, courts have ruled that the employer is under no implied contractual duty of observe the standards of procedural fairness in dismissing its employees.[3] Occasionally, modern courts repeat this proposition.[4] Nevertheless, the fact is that the majority

of courts regularly apply the standards of procedural fairness, generally without mentioning the traditional rule against so doing. Thus, clear warnings of unsatisfactory behaviour must be given to the employee under the corrective discipline philosophy; the doctrines of estoppel, waiver, condonation and laches are applied; the employer generally cannot subsequently alter the grounds of dismissal if the employee would be taken by surprise; and procedurally flawed dismissals may warrant an extension of the reasonable notice period under the *Wallace* doctrine.[5]

1. *Supra*, paras. 306–21.
2. Thus, misconduct must be serious in order to ground justify dismissal e.g. *Colliar* v. *Robinson Diesel Injection Ltd.* (1988) 89 C.L.L.C. 14037, at 12135 (Sask.Q.B.); insubordination must normally involve repeated refusals of an order rather than an isolated refusal to ground dismissal e.g. *Veer* v. *Dover Corp. (Canada) Ltd.* (1999) 99 C.L.L.C. 210037, at para. 141304 (Alta.Q.B.); and incompetence must be seriously inferior to ground dismissal e.g. *Lee* v. *Parking Corp. of Vancouver* (1999) 39 C.C.E.L. (2d) 135, at 146 (B.C.S.C.).
3. *Ridge* v. *Baldwin*, [1964] A.C. 40 (H.L.).
4. E.g. *Higginson* v. *Rocky Credit Union Ltd.* (1995) 162 A.R. 369, at 376 (Alta.C.A.); *Harris* v. *University of Western Ontario* (1998) 98 C.L.L.C. 210026, at para. 141146 (Ont.C.A.).
5. *Supra*, para. 338.

351. The treatment of sexual harassment illustrates the modern approach of the courts to dismissal. Unquestionably, sexual harassment constitutes misconduct, but it will not ground summary dismissal unless the harassment in question is of a serious nature.[1] Furthermore, the employer must comply with the following procedural safeguards:

(1) The employer must conduct personal interviews with the victim, the alleged perpetrator and all key witnesses.
(2) The employer must produce a written account of each interview.
(3) The employer must not pre-judge the credibility of either the victim or the perpetrator but must probe the credibility of both parties.
(4) The employer must make and retain comprehensive records of all aspects of its investigations.
(5) The employer must give the alleged perpetrator notice of the charges against him or her and a reasonable opportunity to respond before invoking dismissal.
(6) The employer must notify its employees of any 'zero tolerance' policy which provides for dismissal for a first offence of harassment.[2]

1. Thus in *Wright* v. *B.C. Trade Development Corp.* (1994) 3 C.C.E.L. (2d) 254 (B.C.S.C.) the employee did commit sexual harassment but his conduct was not so serious as to warrant summary dismissal.
2. E.g. *McIntyre* v. *Rogers Cable T.V. Ltd.* (1996) 18 C.C.E.L. (2d) 116 (B.C.S.C.); *Murrell* v. *Burns International Security Services Ltd.* (1994) 5 C.C.E.L. (2d) 123 (Ont.Gen.Div.); *Quirola* v. *Xerox Canada Ltd.* (1996) 16 C.C.E.L. (2d) 235 (Ont.Gen.Div.).

352. The above description of what constitutes cause for summary dismissal refers to common law cases. The analysis, however, would be the same under Quebec civil law. The Civil Code states that the employer may dismiss an employee for a serious reason.[1] This is generally the case when the employee, either in a culpable or in a non-culpable manner, fails to meet one of the essential obligations of his or her contract of employment.[2] It is culpable when the employee voluntarily enters into an inappropriate pattern of conduct such as insubordination, lateness and voluntary absenteeism, negligence or dishonesty. However, the employee's physical or intellectual inability to perform his or her tasks in a satisfactory manner, although not voluntary, may well amount to a breach of contract and provide the employer with reason for discharge. In all cases, the burden to establish this reason for summary dismissal is placed on the employer's shoulders.

1. C.c.Q., s.2094.
2. For a description of the Quebec case law on this matter, *see* Audet *et al.*, *op. cit.*, ch. 4.

§5. Remedies for Breach of Contract

A. Employer Remedies

1. Summary dismissal

353. As previously described, there are many situations in which an employer will be permitted to exercise a right of self-help in response to a repudiatory breach of contract by an employee by summarily dismissing the employee without notice or wages in lieu. This is by far and away the most potent weapon employers have in their arsenal and the remedy most frequently used by them. According to both the Canadian common law and Quebec civil law, the employer generally does not have the right to use any other form of discipline. For instance, an employer is not entitled to suspend an employee for a period without terminating the contract. If an employer seeks to penalize an employee in this way in response to a breach by that employee, the employer will himself be in breach of contract entitling the employee to remedial action.[1] Of course, an express agreement to the contrary by the parties, or a reliable past practice to the contrary which is implied to be a term of the agreement, overcomes this rule. The rule sharply differentiates the common law of the contract of employment from the jurisprudence applicable to collective agreements. Many of the grounds giving an employer just cause to dismiss employees without notice may give good cause to an employer to discipline employees working under a collective agreement. But, after initial difficulties, it has become legislatively accepted that arbitrators interpreting the agreement have the remedial authority to substitute other forms of discipline for dismissal. In contrast, the Supreme Court of Canada has ruled that an employee's damages for wrongful dismissal cannot be reduced to account for his or her contributory blame.[2] Given the ubiquity of the 'corrective' philosophy[3] of discipline in contemporary industrial relations – unpaid suspensions are the penultimate step to dismissal under this philosophy – the time is ripe for courts to review the rule against unilateral disciplinary suspension.[4]

1. *Hanley* v. *Pease*, [1915] 1 K.B. 698. For Quebec law, *see* Claude D'Aoust, Louis Leclerc and Gilles Trudeau, *Les mesures disciplinaires: Étude jurisprudentielle et doctrinale*, Monographie no. 13, Ecole de relations industrielles (Montreal: Université de Montreal, 1982) 51–8; *see also* *Maheu, Noiseux et Associés* v. *Ronéo Vickers Canada Ltd. et al.* [1988] R.J.Q. 1597 (C.A.).

2. *Dowling* v. *Halifax (City)*, [1998] 1 S.C.R. 22, examined in G. England, '*Dowling* v. *City of Halifax*: the Shortest Hard Case Ever?' (1998) 6 C.L.E.L.J. 455.
3. *Supra*, para. 350.
4. *See*, for example, *Haldane* v. *Shelbar Enterprises Ltd.* (1999) 46 C.C.E.L. (2d) 267, at 272 (Ont.C.A.) where Doherty J.A. stated by way of *obiter dictum* that the courts should consider implying a standard term in all employment contracts allowing the employer to impose unpaid suspensions under 'corrective' disciplinary systems.

354. In the federal jurisdiction, Nova Scotia and Quebec, the standard collective bargaining regime's technique of reviewing the employer's right of summary dismissal has supplanted the common law doctrines. Any employee working under the umbrella of the Canada Labour Code and who has been employed for 12 months by one employer and who does not belong to a group of workers covered by a collective agreement, may complain within 90 days of his or her dismissal. An inspector will be asked to investigate and mediate the problem. Where this does not give the employee satisfaction, the employee may ask for an adjudicator for final determination. The adjudicator has the same powers to settle the dispute as does an arbitrator interpreting a just cause clause of a collective agreement.[1] Unlike at common law, reinstatement can be ordered and damages are based on the make whole method instead of being limited to the contractual notice period. Quebec labour standards legislation provides for a similar recourse for all employees with three years or more of uninterrupted service in the same enterprise.[2] In Nova Scotia, the scheme is similar.[3]

1. Canada, Part III, ss.240–6. *See also* the earlier examination of this legislation in para. 346, *supra*.
2. An Act Respecting Labour Standards, R.S.Q. c.N-1.1, ss.124–31; *see*, for a general overview of both the federal and Quebec recourses, Gerard Hebert and Gilles Trudeau, *Les normes minimales du travail au Canada et au Québec* (Cowansville, Que.: Les Editions Yvon Blais inc., 1987) 160–77.
3. Nova Scotia Labour Standards Code, R.S.N.S., 1989, c.246, s.71(1).

2. *Damages*

355. Where the conduct of an employee does not amount to a breach which warrants the employer terminating the contract without notice, the employer will be entitled to sue for damages incurred. This has occurred, for example, where the employer has incurred costs in fixing up shoddy workmanship.[1] Usually, however, the employee will have insufficient funds to make suing for damages worthwhile. The employer also has the right of suing for damages where the employee leaves without giving appropriate notice.[2] Note here that the notion of agreed upon, reasonable and statutorily provided minimum notice also applies to employees as it does to employer notices of termination. However, the policy interests differ in the context of determining what constitutes reasonable notice of resignation on the employee's part. Here, the objective is to allow an employer sufficient time to hire a substitute for the employee in question. Accordingly, notice periods required of employees are usually much shorter than notice periods required of employers.[3]

1. E.g. *Ferguson* v. *Allstate Insurance Co. of Canada* (1991) 35 C.C.E.L. 257 (Ont.Gen.Div.); *Petrone* v. *Marmot Concrete Services Ltd.* (1996) 18 C.C.E.L. (2d) 170 (Alta.Q.B.).

2. E.g. *Systems Engineering and Automation Ltd.* v. *Power* (1989) 90 C.L.L.C. 14018 (Nfld.Tr.Div.).
3. An exceptional case is *Tree Savers International Ltd.* v. *Savoy* (1992) 39 C.C.E.L. 253, at 259–60 (Alta. C.A.) where 18 months' reasonable notice – as assessed since it took that long for the employer to find a substitute for the highly skilled defendants.

356. The measure of damages to which the employer is entitled is calculated in the same way as damages in general contract law are assessed. There is to be liability for those losses which can be said to arise fairly and reasonably naturally from the breach or for losses which, although they do not arise naturally from the breach, may reasonably be supposed to have been in the contemplation of the parties at the time of contracting as being the likely result of breach. The latter part of this standard formulation means that, where the loss is of an extraordinary kind, to recover damages for it the possibility of its occurrence will have had to be spelled out explicitly when contracting. In Quebec, unless there is fraud or intentional or gross fault on the debtor's part, the damages are limited to those that were foreseen or foreseeable at the time of the formation of the contract.[1]

1. C.c.Q., s.1613.

357. Apart from damage done to inventory or property, it will be rare that the employer will be able to show more than nominal damages. Unless a worker is irreplaceable because of some special knowledge or skill,[1] the requirement that a person suing for damages in contract has a responsibility to mitigate his or her losses, makes it unlikely that great loss will be incurred by an employer. The employer is not entitled to deduct the amount he claims in damages from any wages owing to the employee at the time of the breach. Nor can a term of the contract, which is characterized as a penalty clause, be enforced. It is conceivable that a contract has in it a provision that, in case of breach, a sum certain shall be payable to the aggrieved party. Where a court believes that this term is merely one intended to deter breach as opposed to being an agreed upon estimate of the probable damage caused by a breach, the term will not be enforced. Thus, it is likely that a stated amount for any breach, no matter what its gravity, would be unenforceable.

1. As in *Tree Savers International Ltd.* v. *Savoy* (1992) 39 C.C.E.L. 253, at 259–60 (Alta.C.A.) where $146,200 was awarded for failure to give the proper notice of resignation.

3. Injunctions and specific performance

358. A contract of personal service is not to be specifically enforced. The very personal nature of the relationship dictates that the parties should not be forced to work with each other. As was noted above, an employer cannot discipline employees for a breach by suspending them in order to obtain conformity. The employer cannot positively enforce a particular mode of performance. On the other hand, where an employer has treated the contract as terminated because of the alleged breach by an employee and the employee proves to a court's satisfaction that the employer was wrong in its assessment and, hence, act of dismissal, the court will not force the employer to re-employ the employee.[1] That would be tantamount to forcing the employer to work with an employee whom he may not wish to hire. Once again attention is drawn to the situation under a collective bargaining regime. There, both arbitrators interpreting awards and labour relations tribunals have power to reinstate employees, that is, to enforce contracts of employ-ment specifically. On the other hand, the English Court of Appeal in 1987 granted an injunction to compel an employee who quit without adequate notice to actually work out his notice period.[2] There, the defendant was a highly skilled employee who could not easily be replaced without causing undue hardship to the employer. As yet, the Canadian courts have not followed this approach.

1. The Supreme Court of Canada has suggested it might be possible to do so but carefully refrained from specifying the 'special circumstances' in which it might be done; *see Red Deer College* v. *Michaels and Finn*, [1975] 5 W.W.R. 575, 590 (*per* Laskin, C.J.C.). Quebec civil law provides no greater right for an employee to reclaim his or her job. For an interesting comment on this aspect of Quebec law, *see* Marie-France Bich, 'Du contrat individuel de travail en droit québécois: essai en forme de point d'interrogation' (1986) *Revue generale de droit*, 85; *see also* Pierre Laporte, *La réintégration du salarié: nouvelles perspectives* (Montreal: Wilson et Lafleur Ltée, 1995).
2. *Evening Standard* v. *Henderson*, [1987] I.R.L.R. 64 (C.A.).

359. There are situations which arise under the common law controlling individual contracts of employment which seem to resemble specific performance of contracts of employment. Where a contract explicitly provides that an employee undertakes to render his or her services exclusively for the employer, this clause will not be upheld by the grant of an injunction sought by the employer to prevent an employee from leaving his service by having the court order that the employee perform the contract into which he or she entered. Yet where a similar result is sought by seeking an injunction to prevent breach of a contractual stipulation to the effect that the employee will not, during the term of the contract, render any of the services to be rendered for the employer for any other person, the courts may grant the order restraining an employee from accepting other employment. The distinction made in the cases is between enforcing a positive covenant, that is one requiring performance of the existing contract, and enforcing a negative covenant, that is, requiring the employee not to work in a particular way. The latter is acceptable because it may well leave the employee free not to perform the contract he or she wants to abandon. This assumes that the enforcement of the negative covenant will not, in fact, amount to the enforcement of the existing contract. To require the courts to make distinctions of this kind is to present them with unenviable tasks. To illustrate: the famous actress, Bette Davis, had entered into a contract which both required her to render her acting services exclusively to Warner Brothers, and forbade her from accepting acting work with any other person during the term of the contract. An injunction to force her to render services for the employer was refused; an injunction forbidding her to work as an actress with any other person for the remainder of the contract was granted. This was justified on the basis that the actress was a person of intelligence, capacity and means and that there was no evidence that, were she to refuse to fulfil her contract with Warner Brothers, she would not be able to employ herself both usefully and remuneratively in other spheres of activity. That is, she was not effectively being forced to carry out the contract of employment.[1]

1. *Warner Brothers Pictures* v. *Nelson*, [1937] 1 K.B. 209, *see also Lumley* v. *Wagner* (1852) 42 E.R. 687, *Bell and Atkins* (1956) 56 D.L.L.C. para. 15,285, cf. *Nili Holdings Ltd.* v. *Rose* (1981) 123 D.L.R. (3d) 464 (B.C.S.C.); *Hill* v. *C.A. Parsons & Co. Ltd.*, [1972] Ch. 305 (C.A.) (which gave rise to the Supreme Court of Canada's suggestion that reinstatement might not be precluded; *see Red Deer College, op. cit.*).

B. Employee Remedies

1. Damages

360. Where an employee is able to show that his or her dismissal was wrongful, he or she is entitled to sue for damages. The measure of damages is the amount of wages the employee would have been entitled to receive had the correct period of notice been given. Accordingly, at common law an employee often may not be financially 'made whole' for the actual losses that he or she suffered as a consequence of the fact of having been wrongfully dismissed.[1] For example, a wrongfully dismissed employee aged 55 who will probably never find replacement work, and whose employment contract contains an express three months' notice period, would receive compensation for lost wages and benefits up to retirement age of 65 under the 'make whole' method but at common law would only receive lost wages and benefits for a three-month period. This restriction contrasts starkly with the position under statutory unjust discharge schemes and human rights Acts where the adjudicators are empowered to award make whole remedies. Moreover, at common law the employee is only entitled to receive compensation for contractually binding benefits that would vest during the notice period, not for reasonable expectancies that would usually be given but which do not carry contractual freight. Under a make whole approach, however, such reasonable expectancies would be compensable. In addition, the amount due over the notice period will be reduced if the employer can show that the employee had other suitable employment available before that period of notice would have elapsed. This accords with the general law of contract rule that parties adversely affected by a breach of contract have a duty to mitigate their losses.[2] An employee needs not accept any employment; it must be employment of a roughly equivalent kind to that lost. An offer of alternative employment by the terminating employer may be refused if it is unreasonable. It will be adjudged so if the offer is one of lesser wages, responsibility and/or status, or where there has been a breakdown of the personal relationship between management and the employee.[3]

1. *Vorvis* v. *Insurance Corp. of British Columbia* (1989) 58 D.L.R. (4d) 193 (S.C.C.), [1989] 1 S.C.R. 1085.
2. *Red Deer College* v. *Michaels and Finn*, [1975] 5 W.W.R. 575 (S.C.C.), [1976] 2 S.C.R. 324.
3. *Mifsud* v. *MacMillan Bathurst Inc.* (1989) 70 O.R. (2d) 701 (Ont.C.A.). For a description of the case law in Quebec, where similar rules apply, *see* Audet *et al.*, *op cit.*, ch. 7.

361. Until 1997, Canadian courts had refused to deduct from damages for wrongful dismissal any insurance benefits such as short-term sick pay received by the worker during the notice period so long as it could be shown that the employee 'paid' for the benefits in question either directly by contributing a premium to the insurance plan or indirectly by having the employer discount wages by an amount commensurate with what the employee's share of the premium would have been had he or she been compelled to contribute. This rule was cast into doubt in 1997 by the ruling of the Supreme Court of Canada in *Sylvester* v. *British Columbia* that short-term disability benefits received by the employee during the notice period are deductible from wrongful dismissal damages.[1] The Court stated that the intention of the parties alone decides the issue of deductibility. The Court reasoned that since the employee would not have received his full wages while on sick leave had he not been terminated, the parties must not have intended that he receive his full wages if his sick leave coincided with the reasonable notice period following his wrongful dismissal. However, subsequent decisions have construed the *ratio decidendi* of *Sylvestre* as being a more narrow one, namely that the parties do not intend benefits to be deductible if the employee directly or indirectly makes a financial contribution to the insurance plan.[2] Accordingly, the current position approximates closely to the old law as it was before *Sylvestre*. Regarding unemployment benefits, earlier doubts as to whether or not such benefits such be deducted from wrongful dismissal damages were resolved by express amendment of the Unemployment Insurance Act (as it was then called).[3] The Act states that, where the employee has received unemployment insurance benefits, any damages paid to him or her by an employer in lieu of wages in respect of the benefit period, must be remitted to the Receiver General, or if benefits should be payable for such a period, the employer should deduct the appropriate amount from the damages to be paid to the dismissed employee and remit it directly to the Receiver General.

1. (1997), 146 D.L.R. (4d) 207 (S.C.C.), [1997] 2 S.C.R. 315. *See* J.B. Payne, 'Terminating the Disabled Employee in Ontario – Assessing the Impact of *Sylvestre* v. *British Columbia*' (1998) 6 C.L.E.L.J. 99.
2. E.g. *Stills* v. *Children's Aid Society of the City of Belleville et al.*, (1997) 97 C.L.L.C. 210025 (Ont.Gen.Div.); *McKendrick* v. *Open Learning Agency* (1997) 33 C.C.E.L. (2d) 48 (B.C.S.C.).
3. Currently this is contained in the Employment Insurance Act, S.C., 1996, c.23, s.46.

362. An employee entitled to damages for not having been given appropriate notice may seek to pursue his or her claim under the machinery of the minimum standards legislation, if the notice period for which recovery is sought coincides with the statutory minimum or is unlikely to be much greater. Such procedures are quicker, less formal and less costly than the ones prevailing in the judicial system. All that is required in Ontario, for example, is a complaint by word of mouth or letter; an investigation will ensue and, if an employer appeals an adverse order which is subsequently made, a review will be ordered. In some provinces there are enactments which are descendants of very old English Master and Servant Acts. These English statutes were aimed at restricting employees' freedom and they provided stiff criminal penalties for employees for leaving their masters' employ. One of the aspects of this stringent form of regulation was that it was also provided that masters would be committing a criminal offence if they failed to pay externally imposed remuneration. The modern Canadian equivalents provide a summary criminal procedure for the recovery of wages up to a limited amount. The claiming employee lays a complaint against his or her employer for non-payment of wages in the lowest court with criminal jurisdiction. The judge may discharge the employee from the service of the employer found to be in default and order the payment of wages for a certain period, or a lesser amount. In Alberta, reflecting the legislation's ancestry, the magistrate may impose a penalty on the defaulting employer.[1]

1. The Master and Servant Act, R.S.A. 1980, c.M-8. s.4 (limit: lesser of six months or $500) and s.5 (payment of further amounts subject to limits).

363. For a long time, there was strong English[1] and Canadian[2] authority for the proposition that damages should not be awarded for the manner in which a wrongful dismissal took place. But, gradually, the position is changing. It already has been noted that, contrary to the general rule, work is to be provided where working is more important than remuneration, as it is where an actor needs to perform to enhance his or her reputation. Thus, it is possible in such a case for an employee to recover loss of reputation damages. Also, courts had come to accept that, in some circumstances, a fundamental breach of the employment contract by the employer entitles an employee to treat that breach as a repudiation and, therefore, as a discharge without cause. This has come to be known as a constructive dismissal. In *Cox* v. *Philips Industries*[3] an employee was successful because the employer had, in breach of the agreement, not given the plaintiff an opportunity to do work of a prestigious kind. He had been relegated to being a mere cipher, embarrassing and discomfiting him. As this appears to be contrary to the traditional ruling that hurt and grief at dismissal are not compensable, it may well be that analytically this decision should be read down to a holding that to provide the employee with a certain amount of prestige and pleasure was within the parties' contractual expectations and that, therefore, damages were awarded for a breach of contractual term. Moreover, some courts have awarded damages for mental distress under the doctrine of 'aggravated' damages which states that an employee can receive extra compensation over and above breach of the notice obligation where the employer's conduct compounds the mental or economic harm suffered by the employee.[4] In addition, the Supreme Court of Canada has held that mental distress can be compensated if it is can be causally linked to some other actionable wrong than the failure to give due notice of termination.[5] This has inspired courts to find sometimes innovative tort liabilities on the employer's part such as defamation, 'intentional infliction of nervous shock';[6] 'willful or negligent infliction of harassment or oppression';[7] and 'retaliatory discharge'.[8] However, these tort innovations appear to have been nipped in the bud by the 1997 ruling of the Supreme Court of Canada that no such tort of 'bad faith discharge', or its equivalence, exists.[9] Similarly, some courts founded the independent actionable wrong on breach of another term in the employment contract other than the notice obligation, such as an implied promise on the employer's part to treat the employee fairly and decently, especially when invoking dismissal.[10] Again, the Supreme Court of Canada's 1997 ruling in *Wallace* that there is no implied duty of fairness in the employment contract seems to have blocked this potentially fruitful development. However, the *Wallace* ruling does not appear to prevent the court from implying an independent term of fairness in dismissal or other situations if there is concrete evidence that this represents the parties' *actual* intentions, e.g. personnel memoranda promising to respect the employees' dignity and autonomy.[11] However, today the most important vehicle for compensating mental distress is the *Wallace* doctrine which allows the court to extend the period of reasonable notice to reflect bad faith or unprofessionalism on the employer's part in handling the dismissal.[12] If the employer's conduct causes mental distress and meets the threshold of bad faith or unprofessionalism, the notice period may be extended by up to between five to eight months depending on the degree of the employer's blameworthiness and the severity of the harm to the employee. The major limitation with the *Wallace* doctrine, however, is that it is rendered inoperative by an express notice period in the employment contract since such a clause would prevent the court from implying a reasonable notice period. It would be much easier to compensate mental distress if the courts were simply to imply a standardized implied term into all employment contracts requiring the employer to treat its employees fairly and in good faith in all facets of managerial decision-making, including dismissal.

1. *Addis* v. *Gramophone Company Limited*, [1909] A.C. 488 (H.L.). *See* the important critique of this decision by N. Enonchong, 'Breach of Contract and Damages for Mental Distress' (1996) 16 *Ox. Jo. of Legal Studies* 617.
2. *Peso Silver Mines Ltd. (N.P.L.)* v. *Cropper*, [1966] S.C.R. 673 (S.C.C.).
3. [1976] 3 All E.R. 161 (Q.B.); *see also Saint John Shipbuilding Ltd.* v. *Snyders* (1989) 100 N.B.R. (2d) 14 (N.B.C.A.), *Fisher* v. *Eastern Bakeries Ltd.* (1986) 73 N.S.R. (2d) 336 (N.S.S.C.).
4. *Pilon* v. *Peugeot Canada Ltd.* (1980) 29 O.R. (2d) 711; *Rock* v. *Canadian Red Cross* (1995) 5 C.C.E.L. (2d) 231, at 258 (Ont.Gen.Div.); *Ribeiro* v. *C.I.B.C.* (1992) 44 C.C.E.L. 165 (Ont.C.A.).
5. *Vorvis* v. *Insurance Corporation of British Columbia* (1989) 58 D.L.R. (4d) 193 (S.C.C.), [1989] 1 S.C.R. 1085.
6. E.g. *Clark* v. *Canada* (1994) 94 C.L.L.C. 14028, at para. 12149 (Fed.Tr.Div.).
7. E.g. *Rahemtulla* v. *Vanfed Credit Union*, [1984] 3 W.W.R. 296 (B.C.S.C.).
8. E.g. *Ruggerio* v. *Emco Ltd.* (1994) 6 C.C.E.L. (2d) 57 (Ont.Gen.Div.).
9. *Wallace* v. *United Grain Growers Ltd.* (1997) 97 C.L.L.C. 210029, at para. 141213 (S.C.C.), [1998] 3 S.C.R. 701; *Cassady* v. *Wyeth-Ayerst Canada Inc.* (1998) 163 D.L.R. (4d) 1, at 11–12 (B.C.C.A.).
10. E.g. *Bernardini* v. *Alitalia Air Lines*, D.T.E. 93T-519 (1994) 50 C.C.E.L. 156 (Qu.Sup.Ct.); *Leonard* v. *Wilson* (1992) 41 C.C.E.L. 226, at 240 (Ont.Gen.Div.).
11. E.g. *Ditchburn* v. *Landis and Gyr Powers Ltd.* (1997) 29 C.C.E.L. (2d) 199, at 203 (Ont.C.A.).
12. *Wallace* v. *United Grain Growers Ltd.* (1997) 97 C.L.L.C. 210029, at para. 141213 (S.C.C.), [1998] 3 S.C.R. 701, examined *supra*, para. 338.

364. In Quebec, the manner in which a wrongful dismissal takes place is also relevant in assessing compensation. Quebec courts have been willing to indemnify wrongfully dismissed employees for *dommages moraux* such as mental distress, humiliation, anxiety and damage to reputation. A dismissed employee can claim damages on two different grounds. First, it may be argued that the employer committed a fault in the way the dismissal was handled, giving rise to the employer's civil liability.[1] This could be the case when the employer harms the employee's reputation in such a way that it amounts to a tort. Second, the employee may base his or her claim on the abuse of rights theory.[2] If the employer has a contractual right to dismiss an employee, it cannot be used abusively.[3] Following the ruling of the Supreme Court of Canada in *Banque nationale du Canada* v. *Houle*,[4] an employer may abuse its contractual right to terminate an employee when it uses the right in an unfair or unreasonable fashion. Accordingly, it is sufficient to establish that the employer, when terminating the employee, did not exercise its right in a reasonable manner, i.e. a manner consistent with the conduct of a prudent and diligent individual.[5] Moreover, as in the Canadian common law jurisdictions, the notion of 'constructive discharge' has also been referred to in Quebec for a long time.[6] Such a dismissal will occur when the employer unilaterally changes an essential condition of employment.

1. The employer's liability would be based on s.1457, C.c.Q.
2. For a description of the evolution of Quebec case law on the matter, *see* Georges Audet, Robert Bonhomme, Clément Gascon and Magali Cournoyer-Proulx, *Le congédiement en droit québécois* (Cowansville, Quebec: Les Éditions Yvon Blais Inc., 3rd edn., looseleaf), 2–7 to 2–28.
3. S.2092 of the *Code civil du Québec* explicitly refers to this situation.
4. [1990] 3 S.C.R. 122. In this important decision the Supreme Court of Canada confirmed that: '[t]he doctrine of abuse of contractual rights is consistent with the fundamental principles of Quebec civil law, where good faith and reasonableness permeate the theories of rights and obligations, contractual (Art. 1024 C.C.L.C.) as well as extracontractual' (145). A party to a contract generates his or her contractual liability when breaching this implicit duty of good faith and reasonableness.
5. *See*, for example, *Domtar Inc.* v. *St-Germain*, [1991] R.J.Q. 1271 (Q.C.A.).
6. In *Farber* v. *Compagnie Trust Royal*, [1997] 1 S.C.R. 846, the Supreme Court of Canada clearly stated that the notion of 'constructive discharge' exists in civil law as well as in common law.

365. Punitive damages, which are designed to deter unacceptable behaviour rather than compensate the victim, can be awarded against an employer but only in exceptional cases when the employer's misconduct is of the utmost bad faith.[1] Some very high awards have been given. For example, a bank which fraudulently accused an employee with dishonesty in order to engineer his dismissal was forced to pay the employee $50,000 punitive damages,[2] and an employer who brutally exploited a young, female immigrant whom he hired as a nanny was forced to pay her $175,000 punitive damages.[3] In less egregious instances of employer misconduct where punitive damages would not be awarded, the *Wallace* doctrines fills the gap and the reasonable notice period can be extended to take account of such behaviour.[4] Contrary to the common law, the civil law in force in Quebec does not provide for punitive damages, unless expressly specified in a statute.[5] Aside from this very narrow exception, Quebec courts have no jurisdiction to order any kind of punitive damages, regardless of the circumstances in which the discharge takes place.

1. E.g. *Brennan* v. *Henley Publishing Ltd.* (1997) 29 C.C.E.L. (2d) 180, at 188 (B.C.C.A.).
2. *Ribeiro* v. *C.I.B.C.* (1992) 44 C.C.E.L. 165 (Ont.C.A.).
3. *Mustaji* v. *Tjin* (1998) 98 C.L.L.C. 210051 (B.C.C.A.).
4. *Supra*, para. 338.
5. C.c.Q., s.1621. It is the case in s.49(2) of the Charter of Human Rights and Freedoms, R.S.Q., c.C-12.

366. An employee can sue to recover benefits owed under the employment contract in the civil courts in the usual way. Regarding statutory benefits, the legislation in question typically contains cheap, informal and relatively expeditious enforcement machinery for enforcing and collecting on such rights. In the event that the employer goes into bankruptcy, special considerations come into play by virtue of the federal Bankruptcy Act. These matters must be considered beyond the scope of this essay.[1]

1. For a complete analysis *see* England *et al.*, *op. cit.*, vol. 2, ch.19.

2. Quantum meruit

367. This common law means of recovery was discussed earlier.[1] It will be available where there is no enforceable contract in existence, or where the employer's conduct is of such a kind that the employee is entitled to treat it as a repudiation and, therefore, to rescind the contract. The employee may then recover remuneration for the actual work done. He or she is not entitled to sue for damages on the basis of being entitled to notice and then for a *quantum meruit*. This remedy will seldom be of use to an employee, although it may be a way to recover remuneration for work done under a contract which is interpreted as not requiring pay unless a specified period of employment is completed.

1. *Supra*, paras. 214–15.

3. *Specific performance*

368. Canadian courts have traditionally refused to grant an equitable order such as specific performance or a mandatory injunction which would have the effect of forcing an employer to reinstate a wrongfully dismissed employee or otherwise carry out the terms of the employment contract. Various arguments have been advanced to justify this practice but only one of them has any practical force.[1] The practical problem with reinstating or otherwise forcing an employer to observe a contractual term such as a disciplinary hearing is to ensure full and honest compliance with the order on the employer's part. This is very difficult to do in the non-organized sector where there is no trade union in the workplace to police the order. Nevertheless, there are limited circumstances in which Canadian courts have granted an order to reinstate a wrongfully dismissed employee. One is where the employee derives a substantial element of vocational, professional or psychological value from his or her job, which can only be obtained by actually performing it. For example, a United Church priest who was fired in breach of a dismissal procedure expressly incorporated into his employment contract was reinstated on an interim basis pending the full trial of his wrongful dismissal suit because of the unique benefit he received from actually doing his job.[2] In a similar vein, a Quebec trial court in 1993 granted an interlocutory injunction to prevent the dismissal of a symphony conductor in order to enable him to appear in an important upcoming performance.[3] And in 1994 the Quebec Court of Appeal issued an interlocutory injunction to prevent the discharge of a company president in order to permit him to keep a close eye on the operation of the business in which he was a large majority shareholder.[4] Therefore, it cannot be said that the door to specific performance is permanently locked in Canada. For example, one situation where the remedy could be especially appropriate is if the employer has violated a disciplinary procedure incorporated into the contract and the employee simply wants the court to order the employer to do what it had originally promised to do in any event.

1. The arguments are examined in England *et al.*, *op. cit.*, vol. 2, paras. 16.5–16.17.
2. *McCaw* v. *United Church of Canada* (1991) 38 C.C.E.L. 214 (Ont.C.A.).
3. *Boivin* v. *Orchester Symphonique de Laval 1984 Inc.* (1993) 43 C.C.E.L. 304 (Qu.Sup.Ct.).
4. *Computertime Network Corp.* v. *Zucker* (1994) 11 C.C.E.L. (2d) 102 (Qu.C.A.).

Part II. Collective Labour Relations

Chapter I. Trade Unions and Their Organizations

§1. Trade Union Membership and Characteristics

369. Historically, one of the most important features of the modern Canadian trade union movement has been that much of it was international in nature. International in this context means that the unions are American and Canadian in composition. There is still a significant degree of membership in international unions but there has been a significant trend towards greater membership in non-international unions in recent years, as revealed by the membership statistics discussed below. In Chapter IV of the Introduction (*supra*), some of the major political, economic and social circumstances which gave rise to developments of unionism in Canada were noted.

A. Size and Number of Trade Unions

370. The *Directory of Labour Organizations*, a publication of Labour Canada, reports that at the beginning of 1998, union membership stood at 3,938,000, the lowest level in ten years. This figure represents 32.5 per cent of non-agricultural paid workers and about 25.6 per cent of the total workforce. This represents a significant decline from 1992 when the comparable numbers were membership of 4,089,000 and 37.4 per cent and 30 per cent respectively. The highest rates of unionization in 1998 were found in public sector-dominated industries. In 1998 and 1999 public sector union density stood at approximately 71 per cent. The largest unions at the beginning of 1998 were the Canadian Union of Public Employees (C.L.C.) with 389,300 members, the National Union of Public and General Employees (C.L.C.) with 309,000 members, the National Automobile, Aerospace, Transportation and General Workers Union of Canada (A.F.L.-C.I.O./C.L.C.) with 222,500 members and the United Food and Commercial Workers International Union (A.F.L.-C.I.O./C.L.C.) with 200,000 members. International unions made up 29.9 per cent of total union membership in 1998, a significant decline from levels of 34.6 per cent in 1992 and 44.7 per cent in 1981.

International and National Unions by Size, 1997–8

Membership Range	*International Unions, 1997*	*International Unions, 1998*	*National Unions 1997*	*National Unions 1998*	*Total 1997*	*Total 1998*
Under 999	7	6	81	86	88	92
1,000–9,999	21	19	107	101	128	120
10,000–29,999	10	10	22	23	32	33
30,000–49,999	5	6	13	12	18	18
50,000–99,999	6	5	5	4	11	9
100,000 and over	2	2	5	5	7	7
Total	**51**	**48**	**233**	**231**	**284**	**279**

Union Members in International and National Unions (000s), 1997–8

Membership Range	*International Unions, 1997*	*International Unions, 1998*	*National Unions 1997*	*National Unions 1998*	*Total 1997*	*Total 1998*
Under 999	1	1	32	35	33	36
1,000–9,999	91	73	352	346	444	419
10,000–29,999	152	154	642	388	493	542
30,000–49,999	170	221	495	489	664	710
50,000–99,999	406	348	339	289	745	637
100,000 and over	397	380	1,103	1,009	1,500	1,389
Total	**1,217**	**1,177**	**2,663**	**2,556**	**3,879**	**3,733**

Union Membership in Canada, 1978–1998 (Non-Agricultural Paid Employment and the Labour Force) Total and Average Annual Percentage Changes

	1978–98	*1978–92*	*1992–98*
Union Membership	20.1 (0.9)	24.7 (1.6)	–3.7
Non-Agricultural Paid Employment	37.0 (1.6)	29.6 (1.9)	5.7
Labour Force	41.4 (1.75)	32.7 (2.0)	6.6

All charts above from *Directory of Labour Organizations in Canada*, 1998.

371. Despite significant increases in union density for female workers from 1974 to 1989, in recent years there has been a decline. Between 1974 and 1979 the membership of women in unions increased by 4 per cent; by 1982 their level stood at 32.3 per cent; by 1989, it was 39.1 per cent.[1] However, by 1999 the union density rate for women workers had fallen to just under 30 per cent. This was very close to the union density rate of approximately 31 per cent for men in 1999. The decline in union density has been felt most sharply in the private sector, where it fell from 19.1 per cent to 18.2 per cent from 1998–9. At the same time public sector density remained fairly stable at around 71 per cent, although due to the decline in public sector employment this represented a decline in real numbers of public sector union members. Union density is also much higher among full-time workers (about one in three) than part-time workers (about one in five) or workers with non-permanent jobs (one in four). In 1999 high rates of union density were found among the following types of workers and occupations: employees aged 45–54 (43 per cent); those with university degrees (35.4 per cent); employees in educational services (68.9 per cent), utilities (65 per cent) and public administration (64 per cent); and health care workers (64 per cent). The lowest rates of union density were found among the following groups: youths aged 15–24 (11 per cent); workers in Alberta (22 per cent); agricultural workers (3.8 per cent); professional, scientific and technical industry workers (4.5 per cent); and managers (10 per cent).[2]

1. Corporate and Labour Union Reporting Act, *Annual report*, 1989.
2. Akyeampong, 'Unionization: An Update' (1999) Autumn, *Perspectives* 45 (based on 1999 Statistics Canada Labour Force Survey).

Male and Female Membership, 1998–9

	*1998**			*1999**		
		Union Density			*Union Density*	
	Total Employees '000	*Members* %	*Coverage*** %	*Total Employees* '000	*Members* %	*Coverage*** %
Both Sexes	11,613	30.7	33.3	11,905	30.1	32.6
Men	6,053	31.6	34.4	6,167	30.9	33.5
Women	5,560	29.8	32.0	5,738	29.3	31.6

* January–June average.
** Union members and persons who are not members but are covered by collective agreements.
Source: Statistics Canada – 1999 Labour Force Survey reported in Akyeampong, *supra*.

B. Internationalism and Nationalism

372. A fallacious impression would be given if it was thought that the formal structure of international trade unions meant that Canadian members of such unions were completely dominated by American governing bodies. This may be the case in some unions, but often, regardless of the formal structure, the Canadian branches of international unions have assumed a great deal of autonomy over their everyday affairs. Frequently such branches represent districts of the international unions. For example, the Eastern and Western Canadian branches of the United Steelworkers form Districts 5 and 6 of that union, with all the autonomy of all other districts of that union in the United States. This permits control over bargaining, political and social activity and most internal trade union matters. The National Association of Broadcast Employees and Technicians has a relatively autonomous Canadian division, some former Canadian branches of American unions have formed completely autonomous bodies, such as the Communication Workers and the Canadian Paperworkers Union.

373. In addition, the 8th Canadian Labour Congress Constitutional Conference resolved that, in respect of Canadian autonomy in international unions, certain minimum standards ought to be followed. They included the election of Canadian officers by Canadian members. In some affiliates of the C.L.C., officers of the Canadian sections of the international unions are appointed by the International Executive. Although this C.L.C. guideline is voluntary in nature, it has had an effect. For example, the Seafarers' International Union permits its Canadian membership to elect Canadian officers and the Canadian membership of the United Steelworkers of America elects one national director and three district directors who sit on the international's executive. The C.L.C. Conference also resolved that policies of Canadian concern should be dealt with by Canadian elected officers and that Canadian officers should have authority to speak for their members in Canada. All of this created a climate of consciousness in international affiliates of the C.L.C. of the need to accommodate Canadian national aspirations. Further, as has been noted, the increase in white collar unionism increases the influence of national affiliates in the C.L.C. This too has had some influence in persuading the international unions to give more formal, as well as informal, autonomy to Canadian unions.

§2. The Canadian Labour Congress

374. *Labour Organizations in Canada*, 1998, reported that in 1998, 2,626,740 members were affiliated with the C.L.C. But, this number fell less than total union membership so that the percentage of the C.L.C.'s membership of total union members grew from 65.6 per cent in 1997, to 66.7 per cent in 1998. The second largest central union organization, the Confédération des syndicats nationaux (C.S.N.), declined in membership from 251,420 in 1997 to 242,830 in 1998. Its share of total union membership in Canada was 6.2 per cent in 1998. The Canadian Confederation of Labour (C.F.L.) experienced a rapid decline in membership in the 1990s and ceased to exist in September 1997. Other smaller labour affiliation organizations are referred to in the chart opposite.

Union Membership by Type of Union and Affiliation, 1998

Type and Affiliation	*Unions*	*Locals*	*Membership Number*	*Membership Percentage*
International Unions	**42**	**2,761**	**1,176,980**	**29.9**
(A.F.L.-C.I.O./C.L.C.)	34	2,571	1,090,000	27.7
C.L.C. only	2	29	4,240	0.12
A.F.L.-C.I.O. only	10	153	82,510	2.1
Unaffiliated Unions	2	8	230	0.0
National Unions	**231**	**13,852**	**2,556,400**	**64.9**
C.L.C.	57	7,217	1,531,700	38.9
C.S.N.	9	2,399	242,830	6.2
C.E.Q.[1]	14	305	113,510	2.9
C.C.U.[2]	9	38	17,020	0.4
C.S.D.[3]	2	100	14,070	0.4
Unaffiliated Unions	140	3,793	637,270	16.2
Directly Chartered Unions	**400**		**59,800**	**1.5**
C.S.D.	390		5,900	1.5
C.L.C.	10		800	0.0
Independent Local Organizations	**352**		**144,610**	**3.7**
Total	**1,031**	**16,613**	**3,937,790**	**100.0**

1. Centrale de l'enseignement du Québec (since 2000, Centrale des Syndicats du Québec).
2. Confederation of Canadian Unions.
3. Centrale des syndicats démocratiques.

Source: *Directory of Labour Organizations in Canada*, 1998.

375. The C.L.C. consists, thus, of international and national affiliates. It includes 12 provincial and territorial affiliated federations which look after provincial and territorial jurisdictional matters in respect of the provincial and territorial branches of the affiliates of the C.L.C. It also includes 125 district labour councils. Amongst the major functions of the C.L.C. are the promotion of trade unionism and the protection of its members' rights. It has power to look for more members and has created organizing committees to this end. The C.L.C. has power to directly grant charters to unions, making them C.L.C. affiliates. But, in line with its aim to preserve existing unions, it is not to do so where the grant of a charter would mean the creation of a union whose jurisdiction would conflict with that of an affiliated national or international union. In a similar vein, the constitution of the C.L.C. forbids any of its members from seeking to organize workers where another has existing collective bargaining rights or rights to deal on behalf of certain workers (which is known as having a working relationship). Further where some members agree to merge, thereby blurring jurisdictional lines, the C.L.C. has to approve of the agreement. An impartial umpire may be appointed to this end. In determining whether or not C.L.C. guidelines are being infringed regard can only be had to what the concerned members' jurisdiction has been in the past, not to what it ought to be. The C.L.C. has moral authority, but very few sanctions to enforce these guidelines. It can, where a member has offended the C.L.C. rules (by raiding, espousing totalitarianism, acting discriminatorily, etc.) expel a member union if the majority of members so decide at the C.L.C. convention.

A. Structure of the Canadian Labour Congress

376. Conventions are held every three years. All members and local unions are entitled to send delegates and present resolutions. Approximately 2500 delegates attend the conventions. The triennial convention elects four full-time salaried executive officers, a president, a secretary-treasurer and two executive vice-presidents. Between conventions the governing body of the C.L.C. is the Executive Council, comprised of 42 non-salaried representatives of the unions within the Congress. The resolutions presented at the triennial conventions, if adopted, form the policy to be followed by the C.L.C. The C.L.C. frequently presents submissions to government in line with these policies, the provincial representative federations of the C.L.C. contacting the provincial legislatures, the C.L.C. lobbying the federal Parliament. Such submissions are not restricted to bread and butter labour issues. As well as being related to labour legislation, they may include briefs on the economic situation, wage and price guidelines, regional economic development, bilingualism, consumer affairs, immigration and the like. In recent years the C.L.C. has been quite active in lobbying the federal government concerning its trade policy and the need to incorporate protection for labour standards and freedom of association in both bilateral and multilateral international trade agreements. In addition, there has been a movement in the C.L.C. to assert itself as a major participant in executive decision-making at the national level. The notion is that major employer groupings, the C.L.C. and government should consult and negotiate on a formal, recurring basis in respect of matters affecting their and the nation's interests. This has met with great opposition from some trade unionists who view the development with suspicion because they see it as a potential aggrandization of autonomy for the C.L.C. as a body separate from its member unions. But there has been an increased role for the C.L.C. (and to a lesser extent other trade union umbrella groups) in such consultation processes. In 1985, more than 130 representatives of labour, business and the community participated in the National Economic Conference sponsored by the federal government. At about the same time the federal government agreed to fund the Canadian Labour Market and Productivity Centre, an organization designed to bring together labour, business and government leaders on an ongoing basis to grapple with labour market and productivity issues with the benefit of expert consultation and research. In 1999 the name of the Centre was changed to the Canadian Labour and Business Centre to reflect the fact that it is intended to be a permanent institution to bring together the labour and business communities to deal with common problems with senior government leaders. In 1999 the board of directors was comprised of 37 people, 11 from the C.L.C. and other national labour organizations, 10 representatives of business, 3 representatives of the federal government, 11 representatives of provincial and territorial governments, and 2 representatives of the academic community. The C.L.C. also participates in other consultative bodies.

377. The C.L.C. provides research facilities and publicity for its members. It also has set up extensive educational programmes, including schools on bargaining, administration of agreements and on organizing. Through the International Confederation of Free Trade Unions, the C.L.C. maintains and supports ties with trade unions all over the world. In addition, it has worked closely with the International Labour Organization (United Nations). The C.L.C. has also worked over the years to become actively involved with other social justice groups inside and outside Canada. For example, it has developed close ties with women's groups, seniors' organizations, anti-poverty activists, environmentalists, peace activists, churches and other groups seeking social and economic equality.

1. The international–national debate

378. Canadian trade union development was described in Chapter IV (*supra*, Introduction). It was noted that there has always been both a symbiotic relationship between the American and Canadian trade union movement as well as a tension born out of nationalist and political differences. This remains true as the reasons for the development of international unionism may be reinvigorated by the shift towards a global economy and international competition among multinational corporations. The extent to which globalism lessens the ability of national governments to regulate economic activity to protect workers' interests may shift increasing attention towards international solidarity among workers as a means to protect their interests. It is fair to say that, until relatively recently (most notably the success of the C.A.W.), the best conditions have been obtained by workers represented by major international unions. As times for workers get tougher generally, it may be that the old arguments about a different political role for trade unions will be raised again. That trend was evident in the federal election of 1979, when the union movement in Canada openly set out to support the N.D.P. This development was not without opposition in the labour movement. This opposition argued that non-party politically based alliances had served the business unionism of international unions well. Despite some evidence that such a political role for unions helped elect N.D.P. governments in British Columbia and Ontario in the early 1990s, there has generally not been a consistent unified political approach by trade unions in Canadian elections in recent years.

379. Similarly, the sharpening of Quebec's desire for greater autonomy underscored a potential problem relating to international unionism. Unions in Quebec in which franco-Canadians are not given a primary role have become less viable. The Confédération des syndicats nationaux is the modern descendant of what was a Quebec-based Catholic union movement. The Fédération des Travailleurs du Québec (F.T.Q.) is the numerically dominant trade union representative group. It is associated with the Canadian Labour Congress and, therefore, international unionism. It often complained of the fact that, until fairly recently, international unions were insensitive to the French fact of Quebec by, for instance, publishing their newspapers in English.

380. One of the great attractions of international unionism in Canada is said to be that, because of the huge size of this country, its small scattered population and quite disparate regional needs, it is difficult for a union to provide adequate collective bargaining resources. Being associated with an American-based union which, because of its sheer size can provide coordination, expertise and funds, makes independent, small unions, which are sensitive to local needs, viable. This very benefit has always had the seeds for dissidence inherent in it. Canadian branches of international unions sometimes feel that they are neglected and actually pay more in dues to the international parent than is returned by way of services in the form of advice, administration and strike funds. Sometimes figures in reports made under the Corporations and Labour Unions Returns Act[1] are cited in support of such claims. A somewhat contradictory argument is occasionally raised by people who oppose the presence of international unions. It is that the viability of so many small unions (because of their support by giant American unions) prevents the development of multi-craft, multi-industry Canadian unionism.

1. R.S.C. 1985, c.C-43.

381. Overall, as the reproduced tables show, the dominance of international unionism is waning. Inasmuch as international unions command a declining proportion of the unionized workforce, this is, in part, due to the increase of unionism in the public sectors where American unions are clearly inapposite. So far, however, these emerging national unions have, in the main, affiliated themselves with the C.L.C., the body through which the internationals operate in Canada. They do not seem to feel uncomfortable at all about this co-existence. In the 1980s one of the stalwarts of industrial unionism in Canada, the national branch of the United Automobile Workers, sought more autonomy within the international union. It met with opposition from the international. A bitter disagreement between the Canadian branch and the international's executive arose some time later when the American sections agreed to contract terms which were unacceptable to the Canadian leadership. The Canadians set their own agenda and struck without the support of the international. An agreement was reached which adversely affected some bargaining units in the U.S. This series of events proved to be a catalyst and what had been a demand for more autonomy within the international was transformed into a claim for separation. A separation settlement was reached in March 1985 which gave the Canadian union a proportion of the strike funds, albeit much less than the 10 per cent it had claimed. The significance of this rupture goes beyond the actual case. The automobile workers' union is a central organization, industrially and politically. Its re-organization into a national union has symbolic importance. Morcover, the leadership has set out to promote Canadian nationalism in the trade union movement and it has sought in recent years to merge with some Canadian locals of international unions. In addition, in recent years the Canadian Association of Industrial, Mechanical and Allied Workers, a committed nationalist union which was formed to avow its nationalism, amalgamated with the C.A.W. Canadian national unionism thrived in the 1980s and early 1990s.

382. As has been noted, there has been a dramatic and complete reversal in membership numbers for national and international unions. In 1965, international unions contributed 67 per cent of total union membership. By 1998, this had come down to less than 30 per cent.[1] In the 1980s there was an explosion of new national unions (the C.A.W. being the largest one, of course) so that, between 1986 and 1988, 45 per cent of growth in national union membership was due to new union formation. Since then this movement has settled down. For instance, in 1989, only 15 per cent of growth in national union membership could be attributed to new union formation. Most of the growth was due to the increased membership of existing national unions.[2] Nevertheless, by 1998 national unions comprised almost 65 per cent of total union membership.[3]

1. 'Union Membership by Type of Union and Affiliation' (1998) *Directory of Labour Organizations in Canada*, 1998.
2. Corporations and Labour Union Reporting Act, *Annual Report*, 1992.
3. *Supra*, note 1.

§3. Legal Status of Trade Unions

A. At Common Law

383. Trade unions are groups of people who have come together to further their interest by acting in concert. They intend to combine in the giving and withholding of their members' labour to control the amount and kind of labour available. This will enable them to improve their bargaining position *vis-à-vis* potential employers. This notion of unions as representatives of employees which have interests that are adversarial to those of employers is endorsed by collective bargaining legislation such as that of Ontario which requires that a trade union has a constitution which specifies its objectives in this way.

384. At common law this made trade unions bodies which had purposes in restraint of trade. As such they were illegal bodies and thus were not recognized as legal entities for the purposes of suing and being sued. In addition, not being corporations or natural persons, they were, for the purposes of law, merely unincorporated or voluntary associations. That is, even if their purpose had not been in restraint of trade, they were merely to be treated as clubs were by the law. In nineteenth-century England this meant that trade unionists (but not necessarily trade unions) easily could be attacked as criminals, that they could not enforce agreements they obtained and that they could not protect their property. Despite these barriers, the development of trade unionism blossomed and legislation remedying the situation was passed.

385. In all jurisdictions, including Quebec, the common law position was the same. In 1872, an equivalent of the 1871 English Trade Unions Act was passed.[1] It defined a trade union as a body which, but for the statute, would have been treated as unlawful because its purposes were in restraint of trade. The effect of this has been, as will be shown below, that courts have treated trade unions as entities which can sue and be sued. But, as the Act only applies to registered trade unions and very few unions have ever been registered, it is of minimal effect. In addition, there is a serious question as to whether or not the federal legislation is constitutionally valid. The argument is that inasmuch as it deals with civil rights and property questions, the jurisdiction to legislate is properly vested in provincial legislatures.[2] At the same time as it enacted the Trade Unions Act in1872, Parliament also amended the Criminal Code to declare that the purposes of trade unions were no longer unlawful merely because they were in restraint of trade. However, the amendments did not generally provide unions with protection for the means they used to achieve their purposes.[3]

1. The Canadian Trade Unions Act, 1872, 35 Vict. c.30., now Trade Unions Act, R.S.C. 1985, c.T-14.
2. *Chase* v. *Starr*, [1924] 4 D.L.R. 55; *Polakoff* v. *Winters Garment*, [1928] 2 D.L.R. 277; *Amalgamated Builders' Council* v. *Herman*, [1930] 2 D.LR. 513.
3. Criminal Law Amendment Act, 1872, 35 Vict. c.31; *see* generally the discussion of the history of this legislation in McNeil, Lynk and Engelmann, *Trade Union Law in Canada* (Aurora: Canada Law Book, 1994).

386. The English and Canadian nineteenth-century statutes provided that agreements entered into by trade unions would not be unenforceable merely because they were in restraint of trade, nor were the members of a trade union liable to criminal prosecution merely because the union had such purposes. By registration, trade unions could enable themselves to transfer property from trustee to trustee and empower trustees to bring or defend actions concerned with the property rights and claims of the union. The protection against criminal prosecution proved inadequate. The criminal law was amended to give immunity to a charge of criminal conspiracy if the relevant conduct engaged in took place during a trade dispute as was defined. It also delimited the area of molestation and obstruction which would give rise to criminal responsibility by defining the circumstances in which watching and besetting (commonly referred to as picketing) was an excusable practice.[1]

1. Criminal Code, R.S.C. 1985 c.C-46, ss.422, 423.

387. The upshot of all this was that trade unions had some, but not all, of the attributes with which a legal person such as a corporation or a natural person were endowed. Agreements between trade union members as to how they were to transact business or as to how they were to be employed were unenforceable. Agreements about how trade union funds were to be used, how penalties were to be imposed, how subscriptions were to be raised and paid, were all also unenforceable. This legislation advanced the cause of trade unions inasmuch as they could use concerted action, protect their property and escape some internal financial structures, although they were hampered in their fund-gathering activities and imposition of internal discipline. But the English judiciary, which seemed set on inhibiting trade unionism, used this pro-trade union legislation to do so.

388. The courts had developed the torts of inducing a breach of contract and civil conspiracy. These torts did not present trade unions as such with much of a threat after the passing of the 1871–6 legislative measures. Trade unions had been partially legalized, but had not been made into legal entities which could sue and be sued apart from the statute. In 1901, in *Taff Vale Railway*, the English House of

Lords decided that a trade union could be sued in its registered name.[1] It is not clear from the judgments whether they were merely saying that to hold the union responsible in this way was a convenient way of allowing representative actions or that they could be read as saying that, as a result of the legislation, trade unions had acquired sufficient attributes to become an entity which could sue and be sued as a corporation could. In any event, the threat to trade unions was so great that the English legislature passed a statute in 1906 to overcome the problems presented by the judicial reasoning.[2] In 1901 a precursor of the Bill which finally overcame the effects of *Taff Vale* had been presented in England. A similar Act had been passed in British Columbia in 1902. The effect of this statute was to ban actions of a civil kind against trade unions. This Act was replaced in 1959.[3] Apart from that, Canadian jurisdictions have not passed protective legislation of the English kind. The decision in *Taff Vale* can, theoretically, only burden unions registered under the federal Trade Unions Act 1872, although occasionally courts have held unregistered trade unions capable of suing and being sued, perhaps on a seemingly mistaken notion of the applicability of English doctrine in Canada.[4] It is to be noted, however, that *dicta* in the Supreme Court of Canada suggested that the *Taff Vale* doctrine applies to unregistered unions.[5]

1. *Taff Vale Railway* v. *Amalgamated Society of Railway Servants*, [1901] A.C. 426. Similarly based decisions include *Amalgamated Society of Railway Servants* v. *Osborne* [1910] A.C. 87 and *Bonsor* v. *Musicians' Union*, [1956] A.C. 104.
2. Trade Disputes Act 1906, 6 Edw. VII c.47.
3. Trade Unions Act of 1902 (B.C.) replaced by Trade Unions Act, R.S.B.C. 1960, c.384.
4. *Metallic Roofing Co.* v. *Amalgamated Sheet Metal Workers' International Association* (1903) 5 O.L.R. 424 held: unregistered unions were not suable entities; to the contrary; *Centre Star Mining* v. *Rossland Miners* (1902) 9 B.C.R. 403.
5. *International Longshoremen's Association, Local 273* v. *Maritime Employers' Association* (1978) 89 D.L.R. (3d) 289, 296–302; [1979] 1 S.C.R. 120.

389. Apart from the effect of that federal statute, the question of legal personality of trade unions in common law jurisdictions in Canada is determined by nineteenth- and early twentieth-century English common law as understood in Canada, except where it is varied by collective bargaining regime principles. In Quebec, trade unions encountered similar difficulties and, as will be seen below, legislation was necessary in order to provide them with partial or total legal personality.

B. Under Collective Bargaining

390. It is obviously impossible to treat trade unions as if they were unincorporated or voluntary associations which have no legal personality of their own for the purposes of the legislative collective bargaining schemes in Canada. The essence of those schemes is that trade unions are to be participants in their own right. They are parties to enforceable collective agreements: they are responsible for the administration of the agreements; they may complain and be guilty of unfair labour practices as defined by the schemes; they are fixed with the responsibility of ensuring compliance by their members with statutes and agreements; they are, as trade unions, forbidden from engaging in discriminatory practices contrary to human rights legislation or anti-discriminatory provisions of the collective bargaining statutes. Manifestly, trade unions have been given sufficient legal status under the regimes to accept and enjoy these responsibilities and privileges. But, because of the reluctant judicial acceptance of trade unionism, there is no clear statement that trade unions are legal entities in the same way as corporations or natural persons. Conceptual difficulties remain as various jurisdictions have adopted differing resolutions of intractable problems.

391. Ontario and Saskatchewan, reacting to the common law situation and wishing to put trade unions in a position where they could use concerted conduct to bargain effectively, enacted legislation which defined trade unions as unincorporated associations. That is, they were groups which could neither sue nor be sued as entities, unless the common law permitted it. This meant that a trade union could not be made a party to a court action unless it could be the subject of such an action in the absence of the provisions of labour relations legislation or the rights of labour legislation.[1] But, for the purposes of collective bargaining they were to be treated as entities, capable of enforcing collective agreements, enforcing arbitrators' awards, being subjected to prosecution, forcing the labour relations' board to carry out its functions, etc. Thus, although trade unions are not legal entities for all purposes, they can act as such for many significant ones.

1. Rights of Labour Act, R.S.O. 1990, c.R-33; The Trade Union Act, R.S.S. 1978, c.T-17.

392. Alberta, British Columbia, Manitoba and New Brunswick have directly achieved the above position by making unions legal entities capable of suing and being sued for the purposes of the reigning collective bargaining statutes.[1] In Ontario and Nova Scotia, the collective bargaining legislation provides that trade unions may be prosecuted or prosecute in their own name for violations of the labour relations legislation and for suits for the enforcement of labour board and arbitration orders.[2] The Canada Labour Code is narrower in scope in that it provides only that a trade union has legal status for the purpose of prosecutions under the labour code.[3] The Newfoundland and Prince Edward Island statutes provide that unions should be treated as legal entities in a general sense.[4] In Quebec, too, a similar result has been achieved through legislation. The Professional Syndicates Act,[5] adopted in 1924, allows 15 persons or more, engaged in the same employment or profession, or in similar trades, to form a professional syndicate and to have their association incorporated as such. Professional syndicates may own property, sue and be sued, enter into collective agreements and have those agreements enforced as a regular contract. This incorporation has always been available to trade unions on a voluntary basis. Furthermore, under the Code of Civil Procedure,[6] any group with a common purpose which has no legal personality and is not a partnership, may defend any action at law against it as an entity. It may also institute, as an entity, any legal proceedings provided that it deposits an appropriately authorized certificate stating it is a trade union within the meaning of the Labour Code.

1. Labour Relations Code, S.A. 1988, c.L-1.2, s.23; Industrial Relations Code, S.B.C. c.212, s.154; Labour Relations Act, S.M. 1987, c.L-10, s.150(3); Industrial Relations Act, R.S.N.B. 1973, c.I-4, s.114(2).

2. Ontario Labour Relations Act, 1995, S.O. 1995, c.1, s.107 and s.108; Trade Union Act, R.S.N.S. 1989, c.475, s.79.
3. Canada Labour Code, R.S.C. 1985, c.L-2, s.103.
4. Labour Relations Act, R.S.N. 1990, c.L-1, s.141; Labour Act, R.S.P.E.I. 1988, c.L-1, s.44.
5. R.S.Q., c.S-40. For a complete description of the Quebec law on the matter, *see* Pierre Verge and Gregor Murray, *Le droit et les syndicats* (Sainte-Foy: Les Presses de l'Université Laval, 1991) 112–33.
6. R.S.Q. c.C-25, s.60.

393. As can be seen, the statutory provision of legal personality is, with two exceptions, not of a kind which equates trade unions with natural persons or corporations. It does seem clear that for the purposes of collective bargaining legislation, the courts are to treat trade unions as fully capable legal entities. A Supreme Court of Canada decision has made this explicit in a case concerned with the federal statute.[1] Inasmuch as trade unions are involved in causes of action arising outside the collective bargaining sphere, there is uncertainty.[2] A great deal seems to depend on the context in which the question is posed.[3] It is clear, however, that trade unions may be convicted of criminal contempt;[4] on the other hand, when the principles relating to the governance of internal trade union affairs are examined below, we shall see that trade unions involved in collective bargaining are still treated as unincorporated associations.

1. *International Longshoremen's Association* v. *Maritime Employers* (1978) 89 D.L.R. (3d) 289; [1979] 1 R.C.S. 120.
2. This could even be said about Newfoundland and Prince Edward Island where the statutes simply say trade unions are legal entities. A court could read that as implying that this could only apply to the incidents relating to the empowering statute. *See* generally chapter 1 of McNeil *et al., Trade Union Law in Canada, op. cit.* Note that in *ILA* v. *MEA* it was suggested, *obiter dicta*, that trade unions were entities for all employment related purposes.
3. For example, in *Teamsters, Local 213* v. *Therien* (1960) 22 D.L.R. (2d) 1 (S.C.C.), ([1960] S.C.R. 265), the Supreme Court held that an unregistered union which was subject to B.C. collective bargaining legislation had legal capacity to be sued at common law for tortious interference with business relations by a plaintiff who was refused continued employment with the employer after the union threatened to picket the employer if the plaintiff was retained. However, the Court's ruling that the union had legal status for both statutory purposes and common law actions was based both on the fact it was recognized as a legal entity for the purposes of the Labour Relations Act and on the provisions of the B.C. Trade Union Act which set out circumstances in which a union could not be held liable for damages for actions done for purposes of a labour dispute. The Court inferred from the protection from liability for specified circumstances that there was an intention to allow for liability of other types of common law actions. This latter point undermines the significance of the case for a general finding of legal status for common law actions based simply on recognition of unions as legal entities in general collective bargaining statutes for the purposes of proceedings under those statutes.
4. *United Nurses of Alberta* v. *A.G. Alberta* [1992] C.L.L.C. 14,023 (S.C.C.); [1992] 1 S.C.R. 901.

C. Representative Actions

394. As it is possible that, apart from some specific circumstances, a trade union cannot sue or be sued as an entity in its own right, recourse may have to be had to the use of a representative action. The notion is that unincorporated associations could sue or be sued in their name if certain requirements were met.

These were that, in respect of the right in controversy, the members of the association had a community of interest. Where this could be established, members who were properly constituted representatives of the unincorporated association – union in our case – could appear to bring or to defend an action. The Rules of Court of each jurisdiction provided for this means of conducting a judicial proceeding. What was had to be shown that the members bringing the action comprised a class with identical interests,[1] or that, if a trade union was a defendant, different members of the union did not have separate individual defences. Again, if the trade union initiated proceedings in this form, a defendant would be enabled to defeat the form of the action if s/he could show that s/he would have different defences against different members of the trade union which was bringing the action as a representative. Perhaps the most important limitation when bringing a tortious suit against a trade union in this way is that, should a judgment against the trade union be obtained, a question will arise as to how the judgment is to be satisfied. It has been held that unless the plaintiff can show at the outset that the unincorporated association has set aside a special fund out of which such debts can be paid, a court will not allow a representative action to be brought against the association.[2] But note that, despite these difficulties, injunctions prohibiting picketing have been granted frequently against trade unions on a representative basis.[3]

1. *Ross* v. *C.N.R.*, [1927] 3 W.W.R. 405; *Ackworth & McNair* v. *General Accident Assurance & Edwards* (1962) 31 D.L.R. (2d) 352, and *see* for application *Winnipeg Builders' Exchange* v. *Operative Pasterers* 50 W.W.R. 72.
2. *Body* v. *Murdoch*, [1954] O.W.N. 515; *Smith Transport* v. *Baird*, [1957] O.W.N. 405; *Anderson Block & Tile* v. *Mior*, [1961] O.W.N. 282.
3. *Cotter* v. *Osborne*, [1911] A.C. 137; *Canaday's Apparel* v. *Ross* (1957) 8 D.L.R. (2d) 273.

395. There is some authority for the proposition that where a trade union is a normal legal entity as a result of collective bargaining, it may not be appropriate to allow a representative action to be brought against it.[1] More clearly, in Ontario, where a trade union may not sue or be sued as a result of the 1943 Rights of Labour Act, an attempt to make a trade union liable by way of a representative action was defeated on the basis that this would undermine the objects of that legislation.[2] Nevertheless, Ontario courts have on several occasions upheld the use of representative actions to sue members of a union in tort provided that the plaintiff could establish that there was a trust fund which the representatives could use for payment of any damages that might be awarded.[3]

1. *Sewkin* v. *Utility Glove (1961) Ltd.* (1967) 62 D.L.R. (2d) 48 (Man.C.A.).
2. *Seafarers' International Union* v. *Lawrence* (1980) 97 D.L.R. (3d) 323; 24 O.R. (2d) 257 (Ont.C.A.).
3. *See*, for example, *Anderson Block & Tile Ltd.* v. *Mior* (1961) 62 C.L.L.C. para. 15, 392 (Ont.H.C.; and *National Bolt & Nut Corp.* v. *McDermott* (1974) 51 D.L.R. (3d) 191 (Ont.Div.Ct.).

396. As already said, in Quebec these difficulties have been overcome by the enactment of specific provisions in the Code of Civil Procedure providing that an unincorporated trade union may sue or be sued as an entity. In such a case, it follows that a judgment against a union could be executed against the property of that union.[1] However, the Civil Code of Quebec provides that the directors are liable where the property of the unincorporated association is insufficient. Other members are liable only up 'to the promised contribution and the subscription due for payment'.[2]

1. Code of Civil Procedure, ss.60 and 115.
2. Civil Code of Québec, ss.2274 and 2275.

D. Legal Status and Democratic Rule in Trade Unions

1. The need for democracy and the conceptual difficulty

397. While both the common law and legislation have addressed themselves to the question of the legal personality of trade unions and a gradual evolution of personation has taken place, little has changed in the way law looks at legal problems arising out of the internal organization of trade unions. When such difficulties have to be faced, trade unions are still treated as if they were 'gentlemen's clubs', that is, unincorporated, voluntary associations. Legally, the essence of such groups is that they are an aggregation of individuals who have agreed to effect certain purposes on the basis of agreed upon rules. That is, there is a number of contracts whose terms are the rules or constitution of the association. As such, these rules could have any contents the members desired, provided they were not illegal.

398. But trade unions are not gentlemen's clubs. They have a vital effect on the lives of members and non-members. They affect employers and other sectors of society by the implementation of their rules in order to achieve their objectives. In such a context, it is significant what the contents of trade union rules are. Inasmuch as the main business of trade unions is collective bargaining, it is premised on the notion that the suppression of individuals' desires is worthwhile because all individuals in the group will, eventually, be better served by such suppression. But, in line with societal values, there will be a perceived need to ensure that individuals' rights are not suppressed unduly, that majoritarian principles do not ride roughshod over minority interests. This imports precepts of democratic procedures and doctrines into collective bargaining. Yet, to require a trade union to behave as a democratic institution like a legislature, might derogate from its ability to carry out its tasks. Bargainers must appear to have full authority when sitting at the bargaining table; decisions must be capable of being made without having to go back to the membership for authorization; freedom must exist to bargain away some people's rights to obtain a better overall package, etc. That is, democratic principles will be reached out for, but they must if necessary be compromised. It would be difficult enough to control this even if the relationships within a trade union could be settled by external fiat of those who regulate collective bargaining. It is exceedingly difficult where, for these purposes, a trade union's internal affairs are treated as a matter of private contract-making, as if a trade union were a gentlemen's club with all the rights to restrict and control membership according to its whim. Accommodation of these very different concepts inevitably leads to complexity in the law.

2. The local–parent relationship

399. The pivotal organization for the purposes of collective bargaining is the local bargaining agent or trade union. When discussing the structure of trade unionism in Canada above, the emphasis was on national and international unions and their affiliations. These central bodies, however, are made up of many branches, the locals who usually bargain directly with a particular employer. Where this is the situation, the local may have been created by the central union granting a charter to a local association which seeks to establish itself as a bargaining agent. This gives the local a ready-made constitution. This is important because it enables a labour relations board, familiar with the chartering union, to find that the applicant local is a trade union which satisfies the requirements for certification. In addition, the local obtains the valuable assistance and services of a large, well-organized entity. The C.L.C. can also issue charters. Sometimes a local group's members will agree that they will not become a union until they have obtained such a charter. Sometimes, however, a local seeks affiliation after formation as a trade union and/or certification as a bargaining agent. Other local groups never seek affiliation with anyone else. The concern here is with the situation in which a local–parent relationship has been created. Except for very limited legislative initiatives in Ontario, British Columbia and under the federal labour code, the regulation of parent–local relationships in Canada has generally been left entirely to judicial interpretation of union constitutions and other foundational documents.[1]

1. *See* generally, Lynk 'Trade Union Democracy and the Law In Canada' (2000) forthcoming in 21 *Journal of Labor Research.* The one significant exception is a recent amendment in Ontario which limits the authority of parent unions in the construction industry, mostly located in the U.S. to intervene in the affairs of union locals in Ontario in an oppressive manner. See ss.145–50 of the Labour Relations Act, 1995, S.O. 1995, c.1, which prevent the imposition of trusteeships without just cause. Other less intrusive legislation under Ontario, B.C. and federal labour Acts is discussed below under para. 401a.

400. In such cases, the decision to organize in a particular way was made for collective bargaining purposes. Conceptually this ought to mean that difficulties should be resolved from within the framework of collective bargaining logic. For instance, if the local is merely a creature of the parent in order to bolster its jurisdiction and, hence, power in the industry, it might make sense to say that, should the parent withdraw its charter from the local, the local would cease to exist, or, if the parent sought to merge with another union, that it could dictate what should happen to the local and its assets. But, on the whole, the courts have resisted this approach. They prefer to treat the relationship of local and parent as a contractual one, governed primarily by the union constitution and other foundational documents. If it is seen that, as a matter of contract, there was never any local organization, then they will treat the withdrawal of a charter by the parent as a termination of the local.[1] Where this is not seen to be the contractual relationship, questions of the survival of the local,[2] the splitting-up of assets upon attempted dissolution,[3] the right of a parent to create a competing local[4] and the right of the parent union which puts a local union under its trusteeship (for failure to comply with the parent's and/or collective bargaining rules) to bargain on behalf of the local membership, are all decided by reference to contract principles. That is, the rules of the local, the parent and the terms of their agreed upon relationship are treated as the terms of a contract which require interpretation. This may not adequately reflect the purposes and aims of the various groupings or the needs of the collective bargaining regime, given the fact that the parent union/local union relationship is one concerned with economic and political power and the mechanism to create the relationship, contracting, is merely a legal convenience and is not likely to express the real goals and aspirations of the participants. Let us, by illustration, make these abstractions a little clearer.

1. *Jubilee Lodge No. 6* v. *Carmen's Council Section 'A'*, [1920] 56 D.L.R. 318; *see also Kuzych* v. *White* (1947) 2 D.L.R. 496.
2. *Re International Nickel of Canada, Shedden* v. *Kopinak*, [1949] O.R. 765; *see also Re International Union of Operating Engineers*, 4 W.W.R. (N.S.) 264; *Dionisio* v. *Allain*, [1985] 50 C.P.C. 11.
3. *Lakeman and Barrett* v. *Bruce*, [1950] 3 D.L.R. 146; *see also McMillan* v. *Yandell* (1972) O.R. 146.
4. *Local 1571 I.L.A.* v. *International Longshoremen's Association and Local 1764* I.L.A., [1951] 3 D.L.R. 50.

401. The organizational distribution of power between parent and local which is typically employed by unions has been referred to by one Canadian writer as an 'intriguing paradox'.[1] Under the typical constitution most of the institutional authority to collect and expend finances, make executive and appeal decisions and assume residual and implied or inherent rights is placed in the hands of the parent executive. Yet under the Canadian and American approach to regulation of collective bargaining most of the bargaining power resides at the local plant level and the union local often has a great deal of autonomy on collective bargaining issues.[2] Nevertheless, applying the contractual approach to internal union conflict, courts have generally upheld the constitutional authority of the parent when dealing with intra-union struggles concerning ownership of property or use of resources when dealing with a rebellious local which seeks to defect or otherwise seek greater autonomy. In one case, the majority of a local wished to affiliate with a rival parent union. It was held that the original parent union could, by withdrawing its charter from the local, have all the assets of the local returned to it. That is, the local was blocked from freely exercising its majority's wishes because of the particular contractual relations which had been created.[3] Again, in *Re International Nickel of Canada, Shedden* v. *Kopinak*,[4] the contract of affiliation between local and parent stipulated that, as long as there were 10 members who wanted to remain in the local, the local as such could not transfer its affiliation to another parent union. In that case a large majority wished the local to change its allegiance but was prevented from doing so by the enforcement of this contractual term. More recently, it has been held that defecting locals are barred from hindering the efforts of the parent organization to recover the union's assets as provided for in the constitution,[5] and local union leaders attempting to lead the membership of the local out of the parent organization were prohibited from using the assets and resources of the local to finance their attempt to defect to another union.[6] Thus, democratic principles and central collective bargaining notions may be frustrated by judicial reliance on contract principles pertinent to the rules of gentlemen's clubs.[7]

1. Lynk, 'Trade Union Democracy and the Law In Canada' (2000), *op. cit.*
2. The tension in the distribution of power between the union parent and its locals concerning collective bargaining and management of union affairs is well documented in Diane Veilleux and Renaud Paquet, 'The Degree of Autonomy of Canadian Local Unions of national and International Union', in Magnus Sverke (ed.), *The Future of Trade Unionism* (Aldershot: Ashgate Publishing, 1997) 149–60.
3. *Lakeman and Barrel* v. *Bruce*, n.3, para. 400.
4. N.2, para. 400.
5. *L.C.U.C.* v. *C.U.P.W.*, [1994] 2 W.W.R. 450 (Alta.Q.B.).
6. *McMillan* v. *Yandell* (1971) 22 D.L.R. (3d) 398 (Ont.H.C.).
7. For significant criticism of the contractual approach and its implications for effective collective bargaining policy, *see* MacNeil *et al.*, *op. cit.*, at paras. 5.60–5.80; *see also*, Robert P. Gagnon, Louis LeBel and Pierre Verge, *Droit du travail* (Les Presses de l'Université Laval, 2nd edn., 1991) 323–30; Verge and Murray, *op. cit.*, 167–79.

401a. The other topic of great significance in parent–local relationships is the issue of trusteeships. Most union constitutions provide for imposition of a trusteeship on the local by the parent organization in the event of certain specified events arising, such as a violation of the union constitution or internal corruption or neglect of duty. A trusteeship constitutes a significant interference by the parent union with the autonomy and democratic operation of the local, as it generally allows the parent executive to suspend local governance and appoint an official to directly manage the affairs and finances of the local. However, union trusteeships have been imposed very rarely and for only brief periods of time in Canada. Those who have studied this issue suggest that their infrequent use and the fact they have seldom been used in an oppressive manner is the reason why Canadian labour law has not imposed an extensive regulatory regime similar to that employed in the U.S. to regulate union trusteeships.[1] Ontario and British Columbia have enacted statutory provisions to regulate trusteeships but they are largely procedural in nature.[2] They simply require a parent union that has imposed a trusteeship to file a statement with labour relations board within 60 days of the imposition, setting out the terms of the trusteeship. If the trusteeship is to continue for more than 12 months the parent is required to get the labour board's consent. In such cases the labour board in Ontario has held that it will allow a trusteeship to continue beyond 12 months if there is a legitimate labour relations purpose to be served.[3] Also, under the federal Corporations and Labour Returns Act, unions with 100 or more members in Canada that impose a trusteeship on a local or other subordinate body must submit a report stating the name of each local subject to trusteeship and the date and reasons for the imposition of the trusteeship to the Chief Statistician of Canada.[4] While the imposition of a trusteeship has been challenged in the courts rather infrequently, such challenges have often been successful on the grounds that some procedural provision in the union's constitution has been breached. In *Warner* v. *Kiniak*, frequently identified as a leading decision on this issue, the B.C. Court of Appeal held that a trusteeship was null and void because the international parent union had improperly appointed members to the internal hearing board. The Court noted that it would closely scrutinize constitutional provisions to ensure that a parent's authority to impose a trusteeship was adequately provided and correctly applied.[5] Recognition of this principle plus a general judicial inclination to observe principles of natural justice have meant that Canadian courts have generally required a parent union to meet a high procedural standard to uphold the imposition of a trusteeship.[6]

1. MacNeil *et al.*, *op. cit.*, at paras. 5.240–5.260.
2. Ontario Labour Relations Act, 1995, S.O. 1995, c.1, s.89(1); Labour Relations Act, S.B.C. 1992, c.82, s.150.
3. *See* discussion in Lynk, 'Trade Union Democracy and the Law in Canada' (2000), *op. cit.*
4. R.S.C. 1985, c.C-43, ss.11, 12.
5. (1980), 20 B.C.L.R. 117 (B.C.C.A.).
6. Lynk, 'Trade Union Democracy and the Law in Canada' (2000), *op. cit.*

3. The right to belong to a trade union

402. Perhaps the single most important right trade unions *qua* unions have won is the right to have enforceable security clauses inserted into collective agreements. Closed shop, union shop and the 'Rand formula' are discussed in paras. 578–81. What they import is that in many – most – circumstances, membership in a trade union which has won collective bargaining rights is a prerequisite (subject to the limited right of conscientious objection) to obtaining or retaining a job. In the absence of protection, individuals' rights may be put in jeopardy. Because trade unions are still treated as unincorporated associations when the question of whether or not they can sue or be sued or participate in collective bargaining is not in issue, this area is governed by legal rules which seem to be out of step with the reality of modern labour relations.

403. As the members of an unincorporated association are bound to each other contractually on the basis of the rules of the association, it follows that they have rights against each other should there be a breach of the rules adversely affecting them. It also follows that persons who are not party to the contractual arrangements have no rights under it. Thus, applicants for membership have no standing in law to become members of a trade union. In one well-known English case it was suggested that, where a person had to belong to an unincorporated association to earn a living, such a person could not arbitrarily be denied access to membership. The suggestion was that there was something called a right to work, akin to a property right, which would give such a person legal standing to be considered for membership.[1] This notion has been raised in Canada but not yet accepted. In *Kuzych* v. *White*,[2] it was held by one judge that, if a trade union had the right to have a closed shop, it would amount to unacceptable totalitarianism not to recognize the right of people to work at their trade by giving them access to membership of the trade union. This case went to the Privy Council where this argument was not adumbrated. Another way that the argument supporting a right to work has been advanced[3] is by reasoning that, as the collective bargaining legislation gives employees a right to join a union, whenever a closed shop arrangement is entered into employees must have a right to belong to the trade union concerned otherwise their statutory right to join a union would be rendered meaningless.[4] This argument is bolstered by contrasting the right to join with the right to belong which are the forms of words respectively used in the Ontario and Alberta statutes. But this argument has been judicially rejected, it being argued that if the right to join was intended to mean the absolute right to be a member of a particular union (if occupationally qualified), the legislation would have explicitly stated this. Instead, both labour boards and courts have interpreted this type of provision as one intended to create a collective bargaining right to protect unions and their members against employer interference. In short, it does not create a union democracy right to allow dissident employees to establish statutory claims against unions for denial or termination of union membership.[5]

1. *Per* Lord Denning, *Nagle* v. *Feilden*, [1966] 2 W.L.R. 1027, 1033.
2. *Per* O'Hollaran, J.A., [1940] 4 D.L.R. 187, 191.
3. Refer here to the discussion in paras. 277, 363.
4. All Canadian labour statutes contain a provision similar to that found in the Ontario Labour Relations Act, 1995, S.O. 1995, c.1, s.5, 'Every person is free to join a trade union of the person's own choice and to participate in its lawful activities.'
5. *See Gee* v. *Freeman* (1958) 16 D.L.R. (2d) 65; *Adams Mine, Cliffs of Canada Ltd.* v. *U.S.W.A.* (1982) 1 Can. L.R.B.R. (N.S.) 384 (O.L.R.B.).

404. Some of the disastrous effects of using inapposite common law concepts have been ameliorated by the practices of the labour relations board. As noted, boards will not certify as bargaining agents unions which have rules which would prevent members of the apposite bargaining unit from belonging to the union. Because practices may have modified the rules of admission to membership, boards have been given discretion to interpret the rules so that even rules which on their face might deny membership will not necessarily stop a board from certifying the union.[1] An additional protection is available to prospective employees in that unions and employers are not permitted to enter into agreements which discriminate against people on certain bases. Similarly, some collective bargaining statutes, such as Ontario's, will not grant bargaining rights to trade unions with rules which discriminate on the bases of the grounds proscribed by the Human Rights Code and the Charter of Rights and Freedoms.[2]

1. *See*, for example, s.111(4) of the Ontario Labour Relations Act, 1995, S.O. 1995, c.1, enacted in response to *Metropolitan Life Insurance Company* v. *International Union of Operating Engineers, Local 796* (1970) 11 D.L.R. (3d) 336; the difficulties continue in some jurisdictions; *see Re Construction and General Labourers Working in Construction, Industrial and Commercial, Local 1079A, and Atlantic Wholesalers* (1975) 9 Nfld. and P.E.I.R. 273 (P.E.I.S.C.); *Deware Enterprises Ltd.* v. *Retail, Wholesale and Department Store Union, Local 1065* (1979) 27 N.B.R. (2d) 299 (N.B.C.A.); *Re United Steelworkers of America, Local 6204 and Fahey Building Ltd.* (1981) 128 D.L.R. (3d) 715 (Nfld.C.A.).
2. *See*, for example, s.15 of the Labour Relations Act, 1995, S.O. 1995, c.1. *See also* s.54 of the same Act which prohibits collective agreements from discriminating on grounds prohibited under the Ontario Human Rights Code or the Canadian Charter of Rights and Freedoms.

4. The right to remain in a trade union

405. Trade union security provisions may require dismissal of employees who cease to belong to a trade union. The collective bargaining statutory regimes permit this, but they also provide some safeguards for individuals. Usually the employer will not have to dismiss a person expelled from a trade union if the reason for that expulsion is that that person became a member of another trade union, agitated against the union at a rival union's behest or otherwise dissented in a reasonable manner, etc.[1] Some jurisdictions have gone farther to limit a requirement that an employer discharge an employee who is expelled or suspended from union membership to cases where the employee has failed to pay periodic union dues.[2] In addition, three provinces, Alberta, British Columbia and Saskatchewan, have amended their legislation recently to require that certain procedural safeguards to ensure natural justice are met when members or union officers are the subject of internal union disciplinary proceedings.[3] These provisions give the labour relations boards a role in protecting employees from unfair treatment in internal disciplinary processes. In the absence of such statutory protection, the common law's understanding of the nature of unionism reigns.

1. E.g. Labour Relations Act, 1995, S.O. 1995, c.1, s.51(2) prevents a trade union from requiring an employer to discharge a worker because the employee has been expelled or denied membership in the union due to membership in another union; activity against the union on behalf of another union; participation in reasonable dissent within the union; discrimination against the worker in the application of the union rules; refusal to pay unreasonable fees or dues. *See also* Quebec Labour Code, R.S.Q., c.C-27, s.63.
2. *See*, for example, the Alberta Labour Relations Code, R.S.A. 1980, c.L-12.
3. Labour Relations Code, R.S.A. 1980, c.L-12, s.24; Labour Relations Code, R.S.B.C. 1996, c.244, s.10; Trade Union Act, R.S.S. 1978, as amended, c.T-17, s.36.1(3). *See* discussion of the operation of these provisions in Lynk, *Trade Union Democracy and the Law In Canada op. cit.*

406. The question of whether or not an expelled member has a right of redress against a trade union has been approached by the courts on the basis of interpreting the contract between the members. Consequently, if the rules of the trade union, non-compliance with which led to the expulsion, were illegal in themselves or had illegal purposes, the courts have held the expulsion wrongful.[1] But where the circumstance was not so obviously contrary to enforceable public policy, the judiciary has taken its starting point as being that it ought not to question the contents of the rules. But, because the possible danger to individual rights is high, given the power of trade unions in the labour market, the courts have used several age-old manipulative techniques to provide some remedial processes.[2]

1. *SIU* v. *Stern* (1961) 29 D.L.R. (2d) 29; *Tippett* v. *International Typographers Union* (1976) 63 D.L.R. (3d) 522; *Pollock* v. *Alberta Union of Provincial Employees* (1978) 12 A.R. 398 (Atta.S.C.).
2. The following analysis generally applies also to Quebec. *See* on that matter: Pierre Verge and Gregor Murray, *Le droit et les syndicats* (Sainte-Foy: Les Presses de l'Université Laval, 1991) 211–17.

a. Judges as contract interpreters

407. Courts have been adamant that a domestic tribunal such as, say, a disciplinary body of a trade union, cannot arrogate to itself the right to interpret the contractual terms of the association. The courts are to be the final arbiters of how the contractual terms binding the members, i.e. the rules, should be interpreted. Consistent with this rigid contractual approach to reviewing union disciplinary matters, courts have generally reviewed union conduct under a standard of 'correctness', showing little deference for union decision-making. One recent study of court supervision of internal union disciplinary proceedings has concluded that this allows for frequent intervention on the grounds of inconsistency with union constitutional procedures, even in the case of minor procedural flaws. This resulted in judicial negation of the internal union disciplinary decision in 85 per cent (28 of 33) of the reported cases since the 1940s.[1] In addition, this contractual approach allows them – should they so desire – to imply terms into the contract between the members. Such a tack is most likely to be taken when a court feels moved to protect an individual from the economic power a trade union wields, that is, where a court implicitly has some sympathy for the notion of a right to work. Thus, in one case it was held to be an implied term of the membership contract that, where a hiring hall was operating, the trade union could not discriminate between its members with respect to job opportunities in order to follow an unreasonable policy.[2] But courts are limited in their scope when implying terms. They cannot be too fanciful. In any event, this technique for implementation depends so much on unarticulated premises that its merits are dubious.

1. Lynk, 'Trade Union Democracy and the Law in Canada' (2000), *op. cit.*
2. *Hornak* v. *Patterson* (1966) 58 D.L.R. (2d) 175; *C.P.R.* v. *Building Materials etc. Union* (1972) 2 W.W.R. 535 and Lord Denning in *Lee* v. *Showmen's Guild*, [1952] 2 Q.B. 338, 341.

b. Requirements of good faith

408. The domestic tribunal, set up under the trade union's rules to deal with alleged breaches of the rules, must act without bias. While reasonableness of result is a good indication of a lack of malice, a court should not find a lack of good faith merely because it does not like the determination of the tribunal. Indeed, because it is a domestic tribunal, the mere fact that the members of the tribunal have a view of the policy which they wish to see pursued relating to the matter in dispute will not amount to lack of good faith. What a court will be looking for in the tribunal is an openness to listen to argument, no more.[1]

1. *Gee* v. *Freeman* (1959) 16 D.L.R. (2d) 65; *Bimson* v. *Johnston* (1957) 10 D.L.R. (2d) 11; *Evaskow* v. *International Brotherhood of Boilermakers* (1970) 9 D.L.R. (3d) 715.

c. Natural justice

409. The two previous interpretation devices could have been grouped under this rubric. They frequently are, as they were here, separated for simplicity in presentation. Natural justice seems to imply that there should be a fair hearing. As the courts are to be the arbiters of what is fair, it is not surprising that the procedural safeguards they insist on (in addition to requiring good faith) closely resemble the practices surrounding the judicial processes. Thus, notice must be given to the member under attack.[1] S/he cannot be denied the opportunity to attend union meetings at which her/his fate is to be discussed and determined. Indeed, where a trade union claimed its rules permitted such exclusion, a court held that such terms of the membership contract were not acceptable.[2] The right to cross-examine and other such adversarial process trappings do not necessarily have to be available to the member under attack, but if too many of these tools are denied a court may well determine that there has been a lack of natural justice.[3] Some commentators have suggested that courts have used their role of ensuring fairness in union decision-making to interfere with substantive rulings under the guise of rulings on natural justice.[4]

1. *Re Busche and Nova Scotia Teachers* (1976) 62 D.L.R. (3d) 330.
2. *Hughes* v. *SIU* (1962) 31 D.L.R. (2d) 441.
3. *Gee* v. *Freeman, supra*; *Tippett* v. *International Typographers, supra.*
4. Lynk, 'Trade Union Democracy and the Law In Canada' (2000), *op. cit.*

410. One of the limitations on the right of an aggrieved member to seek redress in the courts is that the member may have to exhaust all remedial avenues available under the trade union's rules. This is certainly so where the union's rules provide so expressly, but a court might be willing to imply such a term where the rules of the union provide a system of appeals. The Privy Council has authoritatively decided that the complaining member should exhaust her/his remedies under the rules first.[1] Althougth this is, therefore, the basic principle it is more honoured in breach than by acceptance. The courts have undermined it in several ways. They have held that if the original disposition was totally unacceptable because the action taken by the trade union was outside the scope of its own rules, there is no need to exhaust the remedies under the rules. Thus, when a union purported to expel a member at a general meeting, without attempting to adhere to its own rules for laying charges and processing them, it was held that the expelled member could get a declaration of her/his rights and damages straight away from a court.[2] Another possible means of circumventing the rule is by holding that, if the union acted in breach of the rules of natural justice, there will be no need for an aggrieved member to exhaust her/his remedies. The reasoning is that, whatever the rules of the union are, they cannot deny natural justice. But the argument is contrary to the founding decision, *Kuzych* v. *White*, where there was a breach of natural justice, yet the plaintiff was held to the obligation of exhausting his remedies. To counter this, it has been noted that in *Kuzych* v. *White* the breach of natural justice could be repaired if the grieving member went through the appeal procedures and that, therefore, it was fair to require him to continue to pursue the internal process. It will not always be fair. This has brought us to the third and most significant way of avoiding the requirement of exhaustion of domestic remedies. It may well be that the appeal procedures provided for in the union rules are inadequate. This is particularly likely in Canada in respect of international unions. These unions can in no way be said to be unfair in respect of the democratic nature of their rules. To the contrary: as their rules may be based on the American parents' which, in turn, have to comply with legislation requiring a good number of protective safeguards for individual members, they are, on the whole, likely to be as satisfactory as any national union's rules. But it may be that the final appeals have to be heard in the United States. This could be treated by courts in Canada as unreasonable. Further, the ultimate appeal may be to a convention of the union which may only be held every two years. In one case, a court held that the plaintiff could be asked to exhaust his remedies in the union because he could not show he would suffer any damages as a result the delay.[3] In another case, where it was not clear when the next union convention – which was the final appeal – would take place, the court did not force a plaintiff to comply with an exhaustion of remedies clause in the trade union's rules.[4]

1. *Kuzych* v. *White*, [1951] 3 D.L.R. 650.
2. *McCrae* v. *Cargo and Gangway Watchmen of St. John, N.B.*, [1953] 1 D.L.R. 327.
3. *Local 471, I.L.A.* v. *International Longshoremen's Association*, [1951] 3 D.L.R. 50.
4. *Gee* v. *Freeman, supra.*

d. Status as a tool

411. From time to time, the absurdity of treating the relationship between members and their trade unions as being contractual in nature leads to an argument that, while it takes the legal concept of contract to set up the relationship, once it exists, it creates rights and duties which are distinct from the contract. That is, the trade union member has a status which is to be recognized by law as giving her/him certain rights which the union cannot erode, regardless of the terms of the original contract. Such a legal concept would enable courts to reflect better the economic and political reality of labour relations. The Supreme Court of Canada has addressed the argument. Only one of the justices accepted the reasoning; it was explicitly rejected by others.[1] This does not mean that this development has no future. It is still open to courts to say the question has not been finally decided and that possibility alone permits courts to make decisions on status-like notions while ostensibly using contract principles. If there are enough decisions of this kind, courts may eventually be able to say that the status of a member of a trade union has been legally recognized. This speculation is offered because it seems a desirable development, but it has yet to be acted upon by courts.

1. *Orchard* v. *Tunney* (1957) 8 D.L.R. (2d) 273 ([1957] S.C.R. 436), Locke, J. supported the notion of status, but Rand, J., whose judgment was a leading one, rejected it.

5. Fair representation

412. As well as the power a trade union has over the employment opportunities of workers, it also has very important influence over the nature of the working conditions workers obtain if employed. As the sole bargaining agent for a group of employees, it is in a position to differentiate between these employees when bargaining with an employer. Collective bargaining principles would be undermined by telling a trade union how to use its economic power. This inhibits the imposition of requirements on how to bargain. But, gradually some rules are developing which oblige trade unions to take into account the needs of individual workers in the unit.

413. The first relevant development took place in the United States. Not surprisingly, it was the judiciary which took up the cudgels for individuals. It is not wedded, conceptually, to the collective aspect of labour relations. The U.S. Supreme Court held that, implicit in a statute giving exclusive bargaining rights, there is a duty to exercise that power fairly, without hostile discrimination against any of the employees represented.[1] Another 18 years elapsed before a labour relations board accepted this notion.[2] This reluctance can be understood because of the labour relations board's inherent respect for freedom in collective bargaining. But now it is a well-established doctrine and can best be described by saying that the bargaining representative has a duty not to draw irrelevant and arbitrary distinctions amongst those it represents. Further, it has been recognized that this duty is applicable to the administration of the collective agreement as this, notionally, is part and parcel of a continuous bargaining process. In Canada, the courts have been more reluctant to develop similar doctrines, but there has been significant statutory and judicial evolution of a duty of fair representation in Canada since 1970. Today the duty of fair representation exists in every jurisdiction in Canada, either under an express statutory obligation or an obligation implied at common law where the relevant labour relations legislation is silent on the issue.

1. *Steele* v. *Louisville and N.R.R.*, 323 U.S. 192 (1944), *Wallace Corp.* v. *N.L.R.B.*, 323 U.S. 248 (1944), *Ford Motor* v. *Huffman*, 345 U.S. 330 (1953).
2. *Miranda Fuel Co. Inc.* 140 N.L.R.B. 181 (1962).

a. Negotiating a collective agreement

Common law

414. There seem to be very few decisions in Canada which impose a common law duty on a union to fairly represent its members during the agreement-making process. In one case it was held that a union should keep its members informed about its proposed actions, such as telling them that picket lines were to be established, boycotts imposed or strikes called.[1] It could be that courts could spell out, as their American counterparts did in respect of similar statutes granting exclusive bargaining agency rights, a duty to fairly represent members in the bargaining process. But note that the American statute had a specific provision allowing for the enforcement of rights under the labour legislation by way of civil remedy, a provision not found in Canadian statutes. Further, the manifest difficulty of assessing what the contents of such a duty ought to be is a powerful dissuader. It is not surprising that the judiciary has so far restricted itself to spelling out that, if there is such a duty, it merely requires a union to abide by procedural safeguards.

1. *Tippett* v. *International Typographers* (1976) 63 D.L.R. (3d) 522, 547.

Statute

415. The Canada Labour Code and labour Acts in Alberta, Manitoba, Newfoundland, Saskatchewan provide for a duty of fair representation with respect to the rights of workers under a collective agreement, but only British Columbia,

Quebec and Ontario have language broad enough to require unions to observe the duty in the course of bargaining for a collective agreement. The statutory obligation generally provides that the bargaining agent is not to act in a manner that is arbitrary, discriminatory or in bad faith in the representation of members of the bargaining unit.[1] For the sake of convenience, when specific legislative references are made, they are to the Ontario statute.[2]

1. Labour Relations Code, S.B.C. 1992, c.82, s.12; Labour Relations Act, 1995, S.O. 1995, c.1, s.74; Labour Code, R.S.Q., c.C-27, s.47.2; Canada Labour Code R.S.C. 1985, c.C-27, s.95.
2. For a useful summary of the legislation see T. Christian, 'The Developing Duty of Fair Representation' (1991) 2 *Lab. Arb. Y.B.* at 3–20.

416. The labour relations boards have been extremely reluctant to second-guess the bargaining strategies and practices of trade unions. Although they may find a violation of the duty of fair representation when the union's procedures effectively stymie any participation in the bargaining by the employees, the boards are loath to do so just because the union made mistakes, creating confusion and alienation in the bargaining unit. Something closer to bad faith may be needed before procedural irregularities will be held to be violations of the duty to fair representation during negotiations.[1] And, when it comes to a question of whether or not the actual provisions of the agreement negotiated constitute a failure to represent fairly, the boards have been even less eager to hold unions responsible. In applying the duty to collective bargaining activity, labour boards have exercised a very minimal level of scrutiny, requiring only a minor degree of procedural fairness, including the canvassing of employee views, but recognizing a broad discretion in the union to fashion and agree to demands that may disregard the interests of individuals or groups of employees in order to get a deal that the union believes serves the interests of the entire bargaining unit.[2] The most likely kind of situation in which they might interfere is where a provision suggests special treatment of employees who are union officials by bargaining for their super-seniority rights and benefits for them.[3] It must be kept in mind that Quebec is the only Canadian jurisdiction where there is no labour relations board to administer the collective bargaining statute. Therefore, an employee wanting to challenge a union's strategies or decisions at the bargaining table would have to sue the union before a court of law.[4] This route, however, places great procedural hurdles in the way of an individual employee who may wish to challenge the union's bargaining strategy.

1. *Manor Cleaners Ltd.* (1983) 83 C.L.L.C. 16,044 (O.L.R.B.); *George Magold*, [1976] 1 C.L.R.B.R. 392 (O.L.R.B.); *Harvey Adams*, [976] 1 C.L.R.B.R. 192 (B.C.).
2. T. Christian, 'The Developing Duty of Fair Representation' (1991) 2 *Lab. Arb. Y.B.* at 17.
3. *Seagrams Employees*, [1978] 1 C.L.R.B.R. (B.C.); *Radenko Bukvich*, [1982] 1 C.L.R.B.R. (O.L.R.B.); *Paul Atkinson*, [1983] O.L.R.B. Rep. 1199 (O.L.R.B.).
4. *See Syndicat des fonctionnaires provinciaux du Québec Inc.* v. *Bastien*, D.T.E. 93T–309 (Q.C.A.).

b. The administration of a collective agreement

Common law

417. There are now some important judicial pronouncements in Canada to the effect that a union has a common law duty to fairly represent a member of the bargaining unit in the grievance process. With few exceptions, the union being the party to the collective agreement has the sole right to bring grievances about the interpretation of that agreement. Thus, an employee could be seriously disadvantaged if her/his bargaining agent chose not to process her/his claim. The duty of fair representation was for the first time expressed by a Canadian court in *Fisher* v. *Pemberton*.[1] In that case, the plaintiff alleged that the union had not treated him fairly because he was a member of a rival union. The court upheld his claim that he had been subject to discriminatory treatment. The American courts had, once they had devised a cause of action on the basis of the implications arising from the statutes, characterized it as a tort action. This entitled the successful plaintiff to damages regardless of her/his rights under the collective agreement. In *Fisher* v. *Pemberton*, the court seemed to take a different approach. Having found that the union had acted improperly, the court then considered whether the plaintiff would have succeeded in an arbitration should it have come to pass. It decided that he would not have and awarded him $1 damages. A few years later, the Supreme Court of Canada confirmed the common law obligation of the certified union to represent fairly any member of the bargaining unit in the grievance procedure where such obligation was not imposed by statute.[2]

1. (1970), 8 D.L.R. (2d) 521.
2. *Canadian Merchant Service Guild* v. *Gagnon and Laurentian Pilotage Authority*, [1984] 1 S.C.R. 509. The S.C.C. has also recently confirmed that where statutory obligations and procedures exist concerning a duty of fair representation these must be resorted to and applicants will not be allowed to pursue court action. *See Gendron* v. *Supply & Services Union, P.S.A.C., Local 50057*, [1990] 1 S.C.R. 1298.

Statute

418. The drafters relied on the American experience in defining the duty of fair representation. Despite some controversy, the dominant theme in the United States is that the weight of a grievance is to be measured in terms of the group interest as assessed honestly by the bargaining agent. Accordingly, the Ontario Labour Relations Board has stated that a complaint under section 74 must be evaluated in light of the industrial realities and practices. It will take into account the fact that trade union officials are not professional advocates and that they do not have much time for reflection when making daily decisions. In the same vein, trade union arguments that they had to weigh the effects of bringing a grievance on future settlements and bargaining are to be given serious weight. The Board has concerned itself with defining arbitrariness, discrimination and lack of good faith from within a very contextualized framework.[1] One academic commentator has summarized the union's obligations under this branch of the duty as follows: to investigate the grievance, hear the grievor's version of events, assess the merits in an unbiased manner, keep the grievor informed of steps being taken by the union to resolve his/her grievance and seek his/her agreement to settlement, avoid acting with serious or gross negligence, and seek such assistance as is reasonable given the resources of the union and the importance of the grievor's interests at risk.[2] It should be noted that while there are a large number of complaints filed by individual employees alleging breach of the duty of fair representation, only a very small percentage, in the range of 1 to 4 per cent are successful.[3]

1. E.g. *Ford Motor*, [1973] O.L.R.B. Rep. 519; *Essex International*, [1971] O.L.R.B. Rep. 104; *Brenda Haley*, [1982] 2 C.L.R.B.R. 121. As will be seen below, in Quebec, the *Tribunal du travail* has jurisdiction to hear the case of an employee claiming that the certified union breached its duty of fair representation in the way her/his grievance contesting a disciplinary measure or a dismissal was treated. The Labour Court's case law on this matter is quite similar to that of the Canadian labour relations boards outside Quebec. *See* Diane Veilleux, 'Le devoir de représentation syndicale: cadre d'analyse des obligations sous-jacentes', (1993) 48 *Rel. Ind.* 661.
2. T. Christian, 'The Developing Duty of Fair Representation' (1991) 2 *Lab. Arb. Y.B.* at 20.
3. One recent commentary estimates a success rate of approximately 2 per cent based on statistics for the Canada Labour Board for 1997–8 showing 170 complaints of which only two were upheld by the labour board. *See* Lynk, 'Trade Union Democracy and the Law In Canada' *op. cit.* Another recent study of fair representation complaints in British Columbia shows that from 1990 to 1994 successful complaints ranged from a low of 1 per cent in 1990 and 1994 to a high of 6 per cent in 1991. *See* T. Knight, 'Recent Developments in the Duty of Fair Representation: Curtailing Abuse in British Columbia' [1996–7] *Lab. Arb. Y.B.* 151, at 152–8.

c. Discrimination and bad faith

419. The Board emphasizes that what is required is a subjective evidencing of hostility or malice. It sees this aspect of the statutory duty of fair representation aimed squarely at eliminating discrimination by the bargaining agent on the basis of race, creed, colour, sex, age, as well as to prevent internal trade union political differences leading to invidious conduct and to inhibit interpersonal breakdown in a trade union.[1] A complainant will have established her/his claim under the statute where it is shown that the benefits of representation are conferred on one member of that bargaining unit and not on her/his co-workers and where the union offers no legitimate reasons for such discrimination.[2] Legitimate reasons are ones which relate to the collective agreement, as the grievance process is seen as an extension of collective bargaining,[3] or to the conduct or skills of the employees involved.[4] A union may be held to have acted in bad faith where there has been no open and frank discussions of the merits of the grievance.[5]

1. *Walter Princesdomu* (1975) O.L.R.B. Rep. 444; *Vancouver General Hospital Employees, and a Group of Employees*, [1978] 2 C.L.R.B.R. 508 (B.C.T.R.B.); *Frank J. Nowotniak and George E. Ostby and Grain Workers*, [1979] 2 C.L.R.B.R. 467 (C.L.R.B.); note that where a union does not press a grievance because it relied on a ground for differentiation prohibited by human rights' legislation it will be in breach of the duty; *see Cameron* v. *Teamsters Local Union 213 and Shuswap Okanagan Dairy Industries Co-op Assc'n* (1982) 82 C.L.L.C. 16,173 (B.C.L.R.B.).
2. *Jim Zorzi*, [1976] 1 C.L.R.B.R. 417 (O.L.R.B.); *Leonard Murphy*, [1977] C.L.R.B.R. 422 (O.L.R.B.).
3. *Rayonier Canada (B.C.) Ltd., and Industrial Woodworkers of America, Local 1–217*, [1975] 2 C.L.R.B.R. 196.
4. *Ford Motor*, [1973] O.L.R.B. Rep. 519; *Napanee Industries* (1972) O.L.R.B. Rep. 353; *Stewart* v. *Teamsters Union, Local 419 and K-Mart Distribution Centre* (1981) 82 C.L.L.C. 16,137 (O.L.R.B.) (arbitrary, discriminatory, defined for negotiation purposes); *see also Bukvich* v. *Canadian Union of United Brewery, Flour, Cereal, Soft Drink and Distillery Workers Local 304* (1982) 82 C.L.L.C. 16,156 (O.L.R.B.).
5. *Ford Motor, supra* note 4.

d. Arbitrariness

420. This head of the duty of fair representation is the one which arises most frequently. It seems that where a union's treatment of a grievance has been perfunctory, a breach of the duty will have been established.[1] The test is an objective one. It requires the union to put its mind to the grievance. Mistakes, if honestly made, even if due to human shortcomings such as laxness, will not make the union's conduct arbitrary.[2] The union must give an opportunity to the employee to present her/his case[3] and where there are internal trade union rules prescribing how a grievance ought to be processed, they must be followed.[4]

1. *Diamond 'Z' Association*, [1975] O.L.R.B. Rep. 791; *The Regional Municipality of Durham*, [1979] O.L.R.B. Rep. 1277; *Westerman* v. *C.U. P.E. Local, 1692*, [1984] O.L.R.B. Rep. 286.
2. *Walter Princesdomu*, [1975] O.L.R.B. Rep. 444; *B.E. Kreber and Douglas Aircraft of Canada, U.A.W.*, [1979] 3 C.L.R.B.R. 235 (O.L.R.B.).
3. *O'Donnell*, [1972] O.L.R.B. Rep. 423; *R.C.A.*, [1974] O.L.R.B. Rep. 60; *Britnell*, [1974] O.L.R.B. Rep. 275.
4. *R.C.A.*, [1974] O.L.R.B. Rep. 60 (O.L.R.B.); *Raynier Canada (B.C.) Ltd.*, [1975] 2 C.L.R.B.R. (B.C.); generally, *see* T. Christian, 'The Developing Duty of Fair Representation' (1991) 2 *Lab. Arb. Y.B.* 1.

e. Procedure

421. The complaint of a breach of the duty of fair representation is made to the Ontario Labour Relations Board under section 99 of the Act. A field officer is sent out to investigate and help attain a settlement. If this fails, a report is made to the Board which, after screening by a panel of the Board, may lead to a hearing. At such a hearing the Board must determine whether there has been a breach of the duty and, if so, what damage the complainant has suffered. In 1998 the Ontario Labour Relations Board promulgated new rules of procedure which expressly refer to the Board's authority to dispose of fair representation complaints without an oral hearing. Similar measures were legislatively in British Columbia in 1993. These measures appear to be a direct result of the fact that the vast majority of fair representation complaints are denied and that factions or individuals within the workplace may misuse the fair representation procedures to further political or personal agendas.[1] In Quebec, although there is no labour relations board, such a complaint may be filed with the Minister of Labour, but only by employees who are grieving a dismissal or a disciplinary measure. If the field investigator fails to work out a settlement, the employee may bring her/his case before the *Tribunal du travail*. Like the Ontario Board, the Tribunal has then to decide whether the union breached its duty of fair representation.[2]

1. *See* Ontario Labour Relations Board Rules of Procedure (August 1998) s.98c and T. Knight, 'Recent Developments in the Duty of Fair Representation: Curtailing Abuse in British Columbia', [1996–7] *Lab. Arb. Y.B.* 151, at 152–8.
2. Quebec Labour Code, R.S.Q., c.C-27, ss.47.3 and 47.4. When the amendments to the Labour Code adopted in June 2001 will come into force, the matter will fall within the jurisdiction of the newly created labour board.

f. Remedies

422. Section 99 of the Ontario Labour Relations Act gives very wide powers to the Board, including recommending reinstatement and awarding compensatory damages. Where there is a breach of duty of fair representation, it will usually mean that the complainant should have had a right to have a claim arbitrated. At this point, the Board will usually defer to the grievance arbitration process under the collective agreement. This can result in an orders ranging from simply sending the grievance to arbitration, to requiring the union to pay for the grievor to retain independent counsel at a subsequent arbitration hearing. In some cases an order might also require the waiver of employer objections to jurisdiction based on time limits and make provision for the union to bear responsibility for part of the grievor's losses if the grievance turns out to be successful at arbitration.[1] This permits honouring the integrity of the collective agreement as well as alleviating the effect of the unfair practice constituted by the breach of the duty of fair representation.[2] In Quebec, when the Tribunal finds that there has been a breach of the duty of fair representation, it may authorize the employee to present her/his claim to a grievance arbitrator. It may also make any other order that it deems necessary.[3]

1. Lynk, 'Trade Union Democracy and the Law in Canada' (2000), *op. cit.*
2. For a full discussion *see Imperial Tobacco Products (Ontario)*, [1974] O.L.R.B. Rep. 418; *Valdi Inc.*, [1980] 3 C.L.R.B.R. 299.
3. Quebec Labour Code, R.S.Q., c.C-27, s.47.5. For an illustration of how this remedy works, *see* the decision of the Supreme Court of Canada in *Centre hospitalier Régina Ltée.* v. *Tribunal du travail*, [1990] 1 S.C.R. 1330.

423. But, sometimes deferral to the grievance process is unsuitable. This will be so where there clearly is a clash between the union's interest and that of the grievor and arbitration might not be an acceptable remedy for the grievor. This can be solved as it was in *Imperial Tobacco.*[1] There had been a complaint under the then section 60 which, if established, would also constitute a breach of the collective agreement. The Board accepted the union's proposal that an arbitrator acceptable to the three parties – the employer, the union and the grievor – should determine whether or not the collective agreement had been breached. If it had not, the Board would have no further interest in the matter. If the collective agreement had been breached, then the complainant had to prove that the breach was caused by a violation of the duty of fair representation. If this was done, the Board would fashion an appropriate remedy. Apart from such unique situations, the Board will provide a remedy where the grievance process could not. This will involve it in interpreting the collective agreement.

1. *Supra*, para. 422 note 2.

424. One of the difficulties is that, in searching for adequate remedies, it may be necessary to make an employer accept a resolution such as reinstatement, a new job assignment, a change in seniority orderings, and the like. The Board has accordingly made employers parties to such proceedings where necessary. Indeed, it may be that failure to notify the employer and to give him standing in the proceedings may amount to a denial of natural justice.

Natural justice again

425. As has just been noted, there will be occasions when a union's interests will conflict with that of some of the employees it represents. It could come about that, when a trade union seeks redress for some of the employees in the unit, the result obtained will be adverse to other persons in the unit. The logic of collective bargaining dictates that, if the union is acting honestly to promote the good of the majority over the long haul, this is a cross that individuals must bear. But there have been some startling judicial developments which give remedies to employees aggrieved in this fashion over and above the jurisprudence relating to the duty of fair representation discussed thus far.

426. In one case, a grievance was brought to interpret the promotion clause of a collective agreement. The arbitrator ordered that a majority of the grievors be given positions filled at that time by other persons in the unit. Three of those incumbents were present at the hearing but played no part in it. Altogether six positions had been contested. The six incumbents claimed, in a judicial hearing, that the arbitrator's ruling should be set aside because they were not given an opportunity to participate in the hearing. The Ontario Court of Appeal agreed with this argument. Acknowledging that a union has to differentiate between employees, it was nonetheless felt that where the interests directly in issue were of a kind which related to substantial employment benefits, the employees whose interests would be so affected were entitled to the safeguards provided by the principle of natural justice. This was so, even though in many cases the union's opponents in the grievance, the employer, would put forward much of the argument that the non-represented employees might make. This, apparently, was not sufficient protection because the employer would only be putting forward those coincidental arguments and evidence which suited his personal interest.[1]

1. *Re Bradley and Ottawa Professional Fire-Fighters' Association*, [1967] 2 O.R. 311; *see also Re Air Canada* (1978) 18 L.A.C. (2d) 187 (Kennedy); *Re La Vevendrye General Hospital* (1978) 20 L.A.C. (2d) 241; *Re Tavener* (1981), 12 Man. R. (2d) 348 (Man.Q.B.); *Syndicat des employées du Centre hospitalier Robert-Giffard et Annexes (C.S.N.)* v. *Syndicat professionnel des Infirmières et Infirmiers de Québec (S.P.I.I.Q.) et al.*, [1979] C.A. 323.

427. This reasoning was reaffirmed by the Supreme Court of Canada in a subsequent case. There the union had sought arbitration in respect of the interpretation of the collective agreement. There was no particular employee whose grievance was processed. In fact, however, the arbitration process was being used by the union to force a recalcitrant bargaining unit employee to pay union dues or be dismissed. The arbitrator knew this full well and made this clear in his ruling. He not only upheld the union's interpretation of the agreement but concluded that the obstinate employee, Hoogendoorn, would have to be dismissed if he continued to refuse to pay union dues. The Supreme Court held that Hoogendoorn should have been allowed to participate in the proceedings.[1] Inasmuch as this case could be treated as that of an individual whose substantial benefits were being directly affected by an arbitration, the decision would merely be an echo of *Bradley*. But this case was not one which concerned an individual's grievance, that is, one relating to the seniority of individuals, promotion, wage rates or opportunity to work overtime, but rather a policy grievance, that is, one in which the parties as part of the ongoing collective bargaining process attempt to mould and shape the collective agreement.

1. *Re Hoogendoorn and Greening Metal Products and Screening Equipment* (1968) 65 D.L.R. (2d) 641; [1968] 1 S.C.R. 30.

428. The need to satisfy the doctrine of natural justice in such cases requires that the affected employees be given notice of the arising of the issue in such a manner and in sufficient time to allow adequate preparation for an appearance to be made. In addition, the employee ought to be permitted to be represented by counsel if this is her/his desire.

429. Manifestly, this development threatens one of the very fundamentals of collective bargaining. It undermines the trade union's right to behave authoritatively and diminishes the possibility of maintaining an informal, expedited means of settling problems which arise during the life of the collective agreement. This latter aspect is serious: there is no right to use the economic sanctions of lockout or strike during this period. The parties, therefore, need to have access to a mechanism which expertly settles disputes on the basis of an understanding that these parties have an ongoing relationship which is best maintained by respecting their autonomy and wisdom. Nevertheless the trend in several arbitration cases in the 1990s dealing with grievances against the employer for harassment based on allegations of wrongdoing against managers or co-workers seems to be to require notice and participation rights to be given to the third party co-workers and managers.[1] The principle affirmed in these recent cases is that where an individual employee has significant interests that could be adversely affected in a final, binding and unchallengeable way by the outcome of the arbitration proceeding and the union has chosen to oppose his or her interests, natural justice requires that both notice and standing be given. These considerations are heightened where there is evidence that the employer may also take a position which is inconsistent with the individual employee's interests.[2]

1. *See*, for example, *Board of School Trustees of School District No. 36 (Surrey) and Surrey Teachers' Assn.* (1998) 75 L.A.C. (4th) 129 (Hope); *The Crown in Right of Ontario (Ministry of Transportation) and Ontario Public Service Employees Union* (1994) 43 L.A.C. (4th).
2. *University of Windsor and University of Windsor Faculty Association* (1997) 70 L.A.C. (4th) 412 (Roach); and *Orillia Soldiers' Memorial Hospital and O.N.A.* (1993) 34 L.A.C. (4th) 315 (Swan); affd. 69 A.C.W.S. (3d) 678.

Chapter II. The Right to Organize

§1. The Need for Statutory Protection

430. With the removal of criminal prohibitions against union organizations in the last quarter of the nineteenth century, workers were, in principle, free to join unions and to participate in their collective bargaining and related activities. However, this theoretical freedom was translated into practice only relatively infrequently, and with great difficulty.

431. Workers who sought to organize a union confronted, first of all, the possibility of economic reprisals by their employer. An employer could, with impunity, refuse to employ unionists, to negotiate with the union, or to abide by any undertakings given to the union. Whether he or she would, as a matter of prudence, actually adopt such a position depended upon the relative power of the parties. If the employer chose to dismiss unionists or to refuse to recognize a union, the union could respond by calling a strike or imposing other economic sanctions. However, the employer, in turn, could seek relief in the civil or criminal courts against such sanctions and, as the law stood down to the 1940s, be reasonably confident of success. Thus, the freedom to organize often amounted, in practical terms, to no more than the freedom to suffer serious adverse legal and economic consequences.

432. Moreover, the absence of effective legal protection for trade union organization imposed at least two significant costs upon the community. First, the resulting weakness of trade unions may have exacerbated the deflationary effects of the great depression of the 1930s. This at least was a premise explicitly adopted in the protective legislation enacted in 1935 in the United States, the National Labor Relations Act (the Wagner Act). Second, again reflecting the American experience, economic conflict over the issue of union recognition was costly and disruptive. Nonetheless, legal protection for the right of workers to organize came to Canada only at a relatively late date.

433. Following the enactment of the Wagner Act in the United States, many Canadian provinces enacted legislation which purported to protect workers' rights to organize and bargain collectively. However, for the most part, this legislation was declaratory and unaccompanied by effective mechanisms for enforcement. An amendment to the federal Criminal Code in 1939 did prohibit refusal of employment, dismissal or threats which were intended to inhibit union membership and organization.[1] However, certain textual difficulties and the inefficacy of criminal prosecution in labour relations matters, largely vitiated this provision.

1. Now Criminal Code, R.S.C. 1985, c.C-46, s.425.

434. Only in the 1940s, in part to avoid disruptions which might damage the war effort, was Canadian legislation which provided for compulsory collective bargaining along the lines of the Wagner Act enacted. The federal Wartime Labour Relations Regulations, otherwise known as P.C. 1003, contained the essential and familiar features of the American Wagner Act: a mechanism for the designation, by majority choice, of one union as the exclusive bargaining agent of the employees; a legally enforceable duty of the employer to recognize, and bargain in good faith with that union; and the prohibition of employer 'unfair labour practices' which might interfere with selection of, or participation in, the union by employees. These Regulations provided the basis for post-war provincial and federal labour relations statutes.

435. The first two of these features – exclusivity of representation and the duty to bargain – will be considered elsewhere. Of immediate concern is the third, protection against unfair labour practices. Within the framework of a basic commitment to the promotion of collective bargaining, the suppression of unfair labour practices involves a balancing of the respective interests of the employee, the union and the employer.

§2. Protection of the Rights of Individual Employees

436. At common law, and also according to Quebec civil law, subject to contractual constraints, an employer might refuse to hire, cease to employ, or otherwise deal with workers more or less as he saw fit. As a practical matter, written employment contracts, and contracts for a fixed term, are very rare, so that most Canadian workers must look to legislation, if anywhere, for protection of their rights. As has been seen, various statutes do establish minimum conditions of work, safety and health standards, and protection against racial, religious, sexual or age discrimination. Workers within the federal jurisdiction, Quebec and Nova Scotia also enjoy statutory protection against unjust dismissal on any grounds.[1] But save to the extent that the employer's common law rights are thus specifically displaced by statute, they remain virtually absolute.

1. Canada Labour Code, ss.240 to 246. In Quebec, ss.124 to 131 of the Act Respecting Labour Standards (R.S.Q., c.N-1.1) provide a remedy to employees with three years of uninterrupted service in the same enterprise where an employee believes that s/he has not been dismissed for good and sufficient cause. The Nova Scotia Labour Standards Code, s.71, also provides statutory protection against unjust dismissal, but limits its protection to employees who have been employed for a minimum of ten years by the same employer.

437. The labour relations Acts provide a further, but limited, incursion into the employer's domain: an employer cannot exercise its rights *vis-à-vis* workers so as to interfere with their right to join a trade union or to participate in that union's lawful activities.[1] Thus, the mere showing that an employee has been arbitrarily dismissed or treated inequitably does not amount to proof that an 'unfair labour practice', in the technical sense, has been committed.[2] Only when the employer's conduct is shown to proceed from an intention to interfere with union organization is it forbidden. However, the apparent narrowness of this protection, with its obvious difficulties of proof, is overcome by statutory or adjudicatively developed presumptions.[3] Unless an employer can demonstrate the contrary, it will be presumed to have dismissed, or otherwise adversely treated, an employee for union activities. This presumption can be rebutted if the employer is able to tender credible evidence as to another motive, particularly if there is no record of other activities exhibiting an anti-union *animus*. On the other hand, the credibility of the employer's alternate explanation may be undermined if it can be shown to be engaging in a series of anti-union manoeuvres.[4]

1. Canada, s.94; British Columbia. s.6; Ontario, s.72; Quebec. s.14.
2. *CKOY* (1976) 77 C.L.L.C. para. 16,067 (C.L.R.B.).
3. Canada, s.98(4); Ontario, s.96(5); British Columbia, s.14(7); Quebec, s.17. And *see National Automatic Vending* (1963) 63 C.L.L.C. para. 16,278 (O.L.R.B.).
4. *Fielding Lumber*, [1976] 1 C.L.R.B.R. 216 (O.L.R.B.).

438. Typical of circumstances which have been held to support a presumption of dismissal for union activity, or to undermine the credibility of an alternative explanation, are the following: the dismissal for 'poor work' of employees of whom no previous complaint has been made, or who have recently been promoted;[1] the selection for discharge on grounds of 'redundancy' only of employees active in the union;[2] and the discharge of employees whose admitted misbehaviour was first condoned or forgiven by the employer, and then relied upon to justify discharge when their union membership was discovered.[3] Typically, it has been held that discharge for union membership or activity need be only one amongst several motives in the employer's mind in order to stigmatize the discharge as an 'unfair labour practice'.[4] Discrimination against union members or activists is similarly forbidden, as is the imposition upon them of monetary or other penalties, or the attempt to secure a promise to abstain from union membership or activities as a condition of employment.[5]

1. *Forano*, [1974] 1 C.L.R.B.R. 13 (B.C.L.R.B.).
2. *Dubois* v. *Distinctive Leather Goods Ltd.*, [1975] T.T. 284, confirmed by the Quebec Court of Appeal, [1976] C.A. 648.
3. *National Automatic Vending, Fielding Lumber, supra.*
4. *R.* v. *Bushnell Communications* (1974) 4 O.R. (2d) 288 (C.A.).
5. Ontario, s.72(b), (c); Canada, s.94(3)(e); British Columbia, s.6(3)(c), (d); Quebec, s.14.

439. The employer is also forbidden, typically, to use threats or promises to induce or coerce workers to abandon union membership or activities.[1] Such promises include both the direct offer of individual bribes and the suggestion that general wage increases would be forthcoming if workers did not organize, and withheld if they did.[2] Moreover, even apart from such overt threats and promises, statutes typically prevent an employer from unilaterally altering terms of employment during critical periods of a union's organizing campaign, to avoid a situation in which employees, either through gratitude or fear, decline to participate in the union.[3]

1. Ontario, ss.70, 72 (c); Canada, s.94(3)(a), (e); British Columbia, s.6(3)(d); Quebec, ss.13, 14.
2. *Martel Lumber*, [1972] O.L.R.B. 811.
3. Canada, s.50; Ontario, s.86(2); British Columbia, s.32; Quebec, s.59; *Spar Aerospace Products*, [1979] 1 C.L.R.B.R. 61 (O.L.R.B.); *Canadian Imperial Bank of Commerce*, [1980] 80 C.L.L.C. para. 16,002 (C.L.R.B.).

440. Finally, some statutes protect employees from victimization by their employer prompted by the fact that they have given adverse testimony in labour relations proceedings.[1] Such statutes generally seek to maintain the integrity of legal mechanisms designed to protect the right to organize.

1. Ontario, s.87 and Canada. s.94(3)(iii) specifically protect the identity of complainants.

441. On the other hand, it must be reiterated that employees involved in union activities do not enjoy complete immunity. They may be disciplined or discharged for acting violently, for example, whether in connection with illegal work stoppages, or in support of a lawful strike.[1] Generally, if the employer can demonstrate a bona fide business reason for a particular activity, the board will not find an unfair labour practice.

1. *International Wallcoverings Limited*, [1983] O.L.R.B.R. 1316.

§3. Protection of Trade Union Rights

442. If a trade union is to represent workers effectively and authentically, it must be completely free of employer control, and deal with the employer at arm's length. The labour relations Acts ensure this effective and authentic representation by forbidding, as unfair labour practices, the participation of management in the formation or administration of a union, its selection by employees, or its representation of them, as a bargaining agent.[1] Even the contribution of financial or other support by the employer to the union is forbidden, except in circumstances where the autonomy of the union is unlikely to be impaired.[2]

1. Ontario, s.70; Canada, s.94(1); British Columbia, s.6(1); Quebec, s.12.
2. *Super City* (1964) 64 C.L.L.C. para. 16,005 (O.L.R.B.) – payment by employer of full-time union staff member unobjectionable because originally provided for in collective agreement and openly undertaken for over 20 years.

443. Thus, for example, an employer is forbidden to infiltrate and spy upon union activities,[1] to interrogate workers regarding their union membership,[2] to support one of two unions competing for members amongst his workers,[3] to pay for a union's legal representation,[4] or to enter into a collective agreement with a union which does not represent his employees.[5] On the other hand, after the employees have freely selected a union as their bargaining agent, the employer may permit it to use plant facilities for meetings, may grant time off to union officers for union business,[6] and may enter into a collective agreement which provides that union membership shall be a condition of employment.[7]

1. Saskatchewan, s.11(1)(h); *Radio Shack*, [1980] 1 C.L.R.B.R. (O.L.R.B.); *Securicor*, [1983] O.L.R.B. 720.
2. *Jones & Laughlin Mining*, [1967–8] O.L.R.B. 202.
3. *Trent Metals*, (1979) 79 C.L.L.C. para. 16,198 (O.L.R.B.).
4. *Norfish*, [1965–6] O.L.R.B. 414.
5. *Sunrise Paving and Construction*, [1972] O.L.R.B. 199.
6. Ontario, s.51(1)(b), (c).
7. *See infra*, para. 448.

444. The exclusion of the employer from union affairs generally extends to the lowest level of management, foremen or supervisors.[1] However, recognizing that their managerial status may be merely temporary and that they may have residual ties to a union, membership by such persons in a union is not automatically suspect. Where their support of the union can be shown to be contrary to the wishes of their employer, foremen and supervisors have occasionally been permitted to participate in union activities,[2] although not legally protected in their right to do so.[3] Where such individuals have been dismissed for union activities, however, it has been held that the union may still seek a remedy on their behalf if the dismissals have improperly interfered with the union's interests.[4]

1. *Infra*, paras. 485–8.
2. *Air Liquide* (1964) 64 C.L.L.C. para. 16,002 (O.L.R.B.).
3. *Jarvis* v. *Assoc. Medical Services* (1964) 44 D.L.R. (2d) 407 (S.C.C.).
4. *A.A.S. Telecommunications*, [1977] 2 C.L.R.B.R. 73 (O.L.R.B.).

445. Under some Canadian collective bargaining statutes unions that are the beneficiaries of illicit employer support are denied status as bargaining agents under and their collective agreements are denied recognition.[1] In Quebec, they are liable to be dissolved by the Labour Court.[2]

1. Canada, s.25; British Columbia, s.31; Ontario, s.53. *See Royal Oak Mines Inc.* (1993) 93 C.L.L.C. para. 16,063 (C.L.R.B.); *Westside Foods and Overwaitea Foods Ltd.* (1997) 97 C.L.L.C. para. 220-066 (B.C.L.R.B.).
2. *Tremblay* v. *F.T.Q.*, [1967] S.C.R. 697; Quebec, s.149.

§4. Reconciling Employee, Employer and Trade Union Rights

446. Labour relations Acts expressly or implied protect trade union rights as a necessary component of the statutorily guaranteed collective bargaining system, but it does not necessarily follow that such rights are always to be preferred when they clash with the interests of individual employees and employers.

447. Collective bargaining legislation also recognizes that there is a need to protect individual workers against abuses of union power. Unions, therefore, are forbidden to use intimidation or coercion to compel employees to join their ranks.

Membership so procured, and union representational claims based on such membership, have no legal effect.[1]

1. *Milnet Mines*, (1953) 53 C.L.L.C. para. 17,063 (O.L.R.B.); *Bradley & Walsh Ltd.* (1993) 93 C.L.L.C. para. 16,080 (N.B.I.R.B.); *Centro Mechanical Inc.* (1997) 97 C.L.L.C. para. 220-035 (O.L.R.B.); *Rossmere Golf and Country Club* (1993) 94 C.L.L.C. para. 16,028 (Man.L.B.); but *see Christian Labour Association, Local 501* (1996) 96 C.L.L.C. para. 220-007 (B.C.L.R.B.).

448. The institutional interests of the union and the exigencies of the labour market are generally accepted as justifying arrangements which require employees, as a condition of employment, either to join the trade union which is their bargaining agent, or to pay a sum to the union in lieu of union dues, in effect as a fee for representation services provided. In some jurisdictions, these arrangements are required by statute,[1] but they may also be the subject of negotiation between the employer and the union and in this way become a provision of the collective agreement.[2]

1. Canada, s.70; Ontario, s.47; Quebec, s.47: British Columbia, s.6(3)(f).
2. Canada, s.68; Ontario, s.51; British Columbia, s.15.

449. The countervailing right of employees to be free from unwanted union membership, and particularly to retain their jobs in the face of union hostility, is protected by a variety of devices. In some jurisdictions, the right of employees to object to union membership, on conscientious grounds, is protected.[1] In others, the union is forbidden to deny membership to employees arbitrarily, or to seek the discharge of members who have been expelled for improper reasons.[2] Unions which practice racial, religious, sexual, or other invidious forms of discrimination, may themselves be denied status under the governing legislation.[3] In general, legislation has sought to strike a balance between the necessary sacrifice of some individual interests to promote a collective regime premised on majority rule, and the countervailing claims of individual non-union employees.

1. British Columbia, s.17; Ontario, s.52; Manitoba, s.76(3).
2. Canada, s.95(e); Ontario, s.51(2); British Columbia, s.10(2); Quebec, s.63.
3. Ontario, s.15; British Columbia, s.31.

450. The Charter of Rights and Freedoms has been invoked to attempt to alter the legislative compromise between the interests of individual employees and the collective interest as represented by the union. A variety of union security arrangements have been challenged on the basis that freedom of association embraces freedom from association. But before the freedom of association question can be addressed, the question of whether or not the Charter applies must be answered. In other words, the preliminary issue is whether or not government action is involved.[1] The British Columbia Court of Appeal held that a statutory provision merely permitting the negotiation of a clause in a collective agreement requiring union membership as a condition of employment did not constitute sufficient government action to trigger the application of the Charter.[2] If the impugned union security provision is negotiated with a government employer, however, the Charter will apply. In such a case the Supreme Court of Canada has held that, even if the compelled dues are used in part for political purposes, this type of arrangement does not violate the Charter.[3]

1. *Retail, Wholesale and Department Store Union Local 580* v. *Dolphin Delivery*, [1986] 2 S.C.R. 573 (S.C.C.).
2. *Re Bhindi and B.C. Projectionists* (1986) 29 D.L.R. 51.
3. *Lavigne and Ontario Public Service Employees' Union* (1991) 91 C.L.L.C. para. 14,029; [1991] 2 S.C.R. 211.

451. On the other hand, the employer is also typically conceded to enjoy important interests, worthy of legal protection, with which trade union interests must be reconciled. For example, an employer is entitled to maintain order and efficiency in his operations, even where the effect of doing so might be to interfere with union organizing campaigns or other activities.[1] These employer rights to manage its operation are not unqualified. A blanket prohibition against the distribution of union literature on the employer's premises at all times, including non-working hours, has been held to constitute an unfair labour practice.[2] Unions normally enjoy no privilege to solicit members or to transact their business on company premises during working hours.[3] However, if an employer chooses to promulgate a rule against all forms of employee solicitation or personal discussion during working hours, the rule must neither explicitly prohibit discussion about unions nor, if phrased generally, be applied discriminatorily only against employees involved in union activities.[4] Nor can such a rule extend gratuitously to innocuous gestures of support for the union, such as the wearing of tiny 'dress pins'.[5] An employer, moreover, may not alter a longstanding practice of allowing a union representative access to its premises unless there is a compelling business reason for refusing access.[6]

1. *Roscoe Metal Products*, (1964) 64 C.L.L.C. para. 16,303 (O.L.R.B.); in *South Peace Home Support Association*, (1995) 95 C.L.L.C. para. 220-071 (B.C.L.R.B.), it was held that a policy prohibiting union members from sitting on the board of directors was not an unfair labour practice.
2. *T. Eaton Co. Ltd.*, [1985] O.L.R.B. 491; *R. Milrod Metal Products* (1964) 64 C.L.L.C. para. 16,007 (O.L.R.B.).
3. Unions, however, are permitted to solicit membership in public areas adjacent to the place of work such as the public areas of shopping malls. *See Cadillac Fairview Corporation Ltd.* v. *Retail Wholesale and Department Store Union et al.* (1990) 90 C.L.L.C. para. 14,003 (Ont. C.A.); *Sobey's Inc.* (1996) 96 C.L.L.C. para. 220-032 (N.B.L.E.B.).
4. *Associated Medical Services*, (1961) 61 C.L.L.C. para. 16,218 (O.L.R.B.); *Canadian Imperial Bank of Commerce* (1985) 85 C.L.L.C. para. 16,021 (C.L.R.B.).
5. *Canadian Imperial Bank of Commerce (North Hills)*, [1979] 1 C.L.R.B.R. 266 (C.L.R.B.); *Ottawa-Carleton Regional Transit Commission*, [1985] 7 C.L.R.B.R. (N.S.) 137.
6. *CFTO-TV Ltd.* (1995) 95 C.L.L.C. 220-045 (C.L.R.B.).

452. Similarly, the normal right of an employer who is the owner or occupier of premises to control access to those premises is generally unimpaired, although it may make it more difficult for the union to reach employees whom it wishes to organize.[1] However, where employees not only work on the employer's premises but also reside there (as for example in mining and logging camps) the denial of access to union organizers so that they may meet the employees after work and in their living quarters, is excessive and improper. Here statutory intervention has created a special right of access for union organizers, so that they can bring the message of collective bargaining to employees in such remote and isolated locations.[2] The federal jurisdiction now gives the Canada Industrial Relations Board a discretion to provide a trade union with the names and addresses of off-site workers and to authorize the union to communicate with these employees by means of the employer's electronic communications system.[3]

1. Canada, s.95(d); Ontario, s.77; British Columbia, s.6(2).
2. Non-employee union organizers attempting to reach such isolated locations have been held to be trespassers: *R.* v. *Labelle* (1964), 48 D.L.R. (2d) 37 (Ont.C.A.). Provisions authorizing entry: Canada, s.109; B.C., s.7(2); Ontario, s.13; Quebec, ss.8, 9. For the application of one of these provisions *see Blackcomb Skiing Enterprise* (1995) 95 C.L.L.C. para. 220-046 (B.C.L.R.B.); *Brewery Creek Mine* (1998) 98 C.L.L.C. para. 220-001 (C.L.R.B.).
3. S.109.1.

453. An employer enjoys the right to close a plant or discontinue or suspend operations for business reasons despite the detrimental effect of such action upon the union and its supporters.[1] If an employer is discontinuing unprofitable operations, moving a plant nearer markets or sources of supply, or consolidating operations to enhance efficiency, its right to do so is uninhibited. However when the resulting interruption of employment cannot be justified by reference to any such business motive, it may well be construed as having an anti-union purpose.[2] And where that purpose is present – even when accompanied by legitimate business motives – an unfair labour practice will have been committed.[3] Nevertheless, the law does not go as far as to force an employer to remain in business, even though the permanent closure of the enterprise is motivated by anti-union reasons.[4]

1. *Alitalia* (1976) 76 C.L.L.C. para. 16,006 (C.L.R.B.); British Columbia, s.6(4)(b); Ontario, s.84. By implication, *Consolidated Bathurst Packaging Ltd.*, [1983] O.L.R.B. 1411 confirms this proposition.
2. *Academy of Medicine*, [1977] O.L.R.B. 783; *EF International Language Schools Inc.* (1997) 97 C.L.L.C para. 220-072 (B.C.L.R.B.).
3. *Westinghouse Canada*, [1980] 2 C.L.R.B.R. 469 (O.L.R.B.); *National Bank*, [1982] 3 C.L.R.B.R. 1 (C.L.R.B.).
4. *City Buick Pontiac (Montréal) Inc.* v. *Roy et al.* (1981) 81 C.L.L.C. para. 14,108 (T.T.). *See*, however, *infra*, para. 466.

454. In all such circumstances, when the motive of anti-unionism can be detected or inferred, otherwise apparently legitimate employer conduct will be found to be illegal.

455. The balance is nowhere more difficult to strike than in connection with appeals by an employer to his employees not to unionize. On the one hand, the employer is generally recognized to possess a right of free speech.[1] Through the exercise of this right, it is hoped, both the attractions and the drawbacks of unionization will be presented for consideration by the employees, so that they can make a rational and informed choice. On the other hand, the exercise of the employer's right of free speech may be so fraught with sinister significance for his employee audience that it will effectively destroy union support. Limits on the employer's right of free speech are thus inevitable. Of course, the employer may not use threats, coercion, intimidation, promises, or undue influence in addressing his employees on the subject of unionization.[2] But the difficult issue in any given case is whether apparently innocuous employer language may reasonably be construed as having such an effect upon employees.

1. British Columbia, s.8; Ontario, s.70; and *see City and Country Radio*, [1975] 2 C.L.R.B.R. 1 (C.L.R.B.); *Ed Klassen Pontiac Buick GMC (1994) Ltd.* (1995) 95 C.L.L.C. para. 220-063 (B.C.L.R.B.).
2. Canada, s.94(3)(e); British Columbia, s.9; Ontario, ss.70, 72; Quebec, s.13, and *see Michelin Tires*, [1979] 2 C.L.R.B.R. (N.S.L.R.B.).

456. Labour relations boards seeking to gauge the true impact of employer appeals have generally accepted that the employer's economic power over his workers, prior to the advent of a union, makes them highly responsive to her/his wishes, especially where her/his message is delivered in a manner or under circumstances which serve to exacerbate this undesirable effect. Labour relations boards will look with suspicion at an appeal to employees who are a 'captive audience', compelled by an order of their employer to attend a meeting on company premises during working hours.[1] They will be similarly concerned with messages which predict, and especially with those which threaten, that employees will lose their jobs or employment benefits if they support the union.[2] Indeed, several jurisdictions have specifically outlawed employer speech which includes threats to move the employer's place of operations, or unilaterally to alter wages and working conditions.[3] One labour board has even held that, where there has been a corporate culture of open communication, a failure by the employer to answer questions as to whether the operation would close if the union became certified amounted to a subtle threat to job security.[4]

1. *Ex-Cell-O*, [1972] 2 C.L.R.B.R. 233 (O.L.R.B.).
2. *Bell and Howell*, [1968–9] O.L.R.B. 695; *Viceroy Construction*, [1978] 1 C.L.R.B.R. 22 (O.L.R.B.); *JAK Electrical Contractors Ltd.* (1998) 98 C.L.L.C. para. 220-001 (O.L.R.B.).
3. Newfoundland, s.26; Saskatchewan, s.11(1)(i).
4. *Wal-Mart Canada Inc.* (1997) 97 C.L.L.C. para. 220-046 (O.L.R.B.); aff'd by (1997) 97 C.L.L.C. para. 220-094 (O.C.J., Gen.Div.).

457. Above all, labour relations boards will be especially vigilant in situations where employer appeals are made against a background of other, overt anti-union behaviour, or as a part of a sustained and egregious campaign of anti-union propaganda.[1]

1. *Dylex*, [1977] O.L.R.B. 357, aff'd. (1977) 18 O.R. (2d) 58 (D.C.).

§5. Remedies

A. Representation Proceedings

458. The occasion for employer interference with the right to organize is usually the union's initial attempt to gain bargaining rights by securing employee membership and support. Once these rights have been secured, either by the granting of a labour relations board certification order or by execution of a collective agreement, the employer will usually acquiesce in the union's existence, and focus his opposition instead upon the union's substantive demands for wages and working conditions. Only if the union's status is subsequently called into question, or if it appears to have a tenuous command of employee loyalties, is the employer likely to be tempted to renew a campaign of serious interference with the union and its members. For this reason, some of the important remedies for employer unfair labour practices are connected with representation proceedings.

459. If the employer has violated the rights of the union and of its members, and thus created a coercive atmosphere in which the true wishes of the employees concerning union representation are unlikely to be ascertained, in some jurisdictions the union may be given bargaining rights, notwithstanding the absence of majority employee support.[1] In addition, labour boards may disregard evidence of opposition to, or resignations from, the union procured by or as a result of employer illegality,[2] and may disqualify one of two competing unions which is the willing beneficiary of improper tactics directed against its competitor.[3] All of these remedies are made available in the context of representation proceedings, and do not require the aggrieved union or individual to launch separate actions.

1. Canada, s.99.1; Nova Scotia s.25(9). Such a remedy is not available in Quebec and is no longer available in Ontario. It is unknown yet if the labour board that will be set up in the near future in Quebec will decide to resort to such a remedy.
2. *Re Clark Leatherdale and Upholsterers' Int'l Union* (1972) 26 D.L.R. (3d) 450 (Man.Q.B.).
3. *Trent Metals* (1979) 79 C.L.L.C. para. 16,198 (O.L.R.B.), but *see Re Brayshaws Steel Ltd. and U.S.W.A.* (1971) 26 D.L.R. (3d) 153 (Ont.C.A.).

B. Administrative Sanctions

460. In the 1970s, labour relations boards acquired additional statutory powers to deal with unfair labour practices.[1] In all jurisdictions except Quebec these procedures conformed to a consistent pattern. Quebec's unfair labour practice procedures, however, are quite distinctive.

1. D.D. Carter, *The Expansion of Labour Board Remedies: A New Approach to Industrial Conflict* (Kingston, 1976); G.W. Adams, 'Labour Law Remedies' in K. Swinton and K. Swan (eds.), *Studies in Canadian Labour Law* (Toronto, 1983).

461. Quebec, since it has no unified body such as a labour relations board to administer its Labour Code as a whole, is the notable exception. Jurisdiction to administer the Quebec Labour Code is divided between administrative officials and a specialized labour court (the *Tribunal du travail*). The administrative officials, the *commissaires du travail* (labour commissioners), play the most important role in the administration of the Labour Code. They have jurisdiction to decide all contested issues relating to certification. In this particular area, they are assisted by the certification agents (*agents d'accréditation*) who conduct the necessary investigations and certify unions in uncontested cases. The *commissaires du travail* also have the jurisdiction to decide unfair labour practice complaints dealing with dismissal, suspension, or any other kind of sanction imposed upon an individual employee who has exercised a protected right under the Labour Code. The *commissaires du travail* may order the employer to cease taking reprisals against the employee, to compensate the employee for the loss of salary and other benefits and, when applicable, to reinstate the dismissed employee in the job.[1] All final decisions of the *commissaires du travail* can be appealed to the *Tribunal du travail*,[2] and this Tribunal's decisions are final.

1. Quebec Labour Code, s.15.
2. *Ibid.*, s.118.

462. The *commissaires du travail*, when dealing with an unfair labour practice complaint, have no power to use the administrative approaches followed by the labour relations boards of the other Canadian jurisdictions. Furthermore, as pointed out above, their remedial powers are quite narrow as they can only provide a remedy to the individual employee and not to the union. For example, they cannot design a 'make whole' remedy that would counterbalance the chilling effect that an unfair labour practice would have on a union's organizing drive. Moreover, they do not have any general power to issue cease and desist orders to restrain breaches of the Code.

463. Rather than emphasizing administrative remedies, the Quebec Labour Code relies heavily on a penal approach. Unfair labour practices directed at the union, or committed by a union, can only be redeemed through penal sanctions. This approach means that such matters as unlawful employer interference with the union, breaches of the duty to bargain in good faith, illegal strikes or employer breaches of the 'anti-scab' provisions can only be dealt with through criminal sanctions administered by the *Tribunal du travail*, since this tribunal has original jurisdiction over any penal prosecution for a violation of the Labour Code. This anachronistic mechanism for administering the Labour Code should be replaced shortly by a new one, much more similar to what is found elsewhere in Canada. In June 2001, the Quebec legislature amended its Labour Code[1] and created a labour board that will exercise the jurisdiction that presently belongs to the *commissaires du travail* and the *Tribunal du travail*. The board will enjoy very broad remedial powers that, when the legislative amendments are effective, should allow the administrative approach to unfair labour practices that prevails in Canada to be implemented in Quebec.

1. An Act to amend to Labour Code, to establish the Commission des relations du travail and to amend other legislative provisions, S.Q. 2001, c.27.

464. In the rest of Canada, different procedures are followed. First, the labour relations board's initial response to a complaint is to attempt to resolve matters by informal processes. A board officer is sent out to investigate and to attempt to settle the complaint. Only if this attempt is unsuccessful is the matter set down for formal adjudication.

465. Second, while carriage of unfair labour practice proceedings rests with the complainant, the board does not make available to the complainant the results of the initial investigation by the board's officer.[1] In view of the importance of motive in assessing employer conduct, and of the notorious difficulty of proving motive, it might be thought that the absence of this report would confront a complainant with an almost impossible task. However, the complainant is assisted, in almost all jurisdictions, by the creation of a legal presumption (either by statute or by labour board decision) that any discharge is for union activity, unless the employer can demonstrate the contrary.[2]

1. *See A. J. (Archie) Goodale*, [1977] 2 C.L.R.B.R. 309 (C.L.R.B.).
2. *Supra*, para. 437.

466. Almost all boards have power to order reinstatement and compensation for employees who are victims of employer unfair labour practices. In addition, most boards have remedial powers framed in very general terms, which include the power to require the cessation of prohibited conduct, and the taking of affirmative action to remedy its effects.[1] In the exercise of this power, labour relations boards have developed, for example, the 'make whole' remedy, by which the employer is required to compensate the union for the entire cost of an organizing campaign frustrated by his unfair labour practice, as well as the costs of litigation leading to the order.[2] Labour relations boards have refused to order employers to re-open operations closed deliberately to forestall unionization, choosing instead to award both 'make whole' damages to the union, and substantial compensation to the employees who lost their jobs.[3] Employees have been awarded compensation for the loss of possible salary increases, due to the employer's failure to bargain with the union,[4] and even interest on such losses.[5]

1. Canada, s.99; British Columbia, s.133; Ontario, s.96(4); Quebec, s.15.
2. *Kidd Bros. Produce*, [1976] C.L.R.B. 304 (B.C.L.R.B.).
3. *Academy of Medicine*, [1977] O.L.R.B. 783, and *see Westinghouse*, [1980] 2 C.L.R.B.R. 469 (O.L.R.B.).
4. *Radio Shack*, [1980] 1 C.L.R.B.R., 99 (O.L.R.B.).
5. *Hallowell House*, [1980] 2 C.L.R.B.R. 469 (O.L.R.B.); *Beckett Elevator Co. Ltd.* (1984) O.L.R.B. 169.

467. Boards have recently been particularly concerned to undo the adverse effects of hostile employer action upon employee attitudes towards unionization. Thus, one board ordered the senior official of a large bank to write to all of its employees rescinding illegal management edicts, apologizing for interference with employee rights, and assuring employees of their right to organize.[1] In another case, a board required that such a statement should also be read to a meeting of employees assembled on company premises for the purpose, following which the union was to be afforded an opportunity to address the meeting.[2] However, the Supreme Court of Canada took strong exception to a board order requiring a senior official to sign such a letter, asserting that 'this type of penalty is totalitarian and as such alien to the tradition of free nations like Canada'.[3]

The courts are, however, evincing an increased willingness to police, and strike down, innovative remedies developed by the boards. The Supreme Court of Canada has manifested an antipathy to proactive remedies designed to deal with the chilling effect on union organization created by employer unfair labour practices. The Court held that the Canada Board has exceeded its jurisdiction by jointly creating a trust fund to be administered by the union and the employer for the purposes of furthering the objectives of the Canada Labour Code.[4]

1. *Canadian Imperial Bank of Commerce* (1980) 80 C.L.L.C. para. 16,002 (C.L.R.B.).
2. *Radio Shack*, [1980] 1 C.L.R.B.R. 99 (O.L.R.B.).

3. *National Bank of Canada* v. *Retail Clerks' International Union* (1984), 9 D.L.R. (4th) 10 at 31 *per* Beetz J; [1984] 1 S.C.R. 269 at 296.
4. *National Bank of Canada, supra.*

468. Of course, specific powers may be conferred which broaden the normal scope of the board's general remedial power. For example, one province authorizes the labour relations board to dissolve a dominated union, rather than merely deprive it of status under its Labour Code.[1] Another province authorizes the labour relations board to award punitive, rather than compensatory, damages to an employee whose rights are interfered with by an employer's unfair labour practice.[2]

1. Quebec, s.149.
2. Manitoba, s.31(4)(e).

469. In any case, remedial orders of the labour relations board are typically made registrable in the provincial supreme court, and are thereafter enforceable as court orders.[1] Continued disobedience of the order following registration may result in a contempt citation by the court, leading to fine or imprisonment for individual contemners, sequestration of corporate contemners, or to enforcement of money judgments by seizure of the assets of the offending party. The Supreme Court of Canada has recently affirmed the authority of the court to punish for criminal contempt any person and/or union for publicly defying a directive of a labour relations' board registered as an order of the court.[2]

1. Canada, s.23; British Columbia, s.135; Ontario, s.96(6); Quebec, s.19.1.
2. *United Nurses of Alberta* v. *Attorney General (Alta.)* (1992) 92 C.L.L.C. para. 14,023.

C. Criminal Prosecution

470. Prosecution in the criminal courts remains a possible, if not favoured, response to employer interference with the right to organize. As has been mentioned such interference constitutes an offence under the federal Criminal Code.[1] However, this provision is seldom resorted to in practice.

1. *Supra*, para. 433.

471. In almost all Canadian jurisdictions, a violation of the provisions of the Labour Relations Act, or disobedience of the orders of any tribunal administering those provisions, is a quasi-criminal offence, typically punishable by a fine which may be imposed after prosecution in the lower level of criminal courts in the province. The fine, again typically, cumulates daily while the offence continues, and is a greater amount in respect of trade union and corporate offences than it is in relation to offences by individuals.[1] However, recourse to prosecution, where available, is discouraged by both practical obstacles and specific statutory provisions.

1. Canada, s.101; British Columbia, s.158; Ontario, s.104; Quebec, s.144, makes no such distinction.

472. As to the practical obstacles, carriage of a prosecution rests with the complainant. Unlike normal criminal prosecutions, the aggrieved party is thus charged with the obligation of gathering the evidence, and presenting it to a criminal court. Of course, the full costs of the prosecution and of any resulting appeals must be borne by the complainant. But if the prosecution is successful any fine imposed goes not to the complainant but to the state. Moreover, conviction does not, of itself, result in an order to terminate the offending conduct; it simply exposes the offender to future prosecution. And finally, except in Quebec, where the Labour Court has jurisdicition to hear penal prosecutions for violation of the Labour Code, the criminal courts are presided over by judges who are largely unfamiliar with labour relations matters, who naturally require the same high standard of proof they impose in other criminal proceedings, and who tend to interpret labour relations statutes without a developed understanding of underlying policies. For all of these reasons, therefore, there are important practical impediments to prosecution as a useful vehicle for enforcing the legislation and the policies it embodies.

473. More important even than the practical problems, are the typical statutory provisions which require that the labour relations board must consent to all prosecutions.[1] While the board may use the application for consent as an occasion for clarifying the rights of the parties and, if possible, securing mutually acceptable solutions, it is in fact loath to give its consent to prosecution. Prosecution is seen as accomplishing little of a positive nature and, on the contrary, as tending to embitter the relationship and to inhibit the resumption of amicable dealing between the parties. Thus, consent to prosecute is given only in the most extreme circumstances.[2]

1. Canada, s.104; Ontario, s.109; neither British Columbia nor Quebec appear to interpose a requirement of consent to prosecute.
2. *A.A.S. Telecommunications*, [1976] O.L.R.B. 751, *Arthur G. McKee*, [1977] 1 C.L.R.B.R. 176 (O.L.R.B.).

D. Other Remedies

474. Some collective agreements echo the statutory prohibition against employer conduct which interferes with the right of the union to represent the employees, or of the employees to be represented by the union. Where the employer in fact takes action during the currency of an agreement which can be so stigmatized, the union is free to seek redress through the grievance procedure and arbitration, as established by the agreement itself.[1] The arbitrator, typically, has sufficient remedial power to give compensation and order reinstatement of employees discharged for union activity, and perhaps has power as well to order the employer to abandon the offending practices.

1. Where arbitration is available, labour relations boards may require the parties to use it rather than seeking relief under statute, *see National Showcase* (1960) 61 C.L.L.C. para. 16,185 (O.L.R.B.), *North Saskatchewan Laundry and Support Services* (1996) 96 C.L.L.C. para. 220-037 (S.L.R.B.), and *contra Ludger Harvey* v. *Cossette*, [1969] C.A. 91.

475. It is notionally possible for employees to frame an action in tort against their employer for conduct which might amount to an unfair labour practice.

However, this possibility is at most a theoretical one.[1] It certainly does not lie within the contemplation of unions confronting employer interference.

1. *Teamsters* v. *Midland Superior Express* (1974) 43 D.L.R. (3d) 540 (Alta.C.A.).

E. Self-help

476. It has quite generally been held that a union or employees, who are themselves the victims of employer unfair labour practices, are not free to visit reprisals upon the employer by means of strikes, picketing or boycotts.[1] If recourse is sought to these self-help remedies, the union and employees leave themselves vulnerable to prosecution, civil suit, or administrative proceedings at the instance of the employer. Only very rarely is a labour relations board given explicit power to deny an employer relief against illegal union or employee conduct on the ground that the employer's unfair labour practices have brought down the offending union or employee conduct upon itself,[2] although it is occasionally assumed to exist.[3] While the courts do possess an analogous discretion to refuse injunctive relief to employers who have provoked their employees into illegal conduct by their own illegality, this discretion is seldom exercised.[4]

1. *Corcoran Foods*, [1964–5] O.L.R.B. 94.
2. British Columbia, s.71.
3. For example, the labour relations board has excercised its discretion in refusing an employer consent to prosecute illegal strikers, because 'prosecution . . . should not be a manifestation of retributive justice', *Savage Shoes* (1953) 53 C.L.L.C. para. 17,060 (O.L.R.B.).
4. *Hiram Walker* v. *Distillery Worker* (1974) 48 D.L.R. (3d) 618 (B.C.S.C.); *Crozier* v. *Western Publishers* (1974) 51 D.L.R. (3d) 96 (Sask.C.A.).

477. Thus, as a practical matter, it can be said that there is no legal privilege to respond to employer unfair labour practices by means of economic reprisals. To this general statement, there is, of course, an overriding exception: if the conduct is not illegal because, for example, it is a timely strike under the Labour Relations Act, the fact that it is mounted in reprisal for the employer's unfair labour practice does not alter its legality.

Chapter III. Legal Recognition of Collective Bargaining Rights

§1. The Source of Collective Bargaining Rights

478. Collective bargaining rights flow from the labour relations legislation enacted by each of the 11 Canadian jurisdictions. The acquisition, transfer and termination of bargaining rights, as well as the definition of the bargaining structure, are all matters covered fully by this legislation. Although the general scheme of these different statutes is the same, there is significant variation in detail between jurisdictions.

479. The federal government and nine of the provinces have established statutory tribunals,[1] commonly known as labour boards, to administer their labour relations legislation. As already seen,[2] Quebec, on the other hand, still divides this responsibility between administrative officials and a labour court.

1. *Supra*, 132–5. *The Role of Government Institutions.*
2. *Supra*, paras. 461 *et seq.*

§2. Acquisition of Collective Bargaining Rights

A. Eligible Employees

480. The benefits and protections provided by collective bargaining statutes extend only to those persons who can be considered to be 'employees',[1] and who have not also been excluded, either expressly or implicitly, from the scope of these statutes. In the context of collective bargaining legislation the term 'employee' has a somewhat different meaning than when it is used in its more general legal sense. Even though certain persons may not be regarded as being employed at common law, they may still be considered as employees as that term is defined in collective bargaining statutes and entitled to the benefits flowing from that legislation.[2] Conversely, there are some persons clearly working under an employment relationship at common law who are expressly or implicitly excluded from the coverage of collective bargaining legislation. The extent of these inclusions and exclusions varies slightly among the different Canadian jurisdictions, reflecting different policy judgments about the appropriate scope of collective bargaining legislation.

1. *Supra*, para. 60.
2. It has been held, however, that retired workers do not fall within the definition of employee. *See Cominco*, [1979] 2 C.L.R.B.R. 322 (B.C.L.R.B.).

481. The Charter of Rights and Freedoms has cast a shadow over at least some of these exclusions. Not only can it be argued that the express exclusion of certain groups of employees from the benefits of collective bargaining legislation is inconsistent with the Charter's guarantee of freedom of association, but such exclusions also have to be measured against its guarantee of equality before and under the law. These broad guarantees are qualified in the Charter itself by the provision that they are 'subject only to such reasonable limits as can be demonstrably justified in a free and democratic society'. While a labour relations rationale may justify some of these exclusions, the continued exclusion from collective bargaining of other groups, such as agricultural employees and domestics, raises interesting constitutional issues.[1] The exclusion from collective bargaining of members of the Royal Canadian Mounted Police, however, has not been regarded as inconsistent with the Charter's guarantees. The Supreme Court of Canada has held that this exclusion does not infringe the Charter's guarantees of freedom of expression, freedom of association, or equality.[2]

1. *Corporation of District of Powell River* (1987) 13 C.L.R.B.R. (N.S.) 289 (B.C.L.R.B.); the General Division of the Ontario Court of Justice has held that the exclusion of agricultural employees from the protection of Ontario's collective bargaining legislation does not violate the Charter, *Dunmore* v. *Attorney General (Ontario) and Highline Produce Ltd.* (1998) 98 C.L.L.C. para. 220-012.
2. *Gaétan Delisle* c. *Le procureur général du Canada et al.*, [1999] 2 S.C.R. 989.

1. Dependent contractors

482. Not all persons work under arrangements exhibiting all the characteristics of a straightforward employment relationship. Some contractual arrangements under which work is performed may display certain features indicating that the worker may be in the business of selling services, and not just performing work for wages. Persons working under such hybrid arrangements have been referred to as 'dependent contractors'.[1] Many of these dependent contractors share the same labour market with employees, raising the question of whether there is a sufficient justification for excluding them from the scope of collective bargaining legislation. A justification put forward for the exclusion of dependent contractors from collective bargaining is that they are entrepreneurs and, as such, prohibited from acting in combination by the public policy found in federal competition legislation.[2] Weighing against this justification for the exclusion of dependent contractors from collective bargaining is the argument that groups in closely analogous economic positions, such as employees and dependent contractors, should receive the same legislative treatment. One particular problem for collective bargaining that stems from a failure to treat employees and dependent contractors alike is that collective bargaining rights may be eroded as employers seek to obtain services on a dependent contractor basis.

1. For a thorough discussion of the problems raised by this type of arrangement, *see* H.W. Arthurs, 'The Dependent Contractor: A Study of the Legal Problems of Countervailing Power' (1964) 16 *University of Toronto Law Journal* 89.
2. It should be noted that the Combines Investigation Act, R.S.C. 1985, c.C-34, while now prohibiting restraints on competition in respect of services, still exempts from such prohibitions 'combinations or activities of workmen or employees for their own reasonable protection as such workmen or employees'.

483. There has been a tendency on the part of labour boards to give a wide interpretation to the term 'employee', bringing within the scope of collective bargaining legislation such workers as owner-drivers of transport trucks who might otherwise be characterized as dependent contractors.[1] The extent to which labour boards can extend the definition of employee, however, has been restricted by the existence of the common law test of employment status. This fourfold test, as it is commonly known, takes into account four factors: the ownership of the tools used to perform the work; the degree of control asserted over the person performing the work; the chance of profit arising from the activity; and the risk of loss that might also result. The appropriateness of this test for determining the extent of coverage provided by collective bargaining legislation has been questioned.[2]

1. For example, *see Pétroles inc. et al.* v. *Syndicat international des travailleurs des industries pétrolières chimiques et atomiques, locaux 9–700 . . .*, [1979] T.T. 209; *Gaston Breton inc.* v. *Union des routiers, brasseries, liqueurs douces et ouvriers de diverses industries, local 1999*, [1980] T.T. 471. (In this case, the trucks were leased from the employer.)
2. Rather surprisingly, the source of this test is *Montreal* v. *Montreal Locomotive Works et al.*, [1947] 1 D.L.R. 101 (J.C.P.C.), a case raising the issue of whether a manufacturer enjoyed immunity from municipal taxation.

484. Some Canadian jurisdictions, by embracing a statutory definition of dependent contractor, have permitted labour boards to take greater account of the economic substance of a relationship when determining the reach of collective bargaining legislation.[1] The widest of these definitions simply requires that a person be in a position of economic dependence, and under an obligation to perform duties analogous to that of the employee. Labour boards have interpreted this definition as bringing within the scope of collective bargaining legislation persons who have made a considerable capital investment in the equipment used to perform their work, and who employ others on a limited basis to assist them in the performance of their work.[2] Such diverse groups as owner-drivers of dump trucks, driver-salesmen employed by dairies, oil-burner servicemen, freelance journalists, homecare workers, and house parents working for welfare agencies have been considered to be dependent contractors. However, if these workers sell their services to a number of purchasers more or less concurrently, they are likely to be considered as independent entrepreneurs.[3]

1. Canada, s.3(1); B.C., s.1(1); Ontario s.1(1).
2. *Fownes Construction*, [1974] 1 C.L.R.B.R. 453 (B.C.L.R.B.); *Adbo Contracting*, [1977] 2 C.L.R.B.R. 1 (O.L.R.B.); *Kelowna Daily Courier*, (1993) 94 C.L.L.C. para. 16,010 (B.C.L.R.B.); *Night hawk Timber Co.*, (1998) 98 C.L.L.C. para. 220-054 (O.L.R.B.); and *Canada Post Corp.*, [1987] 87 C.L.L.C. para. 16,029 (C.L.R.B.); rev'd on other grounds (1988) 88 C.L.L.C. para. 14,006 (Fed.C.A.). There has been considerable debate as to whether the employment of others excludes a person from being treated as a dependent contractor. This issue is discussed in *Superior Sand, Gravel & Supplies*, [1978] 1 C.L.R.B.R. 421 (O.L.R.B.) and *West Fraser Mills Ltd.* (1994) 94 C.L.L.C. para. 16,046 (B.C.L.R.B.).
3. *Craftwood Construction*, [1981] 1 C.L.R.B.R. 155 (O.L.R.B.); in *Ridge Gravel and Paving Ltd.* (1988) 88 C.L.L.C. para. 16,040 and (1989) 89 C.L.L.C. para. 16,030 the British Columbia Industrial Relations Council found persons deriving at least 80 per cent of their income from a single source to be dependent contractors.

2. Managerial employees

485. Persons employed to exercise managerial functions are not included within the concept of employee as it is defined by collective bargaining legislation,[1] effectively preventing managers from bargaining collectively on their own behalf even though under the general law they would be considered as employees. The rationale for excluding them from the benefits of collective bargaining legislation is that the scheme of collective bargaining requires an arm's length relationship between an employer represented by management and those employees represented by trade unions.[2] Their exclusion from collective bargaining serves to keep management and labour insulated from one another, protecting the union from management domination and, on the other side, ensuring that the management presence is not weakened. This rationale has also been used to exclude from the bargaining unit employees related to management,[3] or even employees closely identified with management,[4] even though such persons are still considered to be covered by collective bargaining legislation.

1. *See* Canada, s.3(1); British Columbia, s.1(1); Ontario, s.1(3); Quebec, s.(1)1.
2. *The Corporation of the District of Burnaby*, [1974] 1 C.L.R.B.R. 1 (B.C.L.R.B.).
3. *Bruce Clark*, [1979] 1 C.L.R.B.R. 149 (B.C.L.R.B.); *Feed-Rite*, [1979] 1 C.L.R.B.R. 296 (C.L.R.B.).
4. *Diversey*, [1979] 3 C.L.R.B.R. 77 (B.C.L.R.B.).

486. The identification of management employees is one of the more difficult tasks faced by labour boards. This difficulty is particularly pronounced in larger organizations where authority has become diffused through a number of bureaucratic layers. As management structures become flatter, however, this problem becomes less acute. A distinction has to be drawn between those persons in an organization who exercise control and authority over employees, and those persons who participate in an organization's general decision-making process but have no direct control over other employees.[1] In most Canadian jurisdictions front-line supervisors who exercise a substantial degree of control and authority over other employees are considered to exercise managerial functions.[2] In the case of persons involved in the general decision-making process, however, labour boards have looked to the degree and extent of independent decision-making authority. As well, labour boards often make reference to a person's ability to make effective recommendations, recognizing that managerial authority may be more diffuse in larger organizations.

1. *Carleton University*, [1975] O.L.R.B. Rep. 500; *McIntyre Porcupine Mines*, [1975] 2 C.L.R.B.R. 234 (O.L.R.B.); *Inglis*, [1976] O.L.R.B. 270; *Central Park Lodges* (1997) 97 C.L.L.C. para. 220-005 (Alta.L.R.B.).
2. For example, *see Chrysler*, [1976] 1 C.L.R.B.R. 447 (O.L.R.B.); *Cowichan Home Support Society* (1997) 97 C.L.L.C. para. 220-030 (B.C.L.R.B.).

487. There appears to be no single test that determines whether a person exercises managerial functions. Such factors as the nature of the organization, the manner in which it is organized, a person's position in the organizational structure, the extent of a person's authority over other employees,[1] and the amount of non-managerial work performed by a person are all taken into account. Participation in governance does not necessarily make a person a manager. For example, university faculty involved in a consultative process have not been considered to be managers,[2] nor have employee-directors of a social agency.[3]

1. *Board of Education for the City of Windsor* (1986) 12 C.L.R.B.R. (N.S.) 43 (O.L.R.B.).
2. *Mount Allison University*, [1982] 3 C.L.R.B.R. 284 (N.B.L.R.B.).
3. *Family Services of Hamilton-Wentworth Inc.*, [1980] 2 C.L.R.B.R. 76 (O.L.R.B.); but *see Burnaby Winter Club* (1996) 96 C.L.L.C. para. 220-031 (B.C.L.R.B.).

488. Some Canadian jurisdictions expressly recognize in their legislation the appropriateness of bargaining units of 'supervisory employees'.[1] There appears to have been a greater tendency to extend collective bargaining to persons who in the past might have been regarded as managerial employees where such legislative provisions exist.[2] Even here, however, true managers remain excluded from the benefits of collective bargaining.[3]

1. Canada, s.27(5); B.C., s.29.
2. *B.C. Telephone*, [1976] 1 C.L.R.B.R. 273 (C.L.R.B.); *Tahsis*, [1977] 2 C.L.R.B.R. 452 (B.C.L.R.B.); *Québec-Téléphone* (1998) 98 C.L.L.C. para. 220-006 (Fed.C.A.).
3. *B.C. Ferry*, [1979] 1 C.L.R.B.R. 116 (C.L.R.B.); *Cowichan Home Support Society* (1997) 97 C.L.L.C. para. 220-030 (B.C.L.R.B.).

3. *Confidential employees*

489. Persons employed in a confidential capacity in matters relating to labour relations are expressly excluded from the scope of collective bargaining legislation.[1] This exclusion reflects a clear recognition of the need for management to have some office and technical support when conducting the collective bargaining exercise. Labour boards, however, have been careful about extending this exception too far, since its effect is to exclude from collective bargaining persons who would be in the same economic position as those employees who fall within the bargaining unit. Office and clerical employees in general are often privy to a certain amount of sensitive information that would not be available to their counterparts in the plant, and this fact of life appears to be recognized by labour boards in refusing to give a wide interpretation to the confidential exclusion. In order for an employee to be considered as employed in a confidential capacity in matters relating to labour relations, it must be shown that the confidential matters relate to labour relations and not some other potentially sensitive area for the employer, that the employee has regular access to such confidential labour relations matters, and that these matters are integral to the collective bargaining process.[2]

1. Quebec's Labour Code does not exclude employees because they exercise a confidential capacity relating to labour relations. Quebec's public servants, however, are excluded from collective bargaining if they are employed in any kind of confidential capacity. *See* Labour Code, s.1(1)(3).
2. *Falconbridge Nickel Mines*, [1966] O.L.R.B. 379; *Transair*, [1974] 1 C.L.R.B.R. 281 (C.L.R.B.).

4. Public employees

490. Many public employees are either expressly or implicitly excluded from general collective bargaining legislation. The crown by operation of the rules of interpretation is not bound by legislation unless there is an express provision to the contrary in the statute.[1] Legislative silence has by implication excluded public servants from the general scheme of collective bargaining in many jurisdictions. Express restrictions, however, have been necessary in order to exclude such groups of public employees as policemen, firemen and teachers from collective bargaining legislation. As a general rule, municipal employees (other than firemen and policemen) are not excluded from general collective bargaining legislation, nor are the faculties and staffs of universities. Even where public employees are not excluded (either expressly or implicitly) from general collective bargaining legislation, restrictions may be placed on the exercise of general collective bargaining rights (such as recourse to strike action) by separate and more specific legislation. The general pattern, however, has been to establish special collective bargaining regimes for public employees, reflecting a reluctance to extend fully the private sector collective bargaining model to the public sector.[2] While public employee collective bargaining statutes vary from jurisdiction to jurisdiction, the dominant pattern has been some restriction of the right to strike and a significant limitation upon the range of bargainable issues.[3]

1. In Quebec, Manitoba and Saskatchewan the crown has been expressly included within the definition of employer and is bound by the statute. Quebec, s.1(k); Manitoba, s.3; Saskatchewan, s.2(g).
2. *See* generally, C.G. Simmons and K.P. Swan, *Labour Relations Law in the Public Sector* (Kingston, 1982); J. Finkelman and S. Goldenberg, *Collective Bargaining in the Public Service: The Federal Experience in Canada* (Toronto, 1983); G. Swimmer and M. Thompson (eds.), *Public Sector Collective Bargaining in Canada* (Kingston, 1995).
3. Such restrictions have been held to be consistent with the Charter of Rights and Freedoms. *See Reference re Public Service Employee Relations Act (Alta.)* (1987) 87 C.L.L.C. para. 14,021 (S.C.C.); [1987] 1 S.C.R. 313.

5. Professional employees

491. The exclusion of certain types of professional employees,[1] usually those belonging to the more traditional professions such as law, medicine, dentistry and architecture, is still found in the collective bargaining legislation of some jurisdictions.[2] These exclusions appear to reflect a view that the economic interest of professional employees are best advanced through their own professional associations in the same manner as their self-employed colleagues. As the number of employed professionals has increased, there has been a much greater acceptance of collective bargaining by professionals and, concurrently, a reduction or elimination, of the statutory exclusions for professional employees. Nurses, engineers, para-medical professionals and, to a lesser extent, medical residents and lawyers, have used the collective bargaining structure rather than their own professional associations to assert their economic interests.

1. *See* generally, S.B. Goldenberg, *Professional Workers and Collective Bargaining* (Ottawa, 1970); G.W. Adams *Collective Bargaining by Salaried Professionals*, [1977] 32 *Rel. Ind.* 184.
2. Alberta. s.1(1)(ii); Ontario, s.1(3).

6. Students

492. Whether collective bargaining legislation extends to cover those persons who receive their training on the job is problematical. Such persons may perform some of the work ordinarily performed by employees, but this work forms part of their training programme and may be both supervised and paid for by someone other than the employer. In order for these persons to be considered to be employees for the purpose of inclusion under general collective bargaining legislation their relationship with an employer must possess most of the characteristics of the normal employment relationship.[1] Labour boards have held that residents and interns,[2] prison inmates participating in a rehabilitative programme,[3] persons employed under a publicly subsidized works programme,[4] and student research assistants,[5] can be considered to be employees, and therefore, covered by collective bargaining legislation. Ontario, through special legislation, has now excluded from unionization and collective bargaining those persons working in community participation activities under its workfare programme.[6]

1. *Cranbrook District Hospital*, [1975] 1 C.L.R.B.R. 42 (B.C.L.R.B.).
2. *St Paul's Hospital*, [1976] 2 C.L.R.B.R. 161 (B.C.L.R.B.).
3. *Guelph Beef Centre*, [1977] 1 C.L.R.B.R. 368 (O.L.R.B.).
4. *Kelowna Centennial Museum Association*, [1977] 2 C.L.R.B.R. 285 (B.C.L.R.B.).
5. *Carleton University*, [1978] 1 C.L.R.B.R. 452 (O.L.R.B.).
6. Prevention of Unionization Act (Ontario Works) 1998, S.O. 1998, c.22.

7. Agricultural workers

493. In most Canadian jurisdictions agricultural workers are now covered by collective bargaining legislation.[1] Some jurisdictions, however, effectively exclude those employed in very small agricultural operations by requiring that agricultural bargaining units be a certain size.[2] The growth of 'agribusiness' in Canada, however, has meant that the small farmer is no longer the typical agricultural employer,[3] raising the issue of whether this exclusion has a justifiable labour relations rationale. An Ontario court, however, has held that the exclusion of agricultural employees from Ontario's collective bargaining statute does not violate the Charter of Rights and Freedoms.[4]

1. Ontario, s.3(c) and Alberta, s.4(2)(e), still exclude from collective bargaining employees engaged in most forms of primary agricultural production.
2. Quebec, s.21 requires at least three persons and New Brunswick, s.1(5) requires at least five persons.
3. *See* K. Neilson and I. Christie, 'The Agricultural Labourer in Canada: A Legal Point of View' (1975) 2 *Dalhousie Law Journal* 330; P.J. Moran and G. Trudeau, 'Le salariat agricole au Québec' (1991) 46 *Rel. ind.* 159; I. Mimeault and M. Simard, 'Exclusions légales et sociales des travailleurs agricoles saisoniers véhiculée quotidiennement au Québec' (1999) 54 *Rel.ind.* 388; *South Peace Farms*, [1977] 1 C.L.R.B.R. 441 (B.C.L.R.B.).
4. *Dunmore* v. *Attorney General (Ontario) and Highline Produce Ltd.*, (1998) 98 C.L.L.C. para. 220-012 (O.C.J.Gen.Div.).

B. Eligible Trade Unions

494. Collective bargaining by definition requires that the interests of employees be represented through the collectivity of a trade union. Not every organization of employees, however, has legal status as a trade union as certain qualifications have been imposed by the legislation in order to ensure that the organization is capable of representing the interests of its individual members in collective bargaining. Organizations that do not meet these qualifications are considered to lack status for collective bargaining purposes and cannot acquire bargaining rights or enter into valid collective agreements.

1. Arm's length relationship

495. The scheme of collective bargaining contemplates that there be an arm's length relationship between the trade union and employer. To achieve this end the legislation expressly defines a trade union as an organization of 'employees',[1] and prohibits employers from supporting or interfering with the formation, selection or administration of a trade union.[2] Perhaps even more importantly, if improper domination can be established, the impugned organization does not qualify for legal status as bargaining agent and any agreement made by such an organization would not be considered as a collective agreement.[3] In Quebec, the Labour Court may decree the dissolution of an employer-dominated union.[4]

1. Canada, s.3(1); British Columbia, s.1(1); Quebec, s.1(a); Ontario, s.1(1).
2. *Supra*, paras. 442–5.
3. Canada, s.25(1); British Columbia, s.31; Ontario, s.53.
4. Quebec, s.149.

496. The requirement of an arm's length relationship has not been interpreted rigidly. It has been recognized that the character of an organization may change over time and it is possible for an organization to acquire status as a trade union by purging itself of managerial members.[1] Even more recently it has been held that, in the absence of actual employer domination, an organization could still be considered a trade union even though it included in its membership persons who exercised managerial responsibilities.[2]

1. *Children's Aid Society of Metropolitan Toronto*, [1977] 1 C.L.R.B.R. 129 (O.L.R.B.).
2. *Board of Education for the City of York*, [1984] O.L.R.B. 1279; *Ontario Hydro* (1990) 1 C.L.R.B.R. (2d) 161 and *British Columbia Transit* (1990) 6 C.L.R.B.R. (2d) 1 (B.C.I.R.C.).

497. Problems in applying the requirement of an arm's length relationship may also arise when a person exercising managerial functions, although not a member of a trade union, lends some support to its activities. Such support may not always be regarded as amounting to management domination if it can be established that the person was not perceived by the employees as acting on behalf of the employer.[1] This type of situation may occur where the manager lending support to the union acts under the erroneous belief that he is a member of the bargaining unit, or where that person is clearly acting in opposition to management.

1. *Air Liquide* (1964) 64 C.L.L.C. para. 16,002 (O.L.R.B.); *General Aviation Services*, [1979] 2 C.L.R.B.R. 98 (C.L.R.B.).

498. Not all forms of employer-employee cooperation are treated as being incompatible with collective bargaining. An interesting question is whether employee participation on a board of directors may disqualify a trade union where the employee-director has been active in the union's organizing campaign. In certain circumstances such participation has been held not to taint the union as being management dominated.[1]

1. *S.D. Adams Welded Products*, [1978] 2 C.L.R.B.R. 36 (O.L.R.B.).

499. Moreover, some forms of employer–union cooperation are not considered as impairing the arm's length relationship, especially where there has been a long-standing collective bargaining relationship. It has been recognized that unions may negotiate such benefits as paid leave for employees conducting union business and use of the employer's premises for union business.[1]

1. Canada, s.94(2).

2. *Collective bargaining purpose*

500. The definition of 'trade union' in Canadian collective bargaining legislation expressly contemplates that such organizations have as one of their purposes the regulation of relations between employers and employees. Employees who organize for other purposes such as the encouragement of social and recreational activities might not satisfy this requirement of a collective bargaining purpose,[1] nor would employees who established an organization for the purpose of blocking certification by a valid trade union.[2] This requirement, however, does not preclude the acquisition of bargaining rights by employee organizations not affiliated with national or international trade unions, provided that such organizations have a collective bargaining purpose and do not suffer the taint of employer domination.

1. *Burlington-Nelson Hospital* (1963) 63 C.L.L.C. para. 16,269 (O.L.R.B.).
2. *Graham Cable TV* (1987) 14 C.L.R.B.R. (N.S.) 250 (C.L.R.B.); *Harvest Meats Co. Ltd.* (1991) 8 C.L.R.B.R. (2d) 247 (S.L.R.B.).

501. In British Columbia the legislation takes a slightly more parochial approach imposing the additional requirement that collective bargaining be carried out within the province.[1] Such a requirement would appear to preclude a trade union from bargaining on a strictly national basis where it represents employees falling under that province's jurisdiction.[2] This restriction, however, may not prohibit all forms of national bargaining, provided that the requirements of the provincial legislation are met.

1. S.1(1).
2. *Otis Elevator* v. *International Union of Elevator Constructors* (1973) 35 D.L.R. (3d) 566 (B.C.C.A.).

502. The fact that an organization may conduct bargaining activities under a different legal regime, either in a different jurisdiction or under separate legislation established for public sector employees, does not appear to be given much weight when determining whether that organization has been established for collective bargaining purposes. Although it has been held that an organization formed for the purpose of representing government employees could not properly bargain for employees falling within the private sector,[1] labour boards have also allowed greater latitude for organizations to cross such boundaries.[2]

1. *Oshawa General Hospital*, [1970] O.L.R.B. 765.
2. *Demofsky et al.* v. *Ouvriers Unis des textiles d'Amérique*, [1973] T.T. 158; *Board of Education for City of Windsor*, [1986] 12 C.L.R.B.R. (N.S.) 43 (O.L.R.B.).

503. The requirement of a collective bargaining purpose has been interpreted on occasion as disqualifying from trade union status organizations that have been regarded as having an overriding political purpose,[1] even though the legal justification for such a disqualification appears to be doubtful.[2] Nevertheless, it is clear that the requirement of a collective bargaining purpose has never been interpreted as precluding trade unions from engaging in the usual political activities connected with the advancement of their interests.[3]

1. *Branch Lines* (1950) 52 C.L.L.C. para. 16,622 (C.L.R.B.).
2. *Smith and Rhuland* v. *The Queen*, [1953] 3 D.L.R. 690 (S.C.C.).
3. *Supra*, paras. 101–2.

3. *Formal structure*

504. Canadian collective bargaining legislation appears to contemplate that trade unions operate within at least a rudimentary framework of constitutional organization. Some Canadian jurisdictions provide that a trade union may be required to file its constitution and by-laws with a government agency.[1] In Ontario a proper constitutional framework was once regarded as a pre-condition to certification, but the Ontario Labour Board now appears to be insisting only that the individuals forming a union have agreed to be bound by the terms of an identifiable constitution.[2] In making such determinations Canadian labour boards appear to be concerned only that there be sufficient organizational structure, and not that internal trade union procedures maintain a democratic balance between the union and its members.

1. Ontario, s.91; Quebec, s.26.
2. *Ontario Hydro* (1989) 1 C.L.R.B.R. (2d) 161 (O.L.R.B.).

4. *Restrictions of membership*

505. Even where an organization can establish that it functions within a basic constitutional framework, problems may arise because that constitution restricts those eligible for membership in the organization. Once bargaining rights are conferred upon a trade union, it is required by law to bargain on behalf of all employees in its bargaining constituency. Where the trade union constitution disqualifies some of their employees from membership, there is the possibility that some members of the bargaining unit could find their jobs in jeopardy. If the union were to obtain a union security provision requiring that union membership be a condition for further employment, then those employees not belonging to the union would find themselves out of a job. As a result, labour boards have not granted bargaining rights where membership restrictions would have the effect of disqualifying some members of the bargaining unit.[1]

1. *Gaymer and Oultram* (1954) 54 C.L.L.C. para. 17,017 (O.L.R.B.); *Windsor Raceway Holdings*, [1979] 2 C.L.R.B.R. 89 (O.L.R.B.).

506. This type of constitutional restriction is more prevalent among craft unions operating primarily in the construction industry. Although the problem created by this type of restriction is reduced to some extent by the establishment of craft bargaining units (a bargaining constituency defined in terms of the skills employed by the members of the particular craft union), it still exists where craft unions attempt to organize along industrial lines.

507. Difficulties may also occur where a union has an established practice of not applying the membership restrictions of its constitution. While labour boards generally have overlooked such 'paper' restrictions where *de facto* membership is granted, the courts have been less lenient.[1] As a result, legislation in some Canadian jurisdictions now expressly provides that eligibility requirements contained in union constitutions may be overlooked in determining whether a person is a member of a trade union.[2] Moreover, it is clear that, in the absence of any membership restrictions, trade unions are permitted to organize groups of employees not normally associated with the rest of the membership.[3]

1. *Metropolitan Life Insurance* (1970) 11 D.L.R. (3d) 336 (S.C.C.).
2. British Columbia, s.23(2); Ontario, s.111(4); Quebec, s.36.1. In the federal jurisdiction this problem is overcome by only requiring a determination of the 'wishes' of the employees.
3. In *South Peace Farms*, [1977] 1 C.L.R.B.R. 441 the British Columbia board held that it was not inappropriate for an industrial union to seek to represent agricultural workers; but *see Cravelle Foods*, [1979] 2 C.L.R.B.R. 85 where the Alberta Board held that it was inappropriate for a construction craft union to represent employees in the food processing industry.

508. The extent to which labour boards may regulate the structure of an organization by not granting it status as a trade union has been placed in some doubt by a court decision overruling a board determination that an organization could not be considered as a trade union because the constitution of that organization created a class of provisional members who were barred from holding any office in the organization.[1] The court in quashing this decision indicated that the Board had no legislative mandate to regulate intermembership rights in this manner. While this decision has not been construed by labour boards as restricting their inquiry into the question of whether the organization extends membership to all employees in the bargaining unit, it does appear to have limited the ability of labour boards to regulate internal union affairs when dealing with the issue of trade union status.

1. *Re CSAO National and Oakville Trafalgar Memorial Hospital* (1972) 26 D.L.R. (3d) 63 (Ont.C.A.); *see also R.* v. *N.B. Teachers* (1971) 17 D.L.R. (3d) 72 (N.B.C.A.).

5. Discrimination

509. Canadian collective bargaining legislation provides that trade unions are not to acquire bargaining rights if they discriminate on certain grounds, usually those set out in human rights legislation.[1] While the lack of labour board jurisprudence dealing with these provisions would indicate that this type of discrimination occurs infrequently, instances of racial discrimination have been considered on occasion,[2] as have other forms of discrimination. Discrimination based on creed has been defined in terms of religious belief only and has not been extended to cover adherence to a particular political ideology.[3] As well, discrimination based on national ancestry or place of origin has been held to cover citizenship requirements in union constitutions.[4] The provision relating to discrimination based on age has been qualified by the definition of such discrimination found in human rights legislation,[5] although this definition must now be read in light of the Charter of Rights and Freedoms.

1. British Columbia, s.31; Ontario, s.15. In Quebec, s.17 of the Charter of Human Rights and Freedoms (R.S.Q., c.C-12) prohibits an association of employees, or an employers' association, from discriminating against any person on a number of specified grounds, such as race, colour, sex, in respect of admission, enjoyment of benefits, suspension and expulsion. The federal legislation contains a different kind of provision dealing generally with restrictions on membership (Canada, s.25(2)).
2. *T. Barbesin and Sons*, [1960] O.L.R.B. 80; *John Murdock, Limitée* v. *La Commission des relations ouvrières de la province de Quebec et al.*, [1956] C.S. 30.
3. *Steinbergs*, [1971] O.L.R.B. 329.
4. *Journal Publishing*, [1970] O.L.R.B. 925.
5. *Ontario Hydro*, [1978] 2 C.L.R.B.R. 109 (O.L.R.B.).

510. A more difficult question is whether a trade union with connections to a particular religious denomination can acquire collective bargaining rights. In one case, where the constitution of the union expressly provided that one of its aims was to apply christian principles to collective bargaining, a labour board refused to grant bargaining rights because this type of union would tend to impose a particular religion on all members of the bargaining unit. This decision was overruled by the courts,[1] but this issue may now have to be re-examined in the light of the guarantee of freedom of conscience and religion found in the Charter of Rights and Freedoms.

1. *R.* v. *Trenton Construction Workers' Association, Local 52* (1963) 39 D.L.R. (2d) 523 (Ont.H.C.).

6. Presence within jurisdiction

511. One Canadian jurisdiction has also imposed legislatively the requirement that an organization have some independent presence within the jurisdiction in order to qualify for bargaining rights.[1] Presumably, the rationale for this requirement is that some presence within the jurisdiction is needed in order for the organization to answer both to the general laws of the jurisdiction and also to its own members.[2] The practical effect is not to bar international and national unions from operating within that provincial jurisdiction, but only to require them to charter local unions operated by officials resident within the jurisdiction.[3] In the absence of an express legislative provision, however, other jurisdictions have not required a trade union to have a presence within jurisdiction.[4]

1. British Columbia, s.1(1); *see British Columbia Transit*, (1990) 6 C.L.R.B.R. (2d) 1 (B.C.I.R.C.).
2. *Corcoat Engineering*, [1974] 1 C.L.R.B.R. 530 (B.C.L.R.B.).
3. *Bethlehem Copper*, [1978] 2 C.L.R.B.R. 410 (B.C.L.R.B.).
4. *La-z-Boy*, [1981] 2 C.L.R.B.R. 427 (O.L.R.B.).

7. Councils of trade unions

512. It is also possible under Canadian collective bargaining legislation for a group of trade unions to join together as a council of trade unions and, as a council, acquire bargaining rights.[1] This form of multi-union bargaining often occurs in the situation where a number of trade unions organized along craft lines are faced with a single employer, or a group of employers bargaining as a single industry. In one jurisdiction, British Columbia, the Minister of Labour may refer the question of whether a council of trade unions is the appropriate bargaining structure to the labour board, and the board may in turn impose the council structure upon a group of trade unions.[2] By contrast, in Ontario a council of trade unions cannot obtain certification without first establishing that each of its constituent unions have vested the council with full authority as bargaining agent.

1. Canada, s.32; British Columbia, s.1(1), s.41; Ontario, s.1(1), s.12.
2. *British Columbia Railway*, [1977] 1 C.L.R.B.R. 289 (B.C.L.R.B.); *Construction Labour Relations Association*, [1978] 2 C.L.R.B.R. 203 (B.C.L.R.B.).

C. Method of Acquisition

513. A distinguishing feature of Canadian collective bargaining legislation is that it provides an express method by which trade unions can acquire bargaining rights.[1] The legislation provides that a trade union may make application to the labour board and, if it can establish its representative character and meets all other requirements, it becomes entitled to receive a certificate. The certificate gives the union the exclusive authority to represent employees in the bargaining unit and imposes upon the employer a corresponding obligation to bargain exclusively with that union. This procedure, referred to as certification, was established in order to meet the problems that occurred when unions attempted to obtain employer recognition by strike action.[2] Such recognition strikes, as they are called, have now been proscribed by collective bargaining legislation.

1. Canada, ss.24–36; British Columbia. ss.18–32; Ontario, ss.7–11, s.128 (construction industry); Quebec. ss.21–46.
2. *Supra*. paras. 430–5.

514. While most unions acquire their bargaining rights through the process of certification, it is also possible to do so through the faster and more informal method of voluntary recognition by which an employer simply agrees to recognize a trade union as bargaining agent for his employees.[1] Voluntary recognition is more common in the construction industry where the short duration of many jobs often makes it the more attractive procedure. Bargaining rights acquired in this manner, however, are usually more open to challenge than those acquired through the certification process because of the possibility that employer recognition might constitute a 'sweetheart' arrangement, having the effect of precluding an employee voice in the selection of their bargaining agent.[2] As certification is the more common procedure for acquiring bargaining rights in Canada a number of the more important features of this process will be described.

1. Express reference to this procedure is found in Canada, s.3(1); Ontario, ss.16, 18(3). This procedure was removed from the Quebec Labour Code in 1969.
2. Ontario, s.66; *see also Manitoba Pool Elevators*, [1978] 1 C.L.R.B.R. 161 (C.L.R.B.).

1. Degree of formality

515. Since certification entitles a trade union to employer recognition, it should not be surprising that the certification process has been the focus of considerable labour–management disagreement. One of the more controversial issues is the degree of formality that the certification process should assume. Trade unions take the position that the process should be fast, informal, non-adversarial, and so should be conducted without hearing representations from employers or opposing employees. From the union perspective certification should be a simple matter of determining whether it has sufficient members to meet the criterion of representativeness. The employer position emphasizes due process in the sense of a full opportunity being afforded to any person possibly affected to make representation at judicial-style hearings, and the taking of a vote to determine employee support for the union. Certification procedures in the different Canadian jurisdictions appear to reflect a compromise between these two opposing points of view. In Quebec the statute expressly provides that only the employees and the trade union shall be considered as interested parties where the representative character of a union is the issue.[1] By contrast, Ontario provides a full-scale adjudicative hearing at which the employer has full standing on all issues raised by the certification application.[2] However, because of the need to process construction industry certifications more expeditiously, the Ontario board may make rules to expedite these proceedings.[3]

1. Quebec, s.32. However, if the parties disagree over any matter related to the bargaining unit, or if more than one union is involved, the labour commissioner will hold a full hearing on the question in the presence of the interested unions and the employer.
2. Statutory Powers Procedure Act, R.S.O. 1990, c.S-22.
3. S.110(18).

2. Proof of representativeness

a. Membership evidence

516. For many years the primary method by which trade unions established their representative character in order to acquire bargaining rights was through simple evidence of membership. By establishing that more than a majority of employees in the bargaining unit were union members, trade unions could acquire 'outright' certification without the taking of a vote of the employees.[1] The form of trade union membership evidence had to meet certain standards and, since employers do not have access to this membership evidence, labour boards tended to enforce these standards strictly.[2] Trade unions generally support this procedure for establishing representativeness since, from their point of view, it is faster and more efficacious than an employee vote.[3] More recently, however, a number of Canadian jurisdictions have required that the issue of the representative character of a union be resolved by means of an employee vote.[4]

1. In British Columbia not less than 55 per cent is required for outright certification without a vote.
2. *Webster Air Equipment*, (1958) 58 C.L.L.C. para. 18,110 (O.L.R.B.); but *see W.G. Enterprises Ltd.* (1996) 97 C.L.L.C. para. 220-013 (B.C.L.R.B.).
3. An interesting discussion on the use of membership evidence is found in P.C. Weiler, *Reconcilable Differences* (Toronto, 1980) at 37–49; *see also* P.C. Weiler, 'Promises to Keep: Securing Workers' Rights to Self Organization under the N.L.R.A.' (1983), 96 *Harv. L. Rev.* 1769.
4. Nova Scotia, Alberta, Ontario.

b. Petitions

517. In those jurisdictions where a vote is not required the process of determining membership support without a vote becomes more difficult in those cases where petitions, or statements of desire, have been filed in opposition to the trade union. The problem occurs where employees who earlier have signed membership cards later recant and indicate on the petition that they no longer support the union. Labour boards have treated these 'changes-of-heart' as casting sufficient doubt upon a trade union's membership evidence so as to justify the taking of an employee vote. Petitions are only given weight, however, if it can be established by the petitioner that the petition represents a voluntary expression of the desires of those employees who have signed it.[1] Most petitions founder on this requirement since employer influence tends to be a common feature of these petitions.[2]

1. *Baltimore Aircoil* (1982) 82 C.L.L.C. para. 16,200 (O.L.R.B.).
2. The issue of the extent to which an employer may express his views to employees often arises where the board is assessing the voluntariness of a petition. *Supra*, paras. 455–7.

518. The reception of petitions has been one of the more controversial aspects of the certification process. Not only do petitions tend to prolong the certification process, but they also appear to attract improper employer interference in trade union affairs.[1] In the federal jurisdiction, to protect the integrity of the certification process, membership evidence may even be determined as of a date occurring before the application has been filed in order to eliminate the effect of improper employer interference.[2]

1. *Canadian Imperial Bank of Commerce*, [1979] 1 C.L.R.B.R. 18 (C.L.R.B.); *American Airlines*, [1981] 3 C.L.R.B. 90 (C.L.R.B.).
2. S.17.

c. Votes

519. Trade union opposition to the vote procedure can be explained by the fact that initial membership support is usually greater than the employee support manifested later in a vote. As a result, trade unions usually enjoy a greater success rate where support is determined on membership evidence alone than where the vote is taken. The explanation for this phenomenon may relate to the fact that votes held in the context of the employment relationship are markedly different than the electoral process used to choose governments. The delays resulting from the holding of a vote and the dominant position of the employer are both factors that tend to erode voting support for a trade union.[1]

1. *Plateau Mills*, [1977] 1 C.L.R.B.R. 82 (B.C.L.R.B.); *Cominco Ltd.* (1997) 97 C.L.L.C. para. 220-058 (C.L.R.B.).

520. In order for a certification vote to be held trade unions generally have to establish a certain minimum standard of employee support.[1] Votes are conducted by labour board officials on the employer's premises, and scrutineers representing the union and the employer are appointed. Although a trade union must obtain a majority to gain bargaining rights, what constitutes a majority varies from jurisdiction to jurisdiction.[2] A vote may be set aside by the board if either side has engaged in improper electioneering practices.

1. Canada, 35 per cent; British Columbia, 45 per cent; Ontario, 40 per cent; Quebec, 35 per cent.
2. Canada, a majority of those voting provided at least 35 per cent of employees have voted; British Columbia and Ontario, a majority of those voting; Quebec, a majority of all those in the bargaining unit.

d. Proof of representativeness impaired by employer action

521. Some forms of employer interference in trade union organizing campaigns may actually render it impossible for the true wishes of employees to be ascertained either by means of membership evidence or a vote. Some jurisdictions provide that in these circumstances a trade union may still be certified as bargaining agent despite the lack of proven employee support.[1] These provisions would appear to serve as a disincentive to improper employer conduct by preventing employers from benefiting from their own wrongful conduct.

1. *Supra*, para. 459.

3. Timeliness of application

522. In order to provide some stability for the established collective bargaining structure Canadian collective bargaining legislation places some limits on when applications to acquire (or terminate) bargaining rights may be made. The most important limitation is the one curtailing the making of certification applications when there is already a collective agreement covering the employees in question.[1] Generally, in this situation an application can only be made in the last two or three months of an agreement. The existence of this type of restriction, commonly referred to as the 'collective agreement bar', may give rise to the question of whether certain arrangements are in fact collective agreements. 'Sweetheart' agreements (non-arm's length arrangements between unions and employers) are expressly disqualified by law, and not considered to be collective agreements.[2] Moreover, it must be established that the trade union represented employees in the bargaining unit when the arrangement was first made.[3] An agreement signed in the shadow of another union's organizing campaign, however, has been considered as a valid collective agreement.[4]

1. Canada, s.24(2); Ontario, s.7; Quebec, s.22; in British Columbia, however, an application can be made in the seventh and eighth month of each year of the agreement (s.19).
2. Canada, s.25(1); British Columbia, s.31; Ontario, s.53.
3. *Niagara Crushed Stone* (1958) 58 C.L.L.C. para. 18, 118 (O.L.R.B.).
4. *Brayshaws Steel and U.S.W.A.* (1971) 26 D.L.R. (3d) 153 (Ont.C.A.).

523. Even where there is no collective agreement present, existing bargaining rights may still bar the bringing of a certification application. Canadian collective bargaining legislation generally protects bargaining rights acquired through certification by not permitting any new certification application for a specified time.[1] As well certification applications are often curtailed during the period when parties are negotiating for a collective agreement.[2] In one jurisdiction, Ontario, bargaining rights acquired through voluntary recognition are also given some statutory protection.[3]

1. Canada, s.24(2)(b) – one year; British Columbia, s.18(2) – six months; Ontario, s.7(2) – one year; Quebec, s.22(b.1) – one year.
2. Canada, s.24(3); Ontario, s.67.
3. S.7(3). But employees may apply to terminate bargaining rights acquired through voluntary recognition during the first year of the agreement (s.66).

4. Other bars to certification applications

524. The making of repeated certification applications within a short period of time is not permitted by Canadian collective bargaining legislation.[1] An interval between applications is required in order to protect the work place from the excessive disruption caused by repeated applications.

1. Canada, Regulation s.31; British Columbia, s.19(2); Ontario, ss.7(9), (9.1), (9.2), (9.3), (10), (10.1), (10.2), 10(3), (3.1), (3.2), (4), 111(2)(k), 160(3); Quebec, s.40.

525. Strike action contemporaneous with a certification application may also bar the entertainment of that application. While there is no express legislative provision imposing such a bar, at least one labour board has imposed such a bar in order to enforce compliance with the prohibition against recognition strikes.[1]

1. *Radio Lunch* (1950) 50 C.L.L.C. para. 17,012 (O.L.R.B.).

5. The fluctuating workforce

526. The general requirement of determining employee support as of a specific point of time may cause problems where a workforce is expanding. Balanced against the concern that certification not be delayed is a concern that prospective employees should have a say in the choice of the bargaining agent. Where employees currently employed do not constitute a substantial and representative segment of the workforce to be employed, labour boards have followed the practice of delaying certification and ordering a later vote provided that there is real likelihood that the increase in workforce will take place within a reasonable time.[1] Even though no specific legislative mandate exists for this practice it has nevertheless been approved by the courts.[2] Once bargaining rights have been acquired, however, the additions of new employees is simply considered as an accretion to the existing bargaining unit.

1. *Frant and Waselovich* (1957) 57 C.L.L.C. para. 18,057; *Sears Canada Inc.* (1998) 99 C.L.L.C. para. 220-008 (B.C.L.R.B.); but *see Uranerz Exploration and Mining*, [1978] 2 C.L.R.B.R. 193 (C.L.R.B.). S.121(2) of the Ontario legislation, however, expressly recognizes that this practice may not be appropriate for the construction industry.
2. *Noranda Mines* v. *R.* (1969) 7 D.L.R. (3d) 1 (S.C.C.); [1969] S.C.R. 898. In *Daesung Canada Inc.* (1991)10 C.L.R.B.R. (2d) 161 (B.C.I.R.C.) it was held that the build-up principle did not violate the guarantees of freedom of association and freedom of expression set out in the Charter of Rights and Freedoms.

§3. The Shape of the Collective Bargaining Structure

527. The task of shaping the collective bargaining structure in Canada has been largely left in the hands of the labour boards. Perhaps surprisingly, very little legislative guidance has been given to the boards as to how they should define the appropriate collective bargaining constituency (the bargaining unit) for the trade union, or go about identifying the employer on the other side of the bargaining table. It is in this area, more than any other, that the labour boards formulate policies that are legislative in nature, relying to a large part on their own labour relations expertise.

A. The Collective Bargaining Constituency

528. Bargaining unit determination has been the primary influence shaping the collective bargaining structure in Canada. Labour boards have been given a general power to determine 'the unit of employees appropriate for collective bargaining' qualified only by legislative instructions relating to certain types of employees such as those who belong to established crafts or professions.[1] The general pattern has been the local bargaining unit confined to all employees of a particular employer in a particular municipality. In the federal jurisdiction, however, there can be found bargaining units national in scope covering all employees of such national undertakings as airlines and railways. The bargaining unit pattern for the construction industry is somewhat different, the geographic area being wider than a single municipality in order to take into account the ambulatory nature of construction activity. In the more organized sectors of the construction industry, moreover, there has been a move towards province-wide bargaining on a multi-employer level, and even a multi-union level.[2] Multi-employer bargaining structures are more prevalent in British Columbia where this kind of bargaining structure extends beyond the construction industry.[3]

1. Canada, s.27; British Columbia, ss.21–22; Ontario, s.9; Quebec, s.21.
2. *See* generally P.C. Weiler, *Reconcilable Differences* (Toronto, 1980) c.6.
3. S.43 of the British Columbia legislation provides a general procedure for multi-employer certification. *See Artisan Industries*, [1979] 3 C.L.R.B.R. 518 (B.C.L.R.B.); *Okanagan Federated Shippers Association* (1983) 83 C.L.L.C. para. 16,043 (B.C.L.R.B.). As well, s.34 of the Canada Labour Code provides for multi-employer bargaining for the long-shoring industry. *See St. John's Shipping Association* (1983) 83 C.L.L.C. para. 16,039 (C.L.R.B.); *see also Prince Rupert Grain Ltd.* (1996) 96 C.L.L.C. para. 210-037 (S.C.C.) ([1996] 2 S.C.R. 432) affirming the general jurisdiction of the Canada board to impose a multi-employer bargaining unit.

529. Labour boards must take into account a variety of often competing considerations when determining appropriate collective bargaining constituencies. Reference is often made by labour boards to the rather flexible notion of a 'community of interest' among employees when bargaining unit determinations are being made. Underlying this concept, however, is a basic tension between the desire of unions to organize employees in a manner most beneficial to their interests and the equally strong desire of employers to obtain a bargaining structure most conducive to their interests. Not to be overlooked, moreover, are the interests of employees, not all of whom may support the union. If certification is granted to a union, it then has the exclusive right to represent all employees in the bargaining unit regardless of the fact that a minority of those employees may not wish for union representation. Finally, labour boards must also give some weight to what might be described as the public's interest in the creation of a rational and orderly bargaining structure.

1. Ability to organize

530. The shape and composition of the bargaining unit are factors clearly affecting a trade union's ability to organize employees. Generally trade unions find it easier to organize small, cohesive groups of employees working at a single location and, as a result, propose bargaining units reflecting this fact of life. Where trade unions have been successful in organizing a large group of employees, however, they may be more inclined to request a more comprehensive unit, knowing that existing employee support will be sufficient to sweep other employees into such a bargaining unit. Employers, as a general rule, tend to take the opposite approach, proposing more comprehensive bargaining units when a trade union's support is in doubt and more narrow units where it is clear that a trade union has adequate support for certification.

531. Labour boards in Canada have expressly recognized that the right of employees to organize must be taken into account when defining the appropriate bargaining unit. The most obvious situation where the right to organize had to be considered was in the case of bank employees. Banking in Canada has been dominated by a few large institutions with branches located throughout the country. The large number of employees involved and the geographic distances separating those employees meant that organization of these employees into one national bargaining unit was not a practical reality. Taking this factor into account, the Canada Labour Relations Board, reversing an earlier decision,[1] held that a single bank was a unit appropriate for collective bargaining and opened the door for the organization of banking employees on a local basis.[2] Labour boards in other jurisdictions have also recognized that the ability of employees to organize is a factor influencing bargaining unit determination.[3]

1. *Bank of Nova Scotia* (1959) 59 C.L.L.C. para. 18,152 (C.L.R.B.).
2. *Canadian Imperial Bank of Commerce*, [1977] 2 C.L.R.B.R. 99 (C.L.R.B.). More recently that same board has held that a 'cluster' of branches may also be appropriate; *see National Bank of Canada* (1986) 11 C.L.R.B.R. 257 (C.L.R.B.).
3. *Woodward Stores*, [1975] 1 C.L.R.B.R. 114 (B.C.L.R.B.); *Canada Trustco Mortgage*, [1977] 2 C.L.R.B.R. 93 (O.L.R.B.); *Island Medical Laboratories* (1993) 94 C.L.L.C. para. 16.040 (B.C.L.R.B.).

2. *Viability of bargaining structure*

532. An equally important consideration when determining the appropriate bargaining unit is the establishment of a viable collective bargaining structure for the long term. The primary concern is to avoid 'fragmentation' of the bargaining structure where a number of trade unions end up competing against each other for the same slice of the economic pie.[1] The most obvious example of fragmentation is where employees of the same employer employed at the same location are represented by different unions, a situation likely to create inter-union rivalry in respect of both economic gains and work jurisdiction. Fragmentation sometimes works to the advantage of trade unions, but at times it imposes a handicap upon them. A small bargaining unit of highly skilled employees capable of shutting down an employer's operation possesses considerable bargaining power. On the other hand, if a small bargaining unit of employees is unable to shut down an employer's operation immediately through strike action, then it is unlikely to have the financial resources to carry on sustained strike activity.

1. *See* P.C. Weiler, *Reconcilable Differences* (Toronto, 1980), c.5.

533. The general bias of Canadian labour boards has been in the direction of defining more comprehensive units.[1] Once a bargaining unit is defined, moreover, labour boards have been reluctant to carve out smaller bargaining units from the existing structure.[2] The effect has been to balance trade union bargaining power and to reduce inter-union rivalries. Another effect has been to impose upon trade unions the difficult task of reconciling the divergent interests found within these more comprehensive bargaining units.

1. *Insurance Corporation of British Columbia*, [1974] 1 C.L.R.B.R. 403 (B.C.L.R.B.); *British Columbia Transit* (1990) 6 C.L.R.B.R. (2d) 1 (B.C.I.R.C.); *Mistahia Regional Health Authority*, (1996) 96 C.L.L.C. para. 220-066 (Alta.L.R.B.); but *see Famous Players Inc.* (1990) 7 C.L.R.B.R. (2d) 304 (O.L.R.B.).

2. *Canadian Pacific*, [1976] 1 C.L.R.B.R. 361 (C.L.R.B.); *Syndicat des fonctionnaires municipaux de Montréal, S.C.F.P. section locale 429* v. *Syndicat des professionnels de la ville de Montréal*, [1990] T.T. 147; *MacMillan Bloedel Ltd.* (1997) 97 C.L.L.C. para. 220-071 (B.C.L.R.B.); *Saskatchewan Centre of the Arts* (1995) 96 C.L.L.C. para. 220-016 (Sask.L.R.B.); but *see Canadian Broadcasting Corp.*, [1977] 2 C.L.R.B.R. 481 (C.L.R.B.) and *Air B.C.* (1992) 13 C.L.R.B.R. (2d) 276 (C.L.R.B.).

3. Craft bargaining units

534. There has always been a certain tension within the Canadian trade union movement between those unions organizing employees along craft lines and those that organize employees on an industrial basis.[1] Craft unionism groups together workers who share common skills whereas industrial unionism groups together all employees employed in a particular operation regardless of their skills. Since the skills of their members are often in high demand, craft unions may wield considerable bargaining power. Craft unionism tends to be centred on the construction industry, but may also be found to some extent in the printing industry.

1. *Supra*, paras. 73–107.

535. Organization along craft lines gives rise to a number of problems. For one thing, the unskilled worker may be left outside the protective umbrella of collective bargaining. Just as troublesome is the fact that craft unionism fragments the bargaining structure giving rise to competition between trade unions. Since the craft or skill is the common denominator among its members, the craft union places great emphasis on its own work jurisdiction, and its members feel more closely bound to the craft than to any particular employment relationship. This attachment to a particular work jurisdiction often gives rise to 'jurisdictional disputes' where more than one union makes a claim to the same work. Usually such disputes cannot be resolved by a simple reference to bargaining unit descriptions because such descriptions often overlap[1] and, as a result, some Canadian jurisdictions have established specific procedures for resolving disputes over work jurisdiction.[2]

1. *Toronto Star Newspapers*, [1979] 2 C.L.R.B.R. 423 (O.L.R.B.).
2. Ontario, s.99.

536. In order to protect their work jurisdiction craft unions often rely upon 'sub-contracting' and 'non-affiliation' arrangements. The former type of arrangement, usually made with a general contractor, requires that any sub-contracting of work only be to employers with whom the union and other affiliated craft unions have bargaining rights. Enforcement of this kind of arrangement is often achieved by means of the non-affiliation arrangement that allows the members of the craft union to refuse to work alongside other employees not belonging to their union or another affiliated craft union. Labour boards have regarded the sub-contracting clause as a legitimate method of protecting a union's work jurisdiction,[1] and the British Columbia board has even given its approval to the non-affiliation clause.[2]

1. *Metropolitan Toronto Apartment Builders Association*, [1979] 1 C.L.R.B.R. 197 (O.L.R.B.); aff'd (1979) 79 C.L.L.C. para. 14,222 (Ont.Div.Ct.).
2. *R.M. Hardy*, [1977] 2 C.L.R.B.R. 357.

537. Despite the problems posed by craft bargaining units, it is generally recognized in Canada that employees who have traditionally organized along craft lines are entitled to continue this pattern of organization.[1] Canadian labour boards, however, have been reluctant to extend craft unionism beyond its traditional boundaries.[2] Nevertheless the recent growth in the organization of supervisory and professional employees may be giving rise to a new type of craft unionism to the extent that supervisors and professionals are placed in distinct bargaining units.[3]

1. British Columbia, s.21; Ontario, s.9(3); *Interior Contracting*, [1979] 1 C.L.R.B.R. 248 (C.L.R.B.).
2. *Firestone Tire & Rubber*, [1963] O.L.R.B. 491; *Collegiate Sports*, [1977] 1 C.L.R.B.R. 389 (B.C.L.R.B.); *Atomic Energy of Canada*, [1978] 1 C.L.R.B.R. 92 (C.L.R.B.); *Island Medical Laboratories*, (1993) 94 C.L.L.C. para. 16,040 (B.C.L.R.B.).
3. *Infra*, paras. 542–3.

4. *Agreed upon bargaining units*

538. In many situations unions and employers are able to reach agreement on the appropriate description of the bargaining unit. While such agreements usually serve to expedite certification hearings, they raise the problem of whether labour boards should accept such agreements where they appear to run contrary to prevailing policy. Most labour boards appear to accept such agreements unless they are obviously out of step with established policy.[1] This approach may be influenced by the fact that once bargaining occurs employers and trade unions often negotiate for a unit different than that set out in the certificate and, thereby, redefine their bargaining rights.[2] Such a practice appears to be acceptable provided that there is no encroachment upon other bargaining rights and no breach of the union's duty of fairly representing all the employees in the certified bargaining unit.[3]

1. *Fonthill Lumber* (1964) 64 C.L.L.C. para. 16,305 (O.L.R.B.); but *see CJRP Radio* (1977) 77 C.L.L.C. para. 16,074 (C.L.R.B.). In Quebec, when there is only one union involved, an agreement between the union and the employer on the bargaining unit binds the *agent d'accréditation* (certification agent) dealing with the matter. In such a case, the *agent d'accréditation* certifies the union if s/he comes to the conclusion that the union has the representative character required by the Code. Quebec, s.28(a), (b) and (d).
2. *Beverage Dispensers* v. *Terra Nova Motor Inn* (1975) 50 D.L.R. (3d) 253 (S.C.C.); [1975] 2 S.C.R. 749.
3. *Eastern Provincial Airways*, [1978] 2 C.L.R.B.R. 572 (C.L.R.B.).

5. *Geographic proximity*

539. The general pattern in Canada has been the local bargaining unit described in terms of all employees of an employer employed in a certain municipality, indicating that labour boards give considerable weight to the factor of geographic proximity. This factor, however, may not be determinative in all situations as the boards have at times confined the bargaining unit to a particular location in a municipality even though the employer's operation is conducted at more than one location in that municipality.[1] On other occasions, however, labour boards have described bargaining units embracing locations in the same municipality but several miles apart,[2] and even locations in different municipalities. Influencing these decisions have been such factors as the degree of interchange of employees between locations, the similarity of functions being performed at the different locations, and the difficulties of organizing employees at more than one location.[3] Canadian labour boards have been reluctant to include within bargaining units employees working outside their territorial jurisdiction even though the employer is located within the jurisdiction.[4]

1. *Ponderosa Steak House*, [1975] 2 C.L.R.B.R. 10 (O.L.R.B.).
2. *Usarco*, [1967] O.L.R.B. Rep. 526; *National Bank of Canada* (1986) 11 C.L.B.R. 257 (C.L.R.B.).
3. *Syndicat national des employés de Sicard (C.S.N.) et al.* v. *l'Association internationale des travailleurs de métal en feuilles (116) et al.* and *Sicard Inc.*, [1965] La Revue de droit du travail 353 (Quebec Labour Relations Board). It is to be noted that the Quebec board was abolished in 1969 and replaced by the *commissaires du travail* and the *Tribunal du travail*. This latter structure will in turn be replaced by a new labour board when the amendments to the Labour Code, adopted in June 2001, come into force.
4. *Bell Canada*, [1982] 3 C.L.R.B. 113 (C.L.R.B.); *Hydro Quebec International*, [1982] 3 C.L.R.B.R. 417 (Q.L.C.).

6. *Plant and office bargaining units*

540. Some Canadian jurisdictions separate 'white-collar' and 'blue-collar' workers employed at the same location by placing them in separate bargaining units.[1] It is quite possible, however, that the separate office and plant bargaining units may be represented by the same bargaining agent. Technical personnel are usually included within the office unit. Generally, the larger plant bargaining units tend to fare better in collective bargaining than their office counterparts.

1. *See* W.G. Reed, *White-Collar Bargaining Units Under the Ontario Labour Relations Act* (Kingston, 1969).

7. *Part-time employees and students*

541. In Ontario, for many years, the general practice was to exclude part-time employees and students employed for the school vacation period from bargaining units of full-time employees, leaving this latter group of employees to form their own bargaining unit.[1] Part-time employees in Ontario were defined as persons employed for not more than 24 hours per week. Other Canadian jurisdictions, however, did not draw such a rigid distinction between full-time and part-time employees.[2] Now Ontario has taken a more flexible approach to the issue of whether full-time and part-time employees should be combined in the same bargaining unit.[3] Casual employees who do not work a regular full-time schedule may still be included within bargaining units of regular employees where there is sufficient community of interest between the two groups.[4]

1. *Inter-City Bandag*, [1980] 2 C.L.R.B.R. 302 (O.L.R.B.). For a criticism of this policy, *see* R. Davis, *The OLRB Policy on Bargaining Units for Part-Time Workers: A Crtitique* (Kingston, 1991).
2. *See Serre Rougemont* (1977) 77 C.L.L.C. para. 14,069 (Q.L.C.); *Toronto-Dominion Bank*, [1978] 1 C.L.R.B.R. 156 (C.L.R.B.); *Radio Station CHQM* (1975) 75 C.L.L.C. para. 16,166 (C.L.R.B.).

3. *Caressant Care Nursing Home* (1996) 97 C.L.L.C. para. 220-014 (O.L.R.B.).
4. *Canadian Imperial Bank of Commerce (Powell River Branch)* (1991) 91 C.L.L.C. para. 16,014 (C.L.R.B.); in *Cominco Ltd.* (1997) 97 C.L.L.C. para. 220-058 (C.L.R.B.), however, the Canada board held that indeterminate-term employees and determinate-term employees at a remote mining site should not be included in the same bargaining unit.

8. *Professional employees*

542. Legislation in some Canadian jurisdictions provides separate bargaining units for professional employees.[1] Since professional employees have already organized themselves along professional lines for purposes other than collective bargaining, they generally seem to favour a collective bargaining structure that follows the same pattern. The problem is that bargaining units defined along purely professional lines create a fragmented bargaining structure that could cause the same problems associated with a craft bargaining unit structure. As a result, labour boards have sometimes been reluctant to establish separate bargaining units for professional employees.[2] Nurses, however, have been able to establish a general pattern of organizing in separate bargaining units, and this pattern has been recognized by labour boards.

1. Canada, s.27(3); Ontario, s.9(4).
2. *Bell Canada*, [1976] 1 C.L.R.B.R. 345 (C.L.R.B.); *Stratford General Hospital*, [1977] 1 C.L.R.B.R. 70 (O.L.R.B.); but *see Gitxsan Treaty Society, Nisga'a Valley Health Board* (1997) 97 C.L.L.C. para. 220-055 (B.C.L.R.B.).

9. *Supervisory employees*

543. The trend in some Canadian jurisdictions toward extending bargaining rights to supervisory employees raises the issue of the appropriate bargaining unit for such employees.[1] Labour boards appear to favour separate bargaining units for supervisors in order to reduce the conflict of interest arising from their supervision of other employees.[2] Moreover, such units may flow naturally from the established collective bargaining structure as often hourly-rated employees have organized themselves already in their own bargaining units.[3]

1. Canada, s.27(5), and British Columbia, s.29, expressly recognize this possibility.
2. *British Columbia Telephone*, [1977] 2 C.L.R.B.R. 385 (C.L.R.B.); *Tahsis Company*, [1977] 2 C.L.R.B.R. 452 (B.C.L.R.B.); but *see Québec-Téléphone* (1998) 98 C.L.L.C. para. 220-006 (Fed.C.A.).
3. *British Columbia Transit* (1990) 6 C.L.R.B.R. (2d) 1 (B.C.I.R.C.).

10. *Dependent contractors*

544. Dependent contractors, although having a close resemblance to other employees, can often be distinguished on the basis that they bring to their work a substantial investment in the tools of their trade.[1] The question is whether such differences justify a separate bargaining unit of dependent contractors. One jurisdiction, Ontario, expressly requires a separate unit unless a majority of dependent contractors prefer otherwise.[2] British Columbia, on the other hand, also contemplates placing dependent contractors within existing bargaining units of employees.[3]

1. *Supra*, paras. 482–4.
2. S.9(5).
3. S.28; *see Slocan Forest Products* (1994) 94 C.L.L.C. para. 16,069 (B.C.L.R.B.); but *see Construction Labour Relations Association of British Columbia* (1995) 95 C.L.L.C. para. 220-087 (B.C.L.R.B.) where the issue is whether dependent contractors should be included within craft bargaining units in the construction industry.

11. Security guards

545. The potential conflict of interest resulting from the security guard's responsibility to monitor other employees has meant that this type of employee has usually been placed in a separate bargaining unit.[1] In order for an employee to be considered as a security guard it must be established that the person has responsibilities to monitor and admonish other employees,[2] and is not just a watchman.

1. *St. Vincent's Hospital*, [1974] 1 C.L.R.B.R. 363 (B.C.L.R.B.); *Eastern Provincial Airways*, [1979] 1 C.L.R.B.R. 456 (C.L.R.B.). *See* Ontario, s.14.
2. *Crain & Sons* (1963) 63 C.L.L.C. para. 16,291 (O.L.R.B.).

B. Defining the Employer

546. Collective bargaining contemplates that, on one side of the bargaining table, there is a trade union representing employees and, on the other side, an employer. Collective bargaining legislation generally provides that an employer is simply a person who employs one or more employees,[1] although some Canadian collective bargaining statutes are slightly more restrictive by providing that an employer has to employ more than one person.[2] The fact that an organization may be religious in character does not preclude it from being an employer for collective bargaining purposes despite the guarantee of freedom of religion set out in the Charter of Rights and Freedoms.[3]

1. Canada, s.3(1); British Columbia, s.1(1); Quebec, s.1(k).
2. Trade Union Act, R.S.N.S. 1989, c.475, s.2(1)(1); Trade Union Act, R.S.S. 1978, c.T-17, s.2(g) – at least three employees; the Ontario statute contains no definition of employer, but s.9(1) does provide that a bargaining unit must contain more than one employee.
3. *Swift Current Nursing Home Inc.* (1990) 3 C.L.R.B.R. (2d) 45 (S.L.R.B.).

1. Identifying the employer

547. The functions normally performed by an employer are sometimes spread among more than one person. This spreading of employer functions tends to obscure the employment relationship, giving labour boards some difficulty when determining the person with whom the employees should be bargaining. Often these situations occur where a business has contracted out some of its employment functions to an employment agency. Labour boards have taken the position that they will look beyond the outward trappings of such arrangements in order to identify the person exercising real control over the employees.[1] In doing so the boards must answer such factors as who hires the employees; who controls the employees' work; who effectively establishes wages and working conditions; who controls any negotiations relating to wages and working conditions.[2] The application of these tests makes it difficult for employers to contract out their collective bargaining obligations.

1. *Seafarers Int'l Union* v. *Kent Line* (1972) 27 D.L.R. (3d) 105 (Fed.C.A.); *Welland Country Separate School Board* (1972) 72 C.L.L.C. para. 16,063 (O.L.R.B.).
2. *MacCosham Van Lines*, [1979] 1 C.L.R.B.R. 498 (C.L.R.B.); *Nationair* (1988) 19 C.L.R.B.R. (N.S.) 81 (C.L.R.B.). *See also Le Syndicat des fonctionnaires provinciaux du Québec Inc.* v. *Procureur Général du Québec*, [1987] T.T. 353; *Pointe-Claire (City)* (1997) 97 C.L.L.C. Para. 220-039 (S.C.C.); [1997] S.C.R. 1015. *See* G. Trudeau, 'Temporary Employees Hired Through a Personnel Agency: Who is the Real Employer?' (1997) 5 *Canadian Labour and Employment Law Journal* 359.

2. *Related employers*

548. Another situation where identification of the employer may be a problem is where associated activities are carried on through related businesses operating under common control.[1] A trade union may acquire bargaining rights in respect of a particular employer and then find that these are merely paper bargaining rights as the work being carried on by the employer has been transferred to another entity. This kind of problem often occurs in the construction industry where 'double-breasting' (the carrying on of the same business through more than one company) is a common phenomenon. In order to protect trade union bargaining rights from such changes of form, the legislation in many Canadian jurisdictions provides that labour boards may treat associated employers under common control and direction as a single employer for collective bargaining purposes.[2] This power has also been used, not just to preserve a trade union's bargaining rights, but also to maintain a consolidated, province-wide bargaining structure in the face of franchising.[3] As well, it has been used to prevent an employer from avoiding the obligation of a collective agreement by entering into a contract with an employment agency to supply labour that would displace members of the bargaining unit.[4]

1. *See Industrial Mine Installations*, [1972] O.L.R.B. 1029 for a more detailed description of this problem; *see also Transport Route Canada Inc.* (1998) 17 C.L.R.B.R. (N.S.) 340 (C.L.R.B.); *City of Grand Prairie* (1992) 12 C.L.R.B.R. (2d) 40 (Alta.L.R.B.).
2. Canada, s.35; British Columbia, s.38; Ontario, s.1(4).
3. *Dominion Stores Ltd.* (1985) 8 C.L.R.B.R. (N.S.) 203 (O.L.R.B.); *White Spot Ltd.* (1997) 97 C.L.L.C. para. 220-008 (B.C.L.R.B.); aff'd by the B.C. Supreme Court (1998) 98 C.L.L.C. para. 220-018.
4. *Kennedy Lodge Inc.* (1985) 7 C.L.R.B.R. (N.S.) 159 (O.L.R.B.).

549. In order for labour boards to exercise this discretion it must be established that the two employers are not only under common control or direction but also that the businesses carried on are associated or related. Common control is determined by an examination of such factors as common ownership or financial control;

common management; interrelationships of operation; representation to the public as a single related enterprise; and centralized control of labour relations.[1] Whether businesses are associated or related depends on such factors as the functional integration of the operations and the degree of employee interchange between operations.[2] To meet the evidential problems associated with establishing such factors, one jurisdiction imposes upon employers the duty to adduce all facts within their knowledge relevant to these considerations.[3] A declaration that associated employers constitute a single employer may have retroactive effect and, as a result, could give rise to substantial liability.[4]

1. *Walters Lithographing*, [1971] O.L.R.B. 406; *see also Empire Iron Works Ltd.* (1987) 13 C.L.R.B.R. (N.S.) 161 (Alta.L.R.B.); *Concerned Contractors Action Group* (1987) 13 C.L.R.B.R. (N.S.) 121 (B.C.L.R.B.) and *Ontario Legal Aid Plan* (1992) 6 O.R. (3d) 481 (Ont.C.A.).
2. *Diversey*, [1978] 2 C.L.R.B.R. 535 (O.L.R.B.).
3. Ontario, s.1(5).
4. *Norfolk Hospital Association* (1977) 77 C.L.L.C. para. 14,094 (Ont.Div.Ct); *Caledonian Lands*, [1979] 3 C.L.R.B.R. 12 (B.C.L.R.B.); *Midwest Pipeline Contractors Ltd.* (1991) 10 C.L.R.B.R. (2d) 99 (Alta.L.R.B.).

550. Even where associated or related businesses are being carried on under common direction labour boards in their discretion may refuse to treat these businesses as one employer. Such refusals have occurred where a labour board considered that a union was using the related employer provision as a substitute for obtaining bargaining rights under normal certification procedures,[1] where a trade union delayed unreasonably in seeking this remedy,[2] and where a trade union was attempting to strengthen its hand during bargaining.[3] Labour boards, when exercising their power to treat related businesses as one employer, have been concerned primarily with the erosion of existing union rights and not the establishment of new bargaining rights.[4]

1. *Inducon Construction*, [1975] 2 C.L.R.B.R. 369 (O.L.R.B.).
2. *Farquhar Construction Ltd.*, [1979] 1 C.L.R.B.R. 72 (O.L.R.B.); *Andreynolds Co. Ltd.* (1991) 10 C.L.R.B.R. (2d) 130 (O.L.R.B.).
3. *Calgary Television Ltd.*, [1978] 1 C.L.R.B.R. 532 (C.L.R.B.).
4. *Cyprus Anvil Mining Corp.* (1987) 87 C.L.L.C. para. 16,015 (C.L.R.B.); *Air Canada* (1990), 7 C.L.R.B. (2d) 252 (C.L.R.B.); *Ferretti Forming Inc.* (1996) 96 C.L.L.C. para. 220-041 (O.L.R.B.).

3. Sale or transfer of business

551. Once collective bargaining rights have been acquired by a trade union, it is possible that the identity of the employer may change as the result of a sale or transfer of a business. Since collective bargaining rights are defined in terms of the employees of a particular employer, specific legislative provisions have been enacted in order to preserve collective bargaining rights where a business has been sold or transferred.[1] The effect of these successor rights provisions is to give collective bargaining rights some permanence. Where a collective agreement is in effect the buyer of the business inherits that agreement,[2] and where a union is negotiating for a collective agreement the buyer has the same obligation to negotiate with the union as had the predecessor employer. Only existing bargaining rights are preserved, however, and a union cannot enlarge its bargaining rights by operation of successor rights legislation.[3] The sale of a business, while extending bargaining rights to a buyer, does not necessarily extinguish the original bargaining rights in respect of the seller.[4]

1. Canadas, ss.44–6; British Columbia, s.35; Ontario, s.69; Quebec, s.45.
2. One jurisdiction has treated differently the situation where a collective agreement is entered into between the date of the agreement of sale and the date when the sale is completed. In *Balcom-Chittick*, [1977] 2 C.L.B.R. 336 the Nova Scotia board concluded that the successor employer was not bound by the collective agreement even though a sale had occurred. The Ontario board, however, reached the opposite conclusion in *John Lester Drugs* (1982) 3 C.L.R.B.R. 233 (O.L.R.B.).
3. *Sunnylea Foods*, [1982] 1 C.L.R.B.R. 125 (O.L.R.B.).
4. *Cadillac Fairview Corporation Ltd.* (1997) 97 C.L.L.C. para. 220-074 (O.L.R.B.).

a. The ingredients of a sale or transfer

552. Many transactions raise the question of whether a sale or transfer of the business actually occurred. Labour boards generally have given the successor rights provisions a liberal construction, looking to see if the evidence points to a continuation of the same business function as was carried on prior to the transaction.[1] In taking this approach the boards have tended to look beyond the form of the transaction in order to examine its real essence. The labour boards, however, have drawn a distinction between the continuation of the same business function and the commencement of a parallel business function – the latter not constituting a sale.[2] Emphasis appears to be placed on the extent to which the previous business had been continued.[3] Such factors as the transfer of assets, the continuity of management, the continuity of the work performed by employees, and the continued employment of the same employees are all taken into account.[4] No single factor is determinative as consideration has to be given to the business context in which the transaction occurs.

1. *Thorco Manufacturing* (1965) 65 C.L.L.C. para. 16,052 (O.L.R.B.); *Kelly Douglas*, [1974] 1 C.L.R.B.R. 77 (B.C.L.R.B.); *Radio CJYQ Ltd.*, [1978] 1 C.L.R.B.R. 565 (C.L.R.B.); *Terminus Maritime* (1983) 83 C.L.L.C. para. 16,029 (C.L.R.B.); *United Steelworkers* (1987) 87 C.L.L.C. para. 16,008 (C.L.R.B.); *W W. Lester (1978) Ltd.* (1989) 89 C.L.L.C. para. 14,024 (Nfld. C.A.).
2. *Thunder Bay Ambulance Services*, [1978] 2 C.L.R.B.R. 245 (O.L.R.B.); *Metropolitan Parking*, [1980] 1 C.L.R.B.R. 197 (O.L.R.B.); but *see Riverview Manor* (1984) 5 C.L.R.B.R. (N.S.) 40 (O.L.R.B.).
3. *Cyprus Anvil Mining Corp.* (1987) 87 C.L.L.C. para. 16,015 (C.L.R.B.); *Union des Employés de Service, Local 298*, [1988] 2 S.C.R. 1048; (1989) 89 C.L.L.C. para. 14,045 (S.C.C.); *Sobey's Inc.* (1996) 96 C.L.L.C. para. 220-036 (N.B.L.E.B.); *Curragh Resources Inc.* (1996) 96 C.L.L.C. para. 220-035 (C.L.R.B.); *Starr Schein Enterprises* (1996) 96 C.L.L.C. para. 220-038 (B.C.L.R.B.); *Eagle Forest Products* (1996) 96 C.L.L.C. para. 220-061 (N.B.L.E.B.); *Towne Cinema Theatres (1975) Ltd.* (1997) 97 C.L.L.C. para. 220-076 (Alta.Q.B.); *Atlantic Wholesalers Ltd.* (1998) 98 C.L.L.C. para. 220-064 (N.B.L.E.B.).
4. *Ajax* (1998) 98 C.L.L.C. para. 220-071 (Ont.C.A.).

553. Labour boards have found a sale of a business to have occurred where a retail food store indirectly transferred its lease to a related company in the same business despite a considerable time elapsing before the business was reopened.[1] A receiver appointed by the courts to manage an insolvent business has been regarded as a successor employer,[2] but a privately appointed receiver has been considered to be only the agent of the insolvent company.[3] Where an insolvent business has been purchased from the receiver, however, the purchaser has been treated as a successor employer even where that purchaser is in the process of winding down the business.[4] On the other hand, the replacement of one contractor by another providing the same services has not been treated as the sale of a business,[5] nor have such situations as the transfer of work accompanied by an incidental transfer of assets,[6] the purchase of assets to be put to a different business use,[7] and the loss of a contract to a competitor.[8]

1. *Gordon Markets*, [1978] 2 C.L.R.B.R. 460 (O.L.R.B.).
2. *Uncle Ben's Industries*, [1979] 2 C.L.R.B.R. 126 (B.C.L.R.B.).
3. *Ontario Worldair*, [1981] 2 C.L.R.B.R. 405 (C.L.R.B.); *Price Waterhouse* (1983) 83 C.L.L.C. para. 16,045 (O.L.R.B.); *Weldco-Beales* (1992) 12 C.L.R.B.R. (2d) 133 (B.C.I.R.C.).
4. *Marvel Jewellry*, [1975] O.L.R.B. 733.
5. *K.J.R. Associates*, [1979] 2 C.L.R.B.R. 245 (C.L.R.B.). This question raised an important debate in Quebec's case law that was put to rest by the Supreme Court of Canada's ruling that there will only be an alienation or operation by another of an undertaking triggering the application of the successor right provisions where there is a legal relation between successive employers. Therefore, the replacement of one contractor by another providing similar services cannot be considered as a sale of business. *See Syndicat national des employés de la Commission scolaire régionale de l'Outaouais (C.S.N.)* v. *Union des employés de service, local 298 (F.T.Q.) et al.*, [1988] 2 S.C.R. 1048. For an analysis of the more recent developments in the application of the same provision of the Quebec Labour Code, *see* G. Nadeau, 'Les arrêts de la Cour d'appel concernant l'article 45 du Code du travail: nouvelles controverses?', in *Développements récents en droit du travail* (Cowansville, 2000) 1–20. *See also* the two following recent decisions that bring further precision on the question: *Travailleurs et travailleuses unis de l'alimentation et du commerce, section locale 500 et al.* v. *Ivanhoe Inc et al.*, Supreme Court of Canada, 13 July 2001; *Ville de Sept-Iles* v. *Syndicat canadien de la fonction publique, section locale 2589 et al.*, Supreme Court of Canada, 13 July 2001.
6. *British American Bank Note*, [1979] 2 C.L.R.B.R. 122 (O.L.R.B.): *see also Danfield Security Services Ltd.* (1996) 96 C.L.L.C. para. 220-022 (Alta. L.R.B.); *Marriott Corporation of Canada Ltd.* (1998) 98 C.L.L.C. para. 220-058 (N.S.L.R.B.).
7. *Homco Industries*, [1979] 1 C.L.R.B.R. 453 (C.L.R.B.).
8. *Terminus Maritime* (1983) 83 C.L.L.C. para. 16,029 (C.L.R.B.).

554. The privatization of public enterprises in Canada has given rise to a new round of successor rights problems. It has been held that the successor rights provisions of collective bargaining statutes do not deprive an employee of the common law right to remain the employee of a government agency that has privatized certain of its activities and to exercise bumping rights under the collective agreement with that government agency.[1] Some jurisdictions have enacted special legislation to deal with the transfer of functions outside of the government.[2] Absent such legislation, however, the successor rights provisions of general collective bargaining legislation may still be applicable.[3]

1. *British Columbia Government Employees Union* v. *Industrial Relations Council* (1988) 88 C.L.L.C. para. 14,030 (B.C.S.C.).
2. Successor Rights (Crown Transfers) Act, R.S.O. 1990, c.s.26; *see Ontario (Ministry of Natural Resources)* (1990) 3 C.L.R.B.R. (2d) 161 (O.L.R.B.). Ontario now has exempted the crown from the application of successor rights – Crown Employees Collective Bargaining Act, S.O. 1993, c.38, s.10.
3. The privatization of certain functions of the Canadian postal service has given rise to considerable labour board jurisprudence. *See Canada Post Corp.* (1989) 1 C.L.R.B.R. (2d) 218

(C.L.R.B.); *Canada Post Corp.* (1990) 4 C.L.R.B.R. (2d) 161 (C.L.R.B.); *Canada Post Corp.* (1991) 11 C.L.R.B.R. (2d) 312 (C.L.R.B.). In Quebec, the Court of Appeal ruled that s.45 of the Labour Code was applicable to the transfer of functions outside of the government: *Le Syndicat des fonctionnaires provinciaux du Québec* v. *Centre d'insémination artificielle du Québec (C.I.A.Q.) inc.*, [1988] R.J.Q. 623 (C.A.).

b. Problems of proof

555. Usually the details of a particular transaction are facts peculiarly within the knowledge of the employers privy to that transaction. This fact may give rise to problems of proof when a trade union is attempting to establish that a sale or transfer of a business has occurred. One jurisdiction, Ontario, now imposes upon employers a duty to adduce at the hearing all facts within their knowledge relevant to this issue.[1]

1. S.69(13).

c. Intermingling of employees

556. The sale or transfer of a business may lead to the integration of what were previously separate businesses and the intermingling of employees working for those businesses. Such intermingling of employees gives rise to the question of whether collective bargaining rights attached to the predecessor employer should be continued. Two types of intermingling are possible – the intermingling of the unionized employees of the transferred business with the non-union employees of the successor employer and the intermingling of employees represented by different unions. Where intermingling occurs labour boards may order a vote in order to determine the wishes of employees as to the disposition of bargaining rights.[1] However, this discretion has not been exercised where it is clear that a union represents a substantial majority of the employees in the bargaining unit.[2] As well, one labour board has indicated that it would not terminate an existing collective agreement unless there had been significant intermingling and a continuation of the collective agreement would work substantial and immediate prejudice to the operation of the business of the successor employer.[3]

1. *Silverwood Dairies*, [1981] 1 C.L.R.B.R. 442 (O.L.R.B.).
2. *Seaspan International Ltd.*, [1979] 2 C.L.R.B.R. 213 (C.L.R.B.).
3. *Bermay*, [1980] 2 C.L.R.B.R. 107 (O.L.R.B.).

d. Redefinition of bargaining rights

557. Even if intermingling of employees does not occur, there may still be the question of whether the bargaining rights inherited from the predecessor employer are appropriate as they relate to the successor employer. Labour boards have tended to preserve the bargaining structure established prior to the sale or transfer to the extent that it can be accommodated within the new employer's administrative structure.[1] This approach cuts both ways, however, as labour boards have not interpreted successor rights provisions as expanding the bargaining structure even though the scope clause of the inherited collective agreement may be sufficiently broad as to cover the unorganized employees of the successor employer.[2]

1. *City of Peterborough*, [1979] 2 C.L.R.B.R. 112 (O.L.R.B.); but *see Kelly Douglas*, [1974] 1 C.L.R.B.R. 77 (B.C.L.R.B.).
2. *Bryant Press*, [1972] O.L.R.B. 301; but *see Bermay*, [1980] 2 C.L.R.B. 107 (O.L.R.B.).

e. Change in character of business

558. One jurisdiction, Ontario, appears to qualify the general thrust of its successor rights legislation by giving its labour board a discretion to terminate bargaining rights passing upon a sale or transfer if the buyer has changed its character so that it is substantially different from the business of the predecessor employer.[1] The application of this exception to the general rule has not been without difficulty. While the Ontario Board appeared to apply the exception rather broadly at the outset,[2] a more restrictive approach was taken in later cases. Recognizing that this exception ran against the grain of the general scheme of successor rights, the Board has now taken the approach that for this exception to apply there must be a fundamental change in the business that would make continued representation by the trade union 'inadequate, inappropriate or unreasonable'.[3] Most of the cases where this exemption has been sought have arisen out of the hospitality industry where changes in business format are quite common.[4]

1. S.69(5).
2. In *Man of Aran*, [1973] O.L.R.B. 313 the board held that a conversion from a general tavern to an Irish pub was a change in character sufficient to justify termination of bargaining rights.
3. *Winco-Steak 'n Burger Restaurants*, [1975] 1 C.L.R.B. 296 (O.L.R.B.).
4. *See*, for example, *25168 Holdings*, [1978] 1 C.L.R.B.R. 28 (O.L.R.B.).

f. Extent of liability

559. A purchaser of a business is bound by any existing bargaining rights attached to that business. In the absence of a collective agreement a successor employer is obliged to negotiate with the union holding bargaining rights in respect of the employees of the business that has been purchased. Where a collective agreement already exists that agreement continues to apply to the successor employer, making it liable for any future violations. Moreover, the successor employer has also been held liable at arbitration for violations of the agreement occurring prior to the sale even though it had no knowledge of the collective agreement at the time the grievance arose,[1] and even held liable by the courts for an arbitration award issued against a predecessor employer.[2] The successor employer may also be responsible for the unfair labour practice liability of the predecessor employer. The Canada Board has held a successor employer liable where unfair labour practice orders were pending prior to the sale of business,[3] although the Ontario Board has refused to impose liability where no unfair labour practice order was pending prior to sale[4] or where there has been a bona fide purchase for value without notice of an outstanding unfair labour practice order.[5] However, the Supreme Court of Canada has found a successor employer strictly liable under the Quebec Labour Code for the unfair labour practices of its predecessor.[6]

1. *Man of Aran* (1974) 6 L.A.C. (2d) 238 (Shime); *Woodbridge Hotel* (1976) 13 L.A.C. (2d) 96 (Brown); *Uncle Ben's Industries*, [1979] 2 C.L.R.B.R. 126 (B.C.L.R.B.).
2. *Carpenters* v. *Cassin-Remco* (1980) 105 D.L.R. (3d) 138 (O.H.C.).
3. *Victoria Flying Services*, [1979] 3 C.L.R.B.R. 216 (C.L.R.B.).
4. *Sunnylea Foods*, [1982] 1 C.L.R.B.R. 125 (O.L.R.B.).
5. *Chandelle Fashions*, [1982] 3 C.L.R.B.R. 135 (O.L.R.B.).
6. *Adam* v. *Daniel Roy Ltée*, [1983] 1 S.C.R. 683 (1983) 83 C.L.L.C. para. 14,064 (S.C.C.).

4. Multi-employer bargaining

560. Canadian collective bargaining legislation also recognizes that employers may wish to bargain collectively through associations rather than individually. Multi-employer bargaining, although usually associated with the construction industry, has also been embraced by other industries such as forest products and trucking. While it is common for multi-employer bargaining to occur on a voluntary basis, many Canadian jurisdictions now provide a formal legal structure – often referred to as accreditation – for multi-employer bargaining.[1] Accreditation allows an employer bargaining agency to acquire bargaining rights in respect of unionized employers, and to bargain on behalf of those employers with the union representing their employees. Like the trade union, the employer bargaining agency has exclusive bargaining rights and its individual members are not permitted to strike their own bargains with the union. While accreditation has served to stabilize construction industry collective bargaining by reducing the number of negotiations and strengthening the employer presence at the bargaining table, it has also caused problems by requiring employers regardless of their different interests to operate under a common bargaining structure. Small firms in particular may find it difficult to operate under terms and conditions that are acceptable to larger firms.

1. British Columbia, s.43; Canada, ss.33, 34; Ontario, ss.134, 153, 155, 157; An Act Respecting Labour Relations, Vocational Training and Manpower Management in the Construction Industry, R.S.Q., c.R-20.

§4. Transfer and Termination of Bargaining Rights

A. Transfer of Bargaining Rights

561. The structure of trade unionism in Canada has never been static.[1] Mergers and breakaways occur with sufficient frequency to require that some legal provision be made for the transfer of bargaining rights between trade unions.[2] Affiliation with some other labour body, however, is not regarded as giving rise to a transfer of bargaining rights even where a change of name occurs.[3] Before giving their approval to such transfers of jurisdiction labour boards have required that the transfer be substantially completed, that the predecessor and successor unions have approved the transfer,[4] that the transfer complies with any requirements in the unions' constitution,[5] and that it have the approval of the employees affected.[6]

1. *Supra*, paras. 73-107.
2. Canada s.43; British Columbia, s.37; Ontario, s.68.
3. *Hydro-Electric Power Commission of Ontario* (1957) 57 C.L.L.C. para. 18,080 (O.L.R.B.).
4. *City of Brockville*, [1979] O.L.R.B. 76.
5. *Astgen* v. *Smith* (1970) 7 D.L.R. (3d) 657 (Ont.C.A.); *Brewers' Warehousing*, [1975] 1 C.L.R.B.R. 34 (O.L.R.B.); *Melnor Manufacturing Ltd.* (1989) 2 C.L.R.B.R. (2d) 252 (O.L.R.B.); *A&P Ltd.* (1993) 93 C.L.L.C. para. 16,007 (O.L.R.B.).
6. *Astgen* v. *Smith, supra: British Columbia Ferry and Marine Workers' Union*, [1978] 1 C.L.R.B.R. 17 (B.C.L.R.B.); *Association of Banff Centre Support Employees* (1997) 97 C.L.L.C. para. 220-069 (Alta.L.R.B.).

B. Termination of Bargaining Rights

562. The granting of collective bargaining rights does not always lead to the establishment of a continuing collective bargaining relationship. The failure of collective bargaining rights to take root usually reflects an erosion of employee support often attributable to the employer's continued resistance to collective bargaining. Occasionally, however, the failure of the collective bargaining relationship stems from the union's lack of interest in representing employees. Another possibility is that employee support may switch to another competing trade union so that employees may seek a change of bargaining agents. The procedures for terminating bargaining rights established by Canadian collective bargaining legislation take into account the full range of these possibilities.

1. Decertification

563. All Canadian jurisdictions provide for a review of the representativeness of a bargaining agent.[1] In order to provide some stability to the established collective bargaining structure, however, application for such reviews are subject to the same type of time restrictions as are applications for certification.[2] Labour boards carefully scrutinize such applications for improper employer influence, and will refuse to entertain such applications where there is the taint of employer involvement. The making of such an application following a bitter and protracted labour dispute, however, will not necessarily be considered as tainted.[3]

1. Canada, s.38; British Columbia, s.33; Ontario, s.63; Quebec, s.41.
2. *Supra*, paras. 513–23.
3. *Journal Publishing*, [1978] 1 C.L.R.B.R. 585 (O.L.R.B.).

564. If it can be established (usually by a vote) that a majority of the employees in the bargaining unit no longer support the bargaining agent, a declaration will issue from the board to the effect that the trade no longer represents the employees in the bargaining unit. The effect of such a declaration is to terminate the bargaining rights and put an end to any collective agreement made in respect of that bargaining unit. Applications for decertification may conceal an attempt by another union to 'raid' the incumbent. Often the termination of bargaining rights is closely followed by an application for certification from another union. One labour board, however, has held that decertification is not appropriate where employees wish to continue to participate in collective bargaining.[1]

1. *Hiram Walker*, [1974] 1 C.L.R.B.R. 517 (B.C.L.R.B.).

2. *Displacement*

565. Bargaining rights can also be terminated upon the making of a successful application for certification by another union. The procedures applicable to decertification, as a general rule, also apply to this more open form of raiding. The application must be timely, uninfluenced by the employer, and the representativeness of the applicant union is usually determined by means of a vote. If the displacement application is successful, bargaining rights are taken from the incumbent and given to the challenger.[1]

1. Canada, s.36; Ontario s.62, Quebec, ss.43 and 61.

3. *Union inactivity*

a. Statutory provisions

566. Canadian collective bargaining legislation also provides for the termination of bargaining rights where the trade union has been inactive. British Columbia and Quebec provide that a certificate may be cancelled where the trade union ceases to exist.[1] In Ontario bargaining rights may be terminated for failing to give notice to bargain or failing to commence bargaining.[2] The Ontario board has been reluctant to terminate bargaining rights on these grounds, declining to do so except where no reasonable explanation for the trade union's inactivity is provided.[3] The Canada Labour Code considers trade union inactivity from a quite different perspective, providing that a decertification order may not be made where a collective agreement does not cover the employees in the bargaining unit unless the board is satisfied that the incumbent bargaining agent has failed to make reasonable efforts to enter into such a collective agreement.[4]

1. British Columbia, s.33; Quebec, s.41.
2. Ontario, s.65.
3. *Dominion Stores* (1956) 56 C.L.L.C. para. 18,047 (O.L.R.B.).
4. S.39(2); *see Radio CJYQ936*, [1979] 1 C.L.R.B.R. 180 (C.L.R.B.).

b. Abandonment[1]

567. The statutory provisions do not deal with all situations where a trade union has been inactive. It is possible that a trade union may make a collective agreement providing for automatic renewal but not actively administer that agreement. This agreement would normally stand as a bar to certification application from another trade union. The Ontario Board, however, has taken the position that trade union inactivity can constitute abandonment of bargaining rights so that any subsisting agreement or certificate would not constitute a bar to a certification application.[2]

1. *See* generally, J. Dorsey. 'Abandonment of Trade Union Rights and the Labour Code of British Columbia' (1977) 11 U.B.C.L.R. 40.
2. *Advanced Wire Die* (1971) 71 C.L.L.C. para. 16,033 (O.L.R.B.).

568. Another possibility is that a trade union may wish to return to a bargaining relationship after a considerable period of inactivity. Such a possibility is more likely now that accreditation procedures are becoming more common. Under these accreditation schemes a trade union may attempt to gain access to a multi-employer collective agreement by reclaiming a collective bargaining relationship that it once had with an employer. The doctrine of abandonment has also been applied in these circumstances with the result that trade unions have not been able to reclaim inactive bargaining rights.[1] Underlying this approach appears to be the concern that the trade union, because of its inactivity, may no longer represent the employees in the bargaining unit. The question of whether bargaining rights have been abandoned is essentially a question of fact. The length and degree of the union's inactivity, the reasons for such inactivity, the union's relationship with the employees, and the absence of employees from the bargaining unit are all considered.[2] As well, it is possible for a union to abandon its bargaining rights by a deliberate act of relinquishment.[3]

1. *J.S. Mechanical*, [1979] 2 C.L.R.B.R. 87 (O.L.R.B.); *see also Whitehorse Hotels Ltd.*, [1977] 1 C.L.R.B.R. 477 (C.L.R.B.) and *Marineland of Canada Ltd.* (1991) 10 C.L.R.B.R. (2d) 234 (O.L.R.B.).
2. *Long lake Forest Products* (1994) 95 C.L.L.C. para. 220-033 (O.L.R.B.).
3. *Silverwoods Dairies*, [1981] 1 C.L.R.B.R. 442 (O.L.R.B.).

569. The statutory basis for the doctrine of abandonment is somewhat unclear. Labour boards have been given by statute a wide power to reconsider previous decisions,[1] and this power may be sufficiently wide to justify revocation of bargaining rights previously granted. As well, bargaining rights alleged to flow from a collective agreement could be said to be extinguished along with the agreement where a trade union no longer actively represents the employees covered by such an agreement.[2] At least one Canadian court has approved a labour board determination that bargaining rights had been abandoned.[3]

1. *Genaire* v. *Int'l Machinists* (1958) 14 D.L.R. (2d) 201 (Ont.H.C.); aff'd (1959), 18 D.L.R. (2d) 588 (Ont.C.A.). British Columbia, however, expressly deals with abandonment of bargaining rights in its legislation. *See* s.33(11).
2. In Ontario the definition of collective agreement refers to a trade union 'representing' employees.
3. *Hugh Murray* (1981) 81 C.L.L.C. para. 14,091 (Ont.Div.Ct.).

4. Fraud

570. Two jurisdictions, Canada and Ontario, expressly provide that if a certificate has been obtained through the use of fraudulent evidence, an application to revoke it may be made at any time.[1] Applications to terminate bargaining rights on this ground occur very infrequently.

1. Canada, s.40; Ontario, s.64.

Chapter IV. The Collective Bargaining Process

571. The acquisition of bargaining rights by a trade union can be regarded as a prelude to the main objective of collective bargaining – the negotiation of a collective agreement with the employer. It is at this point that the union and the employer must attempt to work out between them the terms of their collective bargaining relationship. This relationship not only sets the conditions of employment for the employees in the bargaining unit, but it also establishes the arrangement that are to exist between the union and the employer. Underlying these negotiations is the possibility that either party may resort to the use of economic sanctions (the strike or lockout) in support of its bargaining position.

572. Not only do the negotiations determine the terms of any agreement that might be reached by the union and the employer, but they also determine whether any agreement will be reached at all. At stake may be the survival of the union as bargaining agent, the jobs of the employees in the bargaining unit, and even the viability of the employer's operation. The manner in which negotiations are conducted is likely to set the tone for the future relationship of the parties. Long and bitter strikes are often the product of missed opportunities at the bargaining table. At this stage of the collective bargaining relationship common sense and a feel for the proper compromise play a more important role than rules and procedures.[1]

1. *See* generally J.P. Sanderson, *The Art of Collective Bargaining* (2nd edn.) (Toronto, 1989); G. Hébert, *Traité de négociation collective* (Boucherville, 1992).

§1. The Union's Exclusive Authority to Bargain

573. A fundamental principle of Canadian collective bargaining law is that, once a trade union has acquired bargaining rights for a particular bargaining unit, it enjoys exclusive rights to bargain collectively on behalf of the employees in that bargaining constituency. By establishing that it has the support of a majority of the employees in a bargaining unit a trade union gains the exclusive right to bargain for all employees included in that bargaining unit. The trade union's exclusive right to bargain imposes a corresponding obligation on the employer to recognize the trade union as bargaining agent for all employees in the bargaining unit, regardless of whether all of these employees are members of that trade union. A co-relative obligation imposed on the union, however, is the duty to provide fair representation to all members of the bargaining unit.[1] An argument can be made that the principle of exclusivity is inconsistent with the guarantee of freedom of association set out in the Charter of Rights and Freedoms, but it is doubtful whether such a broad challenge to Canada's established industrial relations system would be successful.

1. *See supra*, paras. 412–29.

574. These twin principles of 'majoritarianism' and 'exclusivity' are common threads running through all Canadian collective bargaining legislation. The only jurisdiction to deviate at all from these principles has been Quebec where special legislation establishing a multi-employer, multi-union collective bargaining structure of provincial scope for the construction industry has permitted competing federations of trade unions to share a common bargaining table.[1] Frequent amendments to that legislation attest to the fact that the Quebec experiment has not been free of difficulties.

1. An Act Respecting Labour Relations, Vocational Training and Manpower Management in the Construction Industry, R.S.Q. c.R-20; *see* G. Hébert, *op. cit., supra*, 1034–49.

A. Exclusion of Individual Bargains

575. A corollary of the principle of 'exclusivity' is the illegitimacy of individual arrangements between employer and employee. It has been made clear by the courts that the presence of a collective bargaining relationship excludes 'private' negotiations except where permitted by the agreement itself.[1] One result is that collective agreements in Canada generally establish the actual terms of employment for those in the bargaining unit rather than merely setting minimum terms.

1. *Syndicat catholique des employés des magasins de Québec Inc.* v. *Cie Paquet Ltée* (1959) 18 D.L.R. (2d) 346 (S.C.C.); [1959] S.C.R. 206.

576. Another result has been the wholesale displacement of the law relating to the individual contract of employment by the newer legal regime of collective bargaining.[1] It has been held by the Supreme Court of Canada that the law of the individual contract cannot be applied to relieve an employer from its obligation to make severance payments under a collective agreement to employees engaged in an illegal strike.[2] The strike, and the obligation to pay severance pay, were considered by the court as both being matters to be dealt with according to general collective bargaining law and not by reference to the common law. More recently, the Supreme Court of Canada has confirmed a decision of the Industrial Relations Council of British Columbia that, on termination of a collective agreement, individual contracts of employment do not revive. Therefore, an employer may unilaterally alter terms and conditions of employment after a collective agreement has expired, provided there is no violation of the ongoing duty to bargain in good faith.[3] Canadian courts have also determined that the existence of a collective agreement precludes a dismissed employee from bringing a civil action in the courts in respect of that dismissal.[4]

1. *See infra*, paras. 785–801.
2. *McGavin Toastmaster* v. *Ainscough* (1975) 54 D.L.R. (3d) 1 (S.C.C.); [1976] 1 S.C.R. 718.

3. *Paccar of Canada Ltd.* v. *Canadian Association of Industrial, Mechanical and Allied Workers Local 14 et al.* (1989) 89 C.L.L.C. para. 14,050 (S.C.C.); [1989] 2 S.C.R. 983. It must be noted that the B.C. Labour Code at that time provided for no statutory freeze of working conditions following the termination of a collective agreement.
4. *General Motors* v. *Brunet* (1977) 77 C.L.L.C. para. 14,067 (S.C.C.); [1977] 2 S.C.R. 537; *O'Neill* v. *Canadian National Railway* (1980) 81 C.L.L.C. para. 14,074 (N.S.S.C.); *Campbell* v. *East-West Packers* (1983) 142 D.L.R. (3d) 90 (Man.C.A.); *Maribro inc.* v. *L'Union des employés (ées) de service, local 298 et al.*, [1982] R.J.Q. 572 (Que.C.A.).

B. Prohibition against Bargaining Collectively with Others

577. Canadian collective bargaining legislation protects the union's exclusive authority to bargain by prohibiting employers from bargaining collectively with any person other than the bargaining agent, and also by prohibiting other trade unions from bargaining with the employer in respect of the employees in the bargaining unit represented by the bargaining agent. These prohibitions flow from the general statutory duty to bargain in good faith or, in some jurisdictions, from even more explicit legislative provisions.[1] This kind of prohibition raises the interesting question of the extent to which an employer may communicate directly with his employees during collective negotiations. The answer would appear to be that not all direct communications between employer and employees are prohibited, but only those that constitute an attempt to bargain directly with the employees in the bargaining unit.[2] Employers may attempt to set the record straight by explaining their bargaining position, but they may not disparage the bargaining agent or attempt to undermine its bargaining rights in other ways.

1. Canada, s.94(3)(g); Ontario, s.73.
2. *A.N. Shaw Restoration*, [1978] 2 C.L.R.B.R. 214 (O.L.R.B.); compare *Ottawa Citizen*, [1979] 2 C.L.R.B.R. 251 (O.L.R.B.); *Brewster Transport* (1987) 13 C.L.R.B.R. (N.S.) 289 (C.L.R.B.) and *Ottawa Citizen* (1991) 10 C.L.R.B.R. (2d) 293 (O.L.R.B.). *See also Comcare (Canada) Ltd* (1998) 98 C.L.L.C. para. 220-055 (O.L.R.B.).

C. The Right to Bargain for Union Security Provisions

578. One of the more important incidents of the union's exclusive authority to bargain is the recognition that the union as bargaining agent may bargain for its own financial security. Such arrangements include the 'closed shop' where a person must be a member of the union before being hired,[1] the 'union shop' where a person must join the union upon becoming employed, and the 'dues shop' or 'Rand formula' where a person, although not required to join the union, must pay union dues upon becoming employed.

1. The closed shop is usually found in the construction and longshoring industries where trade unions operate hiring halls.

579. Canadian collective bargaining legislation expressly recognizes the legitimacy of union security provisions.[1] Even more important, the Supreme Court of Canada has now held that 'Rand formula' provisions are not inconsistent with the guarantees of freedom of expression and freedom of association set out in the Charter of Rights and Freedoms.[2] Despite this legislative and judicial approval of union security arrangements, the issue of union security can still be an obstacle in negotiations, especially where the parties are negotiating a first collective agreement. To meet this problem some Canadian jurisdictions now require that 'Rand formula' be included in all collective agreements.[3]

1. Canada, s.68; British Columbia, s.15; Ontario, s.51.
2. *Lavigne* v. *Ontario Public Service Employees Union* (1991) 91 C.L.L.C. para. 14,029 (S.C.C.); [1991] 2 S.C.R. 211.
3. Canada, s.70; British Columbia, s.6(3)(e); Ontario, s.47; the Quebec Labour Code, s.47, requires the deduction of union dues as soon as a union obtains certification.

580. Canadian courts have recognized that the trade union's right to bargain for its own financial security flows from its exclusive authority to bargain. In the leading case on this point it was held that an employer could not refuse to remit union dues to a union after it had agreed to the inclusion of a compulsory check-off provision in the collective agreement.[1] Union security, therefore, is regarded as being a proper matter for collective bargaining and, once bargained for and included in the collective agreement, such arrangements bind both the employer and the employees in the bargaining unit.

1. *Syndicat catholique des employés de magasins de Québec inc.* v. *Cie Paquet Ltée* (1959) 18 D.L.R. (2d) 346 (S.C.C.); [1959] S.C.R. 206.

581. Some jurisdictions, however, do allow employees in the bargaining unit to seek some exemption from union security provisions where they object to supporting a trade union because of their religious convictions or beliefs.[1] The test applied is whether the employee has a sincere religious belief that gives rise to the objection to the trade union.[2] Even if an objection is sincere, an exemption will not be granted if the overall thrust of the objection is not religious.[3]

1. Canada, s.70(2); British Columbia, s.17; Ontario, s.52.
2. *Straub*, [1976] 1 C.L.R.B.R. 261 (B.C.L.R.B.); *Barker* (1986) 86 C.L.L.C. para. 16,031 (C.L.R.B.); *Wasilifsky* (1992) 12 C.L.R.B.R. (2d) 161 (B.C.I.R.C.).
3. *Freedhoff*, [1982] 1 C.L.R.B.R. 433 (O.L.R.B), *Gordon* (1990) 3 C.L.R.B.R. (2d) 245 (C.L.R.B.).

§2. The Statutory Freeze

582. A feature of Canadian collective bargaining legislation is the prohibition against either the trade union or employer unilaterally altering the arrangements existing between them once bargaining begins.[1] While such prohibitions appear to be straightforward on their face value, their application has given rise to some difficulty. The question is whether this type of provision requires that there be no change in the actual state of employment existing at the point when the freeze is imposed, or whether it requires the employer to maintain the established pattern of the employment relationship. This question is particularly important where there has been a past pattern of periodic salary adjustments before the collective bargaining relationship has been established.

1. Canadian, s.50; British Columbia, s.45; Quebec, s.59; Ontario, s.86. Some jurisdictions also impose the same kind of statutory freeze from the filing of the certification application until the certificate is issued.

583. The prevailing approach in Canada is to regard the statutory freeze as requiring an employer to conduct business as before.[1] This approach requires an employer to conduct business according to the pattern established before the freeze was imposed. If that pattern included periodic wage adjustments, then such wage adjustments must be maintained even though an employer is at the same time negotiating with a trade union.

1. *Dallaire* v. *Industrielle Compagnie d'Assurance sur la Vie*, [1978] T.T. 376; *Spar Aerospace Products*, [1979] 1 C.L.R.B.R. 61 (O.L.R.B.); *Bank of Nova Scotia*, [1982] 2 C.L.R.B.R. 21 (C.L.R.B.); aff'd. (1983), 83 C.L.L.C. para. 14,007 (Fed.C.A.); *Simpsons Ltd* (1985) 9 C.L.R.B.R. (N.S.) 343 (O.L.R.B.); *Queensway General Hospital* (1992) 12 C.L.R.B.R. (2d) 80 (O.L.R.B.).

584. The statutory freeze not only refers to the terms and conditions of employment but also to other rights, privileges, and duties. This language has been held to be sufficiently wide to catch all incidents of a collective bargaining relationship, including a union security arrangement.[1] The term 'privilege' has been interpreted as covering such matters as free parking, a waiver of rights under an expired collective agreement,[2] and an expectation that a past pattern of wage review would be continued. A reversion to the pattern of employment conditions prevailing prior to the imposition of the freeze has been considered to fall outside the statutory freeze.[3]

1. *Kodak Canada*, [1977] 1 C.L.R.B.R. 280 (O.L.R.B.).
2. *A.N. Shaw Restoration*, [1978] 2 C.L.R.B.R. 257 (O.L.R.B.).
3. *Parr's Print and Litho*, [1973] O.L.R.B. 597.

§3. Dispute-settlement Procedures

585. A distinctive feature of the Canadian collective bargaining system is its array of dispute-resolution procedures. While some of these procedures have served a useful purpose by reducing industrial conflict, their presence may also have served to protract labour disputes by postponing the time at which the two parties have been able to resort to economic sanctions. Canadian collective bargaining legislation usually requires the parties to exhaust certain dispute resolution procedures before striking or locking out. Because these procedures have been made a pre-condition to the use of economic sanctions, they have often been regarded as being merely indirect restrictions upon the right to strike and lock out. The restrictive side of these procedures, to some extent, has impaired their usefulness in resolving industrial conflict.

A. Conciliation

586. Compulsory conciliation has been a longstanding feature of the Canadian collective bargaining structure.[1] Well before the establishment of a legal structure to provide for the acquisition of collective bargaining rights, Canadian legislators had enacted provisions calling for non-coercive, third-party intervention in labour disputes.[2] While these conciliation procedures did not prevent the employer and trade union from resorting ultimately to economic sanctions, they did have the effect, for better or for worse, of postponing strike and lockout action.

1. For example, Canada, s.89; Ontario, s.79(2); British Columbia and Quebec do not make conciliation a pre-condition to the use of the strike or lockout.
2. *Supra*, paras. 80–1.

1. The conciliation board

587. Conciliation may assume more than one form. In its inception the process was essentially an exercise in fact-finding, contemplating the intervention of a third party to investigate a dispute, make specific recommendations for its settlement, and to report these recommendations to the public. Such an approach assumed that public opinion focused upon the dispute by means of a public report would influence parties to reach agreement. This fact-finding role was given to tri-partite conciliation boards composed of representatives of the two parties and an independent chairperson.

588. The fact-finding technique employed by conciliation boards enjoyed only partial success. The influence of public opinion upon labour disputes has been at the very least unpredictable, and it has not always led to compromise and agreement by the parties. Publicity sometimes may serve to harden bargaining positions rather than soften them. Fact-finding, moreover, is a time-consuming exercise and it may have the effect of postponing the use of economic sanctions for long periods of uncertain duration. Because of the disadvantages of fact-finding, boards of conciliation began to abandon their fact-finding role in order to play a more mediative function. Over time, as the mediative form of conciliation became recognized as being more effective than fact-finding, this latter procedure fell into disuse. In Ontario, for example, conciliation boards are seldom used. In the federal jurisdiction, use of conciliation boards is more frequent, perhaps because labour disputes arising in that jurisdiction tend to receive more public attention.

2. The conciliation officer

589. Fact-finding by tripartite conciliation boards has been largely displaced by mediation conducted by the single conciliation officer. This person is usually a full-time government employee whose function is to act as a channel of communication between the parties. The process contemplates that the parties may be brought to an agreement through the efforts of the conciliation officer (or mediator) rather than by the influence of public opinion. Instead of employing such tools as a public inquiry and a public report, the conciliation officer relies upon private discussions, usually with each party separately. An important factor is the parties' trust in the conciliation officer's ability to keep confidences. The conciliation officer does not prepare public reports, and only makes specific recommendations where it would benefit the parties themselves. Patience, perseverance, diplomacy and discretion are the characteristic qualities of the conciliation officer.

590. The need for confidentiality in the conciliation process has been expressly recognized by the creation of a special statutory privilege.[1] This privilege attaches to the conciliation officer, providing an immunity from giving evidence relating to information acquired in the course of conciliation or, in some jurisdictions, it may also attach to any information furnished to the conciliation officer during negotiations. Problems in applying this kind of privilege often arise when labour boards are dealing with complaints that one or other of the parties have failed to bargain in good faith. The nature of the complaint requires that bargaining conduct be examined, yet much of this conduct may be shielded by the statutory privilege attached to the conciliation process. Labour boards have taken the position that this privilege protects 'private communications' (those made to the conciliator when the other party is not present) but not to 'public statements' (those made to the conciliator in the presence of the other party).[2] Labour boards have also treated the privilege as not belonging to the parties but attaching to the conciliation process itself. A party, therefore, cannot waive the privilege and disclose communications made between it and the conciliator.[3]

1. Canada, s.87; British Columbia, s.146; Ontario, ss.119(2), 120.
2. *CCH Canadian*, [1974] 1 C.L.R.B.R. 388 (O.L.R.B.).
3. *Ibid*; but *see Cheni Gold Mines Inc.* (1990), 7 C.L.R.B.R. (2d) 198 (B.C.I.R.C.).

591. Recourse to the services of the conciliation officer is a pre-condition of the right to strike and lock out in most Canadian jurisdictions. The compulsory aspect of this process has meant that at times it has been treated as a formality to be satisfied in order to gain the right to strike or lock out. Other jurisdictions (for example, British Columbia and Quebec), perhaps recognizing the problems arising from mandatory conciliation, do not stipulate that conciliation is to be a pre-condition of the use of economic sanctions.[1]

1. In particular, it should be noted that, in 1977, Quebec moved from a compulsory conciliation procedure to the present voluntary procedure. *See* Quebec, s.54.

592. In all Canadian jurisdictions, however, there does appear to be a recognition that the mediation function itself performs a particularly useful role in resolving labour disputes. Variations of the basic mediative approach can be found in many Canadian collective bargaining statutes. In addition to compulsory conciliation the legislation may provide for more specialized forms of mediation through the use of industrial inquiry commissioners[1] or mid-contract mediation.[2]

1. Ontario, ss.37, 39; British Columbia, s.79.
2. Ontario, s.38; British Columbia, s.106.

B. Strike Votes and Pre-Strike Notice

593. A number of Canadian jurisdictions make a favourable strike vote a precondition to the exercise of the right to strike.[1] One of the arguments in favour of this procedure is that it acts as a brake upon an over-zealous trade union leadership.[2] Union leaders, however, may not always be in front of the rank and file, and there is some danger that the requirement of a strike vote may lend an unnecessary rigidity to the negotiating process. At the very least such requirements tend to protract negotiations by postponing the use of economic sanctions until a favourable vote has been taken.[3]

1. Alberta, British Columbia, Canada, Manitoba, New Brunswick, Nova Scotia, Ontario, P.E.I., Quebec, Saskatchewan. Ontario (s.42) and B.C. (s.78) also allow employers to require an employee vote on their last offer.
2. *See* P.C. Weiler, *Reconcilable Differences* (Toronto, 1980) at 70–4.
3. *See infra*, paras. 716–37.

594. The procedure for the conduct of such votes varies from jurisdiction to jurisdiction. Only two jurisdictions require that a strike vote be supervised by a governmental official.[1] Usually all employees in the unit affected are considered as eligible voters but one jurisdiction also allows other members of the trade union to vote.[2] As a general rule, the required majority is defined by reference to those who voted.

1. Alberta, Saskatchewan.
2. New Brunswick. However, the union must obtain both a majority of its members and a majority of the employees in the bargaining unit.

595. Some Canadian jurisdictions also require that notice be given prior to the commencement of strike action,[1] making such notice a pre-condition of strike activity. In some jurisdictions notice must be given to the employer; other jurisdictions require that it be given to the Ministry of Labour; and still other jurisdictions require that notice be given to both the employer and Ministry of Labour. In no jurisdiction, however, does the required period of notice exceed 72 hours.

1. Alberta, British Columbia, Canada, New Brunswick, Nova Scotia, Saskatchewan.

C. Arbitration

596. The general approach of Canadian collective bargaining legislation is to permit labour disputes arising in the private sector to be resolved through ultimate recourse to economic sanctions – the strike and the lockout. Third-party intervention has been restricted to fact-finding and mediative functions, and no Canadian jurisdiction provides any general procedure for the ultimate resolution of bargaining impasses in the private sector by means of third-party intervention. Compulsory arbitration of such impasses, while receiving support in some quarters, does not appear to be widely favoured by either employers or trade unions.

597. Interest arbitration,[1] as it is commonly called, requires an arbitration tribunal (usually tripartite in composition) to hear representations from the employer and the union, and then to make the ultimate agreement for them. The procedure gives the appearance of being adjudicative, but the issues being dealt with are usually economic in nature, requiring a particular decision about the allocation of economic resources.

The guidelines provided for the resolution of such disputes, not surprisingly, tend to be general in nature, and are often contradictory.[2] As a result, arbitration awards more often appear to be a compromise between the opposing positions of the parties than to be the result of the application of established principles. The presence of arbitration may also discourage the parties from making concessions prior to arbitration – placing the entire burden of establishing the appropriate compromise upon the arbitrator.[3] The adjudicative format that the process assumes, moreover, makes it slow and expensive – features that do not sit well with either trade unions or employers.

1. *See* generally, J.M. Weiler (ed.), *Interest Arbitration* (Toronto, 1981).
2. For an attempt to formulate more 'rational and objective' criteria, *see Welland County General Hospital* (1965) 16 L.A.C. 1.
3. In order to avoid the problem some commentators have advocated 'final-offer selection', restricting the arbitrator to choosing between the final position of the two parties. This 'all-or-nothing' approach has been adopted to some extent in the educational sector. Problems with this technique may arise, however, where the dispute is complicated by a multiplicity of unresolved issues. For a discussion of these problems *see* Weiler, *op. cit.*, at 231–5.

598. At a more philosophical level, there is the objection that the setting of wages through compulsory arbitration is incompatible with the operation of a free enterprise economy. It has been argued that, if wage levels are to be determined in this manner, then other prices should also be controlled. Unions tend to regard arbitration as an unwarranted intrusion in the free operation of the economy when they receive an unfavourable award, and employers make the same objection when they regard the award as being overly-generous. Given the problems associated with interest arbitration and the general lack of enthusiasm for it, this impasse resolution procedure is not a common feature of private sector collective bargaining, although it is used more frequently to resolve public collective bargaining disputes.

1. Voluntary arbitration

599. Many Canadian jurisdictions expressly provide that, for the purpose of resolving a particular dispute, the parties themselves may agree to be bound by the recommendations of a third party.[1] An interesting question, however, is the extent to which the parties by agreement may bind themselves to a general procedure of interest arbitration for future disputes. While such a procedure leaves open the possibility that future arbitrators might continue this procedure indefinitely, there has been reluctance on the part of the courts to interfere with such arrangements.[2]

1. Canada, s.79; Ontario, s.40; Quebec, ss.74–93.
2. *Haldimand Norfolk Regional Health Unit* (1983) 83 C.L.L.C. para. 14,059 (S.C.C.); [1983] 2 S.C.R. 6.

2. First-agreement arbitration

600. A number of Canadian jurisdictions provide for the arbitration of unresolved first contract disputes.[1] Some of these jurisdictions provide a process to screen requests for first-agreement arbitration,[2] while in others access to first-agreement arbitration is automatic. In the federal jurisdiction, Newfoundland, and Manitoba, the arbitration function is performed by their labour board; in Ontario recourse is to an arbitration board established for the purpose of resolving the dispute or the labour board on agreement of the parties; and in Quebec recourse is to a single arbitrator. First-agreements imposed under these procedures last for only a limited time,[3] and negotiations following their expiry are left to be resolved through the normal collective bargaining process.

1. Canada, s.80; British Columbia, s.55; Manitoba, s.87; Newfoundland, ss.81, 81.1–81.3; Ontario, s.43; Quebec, ss.93.1–93.9; Saskatchewan, s.26.5.
2. Canada – consent of the Minister; Newfoundland – consent of the Minister except for offshore oil platform industry where access is automatic; Quebec – consent of the Minister; Ontario – application to labour board; Manitoba provides automatic access. For Saskatchewan's approach *see Prairie Micro-Tech Inc.* (1996) 96 C.L.L.C. para. 220-033 (Sask.LR.B.).
3. Canada – one year; Manitoba – one year; Newfoundland – one year, Ontario – two years; Quebec – up to two years: Saskatchewan – two years.

601. First-agreement arbitration, has been treated as an unusual remedy to be applied where an employer refuses to deal with a trade union after it has acquired bargaining rights.[1] This remedy, however, may be invoked even when an employer's conduct may not constitute a failure to bargain in good faith.[2] The proponents of first-agreement arbitration argue that, although many imposed first contracts do not mature into a permanent bargaining relationship, this remedy still has a deterrent effect upon other employers who might be tempted to adopt anti-union tactics when bargaining.[3]

1. *London Drugs,* [1974] 1 C.L.R.B.R. 140 (B.C.L.R.B.); *Radio Diffusion Mutuelle,* [1971] 1 C.L.R.B. 332 (C.L.R.B.); *Placer Dome Inc.* (1991) 11 C.L.R.B.R. (2nd) 247 (O.L.R.B.).
2. *Formula Plastics Inc.* (1987) 87 C.L.L.C. para. 16,035 (O.L.R.B.); *Yarrow Lodge Ltd* (1993) 94 C.L.L.C. para. 16,047 (B.C.L.R.B.).
3. *See* Weiler, *op. cit.*, at 52–5; *see also* J. Sexton, 'First Contract Arbitration: A Canadian Invention' and J. McCormack, 'First Contract Arbitration in Ontario: A Glance at Some of the Issues' in W. Kaplan, J. Sack, M. Gunderson (eds.), *Labour Arbitration Yearbook, 1991*, vol. 1 (Toronto, 1991) at 231–64.

602. Reference is made to comparable collective agreements when determining the content of an imposed first-agreement.[1] A study of the Quebec experience concludes that in that jurisdiction a more conservative approach is taken when imposing monetary provisions and a more liberal approach is taken with respect to non-mandatory provisions.[2] Sometimes the bargaining conduct of the parties is also considered and on one occasion a first collective agreement was not imposed on the employer because the union was considered to be using the procedure to gain a strategic advantage in bargaining.[3]

1. *Canada Building Materials Co.* (1991) 9 C.L.R.B.R. (2nd) 71 (O.L.R.B.).
2. J. Sexton, *L'arbitrage de la première convention collective au Québec: 1978–1984* (1987) 42 *Rel. ind.* 272.
3. *Royal Bank,* [1983] 1 C.L.R.B.R. 16 (C.L.R.B.).

3. Ad hoc *intervention*

603. Despite the absence of any general provisions for compulsory arbitration of interest disputes, there has still been in Canada a limited amount of *ad hoc* legislative intervention where unresolved disputes have been considered as being contrary to the public interest. Such intervention usually takes the form of a back-to-work order and provision for the dispute to be resolved by binding arbitration.[1] The service interrupted by the dispute must be regarded as being sufficiently essential to justify such an extraordinary response.

1. It has been held that this kind of legislation does not violate the Charter of Rights and Freedoms. *See Retail, Wholesale and Department Store Union* v. *Government of Saskatchewan* (1987) 87 C.L.L.C. para. 14,023 (S.C.C.); [1987] 1 S.C.R. 460.

604. The question of what constitutes an essential service is not easy to answer.[1] It is generally accepted that at least some of the services provided by governments are essential and, as a result, most Canadian jurisdictions impose at least some restrictions on the use of the strike by government employees.[2] As well, other types of public employees are often regarded as providing services that are essential. Policemen, firemen, school teachers, hospital workers and municipal transit workers may find restrictions upon their use of strike action, either in general legislation or as the result of an *ad hoc* intervention by the legislators. Such disparate groups as railway workers, elevator contractors and loggers have on occasion also discovered that their services are essential. It would appear that the definition of essentiality depends to a great extent upon public tolerance of the inevitable disruptions caused by collective bargaining disputes. As a general observation, Canadians appear to have been more tolerant of a disruption of services in the private sector and less tolerant where there have been disruptions of services in the pubic or quasi-public sectors.

1. *See* generally, H.W. Arthurs, 'Public Interest Disputes in Canada: A Legislative Perspective' (1967) 17 *Buffalo L. Rev.* 39 and Weiler, *op. cit.*, c.7.
2. Most jurisdictions have separate legislation establishing a collective bargaining structure for public employees. For example, Public Service Staff Relations Act, R.S.C. 1985, c.P-35, as am. The Canada Labour Code covering private sector employees within the federal jurisdiction now requires maintenance of services necessary to protect public health and safety and also the maintenance of services affecting grain shipments in the case of work stoppages in the ports – ss.87.4, 87.7.

§4. Conduct of Negotiations

A. Commencement of Bargaining

605. Under Canadian collective bargaining legislation the use of economic sanctions has been restricted in order to provide for periods of labour peace. As a general rule strikes and lockouts are not permitted during the duration of the collective agreements nor are they permitted to be used as a weapon to obtain recognition.[1] Furthermore, the legislation also contemplates a period of negotiation during which the parties are not free to resort to economic sanctions. Resort to certain dispute resolution procedures during this period may also be required in order for the right to strike or lock out to accrue.[2] Given these legislative restrictions, the commencement of bargaining is generally regarded as marking the beginning of the countdown to the time when economic sanctions may be applied.

1. *See infra*, paras. 716–38.
2. *Supra*, paras. 585–605.

1. Notice to bargain

606. Collective bargaining legislation usually provides that bargaining is to commence by the giving of written notice to bargain by one party to the other. Usually it is the union that takes the initiative by serving notice to bargain. The notice is generally regarded as timely if it is given after bargaining rights have been acquired, or during the last months of an expiring collective agreement. Questions sometimes arise as to whether a party is entitled to give notice to bargain. Some of these challenges may raise the issue of the extent of the union's bargaining rights, but others may simply go to the timing of the notice to bargain.

607. In some jurisdictions, particular problems relating to the timing of the notice may arise where the parties are bargaining to renew a collective agreement. Collective bargaining legislation usually provides that notice to bargain may be given within the last months (usually three) of the expiring collective agreement. Where notice is given after this period expires, there is some question as to whether this notice is sufficient to set in motion the negotiation process contemplated by the legislation. Labour boards have held that the time for the giving of notice found in the statute is merely directory, and notice given after that time is sufficient to set the negotiation process in motion.[1]

1. *Peel Memorial Hospital*, [1977] 2 C.L.R.B.R. 211 (O.L.R.B.).

608. A different result would appear to follow, however, where the collective agreement by its own terms provides that it is to continue in effect for a further year. If notice is not given within the time specified in the agreement, the legal result would appear to be that the collective agreement is extended for a further year, having the effect of postponing the time at which notice to bargain may be given under the statute.[1]

1. *Nortex Products*, [1978] O.L.R.B. 1036; [1979] O.L.R.B. 783; *London Generator Service*, [1978] O.L.R.B. 932; *Hield Brothers* (1957) 57 C.L.L.C. para. 18,071; but *see Austin Airways*, [1980] C.L.R.B.R. 393 (C.L.R.B.).

609. Problems may also occur where the expiring collective agreement provides that it is to remain in effect until replaced by a new agreement. Even though such an agreement may also provide for the giving of notice to bargain, there remains the question of whether the parties can ever be free to invoke economic sanctions because of the continuing effect of the collective agreement. The Supreme Court of Canada has held that this type of continuation provision should not be read as perpetually excluding the parties from striking or locking out.[1] The Court viewed the overriding collective agreement provision as being the one providing the notice to bargain. The giving of notice to bargain, therefore, serves to terminate the agreement at the end of its specified term allowing the parties to follow the normal set of procedures for renewal of the collective agreement. One Canadian jurisdiction now expressly allows a party to terminate the continuing operation of such agreements on the giving of 30 days' notice to the other party.[2]

1. *Bradburn* v. *Wentworth Arms Hotel*, (1979) 79 C.L.L.C. para. 14,189, [1979] 1 S.C.R. 846; *see also City of Campbellton* (1982) 134 D.L.R. (3d) 743 (N.B.S.C.).
2. Ontario, s.58 (2); *see Caterpillar of Canada Ltd.* (1990) 5 C.L.R.B.R. (2nd) 307 (O.L.R.B.).

2. Wage re-openers

610. Some collective agreements (usually negotiated during periods of high inflation) may provide for the re-negotiation of the wage scale during the term of the collective agreement. Whether this kind of provision is sufficient to set in motion the full range of negotiation procedures is problematical. Collective bargaining legislation as a rule provides that collective agreements are to be for a term of at least one year. In Ontario, the legislation also provides that if an agreement is for an unspecified term it shall be considered as being for a term of one year.[1] The Ontario board has indicated that where the parties explicitly provide for the early termination of a collective agreement to re-negotiate wages the effect is to create a term of unspecified duration that would be reduced by operation of the statute to one year.[2] A clause merely providing for the re-negotiation of wages during the term of the collective agreement, however, has not been interpreted as being sufficiently express to terminate the agreement prior to specified expiry dates. The Quebec Labour Code allows the parties to strike or lock out during the course of a collective agreement if the agreement contains a clause permitting it to be re-opened.[3] However, the use of economic weapons is restricted to the negotiations of matters falling within the contemplation of the re-opener clause. One jurisdiction, British Columbia, provides for the early termination of collective agreements on the consent of the minister.[4]

1. S.58(1). Quebec has a similar rule, s.66.
2. *Kroehler Mfg.*, [1977] 1 C.L.R.B.R. 107 (O.L.R.B.).
3. Quebec, s.107.
4. British Columbia, s.50(2), (3).

3. Bargaining over technological change

611. The introduction of new technology to the work place may have a very disruptive effect upon labour relations. Not only is it likely to require a reorganization of work assignments and the learning of new work methods, but it is just as likely to involve a reduction in the workforce. Particular problems occur when such changes are made during the term of the collective agreement. Even though the introduction of new technology may have a substantial effect on the arrangements established by collective agreements, legislation in most Canadian jurisdictions does not permit full negotiations over technological change with resort to strike and lockout action until after agreements have expired and the required dispute resolution procedures have been contemplated.[1]

1. *See infra*, paras. 716–18.

612. Some jurisdictions, however, have recognized this problem and have established specific procedures to deal with the introduction of technological change during the collective agreement.[1] Under these procedures it is possible for the bargaining agent to obtain an order preserving the status quo and, in certain circumstances, to open the collective agreement for re-negotiation. Somewhat surprisingly, these procedures do not appear to have had much use, perhaps because of their complexity or perhaps because of the recent trend to shorter collective agreements.[2]

1. Canada, ss.51–5; British Columbia, s.54; Manitoba, ss.83–5; Saskatchewan s.43.
2. For a discussion of these procedures *see Ottawa Carleton Regional Transit Commission*, [1982] C.L.R.B.R. 172 (C.L.R.B.); *Eurocan Pulp & Paper*, [1983] 1 C.L.R.B.R. (N.S.) 63 (B.C.L.R.B.); (1983), 83 C.L.L.C. para. 16,049 (B.C.L.R.B.); *Westfair Foods Ltd* (1992) 12 C.L.R.B.R. 284 (S.L.R.B.).

4. Bargaining and wage controls

613. The imposition of wage controls is becoming an increasingly frequent feature of the Canadian industrial relations system. From 1975 to 1978 the federal government, exercising its power to deal with national emergencies,[1] imposed wage and price controls upon the private sector, throughout Canada as well as imposing wage controls upon its own employees. At the same time all provinces but one either adopted the federal programme or imposed a similar programme for their own public employees. In 1982, the federal government and six provinces legislated a new set of wage controls for public sector employees. These two experiences with economic controls placed severe strain on the collective bargaining process. Even though restraint legislation need does not preclude collective bargaining completely,[2] it is clear that its overall effect is to restrict the collective bargaining process.[3] Despite this incompatibility, it has been held that income restraint legislation is not inconsistent with the Charter's guarantee of freedom of association since this guarantee does not protect either collective bargaining or the right to strike.[4] The severe recession in the early 1990s led a number of Canadian jurisdictions to once again impose wage controls on their public sector employees.

1. *Reference Re Anti-Inflation Act* (1976) 68 D.L.R. (3d) 452 (S.C.C.); [1976] 2 S.C.R. 373.
2. *See* generally P.C. Weiler, *Reconcilable Differences* (Toronto, 1980), c.8.
3. *See* D.D. Carter, P. Kumar, *Recent Public Sector Restraint Programs: Two Views* (Kingston, 1984).
4. *Public Sector Alliance of Canada* v. *The Queen in Right of Canada* (1987) C.L.L.C. para. 14,022 (S.C.C.); [1987] 1 S.C.R. 424.

B. The Duty to Bargain in Good Faith

614. Once notice to bargain has been given the parties are under an express statutory obligation to bargain in good faith and to make every reasonable effort to negotiate a collective agreement.[1] Somewhat surprisingly, there had been until the 1970s very few labour board decisions defining the concept of 'good faith' bargaining in the context of Canadian labour relations. The reason for this lack of jurisprudence can be found in the fact that labour boards have only enjoyed a direct jurisdiction over bargaining complaints since the 1970s. Prior to this extension of the boards' jurisdiction, such complaints had to be brought to the boards in the form of an application for consent to prosecute. If consent was granted, then the matter could proceed in the criminal courts by way of private prosecution. Because of the possibility of subsequent criminal proceedings being pursued, labour boards were reluctant to comment upon the evidence when granting consent to prosecution even though very few of these complaints were taken to the criminal courts after consent to prosecute was given. The result was a singular lack of both board and court decisions defining the duty to bargain in good faith.[2] This vacuum has been rapidly filled by a growing labour board jurisprudence,[3] but the development of this jurisprudence may now be slowed by the increased availability of first-agreement arbitration as a bargaining remedy.

1. Canada, s.50; British Columbia, s.47; Ontario, s.17; Quebec, s.53.
2. *The Canada Labour Code*, s.97(3) still provides that no bargaining complaint may be made to the board except with the consent of the Minister, but in British Columbia and Ontario the complaint may be made to the board directly. In Quebec, where no labour board exists, bargaining complaints can only be the object of a penal prosecution before the Labour Court. This approach should be replaced by a more administrative one when amendments to the Labour Code, adopted in June 2001 and creating a labour board, will come into force.
3. *See* B.L. Adell, *The Duty to Bargain in Good Faith: Its Recent Development in Canada* (Kingston, 1980).

615. The obligation to bargain in good faith poses certain definitional problems. Collective bargaining requires that bargaining impasses be resolved ultimately by pitting the economic strength of the employer against the collective economic strength of the employees. Given the fact that economic strength is the ultimate arbiter of the dispute, it is often asked whether there is room for any concept of 'good faith' in collective bargaining. A closer examination of the nature of collective bargaining provides the answer to this question. Collective bargaining is not merely an economic exercise, being just as much an exercise in human relations. This latter aspect of collective bargaining cannot be carried on successfully if the parties are left free to resort to tactics inherently destructive of the bargaining relationship. The presence of a duty to bargain in good faith serves to control such tactics while still leaving the parties free to resort to legitimate economic sanctions.

616. It should not be surprising, then, that labour boards in administering the duty to bargain in good faith have placed far greater emphasis on the manner in which negotiations have been conducted than upon the content of negotiations.[1] Generally speaking, the boards have not sought to determine whether a particular bargaining proposal should be carried to an impasse – a reticence that appears to reflect a concern that they should not be interfering unduly with the economic forces at play during negotiations. As a result, a great deal of the jurisprudence defining the duty to bargain in good faith deals with the manner in which negotiations are to be conducted.

1. *Noranda Metal Industries*, [1975] 1 C.L.R.B.R. 145 (B.C.L.R.B.); *Journal Publishing*, [1972] 2 C.L.R.B.R. 183 (O.L.R.B.): *CKLW Radio Broadcasting* (1979) 77 C.L.C.C. para. 16,110 (C.L.R.B.); and *Iberia Airlines of Spain* (1992) 13 C.L.R.B.R. (2d) 224 (C.L.R.B.).

1. Duty to meet

617. A primary function of the duty to bargain in good faith is to reinforce the bargaining rights acquired by the trade union. These bargaining rights give the trade union exclusive authority to bargain on behalf of the employees in the bargaining unit. The corresponding obligation upon the employer is to bargain in good faith and make every reasonable effort to reach a collective agreement. It should be self-evident, then, that implicit in the duty to bargain in good faith is an obligation to meet with the other party.

618. The boundaries of this obligation to meet are not capable of precise definition. Where the parties have fully discussed the issues at numerous meetings, a refusal to meet any further until there has been some alteration in position is likely to be legitimate. If such a refusal occurs at the commencement of negotiations, however, it is likely to be regarded as refusal to recognize the other party.[1] Moreover, it is clear that the presence of extenuating circumstances may justify such a refusal to bargain. Where a municipal council took the position that negotiations with the union would be conducted at meetings with the public and press in attendance, a trade union's refusal to meet under these circumstances has been considered to be legitimate.[2] On the other hand, it has been held that an employer was not justified in unilaterally breaking off negotiations simply because of an outstanding dispute under the expiring collective agreement.[3]

1. *De Vilbiss*, [1976] 2 C.L.R.B.R. 101 (O.L.R.B.).
2. *Borough of North York*, [1968] O.L.R.B. 66.
3. *Journal Publishing*, [1977] 2 C.L.R.B.R. 183 (O.L.R.B.).

619. A related question is whether the employer may refuse to meet with the union because it objects to the composition of the union's bargaining committee. Labour boards have held that, since employees are entitled to negotiate through their own freely chosen representatives, an employer's objection to the composition of the union bargaining committee (even where it contains an employee of a business competitor) cannot justify a refusal to meet with the union.[1]

1. *Marshall-Wells* (1955) 55 C.L.L.C. para. 18,002 (S.L.R.B.); *Journal Publishing*, [1977] 2 C.L.R.B.R. 183 (O.L.R.B.); *Mountain Taxi and Tours* (1983) 83 C.L.L.C. para. 16,026 (A.L.R.B.). S.141 of the Quebec Labour Code imposes on the employer an obligation to recognize the bargaining authority of union officials.

2. *Circumvention of bargaining agent*

620. Legal recognition of the trade union as bargaining agent gives it the exclusive right to bargain on behalf of the employees in the bargaining unit. Employees are not permitted to circumvent the bargaining agent by bargaining directly with the employees or with some other union.[1] Moreover, attempts by employers to alter wage and working conditions unilaterally, even after the statutory freeze has expired, have in some circumstances been considered as violations of the duty to bargain in good faith.[2]

1. *Supra*, paras. 573–82; *see also Davidson Rubber* (1969) 69 C.L.L.C. para. 14,190 (Ont.Prov.Ct.). *Nunez* v. *Lloyd's Electronics Limitée*, [1978] T.T. 193.
2. *De Vilbiss*, [1976] 2 C.L.R.B.R. 101 (O.L.R.B.).

3. Requirement of full discussion

621. The duty to bargain in good faith not only requires the parties to acknowledge the collective bargaining relationship between them but also to engage in a full and informed discussion during the course of that bargaining relationship. The requirement of full discussion means that more mature bargaining relationships may come under the scrutiny of labour boards. While lack of recognition is not usually a problem associated with such relationships, difficulties may arise because of a breakdown in communications. Labour boards have made it clear that mutual communication is an essential element of the duty to bargain in good faith.

622. The requirement of mutual communication appears to reflect a concern that negotiations should not break down because of a lack of understanding of the positions taken at the bargaining table. An adamant refusal to discuss alternative interpretations of wage control guidelines has been considered as a failure to bargain in good faith,[1] as has a refusal to explain the rationale underlying a wage offer.[2] An insistence by one party upon discussing an issue to the exclusion of all others have also been regarded as falling short of the required standard,[3] as has a refusal to discuss a particular issue.[4]

1. *Canadian Industries*, [1976] 2 C.L.R.B.R. 8 (O.L.R.B.).
2. *St. Joseph's Hospital*, [1976] O.L.R.B. 255; *Board of Health of Haliburton, Kawartha, Pine Ridge District Health Unit*, [1977] 1 C.L.R.B.R. 221 (O.L.R.B.).
3. *Journal Publishing*, [1977] 2 C.L.R.B.R. 183 (O.L.R.B.).
4. *Governing Council of University of Toronto* (1986) 11 C.L.R.B.R. (N.S.) 219 (O.L.R.B.).

623. Labour boards, however, have recognized that this requirement of mutual communication must take into account the realities of collective bargaining, and some allowance appears to be made for the normal wear and tear of collective bargaining. A mere lack of tact is not by itself sufficient to constitute a failure to bargain in good faith.[1] As well, a refusal to discuss an issue on the periphery of the negotiations may not be considered as bad faith bargaining.[2] It has also been recognized that the parties may reach a point in the bargaining process where further discussions are no longer fruitful. Once such a point is reached, a breaking off of negotiations[3] or the adoption of a 'take it or leave it' position is not likely to be regarded as a failure to bargain in good faith.[4] However, a failure to respond to a union's total capitulation has been considered a breach of the obligation to bargain in good faith.[5]

1. *Board of Health and Haliburton, Kawartha, Pine Ridge District Health Unit*, [1977] 1 C.L.R.B.R. 221 (O.L.R.B.).
2. *Pulp and Paper Industrial Relations Bureau*, [1978] 1 C.L.R.B.R. 60 (B.C.L.R.B.).
3. *CKLW Radio Broadcasting* (1977) 77 C.L.L.C. para. 16,110 (C.L.R.B.).
4. *The Ottawa Citizen*, [1979] 2 C.L.R.B.R. 251 (O.L.R.B.).
5. *General Aviation Services*, [1982] 3 C.L.R.B.R. 47 (C.L.R.B.).

4. Duty to supply information

624. An interesting question arising from the requirement of full discussion concerns the extent to which an employer is obliged to supply wage data and more general financial data about her/his operation to the bargaining agent. While it has been recognized that there is some duty upon the employer to supply information, the full extent of that duty has not been clearly defined.[1] In one case a refusal by an employer to supply existing wage and classification data was taken into account in determining that a failure to bargain in good faith had occurred.[2] In another case an employer's failure to disclose her/his intention to subcontract work amounted to bad faith bargaining.[3] As well, it has been held that a failure to reveal an impending plant closure breached the duty to bargain in good faith.[4]

1. *Noranda Metal Industries*, [1975] 1 C.L.R.B.R. 145 (B.C.L.R.B.); *Forintek Canada Corp.* (1987) 14 C.L.R.B.R. (N.S.) 1 (O.L.R.B.); but *see Marshall-Wells* v. *Retail Wholesale* (1956) 2 D.L.R. (2d) 569 (S.C.C.); [1956] S.C.R. 511; *Starbucks Corp.* (1997) 97 C.L.L.C. para. 220-067 (B.C.L.R.B.).
2. *DeVilbiss*, [1976] 2 C.L.R.B.R. 101 (O.L.R.B.).
3. *Sunnycrest Nursing Home*, [1982] 2 C.L.R.B.R. 51 (O.L.R.B.), but *see Amoco Fibres*, [1982] 2 C.L.R.B.R. 305 (O.L.R.B.).
4. *Consolidated Bathurst Packaging* (1983) 83 C.L.L.C. para. 16,066 (O.L.R.B.); *see also France Film*, [1987] T.T. 374 and *Government of Saskatchewan* (1990) 5 C.L.R.B.R. (2d) 254. (S.L.R.B.).

5. Untimely use of economic sanctions

625. Canadian collective bargaining legislation generally provides that the parties may resort to economic sanctions only after they have had recourse to certain dispute-settlement procedures. The result is that there is a period of negotiation when economic sanctions are proscribed. At times, however, one of the parties may yield to the temptation of 'jumping the gun'. Untimely strikes or lockouts are clearly illegal and a remedy can be sought through the special procedures to deal with such untimely economic action. Picketing at this time, however, may not be illegal *per se*, but its use during this 'quiet' period may be considered as a failure to bargain in good faith.[1]

1. *Nipissing Hotel Ltd.* v. *Hotel & Restaurant Employees* (1962) 36 D.L.R. (2d) 81 (Ont.H.C.).

6. Duty to complete the negotiations

626. Negotiating problems sometimes arise at the very end of the negotiating process. While labour boards appear to have given the parties more leeway at this stage of the negotiations, they have intervened where one of the parties attempted to renege on commitments previously made. A tabling of additional demands by a party after a dispute has been defined has been considered to be a failure to bargain in good faith.[1] Moreover, labour boards have gone so far as to order an employer to execute a formal agreement where a mutual understanding had been reached on all issues.[2]

1. *Graphic Centre*, [1976] 2 C.L.R.B.R. 118 (O.L.R.B.): *Morris Rod Weeder*, [1978] 2 C.L.R.B.R. 232 (S.L.R.B.).
2. *Municipality of Casimir, Jennings and Appleby*, [1978] 2 C.L.R.B.R. 284 (O.L.R.B.); *British Columbia Institute of Technology*, [1976] 2 C.L.R.B.R. 129 (B.C.L.R.B). S.49(2) of the British Columbia Code requires both parties to execute the agreements where an agreement has been reached in bargaining.

7. Supervision of the content of bargaining

627. The development of the duty to bargain in good faith has focused primarily on the manner in which negotiations are to conducted. Despite this emphasis, labour boards on occasion have concerned themselves with the content of negotiations. Unlike the well-developed jurisprudence in the United States, however, the Canada case law does not usually draw a distinction between mandatory and voluntary demands.[1] Nevertheless, Canadian labour boards have considered the making of demands that are tainted by illegality as a failure to bargain in good faith and,[2] going even further, have treated demands that are inconsistent with the scheme of the collective bargaining statute as bad faith bargaining.[3]

1. In *Otis Elevator* (1973) 73 C.L.L.C. para. 14,166 (B.C.C.A.) a distinction was made between mandatory and non-mandatory bargaining proposals.
2. *Board of School Trustees of School District No. 39 (Vancouver)*, [1977] 2 C.L.R.B.R. 201 (B.C.L.R.B.).
3. *Carpenters Employer Bargaining Agency*, [1978] 1 C.L.R.B.R. 50 (O.L.R.B.); *Eastern Provincial Airways Ltd* (1983) 3 C.L.R.B.R. (N.S.) 75 (C.C.L.R.B.). *See* D.D. Carter, 'The Duty to Bargain in Good Faith: Does It Affect the Content of Bargaining?' in K.P. Swan and K.E. Swinton (eds.). *Studies in Labour Law* (Toronto, 1983). *See also Royal Canadian Legion* (1990) 7 C.L.R.B.R. (2d) 291 (S.L.R.B.).

628. A demand may be rendered illegal by legislation other than the collective bargaining statute. For example, the insistence that the collective agreement contain a restriction upon the hiring of members of a particular ethnic group contrary to human rights legislation has been considered to be bad faith bargaining.[1] Labour boards have also indicated that insistence upon a demand in contravention of wage control legislation would amount to a failure to bargain in good faith.[2]

1. *T. Barbesin and Sons*, [1960] O.L.R.B. 80.
2. *Board of School Trustees of School District No. 39 (Vancouver)*, [1977] 2 C.L.R.B.R. 201 (B.C.L.R.B.).

629. The illegality of the demand, however, is more likely to result from a conflict with the collective bargaining legislation itself. A failure to bargain in good faith can occur where a party seeks to bargain for a normal agreement yet the applicable provincial labour legislation requires bargaining to be provincial in scope.[1] An attempt to extend bargaining rights during negotiations has been held to be inconsistent with the scheme of collective bargaining legislation.[2] Employer demands to restrict the scope of a bargaining unit have been considered as illegal, as have demands relating to the assignment of work between competing trade unions.[3] As well, bargaining demands that interfere with the conduct of the internal affairs of a trade union may also be considered to be illegal such as an employer demand that a union not discipline employees who crossed picket lines during a strike.[4] Insistence that a collective agreement be of shorter duration than required by law has also been considered as a failure to bargain in good faith,[5] as has employer insistence on an employee vote when the union has already approved the employer's last offer,[6] and a union's insistence on continuing negotiations after it has lost a last-offer vote required by statute.[7]

1. *Otis Elevator* (1973) C.L.L.C. para. 14,166 (B.C.C.A.); *see also Stelco Inc.* (1991) C.L.R.B.R. (2d) 305 (Alta.L.R.B.).
2. *Carpenters Employer Bargaining Agency*, [1978] 1 C.L.R.B.R. 50 (O.L.R.B.); *Burns Meats Ltd* (1985) C.L.R.B.R. (N.S.) 355 (O.L.R.B.); *Northern-West Elevator Ltd* (1992) 12 C.L.R.B.R. (2d) 308.
3. *British Columbia Telephone*, [1977] 2 C.L.R.B.R. 404 (C.L.R.B.); *Toronto Star Newspapers*, [1979] O.L.R.B. 451; [1979] O.L.R.B. 811; *Beeland Co-operative*, [1982] 3 C.L.R.B.R. 448 (S.L.R.B.); *Abitibi Consolidated Inc.* (1998) 99 C.L.L.C. para. 220-011 (O.L.R.B.).
4. *Morris Rod Weeder*, [1978] 2 C.L.R.B.R. 49 (S.L.R.B.); but *see A.N. Shaw Restoration*, [1977] 1 C.L.R.B.R. 103 (O.L.R.B.).
5. *Canada Bread* (1945) 45 C.L.L.C. para. 16,430 (O.L.R.B.).
6. *Fotomat*, [1981] 3 C.L.R.B.R. 129 (O.L.R.B.).
7. *Canada Cement Lafarge*, [1982] 1 C.L.R.B.R. 300 (O.L.R.B.).

630. Despite these decisions curtailing the scope of bargaining, labour boards in general have allowed a great deal of latitude for the parties to determine the content of their negotiations. For example, issues such as the improvement of the pension benefits for retired employees have been considered as being bargainable.[1] Bargaining demands by themselves, however, may give rise to a failure to bargain in good faith when they conflict with the scheme of the collective bargaining legislation or with some other statute. Bargaining demands may also indicate bad faith bargaining where they stray to far from what has been generally accepted in comparable industries.[2]

1. *Pulp and Paper Industrial Relations Bureau*, [1978] 1 C.L.R.B.R. 60 (B.C.L.R.B.).
2. *Royal Oak Mines Inc.* v. *Canadian Labour relations Board et al.* (1996) 96 C.L.L.C. para. 210-011 (S.C.C.); [1996] 1 S.C.R. 369.

8. Compulsory provisions

631. The latitude given the parties to bargain the content of their collective agreement, however, has been restricted to some extent by legislation requiring that certain types of provisions be included in the collective agreement. Canadian collective bargaining legislation generally requires that there be included in a collective agreement a provision establishing a procedure for final and binding arbitration of any disputes arising from the agreement that cannot be resolved by the parties themselves.[1] In some jurisdictions the collective agreement must also contain a related provision barring strikes and lockouts during its term.[2] Another general requirement is that collective agreements operate for a minimum term of one year.[3] Many jurisdictions also make compulsory a provision recognizing the union as exclusive bargaining agent and may, in addition, require some minimum form of union security.[4] Two jurisdictions require that the collective agreement contain a provision stipulating that dismissal or discipline must be for just cause.[5] In Quebec, the provisions of the Charter of the French Language dealing with language at work are deemed to be an integral part of every collective agreement.[6]

These mandatory provisions have the effect of reducing the scope of bargaining to the extent that they establish a minimum below which the parties cannot bargain.

1. Canada, s.57; British Columbia, s.84; Ontario, s.48.
2. Ontario, s.46.
3. Canada, s.67; British Columbia, s.50; Ontario, s.58; Quebec, ss.65, 66.
4. *Supra*, paras. 573–81.
5. British Columbia, s.84; Manitoba, s.79.
6. Charter of the French Language, R.S.Q. c.C-11, s.50.

9. Duration of the duty to bargain in good faith

632. Some negotiations may drag on over an extended period of time without being resolved. An interesting question is whether the duty to bargain in good faith may be weakened, or even disappear, over the passage of time. It has been recognized that the duty applies even where the law permits the parties to resort to the strike or lockout.[1] Although it would appear that the duty to bargain in good faith cannot be extinguished by the passage of time, it is also apparent that the duty may have a different effect in the situation where extensive negotiations have already taken place.[2] Moreover, if negotiations are too protracted, the bargaining agent may find itself facing a timely application for de-certification. Where bargaining rights are divested by de-certification, then the duty to bargain in good faith is extinguished as a matter of course.

1. *New Method Laundry & Dry Cleaners* (1957) 57 C.L.L.C. para. 18,059 (O.L.R.B.); Quebec's *Tribunal du travail* took a similar approach in *Nunez* v. *Lloyd's Electronics Limitée*, [1978] T.T. 193, but this decision was reversed on appeal.
2. *CKLW Radio Broadcasting* (1977) 77 C.L.L.C. para. 16,110 (C.L.R.B.).

10. Remedies

633. Labour boards have invoked a wide range of remedies when faced with a violation of the duty to bargain in good faith. In some cases labour boards have simply issued a declaration than a violation of the duty has occurred and directed that future negotiations be carried out in good faith[1] but, in other cases, labour boards have gone further. Where one party has carried an illegal demand to impasse, labour boards have directed that party to remove the illegal demand from the bargaining table[2] and where that illegal demand is the only outstanding issue, have even directed the execution of a collective agreement.[3] One labour board has gone so far as to order an employer to agree to a union's proposal on union security in order to rectify a breach of the obligation to bargain in good faith,[4] and another has imposed a provision requiring an employer to take back striking employees.[5] Still another labour board has been prepared to award damages to employees for loss of the opportunity to negotiate a collective agreement,[6] and to an employer where a union has failed to bargain in good faith.[7] Despite the broad remedial mandate given to labour boards, the courts have held that, in the absence of an express legislative mandate, a board cannot go so far as to impose a collective agreement upon the parties.[8]

1. *Journal Publishing*, [1977] 2 C.L.R.B.R. 183 (O.L.R.B.).
2. *Carpenters Employer Bargaining Agency*, [1978] 1 C.L.R.B.R. 50 (O.L.R.B.).
3. *Fotomat*, [1981] 3 C.L.R.B.R. 129 (O.L.R.B.).
4. *Kamloops News*, [1981] 2 C.L.R.B.R. 356 (B.C.L.R.B.).
5. *General Aviation Services*, [1982] 3 C.L.R.B.R. 439 (C.L.R.B.).
6. *Radio Shack*, [1980] 1 C.L.R.B.R. 99 (O.L.R.B.); *aff'd Tandy Electronics* v. *United Steelworkers*, (1980) 80 C.L.L.C. para. 14,017 (Ont.Div.Ct.).
7. *Canada Cement Lafarge*, [1982] 1 C.L.R.B.R. 300 (O.L.R.B.).
8. *Labour Relations Board (Nova Scotia)* v. *Digby Municipal School Board* (1983) 83 C.L.L.C. para. 14,069 (S.C.C.); [1983] 2 S.C.R. 34; but *see Royal Oak Mines Inc.* v. *Canadian Labour Relations Board et al.* (1996) 96 C.L.L.C. para. 210-011 (S.C.C.) ([1996] 1 S.C.R. 369) where a broad remedial order of the Canada board was upheld.

Chapter V. Industrial Conflict

§1. The Role of Conflict in the Canadian System of Industrial Relations

634. It is accepted that the practice of collective bargaining necessarily involves the risk that parties will not successfully conclude negotiations and will not arrive at mutually acceptable terms of agreement. When this risk eventuates, there must be recourse to some method of resolving the impasse. Except in the case of some public servants in several Canadian jurisdictions and a few essential services in the private sector in some jursidictions,[1] or if the parties should so agree[2] (as they virtually never do), the Canadian system does not envisage recourse to arbitration in such circumstances. However, the parties are generally required to have recourse to the services of a mediator or conciliator who will assist them in their negotiations. If agreement is not forthcoming, the parties are free to mount economic pressures in order to force the opposite party to make concessions. The most common forms of pressure are strikes and lockouts, which are treated as notional equivalents under collective bargaining legislation. Strikes are typically supported by picketing and other forms of appeal for sympathetic action against the employer. When an employer conducts a lockout employees are denied the opportunity to work until they are prepared to accept the employer's terms.

1. *Infra.*
2. Ontario Labour Relations Act, 1995, S.O. 1995, c.1, s.40; Quebec, s.74.

635. There are a wide variety of practices in different jurisdictions to the determination of essential services and the manner in which strikes and lockouts are regulated once an area of service is considered to be essential. Alberta and some other provinces have simply denied the right to strike for most public and some quasi-public sector workers. Some jurisdictions, including Saskatchewan, allow almost all workers to strike, including most public servants, but make frequent use of *ad hoc* legislation to stop strikes which are seen to threaten the economy or public safety. Other jurisdictions, such as British Columbia, Quebec, Ontario and the federal government, allow most public servants to strike but give an adjudicative tribunal (usually the labour relations board) the role of regulating essential service work stoppages by giving them the power to designate essential services and require those services to be provided by workers in those services if the parties are unable to agree on essential service designations and arrangements. Some provinces provide additional restrictions on private sector strikes which threaten the economy of the province or the health and safety of its residents. In Saskatchewan the Labour-Management Dispute (Temporary Provisions Act) gives the Lieutenant Governor in Council (the provincial cabinet) the power to prohibit a strike during an election. To trigger this prohibition, the Lieutenant Governor must find that the dispute creates a situation of pressing public importance or endangers the health or safety of any person in the province during an election.[1] British Columbia and Quebec also have legislation to deal with the provision of essential services in the private sector. It is necessary in the private sector in these two jurisdictions because they have banned the use of replacement workers during legal strikes.[2] This legislation generally provides for the designation of essential services where a dispute poses a threat to the health, safety, or welfare of the general public,[3] and these services must be maintained during a labour dispute.

1. S.S. 1981–92, c.L-01, s.14.
2. *See infra.*
3. *See*, British Columbia Labour Relations Code, R.S.B.C. 1996, c.244, ss.72 and 73; Québec, ss.111.0.15 to 111.0.26.

636. The earliest serious efforts at government intervention in labour–management relations centred on the policy of compulsory conciliation. From 1907, with the enactment of the Industrial Disputes Investigation Act,[1] Canadian legislative policy has consistently sought to minimize the incidence of strikes through compulsory, elaborate and time-consuming peacemaking procedures. However, during the 1950s and 1960s, there was a growing consensus that these procedures were dysfunctional, that instead of reducing the number of strikes and minimizing their duration, the procedures were in fact protracting, intensifying, and perhaps actually causing, strikes. Various legislative reforms ensued which were designed to make conciliation or mediation less time-consuming and predictable, more flexible and responsive to the exigencies of particular situations.[2] These reforms have not, however, led to a drastic reduction in the incidence, or severity, of strikes.

1. S.C. 1907, c.20.
2. *See* e.g. H.D. Woods, 'Canadian Collective Bargaining and Dispute Settlement Policy' (1955) 21 *Can. J. Ec. & Poli. Sci.* 447; W.B. Cunningham, 'Conciliation: The End of Compulsory Boards' (1970) 25 *Ind. Rel.* 62.

637. What has not changed has been the determination that economic conflict in labour disputes should be used only to resolve differences over the terms of a new collective agreement. As will be seen,[1] strikes in all other situations are presumptively, if not conclusively, contrary to public policy and illegal.

1. *Infra.*

638. However, although the legitimate occasion for strikes has been very narrowly defined, the number of working days lost per thousand employees is relatively high.[1] And the situation has not improved in recent years. In 1999 statistics released by the I.L.O. showed that Canada led the G7 in time lost to strikes, with unionized workers in Canada spending about four times more days on the picket line than their U.S. counterparts. Between 1986 and 1995, an average of 292 work days annually per 1,000 workers was lost to strikes in Canada. This number was 40 days higher than the average in Italy and was approximately double the average for the 29 countries in the Organization for Economic Cooperation and Development. Although the number of days lost to strikes dipped briefly to 159 per 1,000 workers in the early 1990s due to wage freezes and downsizing in both the public and private sectors, the number was back up to 233 days per 1,000 workers for 1997. Many commentators have attributed this recent increase to increased union militancy as the economy improves. Unions in both the private and public sector seek to catch up when they see rising corporate profits and executive salaries and government surpluses after years of restraint in the compensation offered to organized workers. The result has been numerous lengthy and large-scale strikes, particularly in the public sector. Ontario led the way in the period of increased militancy, perhaps in part due to the confrontational relationship between the pro-business conservative government first elected in 1995 and unions in the province. Between 1996 and 1998 there were 4.9 million work days lost to strikes in Ontario alone, triple the amount lost in the previous three years.[2] In part, this record is due to the fact that Canadian strikes are lengthy compared to those in other countries.

1. (1991) 98 *Employment Gazette* (No. 12) 610 (U.K. Dept. of Employment).
2. 'Canada leads G7 in time lost to strikes', *Globe and Mail*, 5 April 1999, B1 and B4, with references to International Labour Organization, *Yearbook of Labour Statistics 1998*.

639. Apart from these overall, discouraging comparative statistics, certain features of the Canadian strike record should be identified. Obviously, in Canada as in other countries, the strike record is, in part, the product of social, economic, political and demographic factors. Some special features of the Canadian situation should be noted. There have been considerable fluctuations in the growth of the economy, especially during the late 1960s and early 1970s, when expansion encouraged workers aggressively to seek a share of the growing wealth, and a subsequent period of inflation, during the middle 1970s, when government-imposed wage restraints, postponed wage claims, and prompted first a National Day of Protest – a one-day general strike – and then a series of 'catch up' strikes after the end of the period of controls. There was a similar round of catch up strikes following periods of wage restraints and downsizing during the latter half of the 1980s and the 1990s. The proximity of the United States and the intimate connection between the economies of the two countries has provided Canadian workers with a high level of aspiration and collective bargaining claims. The relatively recent advent of public sector unionism graduated into a posture of militancy in the 1970s and 1980s at the very moment when government spending restraints made collective bargaining more difficult. A vivid impact, in a relatively small national labour market, has been made by lengthy strikes by a few, large groups of workers. Social and economic unrest in Quebec had an exacerbating effect, particularly in the 1970s and the early 1980s, which translated into militancy especially amongst public sector unions.

During the economic recessions of the early 1980s and early 1990s, employers were much more willing to lock out employees as part of their strategy to obtain concessions. This contributed to increasingly bitter and lengthy industrial disputes.

640. Certain structural features of the Canadian industrial relations system contribute to the country's poor strike record: the highly decentralized nature of collective bargaining in most industries promotes inter-union competition for wage increases and other benefits; the relative rigidity of complex collective agreements for fixed and lengthy terms, often of two or three years, means that the parties play for high stakes at their periodic negotiations; and the protracted nature of negotiations, in part due to compulsory conciliation procedures, leads to the build-up of resentments and the hardening of positions.

641. For all of these reasons, and no doubt others, there has been considerable concern in Canada in recent years about the cost to the economy both of strikes and of what are sometimes viewed as excessively high wage settlements, secured through the assertion of economic power. In response, during the worst part of the recession in the early 1980s, the federal and several provincial governments temporarily revoked the right of public sector employees to strike and imposed wage controls.[1] The severe recession of the early 1990s brought back similar strategies from several governments. Moreover, Canadian governments have evinced an increasing willingness to introduce *ad hoc* back-to-work legislation substituting compulsory arbitration for private economic sanctions in particular disputes.

1. A.W.R. Carrothers *et al.*, *Collective Bargaining in Canada* (Toronto, 1986) 108–25.

§2. Forms of Conflict

A. The Strike

642. The strike is the most obvious and widely practised form of economic sanction employed in industrial relations. Most labour relations statutes contain a definition of 'strike', which has three components: (1) a refusal to work or cessation of work, which generally includes slowdowns or other concerted activity designed to limit output (2) by employees, (3) in combination or in concert or in accordance with a common understanding.[1] In addition, several provincial statutes introduce a further component: (4) the purpose of compelling an employer to agree to terms and conditions of employment.[2] Each of these components presents certain problems.

1. Canada, s.31(1); Ontario, s.1(1); Quebec, s.1(g).
2. Alberta, s.53(m); Manitoba, s.1(v); Nova Scotia, s.1(v).

643. The 'cessation of' or 'refusal to' work implies that an obligation to work exists. However, it has been held that a strike may include a refusal to work overtime,[1] or to operate new machines,[2] or a slowdown or work to rule,[3] or an attempt by the union to adhere to unilaterally made restrictive work rules.[4]

1. *Mobile Paint*, [1975] 1 C.L.R.B.R. 248 (O.L.R.B.); *Weyerhauser*, [1976] 2 C.L.R.B.R. 41 (B.C.L.R.B.); *MacMillan Bloedel (Alberni)* v. *I.W.A.* (1971) 13 D.L.R. (3d) 741 (B.C.C.A.); *Cardinal River Coals Ltd.* v. *U.M.W., Loc. 1656*, [1982] 3 C.L.R.B.R. 451 (Alta); *Syndicat des Employés de Production du Québec et L'Acadie* v. *C.L.R.B.R.*, [1984] 2 S.C.R. 412 (S.C.C.).

2. *R.* v. *B.C.L.R.B., Exp. Pulp & Paper Workers*, [1964] 45 D.L.R. (2d) 437 (B.C.S.C.).
3. *Pacific Press* v. *Vancouver Typographical* (1970) 15 D.L.R. (3d) 212 (B.C.C.A.); *Transport Labour Relations* v. *Truck Drivers* (1974) 54 D.L.R. (3d) (B.C.S.C.); *Winnipeg Teachers' Assoc.*, v. *Winnipeg School Division No. 1* (1975) 59 D.L.R. (3d) 228 (S.C.C.); *Re C.P. Ltd. and Ash Kennedy Div. No. 657 B.L.E.*, [1981] 1 C.L.R.B.R. 121 (Can.). Many statutes specifically include a slowdown in the definition of strike.
4. *Alps Construction*, [1964–5] O.L.R.B. 131.

644. Significantly, it has been held that a 'strike' may occur notwithstanding a provision in the collective agreement purporting to relieve employees of the obligation to work in specific circumstances, for example, where to do so would require them to cross the lawful picket line of another union. Such a clause is invalid because it would defeat the statutory policy of not permitting employees to strike during the term of their collective agreement.[1] In British Columbia, by contrast, a refusal to work because of the existence of picketing permitted under the collective bargaining legislation does not constitute a strike.[2]

1. *Lacal 273, Int'l Longshoremen's Assoc.* v. *Maritime Employers' Assoc.*, [1979] 1 S.C.R. 120; *Re Otis Elevator and Elevator Constructors* (1973) 36 D.L.R. (3d) 402 (N.S.C.A.); *Nelson Crushed Stone*, [1978] 1 C.L.R.B.R. 115 (O.L.R.B.).
2. British Columbia, s.1(1)(b).

645. An opposing tendency is also discernible, reflecting the desire of some labour tribunals to avoid stigmatizing as a 'strike' concerted conduct which should not be so regarded because of local or industrial custom,[1] special contractual arrangements,[2] or non-culpable motives.[3] However more recent decisions seem to suggest less tolerance for concerted conduct based on motive considerations.[4] However, changes in the statutory definition of 'strike' may influence the degree of flexibility a tribunal exercises in determining whether certain types of collective action are permitted.

1. *MacMillan, Bloedel Packaging*, [1976] 1 C.L.R.B.R. 90 (B.C.L.R.B.) (refusal to go to work behind another union's lawful picket line 'does not fit within the ordinary conception of the nature of a strike').
2. *R.M. Hardy*, [1977] 2 C.L.R.B.R. 357 (B.C.L.R.B.) (affiliation clauses' in construction industry agreements may permit workers to refuse to work with employees who are not members of affiliated unions).
3. *B.C. Telephone*, [1980] 3 C.L.R.B.R. 31 (C.L.R.B.) (refusal to work overtime motivated by desire to share declining work opportunities, rather than by attempt to get specific employer concessions).
4. *See*, for example, *B.C. Terminal Elevator Operators' Assoc. on Behalf of the Saskatchewan Wheat Pool* v. *Grain Workers' Union, Local* 333 (1994) 94 C.L.L.C. para. 16,060 (C.L.R.B.). The Board found that there had been an unlawful strike where it found a concerted refusal to work voluntary overtime following the lay-off of 10 workers. This despite a collective agreement clause that gave all workers the right to refuse overtime work and the absence of any direct evidence of union orchestration of the refusals.

646. Only 'employees' may strike. Hence, in principle, a refusal to accept employment should not amount to a strike. However, the Supreme Court of Canada[1] has held that the refusal of workers to cross picket lines to accept assignments to unload ships was a strike, although there was no subsisting employment relationship between individual workers and the specific stevedoring firms to which they were sent by the union hiring hall from time to time. On the other hand, while the quitting of employment for cause is not *per se* a strike,[2] resignations must be bona fide and not a mere subterfuge.[3]

1. *I.L.A.* v. *Maritime Employers' Assoc.* (1978) 89 D.L.R. (3d) 289 (S.C.C.); [1979] 1 S.C.R. 120.
2. Ontario s.84.
3. *Aubin Plumbing & Heating*, [1967–8] O.L.R.B. 898.

647. Concerted activity is of the essence of a strike. Thus, the refusal by individual employees to cross the picket line of another union to go to work will not be treated as a strike if it can be ascribed to individual motivations, e.g. the fear of violent reprisals,[1] or a bona fide belief that individual employees enjoyed a contractual right to respect the picket line.[2] On the other hand, the mere fact that a large group of employees refuses to work at the same time creates a very strong presumption that they are acting 'in accordance with a common understanding', and hence striking.[3]

1. *MacMillan Bloedel (Alberni)* v. *Swanson* (1972) 26 D.L.R. (3d) 641 (B.C.S.C.).
2. *Nelson Crushed Stone* (1977) 78 C.L.L.C. para. 16,117 (O.L.R.B.).
3. *Strasser* v. *Roberge* (1979) 103 D.L.R. (3d) 193 (S.C.C.); [1979] 2 S.C.R. 953; *Douglas Aircraft* v. *McConnell* (1979) 99 D.L.R. (3d) 385 (S.C.C.); [1980] 1 S.C.R. 245; *B.C. Terminal Elevator Operators' Assoc.*, [1999] C.I.R.B. No. 6 (Q.L.).

648. The special element of 'purpose' found in the British Columbia collective bargaining legislation prior to 1984, and elsewhere, is of potentially great importance. This point is illustrated by a series of cases relating to the National Day of Protest, in effect a one-day general strike, called by the Canadian Labour Congress to protest against the federal government's anti-inflation legislation. A number of unions were charged, in various provinces, with violation of no-strike provisions in collective agreements or statutes. Their defence was that such provisions were not intended to restrict activity which was essentially directed towards political, rather than industrial relations, objectives This argument failed in virtually all forums in which it was advanced,[1] except British Columbia, whose labour relations board relied upon the special statutory requirement of 'purpose' to confine the inhibiting effect of no-strike clauses to situations where the strike was intended to exact concessions from the employer.[2] However, this argument did not prevail in other jurisdictions whose statutes had similar, purposive provisions.[3] But in 1984 the British Columbia definition of strike was amended to delete any reference to purpose.[4] This amendment was brought in by the Social Credit government after the labour board at the time decided that a number of concerted withdrawals of work conducted as part of Operation Solidarity designed to pressure the provincial government did not constitute strikes as defined under the Code.[5] Thus, purpose is no longer significant in any Canadian jurisdiction for determining whether collective action constitutes a strike. In the 1990s there were several attempts to argue that work stoppages conducted for the purpose of political protest should be protected from prohibition during the term of a collective agreement by the protections for freedom of expression and association found in the Charter of Rights and Freedoms. Thus far they have not been successful.[6]

1. *See* e.g. *Domglas*, [1976] 2 C.L.R.B.R. 394 (O.L.R.B.) *aff'd.* (1978), 19 O.R. (2d) 353 (D.C.); *Re U.S.W.A. and Inco.* (1978) 87 D.L.R. (3d) 274 (Ont.H.C.); *Kendall* (1978) 17 L.A.C. 408 and cases cited; but *see contra Dominion Bridge* (1977) 15 L.A.C (2d) 295.
2. *B.C. Hydro & Power Authority*, [1976] 2 C.L.R.B.R. 410 (B.C.L.R.B.).
3. *Re Robb Engineering and U.S.W.A.* (1978) 86 D.L.R. (3d) 307 (N.S.C.A.); *Re Inco and U.S.W.A.* (1978) 86 D.L.R. (3d) 407 (Man.C.A.).
4. Labour Code Amendment Act, S.B.C. 1984, c.24, s.l.
5. *Metro Transit Operating Co.* v. *Independent Can. Transit Union, Loc.* 3 (1983) 83 C.L.L.C. 16,054; *Health Lab. Rel. Assn.* v. *Hosp. Employees' Union Loc-180* (1983) 3 C.L.R.B.R. (N.S.) 390.
6. *General Motors of Canada Ltd.*, [1996] O.L.R.D. No. 2056 (O.L.R.B.). *See* further discussion of the Charter arguments for protection of concerted activity *infra.*

B. The Lockout

649. The 'lockout' is also defined by almost all labour relations statutes.[1] Common elements in these statutory definitions are that the lockout must involve: (1) a closing of a place of employment, the suspension of work, or a refusal to continue to employ, and (2) the purpose of compelling employees to agree to terms and conditions of employment. Thus defined, the lockout is clearly a legitimate employer tactic if exercised in accordance with the procedural requirements which also govern strikes, and if used in aid of the employer's collective bargaining objectives. As long as the lockout is conducted for these purposes and is timely, it has been held that an employer may hire replacement workers during a lockout without committing an unfair labour practice.[2] However, the Ontario statute[3] contains a further element: (3) in the alternative, to compel or induce employees to abandon their rights under the Labour Relations Act. A 'lockout' of this type is an unfair practice, and illegal.[4]

1. Canada. s.3(1); British Columbia, s.1(1); Quebec, s.1(h); the Saskatchewan Trade Union Act contains no definition.
2. *Westroc Industries*, [1981] 2 C.L.R.B.R. 315 (O.L.R.B.). In British Columbia and Quebec, anti-scab breaker legislation prohibits hiring replacement workers during a lockout. *See*, British Columbia, s.68 and Quebec, s.109.1.
3. S.1(k); to the same effect: New Brunswick, s.1(1)(o); Prince Edward Island s.7(1)(k).
4. *C.P.R.* v. *Zambri (Royal York Hotel case)*, (1962) 34 D.L.R. (2d) 654 (S.C.C.); [1962] S.C.R. 609.

650. Although notionally the equivalent of a strike, the common statutory definition of lockout contains both an objective and a subjective element. This means that the critical factor in determining whether a lockout exists is the employer's motive for suspending operations or refusing to continue employment. The employer is free to make legitimate business decisions to suspend or close operations, and these must be distinguished from closures or suspensions designed to force concessions from the union.[1] In fact, explicit statutory recognition is given to the employer's right to manage its affairs and thus to discontinue or suspend operations so long as this does not constitute a lockout.[2]

1. *Humpty Dumpty Foods Ltd.*, [1977] 2 C.L.R.B.R. 248 (Ont.); *Weyerhauser Can. Ltd.*, [1976] 2 C.L.R.B.R. 41 (B.C.). *See also Re Federated Co-op. Ltd. and R.W.D.S.U., Loc. 580*, [1980] 1 C.L.R.B.R. 372 (B.C.) where it was held that the cost of labour is a legitimate consideration in moving a business.
2. Ontario, s.84; British Columbia, s.63(1); Manitoba. s.94; New Brunswick, s.103; Newfoundland, s.100.

C. Picketing

651. While picketing is a familiar feature of strikes and lockouts, and indeed may be encountered even where there has been no work stoppage at all, the term is not one which is, typically, defined with precision. Although Alberta, New Brunswick and Newfoundland[1] define and refer to picketing in their respective labour relations statutes, only the Labour Relations Code of British Columbia purports to contain an authoritative definition.[2]

1. Alberta, s.114; New Brunswick, s.104; Newfoundland, s.124.
2. British Columbia, s.1(1).

652. Generally, picketing is understood to involve these elements: (1) the presence of one or more persons, (2) communication by spoken or written messages, or through behaviour, and (3) an intention by presence or communication to secure a sympathetic response from third persons, e.g. customers who will cease to deal with a struck employer, prospective employees who will decline to accept employment in a struck enterprise, or suppliers who will interrupt shipments of materials required to sustain production in a struck plant.

653. As will be seen,[1] it is the interaction of these elements which creates analytical difficulties. The presence of individual picketers in conflict situations which are often volatile and emotional, may produce, reasonably or otherwise, the fear of illicit reprisal or violence in the minds of customers, prospective employees or suppliers, who refuse to respond sympathetically to the picketers. However, it is not possible to reassure those who are afraid, without at the same time interfering with the freedom of communication and of assembly of the picketers, freedoms which are exercised in all social, economic and political controversies. This is a fact of special significance because the picket line is more than an appeal to third persons. It is, as well, a means of communication and association amongst those picketing. It may provide an occasion for meaningful activity to ease the monotony and idleness of the strike; it may help to stimulate a sense of solidarity and effective action which bolsters morale; and it may serve to discourage those who are considering abandoning the cause.

1. *Infra.*

654. At the same time, there is a sense that communication in the context of an industrial dispute has a greater impact than in other contexts. On the one hand, the solidarity of the labour movement gives an appeal for support special cogency and the consequences of support greater impact. On the other hand, to the extent that occasional incidents of picket line violence do occur, the mere presence of a picket line may induce behaviour on the part of someone contemplating crossing it which is not entirely reasonable. Because of these factors, there is particular concern that picket lines should be mounted only for limited purposes, and not in situations where the impact they might have would be disproportionate to the good they might accomplish. Finally, picketing may involve the invasion of rights of personal security, property and reputation, about which the law traditionally has been especially solicitous. Both courts and legislatures have had considerable difficulty in striking the proper balance between the vindication of these traditional interests, and the newer interests of labour unions implicit in the use of picketing as a legitimate weapon of industrial conflict.

655. Historically, the courts have been unwilling to treat peaceful picketing as an exercise of the right of free speech, and thus protected by law.[1] Rather, they have been much more willing to protect the rights of personal security, property and reputation, which has tended to benefit employers. However, a 1986 decision of the Supreme Court of Canada suggests that peaceful picketing is protected by the Charter of Rights and Freedoms under the guarantee of freedom of expression, subject to demonstrably justified limitations.[2] But that decision also suggests that the Charter will have little effect in furthering legal protection of picketing since the Supreme Court of Canada held that the Charter does not apply to common law actions between private parties. In addition, the Supreme Court indicated that common law and statutory limitations on secondary picketing, picketing of parties other than the employer, were *per se* reasonable limits on the freedom of expression of workers under the Charter of Rights and Freedoms. In Canada, with the exception of British Columbia, picketing is still heavily regulated by the ordinary courts applying common law rules, and the bulk of the regulation of picketing, both statutory and common law, is directed at restricting secondary activity.[3] Although the Supreme Court has more recently expressed a willingness to use the Charter freedom of expression to limit legal restrictions on secondary boycotts and leafleting in support of boycotts, in the same decision the Court seemed to affirm its earlier ruling in *Dolphin Delivery* that restrictions on secondary *picketing* were *per se* reasonable limits which would be upheld under the Charter.[4]

1. *See A.G. Canada* v. *Dupond* (1978) 84 D.L.R. (3d) 420 (S.C.C.); [1978] 2 S.C.R. 770 and *Koss* v. *Konn* (1961) 30 D.L.R. (2d) 242 (B.C.C.A.).
2. *R.W.D.S.U., Local 580* v. *Dolphin Delivery*, [1986] 2 S.C.R. 573.
3. *Infra.*
4. *UFCW, Local 1518* v. *K-Mart Canada Ltd* (1999) 176 D.L.R. (4th) 607 (S.C.C.); [1999] 2 S.C.R. 1083.

D. Boycott

656. A 'boycott' is an invitation to the public to express sympathetic support of the cause of a trade union by avoiding or ending economic involvement with an employer with whom it is in dispute. The term is also broad enough to embrace appeals to workers not to accept employment with that employer, or to handle goods produced by or destined for him, in the course of their employment by some third person. This latter aspect of boycotts will be treated separately.[1]

1. *Infra*, paras. 735–7.

657. A boycott may be solicited by picketing at the employer's place of business or at a place where his products are sold, or by approaches to his customers or suppliers through letters or individual interviews, or simply by appeals to the community at large, or some sympathetic portion of it, by means of leaflets or newspaper advertisements.

658. Except to the extent that such appeals constitute an invitation to violate the law, e.g. an invitation to strike illegally, it might be thought that they should be protected by law as the exercise of the right of free speech. But the trend of the law has historically been otherwise.[1] The earliest decisions of courts under the Charter of Rights and Freedoms suggested that it would have little impact on this historical approach towards leafleting and boycotts. For example, in deciding that picketing by tenants in front of a retail store owned by their landlord was protected under the guarantee of freedom of expression contained in section 2(b) of the Charter, the Nova Scotia Supreme Court specifically distinguished that type of picketing from labour picketing calling for a boycott.[2]

However, in 1999 the Supreme Court of Canada held that statutory restrictions on consumer leafleting by a trade union at secondary locations in support of its dispute with its employer constituted unjustifiable restrictions on the workers' freedom of expression under the Charter. In *UFCW, Local 1518* v. *K-Mart Canada Ltd.*,[3] provisions of the B.C. Labour Code which prohibited secondary picketing, and defined picketing broadly to include leafleting in support of a consumer boycott, were challenged as being contrary to section 2(b) of the Charter. The union's members were leafleting at unorganized store locations operated by their employer in support of their lawful strike at an organized store. In holding that the limitations on consumer leafleting in support of a boycott were unduly broad and could not be upheld as reasonable limits on worker freedom of expression, the Supreme Court stressed the differences between consumer leafleting and picketing as forms of expression deserving protection under the Charter. It suggested that picket lines are inherently coercive and act as a barrier which impedes public access to goods or services and employee access to workplaces, even when peaceful. Consumer leafleting in contrast seeks to persuade members of the public to act through informed and rational discourse, something which is the very essence of freedom of expression. In the Court's opinion, it lacks the coercive element of picketing and does not impede access to premises in any significant manner. Thus leafleting in support of a boycott which is not defamatory or otherwise unlawful, is not conducted in a coercive, intimidating or otherwise unlawful or tortious manner, and does not unduly impede access to leafleted premises or prevent employees of secondary sites from working or interfere with other contractual relations of suppliers to the secondary sites will normally constitute a valid exercise of freedom of expression. Nor can such forms of peaceful leafleting be limited by overbroad prohibitions on secondary activity intended to minimize the harmful effects to third parties that could result from others impeding access to premises or to encourage employees to breach their contracts of employment.

1. *Hersees of Woodstock* v. *Goldstein* (1963) 38 D.L.R. (2d) 449 (Ont.C.A.), discussed, *infra*.
2. *Halifax Antiques Ltd.* v. *Hildebrand* (1985) 22 D.L.R. (4th) 289.
3. (1999), 176 D.L.R. (4th) 607 (S.C.C.); [1999] 2 S.C.R. 1083. A similar result was reached in *UFCW, Local 1288P* v. *Allsco Builiding Products Ltd.* (1999) 176 D.L.R. (4th) 647 (S.C.C.); [1999] 2 S.C.R. 1136. For a more detailed commentary on these decisions see M. MacNeil, 'Labour Picketing and Consumer Boycotts: Judicial Ideology in *K-Mart* and *Allsco*' (2000) 8 C.L.E.L.J. 79.

§3. Lawful Economic Sanctions

A. The Right to Strike

659. It is difficult to identify the juridical nature of the right to strike in Canada. Recently, however, the Supreme Court of Canada decided a trilogy of cases which established that the Charter of Rights and Freedoms does not guarantee the right to strike. The three cases involved union challenges to federal public sector wage control legislation which substituted compulsory arbitration for collective bargaining backed by strikes,[1] a Saskatchewan statute which temporarily prohibited the province's dairy workers from engaging in what had hitherto been a lawful strike during an industry-wide lockout,[2] and a series of Alberta statutes prohibiting a wide range of public sector employees from engaging in otherwise lawful strikes.[3] In each of the cases, the union bringing the challenge sought to persuade the Court that the freedom of association guaranteed by the Charter includes both the right to bargain collectively and the right to strike, and that the various statutes which infringed these rights were not demonstrably justified in accordance with section 1. By a four to two majority, the Supreme Court of Canada held that freedom of association does not include either the right to bargain collectively or the right to strike. The ruling that the freedom of association found in the Charter does not include the right to bargain collectively has been affirmed in two subsequent decisions. In 1990 the Supreme Court held that the government was under no constitutional obligation to bargain collectively or provide a statutory scheme for collective bargaining by recognition or certification. Thus a legislative scheme which limited the right of some public servants to bargain collectively to bargaining only through representation by an association recognized or designated by the government did not infringe their Charter rights.[4] In 1999, the Supreme Court rejected an argument by R.C.M.P officers that their exclusion from collective bargaining under the provisions of both the federal public sector and federal private sector labour relations statutory schemes violated their freedoms of association and expression under the Charter.[5] The freedom of association in section 2(d) of the Charter does not include the right to establish a particular type of association defined in a particular statute, nor does it impose an obligation on the government to provide a particular legislative framework for its employees to exercise their collective rights. Only the establishment of an independent employee association and the exercise in association of the constitutional rights and freedoms and lawful rights of individuals are protected under section 2(d) from government interference.

1. *Public Service Alliance* v. *The Queen*, 87 C.L.L.C. 14,022; [1987] 1 S.C.R. 424.
2. *R.W.D.S.U., Local 544* v. *Gov't of Saskatchewan*, 87 C.L.L.C. 14,023; [1987] 1 S.C.R. 313.
3. *Reference re Public Service Employee Relations Act (Alta.)* 87 C.L.L.C. 14,021; [1987] 1 S.C.R. 460.
4. *Professional Inst. of the Public Service of Canada* v. *Northwest Territories (Comm'r)*, [1990] 2 S.C.R. 367.
5. *Delisle* v. *Canada (Dep. Att.-Gen.)*, [1999] 2 S.C.R. 989.

660. Surprisingly, the right to strike has not even received explicit statutory articulation. Rather, its juridical basis has been variously ascribed to the absence of common law decisions denying its existence ('what is not forbidden is permitted'), or to common law dicta which affirmed the right, or to inferences derived from modern labour relations statutes which, by regulating its exercise, assume that strikes properly conducted are lawful.[1] Whatever its basis, however, a 'right to strike' is now generally thought to exist, and indeed will not even be taken to have been bargained away in the absence of compelling evidence.[2] However, specific legislation relating to certain essential industries and, in a few provinces, to public employment may abrogate this right and compel recourse to such definitive procedures as final and binding arbitration of interest disputes.[3]

1. These positions are taken in various judgments in *C.P.R.* v. *Zambri (Royal York Hotel case)* (1962) 34 D.L.R. (2d) 654 (S.C.C.); [1962] S.C.R. 609.
2. *Re Bradburn and Wentworh Arms Hotel* (1979) 94 D.L.R. (3d) 161 (S.C.C.).
3. *Infra*.

661. In a preliminary way, it is reasonably accurate to state that the only lawful strikes are those which are designed to gain economic objectives, and which are timely in the sense that they follow exhaustion of the compulsory conciliation procedures laid down in the legislation. Even a strike for collective bargaining objectives is unlawful if it is untimely.[1] As well, strikes for recognition,[2] sympathy strikes designed to bring pressure to bear on a secondary employer,[3] strikes designed to force the employer to accept the union's interpretation of an agreement,[4] strikes of political protest,[5] are all unlawful. Not only are such strikes unlawful, but activities conducted in association with them, or in substitution for them, are equally unlawful.

1. Canada, s.89; British Columbia, ss.59, 60; Ontario, s.79; Quebec, s.106.
2. *Gagnon* v. *Foundation Maritime* (1961) 28 D.L.R. (2d) 174 (S.C.C.); [1961] S.C.R. 435.
3. *Canadian Broadcasting Corporation* v. *Canadian Media Guild*, [1999] CIRB No. 11; *The Citizen*, [1976] 2 C.L.R.B.R. 474 (O.L.R.B.); *Mark Fishing* v. *United Fishermen* (1972). 24 D.L.R. (3d) 585 (B.C.C.A.), aff'd (1973) 38 D.L.R. (3d) 316n (S.C.C.); [1974] S.C.R. 435.
4. *Teamsters* v. *Therien* (1960) 22 D.L.R. (2d) 1 (S.C.C.); [1962] S.C.R. 265.
5. *General Motors of Canada Ltd.*, [1996] O.L.R.D. No. 2056 (O.L.R.B.). *See* further discussion of the Charter arguments for protection of concerted activity *infra*.

B. The Effect of a Lawful Strike on Employment Status and Benefits

1. Employment status

662. An employee who participates in a lawful, timely strike does not thereby either resign her/his employment or render herself/himself liable to discharge. In the historic Royal York Hotel decision,[1] the Supreme Court of Canada pointed out that employees who participate in such strikes are exercising a statutorily protected right to participate in the lawful activities of a trade union, violation of which is an unfair labour practice. Moreover, the Court pointed out, the Labour Relations Act in question specifically (but typically) precluded any inference that strikers ceased to be employees 'by reason only of . . . ceasing to work . . . as the result of a lockout or strike'.[2]

This holding, in turn, raises a number of issues, the resolution of which indicates the extent to which the right to strike may or may not be rendered meaningless by employer counter-measures.

1. *C.P.R.* v. *Zambri, supra.*
2. *See* Ontario, s.1(2); to the same effect: British Columbia, s.1(2); Canada, s.3(2); Quebec, s.110.

2. The employer's right to maintain operations and hire replacements

663. It is generally assumed that the employer has the right to maintain operations during a strike or lawful lockout. This may be done by using non-striking employees, supervisors or newly hired replacements.[1] Of course, in any given situation these alternatives may not be available as a practical matter, depending on the number of persons required to maintain operations, their technical skills, etc. In particular, it is assumed that the employer may resort to the labour market in order to keep her/his plant running: her/his ability to do so is in part a test of how realistic the wage proposals of labour and management are. Where there is unemployment, presumably replacements will easily be found at the wages offered by the employer; when there is a labour shortage, s/he will have to offer higher wages, either to arrive at a settlement with the union or to attract new workers. In Quebec this assumption is refuted by law. Legislation in that province not only prevents the employer from using newly hired employees to maintain operations during a strike, but also prevents him from using any employees in the struck bargaining unit for that purpose, or from re-deploying workers amongst her/his struck and non-struck operations. The employer, however, is allowed to use those managers employed at the struck plant to maintain production and may also subcontract some, or all, the operations, provided the work is performed outside the struck establishment.[2] British Columbia has followed Quebec and now severely restricts the use of replacement workers during a strike. British Columbia, however, allows bargaining unit members to be employed during a strike.[3] In Ontario, provisions to prohibit the use of replacement workers were enacted in 1992 but repealed in 1995.

1. *Westroc Industries Ltd.*, [1981] 2 C.L.R.B.R. 315 (O.L.R.B.).
2. Quebec, s.109. 1–3. An employer may take 'necessary measures to avoid the destruction or serious deterioration' of his property.
3. British Columbia, s.68.

664. These 'anti-scab' provisions are perceived as a significant revision of the balance of power, and have no counterpart in other Canadian jurisdictions. However, four other less drastic restrictions upon the employer's freedom of action are found elsewhere. In several provinces, the use of professional strikebreakers is outlawed.[1] There, the employer may not avail herself/himself of the services of firms which maintain a labour pool explicitly for temporary use by struck employers. In Ontario and Manitoba, the employer may not engage in 'strike related misconduct', such as incitement, intimidation or surveillance, designed to thwart the exercise by employees of their right to strike.[2] In several provinces, non-striking employees are permitted to refuse to perform work normally done by strikers.[3] And a recent amendment to the Manitoba Labour Relations Act prohibits the employer from hiring permanent replacement workers.[4] Finally, following the recommendations of a federal task force appointed to review the provisions of the Canada Labour Code regulating collective bargaining in the federal private sector,[5] in 1998 the Canadian government amended the Code to make it an unfair labour practice for employers to use replacement workers for the purpose of 'undermining a trade union's representational capacity rather than the pursuit of legitimate bargaining objectives'.[6] In addition, although there is no general statutory prohibition against the use of replacement workers during a lawful strike, the Code was amended to give the Canada Industrial Relations Board the power to prohibit the use of replacement workers for the duration of a strike where the employer is proven to have used them for the purpose of undermining the representational capacity of the trade union.[7]

1. Ontario, s.78; Manitoba, s.14.
2. Ontario, s.78; Manitoba, s.14(3).
3. Manitoba, s.12; Alberta, s.140(b); Nova Scotia, s.51(3)(c).
4. Manitoba, s.11.
5. *Seeking a Balance: Canada Labour Code Part I Review* (Ottawa: Supply and Services Canada, 1996) (Chair: A. Sims).
6. Canada, s.94(2.1).
7. Canada, s.99(1)(b.3).

3. The striker's right to his or her job

665. Almost inevitably strikes are settled on terms which include the return to work of all strikers.

666. However, not all strikes are won. Sometimes the employer is strong enough to deny any concessions to the union, and *ex hypothese*, to withstand a union claim that all strikers be returned to work. Then a new set of equities comes into play. Senior employees within sight of pension rights may never serve out their few remaining years; employees in their middle years may find themselves on an inhospitable labour market; employees of only a few years service may depend on their job to feed young families. For all of these groups, the consequences of losing their jobs are so severe that they may be prepared to desert the strike and return to work. While there is no authoritative decision on point, it is reasonably clear that the employer cannot deny a striking employee the opportunity to return to work to fill a vacant job, or at least must treat her/his application to do so without discrimination based on strike participation or union membership. However, this general principle might be qualified in two respects.

667. First, it is clear that the striker's right to her/his job will yield to certain economic exigencies. If the employer decides to shut down or suspend an operation for reasons other than anti-unionism, and in response to legitimate business considerations, s/he is entitled to do so even though the result will be to terminate the employment of strikers.[1]

1. *Webster & Horsfall* (1969) 69 C.L.L.C. para. 16,050 (O.L.R.B.).

668. Second, recent legislation guarantees strikers an absolute right to reinstatement in their former jobs, provided that work is still being performed, either for an indefinite period[1] or, in the case of Ontario, for a period of six months.[2]

1. Manitoba, s.11; Quebec, s.110.1; Canada 94(3).
2. Ontario, s.80. The employer may not discriminate against returning strikers, even after the end of the six months' period and must reinstate them if jobs are available; however, he needs not, at that point, discharge replacements to make room for them, *Becker Milk Co.*, [1978] 1 C.L.R.B.R. 175 (O.L.R.B.).

669. An employer's right to hire permanent replacement workers must be balanced against an employee's right to her/his job. An employer who refuses to reinstate striking employees at the end of a strike because s/he does not want to displace replacement workers hired during the strike may be guilty of an unfair labour practice.[1] In such a situation the labour board will either order the employer to reinstate the employees or award monetary damages.

1. *Shaw-Almex Industries Limited* (1986) 15 C.L.R.B.R. (N.S.) 23 (O.L.R.B.) *Canadian Airline Pilots' Ass'n. and Eastern Provincial Airways Ltd* (1984) 5 C.L.R.B.R. (N.S.) 368 (C.L.R.B.).

670. Assuming reinstatement of the striker, there remains the difficult question of what happens to the host of employment benefits which were rooted in the expired collective agreement. If a new agreement is signed, these benefits will usually be renewed by it. If no new agreement is signed, the continued existence of the benefits theoretically is the subject of bargaining between the employer and the individual worker, but practically is unilaterally determined by the former. In theory,[1] if the employer wants to change unilaterally the terms and conditions of employment, including benefits, s/he must first give notice of such proposed changes.

1. *B.C. Hydro* v. *I.B.E.W. Loc. 213* (1986) C.C.E.L. 294 (B.C.C.A.).

4. Employment benefits during strikes

671. Prima facie, an employee who goes on strike thereby forfeits the right not only to her/his regular pay, but also to all other benefits which are associated with her/his employment. So long as a collective agreement is in operation, it will usually provide the employee with a number of such benefits (often building upon a legislatively required minimum): annual vacations, paid holidays, severance pay, pensions, life, accident, health and dental insurance, and preferment in the event of lay-offs or promotions, based on seniority.[1] The Supreme Court of Canada has made it clear that if an employee remains at work when the collective agreement expires, then in the absence of any statutory freeze,[2] an employer may unilaterally alter the terms and conditions of employment, provided that there is no violation of the on-going duty to bargain in good faith. This decision made it clear that individual contracts of employment do not revive on termination of the collective agreement so that there is no contractual obstacle to the employer's unilateral alteration of the existing employment regime. When a strike begins, and work stops, an employer is clearly entitled to cease paying wages to her/his striking employees. By the same token, he may refuse to continue to provide them with employment-based benefits which are, in effect, wages paid in monies' worth.[3]

1. *See supra* paras. 582–4.
2. *Paccar of Canada Ltd.* v. *Canadian Association of Industrial, Mechanical and Allied Workers Local 14* (1989) 89 C.L.L.C. para. 14,050; [1992] 2 S.C.R. 983.
3. It has been held that employees do not accumulate seniority for the duration of a lawful strike, *Volvo Canada* v. *U.A.W. Local 720* (1979) 99 D.L.R. (3d) 193 (S.C.C.); [1978] 1 S.C.R. 178.

672. Thus, with the outbreak of a strike, the employer is free to terminate insurance coverage, pension contributions and benefits, paid vacations and holidays etc.[1] In practice, a union and an employer will often make arrangements whereby contributions may be made by or on behalf of employees to avoid the forfeiture of such benefits. Often, too, after a strike, a collective agreement is signed which relates back to the date of expiry of the previous collective agreement, and retroactivity restores the *status quo ante*. Pursuant to the terms of such an agreement, the employer may make up any deficiency in payment of premiums or pension contributions, and rectify any violation of seniority.

1. *Crown Life Insurance*, [1981] 3 C.L.R.B.R. 227 (B.C.L.R.B.).

673. But, in the heat of battle, an employer may refuse to agree to any such arrangements, and thereby generate considerable pressure on his striking employees, for example, by threatening them with loss of pension benefits when they are very close to retirement age. While this situation was the subject of sympathetic comment in the *Royal York Hotel* decision in the lower courts,[1] and has been to a limited extent addressed by specific legislation,[2] the position remains essentially as stated. The Supreme Court of Canada has been unable to find any foundation upon which to ground the protection of benefits which had been provided by the expired collective agreements.[3] And various arbitration decisions have held that (subject always to the specific terms of a subsequent collective agreement) strikers forfeit sick pay and severance pay and pay for holidays and annual vacations which occur during the strike.[4]

1. *R.* v. *C.P.R.* (1962) 31 D.L.R. (2d) 209 at 220 *per* McRuer, C.J.H.C. (Ont. H.C.), aff'd, sub nom. *C.P.R.* v. *Zambri*, *supra*.
2. Canada, s.94(3)(d); Alberta. s.171(3)(c); Manitoba, ss.14(a), 14.1; Newfoundland, s.24(2); Nova Scotia, s.51(3)(d); Saskatchewan, s.11(1)(1).
3. *C.P.R.* v. *Zambri*, *supra* at 666 (*per* Judson, J.).
4. *See* generally, G. England, 'The Legal Response to Striking at the Individual Level in the Common Law Jurisdictions of Canada' (1976) 3 *Dalhousie L.J.* 440.

674. Obviously, if benefits are to be protected during a strike, legislative intervention is required. In several jurisdictions,[1] this has already happened in regard to pension benefits and in Saskatchewan,[2] and Manitoba[3] in regard to health benefits and insurance schemes respectively. In addition, in 1998 the federal government amended the Canada Labour Code to require employers to maintain health benefit plans and insurance plans during lawful strikes as long as the union tenders any premiums required to maintain the plans.[4] But such protection is not widespread.

1. Canada, s.94(3)(d); Alberta, s.137(3)(c); Manitoba, s.14(1); Newfoundland, s.24(2); Nova Scotia, s.51(3)(d).
2. Saskatchewan, s.11(1)(1), prevents employer interference with 'pension rights or health rights or benefits or medical rights or benefits'.
3. Manitoba, s.14.1.
4. Canada, s.94(3)(d.1)(d.2).

675. Finally, assuming that a striker is disentitled to various employment-related benefits during a strike, to what extent is this loss offset by eligibility to receive benefits under various state-sponsored schemes? Under employment insurance legislation,[1] strikers are disqualified from receiving benefits for the duration of the labour dispute. Likewise, they may be ineligible even for social assistance benefits, because they are not considered to be 'persons in need' within the contemplation of welfare legislation.[2] However, co-workers who are not in the striking bargaining unit but nevertheless are put out of work as a consequence of the work stoppage will be entitled to employment insurance benefits, provided they can prove they are not financing, participating in, or directly interested in the labour dispute that caused the stoppage of work.[3]

1. Employment Insurance Act, S.C. 1996, c.23 as amended, s.36; *see* M.A. Hickling, Labour *Disputes and Unemployment Insurance in Canada and the United Kingdom* (Toronto, C.C.H., 1975). Failure to cross a picket line on account of fear of personal safety does not disentitle workers to unemployment benefits; *see Valois* v. *A.G.–Can.*, 86 C.L.L.C. 14,057 (S.C.C.); [1986] 2 S.C.R. 439.
2. The provinces administer welfare programmes funded (in part) by federal grants, and subject to general federal standards and policies. *See* Canada Assistance Plan, R.S.C. 1985, c.C-l, s.2. However, the provinces have considerable latitude in defining eligibility for benefit, and some have done so in such a way as to exclude strikers, *see Alden* v. *Gaglardi* (1973) 30 D.L.R. (3d) 760 (S.C.C.); [1973] S.C.R. 199.
3. Employment Insurance Act, S.C. 1996, c.23 as amended, s.36(4). *See also Hills* v. *Canada*, [1988] 1 S.C.R. 513 and *White* v. *Canada*, [1994] 2 F.C. 233 (FCA).

676. Deprived of income by both her/his employer and the state, the striking employee is left largely to her/his own resources. These are, at least minimally, supplemented by payments from the strike funds established by most unions. Such payments are, however typically meagre, and their duration limited by the union's ability to renew its resources through contributions from non-striking members in other enterprises, and from other unions. Beyond this, unions are occasionally able to borrow funds by pledging their capital assets, but are obviously reluctant to do so.

677. In sum, a striking employee is almost certain to confront severe economic loss, both of her/his regular wages, and of 'fringe benefits'.[1]

1. *See* G. England, 'Employee Finances During Strikes and Lockouts: A Case Study' (1995) 3 C.L.E.L.J. 475.

5. *Employee obligations during a strike*

678. Obviously, an employee is not bound to report for work during a strike. S/he is not, however, relieved of all obligations towards her/his employer. While a worker does not terminate her/his employment relationship, 'by reason only of participating in a lawful strike' s/he is not thereby completely insulated from discharge.

679. Specifically, an employer has a right to dismiss and discipline employees for cause, without committing an unfair labour practice, for such serious misconduct as sabotage against plant property or violence on the picket line.[1] There is, however, some controversy over the existence of the employer's disciplinary authority during a strike. At least one arbitrator has held that because the employer–employee relationship ceased during a strike, the employer had no disciplinary power left to exert.[2] The Supreme Court of Canada declined to resolve this controversy.[3] However, the dominant position among arbitrators and labour boards is that the employer retains the authority to discipline for just cause during a strike, provided its disciplinary action is not tainted by anti-union animus.[4]

1. *See* e.g. *Re Canadian Gypsum and Nova Scotia Quarryworkers* (1960) 20 D.L.R. (2d) 319 (N.S.S.C.); *Inmont*, (1970) 21 L.A.C. 411; *Gates Rubber* (1978) 18 L.A.C. (2d) 412; *Becker Milk Co.*, [1978] 2 C.L.R.B.R. 252 (O.L.R.B.); *Rogers Cable T.V. (British Columbia) Ltd., Vancouver Division* v. *I.B.E.W., Local 213* (1987) 16 C.L.R.B.R. (N.S.) 71. *See also* Quebec, s.110.1.
2. *Re British Columbia Telephone Co. and Telecommunication Workers Union*, 2 April 1981 (Hope).
3. *British Columbia Telephone Co.*, [1988] 2 S.C.R. 564, where the Court held that the arbitrator's decision was within his jurisdiction and was therefore unreviewable, whether or not it was wrong.
4. *See Allsco Building Products Ltd.*, [1998] N.B.L.E.B.D. No. 24.

680. While there is little debate over the employer's right to discharge employees for such serious acts of misconduct, the application of the principle poses certain problems. Foremost amongst these is the difficulty of assessing employee conduct in the volatile atmosphere of a strike. Provocative employer action, for example, may actually be designed to elicit misconduct on the picket line for the very purpose of affording the employer a convenient excuse for the discharge of strikers. Moreover, the usual forum for adjudication of discharge grievances is arbitration. But, by definition, arbitration which is established by a collective agreement, is not available during the course of a strike. Thus, if the discharge of employees for alleged misconduct during the strike is to be arbitrated, the parties must almost inevitably make some provision for such arbitration when they execute a new collective agreement following the termination of the strike. If the parties fail to do so, an arbitrator has no jurisdiction to hear a grievance for dismissal which occurred during a strike after the collective agreement had expired.[1] In such cases, often the only recourse for the discharged employees is to bring a complaint to the labour board alleging that the discipline constituted an unfair labour practice.[2]

1. *Re Precious Plate and Communication Workers* (1987) 27 L.A.C. (3d) 329 (Ont.). S.110.1 of the Quebec Labour Code provides that an employer does not have to recall to work an employee at the end of a strike if it has a good and sufficient reason not to do so. The section stipulates also that any disagreement on such a matter must be referred to an arbitrator as if it were a grievance.
2. *Canadian Paperworkers Union* v. *International Wallcoverings*, [1983] O.L.R.B. Rep. 1316.

6. The duration of the employment relationship

681. To hold that neither a strike nor the illegal discharge of the strikers severs the employment relationship throws up the obvious questions: how long does the relationship last and what will sever it? The questions are important for psychological and legal reasons. As to the former, when there are no more striking 'employees', the strike is over. Thus announcement that no more strikers are employed may destroy union morale, just as continued assertion that the strikers are 'employees' bolsters it. As to the latter, employment status may determine entitlement to various welfare benefits and may affect the continued existence of the union's bargaining rights.

682. Obviously, if a striker dies or becomes unemployable, or clearly renounces her/his employment status, s/he ceases to be a striking 'employee'.[1] But usually matters are not so clear. For the duration of the conflict, strikers may take full-time or part-time jobs in order to supplement their meagre strike pay. Can it be said that by so doing they are acting inconsistently with continued employment by the struck employer, and thus that they have renounced their jobs as well? While in principle this might be a sound position, in practice it is not. The relative frequency with which workers move from job to job throughout the economy suggests the striker is unlikely to regard her/his new job as 'permanent'. Especially if the former job is one in which the striker is experienced and has seniority, and in which there is a prospect of renewed pension and other benefits, s/he is likely to regard her/his new job as only 'temporary'.

1. *R.* v. *C.P.R.*, *supra*, at 220 *per* McRuer, C.J.H.C.; but this position was challenged in the Supreme Court of Canada (1962) 34 D.L.R. (2d) 654 at 657, *per* Locke J., dissenting; [1962] S.C.R. 609. *See also* England, *op. cit.*, at 449.

683. While some indication of continued interest by the striker in her/his former employment can be demonstrated through such activities as picketing, their absence is not necessarily conclusive; all aspects of the employee's behaviour must be examined in order to determine whether the employment status survives a protracted strike in any individual instance.[1] In some cases striking employees have been held to have the right to return to work after prolonged strikes which have lasted for several years.[2]

1. England, *op. cit.*, at 449.
2. *See*, for example, *Shaw-Almex Industries Limited* (1986) 15 C.L.R.B.R. (N.S.) 23 (O.L.R.B.).

C. Ancillary Tactics in support of Lawful Strikes

1. Picketing as the exercise of fundamental civil liberties

684. As indicated above, the phenomenon of picketing poses conceptual or analytic difficulties of legal characterization, as well as a prescriptive problem in determining the appropriate balance between competing rights and interests recognized by law. On the one hand, picketing is both a tactic used to support workers' demands during a strike and a means for workers to express their solidarity and their aspirations. On the other hand, picketing potentially involves intimidating third parties and infringing the rights and freedoms of such parties in addition to those of employers. Historically, ordinary courts applying the common law to regulate picketing have tended to emphasize the coercive aspect of picketing and to protect third-party and employers' rights and interests at the expense of those of the picketers. To counter this tendency an attempt has been made to claim protection for peaceful picketing appeals as the exercise of freedom of speech, and for the physical presence of picketers as the exercise of freedom of assembly and association.

685. Prior to the adoption of the Charter of Rights and Freedoms in 1982, civil liberties were treated as having no independent constitutional value. They were subject to regulation by whichever level of government, provincial or national, had jurisdiction over the subject matter with which the 'civil liberty' was associated. The Supreme Court of Canada has held that parades and demonstrations might be banned by a municipality (acting under provincial legislation) because the highways and parks upon which such manifestations occurred fell under provincial legislative jurisdiction.[1] Similarly, it was held that a province could competently enact a statute which forbade all picketing not associated with a lawful strike (and presumably such picketing as well, if it desired) even though the picketers whose presence was prohibited in the particular case were not shown to be acting on behalf of a union.[2] Thus, either the provinces or the federal government were free to expand or contract freedom of speech and assembly in the context of a labour dispute to any extent, so long as the dispute itself occurred in an enterprise which that level of government was constitutionally competent to regulate.

1. *A.G. Canada* v. *Dupond* (1978) 84 D.L.R. (3d) 420 (S.C.C.); [1978] 2 S.C.R. 770.
2. *Koss* v. *Konn* (1961) 30 D.L.R. (2d) 242 (B.C.C.A.).

686. However, even in the absence of constitutional protection, the basic libertarian aspects of picketing were not entirely ignored. For example, the federal Criminal Code expressly protects informational picketing,[1] a Manitoba statute protects 'communication . . . on a public thoroughfare' as 'the exercise of . . . freedom of speech' which is not subject to restraint by injunction,[2] while legislation in British Columbia specifically excepts general public appeals from prohibitions against illegal picketing 'at or near' the employer's place of business.[3]

1. Criminal Code, s.423(2).
2. Queen's Bench Act, C.C.S.M., 1987, c.C-280, s.58(2).
3. British Columbia, ss.1(1) and 66, New Brunswick, s.104(3) and Newfoundland, s.124(3) protect such appeals provided they are not conducted by means of picketing, no matter where located.

687. Of somewhat greater potential importance than these relatively rare legislative attempts to protect picketing as free speech was the willingness of some judges implicitly to recognize that a residuum of picketing should be preserved. A few judges were prepared, indeed, to be explicit on this point,[1] but others merely relied upon the general legal presumption that what is not forbidden by law is permitted.[2]

1. *General Dry Batteries* v. *Brigenshaw*, [1951] 4 D.L.R. 414, *per* McRuer, C.J.H.C. (Ont. H.C.); *Williams* v. *Aristocratic Restaurants*, *supra* at 790, *per* Rand, J; *Channel Seven Television* v. *Broadcast Employees & Technicians* (1971) 21 D.L.R. (3d) 424 at 441, *per* Hall, J.A. (Man. C.A.).
2. *Canada Dairies* v. *Seggie*, [1940] 4 D.L.R. 725 (Ont. H.C.).

688. But, by and large, even while conceding that there was a free speech aspect to picketing, courts generally held that it was outweighed by other, competing interests such as the preservation of commercial activity,[1] of traditional property rights,[2] and of industrial peace.[3] The most that can be said is that the courts generally did not interfere with peaceful informational picketing at an employer's place of business, by small numbers of picketers, in support of a lawful strike.

1. *Hersees of Woodstock* v. *Goldstein* (1963) 38 D.L.R. (2d) 449 (Ont. C.A.).
2. *Harrison* v. *Carswell* (1976) 62 D.L.R. (3d) 68 (S.C.C.); [1976] 2 S.C.R. 200; *Canadian Gypsum Co. Ltd.* v. *Confédération des Syndicats Nationaux.*, [1973] C.A. 1075.
3. *Winnipeg Builders' Exchange* v. *I.B.E.W.* (1967) 65 D.L.R. (2d) 242 (S.C.C.); [1967] S.C.R. 628.

689. The entrenchment of the Canadian Charter of Rights and Freedoms has done little to extend the scope of permissible peaceful picketing. In its first significant Charter decision on picketing, the Supreme Court of Canada stated that peaceful picketing is prima facie protected under the Charter's guarantee of freedom of expression contained in section 2(b). But the Court went on to indicate that limitations on secondary picketing affecting third parties would constitute a reasonable limitation under section 1 on the freedom of expression guaranteed by the Charter.[1] In any event, this statement regarding the scope of protected picketing was not necessary to dispose of the case which turned upon the answer to the question of whether or not the Charter applied to injunctions issued by courts on the basis of common law rules. The Supreme Court of Canada unanimously asserted that an element of governmental activity was necessary for the Charter to apply, and it held that a court order giving effect to a common law rule between two private parties did not trigger the application of the Charter.[2] Since common law rules constitute by far the largest source of the legal regulation of picketing in Canada, the Charter is virtually irrelevant for extending the scope of picketing. Moreover, in British Columbia where the regulation of picketing is legislatively based,[3] it is unlikely that the Charter will expand the scope of permissible picketing since the Supreme Court of Canada indicated, albeit in *obiter*, that limitations on peaceful picketing such as those contained in the British Columbia legislation would be saved by virtue of section 1.

The question that remains is whether this limited view of the impact of the Charter freedom of expression will be maintained following the Supreme Court's 1999 decision in *UFCW, Local 1518* v. *K-Mart Canada Ltd.*,[4] on consumer leafleting. The Supreme Court of Canada held that statutory restrictions on peaceful consumer leafleting by a trade union at secondary locations in support of its dispute with its employer constituted unjustifiable restrictions on the workers' freedom of expression under the Charter. The union's members were leafleting at unorganized store locations operated by their employer in support of their lawful strike at an organized store. However, in holding that the limitations on consumer leafleting in support of a boycott could not be upheld as reasonable limits on worker freedom of expression, the Supreme Court stressed the differences between consumer leafleting and picketing as forms of expression deserving protection under the Charter. It suggested that picket lines are inherently coercive and act as a barrier which impedes public access to goods or services and employee access to workplaces, even when peaceful. The decision seemed to indicate that the Court's prior legitimation of restrictions on secondary picketing in *Dolphin Delivery* would continue to be followed.

1. *R.S.D.W.U., Local 580*, v. *Dolphin Delivery*, [1986] 2 S.C.R. 573.
2. *Infra*.
3. British Columbia, ss.65–7.
4. 176 D.L.R. (4th) 647 (S.C.C.); [1999] 2 S.C.R. 1083.

690. Moreover, the Supreme Court's assumptions in *Dolphin Delivery* regarding the scope of permissible secondary picketing reflected those of lower courts and labour boards which were called upon to decide whether a particular restriction on picketing infringes the Charter before the authoritative decision in *Dolphin* was issued. Although not addressing whether the Charter applies to the legal restriction being attacked (whether it be an injunction based on the common law or on a labour relations statute), lower courts and labour boards have decided that the Charter does not extend the scope of permitted picketing beyond what existed before the Charter's enactment. Prohibitions on informational picketing to further a jurisdictional dispute,[1] picketing taking place in a shopping mall,[2] picketing for political purposes conducted during the currency of a collective agreement,[3] mass picketing,[4] secondary picketing,[5] picketing in violation of the provisions of the labour relations code[6] and picketing by public sector workers in front of provincial courts during a lawful strike against the government employer[7] have all been upheld, regardless of whether the prohibition was based on doctrines of the common law labour relations statutes, or issued to protect the public interest in general.

However, there are some recent decisions from the Saskatchewan Court of Appeal which suggest Canadian courts may have been influenced by the Charter to become more willing to accept the legality of secondary picketing which is peaceful and informational. Most notable is its 1998 decision in *R.W.D.S.U., Local 558* v. *Pepsi-Cola Canada Beverages* (West) Ltd.[8] The Saskatchewan Court of Appeal rejected the notion that secondary picketing was *per se* illegal. It also went on to reject claims that peaceful secondary picketing intended to dissuade secondary retailers and customers from purchasing the products of the struck employer satisfied the requirements for the torts of nuisance, inducing breach of contract, interference with economic relations, and intimidation. In doing so the Court indicated that it should be reluctant to make policy choices concerning the application of the common law to picketing that failed to take into account the importance of picketing as a constitutionally recognized form of expression under the Charter.

1. *Horton C.B.I. Limited* v. *Int'l. Ass'n. of Bridge, Structural and Ornamental Ironworkers, Local 759* (1985) 85 C.L.L.C. 16,044 (O.L.R.B.).
2. *281856 B.C. Limited* v. *Kamloops, Revelstoke Okanagan Building Trades Union* (1986) 86 C.L.L.C. 14,056 (B.C.C.A.). The B.C. Court of Appeal refused to decide the freedom of expression issue on the ground that the Supreme Court of Canada decision in *Harrison* v. *Carswell* (1975) 75 C.L.L.C. 14,486, [1976] 2 S.C.R. 200 was controlling.
3. *University of British Columbia* (1983) 4 C.L.R.B.R. (N.S.) 158 (B.C.L.R.B.).
4. *Commonwealth Construction Company Limited* v. *Wright* (1982) 82 C.L.L.C. 14,205 (Sask. Q.B.).
5. *Imperial Oil* v. *Wright*, [1982] 1 C.R.D. 525. 10–01 (Sask. Q.B.) and *Re United Assn. of Plumbing Industry and Pitts Construction* (1984) 7 D.LR. (4th) 609 (Nfld. C.A.).
6. *Overwaitea Foods Division of Jim Pattison Ind. Ltd* (1987) 14 C.L.R.B.R. (N.S.) 268 (B.C.L.R.B.).
7. *British Columbia Government Employees Union* v. *Attorney-General of British Columbia* (1988) 88 C.L.L.C. para. 14,047 (S.C.C.); [1988] 2 S.C.R. 214.
8. [1998] S.J. No. 727, leave to appeal to SCC granted.

2. *The legal rules governing picketing*

691. The law governing picketing, in all Canadian jurisdictions, is essentially the ordinary law of tort or delict, administered by the regular courts. Exceptions to this generalization can be easily identified and will be dealt with in detail elsewhere: the federal Criminal Code controls coercive and excessive forms of 'watching and besetting';[1] British Columbia integrates the law of picketing with its general code of labour relations, administered by the Labour Relations Board;[2] and several provinces have modified common law principles by either protecting conduct which might otherwise constitute a civil wrong,[3] or forbidding conduct which would not.[4]

1. Criminal Code, s.423.
2. British Columbia, ss.65–7.
3. E.g. The Petty Trespass Act, C.C.S.M. 1987, c.P-50, s.2 as am. By S.M. 1992, c.21; The Queen's Bench Act, C.C.S.M. 1987, c.C-280, s.60.2; Rights of Labour Act, R.S.O. 1990, c.R-33; British Columbia, s.66.
4. *Infra.*

692. In Quebec, the general provisions of the Civil Code concerning intentional wrongs are applied to conduct in labour disputes. In common law jurisdictions, several torts, largely developed in nineteenth-century England to regulate trade union activity, are relied upon: conspiracy, inducing breach of contract, and wrongful interference with economic relations. These torts can be briefly defined, although extensive doctrinal analysis is, in this context, neither possible nor useful.[1]

1. *See* H.W. Arthurs, 'Tort Liability for Strikes in Canada: Some Problems of Judicial Workmanship' (1960) 38 *Can. B. Rev.* 346; A.W.R. Carrothers, *Collective Bargaining Law in Canada* (Toronto, 1965) esp. Part III *The Limits of Lawful Picketing and Boycotting*; I.M. Christie, *The Liability of Strikers in the Law of Tort: A Comparative Study of the Law in England and Canada* (Kingston, 1967); S. Tacon, *Tort Liability During the Various Phases of the Collective Bargaining Relationship* (Toronto, 1980); R.P. Gagnon, L. LeBel and P. Verge, *Droit du travail* (Sainte-Foy, 1991), 673–81.

693. Conspiracy, as a civil wrong, involves the agreement of two or more persons to accomplish a wrongful purpose, or a proper purpose through the use of wrongful means. 'Wrongful' in this sense is not confined to means or ends explicitly proscribed by the positive law; it includes all conduct which a judge might stigmatize as 'wrongful'. However, as the case law has developed, if a union has as its predominant purpose the pursuit of its own economic self-interest, that purpose will not be found to be unlawful.[1] And, as for 'means', these are increasingly tactics which are proscribed by the Labour Relations Act,[2] as well as by the various doctrines described below.

1. *Crofter Hand Woven Harris Tweed* v. *Veitch*, [1942] A.C. 435 (H.L.).
2. *Gagnon* v. *Foundation Maritime* (1961) 28 D.L.R. (2d) 174 (S.C.C.); [1961] S.C.R. 435; *Jacobsen Bros.* v. *Anderson* (1962) 35 D.L.R. (2d) 746 (N.S.S.C.).

694. It is wrongful for a third person to interfere in existing contractual relationships either by persuading one of the parties to a contract to break it, or by using illegal means to prevent her/him from performing. In principle, any such interference by means of picketing or otherwise should involve a union in liability; there is a very limited privilege to induce breaches of contract and it has never been extended to cases where a union is vindicating its own economic interests. But in practice, the tort is not applied in ordinary situations where picketing takes place at the premises of a lawfully struck employer.[1] However, along with other torts, it is one of the bases upon which courts rely in prohibiting labour union activity which is thought to violate the Labour Relations Act.[2] The tort does not apply in relationships where there is no existing contract, nor to interference by means of appeals to one of the parties to exercise a right not to enter into, or to withdraw from, a contract with another, rather than to break it.[3]

1. This result has been accomplished by specific legislation in Newfoundland, s.99.
2. *Smith Bros.* v. *Jones*, [1955] 4 D.L.R. 255 (Ont. H.C.), *Mark Fishing* v. *United Fishermen* (1972), 24 D.L.R. (3d) 585 (B.C.C.A.) aff'd (1973), 38 D.L.R. (3d) 316 (S.C.C.); [1973] S.C.R. vii.
3. *Newell* v. *Barker & Bruce*, [1950] 2 D.L.R. 289 (S.C.C.); [1950] S.C.R. 385.

695. Wrongful interference with economic relationships does not depend upon the existence of a contract, but protects such economic interests as a course of dealing, past or prospective. In determining what interference is 'wrongful', the courts have expressed a willingness to be guided by either common law or statute law. In effect, the courts rely upon violations of the Labour Relations Act as important indicators of unlawfulness.[1]

1. *Teamsters* v. *Therien* (1960) 22 D.L.R. (2d) 1 (S.C.C.); [1962] S.C.R. 265.

696. It has become clear that, apart from any other sources of law upon which they might rely, the courts in purporting to apply common law doctrine are in fact enforcing what they conceive to be the policies and express requirements of the Labour Relations Act. Beginning in the 1970s, there has been a growing tendency to do so directly and without obfuscating references to common law doctrine.[1]

1. *See* e.g. *I.B.E.W.* v. *Winnipeg Builders' Exchange* (1967) 65 D.L.R. (2d) 242 (S.C.C.); [1967] S.C.R. 628; *I.L.A.* v. *Maritime Employers' Assoc.* (1979) 89 D.L.R. (3d) 289 (S.C.C.); [1979] 1 S.C.R. 120. More recently *see St. Anne Nackawic Pulp & Paper Co.* v. *CPWU, Local 219*, [1986] 1 S.C.R. 704.

697. This trend, while perhaps defensible on jurisprudential grounds, has attracted negative comment on the grounds that courts are extrapolating provisions of labour relations statutes beyond the contemplation and intention of the legislature that enacted them, that judges are insufficiently familiar with industrial relations policies and practices to apply such statutes in a sophisticated and constructive way, and that the intervention of the courts in policing the rules of industrial conflict impedes the development of an integrated scheme of enforcement under the aegis of the labour relations board.

698. In the discussion that follows, no attempt will be made to explain the doctrinal bases of the courts' decisions. For the most part, the doctrines outlined above have little application in the context of 'lawful' strikes, apart from their use to regulate secondary picketing; they are more typically used to render unlawful conduct which supports, or is in substitution for, illegal strike action.[1]

1. *Infra*, §4 Unlawful Industrial Action.

3. *Timeliness*

699. As has been indicated, the essential test of the legality of a strike is whether or not it is timely, i.e. whether it follows exhaustion of the negotiation and conciliation procedures prescribed by statute. Although not all labour relations statutes specifically address the use of 'ancillary' tactics such as picketing,[1] it can generally be said that where a strike would be unlawful, so will ancillary activity be forbidden.[2] Conversely, where a strike is lawful, picketing is presumptively lawful.[3]

1. British Columbia, ss.65–7; Alberta, s.114; New Brunswick, s.101; Newfoundland, s.124.
2. Ontario and Quebec legislation, for example, contains no direct reference to picketing. However, in Ontario, judicial decisions have generally concluded that picketing is forbidden when the strike is itself illegal. In Quebec, the case law is divided on that question. *See* Morin and Brière, 941–2. *See infra*.
3. *Williams* v. *Aristrocratic Restaurants*, [1951] 3 D.L.R. 769 (S.C.C.); [1951] S.C.R. 762.

4. *Behaviour on the picket line*

700. This presumption in favour of picketing in support of a lawful strike will yield to a showing that behaviour on the picket line is improper. An earlier view that peaceful picketing is 'a negation in terms'[1] is now obsolete, and peaceful picketing is prima facie lawful.[2] But the courts will not permit picketing which is perceived to interfere with the personal security, property rights or reputation of either the employer who is its primary target, or other persons to whom appeals for support are directed.

1. *Hollywood Theatres* v. *Tenney*, [1940] 1 D.L.R. 451 at 459 *per* O'Halloran, J.A. (B.C.C.A.).
2. *Williams* v. *Aristocratic Restaurants, supra.*

a. Personal security

701. Anyone has the right to pass through a picket line without being subjected to violence or threats of violence. Violent picketing may well constitute the crime of assault, or of watching and besetting, although the latter offence specifically excludes mere 'attending for the purpose only of obtaining or communicating information'.[1] In addition, such picketing may give rise to an action for an injunction, which will not only restrain violence *per se*, but, if it is egregious, will completely, or virtually, forbid all picketing.[2] The courts are relatively quick to detect such threats even where picketers, for example, merely point, grimace or stare,[3] or congregate in large numbers in a confined area.[4] Thus, the courts routinely limit the numbers of picketers who may be present at any one time at each entrance to a plant and the number of minutes they may hold up vehicles entering or leaving a struck plant,[5] and police are generally able to assure access to struck premises by means of informal agreement with the picketers, rather than by bringing charges.

1. Criminal Code, s.423(2).
2. *Hallnor Mines* v. *Behie*, [1954] 1 D.L.R. 135 (Ont. H.C.); *Canadian Gypsum Co. Ltd.* v. *Confédération des Syndicats Nationaux*, [1973] C.A. 1075; *Bulk-Lift Systems* v. *Drivers* (1976) 64 D.L.R. (3d) 208 (Ont. H.C.).
3. *Hammer* v. *Kemmis*, [1956] 3 D.L.R. (2d) 565 (B.C.S.C.).
4. *Hanes* v. *McConnell*, [1969] 2 O.R. 782 (H.C.).
5. *See*, for example, *Blue Cirle Canada Inc.* v. *Fielder* (1998) 1998 Carswell Ont 1689 (O.C.J. Gen. Div.) (ten minutes) and *Cargill Foods Toronto Ltd.* v. *Suppa-Magee*, [1995] O.J. No. 3203 (O.C.J. Gen. Div.) (three minutes).

702. On the other hand, there have been situations where serious violence has broken out, either as a result of union frustration, or as a result of deliberate employer provocation. In these situations, recourse may be had to both the criminal law and the courts' injunctive powers.

b. Property rights

703. Normally, picketing takes place on a sidewalk or roadway in front of struck premises. However, the Criminal Code prevents the blocking or obstructing of a highway,[1] so that picket line activity is not permitted to interfere with the flow of supplies into the plant, or of goods departing. Interference with ingress or egress may also be treated as a civil wrong, subject to injunction.[2]

1. Criminal Code, s.423(1)(g).
2. *See* para. 701 *supra*.

704. Where a struck enterprise is located on land owned by a third person, and shared with other tenants, e.g. shopping centre, picketers are confronted with an awkward situation. If they picket on the sidewalk or road surrounding the entire premises, there is a risk that neutral employers who share those premises but have nothing to do with the dispute may be injured, and have good grounds for complaint. On the other hand, although picketing may be confined to the immediate vicinity of the struck enterprise, if it occurs on privately owned land, e.g. on the sidewalk of a shopping centre, the owner of the land will probably be able to vindicate his property rights by a trespass action.[1]

1. *Harrison* v. *Carswell* (1976) 62 D.L.R. (3d) 618 (S.C.C.); [1976] 2 S.C.R. 200. Relying on *Harrison* v. *Carswell*, the British Columbia Court of Appeal refused to consider whether the law of trespass infringed peaceful picketers' freedom of expression as guaranteed by s.2(b) of the Charter, 281865 *B.C. Limited* v. *Kamloops, Revelstoke, Okanagan Building Trades Union* (1986) 86 C.L.L.C. 14,056. Note that the Ontario Court of Appeal has recognized that the mall owner's property rights must be balanced against the rights of workers to organize under labour relations legislation in *Cadillac Fairview Corp.* v. *R.W.D.S.U.* (1989), 90 C.L.L.C. Para. 14,003 (Ont. C.A.). It held it was an unfair labour practice for the mall owner to prohibit any organizing activity by the union in front of the store that was the target of a certification drive. It seems feasible to extend a similar analysis to peaceful picketing activity in support of a lawful strike.

705. This dilemma, which virtually immunizes employers in such circumstances from picketing, has been resolved in some provinces by legislation which in effect confers upon the picketers a licence to go on to privately owned land, such as shopping centres, to which the public is ordinarily admitted.[1]

1. British Columbia, s.66; Trespass Act, C.C.S.M. 1987 c.P-50, s.5. Ontario enacted a similar provision in 1993 but it was repealed in 1995.

c. Reputation

706. Early cases had held that such pejorative terms as 'unfair' or 'scab' amounted to defamation of the persons at whom they were directed. However, these terms have now become sufficiently commonplace to be accepted as part of the permissible – if unpleasant – vocabulary of the picket line.

707. But, in one special sense, the courts remain concerned to control messages conveyed by picket signs. Under the general rubric of defamation, the courts have enjoined false and misleading statements by unions against management. For example, the courts have prevented a union from displaying a sign which might have conveyed the impression that a dispute was at the picketed location, rather than another, although the true location was stated accurately, albeit in smaller-sized, less easily noticed, letters on the picket sign.[1]

1. *F.W. Woolworth* v. *Retail Clerks* (1961) 30 D.L.R. (2d) 377 (B.C.S.C.).

5. The scope of ancillary activities: secondary pressure

a. Definition

708. If it is reasonably clear that a union may peacefully picket the premises of an employer against whom it is lawfully on strike, it is by no means clear what other economic sanctions it may bring to bear against him. Specifically, union attempts to secure sympathetic action by other means may well be categorized as 'secondary', and illegal.

709. 'Secondary' pressure is not a term of art. However, it is generally taken to include any situation where the union brings pressure to bear against the primary employer by actual or threatened sanctions mounted against third persons. For example, a union may picket a retail store selling goods produced by the struck primary firm, or may picket the supplier of materials or services to the struck primary firm to persuade the retailer's or supplier's employees not to perform their duties for their own employer, until his relations with the struck firm are abandoned. Also treated as 'secondary' pressures are more generalized appeals to the public not to purchase goods from a struck firm, or to the labour movement, not to handle goods moving to or from the struck firm.

b. The legality of secondary picketing and boycotts[1]

710. The legal reaction to secondary pressure has generally been to prohibit or restrict it. However, the legal technique used and the actual extent of the restriction has varied somewhat from one Canadian jurisdiction to another. The particular rationale (if any) accepted by a court or legislature for regulation of such pressure will obviously determine the form and extent of the prohibition it adopts against it.

1. *See* generally A.W.R. Carrothers, 'Secondary Picketing' (1962) 40 *Can. B. Rev.* 57; J.C. Paterson, 'Union Secondary Conduct: A Comparative Study of the American and Ontario Positions' (1973) 8 U.B.C.L. Rev. 77; D. Beatty, 'Secondary Boycotts: A Functional Analysis' (1974) 52 *Can. B. Rev.* 388; J. Manwaring, 'Legitimacy in Labour Relations: The Courts, the British Columbia Labour Board and Secondary Picketing' (1982) 20 *Osgoode Hall L.J.* 274; P. Macklem, 'Secondary Picketing, Consumer Boycotts and the Charter' (2000) 8 C.LE.L.J. 1.

711. Three reasons have been relied upon to justify complete or partial judicial or legislative restrictions upon the use of secondary pressures. First, the potential harm to the primary employer of a secondary boycott may be much greater than that of a strike and picketing at his premises. It may be argued that the use of secondary pressures thus disturbs the balance of power and should for that reason alone be forbidden. In the absence of any authoritative standards for measuring the appropriate balance of power, this is an unacceptable rationale. Second, secondary pickets and boycotts can have significant harmful consequences for the interests of other businesses and of consumers, who may be injured by the dispute although not a party to it. Such consequences are to some extent inevitable even as a result of primary strikes and picketing but, it is argued, they should be confined so far as possible.[1] Third, where secondary pressure takes the form of appeals to other workers to cease work, such action not only invites widespread industrial disruption, but involves as well violations of various no-strike provisions in statutes or collective agreements. The Supreme Court of Canada has indicated its willingness to consider legal restrictions on picketing based upon such reasons as acceptable limitations on Charter protected rights and freedoms.[2]

1. This is the rationale for legislative restrictions on secondary activity which was recognized by the Supreme Court of Canada in *UFCW, Local 1518* v. *K-Mart Canada Ltd* (1999) 176 D.L.R. (4th) 647 (S.C.C.); [1999] 2 S.C.R. 1083.
2. *R.W.D.S.U., Local 580* v. *Dolphin Delivery*, [1986] 2 S.C.R., 573. The Supreme Court's recent decision in *UFCW, Local 1518* v. *K-Mart Canada Ltd* (1999), *supra*, indicated that the Court's legitimation of restrictions on secondary picketing in *Dolphin Delivery* would continue to be followed.

712. The response of common law courts has essentially been divided into two phases. A series of decisions concerning secondary picketing prior to 1963 had exhibited, for reasons which were peculiar to each case, a 'fundamental indisposition' to such picketing.[1] In 1963, however, the Ontario Court of Appeal in the well-known *Hersees* decision held that secondary picketing was 'illegal *per se*', because it sought to 'benefit . . . a particular class only' while the right of a neutral retailer handling struck products was 'a right far more fundamental and of far greater importance as one in which its exercise affects and is for the benefit of the community at large'.[2] This conclusion, however opaque, has generally prevailed in subsequent decisions. However, there are some recent decisions by provincial courts of appeal which have rejected the balancing of interests accepted in *Hersees*.

1. Carrothers, *supra*, at 74.
2. *Supra*, at 454.
3. Most notable is the decision in *R.W.D.S.U., Local 558* v. *Pepsi-Cola Canada Beverages (West) Ltd.* [1998] S.J. No. 727 (Sask. C.A.), leave to appeal to SCC granted. The Saskatchewan Court of Appeal rejected the notion that secondary picketing was *per se* illegal. In doing so the Court indicated that it should be reluctant to make policy choices concerning the application of the common law to picketing that failed to take into account the importance of picketing as a constitutionally recognized form of expression under the Charter.

713. Legislatures, however, have reacted in a more limited and specific way to secondary picketing. Ontario, for example, only prohibits conduct which might, as a reasonable and probable consequence, cause an unlawful, sympathetic strike.[1] Furthermore, the Labour Relations Board of that province has recently asserted jurisdiction to regulate picketing in support of strike activity.[2] Alberta has specifically outlawed boycotts in the transportation of goods.[3] British Columbia, New Brunswick, and Newfoundland, while generally forbidding picketing except where conducted at an employer's place of business operations, specifically preserve the right to make public appeals by means other than picketing.[4]

1. S.83.
2. *Consolidated-Bathurst Packaging and Canadian Paperworkers Union, Local 595*, [1982] 3 C.L.R.B.R. 324 and *Sarnia Construction Association*, [1982] 3 C.L.R.B.R. 60. The Labour Relations Act was subsequently amended in 1984 to ensure the board's jurisdiction to regulate picketing used in support of strikes. *See* S.O. 1995, c.1, s.100.

3. S.100.
4. British Columbia. ss.1(1), 64; New Brunswick, s.104(3) and Newfoundland. s.124(3).

714. The difficulty is that, save for the Labour Relations Code of British Columbia which considerably limits the courts' role,[1] legislation – whether specific or merely silent – is largely ignored by judges as they reach their conclusion concerning the legality of secondary picketing on common law grounds. Thus, for example, in the *Hersees* case, the Court of Appeal pronounced a complete ban on secondary picketing, although the legislature had only a few years earlier specifically declined to follow the recommendation of a legislative committee to the same effect, and had instead adopted the much narrower prohibition referred to above.[2]

1. Ss.136 and 137. The courts retain only a vestigial jurisdiction under s.137(4) to award damages if the labour relations board finds that the Act has been violated.
2. H.W. Arthurs, 'Comment' (1963) 41 *Can. B. Rev.* 573.

c. Problems of characterization: primary versus secondary

715. Jurisdictions which legislatively confine picketing to the employer's place of business operations, as well as those which judicially prohibit all secondary picketing, are confronted with a difficult task of determining whether, in a given case, picketing does fall within permissible limits.[1] For example, in some industries such as taxi-cabs, the primary employer's place of business is ambulatory, and unless pickets are permitted to follow the employer from place to place, wherever he makes contact with customers, the right to picket would be entirely negated. Again, in other industries such as construction, the employer's place of business is typically shared with a number of other firms, each of which employs workers who belong to different unions. There is a risk that if the primary employer's striking employees are permitted to picket the common workplace, the picket line will cause a work stoppage by the unionized employees of all other firms. Yet it would be unfair, for that reason, to deny them a right to picket which they would otherwise enjoy. A compromise position, adopted in some cases, is to permit picketing but to confine its undesired effects by requiring the picketers to clearly identify their primary target, and to avoid interfering with employees of other firms. A more difficult question relates to the right of a union to picket businesses which have a close connection with that of the primary employer. Unions are entitled to picket all locations at which the primary business is conducted, although they may represent workers at only some of the locations, because the employer draws strength from his entire enterprise. The position in relation to corporate affiliates of the struck firm is somewhat more ambiguous, but some recent decisions suggest a greater willingess to look beyond surface corporate structures to make the distinction between primary and secondary activity. Where the struck entity and the putative 'secondary' employer are related through common corporate ownership or control the picketing may not be held to be secondary.[2] But the real difficulty is to identify those firms which are active allies of the primary employer in the industrial conflict. It has been recognized both by courts and at least one legislature[3] that a firm which knowingly intermeddles in a dispute to assist the struck employer is no longer a neutral deserving protection, and is itself liable to be picketed. This 'ally' doctrine extends at least to firms whose assistance is active, as for example the performance of work on behalf of the struck firm, rather than passive, as for example a public warehouse continuing to provide storage facilities used by the primary employer prior to the strike.[4]

1. The cases discussed in this paragraph are conveniently collected and analysed in Beatty, *op. cit.* and Tacon, *op. cit.*; *see also* R. Brown, 'Picketing: Canadian Courts and the Labour Relations Board of British Columbia' (1981) 31 U.T.L.J. 153.
2. *See O.K. Economy Stores* v. *R.W.D.S.U., Local 454* (1995) 118 D.L.R. (4th) 345 (Sask. C.A.), which suggested a more restricted view of what constitutes secondary picketing in cases involving picketing of sister or subsidiary divisions of the struck employer entity.
3. British Columbia, s.65(2).
4. *See Consolidated-Bathurst Packaging and Canadian Paperworkers Union, Local 595*, [1982] 3 C.L.R.B.R. 324 on the definition of an ally employer.

§4. Unlawful Industrial Action

A. Generally

716. In Canada, a strike which is 'timely' is almost always lawful, and one which is 'untimely' is almost always not. Timeliness is the touchstone of the lawfulness of a strike. Moreover, as will be seen, by a process of judicial extension to the development of common law tort doctrines, the courts have held that picketing and other conduct which induces, supports, or is in substitution for, an untimely strike is similarly unlawful.

717. Whether framed in terms of compulsory recourse to conciliation procedures,[1] or of specific time delays during which negotiations may run their course,[2] or of compliance with strike notice and strike vote requirements,[3] Canadian labour legislation generally provides that all lawful strikes must be postponed until various peace-keeping measures have been exhausted.[4] But to introduce this requirement of timeliness is also to define the purposes of the strike itself since such measures are provided only in specific circumstances.

1. Ontario, s.79; Canada, s.89.
2. Quebec, s.58
3. British Columbia, s.59.
4. Conciliation is no longer a mandatory step in Quebec in order to acquire the right to strike or lock out. *See* Quebec, s.54.

718. First, conciliation is available only to certain unions – those which have already secured the right to represent employees and therefore to call upon the employer to enter upon negotiations. Second, conciliation is available only for certain kinds of disputes – those which involve conflicts of interests arising upon the expiry of the collective agreement (whose term is of fixed duration), and not those which involve conflicts of rights arising out of the administration of the agreement. Third, conciliation is available (at least arguably; the point has not been decided) only to resolve certain kinds of interest disputes – those whose subject matter falls within the statutorily defined scope of collective bargaining. And, finally, while strike notice and strike vote requirements help to safeguard important employer and employee interests, it is questionable whether non-compliance with them should result in open-ended liability for resulting damage to both those interests and all others. Each of these points must now be be considered in detail.

B. Strikes for Union Bargaining Rights

719. Canadian law contains elaborate administrative procedures, known as certification,[1] by which a union's claim to act as the bargaining agent of employees may be tested and validated, if an employer declines to accept that claim at face value. In principle, it is not surprising that the courts should take the view that any economic pressure designed to secure union bargaining rights amounts to an attempt to 'short circuit' the statutory certification mechanism.[2] Indeed, the desire to avoid industrial action to secure recognition was a prime objective of the original American and Canadian labour relations statutes. However, it must be noted that in some jurisdictions legislation does not explicitly restrict activity other than strikes, so that in this situation the courts may arguably be said to be extending the reach of the statutory prohibition. Moreover, the premise of these cases is that the availablility of certification makes impermissible any recourse to economic sanctions. While it might be argued that, if in given circumstances there are practical obstacles to certification, the use of economic sanctions should be permitted, this position has not been accepted.[3]

1. *Supra.*
2. *Smith Bros. Construction* v. *Jones*, [1955] 4 D.L.R. 255 (Ont.H.C.), *Gagnon* v. *Foundation Maritime* (1961) 28 D.L.R. (2d) 174 (S.C.C.); [1961] S.C.R. 435.
3. This was, for some years, a particular problem in the construction industry. The time required to gain certification often exceeded the duration of the job, after which the workforce would be disbanded. As a result, unions often felt obliged to use strikes and picketing to gain recognition. Reform and acceleration of certification in the construction industry significantly alleviated the problem.

720. The general question of civil, criminal and administrative sanctions for illegal conduct will be canvassed below. A special issue arises, however, in the context of economic pressure to secure bargaining rights. On occasion, a union which resorts to such pressure may simultaneously seek to win bargaining rights through certification. The Ontario Labour Relations Board has used its control over certification procedures as a lever to bring illegal strikes to an end by adjourning the application for certification until the strike has terminated.[1] It has, moreover, declared invalid collective relationships whose origins were tainted by the assertion of illegal economic pressure.[2] In Alberta this result is achieved through legislative proscription, rather than by administrative discretion, as the statute specifically states that no trade union shall be certified where membership in the union is a direct result of picketing the place of employment.[3]

1. *Robert McAlpine* [1961–2] O.L.R.B. 178; the Board's early policy was to dismiss outright any application for certification by a striking union, *Radio Lunch* (1950) 52 C.L.L.C. para. 17,012 (O.L.R.B.).

2. *Traugott Construction*, [1982] 1 C.L.R.B.R. 152 (O.L.R.B.); *Folgar Construction*, [1982] 2 C.L.R.B.R. (O.L.R.B.).
3. S.39(2).

C. Industrial Action during a Collective Agreement

721. Legislation in all Canadian jurisdictions, provides procedures by which disputes concerning the interpretation, administration or violation of a collective agreement may be adjudicated. By much the same reasoning as in cases concerned with bargaining rights, the courts have relied upon such provisions to prohibit industrial action to enforce the collective agreement.[1]

1. *Teamsters* v. *Therien* (1960), 22 D.L.R. (2d) 1 (S.C.C.); [1962] S.C.R. 265.

722. However, at least some controversies which arise during the term of the collective agreement do not fall neatly into the categories of disputes which are intended to be adjudicated. An example of such controversies are those which arise out of a radical technological change, requiring fundamental revision of the collective agreement rather than the application of its provisions. In effect, disputes about wages and working conditions premised upon a now-obsolete assumption concerning the nature of the work performed can hardly be decided by reference to the terms of the former agreement. The parties are left with the problem of resolving an interest dispute – whether such a change shall be instituted and, if so, with what consequences – through an adjudicative procedure designed for rights disputes. The intractability of this situation has led, from time to time, to the use of strikes, both legal and illegal, by frustrated unions. These, in turn, have led to public inquiries,[1] and to legislative attempts to deal specifically with the consequences of mid-agreement industrial change, by permitting the use of strikes in certain circumstances.[2] Except as provided by such legislation, however, mid-agreement strikes are forbidden, even though the parties confront problems which cannot be resolved through adjudication. In such circumstances, the employer's initiative is allowed to prevail unless and until it is revised at subsequent negotiations, following the expiry of the agreement.

1. *Report of the Industrial Inquiry Commission on Canadian National Railways 'Run-throughs'* (Ottawa, 1965).
2. Manitoba ss.72–5; Canada ss.51–4; Saskatchewan, s.43.

723. Safety problems present another example of controversies which cannot easily be resolved within the adjudicative mechanism of the collective agreement. Here, the concerns of workers may be too urgent and the mechanisms of decision too slow-moving to justify a total prohibition of work stoppages. Recent legislation has conferred upon workers a right to stop work during the currency of a collective agreement where there is a bona fide reasonable belief that they are in imminent danger.[1]

1. Occupational Health and Safety Act, R.S.O. 1990, c.O-1, ss.43–9, as amended by S.O. 1997, c.4, s.84, S.O. 1998, c.8, s.5, 54, 55; British Columbia, s.63(3)(a); An Act Respecting Occupational Health and Safety, R.S.Q., c.S-2.1, ss.12–31.

724. Save where expressly permitted, then, strikes and ancillary activity during the term of a collective agreement may give rise to civil, criminal or administrative proceedings. In addition, however, there are three distinctive consequences of such strikes which must be addressed as a result of the fact that collective agreements (whether by legislative compulsion or by free choice) generally contain a 'no-strike' clause.[1]

1. Ontario, ss.46; Canada, s.57; British Columbia, s.58. (Quebec, s.107 forbids strikes during a collective agreement, unless the parties have included in it a clause permitting renegotiation of its terms.)

725. First, the question immediately arises as to whether breach of a no-strike clause by the union or its members constitutes such a fundamental breach of the collective agreement as to relieve the employer of his obligation further to be bound by it. The Supreme Court of Canada has answered this question in the negative.[1] A strike in violation of a collective agreement does not bring it to an end.

1. *McGavin Toastmaster* v. *Ainscough* (1975) 54 D.L.R. (3d) 1 (S.C.C.); [1976] 1 S.C.R. 718.

726. Second, given that the agreement remains in force for its full term, what recourse does the employer have against the union for such violations? That the union should be made to answer before an arbitrator or other adjudicative forum for breach of its promise not to strike is apparent, since all other breaches of the agreement are similarly subject to adjudication. But it has also been held that a union is answerable for failing to take reasonable measures to bring to an end a spontaneous work stoppage which it did not officially promote or condone.[1] In either case, a union is liable for any financial loss suffered by the employer by reason of the illegal strike,[2] but the employer must seek damages in the grievance arbitration forum rather than by civil action. However, the courts remain available to provide an injunction to bring an end to the unlawful work stoppage where labour board procedures are inadequate to provide such relief.[3]

1. *Re Polymer* (1958) 10 L.A.C. 31 aff'd *Imbleau* v. *Laskin* (1962), 33 D.L.R. (2d) 124 (S.C.C.); [1962] S.C.R. 338. *See also Int'l. Longshoremen's Assoc., Local 273* v. *Maritime Employers Assoc.* (1979) 89 D.L.R. (3d) 289 (S.C.C.); [1979] 1 S.C.R. 120; *A.G. Nfld.* v. *Nfld. Ass. of Public Employees* (1976) 74 D.L.R. (3d) 195 (Nfld.T.D.).
2. *Re New Brunswick Power Commission and I.B.E.W.* (1976) 73 D.L.R. (3d) 94 (N.B.C.A.).
3. *St. Anne Nackawic Pulp & Paper Co.* v. *CPWU, Local 219*, [1986] 1 S.C.R. 704.

727. Third, although employees do not cease to be employed by reason only of striking (either legally or illegally)[1] they do expose themselves to employer sanctions, including discharge.[2] However, that discharge may itself be questioned as a violation of the usual requirement in a collective agreement that employees should only be disciplined or discharged for 'just cause'. Arbitrators have held that discharge is too harsh a penalty for employees whose strike was, in effect, provoked by the employer.[3] On the other hand, arbitration decisions have held union stewards and officers to a particularly high standard of conduct, and held them strictly liable for organizing work stoppages.[4]

1. *McGavin Toastmaster* v. *Ainscough, supra; Praesto Aluminium Products* (1959) 59 C.L.L.C. para. 18,137 (O.L.R.B.).

2. *Dresser Electric*, [1966–7] O.L.R.B. 906; *Berlet Elecrronics* (1968) 19 L.A.C. 152; *Re Canadian Gypsum and Nova Scotia Quarryworkers* (1959), 20 D.L.R. (2d) 319 (N.S.S.C.).
3. *Aerocide Dispenser* (1965) 16 L.A.C. 57; *Radio Shack*, (1980) 26 L.A.C. (2d) 227.
4. *Douglas Aircraft* v. *McConnell* (1979) 99 D.L.R. (3d) 385 (S.C.C.); [1980] 1 S.C.R. 245. More recently *see Mill & Timber Products Ltd. and I.W.A. Local 1–3567* (1996) 61 L.A.C. (4th) 52 (Munroe) which indicates that the decision to impose greater discipline on union officials should be based on a finding that the combination of the official's conduct and office was likely to affect the conduct of other employees.

D. Industrial Action for Improper Purposes

728. As has been suggested, strikes may lawfully occur only following collective bargaining and conciliation. However, there is some authority for the proposition that even when these requirements of timeliness are met, strikes for certain purposes extrinsic to, or inconsistent with, the Labour Relations Act, are unlawful.

729. Politically motivated strikes have almost inevitably been held unlawful (although admittedly in cases where they were also untimely),[1] as has industrial action to secure changes in government policy,[2] or to support the struggle of foreign workers involved in a labour dispute.[3] Sympathetic strikes to aid other workers within the same industry are also unlawful.[4] There is some suggestion, as well, that industrial action, albeit for collective bargaining purposes, may become unlawful if the particular concessions sought are contrary to the policy of the Labour Relations Act,[5] although this suggestion has not received authoritative approval.

1. *R.* v. *Russell* (1920) 51 D.L.R. I (Man.C.A.); In *General Motors of Canada Ltd.*, [1996] 96 C.L.L.C. 143, 580, the Ontario Labour Relations Board reaffirmed these principles in the face of union arguments that they should be reconsidered in the context of the Canadian Charter of Rights and Freedoms. The union argued that the provisions of the Ontario Labour Relations Act, 1995 which prohibited strikes during the term of a collective agreement were contrary to the Charter and of no force or effect insofar as they prohibited political protest strikes. The Ontario Board recognized that political protest strikes fell within the meaning of expression protected by s.2(b) of the Charter, but held that the blanket prohibition on all strike activity during the term of a collective agreement was a reasonable limit which was demonstrably justifiable under s.1 of the Charter.
2. *Ellis* v. *Willis* (1972) 30 D.L.R. (3d) 397 (Ont.H.C.); *B.C. Ferry Corp.* [1981] C.L.R.B.R. 457 (B.C.L.R.B.).
3. *Pietro Culotta Grapes* v. *Moses*, [1968] 1 O.R. 89 (H.C.); *Darrigo's Grape Juice* v. *Masterson* (1971) 21 D.L.R. (3d) 660 (Ont.H.C.); *Slade & Steward* v. *Retail Wholesale* (1969) 5 D.L.R. (3d) 736 (B.C.S.C.).
4. *Antonsen* v. *United Fishermen* (1963) 64 C.L.L.C. para. 15,497 (B.C.S.C.); *The Citizen*, [1976] 2 C.L.R.B.R. 474 (O.L.R.B.).
5. *Otis Elevator* v. *Constructors* (1973) 35 D.L.R. (3d) 566 (B.C.C.A.); *Carpenters Employer Bargaining Agency*, [1978] 2 C.L.R.B.R. 501 (O.L.R.B.).

730. Finally, there has been some attempt specifically to outlaw so-called 'jurisdictional' or 'demarcation' strikes and picketing. Such tactics are employed when a union demands that work be assigned to its members rather than to workers associated with some other union, trade, craft or class. Typically, such disputes arise in the construction industry which is organized on a craft union basis, with each union representing workers of only a single craft, and each employer typically employing workers associated with that craft and union. In effect, disputes over jurisdiction or demarcation amount to a contest for available work or employment opportunities, between groups of workers, claiming supposed rights based upon traditional skills, industrial custom, or 'job property'.

731. Being essentially multilateral, involving two unions and two or more employers, such disputes do not yield easily to adjudication in traditional forums. Several solutions have evolved. On the one hand, a variety of permanent and *ad hoc* tribunals have been established on a purely consensual basis by various employer and union initiatives.[1] On the other hand, in several provinces the labour relations board is specifically empowered to terminate jurisdictional strikes and picketing, and to settle the underlying controversy which gives rise to such industrial action.[2]

1. J.H.G. Crispo and H.W. Arthurs, *Jurisdictional Disputes in Canada: A Study in Frustration*, E.E. Palmer (ed.), III *Current Law and Social Problems* (Toronto, 1963).
2. Ontario, s.99; Alberta, s.144; Nova Scotia, s.52(1); Prince Edward Island, s.38; New Brunswick, ss.82–9. These statutes, in varying degrees, contemplate resort by the parties to procedures of their own creation.

E. Compliance with Notice and Strike Vote Procedure

732. Various Canadian jurisdictions provide that notice of strike must be given to an employer,[1] or that a secret ballot vote of employees must be held,[2] prior to the commencement of a strike. These provisions are, respectively, designed to protect the interests of the employer against the precipitate strike action, and of individual workers against strikes which are not democratically mandated. However, they also serve the latent function of delaying strikes because of the formalities involved and the time consumed.[3] Ontario has two unique provisions, one which permits the Labour Minister to require a vote by employees on the employer's last offer,[4] and another which gives the employer the right to have the employees vote on its final offer once, either before or after commencement of a strike.[5] The Saskatchewan legislation enables a trade union, an employee or an employer to apply to the labour board to conduct a vote on the employer's final offer where a strike has continued for 30 days.[6] This provision is designed to test employee wishes during a protracted strike.

1. Alberta, s.90; New Brunswick, s.97; British Columbia, s.60; British Columbia also provides for greater notice where the strike involves perishable goods, s.61(4)–(6).
2. British Columbia, s.60; Alberta, s.88; New Brunswick, s.94(1); Saskatchewan, s.11(2)(d); Quebec, s.20.2; Ontario, s.79(3) and (4). The Ontario provisions requiring a strike vote were added in 1995 but they do not apply to the construction industry.
3. The experience with strike votes has been that they almost always are in the affirmative, and that their effect may be to heighten the possibility of strikes by making rank-and-file support more visible. F.R. Anton, *Government Supervised Strike Votes* (Toronto, 1961).
4. Ontario, s.41.
5. Ontario, s.42. In the construction industry the Labour Minister has discretion to order a final offer vote at the employer's request but in all other cases the legislation requires the ministry to conduct a vote on a final offer (once) following an employer request.
6. Saskatchewan, s.45.

733. Non-compliance with these provisions is obviously at least a minor a violation of the statute, in principle giving rise to a quasi-criminal sanction.[1] However, some Canadian courts have also treated non-compliance as rendering illegal not only the strike – a sufficiently significant conclusion – but all activities associated with the strike, including otherwise innocuous picketing.[2] And they have done so even when the statutory provisions themselves were obscure and the breaches of a highly technical nature. Similarly, it has been held, under the Ontario legislation referred to, *supra*, that a vote by striking employees to accept the employer's last offer has the effect of bringing the strike to an end.[3] However, the Quebec legislation expressly states that non-compliance with the strike vote provision may only give rise to penal prosecution. Consequently, the legality of the strike is not affected by such a failure.[4]

1. *Industrial Wire and Cable* [1960–1] O.L.R.B. 451; *Keddy* v. *R.* (1961) 130 C.C.C. 226 (N.S.S.C.).
2. *Contractors Equipment & Supply* v. *Teamsters* (1965) 54 D.L.R. (2d) 726 (Man. C.A.); *Jacobson Bros.* v. *Anderson* (1962) 35 D.L.R. (2d) 746 (N.S.S.C.); *Culinary Workers* v. *Terra Nova Motor Inn* (1974) 50 D.L.R. (3d) 253 (S.C.C.); [1975] 2 S.C.R. 749; *Waterford Hospital* v. *Newfoundland Ass. of Public Employees* (1979) 99 D.L.R. (3d) 189 (Nfld. C.A.).
3. *Canada Cement Lafarge*, [1981] 1 C.L.R.B.R. 236 (O.L.R.B.).
4. Quebec, s.20.4.

734. Of special interest is the extent to which other forms of industrial action may be permitted at a time when strikes are not, specifically when such action is intended to spur current negotiations. In an early case, the Supreme Court of Canada had noted that, although strikes were forbidden prior to compliance with the strike vote procedures, no such restraints were imposed upon 'ancillary means of advancing the interests of either party'.[1] In that case, picketing was permitted even though the required strike vote was not held, and no strike had been called. However, a later decision held that picketing of their employer's premises by off-duty employees, in an effort to stimulate bargaining concessions, was illegal because they were not yet entitled to strike.[2]

1. *Williams* v. *Aristocratic Restaurants, supra* at 791, *per* Rand J.
2. *Nipissing Hotel* v. *Hotel and Restaurant Employees* (1962) 36 D.L.R. (2d) 81; (1963) 38 D.L.R. (2d) 675 (Ont.H.C.). The precise grounds of decision are unclear: Landreville J., dealing with a preliminary motion, held that any pressure asserted during negotiation violated the obligation of the parties to negotiate in good faith. Spence J., not primarily addressing himself to that point, held at trial, that a common law duty of fidelity precludes employee conduct which may injure the employer.

F. Boycotts

735. Reference has already been made to the use of consumer and other boycotts in the context of secondary picketing following a lawful strike.[1] They may also be treated as conduct utilized in substitution for other industrial action in circumstances when such action would be unlawful. Where the boycott is conducted by means of an unlawful work stoppage it is actionable.[2] Moreover, the courts have been prepared to extend a statutory prohibition on untimely picketing to all forms of appeal, including newspaper advertisements handbills, and letters.[3] In several jurisdictions, however, the legislature has countered such judicial extensions by specifically providing that public expressions of sympathy, other than by picketing, are permitted.[4] Only in Manitoba is peaceful secondary picketing, regardless of its object, expressly permitted.[5] Nor will a union be allowed to institute a boycott by means of provisions in its collective agreement precluding the employer from dealing with the party at whom the boycott is aimed, whether an employer or a rival trade union[6] unless, arguably, it is protecting its existing bargaining rights.[7]

1. *Supra.*
2. *Mark Fishing* v. *United Fishermen* (1972) 24 D.L.R. (3d) 585 (B.C.C.A.), aff'd. (1973) 38 D.L.R. (3d) 316*n* (S.C.C.); [1973] S.C.R. 749.
3. *Sonoco* v. *I.B.P.W.* (1970) 13 D.L.R. (3d) 617 (B.C.C.A.); *Coles Bakers* v. *Bakery Workers*, (1962) 36 D.L.R. (2d) 772 (B.C.S.C.). (The specific holding in these cases was overruled by the enactment of British Columbia, s.84.)
4. New Brunswick, s.104(3); Newfoundland, s.124(3), which permits endeavours to persuade by the use of circular, press, radio or television.
5. Queen's Bench Act, C.C.S.M., 1987, c.C-280, s.58(2).
6. *Int'l Iron Workers* v. *Canadian Ironworkers* (1971) 21 D.L.R. (3d) 469 (S.C.C.); [1972] S.C.R. 295; *C.P.R.* v. *Teamsters* (1975) 60 D.L.R. (3d) 249 (B.C.C.A.).
7. *R. M. Hardy*, [1977] 2 C.L.R.B.R. (B.C.L.R.B.), and of *Oakmount Industries*, [1983] 1 C.L.R.B.R. (N.S.) 367 (B.C.L.R.B.).

736. Despite earlier indications to the contrary, the Charter of Rights and Freedoms could, conceivably, provide considerable additional constitutional protection for boycotts. In 1999 the Supreme Court of Canada held that statutory restrictions on consumer leafleting by a trade union at secondary locations in support of its dispute with its employer constituted unjustifiable restrictions on the workers' freedom of expression under the Charter. In *UFCW, Local 1518* v. *K-Mart Canada Ltd.*,[1] provisions of the B.C. Labour Code which prohibited secondary picketing, and defined picketing broadly to include leafleting in support of a consumer boycott, were challenged as being contrary to section 2(b) of the Charter. The union's members were leafleting at unorganized store locations operated by their employer in support of their lawful strike at an organized store. The Court held that the limitations on consumer leafleting in support of a boycott were unduly broad and could not be upheld as reasonable limits on worker freedom of expression. The Supreme Court stressed the differences between consumer leafleting and picketing as forms of expression deserving protection under the Charter. Picket lines were deemed to be inherently coercive and seen as barriers which impeded public access and employee access to workplaces, even when peaceful. Consumer leafleting in contrast sought to persuade members of the public to act through informed and rational discourse, something which is the very essence of freedom of expression. Thus leafleting in support of a boycott which is not defamatory or otherwise unlawful, is not conducted in a coercive, intimidating or otherwise unlawful or tortious manner, and does not unduly impede access to leafleted premises or prevent employees of secondary sites from working or interfere with other contractual relations of suppliers to the secondary sites will normally constitute a valid exercise of freedom of expression. Nor can such forms of peaceful leafleting be limited by overbroad prohibitions on secondary activity intended to minimize the harmful effects to third parties that could result from others impeding access to premises or to encourage employees to breach their contracts of employment.

1. (1999) 176 D.L.R. (4th) 607 (S.C.C.); [1999] 2 S.C.R. 1083. A similar result was reached in *UFCW, Local 1288P* v. *Allsco Builiding Products Ltd.* (1999) 176 D.L.R. (4th) 647 (S.C.C.); [1999] 1 S.C.R. 1136.

737. The potential impact of the *UFCW, Local 1518* v. *K-Mart Canada Ltd.* decision for broader protection of other secondary activity, including activity in support of a boycott other than leafleting, is very uncertain. The Court could later be taken to have merely carved out very limited protection for low key consumer leafleting which leaves it open for other forms of boycott activity, such as waving placards or the use of a hot cargo or struck work declaration, to be characterized as coercive or illegitimate forms of social pressure which are less deserving of constitutional protection, much like the characterization of peaceful secondary picketing in *K-Mart* itself.[1]

1. *See* MacNeil, 'Labour Picketing and Consumer Boycotts' *op. cit.*

§5. Remedies for Unlawful Industrial Action

A. Employer Self-help

738. An employer confronted with an illegal strike by his employees, or by unlawful conduct on the picket line during the course of a lawful strike may impose appropriate discipline, including outright dismissal.[1] However, the mere occurrence of unlawful industrial action does not of itself bring to an end any existing collective agreement.[2] Thus, the employer's self-help measures are liable to be tested in arbitration by employees who claim that they have been disciplined or discharged without just cause.[3] If no collective agreement is in force, the employer's action may still be tested under the unfair labour practice provisions of the Labour Relations Act, to determine if it is discriminatory or designed to interfere with the rights of employees,[4] rather than to vindicate the employer's legitimate business interests.[5]

1. *Supra.*
2. *McGavin Toastmaster* v. *Ainscough* (1975) 54 D.L.R. (3d) 1 (S.C.C.); [1976] 1 S.C.R. 718.
3. *See* generally C. D'Aoust, L. Leclerc and G. Trudeau, *Les mesures disciplinaires: Étude jurisprudentielle et doctrinale* (Montreal: Ecole de relations industrielles, Université de Montréal, 1982) 393–400; D.J.M. Brown and D.M. Beatty, *Canadian Labour Arbitration* (Aurora: Canada Law Inc., 3rd edn., 1992) para. 9.2400.
4. *Praesto Aluminium Products*, (1959) 59 C.L.L.C. para. 18,137 (O.L.R.B.); *Robinson, Little*, [1975] 2 C.L.R.B.R. 81 (B.C.L.R.B.); *Central Broadcasting*, [1975] 2 C.L.R.B.R. 65 (C.L.R.B.); *Hydro Electric Power Commission of Ontario*, [1969] O.L.R.B. Rep. 249, *aff'd* (1970), 70 C.L.L.C. para. 14,031 (Ont.C.A.).
5. *Perley Hospital*, [1981] 3 C.L.R.B.R. 1 (O.L.R.B.); *Lafrance* v. *Commercial Photo Service* (1980) 111 D.L.R. (3d) 310 (S.C.C.); [1980] 1 S.C.R. 536.

B. Legal Remedies: Introduction

739. As has been mentioned, a given instance of industrial action may be viewed from the perspective of several different legal regimes. For example, a strike which occurs during the currency of the collective agreement may be viewed (i) as a violation of the Labour Relations Act which prohibits such strikes (giving rise to possible administrative sanctions by the labour relations tribunal or to prosecution in the criminal courts); or (ii) as a violation of the no-strike clause in the agreement itself (giving rise to the possible award of damages by an arbitrator); or (iii) as a tort or delict (giving rise to an action for damages or an injunction in the ordinary civil courts).

740. There are, in general, no clear-cut legislative guidelines which force an aggrieved party to choose one avenue of recourse rather than another. Even in British Columbia, which purports to assign exclusive jurisdiction over most aspects of industrial conflict to the labour tribunal,[1] the courts have managed to find a basis for reasserting, and exercising their jurisdiction in tort.[2]

1. *See supra.*
2. *Better Value (chwk) Ltd.* v. *Vancouver Distribulion Centre* (1981) 122 D.L.R. (3d) 12 (B.C.C.A.).

741. For a long time it appeared that so long as a plaintiff found a way of framing her/his action in terms which were justiciable in the particular forum, that forum might take jurisdiction and deal with the matter on its merits. However, recently the Supreme Court of Canada deferred to arbitration for the assessment of damages for illegal strikes,[1] although it sustained a judicial right to grant injunctions.[2] The jurisprudential basis for the distinction between the power to award damages as opposed to the power to grant an injunction is questionable, but the decision indicates a willingness on the part of the highest court to defer to the special tribunals and mechanisms involved in regulating industrial conflict. This notion of a reluctance on the part of courts to take jurisdiction over unlawful concerted activity until specialist labour tribunal enforcement mechanisms have been tried and found lacking was reinforced in *Attorney General for Ontario* v. *O.T.F.*[3] Nevertheless, it is fair to say that not all civil court judges share the same degree of reluctance to exercise their jurisdiction when dealing with allegations of unlawful concerted activity.[4]

1. *St. Anne Nackawic Pulp and Paper Ltd.* v. *Canadian Paperworkers Union, Local 219*, [1986] 1 S.C.R. 704. Note that there may still be some room for the courts to entertain claims for damages arising out of illegal strikes in situations where arbitration is not available, such as recognition or jurisdictional strikes.
2. *I.B.E.W.* v. *Winnipeg Builders' Exchange*, [1967] S.C.R. 628 (S.C.C.). *Brotherhood of Maintenance and Way Employees* v. *C.P. Ltd.*, [1996] 2 S.C.R. 495.
3. (1997), 36 O.R. (3d) 367 (Ont.C.J.Gen.Div.). The Court refused to grant the government's request for an interlocutory injunction to bring an end to an unlawful province wide teacher's strike, in part because there had been no attempt to use the Ontario Labour Relations Board procedures to bring an end to the work stoppage before seeking the court injunction.
4. *See* the discussion of *Weber* v. *Ontario Hydro*, *infra*, at para. 756, concerning areas of overlapping jurisdiction between arbitration and civil courts when dealing with common law and Charter claims.

742. In the result, although each legal regime may tend towards a degree of internal coherence, there is no necessary predictability or consistency of outcome on any given set of facts when all possible avenues of redress are taken into account.

C. Administrative Remedies[1]

1. Declaration

743. Several labour relations tribunals have power to declare that a strike or lockout is unlawful. Originally a remedy with no compulsive effect, the declaration was nonetheless a useful device for educating the parties as to their rights in situations in which there was some doubt about the legality of a strike. Moreover, a mere declaration, unaccompanied by other sanctions, sometimes brought a strike to an end because it amounted to a useful prediction as to how a court would react to the legality of such conduct in a subsequent proceeding. During the 1970s, however, the declaration became increasingly the prelude to authoritative labour relations tribunal orders requiring cessation of illegal activity,[2] or triggering other important remedies.[3]

1. *See* generally: P.C. Weiler, 'The Administrative Tribunal: A View from the Inside' (1976) 26 U.T.L.J. 193; D.D. Carter, *The Expansion of Labour Board Remedies: A New Approach to Industrial Conflict* (Kingston, 1976); G.W. Adams, 'Labour Law Remedies', in Swan and Swinton *op. cit.*, c.3. In Quebec, where no labour relations board exists, no administrative remedies are available in case of unlawful industrial action. This situation will change in the near future when the amendments to the Labour Code that create a labour board will come into force.
2. Canada, s.91, as am. by S.C. 1991, c.39, s.3, S.C. 1998, c.26, s.45; Ontario, ss.100, 101.
3. Ontario, s.103, provides that following the making of a declaration, a claim for damages may be pursued though a special arbitration mechanism.

2. Investigation and settlement

744. Typically, labour relations tribunals which enjoy power to issue authoritative orders against illegal industrial action do so only after making preliminary efforts to solve the underlying industrial relations problems. Upon the filing of a complaint seeking the intervention of the tribunal, it usually despatches an official who meets informally with the parties and seeks to bring unlawful conduct to an end without recourse to further, formal proceedings. This effort may involve not merely pointed reminders to the employees of the consequences of continued illegality, but as well resolution of the differences which initially provoked it.

3. Cease and desist orders

745. Generally, labour relations tribunals have power to order an offending party to cease and desist from its illegal conduct.[1] This power is amplified, in some statutes, by explicit language permitting the tribunal to rectify underlying problems,[2] to withhold or attach conditions to such remedies in order to achieve equitable results,[3] to provide relief on an emergency basis,[4] and to modify any order in the light of subsequent developments.[5]

1. Canada, s.99, as am. by S.C. 1991, c.39, s.3, S.C. 1998, c.26, s.45; British Columbia, s.133; Ontario, ss.100, 101, 144.
2. Ontario, ss.100, 101; British Columbia, s.133.
3. British Columbia, s.133.
4. Nova Scotia, s.51, Ontario, s.98.
5. Nova Scotia, s.51(11); Canada, s.93(2).

4. *Enforcement*

746. Labour relations tribunals cannot enforce their own orders. That is why labour relations statutes typically provide that, once a board order or directive is filed with the appropriate court, it is to be enforced as if it were a court order.[1] Failure to conform to the order puts the union, its leaders and its members in jeopardy of being held in either (or both) civil or criminal contempt of court.[2]

1. Alberta, s.17(6); Ontario, s.102, 108; Manitoba, s.143(11).
2. *United Nurses of Alberta* v. *Attorney General (Alta.)* (1992), 92 C.L.L.C. para. 14,023 (S.C.C.); [1992] 1 S.C.R. 901.

D. Criminal and Quasi-criminal Sanctions

1. *Criminal Code*

747. The federal Criminal Code contains several offences pertinent to industrial conflict, commission of any one of which may result in prosecution, leading to fines or imprisonment. These offences include 'watching and besetting', i.e. coercive and obstructive picketing,[1] assault,[2] unlawful assembly,[3] criminal conspiracy,[4] and criminal breach of contract involving public utility workers.[5] In addition, two provisions of the Code of general application provide penalties for disobeying the order of a court,[6] and for violating a law for which no penalty is elsewhere expressly provided.[7]

However, as a practical matter, only assault charges are laid with any frequency, and then only following violent episodes on a picket line.

1. Criminal Code, s.423.
2. S.266.
3. S.63.
4. Ss.465, 466.
5. S.422.
6. S.127.
7. S.126.

2. *Labour Relations Acts*

748. Violation of the provisions of a Labour Relations Act or in some cases of orders made under the Act, is an offence punishable by summary procedure in the lower criminal courts.[1] In most jurisdictions there are particular fines for illegal strikes and lockouts, the amount of which depends upon the person charged and the length of the offence. Initiation of prosecutions for offences under the Labour Relations Act may require the prior consent of the labour relations tribunal.[2] The decision by a labour relations tribunal to allow prosecution is discretionary, and consent will not lightly be given. For example, the Ontario board has said that it will not allow prosecution to be used as 'a vehicle of retributive justice',[3] when strikers have been fired,[4] or selected randomly for prosecution,[5] or where the strike resulted from a genuine mistake as to the legal position of the union,[6] or has already been ended with no pattern of prior illegality or likely prospect of resumption.[7] Moreover, as with all labour relations tribunal proceedings, an application for consent to prosecute is usually the occasion for formal and informal settlement efforts. Prosecution itself is seen as the remedy of last resort.[8]

1. Ontario, s.98; Canada, ss.100, 101; Quebec, s.142.
2. Ontario, s.104; Canada, s.104.
3. *Savage Shoes* (1953) 53 C.L.L.C. para. 17,060 (O.L.R.B.).
4. *Canal Cartage*, [1961–2] O.L.R.B. 251; *Joyce and Smith Plating* (1956) 56 C.L.L.C. para. 18,049 (O.L.R.B.); *Toronto Western Hospital*, [1972] O.L.R.B. 1018.
5. *Canadian Elevator Manufacturers*, [1975] O.L.R.B. 722; *Arthur G. McKee*, [1976] O.L.R.B. 637.
6. *Savage Shoes* (1953) 53 C.L.L.C. para. 17,060 (O.L.R.B.).
7. *Foundation Co.*, [1971] O.L.R.B. 29.
8. *National Harbours Board*, [1979] 3 C.L.R.B.R. 513 (C.L.R.B.).

749. As a practical matter, apart from the reluctance of the labour relations tribunal to encourage prosecution, it is not a remedy much favoured by the parties as a means of enforcing their rights under labour legislation.[1] Criminal proceedings are slow and technical; proof to the standard of 'beyond a reasonable doubt' required in criminal cases is difficult; judges are generally unfamiliar with industrial relations or labour law; the effect of even a successful prosecution is likely to be a rather small fine – not an order prohibiting continuation or repetition of the offence; and the burden of the whole prosecutorial function is borne by the complainant rather than the state, which normally conducts prosecutions.

1. A.M. Minsky, *A Study of Consent to Prosecute Applications Disposed of by the Ontario Labour Relations Board from April 1, 1965 to March 31, 1968*, [1969–70] Pt. 1 O.L.R.B. (Supplement).

E. Civil Remedies

1. General

750. In affording relief to persons injured by unlawful industrial action, the courts ostensibly apply the ordinary law of civil wrongs – tort or delict and occasionally contract – although they increasingly place reliance upon labour relations legislation as the ultimate basis of liability.[1] The usual remedies in civil litigation are money damages and injunctions (prohibitory or mandatory orders). While occasionally civil remedies are sought by unions or employees against employers, typically it is employers who institute such proceedings. The following analysis assumes, unless otherwise noted, that the union is the defendant.

1. *Supra.*

2. *Problems of suing unions*

a. Union responsibility

751. When a wrong is committed during a labour dispute, liability may of course fall on the individual worker who has committed the act complained of – assault, defamation, inducing breach of contract, etc. But that individual's identity may be difficult to establish, her/his degree of participation obscure and, in any event, her/his assets so limited that a damage award against her/him would be worthless. Hence, the employer may prefer to proceed against the union. But whether the union or individual employees are to be named as defendants, if the dispute which is the cause of the claim can be said to arise expressly or inferentially from the collective agreement, grievance arbitration has exclusive jurisdiction over the claim, albeit that the conduct of the defendant might also comprise all the requirements for a successful action in tort or contract or for breach of the Charter.[1]

1. *See Weber* v. *Ontario Hydro*, [1995] 2 S.C.R. 929; and *New Brunswick* v. *O'Leary*, [1995] 2 S.C.R. 967. In the latter case the employer was barred from maintaining an action in negligence against one of its employees for damage caused to machinery at work. *See* additional discussion of *Weber* at para. 756 *infra*.

752. The question thus arises as to when the union itself can be made responsible. Clearly, a union will be held liable for conduct which it officially authorizes, encourages or directs, or in which its responsible officials participate.[1] However, insofar as wrongful conduct is that of mere rank-and-file members or of stewards or other junior union officials, the union's responsibility is more difficult to establish. Essentially, the union itself will be held liable for unauthorized and illegal industrial action only if it fails to take reasonable measures to dissociate itself from such action, and to bring any unlawfulness to an end.[2] Such action by the union includes publicly broadcasted directives to the union members to return to work and discipline.[3] However, in practice this question is not always addressed. The union will often feel obliged to stand behind its members and officers if they are sued in their personal capacities, although no question arises of the union's direct or vicarious liability.

1. *U.S.W.A.* v. *Gaspé Copper Mines* (1970) 10 D.L.R. (3d) 443 (S.C.C.); [1970] S.C.R. 362, but *cf. Western Construction & Lumber* v. *Jorgensen* (1973) 40 D.L.R. (3d) 613 (S.C.C.); [1974] S.C.R. 826. For a recent statement that trade unions are to be held legally responsible for unlawful strike activity see *United Nurses of Alberta* v. *Attorney General* (Alta) (1992) 92 C.L.L.C. para. 14,023 (S.C.C.); [1992] 1 S.C.R. 901. *See also* C. D'Aoust and L. Verschelden, *Le droit québécois de la responsabilité civile des syndicats en cas de grève illégale* (Montreal: Ecole de relations industrielles, Université de Montréal, 1980).
2. *Re New Brunswick Electric Power Commission and I.B.E.W.* (1976) 73 D.L.R. (3d) 94 (N.B.C.A.); *Oliver Sawmills* v. *I.W.A.* (1969) D.L.R. (3d) 48 (B.C.C.A.).
3. *A.G. for Newfoundland* v. *Newfoundland Association of Public Employees* (1976) 74 D.L.R. (3d) 195 (Nfld.S.C.).

b. The juridical status of unions

753. Most labour relations statutes implicitly or explicitly make unions legal entities for purposes of proceedings under those statutes. But, at common law, a union was simply an unincorporated collection of individuals with no legal personality; it could neither sue nor defend in its own name in ordinary civil proceedings.[1]

1. D.J. Sherbaniuk, 'Actions by and against Trade Unions in Contract and Tort' (1957–8), 12 U.T.L.J. 151.

754. The inconsistency between these two views of the union's status had to be resolved, especially in cases where the substantive basis of liability was framed as a common law action, although in fact heavy reliance was placed on the union's alleged contravention of the letter or spirit of a labour relations statute. In the pivotal case of *Therien*,[1] the Supreme Court of Canada held that a union had wrongly interfered with the economic interests of the plaintiff by threatening to picket a construction project on which he was engaged, in order to enforce its view that the collective agreement precluded his presence; 'wrongfulness' resided in the union's failure to seek arbitration of the relevant provisions of the collective agreement, contrary to its terms, and the provisions of the Labour Relations Act. The Court went on to hold that the union was itself answerable in damages, on the grounds that the Labour Relations Act had conferred rights and obligations upon unions, thus impliedly endowing them with juridical status sufficient to make them subject to civil suits, although such an intention was not expressly manifested by the words of the statute. Although criticized in the literature, this decision now prevails in all Canadian jurisdictions,[2] except Ontario and Saskatchewan where legislation[3] expressly preserves the union's former common law immunity from suit.[4] In Quebec, legislation predating the *Therien* decision, expressly gave legal status to unions. *See supra*, paras. 391–3.

1. *Teamsters* v. *Therien* (1960) 22 D.L.R. (2d) 1 (S.C.C.); [1962] S.C.R. 265.
2. Most recently, in the federal sphere: *I.L.A.* v. *Maritime Employers' Assoc.* (1978) 89 D.L.R. (3d) 289 (S.C.C.); [1979] 1 S.C.R. 120.
3. Rights of Labour Act, R.S.O. 1990, c.R-33, s.3(2); The Trade Union Act, R.S.S. 1978, c.T-17.
4. *Nipissing Hotel* v. *Hotel & Restaurant Employees* (1963) 38 D.L.R. (2d) 675 (Ont.H.C.).

755. Even before the *Therien* decision, however, unions did not, and now do not, enjoy complete immunity from suit. First, as mentioned, they often choose to stand behind individual members who are sued and to pay for their legal representation and any damage awards that might be made against them. Second, court rules in many jurisdictions provide that a member of an unincorporated group may be appointed by the court to act as its representative for purposes of litigation.[1] By this device of a 'representative action' a union might in effect be sued, although this possibility was diminished by a judicial gloss restricting representation orders to cases where the group has a common interest in a fund specifically designated as being available for the payment of damages;[2] few unions obligingly maintain such funds. Third, in injunction proceedings, an employer is entitled to seek relief against named individual defendants, but as well against 'their servants and agents, and anyone acting with knowledge' of the court's order, in effect all other members of the union.[3] And finally, some statutes specifically make unions suable entities.[4] *See* paras. 394–6, *supra*.

1. E.g. *Supreme Court of Ontario Rules of Practice*, R.R.O. 1980, Reg. 540 Rule 12. Note, however, that where the Rights of Labour Act prevents a union from suing or being sued a representative form cannot be used to do indirectly what the statute prevents from being done directly: *Seafarers' Int'l. Union* v. *Lawrence* (1980) 97 D.L.R. (3d) 324 (Ont.C.A.).
2. *Body* v. *Murdoch*, [1954] O.W.N. 658 (H.C.).
3. *I.L.A.* v. *Maritime Employers Assoc.*, *supra*.
4. Alberta, s.25(1)(b); Manitoba, s.127(3); Prince Edward Island, s.44(1); New Brunswick, s.114(2); Newfoundland, s.137(1). An old, unrepealed, federal statute, Trade Unions Act, S.C. 1872, c.30, afforded trade unions the opportunity to register if they wished to hold property; if they chose to register, they would also be liable to suit. Virtually no trade unions registered.

3. Common law actions to enforce collective agreements[1]

756. Collective agreements could not be sued upon at common law.[2] This position was called into question in a lower court judgment on the grounds that the Labour Relations Act was tantamount to legislative recognition of the collective agreement, and the reversal of the common law position,[3] an inference clearly precluded in Ontario.[4] This was followed by the Supreme Court of Canada's holding that it should not enter upon the interpretation of collective agreements where arbitration is established as the exclusive forum for their enforcement.[5] It might be assumed, therefore, that the employer could not bring an action in the regular courts to enforce the no-strike provisions of a collective agreement. However, without clearly addressing its own self-imposed rule against interpreting a collective agreement, the Supreme Court later granted injunctive relief against industrial action which violated the no-strike provisions of a collective agreement.[6]

Commencing with its 1986 decision in *St. Anne Nackawic Pulp and Paper Ltd.* v. *Canadian Paperworkers Union, Local 219*, the Supreme Court of Canada has moved toward a position of strong deference to arbitration as the appropriate forum to deal with all claims arising out of the collective agreement.[7] In that case the Court said arbitrators should have exclusive jurisdiction to consider claims for damages for violation of the collective agreement, including claims for damages arising from an unlawful strike. This ruling was extended considerably in the Court's 1995 decision in *Weber* v. *Ontario Hydro*.[8] The majority held that if the differences between the parties creating the dispute expressly or inferentially arise out of the collective agreement, arbitration is the exclusive remedy, and courts are precluded from entertaining the action. The question in each case is whether the dispute, viewed with an eye to its essential character, arises from the collective agreement. One should consider the dispute and the ambit of the collective agreement to decide whether the dispute, in its essential character, can be said to arise out of the collective agreement. The test is one which focuses on the factual nature and context of the dispute, not the legal characterization of issues or forms of pleading. This applies to claims alleging violation of Charter rights as well as claims in contract and tort. However, where arbitrators lack the power to provide an appropriate remedy, courts may exercise their inherent jurisdiction so that the grievor will not be deprived of an ultimate and effective remedy.[9] However, *Weber* has created considerable confusion and inconsistency in lower court decisions concerning the expansion of jurisdiction of arbitrators to apply common law doctrine and remedies to disputes arising from the workplace and retraction of court jurisdiction. The ultimate implications of *Weber* for the boundaries of exclusive arbitral jurisdiction remain very uncertain and have been the subject of considerable academic comment.[10]

1. *Supra.*
2. In *Young* v. *Canadian Northern Railway*, [1931] A.C. 83 (P.C.), the Privy Council – then Canada's final appellate court – held that if the employer violated the collective agreement 'the effective sequel would be, not an action by any employee, not even an action by [the union] against the employer for specific performance or damages, but the calling of a strike until the grievance was remedied' (at 89). A 1924 statute, the Professional Syndicates Act, R.S.Q. c.S-40, resolved this problem partially in Quebec.
3. *Nelsons Laundries Ltd.* v. *Manning* (1965) 51 D.L.R. (2d) 537 (B.C.S.C.). This result was specifically accomplished by statute in Manitoba, s.127(2).
4. Ontario Rights of Labour Act, R.S.O. 1990, c.R-33, s.3(3).
5. *Hamilton Street Railway* v. *Northcott* (1966) 58 D.L.R. (2d) 708 (S.C.C.); [1996] S.C.R. 3.; *General Motors* v. *Brunet*, [1977] 2 S.C.R. 537.
6. *I.B.E.W.* v. *Winnipeg Builders' Exchange* (1967) 65 D.L.R. (2d) 242 (S.C.C.); [1967] S.C.R. 628; *I.L.A.* v. *Maritime Employers' Assoc.* (1978) 89 D.L.R. (3d) 289 (S.C.C.); [1979] 1 S.C.R. 120.
7. *Supra.*
8. [1995] 2 S.C.R. 929.
9. *See*, for example, *Brotherhood of Maintenance and Way Employees* v. *C.P. Ltd.*, [1996] 2 S.C.R. 495, concerning the continuing jurisdiction of courts to issue injunctions to prevent irreparable harm pending the outcome of grievance arbitration where arbitrators lack authority to provide injunctive relief.
10. *See* Adell, 'Jurisdictional Overlap Between Arbitration and Other Forums: an Update'; Carter 'Looking at *Weber* Five Years Later: Is It Time for a New Approach?'; and MacDowell, 'Labour Arbitration – The New Labour Court?'; all in (2000) 8 C.L.E.L.J. 121–252.

4. *Damages*

a. Compensatory damages

757. Damages are primarily intended to restore the injured party to the *status quo ante*. However, courts have not been willing to scrutinize with excessive care the causal relationship between the wrong done by the defendant and the loss suffered by the plaintiff. For example, in one case, the court held that a technical breach of strike vote procedures not only made the strike itself unlawful, but fixed liability upon the union for all business loss subsequently suffered by the employer due to either the strike or to activities supporting it.[1] However, arbitrators have been more careful to require that the employer's entitlement to damages depends on its ability to meet the burden of proving the existence of a loss and a sufficient causal connection between the union's breach of the agreement and the loss claimed.[2] In this regard, it is important to note that following *St. Anne Nackawic*, *supra*, and *Weber*, *supra*, courts will seldom take jurisdiction to award damages for illegal strikes. Arbitrators now have exclusive jurisdiction over such claims where there is a collective agreement in place and labour legislation in several jurisdictions provides a mechanism for addressing damage issues following a declaration that a strike is illegal without recourse to courts.[3]

1. *Jacobson Bros.* v. *Anderson* (1962) 35 D.L.R (2d) 746 (N.S.S.C.).
2. *City of Waterloo and C.U.P.E., Local 1542* (1995) 50 L.A.C. (4th) 197 (Williamson).
3. Ontario, s.103.

b. Punitive or exemplary damages

758. Where there is a deliberate or calculated infliction of harm,[1] rather than a mere failure, to bring an illegal strike to an end,[2] in addition to any compensatory damages, a court may also award a sizeable, discretionary sum to punish the defendant for high-handed conduct, and to discourage repetition of the act in the future. However, punitive damages should only be awarded where the defendant's misconduct is so malicious, oppressive and high-handed that it offends the court's sense of decency.[3] It must be noted, however, that except in some exceptional situations, punitive damages cannot be awarded under the Quebec civil law since civil damages must always be compensatory.[4] It should also be noted that in declaring arbitral authority to award damages for unlawful strikes in *Polymer and Oil, Chemical and Atomic Workers*,[5] Professor Laskin stressed that arbitrators did not have a punitive function or sit in some quasi-criminal capacity. They should award damages on a compensatory basis, attempting to put the innocent party in the position it would have been if there had been no breach of the agreement, in so far as that was possible. While there is some suggestion in arbitral jurisprudence that arbitrators have a very limited authority to award punitive damages in rare cases,[6] the more prevalent view is that arbitrators should refuse to award punitive damages for unlawful work stoppages.[7]

1. *Johnston Terminals & Storage* v. *Miscellaneous Workers* (1975) 61 D.L.R. (3d) 741 (B.C.S.C.); *Canadian Ironworkers* v. *Int'l. Ironworkers* (1973) 31 D.L.R. (3d) 750 (B.C.S.C.), aff'd. (1947) 45 D.L.R. (3d) 768n (B.C.C.A.).
2. *Weins Contracting* v. *MacMillan Bloedel (Alberni)* (1973) 40 D.L.R. (3d) 593 (B.C.S.C.).
3. *Matusiak* v. *B.C. and Yukon Building and Construction Trades Council*, [1999] B.C.J. No. 2416 (B.C.S.C.); citing *Hill* v. *Church of Scientology*, [1995] 2 S.C.R. 1130.
4. *See* s.1621 C.c.Q.; J.-L. Baudouin and P. Deslauriers, *La responsabilité civile*, 5th edn. (Cowansville: Les Editions Yvon Blais Inc., 1999) 177–98.
5. (1959), 10 L.A.C. 51.
6. *Ontario Hydro and C.U.P.E., Local 1000* (1990) 16 L.A.C. (4th) 264 (Kates).
7. *City of Waterloo and C.U.P.E., Local 1542* (1995) 50 L.A.C. (4th) 197 (Williamson).

c. Mitigation or diminution of damages

759. As a matter of general principle, any plaintiff is under a duty to act in her/his own self-interest in order to minimize her/his loss. S/he cannot simply stand by following the defendant's wrong, and allow financial consequences to multiply. This general principle presumably applies to tort actions arising out of industrial action as well. Moreover, it has been argued that the courts ought to reduce damages to which a plaintiff employer would otherwise be entitled if he has acted improperly in such a way as to provoke the illegal industrial action of which he complains. The Supreme Court of Canada has rejected this argument on the particular facts of a case in which it was raised, but not as a matter of principle.[1] The principle of mitigation is also applied by arbitrators.

1. *U.S.W.A.* v. *Gaspé Copper Mines* (1970) 10 D.L.R. (3d) 443 (S.C.C.); [1970] S.C.R. 362, *cf. Brown's Bread* v. *Bakery Workers*, [1971] W.W.R. 577 (Man. Q.B.).

d. Extended liability

760. Normally, a wrongdoer is civilly liable only to someone whom s/he deliberately or foreseeably injures by her/his wrong. A strike, or other industrial action, however, may trigger a chain of consequences by which a struck employer is, for example, unable to supply promised goods to her/his customers, and they to theirs. A union will presumably, not be liable for such extended consequences, so long as its strike is a lawful one.[1] However, when the strike is unlawful, it is at least possible that a union may be fixed with liability.[2]

1. This principle seems generally to be accepted at common law, and is made explicit in Newfoundland, s.99.
2. Manitoba, s.127(1) imposes liability upon anyone violating the Act 'for general or special damages, or both, to *anyone* who is injured or suffers damages by the violation'. *See also Canadian Ironworkers* v. *Int'l. Iron Workers* (1970) 13 D.L.R. (3d) 559 (B.C.C.A.).

5. Injunctions

a. General[1]

761. The injunction has been by far the most frequently sought remedy in conflict situations. It has the attraction of being available speedily with relatively little formality of proof or pleading, and of stopping illegality and the resulting loss or damage, rather than attempting to compensate for it.

1. A classic American work on this subject, F. Frankfurter and N. Greene, *The Labour Injunction* (New York, 1930) contains much historical and scholarly criticism which would apply to Canadian injunction law. Two important Canadian studies are A.W.R. Carrothers, *The Labour Injunction in British Columbia* (Toronto, 1956) and A.W.R. Carrothers and E.E. Palmer, *Report of a Study on the Labour Injunction in Ontario*, esp. Part I, H. Krever, *The Labour Injunction in Ontario: Procedures and Practice* (Toronto, 1966). In Quebec, a similar study was conducted by F. Morin, '*L'injonction en temps de grève*' (1977) 32 *Rel. Ind.* 414.

762. On the other hand, the injunction has also given rise to great political and social controversy. First, the very virtues of speed and informality have been seen to involve an undue sacrifice of procedural fairness. Second, the courts' intervention is limited to the suppression of illegality (itself defined according to rather vague common law standards) and is not directed to the underlying causes of conflict. Third, there has been the appearance of anti-unionism in the reaction of some judges to strikes and picketing. As a result, reforms during the 1970s in various Canadian jurisdictions have either entirely displaced the injunction or radically altered the procedure by which it is obtained. Despite this, it is still relatively easy to obtain an injunction to restrict collective action by workers in most Canadian jurisdictions.

b. Procedural problems

763. Injunctions may be granted either temporarily (interlocutory injunctions) or permanently. Permanent injunctions are granted only after a full-scale trial, but because of delays in mounting such trials, they are almost never sought. Temporary injunctions are granted, typically, upon motion, supported only by affidavit evidence, on brief notice or no notice, and on the explicit understanding that they will last only for a fixed period of days, or until the trial of the action. While summary procedures are the key to the usefulness of temporary injunctions, they do undoubtedly pose problems.

764. Where an injunction against picketing is given without notice (*ex parte*) even for a few days, the effect may be to disrupt and demoralize the union's activities. If it should turn out that the injunction was wrongly obtained, and even though it is ultimately dissolved, the employer will still have won a tactical advantage. Even when an injunction is given on notice, typically only of two days' duration, a union's chance to prepare reply evidence is very limited. Moreover, the use of affidavit evidence offers the employer an opportunity for artful equivocation or distortion of the facts in order to elicit the judge's sympathy. It is very difficult, as a practical matter, to either cross-examine or rebut witnesses (deponents) whose affidavits are the only evidence before the court. Because motions are hurriedly scheduled, usually in courts crowded with other business, and heard in an atmosphere of urgency, the opportunity for extended argument and calm deliberation is not easily achieved. And because, in principle, the injunction is only temporary and in prospect of a future full-scale trial (which, however, seldom occurs) rights of appeal against the granting of a temporary injunction are severely limited. Finally, although the plaintiff must promise to indemnify the defendant if it should turn out that the injunction has been wrongly obtained, in practice the defendant almost never has a chance to enforce this promise, since the matter becomes moot after the injunction has run for even a limited period.

765. Added to all of these problems are the facts that courts of general jurisdiction contain relatively few judges who have specialist knowledge of industrial relations or labour law; that such courts lack power to make an independent investigation of the facts or to probe, let alone resolve, the underlying controversies; and that ordinary doctrines of tort, delict or contract administered by them are somewhat obscure and not necessarily consistent with contemporary industrial relations policies and realities.

766. As will be seen, some of these problems have been addressed by reforming legislation.

c. The scope of injunctions: conduct and persons

767. A temporary injunction is, in theory, intended to hold matters in status quo pending trial. It is thus essentially negative in character, and orders that wrongful conduct should cease. Because such an order interferes with the defendant's freedom of action, certain doctrines had emerged in non-labour situations which were designed to avoid overreaching. A plaintiff, for example, was required to show that he had a strong prima facie case which would likely prevail at trial; that the balance of convenience lay in favour of restricting the defendant rather than allowing him to continue her/his conduct; and that any harm done by the defendant would be irreparable in the sense that it could not be compensated by the payment of money damages. In the light of such doctrines, it is rather surprising, for example, that an injunction has been given anticipatorily to restrain possible future unlawful behaviour, the occurrence of which is neither imminent nor certain.[1] Indeed, none of these limiting doctrines is rigorously adhered to in the context of labour injunction litigation, although all of them are occasionally reaffirmed by *dicta* in the higher courts.[2] Some courts take the view that in the case of injunctions to prevent or stop an illegal strike all that is required is proof of a prima facie case and proof that the conduct is or will be a violation of the applicable labour law statute.[3] On the rare occasions when the three criteria for an interlocutory injunction are applied rigorously the case stands out as an exception to the norm.[4]

1. *Foundation Co.* v. *McGloin* (1964) 42 D.L.R. (2d) 209 (Ont.H.C.). For a more recent example *see R.S.D.W.U., Local 580* v. *Dolphin Delivery*, [1986] 2 S.C.R. 573.
2. E.g. *Trus Joist* v. *United Carpenters, Local 1598*, [1982] 6 W.W.R. 744 (B.C.S.C.).
3. *See*, for example, *Corner Brook Pulp and Paper Ltd.* v. *C.E.P.U., Local 60N*, [1999] N.J. No. 223 (Nfld.S.C.T.D.).
4. *Attorney General for Ontario* v. *O.T.F.* (1997) 36 O.R. (3d) 367 (Ont.C.J.Gen.Div.).

768. Because injunctive relief was, historically, administered by the courts of equity, in principle, a plaintiff seeking such relief must come to the court 'with clean hands', i.e. he or she must not himself or herself be guilty of conduct which is unconscionable or improper. On occasion, the argument has been made that an employer, seeking an injunction, ought not to receive it, although otherwise entitled, because he or she has behaved unacceptably in the conduct of his or her relationship with his or her employees or their union. This argument has seldom persuaded courts to exercise their discretion to withhold the relief sought.[1]

1. *A.G. Canada* v. *Whitelock* (1973) 37 D.L.R. (3d) 757 (B.C.S.C.). More recently *see Corner Brook Pulp and Paper Ltd., supra.*

769. Moreover, because the injunction is sought at the instance of a private party, the plaintiff must normally sue to vindicate some interest of her/his own. An injunction will not, in principle, lie at the suit of a private party to enforce the criminal law or other statutes protecting the public interest.[1] This doctrine has also been abandoned in practice in the context of labour injunction litigation, and the courts will in fact enjoin conduct upon an allegation of injury by the plaintiff, merely because it amounts to a violation of the Labour Relations Act[2] or the Criminal Code, and without regard to whether the plaintiff actually pleads a cause of action based on the violation of some right personal to herself/himself. Recently the Supreme Court of Canada has held that superior courts have jurisdiction to grant interim injunctions even where there is no cause of action or claim for final relief that will be ultimately determined by those courts. In *Brotherhood of Maintenance and Way Employees* v. *C.P. Ltd.*, the Court held that courts have jurisdiction to grant an injunction wherever there is a justiciable right, regardless of where that right might ultimately fall to be determined. In that case an injunction was granted to preserve the status quo until the ultimate issue of the authority of the employer to implement a new shift schedule could be resolved in grievance arbitration.[3]

1. *Robinson* v. *Adams*, [1925] 1 D.L.R. 359 (Ont.C.A.).
2. *I.L.A.* v. *Maritime Employers, supra.*
3. [1996] 2 S.C.R. 495. A determination that the arbitrator lacked authority to provide interim injunctive relief to prevent irreparable harm was critical to the Court's decision.

770. Injunctions are, in principle, designed to restrict unlawful conduct. In the context of picketing, especially, the labour injunction has become a rather refined instrument. For example, the courts will often stipulate by injunction that a union is limited in its picketing to a fixed number of persons patrolling a designated area, that particular offending words on a picket sign be removed, that picket line conduct be modified in stipulated ways, or that union officers issue statements to their members to ensure compliance with the court's orders. In effect, the courts have become intimately involved in the case-by-case development of a detailed code of picketing, a task for which, critics argue, they are ill equipped.

771. The issuance of injunctions requiring strikers to return to work has been an especially radical development in the scope of the injunction, given that its traditional role was to preserve existing situations by stopping unlawful conduct. Also such injunctions are even more surprising in view of the historic reluctance of the law to require performance of employment contracts, except by providing damages upon breach. But the Supreme Court of Canada has clearly set aside any such traditional inhibitions, and has authorized the issuance of such orders.[1]

1. *I.B.E.W.* v. *Winnipeg Builders' Exchange, supra.*

772. Finally, an injunction is in principle directed against a named wrongdoer. That defendant thus has the opportunity to challenge factual allegations against her/him and to persuade the court that her/his conduct does not constitute an actionable wrong. But labour injunctions are typically directed to a named defendant, 'his servants or agents, and anyone having knowledge of the order'. There can be little objection to an order which binds persons acting on behalf of the named defendant. However, the restriction upon the rights of 'persons having knowledge' is more questionable, and not merely because such an order was unknown in traditional injunction practice. A general order of this sort binds people who have no advance knowledge of the proceeding, and thus no chance to influence the scope of the order as it might affect them. Not being parties to the action, they lack standing either to seek modification of the original or to appeal it. And, of course, their interests or circumstances may differ from those of the named defendants. Nonetheless, the practice of framing injunctions in this way has received the *imprimatur* of Canada's highest court.[1]

1. *I.L.A.* v. *Maritime Employer's, supra.*

d. Enforcement

773. Disobedience of an injunction is contempt of court, so-called 'civil' contempt. But any conduct, including disobedience, by any person, whether a party to the proceeding or not, amounts to the much more serious offence of 'criminal' contempt, if it interferes with the administration of justice. In either case, a court whose order has been disobeyed has the power summarily to try the contemnor and impose sanctions in its discretion.[1] These sanctions may include imprisonment until the contempt is purged by compliance, or penalties such as fixed terms of imprisonment and heavy fines imposed upon both unions and individuals.

1. For a discussion of the relationship between civil and criminal contempt and the appropriate role of the criminal contempt in industrial disputes *see* the majority and dissenting decisions in *United Nurses of Alberta* v. *Attorney General (Alta), supra.* The majority of the Court held that the offence of criminal contempt does not infringe the Charter.

774. At various periods in recent Canadian labour history, the use of the contempt power to enforce labour injunctions has aroused great political controversy[1] and, ultimately, led to various projects of law reform.

1. Amongst the more controversial examples of the use of the contempt power are its invocation against an alleged political demonstration against injunctions, *Re Tilco Plastics* v. *Skurjat* [1966] 2 O.R. 547 (H.C.), the jailing of 44 senior leaders of *le front commun* of public service unions in Quebec, *A.G. Quebec* v. *Charbonneau* (1974) 40 D.L.R. (3d) 65 (Que.C.A.), and the jailing of postal union leaders following their failure to obey legislation, and a supporting court order, requiring them to end a strike, *R.* v. *Parrot* (1979) 106 D.L.R. (3d) 296 (Ont.C.A.).

e. Law reform

775. Given the intensity of resentment against labour injunctions and the apparent validity of some of the criticisms made against them, it is not surprising that several Canadian jurisdictions have adopted reforming statutes.

776. The most far-reaching of these is the Labour Relations Code of British Columbia[1] which specifically deprives the civil courts of the power to issue injunctions against strikes or picketing, except in cases involving immediate and serious danger to individuals, or physical damage to property.[2] In place of the courts' injunction jurisdiction, the Labour Relations Board is given full remedial powers in relation to industrial action.[3]

1. H.W. Arthurs, '"The Dullest Bill": Reflections on the Labour Code of British Columbia' (1974) 9 U.B.C.L. Rev. 280 discussing an earlier statute, which does not significantly modify the tribunal's jurisdiction to regulate industrial action.

2. Labour Relations Code R.S.B.C. 1996, c.244, s.137(2).
3. B.C., ss.133–6.

777. Ontario has adopted a more tentative approach. Injunction procedures have been substantially reformed, particularly in relation to problems of proof, notice, and other aspects of fairness.[1] Indeed, there is some suggestion that so long as the controversy involves a 'labour dispute', as that term is statutorily defined,[2] no injunction may issue except after unsuccessful recourse to police action.[3] By implication, such a holding would confine the issuance of labour injunctions to cases involving violence and obstruction and other matters of a criminal nature, leaving the remaining aspects of illegality to be dealt with by the labour relations board. The labour relations board, in turn, has acquired extensive new remedial powers in relation to industrial action which is forbidden by the Labour Relations Act.[4] However, the Labour Relations Act does not purport to be an integrated and complete code, as does the Labour Relations Act of British Columbia, and there is conduct to which it is apparently not addressed. It would seem unlikely, therefore, that the courts will ultimately be prepared (in the absence of express legislation such as the Labour Relations Act of British Columbia) to concede to the labour relations board plenary and exclusive jurisdiction over industrial action.[5] However, as the courts exercise greater restraint when it comes to granting injunctions to restrict secondary picketing, the labour board has extended its remedial powers in order to regulate such behaviour.[6]

1. Courts of Justice Act, R.S.O. 1990, s.102. *See also* Newfoundland, s.130; Albert, s.112.
2. Courts of Justice Act, s.102(1). *Darrigo's Grape Juice* v. *Masterson*, [1971] 3 O.R. 772 (H.C.), held that secondary picketing was not a 'labour dispute'.
3. Courts of Justice Act, s.102(3); *Charterways Transportations* v. *Alexander* (1975) 9 O.R. (2d) 198 (H.C.); *Sasso Disposal* v. *Webster* (1975) 10 O.R. (2d) 304 (H.C.); *Blue Circle Canada Inc.* v. *Felder*, [1998] Carswell Ont 1689 (O.C.J.Gen.Div.).
4. *Supra.*
5. But *see Re C.J.M.S. Radio Montreal* v. *C.L.R.B.* (1978) 91 D.L.R. (3d) 388 (Fed.T.C.); *McKinlay Transport* v. *Goodman* (1978) 90 D.L.R. (3d) 689 (Fed.T.C.); *Chevron* v. *Teamsters* (1978) 91 D.L.R. (3d) 649 (B.C.S.C.); *NABET* v. *A.G. Canada* (1979) 79 C.L.L.C. 14,231 (Fed.C.A.). *See also A.B. McLean Ltd.* v. *U.S.W., Local 2251*, [1991] 91 C.L.L.C. 14,018 (Ont.Ct.(Gen.Div.))
6. *Consolidated-Bathurst Packaging*, [1982] 3 C.L.R.B.R. 324 (O.L.R.B.) and the subsequent amendment to then s.92 (now s.100) C.34, s.2.

778. Manitoba is unique among Canadian jurisdictions in that it defines picketing as the exercise of free speech,[1] and specifically prohibits a court from issuing an injunction which restrains a person from exercising her/his right to free speech.[2] Consequently, peaceful picketing, regardless of its object, is permitted.[3]

1. Queen's Bench (Court of) Act, C.C.S.M. 1987, C.280, s.58(2).
2. S.60.2(1).
3. There are, however, certain enumerated exceptions contained in s.60.2(3). Note also that a claim for damages is still available.

F. Arbitration

779. Collective agreements, usually by compulsion of statute, contain a promise that there will be no strike or lockout for the duration of the agreement. They also contain, again usually by compulsion of statute, a provision for arbitration of all alleged violations of the no-strike clause. It follows that, if a strike occurs in violation of a no-strike clause, the aggrieved employer may have recourse against the union in arbitration. And following the Supreme Court of Canada decisions in *St. Anne Nackawic*, *supra*, and *Weber*, *supra*, arbitrators have exclusive jurisdiction over claims for damages for illegal strikes in contravention of a collective agreement.

780. The arbitrator has effective remedial powers. Most importantly, he may award money damages for an unlawful strike. The leading authority on the remedial jurisdiction of arbitrators, and in particular their jurisdiction to award damages for breaches of the collective agreement including unlawful strikes, is the decision by Professor Laskin in *Polymer and Oil, Chemical and Atomic Workers.* Professor Laskin rejected the union argument that arbitrators lacked jurisdiction to award remedies which were not expressly authorized by the collective agreement. Instead, he ruled that the legislative policy of requiring the parties to submit to grievance arbitration for final and binding resolution of their disputes would be undermined if arbitrators were denied the jurisdiction to order the remedies necessary to provide a final and binding resolution.[1] Damages may include all business loss incurred by the employer as a result of the interruption of work,[2] although the sum may be reduced if the employer has, in some way, contributed to her/his own loss by provocative or inept response to the union's concerns.[3] It is also possible that the arbitrator may have authority to enjoin future violations of the agreement.[4]

1. (1959), 10 L.A.C. 51. Upheld in *Re Polymer and Oil Workers Union* (1962) 33 D.L.R. (2d) 124 (S.C.C.); [1962] S.C.R. 338.
2. *Maritime Employers' Assoc.* (1975) 10 L.A.C. (2d) 225; *Windsor Star* (1974) 4 L.A.C. (2d) 207; *Canadian Kenilworth* v. *C.A.I.M.A.W. Local 14* (1982) 82 C.L.L.C. para. 14,173 (B.C.C.A.).
3. *Lake Ontario Steel* (1968) 19 L.A.C. 260.
4. *Re Samuel Cooper and Ladies' Garment Workers* (1973) 35 D.L.R. (3d) 501 (Ont.H.C.).

781. Of course, recourse to arbitration generally assumes the existence of a collective agreement, and is available only when the employer alleges violation of the no-strike clause, one of the terms of the agreement. If there is no agreement in force, or if the industrial action took some form other than a strike, arbitration is not normally available. However, the relative attractions of arbitration as a forum for determining the consequences of illegal strikes has led Ontario to provide access to arbitration to deal with damage claims arising out of illegal strikes, even when there is no collective agreement in effect.[1]

1. Ontario, s.103.

Chapter VI. Collective Agreements

782. The making of a collective agreement represents the culmination of the collective bargaining process. At this stage the union and the employer have not only defined their future relationship but they have also established the terms and conditions of employment for all of the employees in the bargaining unit. The legal incidents flowing from the collective agreement and its administration now form a very large part of Canadian labour law.

§1. The Collective Agreement

A. Legal Requirements

783. In order for arrangements between an employer and trade union to be considered as collective agreements they must be sufficiently formalized. Canadian collective bargaining law generally requires that such arrangements be in writing,[1] and that the assent of the trade union and employer be evidenced by the signatures of persons having the authority to act on their behalf.[2] An unconditional memorandum of settlement reached upon the completion of negotiations would appear to be considered as a binding collective agreement provided that it sets out the agreement of the parties with sufficient particularity, even though the parties might intend to replace it with a more formal document at some later date.[3] Where the agreement is made subject to ratification, however, it would not be treated as binding until the fact of ratification has been established.[4]

1. Canada, s.3(1); British Columbia, s.1(1); Ontario, s.1(1); Quebec, s.1(d).
2. *Graphic Centre*, [1976] 2 C.L.R.B.R. 118 (O.L.R.B.).
3. *John Inglis*, [1974] 1 C.L.R.B.R. 481 (B.C.L.R.B.); *Ferranti-Packard*, [1977] 1 C.L.R.B.R. 503 (O.L.R.B.).
4. *Ibid.*

784. Some Canadian jurisdictions have legislative provisions allowing only one collective agreement to be made for a bargaining unit during any particular period of time.[1] This requirement, however, does not prohibit the parties from entering into supplementary agreements relating to such matters as pension and insurance plans provided that such arrangements do not contradict the terms of the collective agreement. Such supplementary arrangements are not considered as being part of the collective agreement unless it can be established that they have been incorporated by reference into the agreement.

1. Ontario, s.55; Quebec, s.67.

B. Unique Legal Effect

785. A collective agreement creates a unique legal arrangement, not only defining the rights and obligations of the two principle parties (the trade union and the employer), but also setting the terms and conditions of employment for all of the employees in the bargaining unit regardless of whether they happen to be members of the trade union.[1] This first aspect of the collective agreement has been referred to as the 'contractual effect', while the latter aspect has been described as the 'normative effect'.

1. *See* generally, B.L. Adell, *Legal Status of Collective Agreements in England, the United States and Canada* (Kingston, 1970).

1. Contractual effect

786. Collective agreements define the relationship between the trade union and the employer in a variety of ways. For one thing, a description of the bargaining unit is a feature of all collective agreements. It is generally accepted that, once a collective agreement is reached, the union's bargaining rights flow from the collective agreement and not from the earlier certificate.[1] It is quite possible that the parties through bargaining may redefine the bargaining constituency by agreeing upon a different description of the bargaining unit. Such a practice appears to be acceptable provided that it does not involve a breach of the duty of fair representation on the part of the union in relinquishing its bargaining rights, or a beach of the duty to bargain in good faith on the part of either the union or employer by insisting on re-defining the bargaining unit during negotiations.

1. *Culinary Workers* v. *Terra Nova Motor Inn.* (1974) 50 D.L.R. (3d) 253 (S.C.C.); [1975] 2 S.C.R. 149.

787. Even more importantly, the collective agreement is likely to contain some sort of language requiring as a condition of further employment that the employees falling within the bargaining unit either join the union or support it financially. Such arrangements, known as union security provisions, are a common feature of Canadian collective agreements.[1] As well as bargaining for its own financial security, a trade union may bargain for and obtain other provisions of direct benefit to itself, such as provisions permitting union officials to take time off work to conduct union business or provisions providing greater job security to union officials in the event of a reduction of the workforce.

1. *Supra*, paras. 578–81.

788. An almost universal feature of Canadian collective agreements is a provision establishing informal settlement mechanisms for disputes arising from the agreement with binding arbitration as the final step. All jurisdictions prohibit resort to the strike and lockout during the term of the collective agreement and many require that the parties include in their collective agreement a provision explicitly promising not to resort to economic sanctions during the term of the agreement. The *quid pro quo* for this restriction is generally considered to be the legislative stipulation that grievance arbitration be the means of finally resolving collective agreement disputes.[1] Nevertheless the parties may design their own arbitration procedure through bargaining provided that this procedure meets the requirements for arbitration found in the legislation.

1. Canada, s.57; British Columbia, s.84(2); Ontario, s.48; Quebec, s.100.

789. Despite the general prohibition against striking or locking out during the term of the agreement, the parties may still include in their collective agreement other provisions affecting the use of economic sanctions. They may, for example, agree that the members of the bargaining unit are not to be disciplined for refusing to cross picket lines,[1] or they may agree following a strike or lockout that neither party is to take the disciplinary action in respect of incidents arising from the dispute.[2]

1. *See Nelson Crushed Stone*, [1978] 1 C.L.R.B.R. 115 (O.L.R.B.).
2. Such a specific agreement dealing with the consequences of a strike or lockout is not always a part of the collective agreement. *See* generally: C. D'Aoust and L. Leclerc, *Les protocoles de retour au travail: une analyse juridique* (Montreal: Ecole de relations industrielles, Université de Montréal, 1980).

790. The fact that the collective agreement serves to define the relationship between the trade union and the employer raises a question as to the extent to which the traditional prerogative of the employer to manage has been curtailed by the establishment of a collective bargaining relationship. Most collective agreements contain a broadly worded provision recognizing the general right of the employer to manage the enterprise, and, where such provisions have been absent, arbitrators usually have read into the collective agreement a general right to manage. On the other hand, collective agreements also contain specific provisions dealing with such matters as discharge and discipline, seniority, job classification, wages, and hours of work that clearly limit the general power of the employer to manage. The potential conflict between these two types of provisions has given rise to some debate as to how this contractual language should be read.

791. One approach would treat the collective agreement as only restricting the traditional prerogative of the employer to manage to the extent that it does so through specific contract language. This approach, often called the 'reserved rights' approach is premised on the assumption that management when entering the collective bargaining relationship does not surrender its traditional right to manage. The other approach, however, would treat the collective agreement as creating a new legal regime that puts the trade union and employer on an equal footing.[1] Under this approach fundamental changes affecting the bargaining unit could not be made unilaterally by the employer but would have to be the subject of mutual agreement. Neither approach has received general acceptance by Canadian labour arbitrators who appear to prefer less philosophical, and more pragmatic, approaches toward the resolution of collective agreement disputes.[2]

1. *Peterboro Lock* (1953) 4 L.A.C. 1499.
2. *Russelsteel* (1966) 17 L.A.C. 253.

2. Normative effect

792. It has now been authoritatively recognized that the collective agreement dictates the terms and conditions of employment for all the employees in the bargaining unit. The trade union, as bargaining agent, has the exclusive authority to bargain for such employees, leaving no room for private negotiations between the employer and individual employee.[1] The terms negotiated between the union and employer, moreover, are by operation of law binding upon all the employees in the bargaining unit.[2] It is the collective agreement that establishes the norms of the employment relationship for the individual employees in the bargaining unit, operating in much the same manner as legislation.

1. *Supra*, paras. 573–7.
2. Canada, s.56; British Columbia, s.48; Ontario s.56; Quebec, s.67.

3. Exclusion of common law principles

793. There exists in Canada a body of common law principles dealing with the individual employment relationship.[1] Where a collective bargaining relationship exists, however, the legal arrangements between the employer and the employee have been dictated by negotiations between the union and the employer rather than by any direct bargaining between employer and employee. Recognizing this 'reality', the Supreme Court of Canada has clearly indicated that the common law of employment, as a general rule, is no longer relevant to the determination of the rights and obligations of employees covered by collective agreements.[2] The practical result of this ruling is to leave the legal position of such employees to be defined by reference to the law of the collective agreement rather than by reliance upon imported common law principles.

1. *Supra*, paras. 152–368.
2. *McGavin Toastmaster Ltd.* v. *Ainscough* (1975) 54 D.L.R. (3d) 1 (S.C.C.); [1976] 1 S.C.R. 718.

4. Limited standing in the courts to enforce the collective agreement

794. The trade union's exclusive authority to represent the employees in the bargaining unit encompasses not only the negotiation of the collective agreement but also its administration. Except where specific provision is made for the involvement of individual employees, it is the union as bargaining agent that has the exclusive right to take any matter through the grievance and arbitration procedures. An individual employee cannot turn to the courts in order to enforce the terms of the collective agreement as any matter that requires the interpretation or application of the collective agreement must be resolved through the grievance and arbitration procedures provided in the collective agreement.[1] If the essence of a dispute arises from the collective agreement, it falls within the exclusive jurisdiction of the arbitrator even though the claim itself may be framed as a breach of tort law or even as a violation of the Charter of Rights and Freedoms.[2]

1. *General Motors* v. *Brunet* (1976) 77 C.L.L.C. para. 14,067; [1977] 2 S.C.R. 537; *St. Anne Nackawic Pulp & Paper Ltd.* v. *Canadian Paperworkers Union, Local 219* (1986) 86 C.L.L.C. para. 14,037 (S.C.C.); [1986] 1 S.C.R. 704; *Young Estate* v. *Transalta Utilities Corp.* (1998) 98 C.L.L.C. para. 220-032 (Alta.C.A.); the Rights of Labour Act, R.S.O. 1990, c.R-33, s.3(3), expressly provides that 'a collective bargaining agreement shall not be the subject to any action in any court unless it may be the subject of such action irrespective of any of the provisions of this Act or of the Labour Relations Act'.
2. *Weber* v. *Ontario Hydro* (1995) 95 C.L.L.C. para. 210-027; [1995] 2 S.C.R. 929; *O'Leary* v. *Her Majesty the Queen* (1995) 95 C.L.L.C. para. 210-028 (S.C.C.); [1995] 2 S.C.R. 967; but *see* *Piko* v. *Hudson's Bay Co.* (1998) 99 C.L.L.C. para. 220-007 (Ont.C.A.).

5. *Potential legal vacuum upon expiry of the collective agreement*

795. Collective agreements, unlike many individual contracts of employment, are not of indefinite duration and must be renewed at periodic intervals. Negotiations for renewal may be protracted and often extend past the expiry of both the collective agreement and the period of the statutory freeze. Where employees continue to work beyond the expiry of the collective agreement and the freeze period a question may arise as to whether their terms and conditions of employment are still governed by the expired collective agreement.

796. It appears to be recognized that the provisions of the collective agreement relating to the terms and conditions of employment of the employees in the bargaining unit survive both the expiry of the collective agreement and the period of the statutory freeze.[1] At that point the right to alter unilaterally these terms of employment is not entirely unqualified, since in some circumstances a unilateral alteration might be interpreted as a breach of the obligations to bargain in good faith. Moreover, at this stage, there is a question of how the surviving terms and conditions of employment might be enforced. One court has held that the grievance and arbitration procedures become part of the individual contracts of employment between the employer and the employees upon the expiry of the collective agreement.[2] Some doubt has been expressed, however, as to whether this type of provision, which is integral to the relationship between union and employer, is consistent with the terms found in individual contracts of employment.

1. *Telegram Publishing* v. *Zwelling* (1976) 76 C.L.L.C. para. 14,047 (Ont.C.A.); *see* now *Paccar of Canada Ltd.* v. *CAIMAW* (1989) 89 C.L.L.C para. 14,050 (S.C.C.); [1989] 2 S.C.R. 983.
2. *Re Prince Rupert Fishermen's Co-operative Association and United Fishermen* (1967) 66 W.W.R. 43 (B.C.S.C.); *Caribou College* (1984) 4 C.L.R.B.R. (N.S.) 320 (B.C.L.R.B.); but *see* *Communications Union* v. *Bell Canada* (1979) 97 D.L.R. (3d) 132 (Ont.Div.Ct.).

797. The legal vacuum created by the expiry of the collective agreement usually poses a problem only where there has been a failure to renew the collective agreement. In those cases where the collective agreement is renewed the parties are likely to make the new agreement retroactive to the expiry date of the previous agreement. These retroactive provisions, however, have sometimes been interpreted by arbitrators as not touching all terms of the collective agreement. Where full retroactivity would lead to impractical and unintended results, then certain terms of the agreement may not be given retroactive effect.[1] Arbitral authority appears to be divided on the more specific question of whether persons who leave their employment prior to the signing of the collective agreement may still benefit from a retroactive wage increase.[2]

1. *Penticton and District Retirement Service* (1978) 16 L.A.C. (2d) 97 (B.C.L.R.B.); *Salvation Army Grace Hospital* (1980) 25 L.A.C. (2d) 235.
2. *See Ontario Federation of Labour* (1978) 16 L.A.C. (2d) 265. The Quebec Superior Court has ruled that such persons are not entitled to benefit from a retroactive wage increase. *See O'Rully* v. *Communauté urbaine de Montréal*, [1980] C.S. 708.

6. *Status of the collective agreements in the courts*

798. The primary method of enforcing collective agreements is the grievance arbitration procedure established in the agreement itself. The existence of this special procedure for enforcement is at least partially a result of an earlier reluctance on the part of the courts to recognize trade unions as legal entities as well as a judicial unwillingness to treat collective agreements as legally enforceable arrangements.[1] Moreover, the union's role of exclusive bargaining agent virtually eliminates any possibility of individual employees being able to use the courts in order to enforce the terms of employment established by the collective agreement. The result is that the courts in Canada have not played a direct role in the enforcement of collective agreements.

1. *See supra*, paras. 753–5.

a. Standing of trade unions in the courts

799. Even after the repeal of the laws of criminal conspiracy relating to trade unions, the common law of restraint of trade was still recognized by the courts as applying to trade unions. The survival of this common law doctrine until the advent of present-day collective bargaining legislation meant that trade unions found to be operating in restraint of trade were denied standing in the courts to enforce their collective agreements.[1] While present-day collective bargaining legislation has had the effect of legitimating trade unions,[2] other means of enforcing the collective agreement had already been established by the time that this incident of collective legislation was recognized by the courts.

1. *Polakoff* v. *Winters Garment*, [1928] 2 D.L.R. 277 (Ont. H.C.).
2. *I.B.E.W.* v. *Town of Summerside* (1960) 23 D.L.R. (2d) 593 (S.C.C.); [1960] S.C.R. 591.

800. Even after the demise of the restraint of trade bar there remained a further obstacle to judicial recognition of the trade union as a legal entity. Initially, the trade union was regarded by the courts as just another unincorporated association and, as such, was not treated as a legal person in its own right. The result was that the trade union could only sue or be sued in the courts through the cumbersome procedure of the representative action.[1] This disability was not regarded as being entirely disadvantageous by trade unionists who harboured some distrust of the courts, and who feared the potential consequences of a damage action in the courts. In fact, some jurisdictions expressly preserved this disability even after the enactment of Wagner-style collective bargaining legislation,[2] but most jurisdictions came to treat trade unions as having status to sue and be sued in the courts.[3] By this time, though, grievance arbitration had become firmly entrenched as the method by which collective agreements were enforced by and against trade unions.

1. *Supra*, paras. 753–5; *see also S.I.U.* v. *Lawrence* (1979) 24 O.R. (2d) 257 (Ont.C.A.).
2. *See* Rights of Labour Act, R.S.O. 1990, c.R-33, s.3(2).
3. *I.L.A.* v. *Maritime Employer's Assoc.* (1978) 89 D.L.R. (3d) 289 (S.C.C.); [1979] 2 S.C.R. 120. As early as 1924, the Province of Quebec enacted The Professional Syndicates Act, allowing trade unions incorporated under the Act to appear before the courts of the Province. The incorporation has always been available to unions on a voluntary basis. This statute is still part of the Quebec legislation. *See* R.S.Q. c.S-40.

b. Unenforceability of the collective agreement at common law

801. A further impediment of the enforcement of the collective agreement in the courts was an earlier judicial unwillingness to recognize collective agreements as giving rise to legally enforceable obligations. The courts took the view that parties to the collective agreement had not intended to create legally enforceable obligations, and that any disputes arising from the agreement could only be resolved through negotiation and, if necessary, the use of economic sanctions.[1] The enactment of present-day collective bargaining legislation rendered this approach obsolete. One of the primary thrusts of this legislation is to limit economic conflict to the period when the collective agreement is being negotiated. Since the use of the strike or lockout to resolve problems arising during the term of a collective agreement is expressly prohibited, the collective agreement cannot be the subject of continuous negotiation and must be treated as being enforceable during its term.[2] The procedure for enforcing the collective agreement is grievance arbitration – a procedure that is mandatory in almost all Canadian jurisdictions.

1. *Young* v. *Canadian Northern Railway*, [1931] 1 D.L.R. 645 (P.C.). *See supra*, para. 756.
2. Some Canadian jurisdictions expressly provide that the collective agreement is binding upon both the bargaining agent and the employer – Canada, s.56; British Columbia, s.48; Ontario, s.56.

§2. Administration and Enforcement of the Collective Agreement

802. The collective agreement establishes a continuing relationship between the employer, union, and the employees represented by the union. In a sense these parties are partners in the operation of the enterprise. The administration of the collective agreement is very much a continuing process requiring the parties to work out within the framework of the agreement the numerous problems, some small and others large, arising from the day-to-day running of the enterprise. Most of these problems are resolved on a very informal basis by the parties themselves, sometimes without reference to the collective agreement. Where informal adjustment is unsuccessful more formal procedures for the administration and enforcement of the collective agreement can usually be found in the agreement itself.

A. Grievance Procedure

803. Most collective agreements contain some sort of grievance procedure designed to resolve collective agreement disputes by means of discussion and agreement between the parties. The complexity of such procedures usually depends on the nature and size of the enterprise. In the small enterprise only a single meeting between the union representative and the owner may be called for. A more structured, multi-stage, procedure is likely to be found in the larger enterprise, each additional stage requiring the participation of management and union officials having greater authority than those participating in the preceding stage. These more complex grievance procedures have been designed to allow minor grievances to be settled at the earlier stages (or steps) of the grievance procedure, and to have more important grievances settled at a more senior level.

804. Carriage of a grievance through the grievance procedure is usually the function of the union, and not of the individual employee. Collective bargaining legislation in some jurisdictions, however, does contemplate that employees may initiate their own grievances.[1] In the absence of such legislative provisions, or an express provision in the collective agreement allowing employees to have access to the grievance procedure, it is only the union and the employer who may set the grievance procedure in motion.

1. For example, Manitoba, s.130. It is clear, however, that this type of provision does not permit an employee to carry a grievance through to arbitration.

805. Many collective agreements establish time limits for both filing the grievance and moving it through the various steps in the grievance procedure. As well, the collective agreement may also stipulate that the grievance be in writing and signed by the grievor. A distinction may also be drawn in the collective agreement between individual and policy grievances. Although all of these procedural requirements can be waived by the parties in the interests of settling a grievance, they can become an issue at arbitration where one of the parties wishes to resist the grievance on procedural grounds.[1]

1. *Infra*, paras. 832–40.

B. Grievance Arbitration

806. Those grievances that cannot be settled by the parties themselves are generally resolved through grievance arbitration. Grievance arbitration is mandatory in all jurisdictions but Saskatchewan, and even in that jurisdiction arbitration procedures are usually found in collective agreements. While only a small proportion of grievances go to arbitration, the process itself has a substantial impact upon the administration of the collective agreement. Over the years arbitral decision-making has given rise to a comprehensive body of principles relating to the rights and duties created by a collective agreement.[1] This law of the collective agreement undoubtedly influences decisions made at the earlier stages of the grievance procedure as to whether to proceed to arbitration. Moreover, the effectiveness of the grievance arbitration process itself, both in terms of cost and speed, has some bearing on whether a matter will be taken to arbitration or withdrawn at an earlier stage.

1. *See* generally, D.J.M. Brown and D.M. Beatty, *Canadian Labour Arbitration* (3rd edn.) (Aurora, 1991); E.E. Palmer and B.M. Palmer, *Collective Agreement Arbitration in Canada* (3rd edn.) (Toronto, 1991). For Quebec's arbitration system, which is similar to that found in other Canadian jurisdictions, *see* R. Blouin and F. Morin, *Droit de l'arbitrage de grief*, 4th edn. (Cowansville, 1994). The close similarity between Quebec and other Canadian jurisdictions is discussed in M.-F. Bich, 'Labour Arbitration in Quebec', in *Labour Arbitration Yearbook*, W. Kaplan, J. Sack and M. Gunderson (eds.) (Toronto, 1993) 93–114.

1. Nature of the process

807. Grievance arbitration is a hybrid process – containing both public and private elements.[1] Although the process is mandatory in all but one jurisdiction, the parties still have a wide latitude to define the process on their own terms. The legislative requirement establishes only a minimum procedure, leaving the parties free to improve upon this basic model by devising procedures suited to their own particular needs. There exists in Canada a number of variations from the standard model of arbitration as evidenced by the rail, longshoring, trucking, mining and garment industries, which have each devised their own special procedures for the final resolution of grievances.[2]

1. *See* generally Weiler, *op. cit.*, c.3.
2. *See* Labour Canada Study, *Industry and Expedited Arbitration Alternatives to Traditional Methods* (Ottawa, 1977).

808. Grievance arbitration, moreover, is procedure separate and distinct from commercial arbitration. Recognizing this fact, all but two provinces[1] exclude grievance arbitration from the scope of the statutory structure established for the arbitration of commercial disputes.

1. Newfoundland and Nova Scotia.

a. Constitution of the arbitration tribunal

809. The parties themselves are initially responsible for the establishment of the arbitration tribunal, an exercise usually performed on *ad hoc* basis. Where a grievance is to be taken to a three-person board of arbitration, the general practice is for the union and employer each to nominate a representative member to sit on the board with the chair being chosen by mutual agreement of the union and employer. Increasingly, however, unions and employers are using sole arbitrators chosen by mutual agreement. In many cases the arbitration tribunal or sole arbitrator is chosen only after the grievance is referred to arbitration, although some collective agreements provide for less *ad hoc* procedures by establishing a panel of arbitrators to be used in rotation or, more exceptionally, a permanent umpire. The arbitration tribunal is only appointed by the government where the parties have failed to constitute the tribunal themselves or where one of the parties chooses to use statutory expedited arbitration procedures now available in some Canadian jurisdictions.[1]

1. The Ontario legislation, however, permits either party to apply immediately to the minister for the appointment of an arbitrator even though the collective agreement may establish a different procedure for the selection of the arbitrator (s.49). New Brunswick now provides a very similar procedure (s.55.01). S.107 of the Nova Scotia legislation goes even further for construction industry arbitrations, providing a mandatory statutory procedure for the expeditious appointment of a single arbitrator.

b. Costs of proceedings

810. As a general rule the parties by agreement bear the costs of the arbitration tribunal equally. Where a board of arbitration is used, each party pays the fees and expenses of its own nominee to the board and the fees and expenses of the chairman are divided equally between them. In the case of a sole arbitrator, the fees and expenses of the arbitrator would again be divided equally. Each party bears its own costs of presenting the grievance to the arbitration tribunal as it is the prevailing practice of arbitrators not to award costs against the losing party.

c. Openness to public

811. There is some question as to whether arbitration tribunals are sufficiently private in nature so as to justify the exclusion of the general public and the media from their hearings. Legislation in both Ontario and the federal jurisdiction appears to treat grievance arbitration tribunals as being different from statutory tribunals.[1] On the other hand, an arbitral ruling to the effect that the essentially private nature of the arbitration process precluded the opening of an arbitration hearing to the public has not met with judicial approval.[2] The result is that an arbitration tribunal now appears to have a discretion as to whether to exclude members of the public, including the media, from its proceedings.[3] This discretion has been exercised to exclude the public from an arbitration hearing where it was necessary to ensure the fairness of the hearing itself.[4]

1. Statutory Powers Procedure Act, R.S.O. 1990, c.S-22; *Canada Labour Code*, s.58(3).
2. *Toronto Star* (1975) 9 L.A.C. (2d) 193; overruled by (1977) 14 O.R. (2d) 278 (Ont.Div.Ct.).
3. *Toronto Star* (1977) 14 L.A.C. (2d) 155. *See also* Quebec, s.100.4.
4. *Malaspina University College* (1996) 53 L.A.C. (4th) 93; *Fraternité des policiers de Val-d'Or inc.* et *Ville de Val-d'Or*, [1998] R.J.D.T. 1363.

d. The problem of bias

812. The *ad hoc* and representative nature of arbitration tribunals raises a question of whether the nominees to a board of arbitration may be so closely connected with their nominating party so as to be disqualified on the ground of bias. The appointment as nominee of an official of a trade union party to an arbitration or, on the other side, of an employee of an employer party may sometimes occur. In most of these situations no objection is taken to the constitution of the arbitration board and the problem of bias is effectively avoided. Where objection to the constitution of a board is made at the outset of the hearing, however, consideration has to be given to the relationship between a party and its nominee. The courts have indicated that they are not willing to approve of a nominee with too close a relationship with one of the interested parties, such as an official of the union which is itself a party to the arbitration.[1] In order to prevent such a problem, the Quebec Labour Code now stipulates that an arbitration tribunal is to be a single arbitrator but, if the parties wish, an assessor may be appointed by each party. The assessors do not take part in the final decision even though they participate in the deliberations.[2]

1. *Canadian Shipbuilding and Engineering* (1973) 73 C.L.L.C. para. 14,185 (Ont.Div.Ct.); but *see Gainers and Packinghouse Workers* (1964) 47 W.W.R. 544 (Alta.S.C.) and *J.K. Campbell & Association* (1979) 21 L.A.C. (2d) 16; *see* now T.S. Kuttner, 'Bias and the Arbitral Forum' in W. Kaplan, J. Sack. and M. Gunderson (eds.). *Labour Arbitration Yearbook, 1991*, Vol. 1 (Toronto, 1991) at 23.
2. Quebec, s.100.1.1.

e. Conduct of hearings

813. Once constituted the arbitration tribunal usually convenes a hearing of the grievance at a time and place agreed upon by the parties. Hearings are almost always held in a neutral location away from the place of work such as a hotel conference room or a special facility catering to arbitration proceedings. The format of the arbitration hearing is usually informal. Often the parties are able to agree upon a statement of facts avoiding recourse to more formal evidential procedures. In some cases, the parties (more often trade unions) do not use lawyers to present their case but, instead, make use of the services of their own officials. Many cases are settled by the parties, either before the hearing commences or during the course of the hearing. Despite this informality, it would appear that the courts still require arbitration tribunals to adopt an adjudicative format and to adhere to basic principles of judicial procedure. All parties having any interest in the outcome of the proceedings are required to be notified.[1] Parties are entitled to be represented by counsel,[2] and entitled to cross-examine the evidence of the other party at the hearing.[3] These procedural requirements imposed by the courts have introduced a substantial legal element into the process – a factor that may explain why many Canadian arbitrators have legal backgrounds.

1. *Hoogendoorn and Greening Metal Products and Screening Equipment Co.* (1968) 65 D.L.R. (2d) 641 (S.C.C.); [1968] S.C.R. 30. Quebec, s.100.5.
2. *Men's Clothing Manufacturers Association of Ontario* (1979) 79 C.L.L.C para. 14,224 (Ont.Div.Ct.).
3. *Girvin and Consumers' Gas Co.* (1974) 40 D.L.R. (3d) 421 (Ont.Div.Ct.).

f. Sources of arbitral standards

814. Grievance arbitration is essentially an adjudicative process requiring the arbitration tribunal to make findings of fact and then to apply appropriate standards to these facts.[1] The primary source of the standards applied by the arbitrator is the collective agreement itself. Initially the arbitrator looks to the language of the collective agreement in order to determine whether the parties have formulated a rule that can resolve the immediate dispute. This exercise is not as easy as it would appear at first glance. Some collective agreements may contain language of so general a nature as to make it virtually impossible for the arbitrator to find a specific rule to deal with the particular problems. Even where contract language is more specific, collective agreement provisions may conflict with each other, making it equally difficult for the arbitrator to resolve the dispute by reference to the language of the collective agreement alone.

1. *See* generally, P.C. Weiler, 'The Role of the Labour Arbitrator: Alternative Versions' (1969) 19 U.T.L.J. 16.

815. The nature of the negotiation process is such that it is impossible for the parties to provide for every eventuality in their collective agreement. The crisis atmosphere of negotiations means that collective agreements are often drafted in haste, and that language may be deliberately left unclear in order to mask those issues on which complete agreement has not been reached.[1] Even where the greatest care is taken in drafting a collective agreement, the contract language may still not be adequate to resolve the grievance simply because of the limits of human foresight.

1. Collective agreements, however, are not treated as being void because of a lack of consensus *ad idem. See Northwest Drywall and Building Supplies Ltd.* (1991) 10 C.L.R.B.R. (2d) 180 (B.C.I.R.C.).

816. In those situations where the language of the collective agreement does not clearly reveal a standard for the resolution of the case, the arbitrator may look outside the collective agreement. It has been recognized that where a collective agreement is ambiguous, arbitrators are permitted to rely upon extrinsic (or parole) evidence as an aid to interpreting the language of the contract.[1] Such extrinsic evidence usually takes the form of testimony as to the practice of the parties in previous cases of a like nature, or testimony as to the history of the negotiations that led up to the making of the collective agreement. Whether a collective agreement is sufficiently ambiguous to justify the use of extrinsic evidence will depend upon the relative plausibility of the conflicting interpretations given to the collective agreement.[2] If the language of a collective agreement supports more than just one plausible interpretation it can be said to be patently ambiguous. An ambiguity, however, may also be latent, occurring where the application to the facts of what appears to be unequivocal language is uncertain or difficult.[3]

1. *John Bertram* (1967) 18 L.A.C. 362.
2. *University of British Columbia*, [1977] 1 C.L.R.B.R. 13 (B.C.L.R.B.); *Noranda Metal Industries*, (1984) 84 C.L.L.C. para. 14,024 (Ont.C.A.).
3. *Leitch Gold Mines* v. *Texas Gulf Sulphur* (1969) 3 D.L.R. (3d) 161 (Ont.H.C.); but *see R.* v. *Barber, Ex parte Warehousemen's Union* (1968) 68 D.L.R. (2d) 682 (Ont.C.A.).

817. In cases where the language of the collective agreement does not supply a ready answer arbitrators may also rely upon the arbitral jurisprudence. Although arbitrators are not strictly bound to follow prior arbitration decisions, the very well-developed body of arbitral case law in Canada does have a substantial influence on the process. Arbitrators tend to assume that the parties have entered into their collective agreement with knowledge of the basic themes running through this jurisprudence.[1] Moreover, where there has been a previous decision relating to a similar provision in the collective agreement, arbitrators have taken the approach that they will follow the previous award unless convinced that the earlier interpretation is clearly wrong.[2] The extensive use of arbitral jurisprudence by Canadian arbitrators has meant that the parties now rely heavily upon previous decisions when presenting their cases at arbitration.

1. *Russelsteel* (1966) 17 L.A.C. 253.
2. *See* J.F.W. Weatherill, 'The Binding Force of Arbitration Awards' (1958) 8 L.A.C. 323.

818. Even though the collective agreement is regarded as the primary source of the arbitrator's jurisdiction, it may still be necessary for the arbitrator to take into account relevant statutory provisions. The roots of the grievance arbitration process can be found in general collective bargaining legislation, and arbitrators may refer to this legislation in order to avoid giving the collective agreement an interpretation that would be inconsistent with this legislative scheme. Arbitrators may go even further and refuse to enforce language in the collective agreement that is in direct conflict with collective bargaining legislation. It has been recognized, for example, that in the face of legislative provisions making mandatory the arbitration of all disputes arising from the collective agreement arbitrators may ignore language in the collective agreement intended to restrict access to arbitration.[1]

1. *Cassiar Asbestos*, [1974] 1 C.L.R.B.R. 428 and [1975] 1 C.L.R.B.R. 212 (B.C.L.R.B.); *Transair*, [1978] 2 C.L.R.B.R. 354 (C.L.R.B.); *Larry Elliston*, [1982] 2 C.L.R.B.R. 241 (C.L.R.B.); *Re Toronto Hydro and CUPE* (1980) 80 C.L.L.C. para. 14,035 (Ont.Div.Ct.); *Re City of Halifax and I.A.F.* (1982) 131 D.L.R. (3d) 426 (N.S.C.A.); *Ontario Hydro and CUPE* (1983) 147 D.L.R. (3d) 210 (Ont.C.A.).

819. External legislation in general, but particularly human rights legislation, is now having a much greater impact upon the grievance arbitration process.[1] It is now well accepted in most Canadian jurisdictions that arbitrators are required to apply external legislation to collective agreements even where the effect is to override the express language of the collective agreement.[2] Where the provisions of a collective agreement clearly conflict with a statute, the arbitrator is obliged to take the statute into account even if it means having to treat the language of the collective agreement as a nullity.[3] If the language of the agreement is open to alternative interpretations, however, the arbitrator can adopt the interpretation that is consistent with the statute by assuming that the parties did not intend to agree on language that would be in conflict with the general law. The overall effect of external legislation has been to qualify the negotiated internal value systems articulated in the express language of collective agreements.

1. *See* D.D. Carter, 'The Duty to Accommodate: Its Growing Impact on the Grievance Arbitration Process' (1997) 52 *Rel. Ind.* 185.

2. *See generally*, P.C. Weiler, 'The Arbitrator, the Collective Agreement and the Law' (1972) 10 *Osgoode Hall L.J.* 141; Canada, s.60(1)(a.1); Ontario (s.48(12)(j)), British Columbia (s.89(g)) and Quebec (s.100.12(a)) provide arbitrators with an express power to interpret and apply statutes.
3. *McLeod* v. *Egan* (1974) 46 D.L.R. (3d) 150 (S.C.C.); [1975] 1 S.C.R 517.

820. The Charter of Rights and Freedoms has had a similar effect on the negotiated internal value systems set out in collective agreements to which government is a party as employer. The Supreme Court of Canada has now made it clear that the Charter applies directly to collective agreements between unions and government agencies, and that arbitrators have the authority to apply the Charter to these collective agreements.[1] Even where government is not a party to a collective agreement the Charter may still have an indirect impact because human rights legislation applies to all collective agreements, and human rights legislation itself must conform to the requirements of the Charter.[2] The Charter has also had an impact upon arbitration procedure because the procedural powers of arbitrators are derived from collective bargaining legislation, making their exercise subject to the Charter.[3]

1. *Douglas College* v. *Douglas/Kwantlen Faculty Association* (1991) 91 C.L.L.C. para. 17,002 (S.C.C.), [1990] 3 S.C.R. 211; *Lavigne* v. *Ontario Public Service Employees Union* (1991) 91 C.L.L.C. para. 14,029 (S.C.C.), [1991] 2. S.C.R. 211.
2. *Vriend* v. *Attorney General (Alta)* (1998) 98 C.L.L.C. para. 230-021 (S.C.C.) (1998) 156 D.L.R. (4th) 385 (S.C.C.) [1998] 1 S.C.R. 493.
3. *Canada Post* (1985) 19 L.A.C. (3d) 361; *Greater Niagra Transit Commission* (1987) 26 L.A.C. (3d) 1.

821. To some extent arbitrators also rely upon general notions of equity when deciding grievances. Although the primary assumption is that the arbitrator must be faithful to the language of the collective agreement, there is still some latitude allowed for the introduction of particular equitable doctrines.[1] At times arbitrators have invoked a concept of equitable estoppel to prevent one party from claiming its strict rights under a collective agreement where it has led the other party to believe that such rights would not be enforced and that other party has relied on the representation to its detriment.[2] This approach to collective agreement interpretation permits greater weight to be placed upon the practice of the parties and less upon the language of the collective agreement itself. An estoppel may continue to operate until the party relying upon it has had an opportunity to renegotiate the collective agreement,[3] and in some circumstances it may even extend beyond the life of a current collective agreement.[4]

1. *See* R. Blouin, 'L'apport de l'équité en contexte d'arbitrage de grief', in G. Trudeau, G. Vallée and D. Veilleux (eds.) *Études en droit du travail à la mémoire de Claude D'Aoust* (Cowansville) (1995) 25–50.
2. *CN/CP Telecommunications* (1982) 4 L.A.C. (3d) 205; *aff'd.* (1982) 82 C.L.L.C. para. 14,163 (Ont.Div.Ct.). *See* C. D'Aoust and L. Dubé, *L'estoppel et les laches en jurisprudence arbitrale* (Montreal: Ecole de relations industrielles, Université de Montréal, 1990).
3. *Outboard Marine* (1982) 4 L.A.C. (3d).
4. *Ford Motor Co. Of Canada* (1997) 56 L.A.C. (5th) 257.

822. Another equitable doctrine sometimes invoked by arbitrators is that of laches or undue delay. If a party delays unduly in processing a grievance and this delay results in some detriment to the other party, the arbitrator may refuse to hear the grievance even though it might be timely under the grievance procedure in the collective agreement.[1] This equitable doctrine has been used infrequently as arbitrators appear to be reluctant to disqualify a grievance simply because of the passage time.

1. *Governing Council of U. of T.* (1976) 10 L.A.C. (2d) 417.

823. The equitable approaches discussed above have their origins in doctrines developed by the courts and have been generally accepted by arbitrators. There has also been considerable debate as to whether arbitrators may also read into collective agreements a concept of substantive fairness that would qualify the exercise of management rights, requiring management to act fairly and reasonably when administering the collective agreement. The courts have allowed arbitrators to read into collective agreements an implied duty of reasonable contract administration,[1] but arbitrators still prefer to base such a duty on the express language of the collective agreement.

1. *Re Wardair Canada Ltd. and Canadian Air Line Flight Attendants* (1988) 63 O.R. (2d) 471 (Ont.C.A.); *see also Municipality of Metropolitan Toronto* (1990) 74 O.R. (2d) 239 (Ont.C.A.).

g. Remedial authority

824. The hybrid nature of the arbitration process has given rise to considerable debate about the proper limits of the arbitrator's remedial authority.[1] Those who characterize the arbitration process as being merely a creation of the collective agreement argue that the arbitrator's remedial power cannot extend beyond those powers expressly conferred by the terms of the collective agreement. On the other hand, those who regard the arbitration process as being primarily the product of collective bargaining legislation take the position that a full range of remedial powers can be implied from the statutory language requiring final and binding settlement of grievances by means of arbitration.

1. *See* generally, P.C. Weiler, 'Remedies in Labour Arbitration: Revised Judicial Version' (1974) 52 *Can. Bar Rev.* 29.

825. In the early stages of grievance arbitration in Canada there was some doubt as to whether, absent specific language in the collective agreement, an arbitration tribunal could do more than make a declaration as to the respective rights of the parties under the collective agreement. Judicial approval, however, was later given to an arbitral damage award, indicating that the courts were prepared to treat the legislative framework as providing the arbitrator with at least some authority to fashion an appropriate remedy.[1] It is clear that arbitrators have a wide authority to award damages for a breach of the collective agreement provided that the damages are essentially compensatory in nature.[2] Arbitrators have also been prepared to recognize that interest on the damages may be awarded to a grievor in appropriate circumstances.[3] It now appears that arbitrators may award damages based on tort if the facts giving rise to the claim relate to the administration of the collective agreement.[4]

1. *Polymer* (1959) 10 L.A.C. 51; *aff'd* (1962) 33 D.L.R. (2d) 124 (S.C.C.); [1962] S.C.R. 338.
2. In *Blouin Drywall Contractors and Carpenters & Joiners* (1976) 57 D.L.R. (3d) 199 (Ont.C.A.) the court upheld their authority of an arbitrator to award damages to a union for beach of a hiring hall provision in a collective agreement.
3. *British Columbia Hydro*, [1982] 3 C.L.R.B.R. 87 (B.C.L.R.B.); *Air Canada* (1981) 29 L.A.C. (2d) 142; but *see Newport Sportswear* (1981) 30 L.A.C. (2d) 149; *Keeprite* (1983) 8 L.A.C. (3d) 35. *See also* Quebec, s.100.12(c).
4. *Pacific Press* (1998) 73 L.A.C. (4th) 35.

826. In other situations, however, the courts have been less willing to recognize the remedial authority of the arbitrator. In the case of an improper discharge the usual remedy is a direction to the employer to reinstate the employee without loss of seniority and to compensate the employee for wages and fringe benefits lost during the period of discharge. While the power of the arbitrator to order full reinstatement has never been seriously challenged, the order of an arbitrator substituting a lesser penalty for discharge has been overturned by the courts on the basis that in making this remedial order the arbitrator exceeded the jurisdictional limits established by the collective agreement.[1] The effect of this judicial decision was to curtail the power of arbitrators to fashion a remedy falling somewhere between the two extremes of full reinstatement or dismissal of the grievance. Recognizing the problems created by this restriction, collective bargaining legislation in most Canadian jurisdictions has been amended to provide the arbitrator with a wide remedial authority in cases of discharge.[2] Despite these provisions, however, there is still considerable debate within the Canadian labour relations community as to whether arbitrators can take into account evidence arising after the discharge when exercising this remedial authority.[3]

1. *Port Arthur Shipbuilding* v. *Arthurs* (1968) 70 D.L.R. (2d) 693, but *see* now *New Brunswick Electric Power Commission* (1979) 79 C.L.L.C. para. 14,200 (S.C.C.); [1979] 2 S.C.R. 768.
2. Canada, s.60(2); British Columbia, s.89(d); Ontario, s.48(17); Quebec, s.100.12(f); a perceptive review of the evolution of the arbitrator's jurisdiction in this area is found in William Scott, [1977] 1 C.L.R.B.R. 1 (B.C.L.R.B.).
3. *See Cie minière Québec Cartier* v. *Quebec (Grievances arbitrator)*, [1995] 2 S.C.R. 1095; *Westmin Resources Ltd.* (1997) 63 L.A.C. (4th) 134; *Newtel Communications* (1998) 71 L.A.C. (4th) 73; *Westmin Resources Ltd.*, (1998) 98 C.L.L.C. para. 220-060 (B.C.L.R.B.).

827. The power of the arbitrator to relieve against provisions in the collective agreement restricting the time for the processing of grievances experienced a somewhat similar evolution. Attempts by arbitrators to provide relief against the harsh consequences of a missed time limit did not meet with judicial approval.[1] Some Canadian jurisdictions, recognizing the undesirability of grievances being forfeited on technical grounds, have now amended their legislation to give arbitrators the explicit power to relieve against the forfeiture of a grievance because of a failure to meet contractual time limits.[2]

1. *See*, for example, *Truck Drivers* v. *Hoar Transport Co. Ltd.* (1969) 4 D.L.R. (3d) 449 (S.C.C.); [1969] S.C.R. 634.
2. British Columbia, s.89(e); Ontario, s.48(16).

828. Whether an arbitrator has the power to rectify a collective agreement when there has been a mistake made in reducing the actual agreement reached by the parties into final written form is problematical. Although the courts themselves exercise such a power, they have been reluctant to recognize the arbitrator's authority to perform the very same remedial role.[1] Arbitrators themselves appear to be divided on the question of whether they have the authority to order rectification.[2] This reluctance to order rectification may be explained in part by the difficulty of determining what constitutes the actual agreement of the parties when it has not been reduced into final written form.

1. *Metropolitan Toronto Board of Commissioners of Police and Metropolitan Toronto Police Assoc.* (1972) 26 D.L.R. (Ont.C.A.); *Canadian National Railway Co.* v. *Beatty* (1982) 82 C.L.L.C. para. 14,163 (Ont.Div.Ct.).
2. *See British Columbia Transformer* (1976) 11 L.A.C. (2d) 233; *Okanagan Federated Shippers Association*, [1977] 1 C.L.R.B.R. 21 (B.C.L.R.B.); *Prince Albert Pulp* (1975) 7 L.A.C. (2d) 345; *Alcan* (1982) 5 L.A.C. (3d) 1.

829. The power of arbitrators to make affirmative orders to remedy breaches of the collective agreement appears to be more clearly established. These compliance orders, as they have been called, have been used not only to remedy past breaches of a collective agreement but also to restrain future anticipated breaches.[1] This type of relief, however, may be difficult to enforce and, as a result, arbitrators may not consider it to be appropriate in all circumstances.

1. *Polax Tailoring* (1972) 24 L.A.C. 201; aff'd by *Re Samuel Cooper and Ladies Garment Workers* (1973) 35 D.L.R. (3d) 501 (Ont.Div.Ct.).

830. Despite their approval of the general arbitral power to make compliance orders, the courts have been less inclined to recognize the power of the arbitrator to make a specific order awarding a job to a grievor where it has been found that an employer has improperly exercised its power to promote.[1] More recently, however, the courts have recognized that in some circumstances a specific order may be a more appropriate arbitral response than remitting the matter back to the employer for reconsideration.[2]

1. *Falconbridge Nickel Mines and U.S.W.A.* (1972) 30 D.L.R. (3d) 412 (Ont.C.A.).
2. *R.* v. *Ontario Public Service Employee Union* (1982) 82 C.L.L.C. para. 14,182 (Ont.Div.Ct.).

831. Finally, it is interesting to note that arbitrators have not followed the practice of the courts of awarding the costs of the proceedings against the losing party, even in the situation where it is clear that one of the parties has been responsible for prolonging the proceedings. This arbitral reluctance to assume a jurisdiction to award costs by deviating from the general understanding that each party assumes an equal share of the costs of the process may be partly attributed to the consensual element of grievance arbitration. Arbitrators, being chosen and paid by the parties, do not enjoy the same position of authority as a judge or a member of a public tribunal, a factor that may explain their reluctance to single out one of the parties to bear all of the costs of the proceedings.

2. Arbitrability of grievances

832. At the outset of arbitration proceedings certain questions may arise as to whether the grievance should even have been brought to arbitration. It may be argued that a collective agreement was not in effect when the grievance arose, that the grievor was not covered by the collective agreement (perhaps because of probationary status), that the issue raised fell outside the ambit of the collective agreement, that the grievance was improperly submitted to arbitration, or that the grievance must be forfeited because of a failure to comply with the time limits contained in the collective agreement. All of these issues are generally regarded as going to the arbitrability of the grievance, and collective bargaining legislation in all jurisdictions provides arbitrators with a full jurisdiction to resolve this type of issue. While arguments contesting the arbitrability of a grievance usually raise issues that are preliminary in nature, in some cases the issues raised by a preliminary objection may be closely connected with the merits of the grievance. Some disagreement exists among arbitrators as to whether issues relating to the arbitrability of the grievance should be disposed of before proceeding to hear the merits.[1] As a general practice, any serious objection to the arbitrability of the grievance is usually dealt with before the arbitrator proceeds to the merits.

1. *Hiram Walker* (1973) 3 L.A.C. (2d) 203; *cf. Alcan* (1974) 5 L.A.C. (2d) 300.

a. Submission to arbitration

833. Union grievances submitted to arbitration generally fall into two categories – those that relate to a particular problem of an individual employee (the individual grievance) and those of a more general nature with implications extending beyond the particular situation of a single employee (the policy grievance). Arbitrators at first tended to draw a rigid distinction between these two types of grievances by not permitting matters that were in essence individual grievances to be brought to arbitration as policy grievances. Latterly, however, arbitrators have modified this approach by drawing this distinction only where the language of the collective agreement explicitly limits the use of policy grievances.[1] Despite this change of approach, arbitrators still recognize that a policy grievance cannot be used as a device to circumvent the time limits established for the processing of individual grievances.[2]

1. *Weston Bakeries* (1970) 21 L.A.C. 308; *Toronto Star Newspaper* (1978) 20 L.A.C. (2d) 392.
2. *Hydro Electric Commission of Borough of North York* (1974) 6 L.A.C. (2d) 113.

b. Carriage of the grievance

834. The general rule is that, regardless of whether a grievance may be an individual grievance, it is the union that has the right to take the grievance to arbitration. Individual employees are not permitted to take their grievance to arbitration on their own even where they are prepared to assume the costs of the process.[1] It is only possible for employees to have access to arbitration in their own right where the language of the arbitration provisions in the collective agreement expressly so provides. Language to this effect is not commonly found in Canadian collective agreements, and the usual situation is that the trade union has the exclusive right to bring employee grievances to arbitration.

1. *The Danby Corporation* v. *Clément et al.*, [1978] C.S. 746. *See also Venditelli* v. *La Cité de Westmount*, [1980] C.A. 49.

835. Two consequences of some importance flow from trade union control over the carriage of the grievance. First, a trade union may settle or withdraw the grievance at any time without the consent of the individual grievor.[1] A second consequence is that the union may take a grievance to arbitration even where the individual is no longer interested in pursuing it any further.[2]

1. *Governing Council of U. of T.* (1974) 5 L.A.C. (2d) 304. In exercising this right, however, the union must be careful not to violate its duty of fair representation. *See Centre hospitalier Régina Ltée* v. *Prud'homme et al.*, [1990] 1 S.C.R. 1330.
2. *International Nickel* (1975) 9 L.A.C. (2d) 83.

c. Timeliness

836. Grievance procedures contained in most collective agreements stipulate certain time limits for the taking of each step in the procedure, including the submission of the grievance to arbitration and the constitution of the arbitration tribunal. A failure to comply with these time limits may often give rise to an objection that the grievance is no longer arbitrable. In dealing with this kind of objection arbitrators have drawn a distinction between time limits that are 'mandatory' in that they dictate the forfeiture of the grievance for non-compliance, and those time limits that are merely 'directory' and which do not by themselves invalidate the grievance.[1] The nature of a time limit is determined by an examination of the language used by the parties when drafting the grievance procedure and by consideration of the purposes intended to be served by the use of this language. The use of the word 'shall' does not necessarily make a time limit mandatory. However, where the grievance procedure provides an express penalty for non-compliance, the time limit is generally considered to be mandatory. It does not follow, though, that the lack of penalty provision makes a time limit directory. In all cases the language used must be interpreted in the context of the overall grievance procedure.

1. For a review of these decisions *see Municipality of Metropolitan Toronto* (1973) 3 L.A.C. (2d) 126.

837. Arbitrators have recognized that relief against the strict operation of mandatory time limits may be justified in some cases. While arbitrators do not have any general power to relieve against time limits in the absence of an explicitly statutory mandate,[1] they have nonetheless been able to provide some relief in certain types of situations. One situation is where the time limit (or other procedural irregularity) has been clearly waived by the party otherwise entitled to insist upon its observance.[2] Another situation is where the grievance can be characterized as a continuing grievance in the sense that the conduct giving rise to the grievance is of a recurring nature. Here arbitrators have treated time limits as operating only to limit grievances relating to earlier breaches of the collective agreement, and not as restricting a grievance relating to a fresh recurrence.[3]

1. *Supra*, para. 827.
2. *Regency Towers Hotel* (1973) 4 L.A.C. (2d) 440.
3. *Parking Authority of Toronto* (1974) 5 L.A.C. (2d) 150.

838. In some jurisdictions legislation explicitly gives arbitrators a power to relieve against time limits.[1] This power is a discretionary one and when exercising it arbitrators consider such matters as the reason for the delay in processing the grievance, the length of the delay, the nature of the grievance, and the extent of prejudice to the other party if relief against the time limit were to be granted.[2] The existence of an explicit statutory power to relieve against time limits in these jurisdictions makes the distinction between mandatory and directory time limits much less significant.

1. British Columbia, s.89(e); Canada, s.60(1.1); Ontario, s.48(16). In Ontario the power to relieve against time limits does not extend to the limits on the referral of a grievance to arbitration; *see S.E.I.U., Local 204* v. *Leisureworld Nursing Homes Ltd.* (1997) 99 O.A.C. 196.
2. *Pamour Porcupine Mines* (1977) C.L.C.C. para. 14,078 (Ont.Div.Ct.); *Becker Milk* (1979) 19 L.A.C. (2d) 217.

839. Late grievances, on the other hand, may not be arbitrable even where strict time limits are not found in the collective agreement. Arbitrators on occasion have applied the equitable doctrine of laches, refusing to hear the grievance on the ground that unreasonable delay in bringing the grievance has caused prejudice to the other party.[1]

1. *Supra*, para. 822.

d. Settlement, withdrawal and abandonment

840. The settlement, withdrawal, or abandonment of a grievance generally has the effect of rendering the grievance no longer arbitrable. Moreover, the disposition of a grievance in this manner usually precludes a party from bringing to arbitration another grievance raising the same matter as the earlier grievance. Arbitrators have recognized that the integrity of the earlier settlement process must be maintained, and have been reluctant to re-open issues where they appear to have been settled by the parties at an earlier stage in the process.

3. Discharge and discipline

841. The largest category of grievances carried to arbitration arises from those situations where employees have been disciplined or discharged by their employer.

Discipline covers such matters as suspension with pay, formal warnings and, in some cases, demotion. Discharge, the most severe form of disciplinary sanction, is often considered as being distinct from other disciplinary sanctions.[1]

1. On discipline in arbitration, *see* generally C. D'Aoust, L. Leclerc and G. Trudeau, *Les mesures disciplinaires: étude jurisprudentielle et doctrinale* (Montréal, 1982).

842. Discipline and discharge cases raise questions concerning the extent to which the traditional prerogative of employers to manage has been restricted by collective agreement provisions requiring that the disciplinary sanctions only be imposed for just cause. Viewed from the employee perspective discharge and discipline can be regarded as sanctions that have been imposed for wrongful conduct, and the argument is that such cases must be resolved by reference to principles analogous to those found in the criminal law. Employers, on the other hand, tend to resist this analogy to the criminal law, arguing that the power to discharge and discipline is simply one facet of their general responsibility to manage the enterprise as efficiently as possible. A decision to discharge or discipline, according to this view, amounts merely to the enforcement of the contractual bargain with the employees – a function that is not analogous to the imposition of sanctions under the criminal law. The true nature of discharge and discipline probably lies somewhere between these two extreme positions. In some situations employers appear to be attempting to regulate the conduct of their employees by reference to what is often an unwritten code of employment conduct. Theft, dishonesty, participation in illegal strikes, fighting on the job, sexual harassment and insubordination are usually regarded as the more serious offences, and often result in discharge. On the other hand, employees may be discharged or otherwise disciplined simply because their work performance is inadequate. Inadequate work performance may occur for such diverse reasons as incompetence, excessive absenteeism, ill health, or the inability to get along with fellow employees.

843. Most collective agreements provide that the employer can only discharge or discipline an employee for just cause. In the absence of such a restriction, arbitrators have been reluctant to review management decisions to discharge or discipline, especially where there exists in the collective agreement a clause giving management a general right to discharge or discipline.[1] Two Canadian jurisdictions, however, make it mandatory for the parties to include in their collective agreement a clause requiring that discharge or discipline be for just and reasonable cause.[2]

1. *See* C. D'Aoust, L. Dubé and G. Trudeau, *L'intervention de l'arbitre de grief en matière disciplinaire* (Montréal, 1995).
2. British Columbia, s.84(1); Manitoba, s.79(2).

a. Resignation

844. The term 'discharge' is not considered as including all terminations of employment. Where the employment relationship is terminated by the voluntary actions of the employee, such a termination is regarded as a resignation (or a quit) and is not arbitrable as a discharge. Arbitrators, however, have been cautious when characterizing employee conduct as a quit, requiring that there not only be evidence of an employee's intention to quit but also proof of conduct indicating that this intention has been carried out.[1] Both of these elements must be established clearly before arbitrators have concluded that the employee has voluntarily terminated the employment relationship.[2]

1. *Anchor Cap and Closure* (1949) 1 L.A.C. 222.
2. For a review of the arbitral jurisprudence, *see University of Guelph* (1973) 2 L.A.C. (2d) 351.

b. Retirement

845. The retirement of an employee, regardless of whether it is involuntary, has not been considered to be the same kind of termination as a discharge.[1] The characterization of retirement as being different from discharge means that a compulsory retirement cannot be dealt with by an arbitrator in the same manner as other terminations of employment. While arbitral review of involuntary retirement is not entirely absent, the usual standard of 'just cause' is not applicable. The arbitral case law indicates, however, that an involuntary retirement cannot be made in an arbitrary, discriminatory, or unreasonable manner.[2] In applying this standard arbitrators have taken into account such considerations as the prevailing retirement age, equality of treatment in the application of a retirement policy, the amount of notice of a retirement policy given to the employee, non-discrimination clauses in the collective agreement,[3] and applicable human rights legislation.[4] In some situations arbitrators have found the involuntary retirement of an employee to be improper but, in general, it would appear that they have been reluctant to interfere with the application of compulsory retirement policies. The Supreme Court of Canada has now held that mandatory retirement policies can be justified as a reasonable limit upon the guarantee of equality set out in the Charter of Rights and Freedoms.[5]

1. *Bell Canada* (1973) 37 D.L.R. (3d) 561 (S.C.C.).
2. The case law is discussed in some detail in *Electrical Power Systems Construction Association* (1978) 18 L.A.C. (2d) 205 (O.L.R.B.). In Quebec, compulsory retirement because of the employee's age or number of years of service is forbidden. *See* An Act Respecting Labour Standards, R.S.Q., c.N-1.1, ss.84.1 and 122.1.
3. *Oshawa Times* (1977) 14 L.A.C. (2d) 375.
4. *Prince Rupert Fisherman's Co-operative Association* (1979) 19 L.A.C. (2d) 308; but *see Crestbrook Forest Industries* (1979) 22 L.A.C. (2d) 25; aff'd. (1980) 80 C.L.L.C. para. 14,037 (B.C.C.A.); *United Steelworkers* (1983) 8 L.A.C. (3d) 71.
5. *Harrison* v. *University of British Columbia* (1991) 91 C.L.L.C. para. 17,001; [1990] 3 S.C.R. 451; *Douglas College* v. *Douglas/Kwantlen Faculty Association* (1991) 91 C.L.L.C. para. 17,002; [1990] 3 S.C.R. 570; *Vancouver General Hospital* v. *Stoffman* (1991) 91 C.L.L.C. para. 17,003; [1990] 3 S.C.R. 483; *McKinney* v. *University of Guelph* (1991) 91 C.L.L.C. para. 17,004; [1990] 3 S.C.R. 229.

c. Probationary employees

846. One of the most difficult problems facing arbitrators concerns the position of the probationary employee whose employment has been terminated prior to the expiry of the probationary period. Many collective agreements expressly provide that the discharge of a probationary employee is not to be judged by reference to as high a standard as that of the employee who has acquired seniority. Other agreements expressly preclude the matter from being arbitrated at all but such language has usually been considered as being incompatible with the legislative provision making mandatory arbitration of all outstanding grievances.[1] Even where the collective agreement does not explicitly deal with the situation of the probationary employee who has been terminated, arbitrators have generally taken the approach that in this type of situation the management decision to terminate the employment relationship will be subject to a less onerous standard of arbitral review.[2] The result is that the probationary employee, although generally entitled to all other benefits of the collective agreement, has far less job security under the collective agreement than the employee with seniority.

1. *Supra*, paras. 806–7.
2. *Porcupine Area Ambulance Service* (1974) 7 L.A.C. (2d) 182.

d. Loss of seniority

847. Some collective agreements may also provide for the loss of seniority where certain events occur such as the absence of an employee without leave for a specified number of days. A loss of seniority need not be treated as a termination of employment.[1] Nevertheless some arbitrators have still treated a loss of seniority as justifying an employee's discharge[2] even though others have regarded it as having less severe consequences.[3]

1. *Re Dwyer and Chrysler* (1978) 78 C.L.L.C. para. 14,160 (Ont.Div.Ct.).
2. *Rio Algom* (1983) 6 L.A.C. (3d) 164.
3. *Gates Rubber* (1979) 20 L.A.C. (2d) 229; *Collingwood Shipyards* (1982) 4 L.A.C. (3d) 132.

e. Demotions

848. There is some question as to whether demotions should be treated as a form of discipline. Arbitrators have drawn a distinction between those demotions which are in essence disciplinary measures and those that are not a form of discipline. A disciplinary demotion occurs where an employee, because of some misconduct, has been transferred to a lower-rated job. A non-disciplinary demotion occurs where the transfer to the lower-rated job does not relate to employee misconduct, such as where the employee is incapable of performing the job or where a lack of work requires a reassignment of the workforce.[1] Arbitrators have applied a different standard to non-disciplinary demotions, usually restricting their inquiry to the question of whether the employer has acted in a manner that was arbitrary, discriminatory, or in bad faith.[2] In cases of disciplinary demotion, arbitrators initially tended to regard demotion as being an inappropriate form of penalty, although some arbitrators have recognized that a demotion may be appropriate where the employee misconduct relates to that person's suitability to perform the job.[3]

1. *Cominco* (1975) 9 L.A.C. (2d) 233 (B.C.L.R.B.).
2. *Canadian Canners* (1975) 9 L.A.C. (2d) 132.
3. *Stelco* (1974) 7 L.A.C. (2d) 132.

f. Onus and standard of proof

849. It is now generally accepted that the employer bears the ultimate onus of establishing that discharge of discipline is for just cause.[1] This approach recognizes that it is the employer who has access to the reasons for the discharge or discipline and is in the better position to be able to introduce proof of these reasons. Because the employer bears the ultimate onus of proof in these cases, it is the usual practice for the arbitrator to have the employer adduce evidence of cause for discharge or discipline before calling upon the union to present its case.

1. *International Nickel* (1964) 20 L.A.C. 51.

850. The standard of proof required of the employer in cases of discharge and discipline is that which applies in other civil matters – that the case be established on the balance of probabilities. While the application of the standard does not usually give rise to difficulty, problems can occur where the misconduct giving rise to the disciplinary sanction also constitutes a criminal offence. In these circumstances the issue is whether the civil standard of proof is still applicable, or whether a more stringent standard (approaching that of the criminal standard of proof beyond a reasonable doubt) should be applied.[1]

1. The Quebec Court of Appeal has rejected the more stringent standard. *Syndicat national des travailleurs des pâtes et papiers d'Alma Inc.* v. *Compagnie Price Ltée.*, D.T.E. 91T-690 (C.A.).

g. Alteration of grounds

851. On occasion employers advance at the hearing a justification that had not been relied upon when the disciplinary sanction was first imposed. As a general rule, arbitrators have been reluctant to receive this subsequent justification even though it might serve to support the employer's decision to impose discipline.[1] However, where it can be established that the employer was unaware of these alternative grounds at the time disciplinary action was taken, there appears to be greater arbitral willingness to allow the employer to raise such grounds at a later stage in the proceedings. In those situations where alternative grounds are received at the hearing, the usual is to adjourn the hearing to allow the union the opportunity to prepare a response.

1. *Aerocide Dispensers* (1965) 15 L.A.C. 416.

h. Culminating incident

852. Employers may sometimes attempt to justify disciplinary action by reference to the employee's previous unfavourable employment record. Such a justification can only be used where the event precipitating the imposition of the sanction by itself warrants the imposition of some kind of discipline.[1] Once this culminating incident, as it is called, has been established arbitrators have been prepared to consider previous incidents of misconduct as being relevant to the issue of just cause, provided that these incidents have been the subject of disciplinary action which have been brought to the employee's attention and placed on the employment record.

1. *Canadian Lukens* (1976) 12 L.A.C. (2d) 439.

i. Insubordination

853. Insubordination is one of the primary grounds for the imposition of disciplinary sanctions by employers. Employers place a high priority upon being able to run their enterprises in an orderly and disciplined manner and, not unnaturally, view employee challenges to their managerial authority in a serious light. From the employee and union perspective, however, some of these challenges to managerial authority raise important questions concerning the extent of an employee's civil rights in the work place.

854. Arbitrators when reviewing cases of insubordination have generally placed greater emphasis upon the employer's right to direct its workforce and to take immediate disciplinary action where such directions are not followed. The general rule is that the employee is expected to comply with the order of the employer even where that order appears to be in violation of the collective agreement. This approach, however, does not leave the union and employee without redress where the employer's conduct constitutes a violation of the collective agreement since the dispute can be resolved subsequently through the grievance and arbitration procedure. This 'comply-now, grieve-later' rule is one that has received wide acceptance by Canadian arbitrators.[1]

1. This approach appears to have its origin in an American arbitration award, *Ford Motor* (1944) 3 L.A 799. Its application in Quebec and Canada is discussed in C. D'Aoust and G. Trudeau, *L'obligation d'obéir et ses limites dans la jurisprudence arbitrale québécoise* (Montréal, 1979) and in W. Kaplan, J. Sack and M. Gunderson, *Labour Arbitration Yearbook*, 1991, Vol. 1 (Toronto, 1991) at 187–222.

855. Like any rule, the 'comply-now, grieve-later' rule has certain recognized exceptions. Arbitrators take into account the fact that in some situations the grievance and arbitration procedure is not likely to provide the employee with adequate redress. Conduct that would ordinarily be considered as insubordinate has been excused when influenced by a legitimate concern for personal health and safety,[1] where compliance would require the employee to perform an illegal act,[2] where a union official is pursuing the legitimate interests of the union and its members,[3] and in some circumstances where there is an objection to a rule relating to the personal appearance of employees.[4] In Quebec, arbitrators have even ruled that an employee was not bound by the 'comply-now, grieve-later' rule when the order was in violation of the collective agreement.[5]

1. *Stelco* (1973) 4 L.A.C. (2d) 315.
2. *International Nickel* (1974) 6 L.A.C. (2d) 172.

3. *Stancor Central* (1970) 22 L.A.C. 184.
4. *Borough of Etobicoke* (1974) 6 L.A.C. (2d) 251.
5. The decision by arbitrator André Rousseau in *Alliance des infirmières de Montréal* v. *L'Hôpital St-Eusèbe de Joliette* (1973) Sentences Arbitrales de Griefs, 1235, is often considered as the precedent on this matter.

j. Misconduct outside the work place

856. At times misconduct of an employee occurring away from the work place may be brought to the attention of the employer, usually where such misconduct has resulted in the machinery of criminal justice being put into motion. Where an employee has been charged with a criminal offence for conduct occurring away from work, arbitrators have considered that the suspension of the employee from work to be justified only where the employer can establish that the continued employment of that employee would prejudice the employer's interests in some material way.[1] This approach takes into account such employer concerns as the security of its own property and its reputation in the eyes of the public.

1. *Dorr-Oliver-Long* (1973) 3 L.A.C. (2d) 193.

857. Much the same approach is taken by arbitrators where off-duty misconduct results in a criminal conviction. Again the question is whether the conviction is sufficiently prejudicial to the interests of the employer so as to justify the employer taking the disciplinary action (in most cases discharge).[1] If the conviction carried with it a penalty or imprisonment, however, the employer may be justified in terminating the employment relationship simply because the employee is no longer available for work.[2]

1. *Borough of Scarborough* (1973) 3 L.A.C. (2d) 219.
2. *Canadian Westinghouse* (1956) 7 L.A.C. 94; but *see Alcan* (1974) 6 L.A.C. (2d) 386; *Stelco* (1984) 11 L.A.C. (3d) 388; *Zellers Inc.*, D.T.E. 90T-452 (T.A.).

k. The appropriate penalty

858. Even where it can be established by the employer that just cause exists for the imposition of some form of discipline, there still remains a question of whether the disciplinary sanction chosen by the employer is appropriate in the circumstance of the particular grievance.[1] Arbitrators have taken a wide variety of factors into account when reviewing the appropriateness of the penalty, including the previous record and service of the grievor, the nature and seriousness of the offence,[2] and equality of treatment among employees.[3] Moreover, arbitrators now take into account the desirability of corrective discipline,[4] and have even considered the rehabilitative potential of the employee.[5]

1. *See supra*, para. 826, for a discussion of the extent of the arbitrator's remedial authority to substitute a lesser penalty.
2. *Steel Equipment* (1964) 14 L.A.C. 356.
3. *Julius Resnick* (1973) 3 L.A.C. (2d) 247.

4. *Ontario Produce* (1976) 12 L.A.C. (2d) 235.
5. *Toronto East General Hospital* (1975) 9 L.A.C. (2d) 311; but *see Northern and Central Gas Corp. Ltd.* (1978) 16 L.A.C. (2d) 395.

4. Seniority

859. Just as important as the discharge and discipline cases are those grievances claiming that the employer has not acted with proper regard to the seniority of the employee. Employee seniority rights substantially qualify the general right of the employer to manage the enterprise. Length of service is not only a factor that may affect entitlement to benefits such as vacations and pensions, but, even more importantly, it is usually a factor affecting employee claims to job opportunities and job security. Most collective agreements provide that the employer cannot promote, demote, transfer, lay off or recall without giving at least some consideration to the relative seniority of the employees.[1] Arbitrators are divided on whether seniority is defined by length of employment with the employer or, more narrowly, by length of employment within the bargaining unit. The distinction is important for those employees who seek to return to the bargaining unit after having worked in a position falling outside of it.

1. *See* generally: C. D'Aoust and F. Meunier, *La jurisprudence arbitrale québécoise en matière d'ancienneté* (Montréal, 1980); C. Vézina, *Les clauses d'ancienneté et l'arbitrage de grief* (Ottawa, 1979); Hébert, *op. cit.* ch. 9, 277–329.

a. Types of seniority provision

860. Although there exists a great variation in the wording of seniority clauses from agreement to agreement, such provisions are usually characterized by reference to two basic models – the competitive clause and the non-competitive clause.[1] The former type of clause, which is more common, requires the employer to consider seniority as the deciding factor only where the skill and ability of the competing employees is relatively equal. The latter type of clause, however, places much greater emphasis on seniority, making it the deciding factor so long as the more senior employee can perform the job competently. Both types of clause may give rise to a grievance alleging that the employer has either established the qualifications for the job in an improper manner, or has improperly assessed the abilities of the more senior employee.

1. *Westeel Products* (1960) 11 L.A.C. 199.

b. Scope of arbitral review

861. Grievances relating to the establishment and assessment of job qualifications raise the vexing question as to the extent to which the arbitrator may properly review this type of managerial judgment. Although it is clearly recognized that it not appropriate for arbitrators to usurp the functions of management, it is equally apparent that arbitrators must give meaning to seniority provisions contained in collective agreements. There has been no lack of arbitral effort spared in attempting to reconcile these competing concerns as evidenced by the numerous decisions that have attempted to formulate an appropriate approach.[1]

1. For a review of some of this jurisprudence, *see Hydro-Electric Power Commission of Ontario* (1976) 11 L.A.C. (2d) 36.

862. Arbitrators in general have not applied the same scrutiny to a management decision respecting employee qualifications as they have to disciplinary decisions. Unless it can be established by a grievor that an employer has acted in bad faith arbitrators have not been prepared to interfere with the setting of the qualifications for jobs.[1] Even more important, employer assessments of employee qualifications have been usually respected by arbitrators. Nevertheless, there is some indication from the courts that arbitrators may have been taking too narrow a view of their authority to review this type of employer decision by simply asking whether an employer acted honestly and reasonably.[2]

1. *Reynolds Aluminium* (1974) 5 L.A.C. (2d) 251 (Schiff).
2. *Great Atlantic and Pacific* (1976) 76 C.L.L.C. para. 14,056 (Ont.Div.Ct.).

c. Job posting

863. A usual incident of seniority provisions is a requirement in the collective agreement that job vacancies be publicly posted. In this way employees can be made aware of the job opportunities to which their seniority gives them some claim. Job posting requirements have been interpreted by arbitrators as binding employers only where the employer has actually determined that there is sufficient work available to justify the creation of the job.[1] Moreover, it is usually only the jobs described in the collective agreement that are considered to be subject to the posting requirement so that transfers within job classifications have been regarded as falling outside this requirement.[2]

1. *Tidewater Oil* (1963) 14 L.A.C. 233.
2. *Kysor of Ridgetown* (1967) 18 L.A.C. 63.

5. *Assignment of work*

864. The general right of the employer to assign work as s/he sees fit may be qualified by restrictions other than a requirement to consider the relative seniority of employees. Certain other qualifications, either explicit or implicit, upon the right of management to assign work may be found in the collective agreement.

a. Bargaining unit work

865. Arbitrators have recognized that there is a core of work that is customarily performed by members of the bargaining unit. While the bargaining agent does not have any absolute right to claim this work for its employee constituents, it would appear that an employer is not allowed to make any substantial assignment of this core of bargaining unit work to either its supervisory employees, or to its non-supervisory employees not included in the bargaining unit. Arbitrators have recognized that this type of work assignment would substantially erode the seniority, classification, and wage structure created by the collective agreement.[1]

1. For a review of these decisions *see Westroc Industries* (1974) 5 L.A.C. (2d) 61; *see also Irwin Toy* (1983) 6 L.A.C. (3d) 328.

866. A less restrictive approach, however, has been taken by arbitrators toward the contracting-out of work by an employer. The general arbitral approach is that, in the absence of any explicit limitation in the collective agreement, an employer may enter upon a legitimate contracting-out of work.[1] Not all agreements giving the appearance of a contracting-out have been regarded by arbitrators as being legitimate. Where an employer still retains substantial control over the employees of the person to whom the work has been allegedly contracted out, the agreement made by the employer is likely to be regarded by an arbitrator as something less than a *bona fide* contracting-out of work.[2]

1. *Russelsteel* (1966) 17 L.A.C. 253.
2. *Wean-McKay* (1971) 23 L.A.C. 27.

b. Classification structure

867. Many collective agreements contain a fairly elaborate system of job classification, setting out both descriptions of the job and the wage to be paid for the work falling within that job description.[1] Such job classification systems serve the purpose of creating an equitable wage structure where remuneration bears some relation to the effort and skill required by the job. Although arbitrators have regarded job classification structures as creating a restriction upon the employer's discretion to determine the wage to be paid an employee, they have not treated such structures as restricting management's right to assign work.[2] As a general rule, management can create new job classifications and add to the job content of existing classifications.

1. *See* Hébert, *op. cit.*, ch. 11, 361–93.
2. *Algoma Steel* (1968) 19 L.A.C. 236; *Windsor Public Utilities Commission* (1975) 7 L.A.C. (2d) 380.

c. Overtime

868. In the absence of an express provision in the collective agreement making overtime voluntary, arbitrators have taken the view that management has the right to require an employee to work overtime.[1] The employer's right to assign overtime on a compulsory basis, however, may be qualified by operation of minimum standards legislation. It is now clear that arbitrators must have regard to such legislation when determining the extent of an employer's right to assign overtime under the collective agreement.[2]

1. *Bridge and Tank* (1976) 11 L.A.C. (2d) 301.
2. *McLeod* v. *Egan* (1974) 46 D.L.R. (3d) 150 (S.C.C.); [1975] 1 S.C.R. 517.

869. Overtime is not always regarded by employees as a burden since many collective agreements provide premium pay for overtime work. As a result, collective agreements often contain provisions requiring the employer to distribute overtime so as to give all employees an equal chance to benefit from the extra work. Where such provisions have been breached, the employee may be awarded compensation for the lost overtime opportunity or, where appropriate, may receive a remedy 'in kind' providing the employee with an overtime opportunity to make up for the opportunity previously lost.[1]

1. *Canadian Johns Manville Co. Ltd.* (1971) 22 L.A.C. 396.

6. *Monetary grievances*

870. An essential part of any collective agreement are those provisions establishing the compensation package for the employees in the bargaining unit. Collective bargaining in Canada is very much an economic exercise, and Canadian trade unions place great emphasis upon representing the economic interests of their members. As a result, many collective agreements not only provide for an elaborate wage structure,[1] but they also provide a comprehensive system of fringe benefits, including such items as paid holidays, paid vacations, sick pay, medical and hospital insurance, disability insurance, pensions, and supplementary unemployment benefits.[2] When the rate of inflation accelerated in the 1970s and 1980s, a number of collective agreements provided for the periodic adjustments of wages to take into account increases in the cost of living. Such clauses are now less common as inflation as Canada experiences a period of low inflation.

1. *See* Hébert, *op. cit.*, ch. 13, 445–97.
2. *Ibid.*, ch. 14, 499–547.

7. *Union rights and liabilities under the collective agreement*

871. The trade union as one of the two principal parties to the collective bargaining relationship may bargain on its own behalf as well as for the members of the bargaining unit. Certain clauses of the collective agreement may create special rights for the union, and for its officials. By the same token, however, arbitrators have recognized that the special position of the union and union officials may carry with it greater obligations than those imposed upon the members of the bargaining unit.

a. Enforcement of union security provisions

872. Union security provisions are a common feature of Canadian collective agreements.[1] Most of these provisions make the payment of regular union dues a condition of employment, and some go further by making continued employment conditional upon union membership. Such provisions are enforced through the grievance and arbitration process in the same manner as any other clause of the collective agreement.

1. *Supra*, paras. 578–81. *See also* Hébert, *op. cit.*, ch. 4, 99–133.

873. The enforcement of a union security provision through arbitration brings into conflict the interests of the trade union and those of the individual employee. While trade unions usually place great emphasis upon the protection of employment, in this situation they find themselves in the unusual position of insisting upon the termination of the employment relationship. Union security provisions have been recognized as being quite legal, and arbitrators have enforced them by ordering employers to terminate the employment relationship of employees who have not complied with the requirement of such provisions.[1] However, these employees, since they would be directly affected by the disposition of the union's grievance at arbitration, are entitled to notice of the arbitration hearing, and also entitled to participate fully in the hearings.[2] The enforcement of a union security provision at arbitration may also entail an examination of the internal affairs of the trade union in order to determine the circumstances under which union membership has been divested or withheld.[3]

1. S.63 of the Quebec Labour Code severely restricts the impact of union security provisions upon individual employees by limiting the circumstances under which an employee can be dismissed by operation of such provisions.
2. *Hoogendoorn* v. *Greening Metal Products and Screening Equipment* (1968), 65 D.L.R. (2d) 641 (S.C.C.); [1968] S.C.R. 30.
3. *Orenda Engines* (1958) 8 L.A.C. 116.

874. Union security provisions not only impose an obligation upon employees to contribute financially to the trade union, but they also impose an obligation upon the employer to collect such funds on behalf of the bargaining agent. Employers have not been permitted to impound these funds in order to satisfy some other financial obligation that might be owed to the employer by the trade union.[1] Where a union security provision requires, not only the collection of union dues, but also the hiring of union members, employer liability for breach of such a provision is likely to be even more extensive. A breach of a 'hiring hall provision gives the union the right to claim damages, not just for lost dues, but also for lost contributions to its welfare and vacation funds, and for the wages that its members would have earned had the clause been honoured'.[2]

1. *Brooks Manufacturing* (1969) 20 L.A.C. 298.
2. *Blouin Drywal Contractors and Carpenters and Joiners* (1975) 57 D.L.R. (3d) 199 (Ont.C.A.).

b. Special position of union officials

875. The collective agreement may also confer certain privileges upon union officials. Time-off for union business may be provided for in the collective agreement, permitting union officials to carry out their functions on the employer's time. Many collective agreements provide that the union official is to be indemnified for any loss of earnings resulting from performing union business during working hours. The right of a trade union official to take time-off for union business, however, is not an absolute right, and arbitrators have held that an employer may discipline a union official for abusing this right.[1] Union officials may also acquire super seniority under the collective agreement, giving them greater job security in the event of lay-off than that enjoyed by the other members of the bargaining unit and, sometimes, a better claim to overtime work. Arbitrators have also recognized that union officials should not be denied opportunity for promotion simply because they may have to spend some time performing their union responsibilities. However, employers are permitted to consider whether an official's union responsibilities would interfere substantially with performance of the job.[2]

1. *Massey-Ferguson Industries* (1970) 21 L.A.C. 244.
2. *Northern Electric* (1976) 11 L.A.C. (2d) 208; *Toronto Star* (1977) 15 L.A.C. (2d) 326.

876. Union officials may also be allowed more latitude than other employees in their relationship with management. Emotions may run high in meetings between union and management giving rise to conduct that would normally be considered as insubordinate. Arbitrators, however, have not treated such conduct as justifying discipline where it is clear that the conduct occurred in circumstances where the union official was acting in a representative capacity.[1]

1. *St. Lawrence Seaway Authority* (1979) 20 L.A.C. (2d) 24.

c. Union obligations

877. Collective agreements usually contain a provision stipulating that there are to be no strikes or lockouts during the term of the agreement. Most grievances brought to arbitration by employers relate to the breach of this particular obligation.[1] Arbitrators have generally characterized conduct as strike action in the same way as have the labour boards when dealing with the legislative strike prohibition. Where a strike occurs, an onus is placed upon the trade union to establish that it did not authorize or condone such activity.[2] Although arbitrators have interpreted the 'no-strike' obligation as requiring the union and its officials to make their best effort to end the strike, they have not imposed absolute liability upon the trade union, recognizing that a trade union and its officials may not always be able to control spontaneous or 'wildcat' strikes. If a trade union is found to be responsible for strike action occurring during the term of the collective agreement, the arbitrator has the power to award damages for losses flowing from breach of the no-strike provision in the collective agreement.[3]

1. *Supra*, paras. 779–81.
2. *Canadian General Electric* (1951) 2 L.A.C. 608.
3. *Re Polymer and Oil Workers* (1962) 33 D.L.R. (2d) 124 (S.C.C.); [1962] S.C.R. 338.

d. Obligations of union officials

878. There has been considerable debate over the extent to which union officials have a greater responsibility to an employer that other members of the bargaining unit. This issue usually arises in the context of an illegal strike, the question being whether the participation of union officials in a walk-out should draw more severe discipline than that meted out to other striking employees. Judicial authority now clearly suggests that, although more severe discipline may be warranted where a union official played a larger role in the breach of the collective agreement, greater discipline cannot be justified simply by virtue of the fact of holding union office.[1] Where a trade union official assumes only a passive role in the particular incident drawing disciplinary sanctions, then the responsibility of that official is no greater than that of the ordinary employee.

1. *Douglas Aircraft* v. *U.A.W.* (1979) 79 C.L.L.C. para. 14,221 (S.C.C.); [1980] 1 S.C.R. 245.

879. The disciplining of union officials also raises the question of the appropriate sanctions to be imposed in such circumstances. In one case, where a union official had been discharged for irresponsible behaviour, the arbitrator ordered that the official be reinstated on the condition that the person not hold union office.[1] The imposition of this condition, however, was considered by the courts as being inconsistent with those provisions of collective bargaining legislation protecting employee freedom of association, and the arbitrator's award was quashed.[2]

1. *Inglis* (1976) 12 L.A.C. (2d) 435.
2. *Inglis* (1977) 8 C.L.L.C. para. 14,089 (Ont.Div.Ct.).

§3. The Limited Role of the Courts

880. The existence of a well-developed system of grievance arbitration, and the legal barriers to the direct enforcement of collective agreements in the courts,[1] has meant that the judiciary has not played a major role in the enforcement of Canadian collective agreements. Nevertheless, the courts have influenced the development of Canadian arbitral jurisprudence through the exercise of their prerogative to review the decisions of lower tribunals. As well, the enforcement process of the courts has had to be brought into play occasionally in order to ensure compliance with arbitral awards.

1. *Supra*, paras. 794–801.

A. Judicial Review

881. Canadian courts have made it clear that their authority to review the decisions of lower tribunals extends to grievance arbitration tribunals.[1] While at one time the courts appeared to attach some significance to the difference between statutory grievance arbitration and consensual grievance arbitration when determining the scope of the judicial review, more recent cases would indicate that this distinction can no longer be maintained.[2] Now the scope of judicial review is more likely to be influenced by whether the applicable collective bargaining legislation has expressly restricted judicial review of grievance arbitration.[3] Such legislative provisions referred to as privative clauses, have been held to preclude review where the alleged error does not go to an arbitrator's jurisdiction.[4]

1. *See* generally, K.P. Swan, 'The Supreme Court of Canada, Judicial Review and Labour Arbitration' in Swan & Swinton *op. cit.*; *see also* D. Pothier, 'Judicial Review of Labour Arbitrators' in W. Kaplan, J. Sack, and M. Gunderson (eds.), *Labour Arbitration Yearbook, 1991*, Vol. 1. (Toronto, 1991) at 55.
2. *Volvo Canada*, (1979) 79 C.L.L.C. para. 14,210 (S.C.C.); [1980] 1 S.C.R. 178; *Roberval Express* (1983) 83 C.L.L.C. para. 14,023 (S.C.C.); [1982] 2 S.C.R. 888.
3. Canada, s.58; Quebec, s.139; British Columbia, s.101. In British Columbia, moreover, s.99 expressly gives a power of review to the labour relations board.
4. *Canadian National Railway and Telecommunications Union* (1970) 63 D.L.R. (3d) 385 (Ont.C.A.); *Communications Union and Bell Canada* (1979) 97 D.L.R. (3d) 132 (Ont.Div.Ct.). *See also*, 'L'erreur juridictionnelle en arbitrage de grief: les arrêts récents de la Cour d'appel et de la Cour suprême', in *Études en droit du travail à la mémoire de Claude D'Aoust*, G. Trudeau, G. Vallée and D. Veilleux (eds.) (Cowansville: 1995) 255–301.

882. Even where no privative clause is in force, however, the courts have demonstrated some deference to arbitral decision-making. On matters of collective agreement interpretation, the courts have indicated that they are not prepared to overrule an arbitrator where they simply disagree with the interpretation to the agreement given by the arbitrator, and that an arbitral award will be quashed only where an arbitrator has given the language an interpretation that it cannot reasonably bear.[1] The courts have been less deferential, however, where the arbitrator has had to construe a general statute or other matters of general law[2] or where the decision relates to the arbitrator's jursidiction.[3]

1. *Hudson Bay Mining and Smelting* (1968) 66 D.L.R. (2d) 1 (S.C.C.); [1968] S.C.R. 113.
2. *McLeod* v. *Egan* (1974) 46 D.L.R. (3d) 150 (S.C.C.); [1975] 1 S.C.R. 517; *Retail, Wholesale Union and Dominion Stores* (1982) 37 D.L.R. (3d) 524 (Sask.C.A.).
3. *Dayco (Canada) Ltd.* v. *C.A.W.-Canada*, [1993] 2 S.C.R. 230.

B. Enforcement of Arbitration Awards

883. Arbitrators do not themselves have the coercive powers to enforce their awards, and collective bargaining legislation in Canada usually provides that arbitration awards are to be filed with the courts and enforced in the same manner as a judicial decision. The result is that the contempt power of the court is ultimately available to enforce compliance with the arbitrators award. Generally speaking, non-compliance with arbitration awards does not appear to be a serious problem in Canada.

§4. The Role of Labour Boards

884. Until quite recently labour boards have played only a minor role in the grievance arbitration process. The adjudication of disputes arising under collective agreements was generally regarded as being the function of arbitrators with the labour boards playing only a supporting role. Only such ancillary functions as ensuring whether a grievance arbitration provision met the statutory standard, and advising on whether there was any authority to constitute an arbitration tribunal, were given to labour boards by the legislation.[1] Even in situations where a violation of the collective agreement might also be construed as a violation of the collective bargaining statute itself, labour boards were still generally content to have the matter dealt with through the arbitration process.[2]

1. For example, s.48(3) and s.115(1) of the Ontario legislation.
2. This general policy of deferral to arbitration can be found in *United Gas* (1965) 65 C.L.L.C. para. 16,056 (O.L.R.B.); but *see Valdi*, [1980] 3 C.L.R.B.R. 299 (O.L.R.B.).

A. Direct Jurisdiction

885. In Ontario the labour board has been given a direct jurisdiction to arbitrate disputes arising from construction industry collective agreements.[1] Either party to such a collective agreement may refer a grievance to the labour board, even though the collective agreement may contain its own arbitration procedure, and this referral gives the board exclusive jurisdiction to deal with the matter. The board, however, now has a discretion to refuse to accept such a referral.

1. S.133.

886. If the board does decide to proceed, it may appoint an official to attempt to settle the dispute prior to the hearing. If the grievance remains unresolved it then goes to a formal board hearing, which by statute must be fourteen days after the grievance is first referred to the board. Both parties must pay a fee established by regulation for the use of this alternative to conventional arbitration.

887. British Columbia provides its labour board with a jurisdiction to deal with differences arising during the term of the collective agreement.[1] The board's jurisdiction, however, is restricted to inquiring into the difference and making recommendations for settlement. If the difference is arbitrable, the board can order that it be submitted to a specified step in the grievance procedure under the collective agreement. In all cases, however, the board can request the minister to appoint a special officer and this special officer could, among other options, arbitrate the dispute.[2]

1. S.88.
2. S.106.

B. Review Jurisdiction

888. In addition to its direct jurisdiction over grievance arbitration the British Columbia labour relations board, alone among Canadian labour boards, has been given a power to review the decision of arbitrators.[1] This jurisdiction has not been interpreted as giving a full appellate power to overrule the arbitrator's award, but has been defined as a power to review arbitration proceedings to ensure fairness of procedures and to ensure that the arbitrator has taken into account the principles established by the collective bargaining statute.[2]

1. S.99.
2. *Simon Fraser University*, [1976] 2 C.L.R.B.R. 54 (B.C.L.R.B.).

C. Concurrent Jurisdiction

889. Some breaches of the collective agreement may also constitute violations of collective bargaining legislation, giving rise to an overlap of jurisdiction between an arbitrator and a labour board. While as a general rule labour boards have deferred to the jurisdiction of the arbitrator,[1] there appears to be increasing recognition by the boards that this policy of deferral may not be appropriate in all situations. One exception to this general policy of deferral are those situations where a labour board considers that the arbitration process cannot deal effectively with the matter.[2] Such a situation might occur where there is a direct conflict between the interests of the union and those of the grievor, or where there is some form of collusion between the union and the employer to be prejudice of the employee grievor.[3] A second exception to the general policy of deferral are those matters raising issues extending beyond the interpretation and administration of the collective agreement by affecting the general structure of collective bargaining.[4] Labour boards have indicated that they now regard it as their function to deal with such broader issues and have not been content to have this type of issue settled by grievance arbitration.[5]

1. *Supra*, para. 474.
2. *Bell Canada*, [1978] 1 C.L.R.B.R. 1 (O.L.R.B.); *Valdi*, [1980] 3 C.L.R.B.R. 299 (O.L.R.B.); *see also City of Saskatoon* (1991) 8 C.L.R.B.R. (2d) 310 (S.L.R.B.) and *Canada Post Corp.* (1992), 12 C.L.R.B.R. (2d) 117 (C.L.R.B.).
3. *Imperial Tobacco Products (Ontario) Ltd.*, [1974] 1 C.L.R.B.R. 1 (O.L.R.B.).
4. *Kodak Canada Ltd.*, [1977] 1 C.L.R.B.R. 280 (O.L.R.B.); *Northern Loram* (1985) 9 C.L.R.B.R. (N.S.) 218 (C.L.R.B.); *Canadian Museum of Civilization Corporation* (1996), 96 C.L.L.C. para. 220-067 (C.L.R.B.).
5. Quebec has not adopted a policy of deferring to arbitration. The recourse before the Labour Commissioner and grievance arbitration are different and distinct recourses that can be exercised simultaneously. For example, *see Clément* v. *La Société des Alcools du Québec*, [1982] 2 C.L.R.B.R. 1 (Q.L.C.).

Index

The numbers refer to paragraphs.

Index

www.ingramcontent.com/pod-product-compliance
Lightning Source LLC
Chambersburg PA
CBHW071559040526
44394CB00004B/679
9789041117502